RAC
Road Atlas
Britain & Ireland

CONTENTS

Key to map pages — ii

Britain distance chart — iii

Key to map symbols — iv-v

Route planning map — vi-vii
(40 miles to 1 inch)

Road map section — 2-109
Britain (4.2 miles to 1 inch)

Ireland road maps — 110-113
(15.8 miles to 1 inch)

M25 London orbital motorway map — 114-115

London urban map — 116-117
(1.1 miles to 1 inch)

London central map — 118-119
(5.1 inches to 1 mile)

Urban area maps and city centre plans — 120-133
(1.25 miles to 1 inch)
Southampton and Portsmouth — 120-121
Cardiff and Newport — 122
Bristol — 123
West Midlands — 124-125
Merseyside — 126-127
Greater Manchester — 128-129
Newcastle upon Tyne — 130
Edinburgh — 131
Glasgow — 132-133

Index to place names in Britain — 134-162

Index to place names in Ireland — 162

Published by Collins
An imprint of HarperCollinsPublishers
77-85 Fulham Palace Road, Hammersmith, London W6 8JB

www.collins.co.uk

Copyright © HarperCollinsPublishers Ltd 2003

Collins® is a registered trademark of HarperCollinsPublishers Limited

Mapping generated from Collins Bartholomew digital databases

The grid on this map is the National Grid taken from the Ordnance Survey map with the permission of the Controller of Her Majesty's Stationery Office.

The contents of this publication are believed correct at the time of printing. Nevertheless, the publisher can accept no responsibility for errors or omissions, changes in the detail given, or for any expense or loss thereby caused.

The representation of a road, track or footpath is no evidence of a right of way.

Printed in Great Britain

ISBN paperback 0 00 717338 5 imp 001
wiro 0 00 717339 3 imp 001

QCI1660 / QCI1661 BDM

e-mail: roadcheck@harpercollins.co.uk

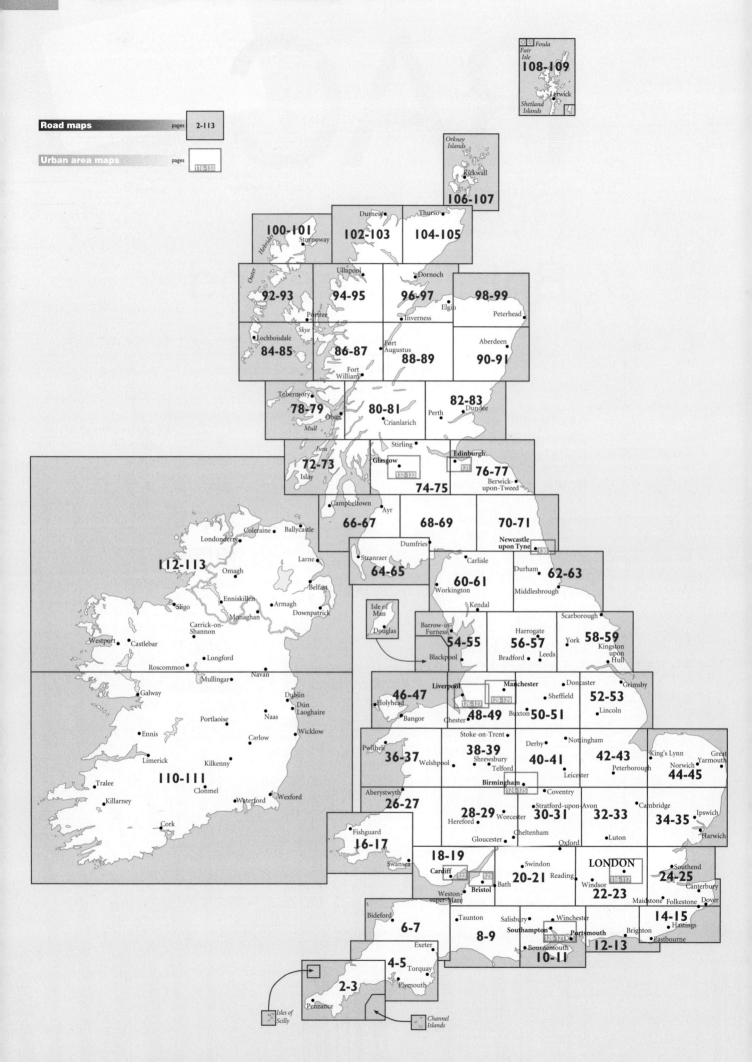

Distances between two selected towns in this table are shown in miles and kilometres. In general, distances are based on the shortest routes by classified roads.

DISTANCE IN KILOMETRES

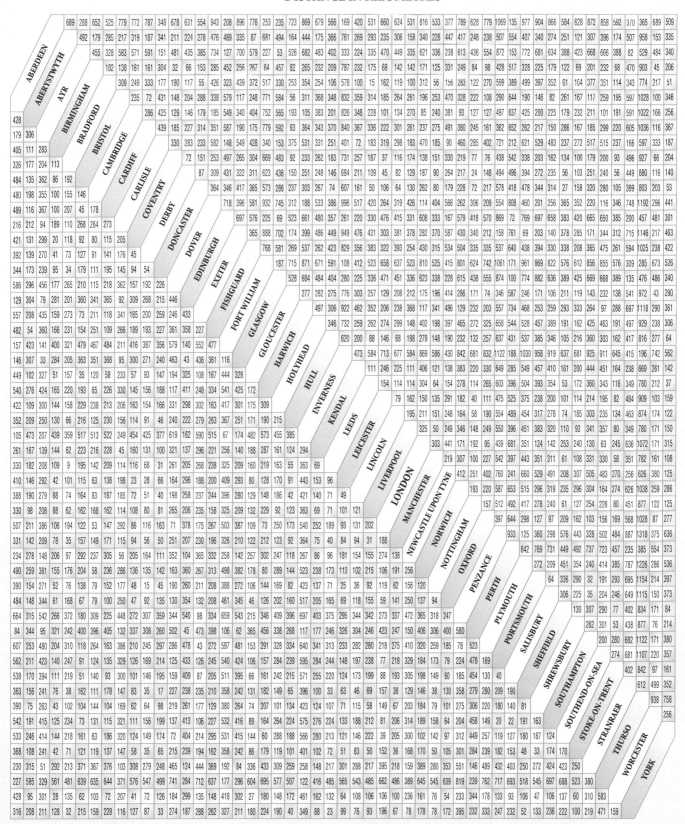

DISTANCE IN MILES

KEY TO MAP SYMBOLS

Road maps (pages 2-109)

ROAD INFORMATION

M5	Motorway
30 29	Motorway junction with full / limited access
Maidstone Birch Sarn	Motorway service area with off road / full / limited access
A48	Primary dual / single carriageway
	With passing places
A30	'A' road dual / single carriageway
	With passing places
B1403	'B' road dual / single carriageway
	With passing places
	Minor road
	Restricted access due to road condition or private ownership
	Road proposed or under construction
24	Multi-level junction (occasionally with junction number)
	Roundabout
10	Road distance in miles between markers
	Road tunnel
	Steep hill (arrows point downhill)
Toll	Level crossing / Toll

OTHER TRANSPORT INFORMATION

	Car ferry route with journey times; daytime and (night-time)
	Railway line / Station / Tunnel
	Airport with scheduled services
	Heliport
	Park and Ride site (operates at least 5 days a week)

CITIES, TOWNS & VILLAGES

	Built up area
□ ▫ ▫	Town / Village / Other settlement
Peterhead	Primary route destination

Primary route destinations are places of major traffic importance linked by the primary route network. They are shown on a green background on direction signs.

St Ives	Seaside destination

OTHER FEATURES

	National boundary
	County / Unitary Authority boundary
	National / Regional park
	Forest park boundary
Danger Zone	Military range
	Woodland
•468	Spot height in metres
▲941	Summit height in metres
	Lake / Dam / River / Waterfall
	Canal / Dry canal / Canal tunnel
	Beach
14	Adjoining page indicator

TOURIST INFORMATION

A selection of tourist detail is shown on the mapping. It is advisable to check with the local tourist information office regarding opening times and facilities available.

i i	Tourist information centre (all year / seasonal)
m	Ancient monument
⚔ 1738	Battlefield
🏰	Castle
	Country park
✝	Ecclesiastical building
✿	Garden
⚑	Golf course
🏛	Historic house
£	Major shopping centre / Outlet village
	Major sports venue
	Motor racing circuit
🏛	Museum / Art gallery
	Nature reserve
	Preserved railway
	Racecourse
🎋	Theme park
	Wildlife park or Zoo
★	Other interesting feature
(NT)	National Trust property
(NTS)	National Trust for Scotland property

London central map (pages 118-119)

Dual A4	Primary route	Main / Other railway station		Tourist information centre	
Dual A302	'A' road	LRT / Bus or coach station		Cinema / Theatre	
B240	'B' road	Leisure and tourism		Major hotel	
	Other road / Track / Path	Shopping		Embassy	
	Street market / Pedestrian street	Administration and law		Church	
	Congestion Charging Zone	Health and welfare		Mosque	
	One way street / Access restriction	Education		Synagogue	
	Ferry	Industry and commerce		Other place of worship	
	Borough boundary	Public open space		Car park / Public toilet	
	Postal district boundary	Park / Garden / Sports ground		Police station / Fire station / Post office	

Urban area maps (pages 120-133)

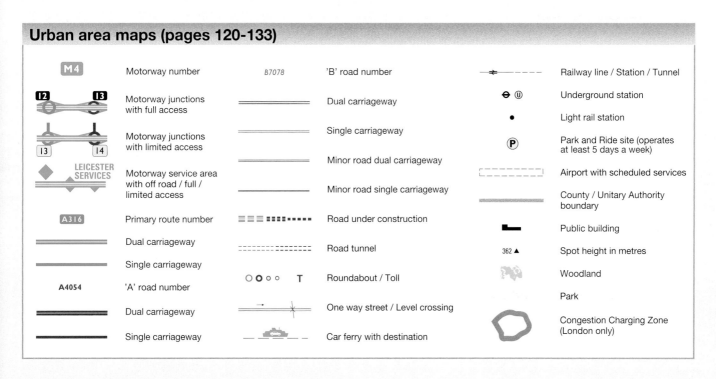

M4	Motorway number	B7078	'B' road number	Railway line / Station / Tunnel	
12 13	Motorway junctions with full access		Dual carriageway	Underground station	
13 14	Motorway junctions with limited access		Single carriageway	Light rail station	
LEICESTER SERVICES	Motorway service area with off road / full / limited access		Minor road dual carriageway	Park and Ride site (operates at least 5 days a week)	
A316	Primary route number		Minor road single carriageway	Airport with scheduled services	
	Dual carriageway		Road under construction	County / Unitary Authority boundary	
	Single carriageway		Road tunnel	Public building	
A4054	'A' road number		Roundabout / Toll	362 ▲ Spot height in metres	
	Dual carriageway		One way street / Level crossing	Woodland	
	Single carriageway		Car ferry with destination	Park	
				Congestion Charging Zone (London only)	

City and town centre plans (pages 120-133)

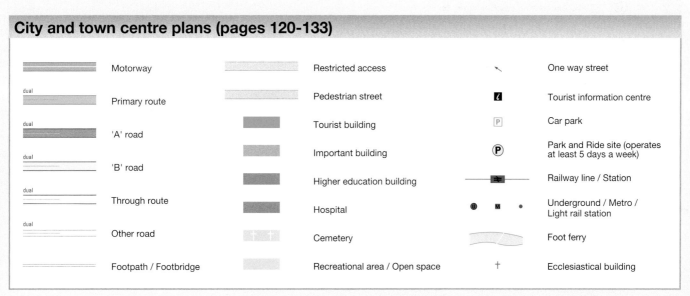

	Motorway		Restricted access	One way street	
dual	Primary route		Pedestrian street	Tourist information centre	
dual	'A' road		Tourist building	Car park	
dual	'B' road		Important building	Park and Ride site (operates at least 5 days a week)	
dual	Through route		Higher education building	Railway line / Station	
dual	Other road		Hospital	Underground / Metro / Light rail station	
	Footpath / Footbridge		Cemetery	Foot ferry	
			Recreational area / Open space	Ecclesiastical building	

ROUTE PLANNING MAP OF GREAT BRITAIN AND IRELAND

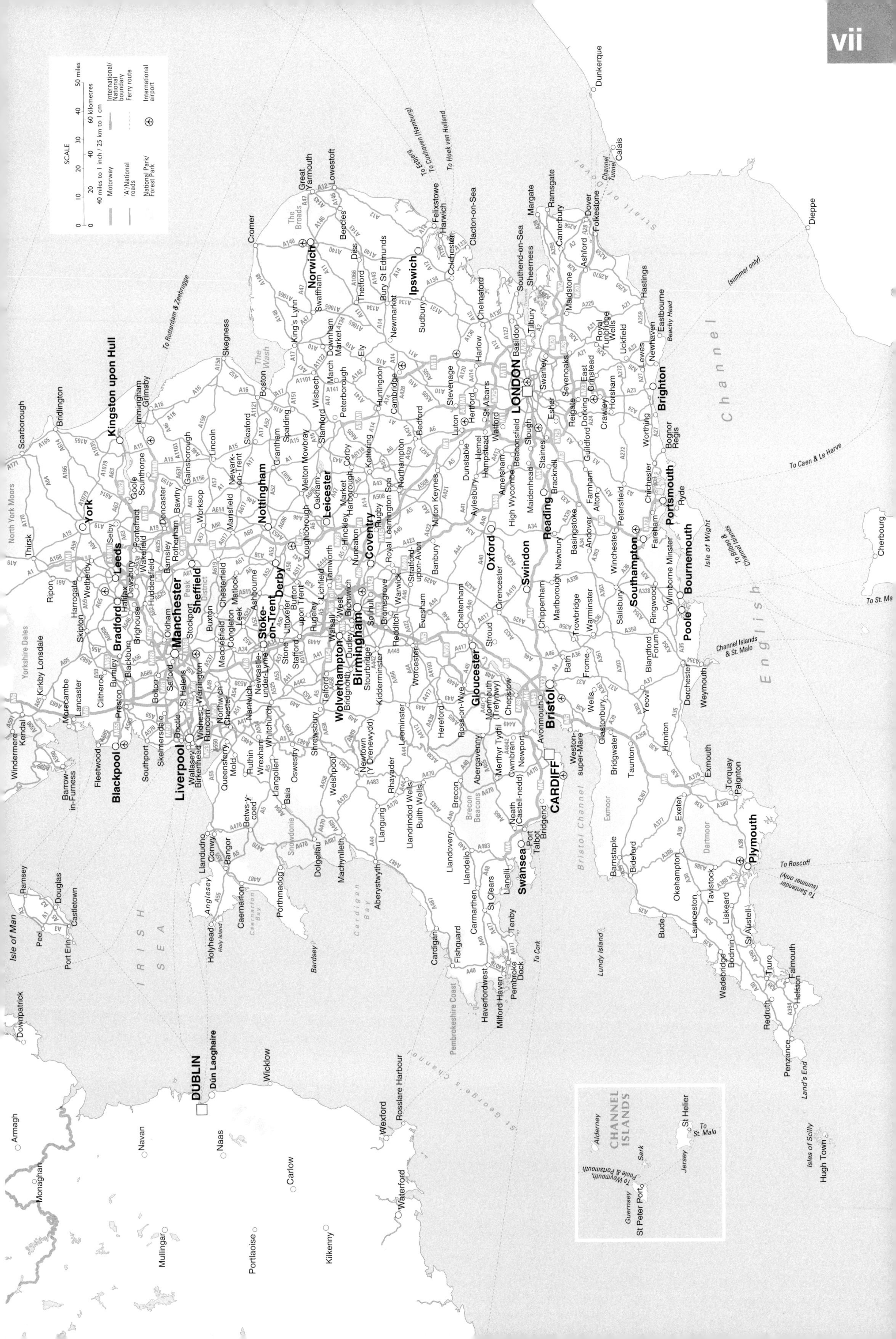
SCALE
0 10 20 30 40 50 miles
0 20 40 60 kilometres
40 miles to 1 inch / 25 km to 1 cm
Motorway
'A'/National roads
National Park/ Forest Park
International/ National boundary
Ferry route
International airport
LONDON
CARDIFF
DUBLIN
Birmingham
Manchester
Liverpool
Leeds
Sheffield
Bristol
Nottingham
Leicester
Coventry
Kingston upon Hull
York
Norwich
Ipswich
Cambridge
Oxford
Reading
Southampton
Portsmouth
Brighton
Bournemouth
Plymouth
Swansea
Gloucester
Wolverhampton
Stoke-on-Trent
Derby
Bradford
Blackpool
Poole
Swindon
IRISH SEA
English Channel
Bristol Channel
St George's Channel
Strait of Dover
Cardigan Bay
Caernarfon Bay
The Wash
The Broads
Isle of Man
Isle of Wight
Isles of Scilly
Lundy Island
Anglesey
Holy Island
Bardsey
North York Moors
Yorkshire Dales
Peak District
Snowdonia
Brecon Beacons
Exmoor
Dartmoor
Pembrokeshire Coast
CHANNEL ISLANDS
Alderney
Guernsey
Sark
Jersey
St Peter Port
St Helier
To St. Malo
To Weymouth, Poole & Portsmouth
Dunkerque
Calais
Dieppe
Cherbourg
To Rotterdam & Zeebrugge
To Esbjerg
To Cuxhaven (Hamburg)
To Hoek van Holland
To Caen & Le Havre
To Roscoff
To Santander (summer only)
To Bilbao & Channel Islands
To Cork
Channel Islands & St. Malo
(summer only)
Channel Tunnel
Beachy Head
Land's End

ISLES OF SCILLY

same scale as main map

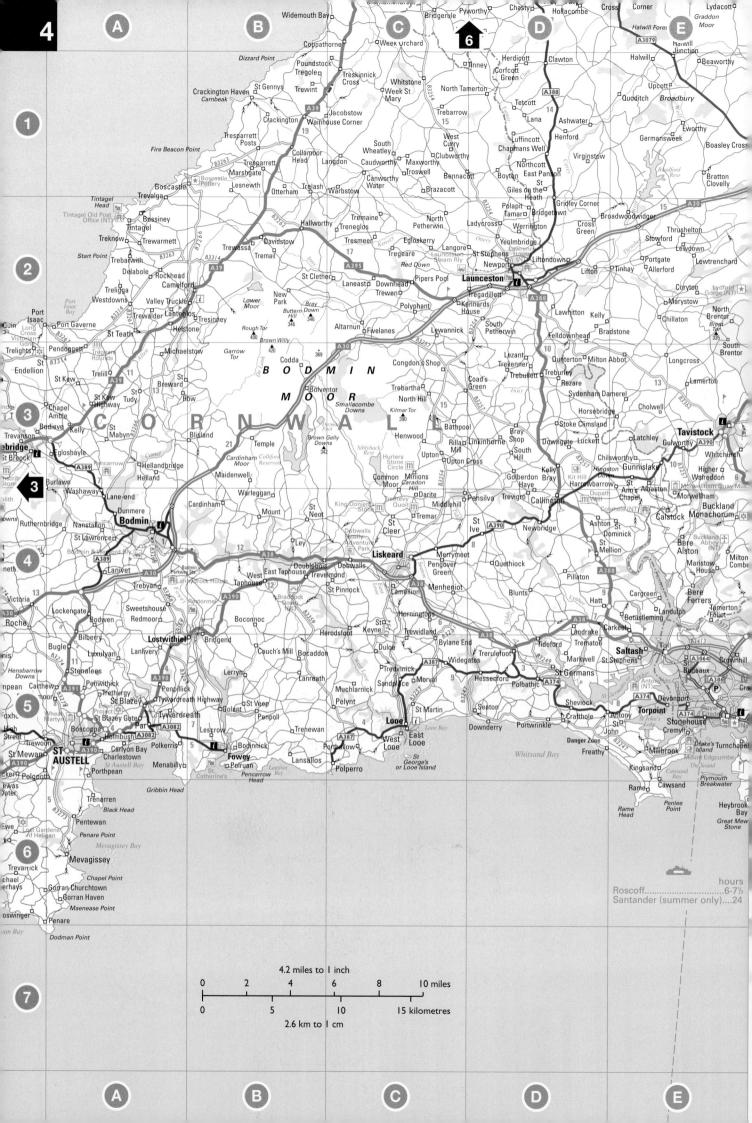

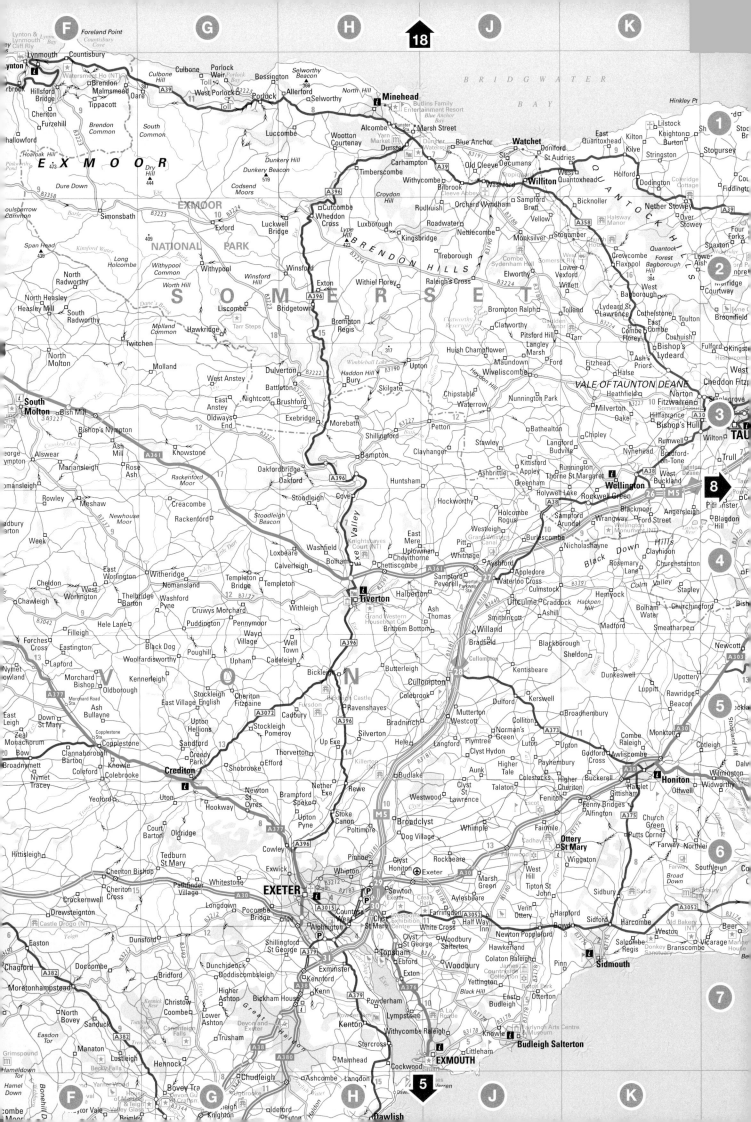

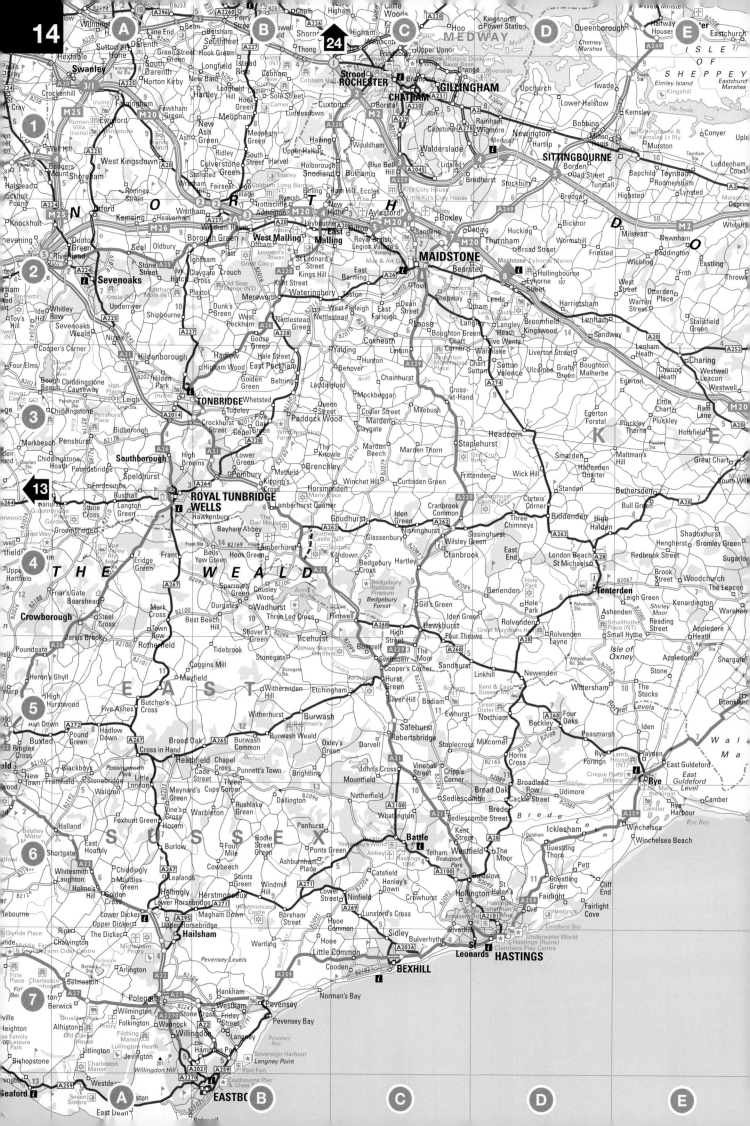

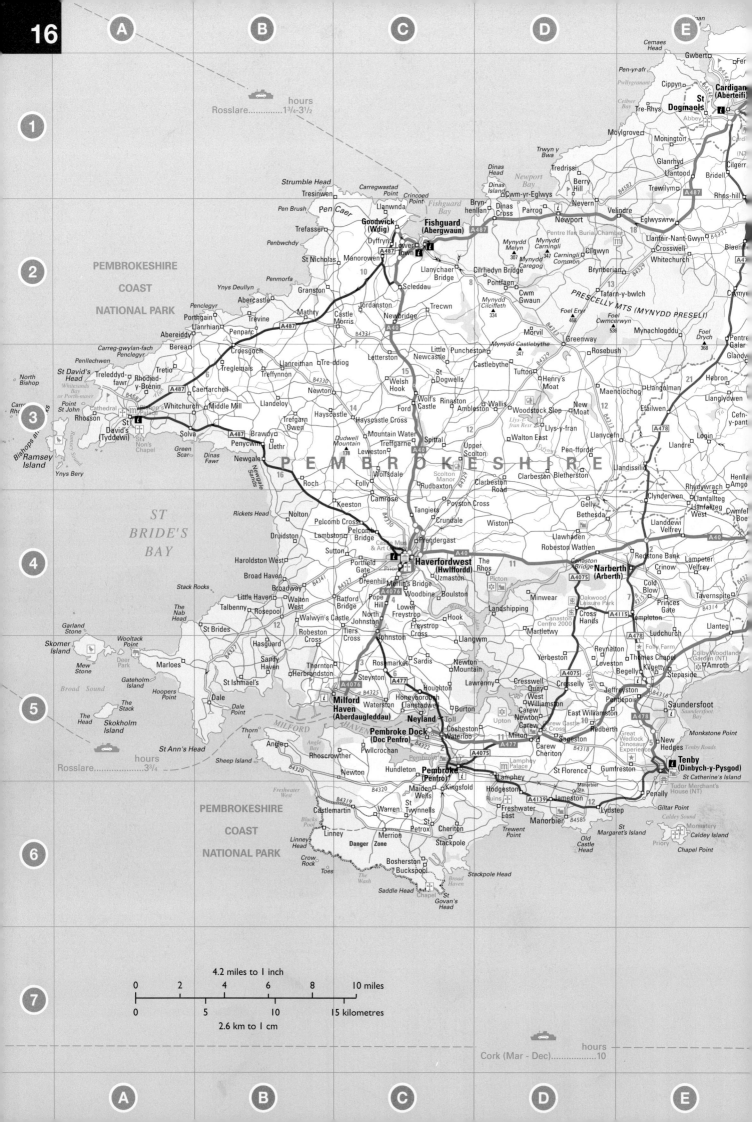

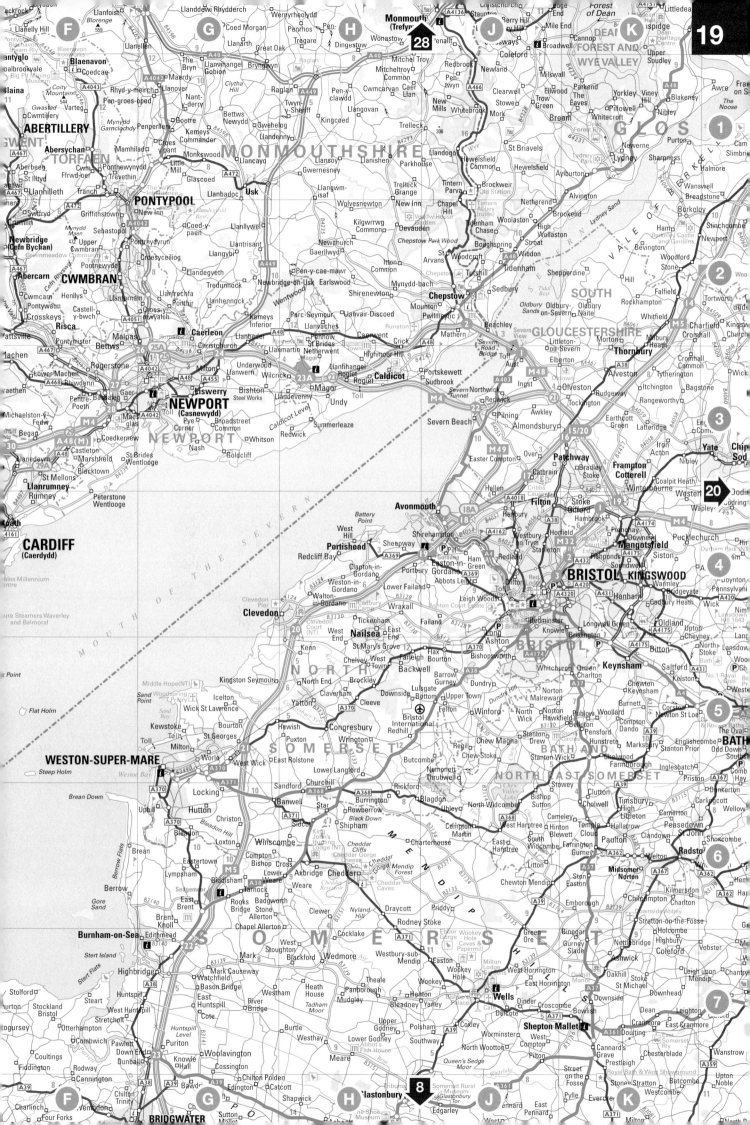

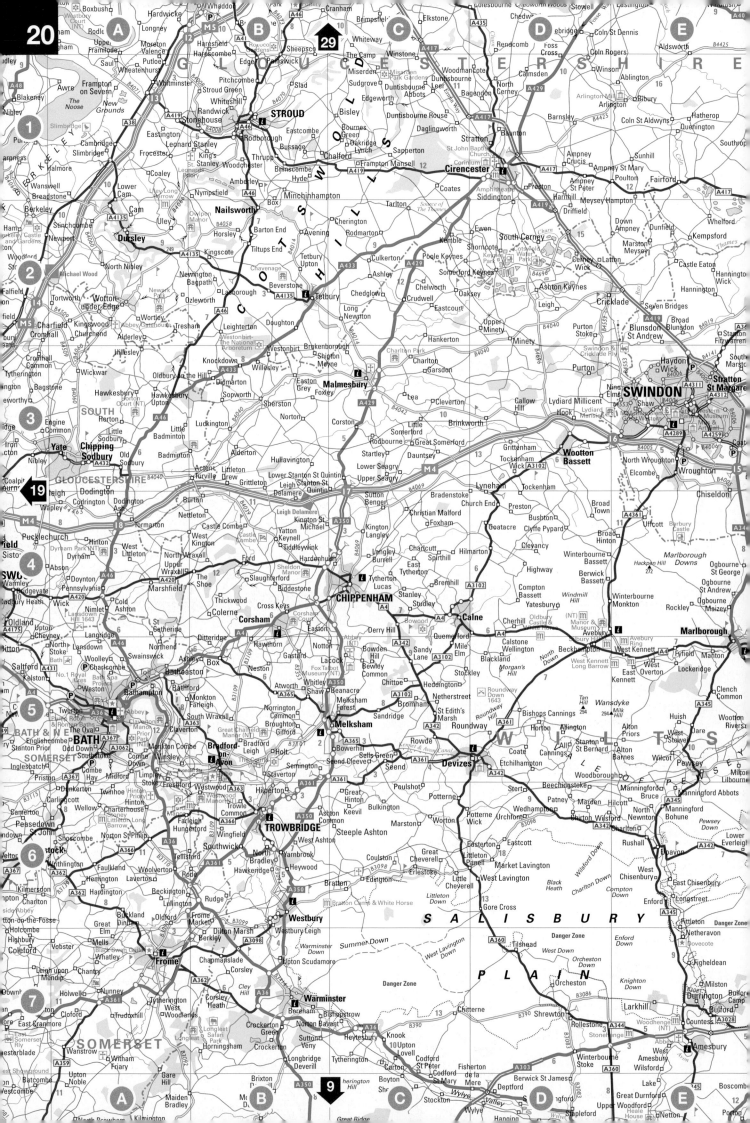

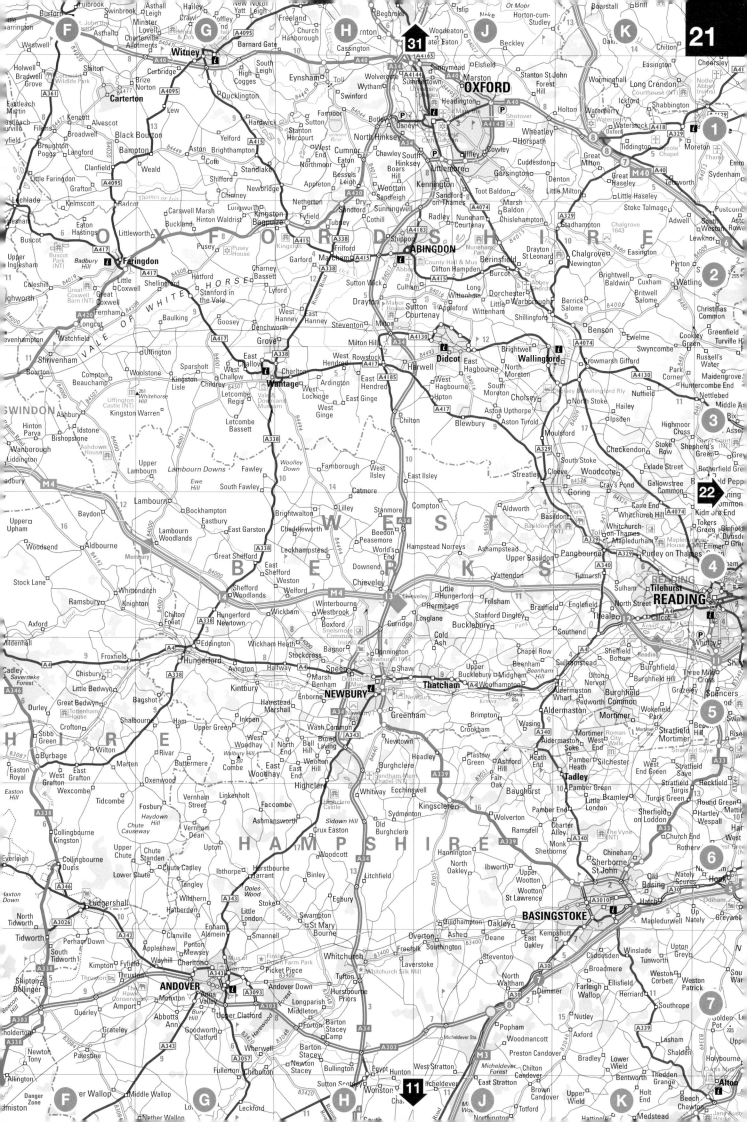

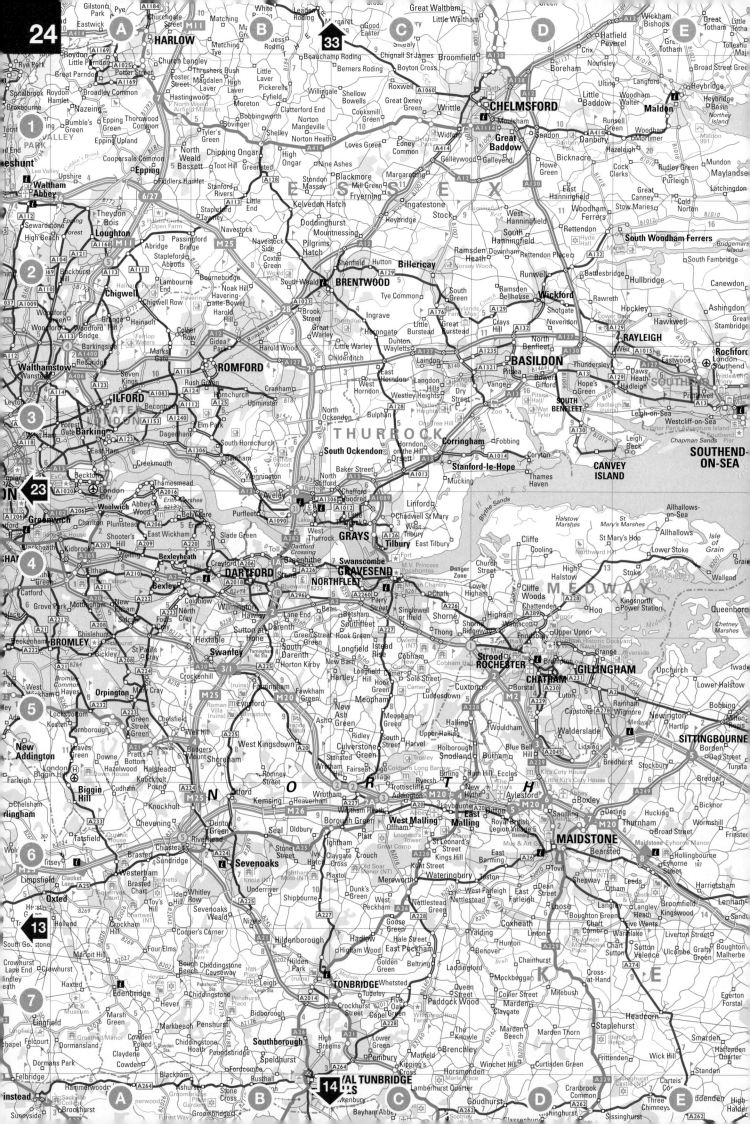

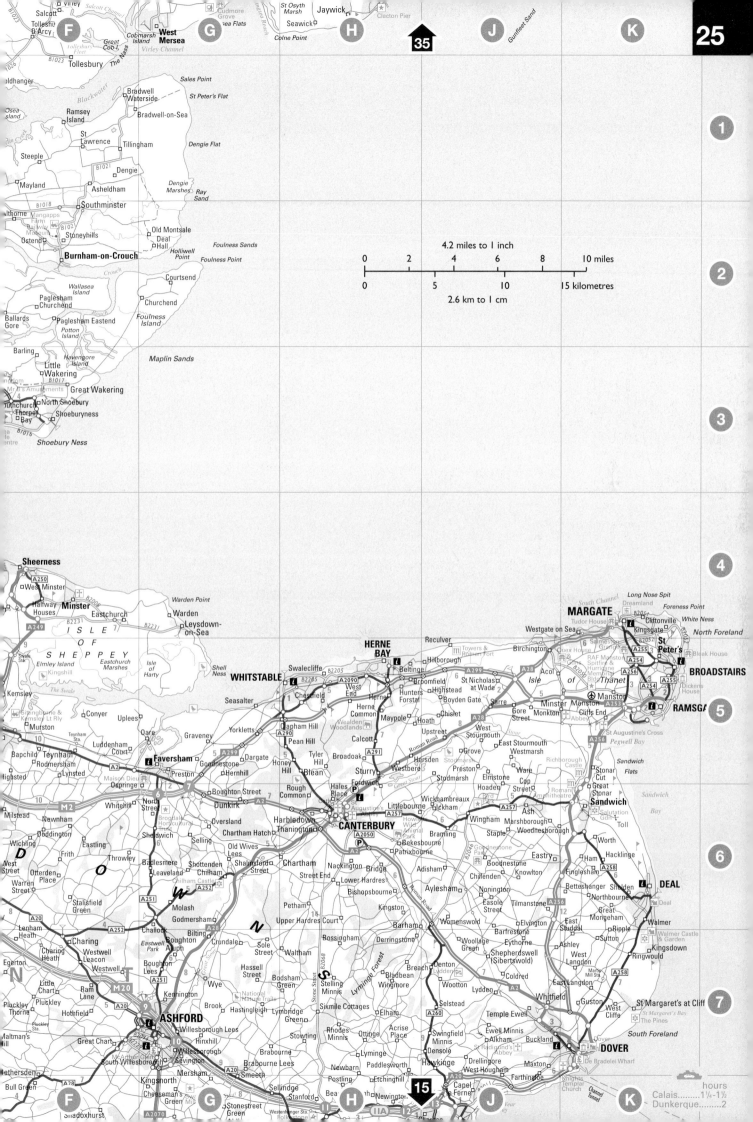

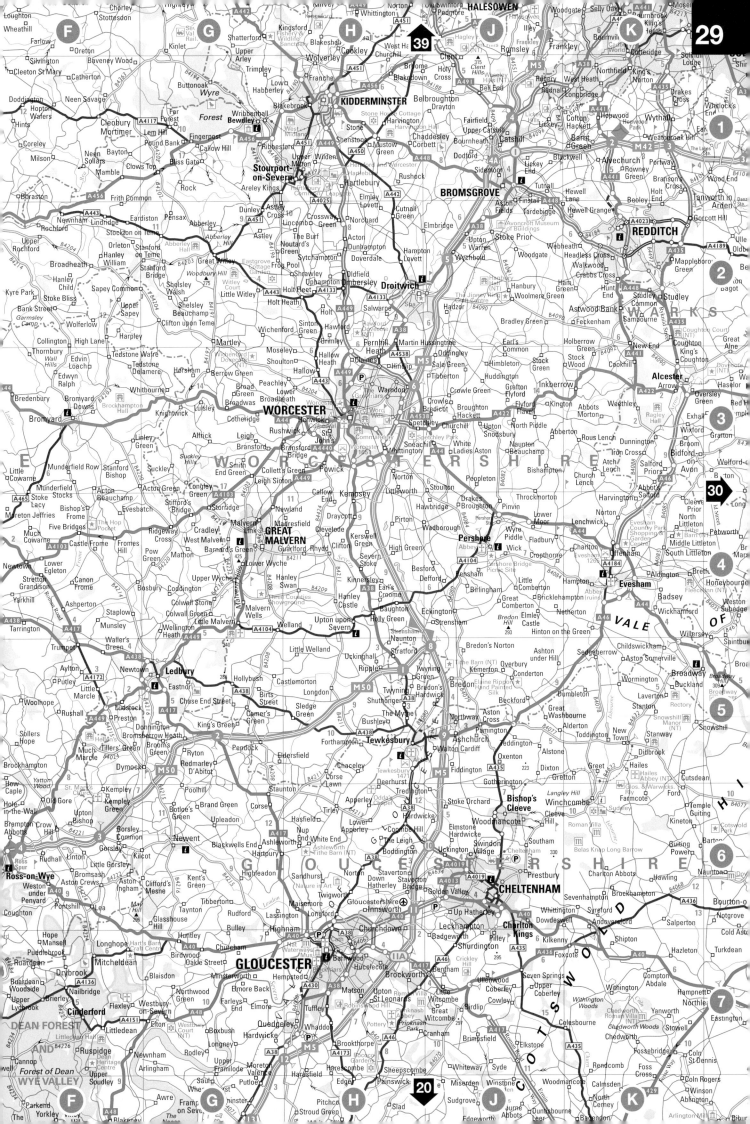

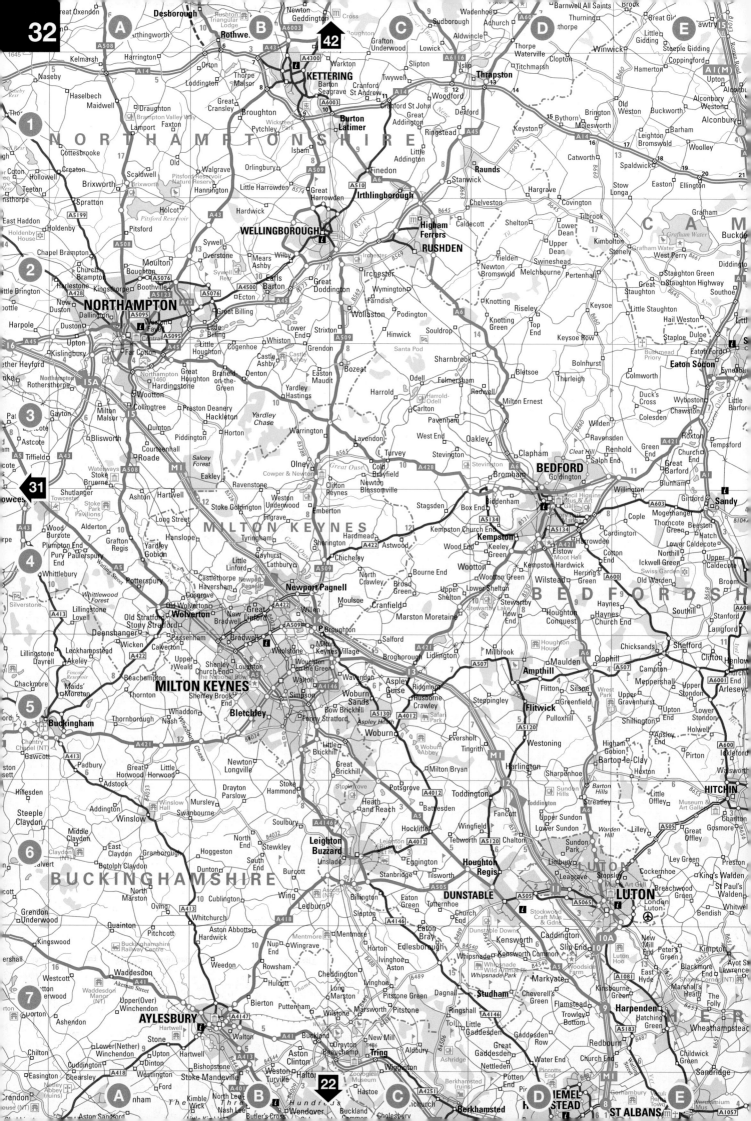

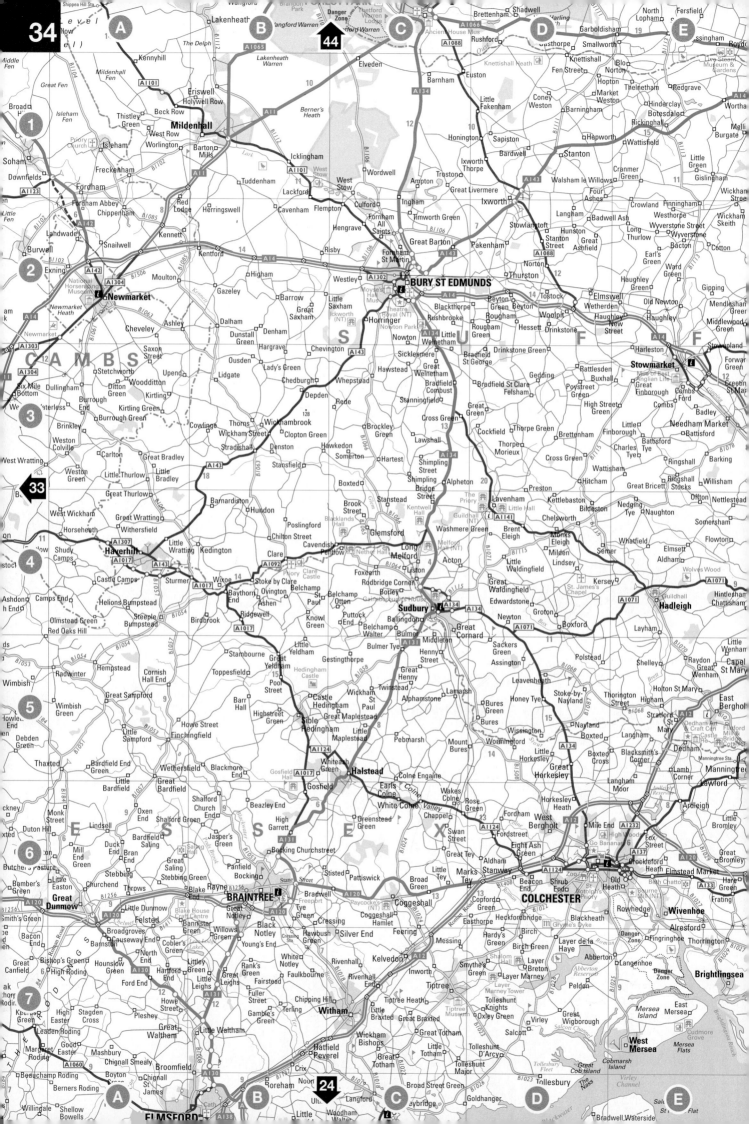

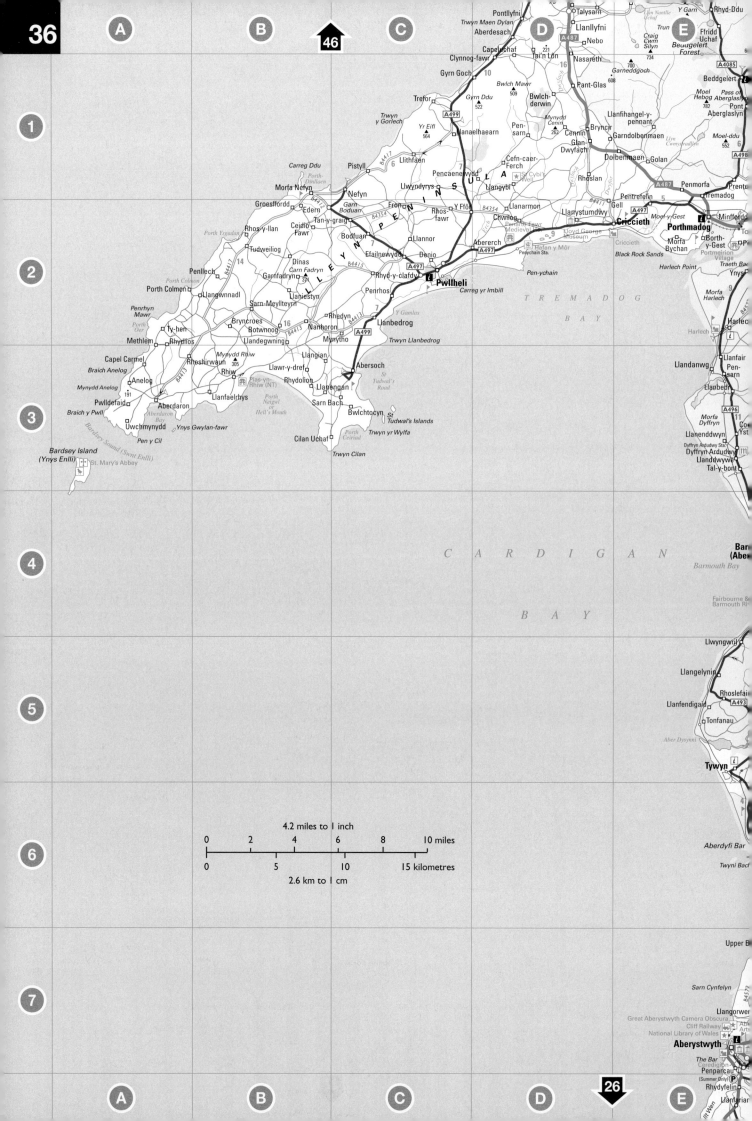

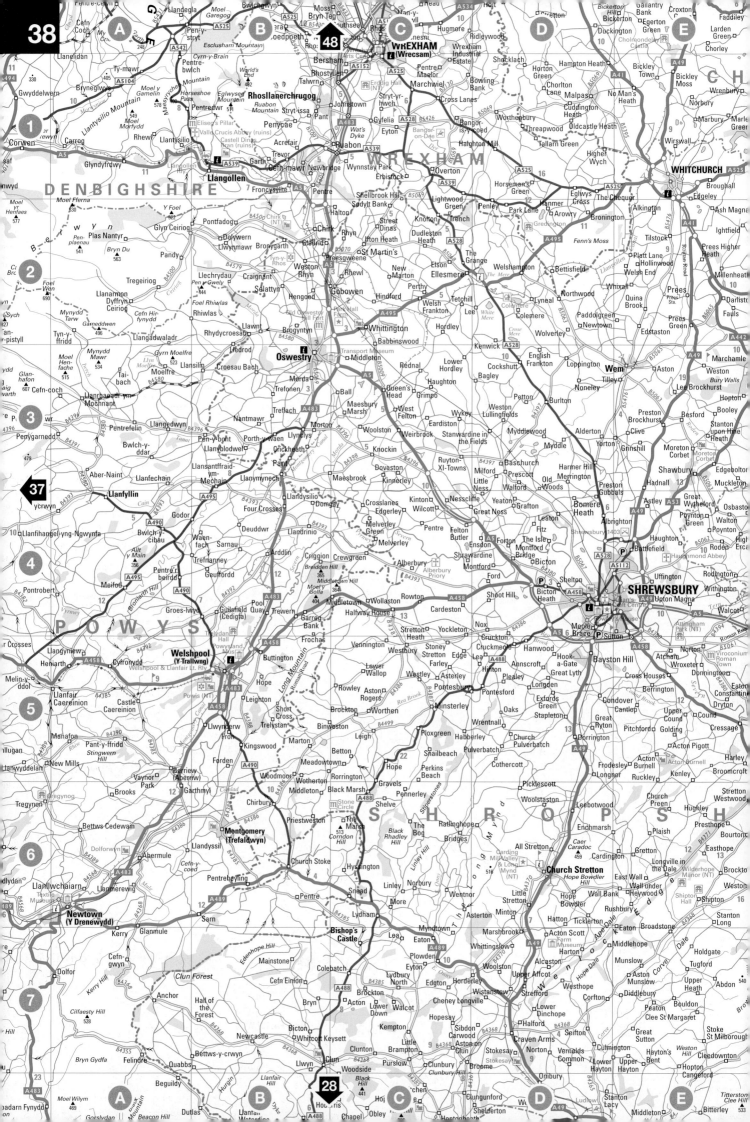

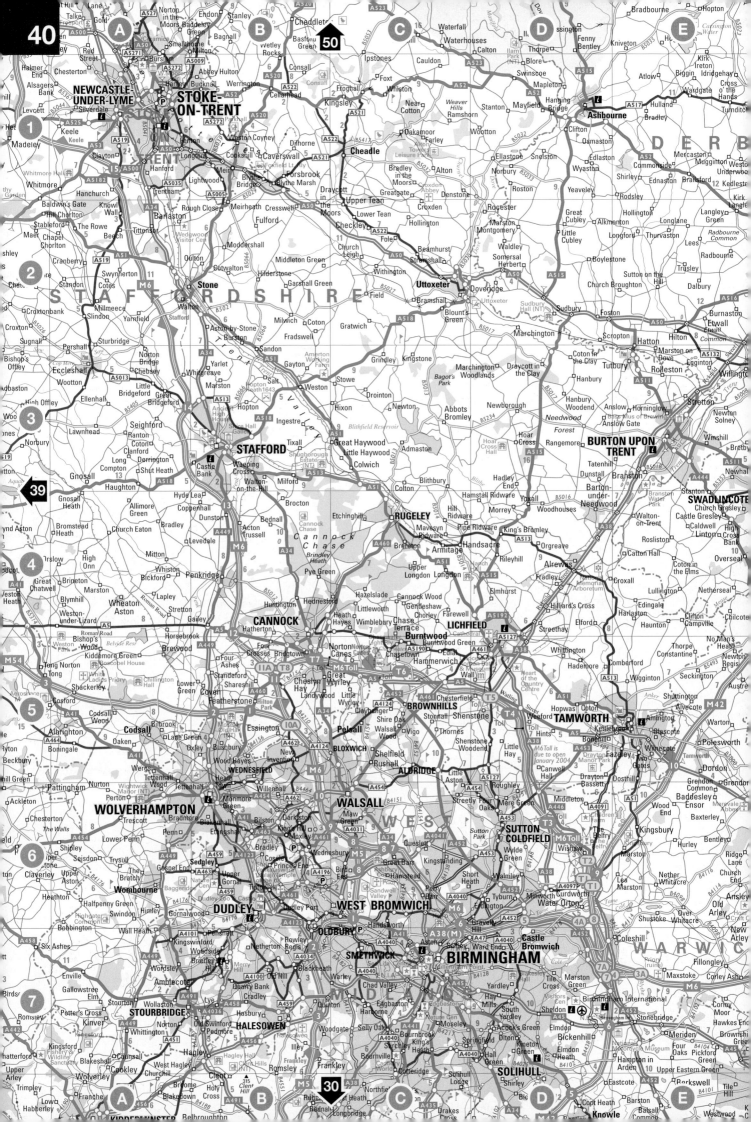

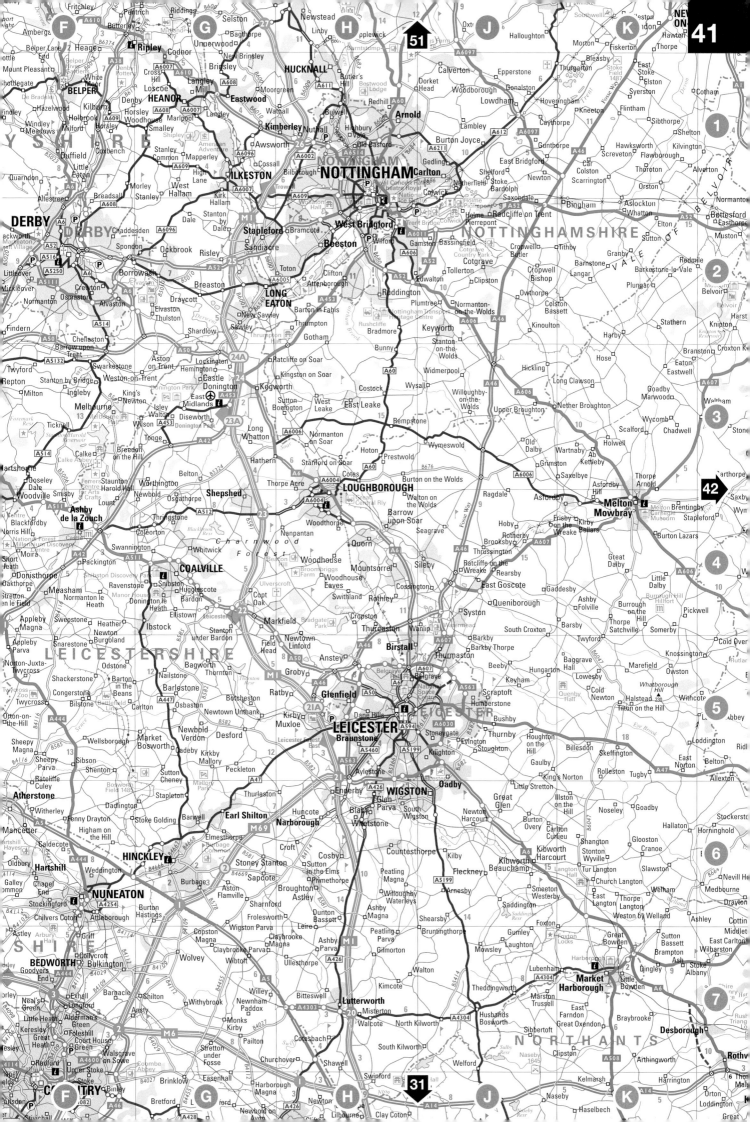

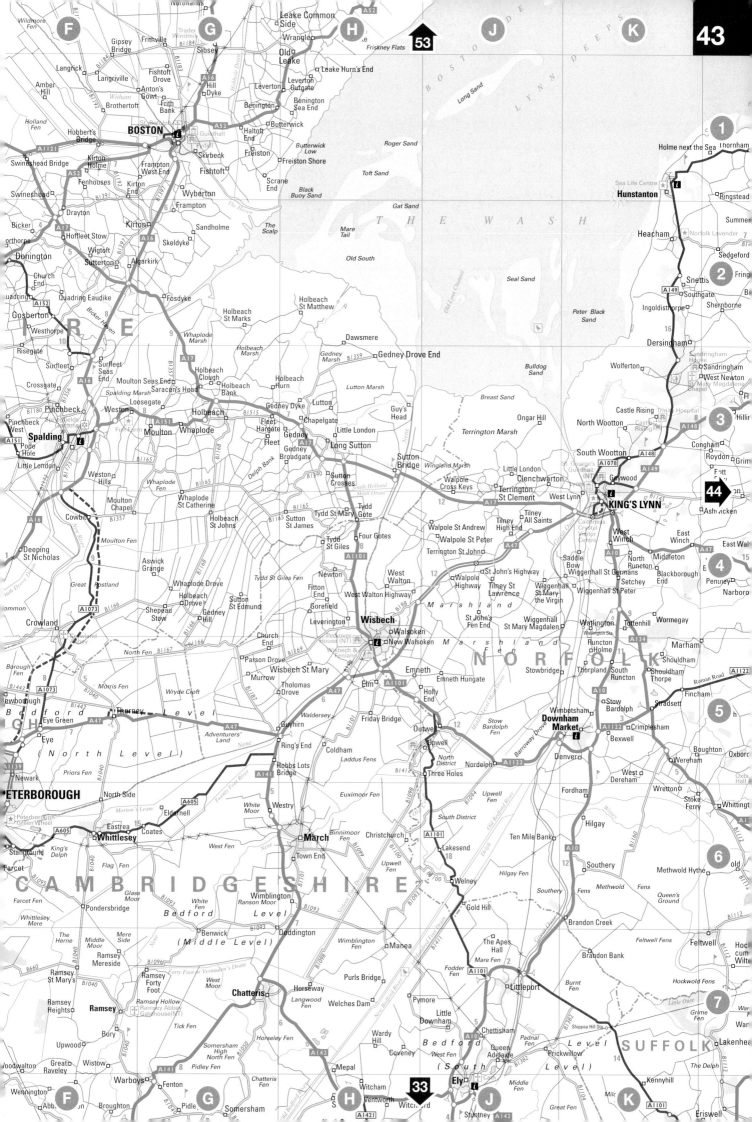

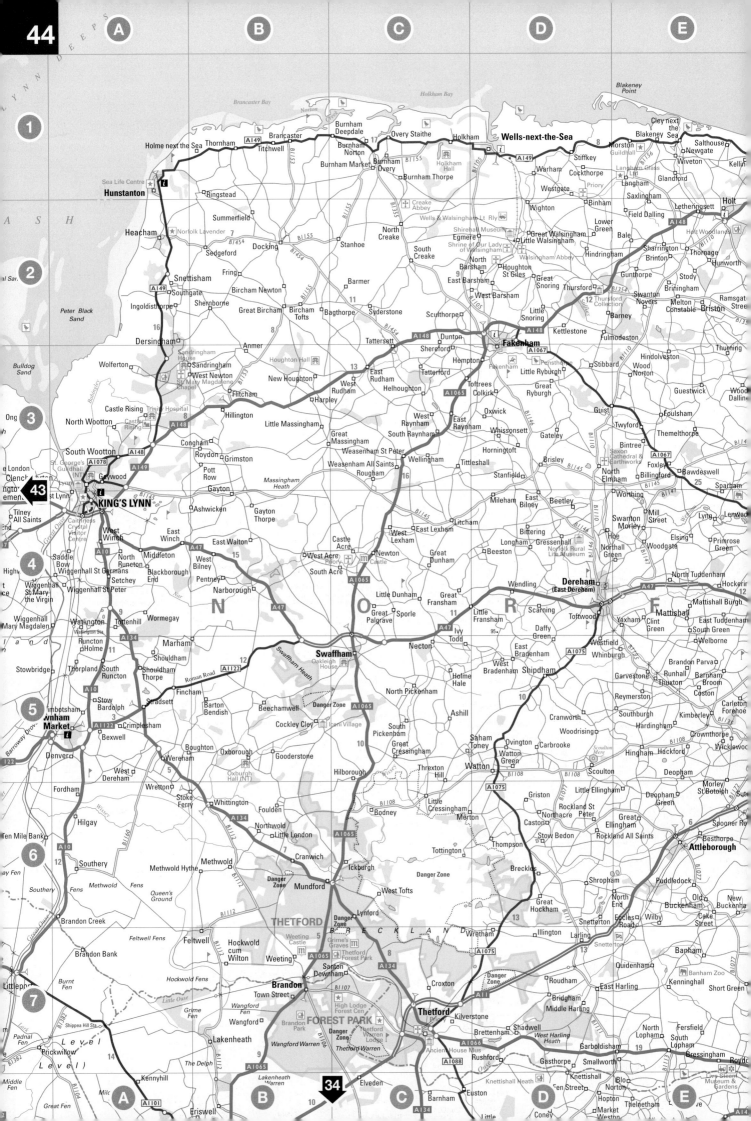

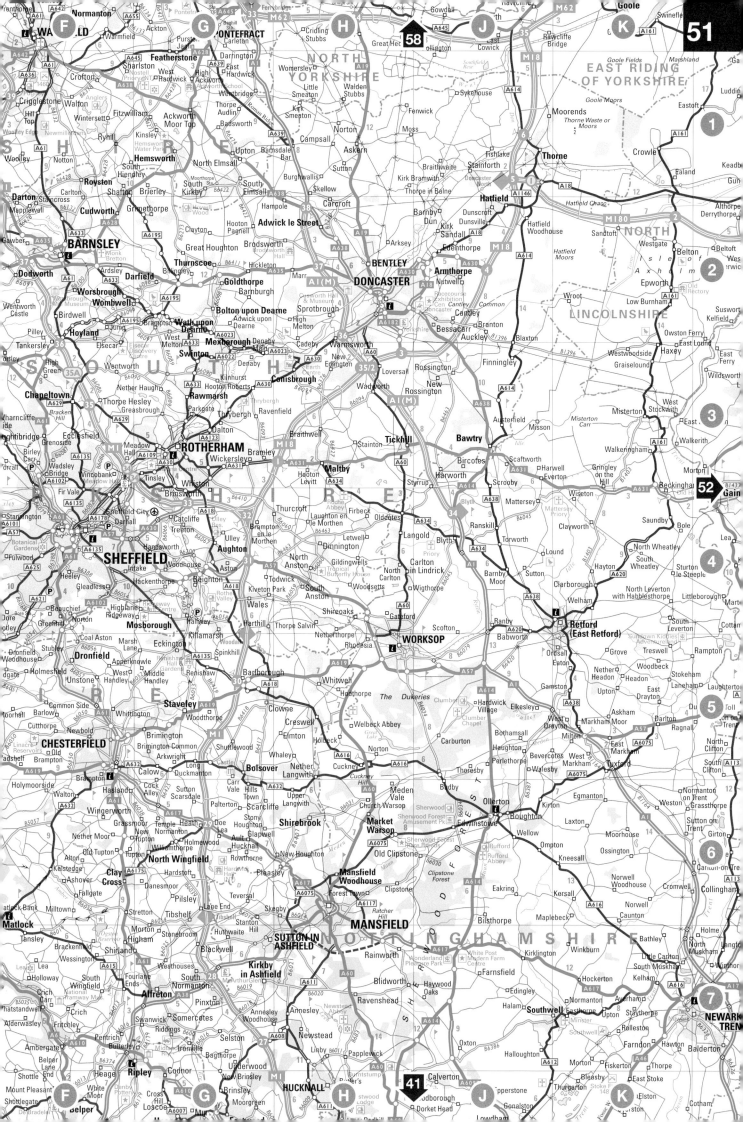

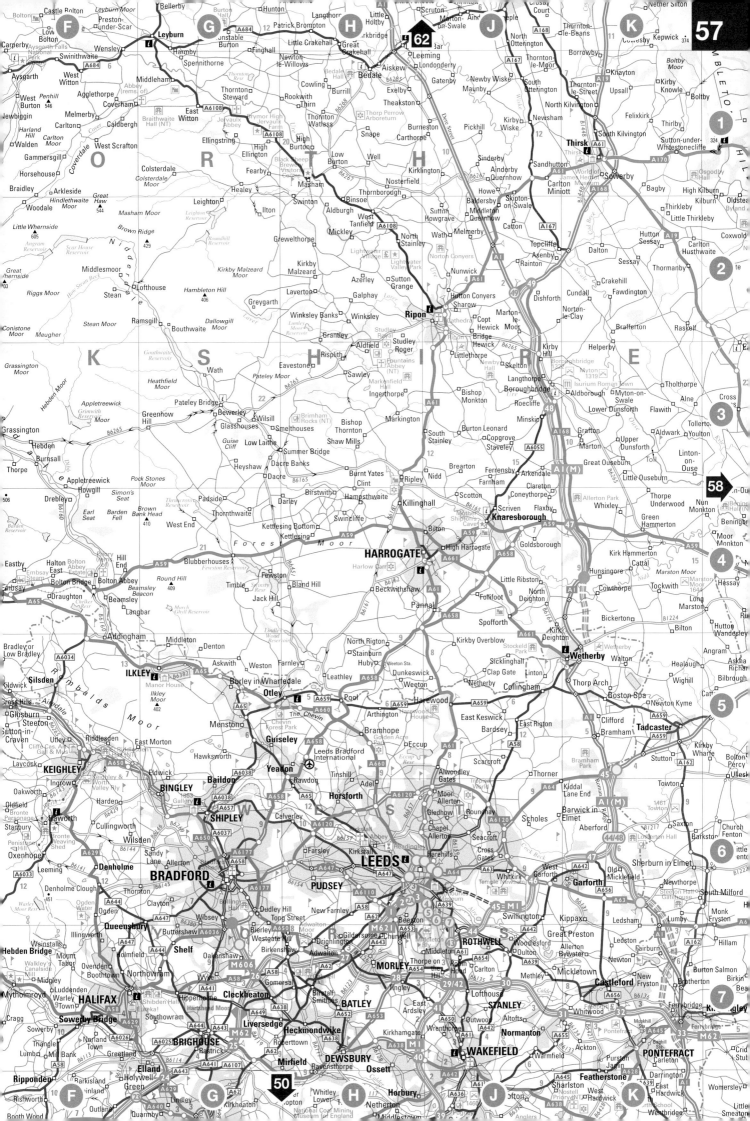

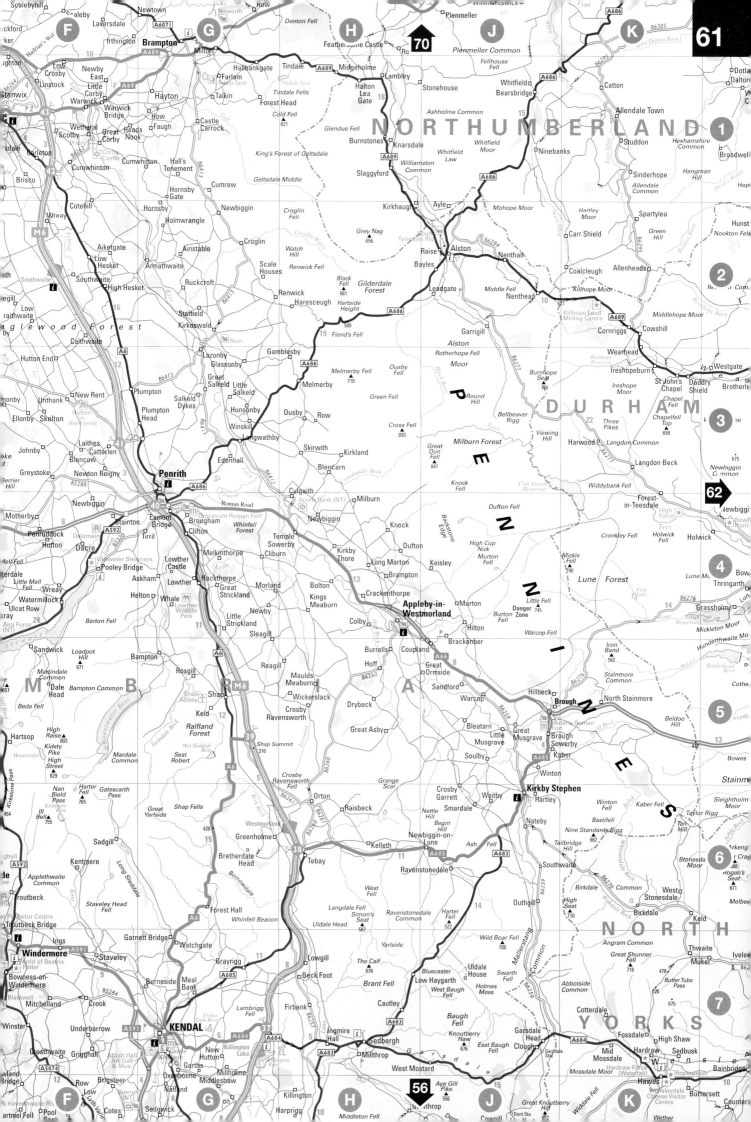

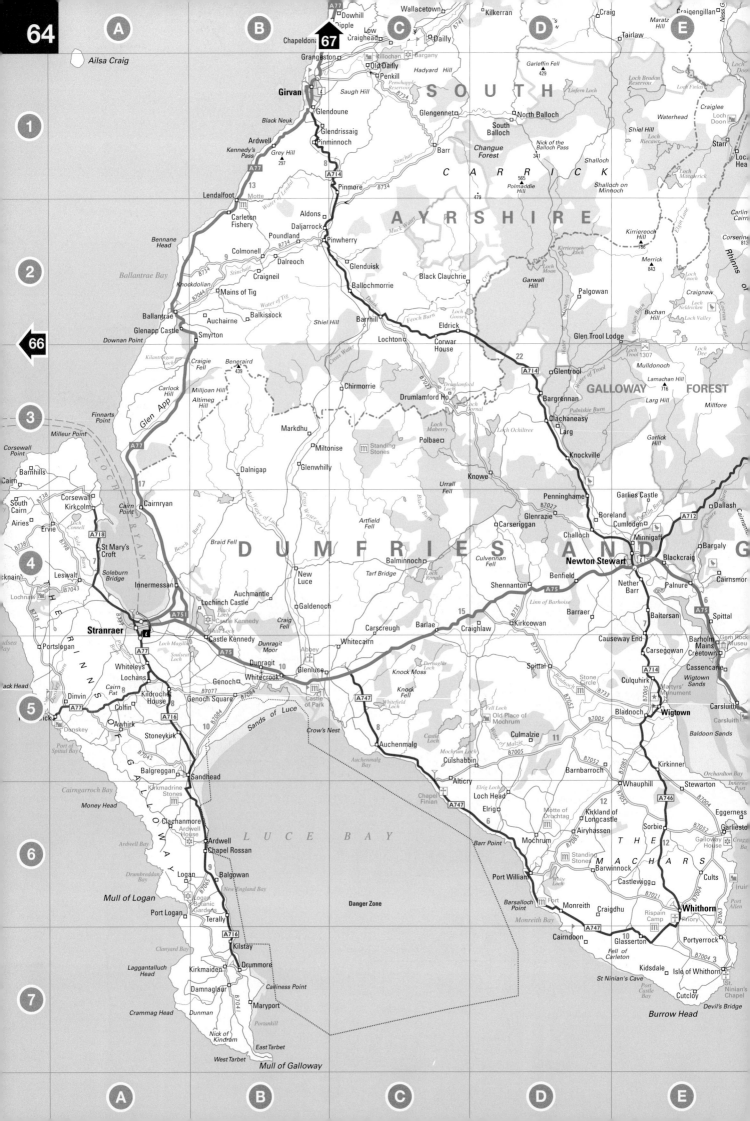

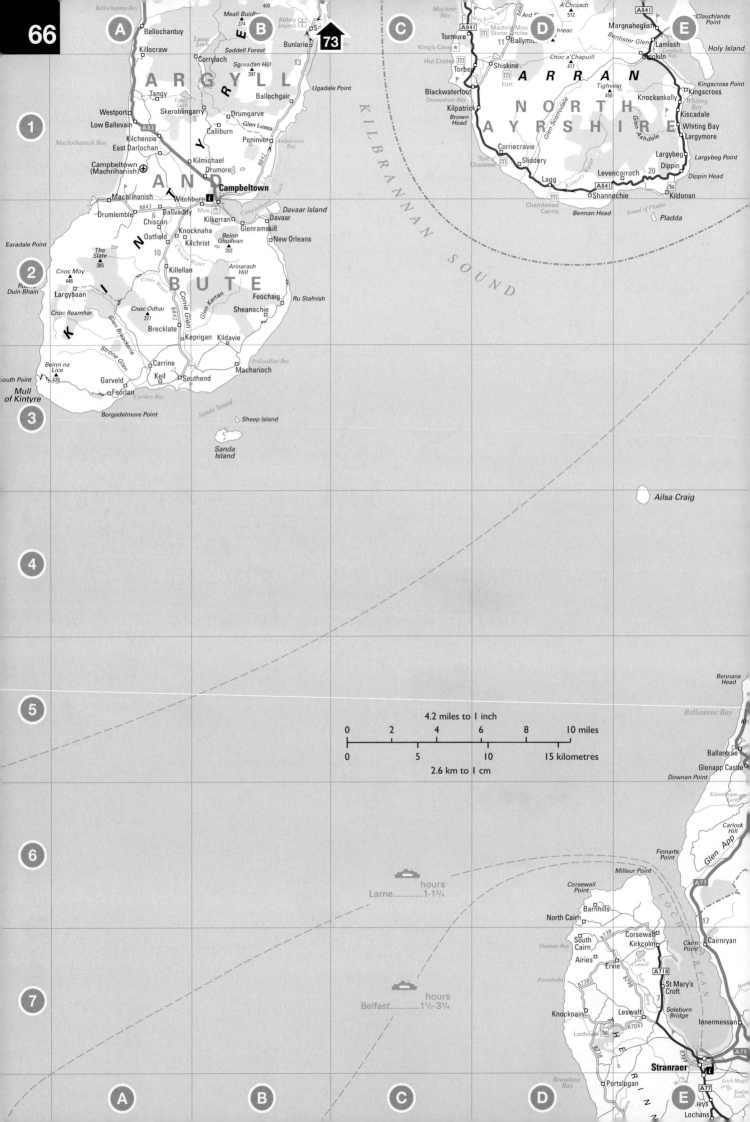

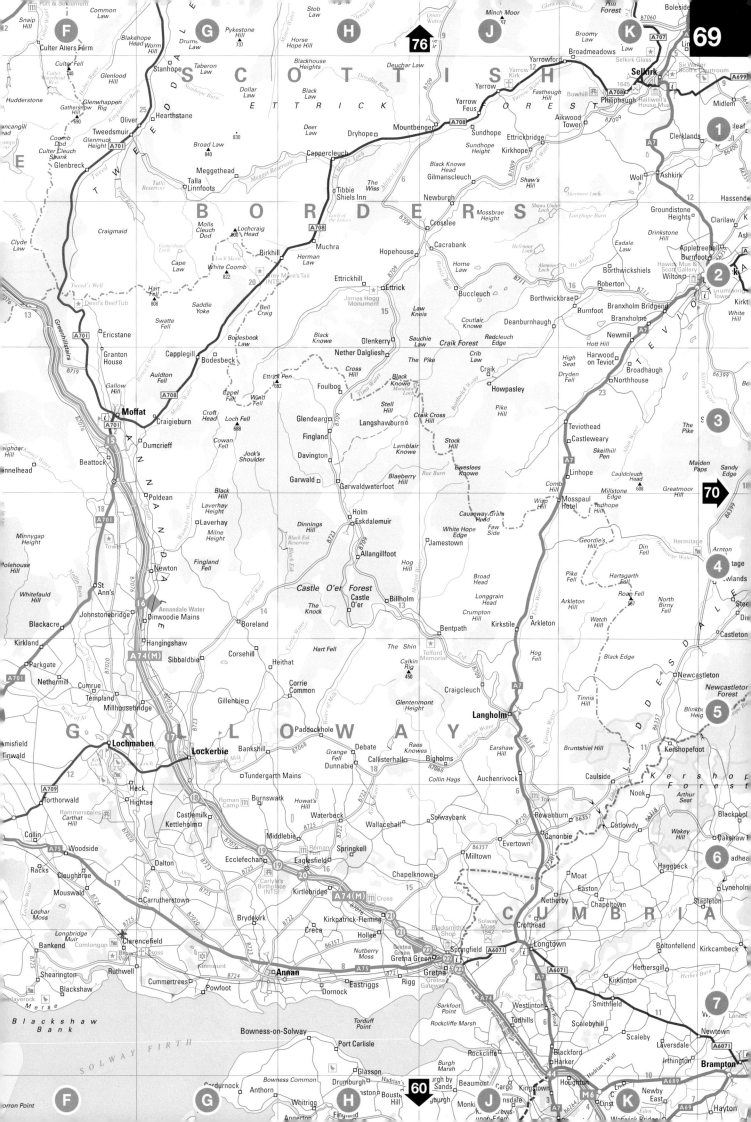

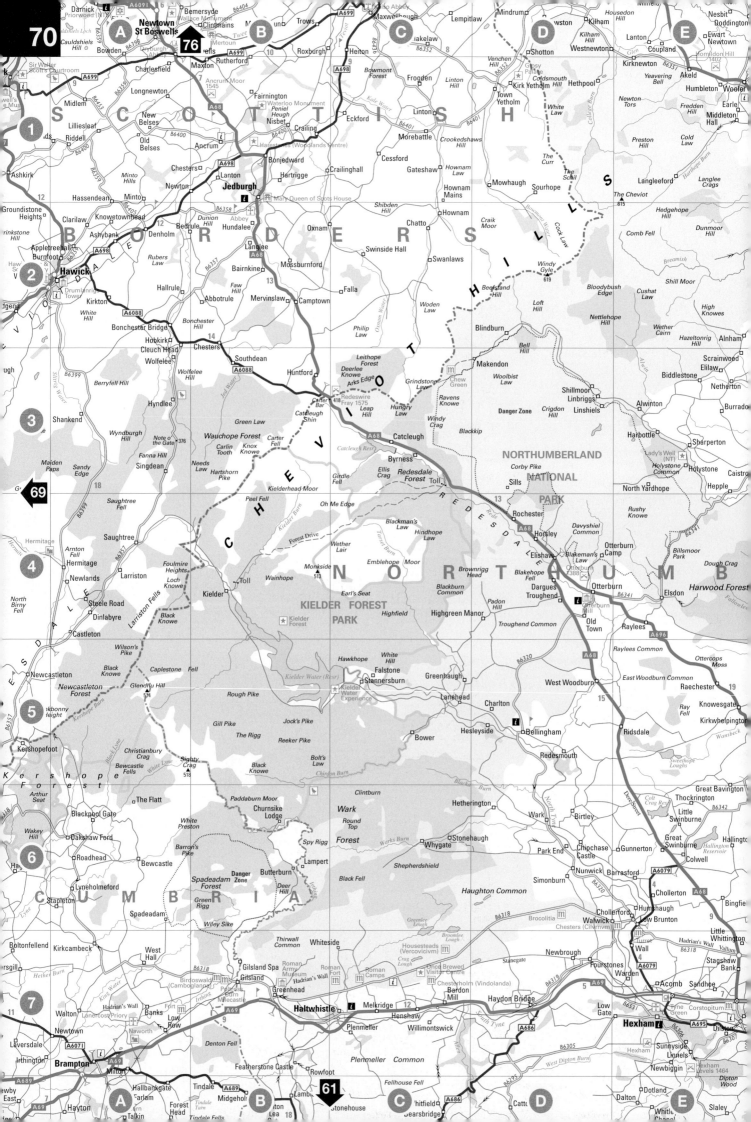

A map page covering the Northumberland and Tyne and Wear coast including:

Grid references (top): F G H J K

Grid references (right side): 1 2 3 4 5 6 7

Major places shown:
Seahouses, Beadnell, Benthall, Embleton, Craster, Howick, Boulmer, Alnwick, Alnmouth, Amble, Warkworth, Widdrington, Cresswell, Lynemouth, Newbiggin-by-the-Sea, ASHINGTON, Morpeth, BLYTH, Bedlington, Cramlington, WHITLEY BAY, Seaton Delaval, TYNEMOUTH, NORTH SHIELDS, SOUTH SHIELDS, Ponteland, Gosforth, Longbenton, Wallsend, Jarrow, NEWCASTLE UPON TYNE, GATESHEAD, FELLING, WHICKHAM, Prudhoe, Newburn, Blaydon, BOLDON, SUNDERLAND

Scale:
4.2 miles to 1 inch
0 — 2 — 4 — 6 — 8 — 10 miles
0 — 5 — 10 — 15 kilometres
2.6 km to 1 cm

Ferry times:
	hours
Bergen	22-26
Göteborg	25
Haugesund	21½
Kristiansand	17
Stavanger	19

	hours
Amsterdam	15

77

62

78

A B C D E

1
2
3
4
5
6
7

COLONSAY

Rubh' a'Geodha
Balnahard Bay
Eilean Dubh
Balnahard
Port Ceann a'Gharraidh
Kiloran Gardens
Kiloran
Loch an Sgoltaire
Colonsay
Oban............2¼ hours
Upper Kilchattan
Lower Kilchattan
Loch Fada
Scalasaig
Machrins
B8086
B8085
Port Mor
Port Lotha
Baleromindubh
Garvard
Balerominmore
Rubha Dubh
Sguide Loinne
Eilean Mhucaig
Priory
Dubh Eilean
Eilean nan Ron
Caolas Mor
Eilean Ghaoideamal
Oronsay
Rubha Ban

same scale as main map

ISLAY

Tormisdale
Lossit
Kelsay
Rubha na Faing
East Ellister
Portnahaven
Port Wemyss
Orsay
Rinns
continued in main map square A5

1¼ hrs (summer only)

Rubh a'Mhail
Rubha Bholsa
Sgarbh Breac 364
Margadale Hill
Na Peileirean
Nave Island
Ardnave Point
Gortantaoid Point
Killinallan Point
Killinallan
Ardnave
Tayovullin
Kinave
Ardnave Loch
Loch Gruinart
Bunnahabhainn
Giur-bheinn 316
Ardnahoe
Loch Staosnaig
Beinn Bhreac 286
Loch Finlaggan
Balulive
Port Askaig
Keills
Feolin Ferry
Sanaigmore
Eilean Mor
Rubha Lamanais
Bratgo
Smaull
Ballinaby
Carnduncan
Leckgruinart
Aoradh
Craigens
Gruinart Flats
Ballygrant
8 A846
Loch Ballygrant
Loch Lossit
Keills
Saligo Bay
Coul Point
Machrie
Aruadh
Grainel
Lyrabus
Foreland
Blackrock
Redhouses
Moin'a'choire
Esknish
Rockside
Kilchoman
Conisby
Islay Ho.
Bridgend
Cachlaidh Mhor
Barr
Beinn Dubh
Machir Bay
Bruichladdich
Gartnatra
Neriby
Cattadale
Cladville
Kilchiaran
Kilchiaran Bay
Port Charlotte
Bowmore
Ronnachmore
Cruach
Cluanach
Sgorr nam Faoileann
Tormisdale
Gearach
Gartbreck
Kilennan
Beinn na Caillich
Glas Bheinn 471
McArthur's Head
2 hrs
Beinn Tart a'Mhill 232
Carn
Laggan
Laggan
Beinn Bhan 471
Beinn Bheigeir 491
Proaig
Rubha Liath
Nerabus
A847
Easter Ellister
13
B8016
11
A846
Beinn Uraraidh 454
Loch Uraraidh
Ardtalla
Claggain Bay
Rinns Point
Islay
Glenegedele
Machrie
Kintra
Leorin
Sgorr Bhogachain
Kintour
Ardmore Point
Ardmore
Kildalton Church & Crosses
Rubha Mor
Leorin Lochs
Beinn Sholum 347
Lagavulin
Ardbeg
Rubha na Gainmhich
2¼ hrs
Cornabus
Carnmore
Port Ellen
Laphroaig
Eilean a'Chuirn
Eilean Bhride
Maol Buidhe 165
THE OA
Risabus
The Ard
Caolas an Eilein
Texa
Lower Killeyan
Inerval
Loch Kinnabus
Port Chubaird
Mull Of Oa
Rubha nan Leacan

JURA

Beinn nan Capull
Glengarrisdale Bay
Cruach nan Seilcheig
Glengarrisdale
Bagh Gleann Speireig
Glendebadel Bay
Ben Garrisdale 365
Cruach Iannastail
Lealt
Corpach Bay
Beinn Bhreac 467
Dubh Bheinn
Tramaig Bay
Ardlussa
Inverlussa
Lussa Point
Eilean an Rubha
Lussagiven
A846
Beinn Sgaillinish
Shian Bay
Rainberg Mor 453
Cruach Sganadail
Tarbert
Tarbert Bay
Creag Nam Fiadh Mor
Keillmore
Loch Tarbert
Rubh' a'Chrois-aoinidh
Sgeir Mhor a'Bhrein-phuirt
Rubh' an t-Sailein
Loch Tarbert
Danna Island
Glenbatrick
Lagg
Rubh' a'Chamais
Scrinadle
Beinn Bhreac 439
Gate House
A846
Eilean Mor
Corr Eilean
Jura Forest
Beinn an Oir 785
Beinn Shiantaidh 755
Beinn Tarsuinn
Achamore
Eilean Mor Chapel
Kilmo
Beinn a'Chaolais 734
Paps of Jura
Loch an t-Siob
Loch a'Chnuic Bhric
Corran
Ardmenish
An Dunan
Rubh' an Leim
24
Point of Kna
Gleann Asdale
Glas Bheinn 561
Loch na Mile
Knockrome
Leargybreck
Rubh' an Leanachais
Feolin
Keils
Lowlandman's Bay
Eilean Bhride
Dubh Bheinn
Small Isles
Craighouse
Eilean nan Gabhar
Brat Bheinn 342
Rubha na Caillich
A846
Crackaig
Cabrach
Ardfin
Sannaig
Na Cuiltean
Kilberry Hea
Jura Ho.
Am Fraoch Eilean
Rubha na Traille
Brosdale Island

Port Mor
West Tarbert Bay
East Tarbert Bay
Tarbert
Creag Bhan 100
Druimyeon Bay
GIGHA ISLAND
Ardaily
Rhunahaorin Point
Ardminish Bay
Ardminish
Achamore Gardens
½ hr
Craro Island
Grob Bagh
Cara Island
Mull of Cara
Tayinloan
Killean
Muasdale
Glenacardoch Point
33
Belloch
Glenbarr
Bellochantuy Bay
Bellochantuy
Killocraw
Tangy

Str. of Corryvreckan
Sca
3

SOUND OF ISLAY
SOUND OF JURA

A R G Y L L

ISLAY

RINNS OF ISLAY

LOCH INDAAL

4.2 miles to 1 inch
0 2 4 6 8 10 miles
0 5 10 15 kilometres
2.6 km to 1 cm

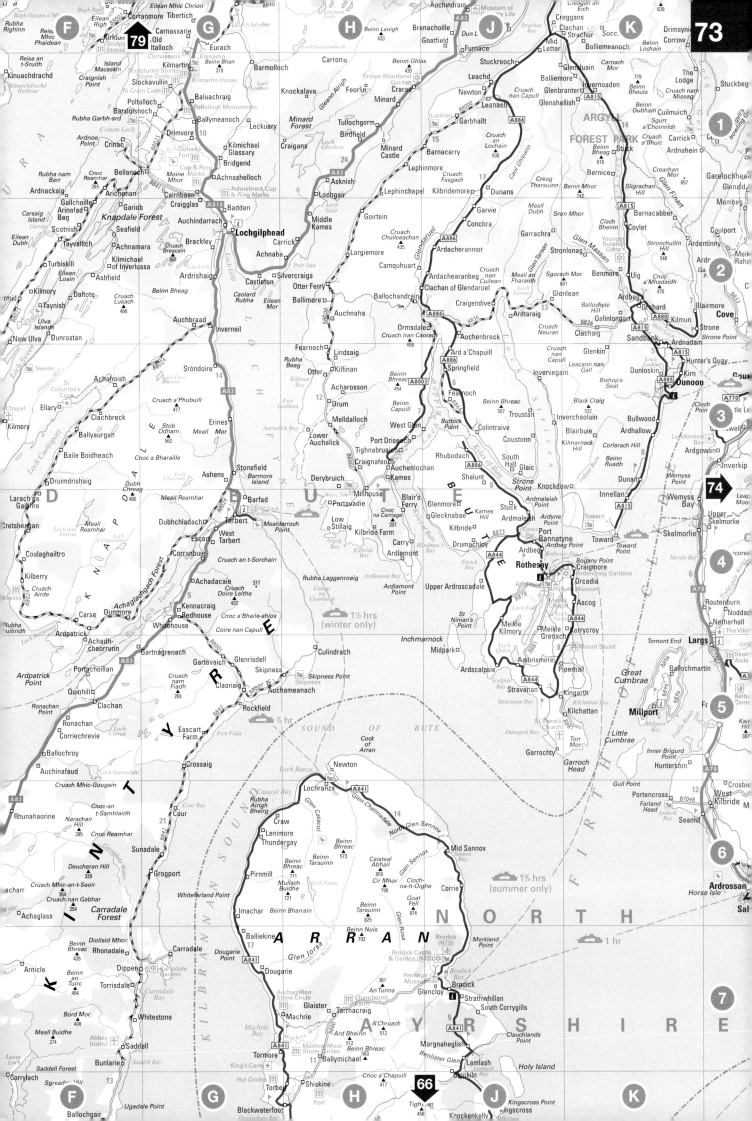

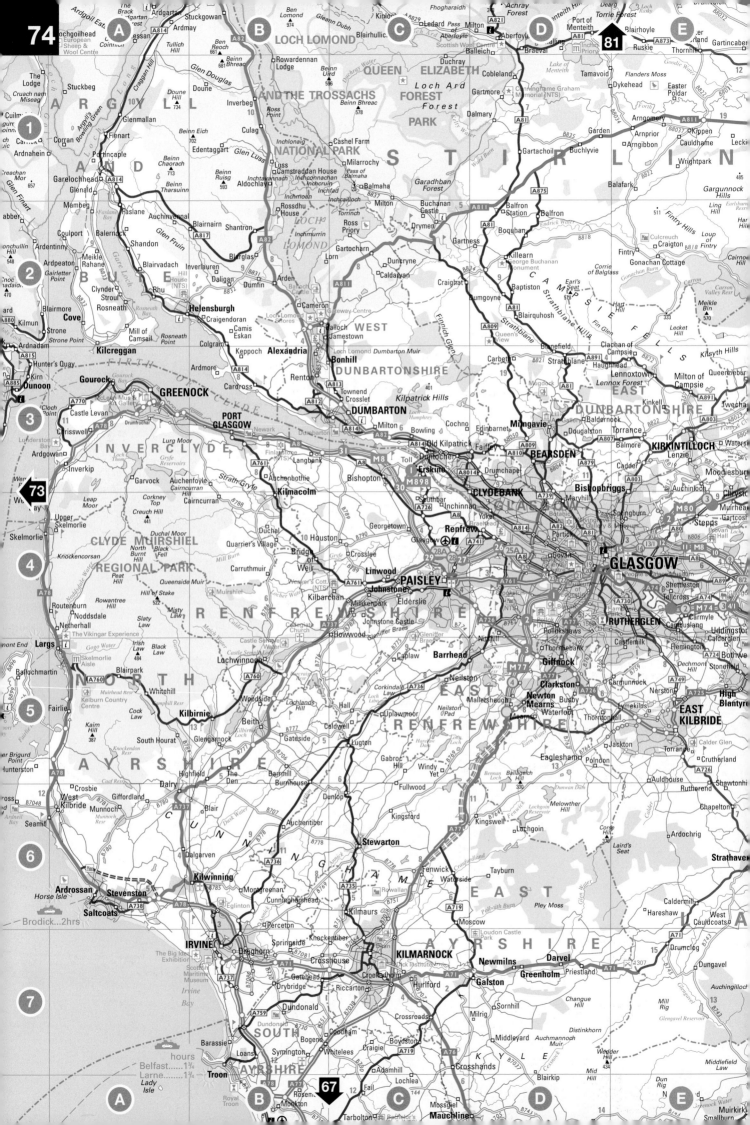

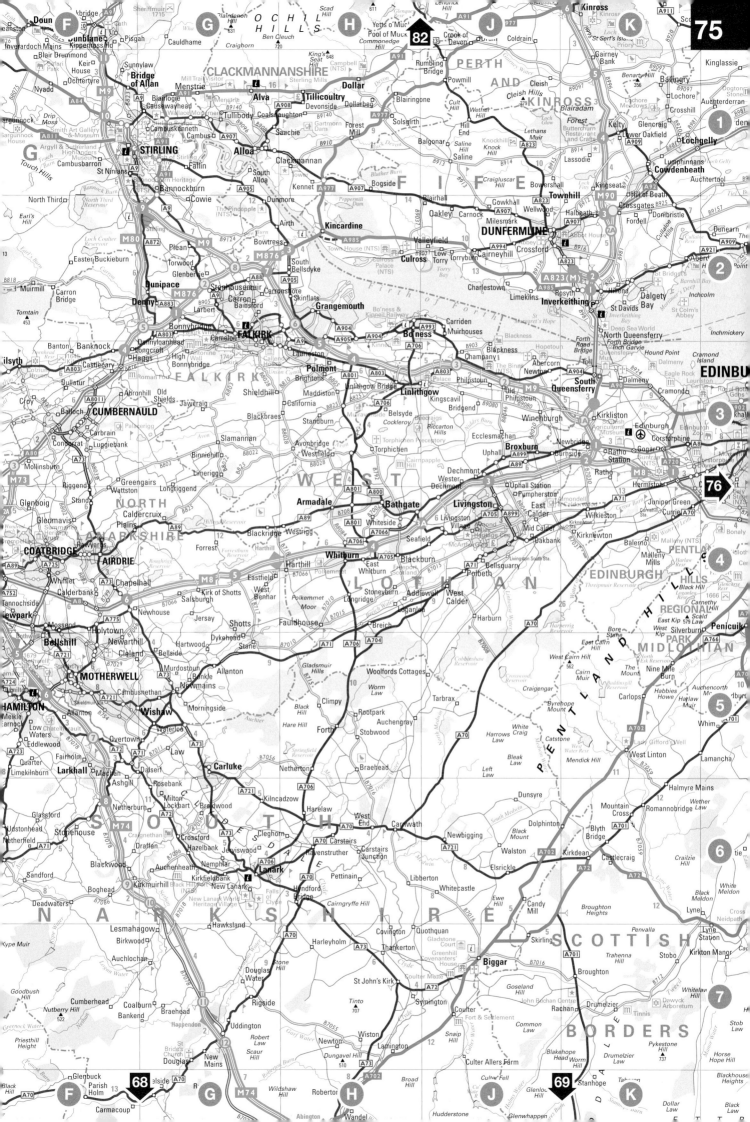

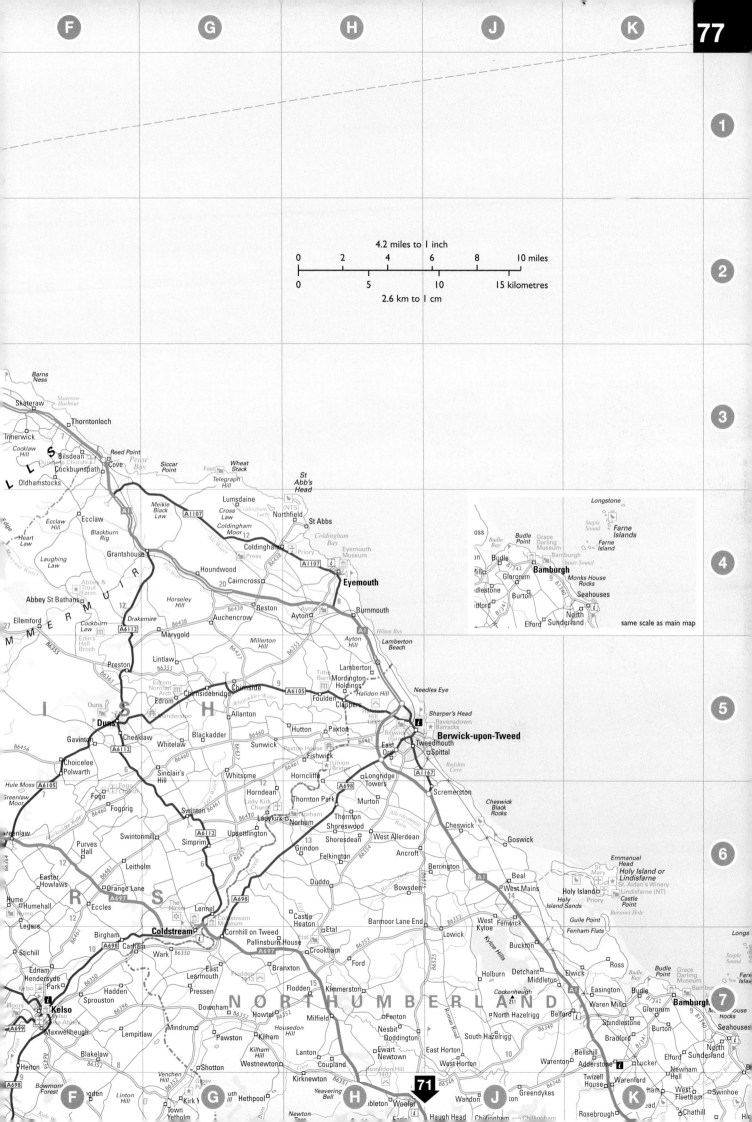

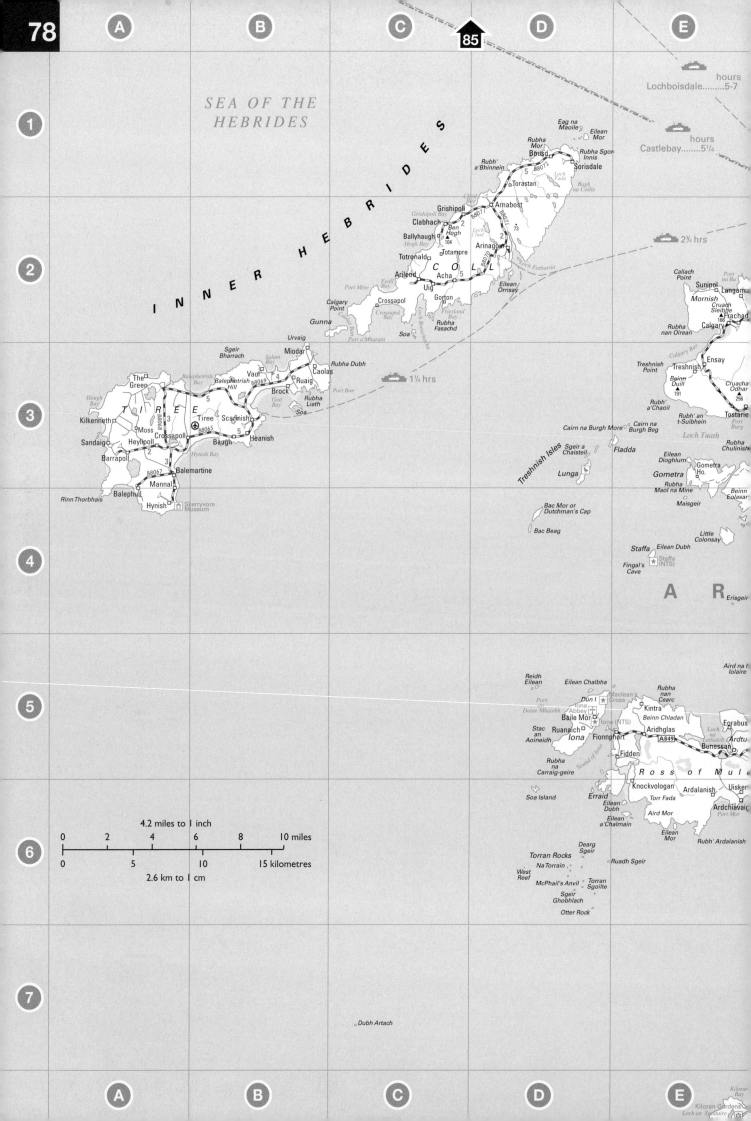

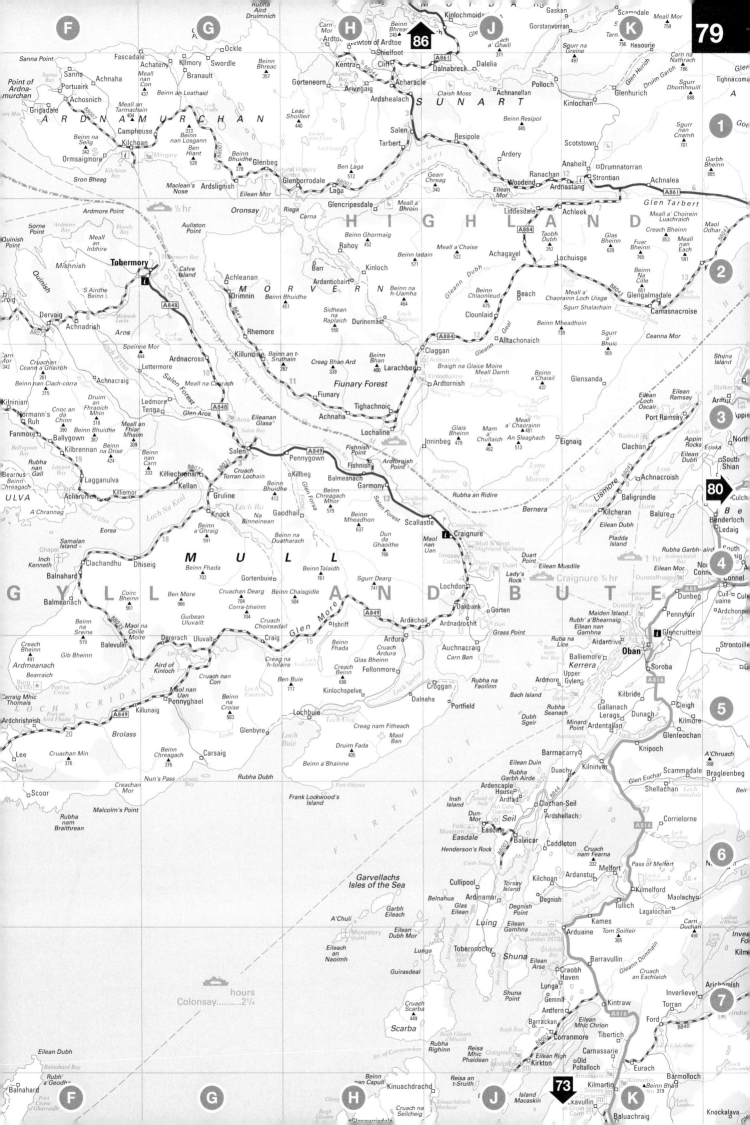

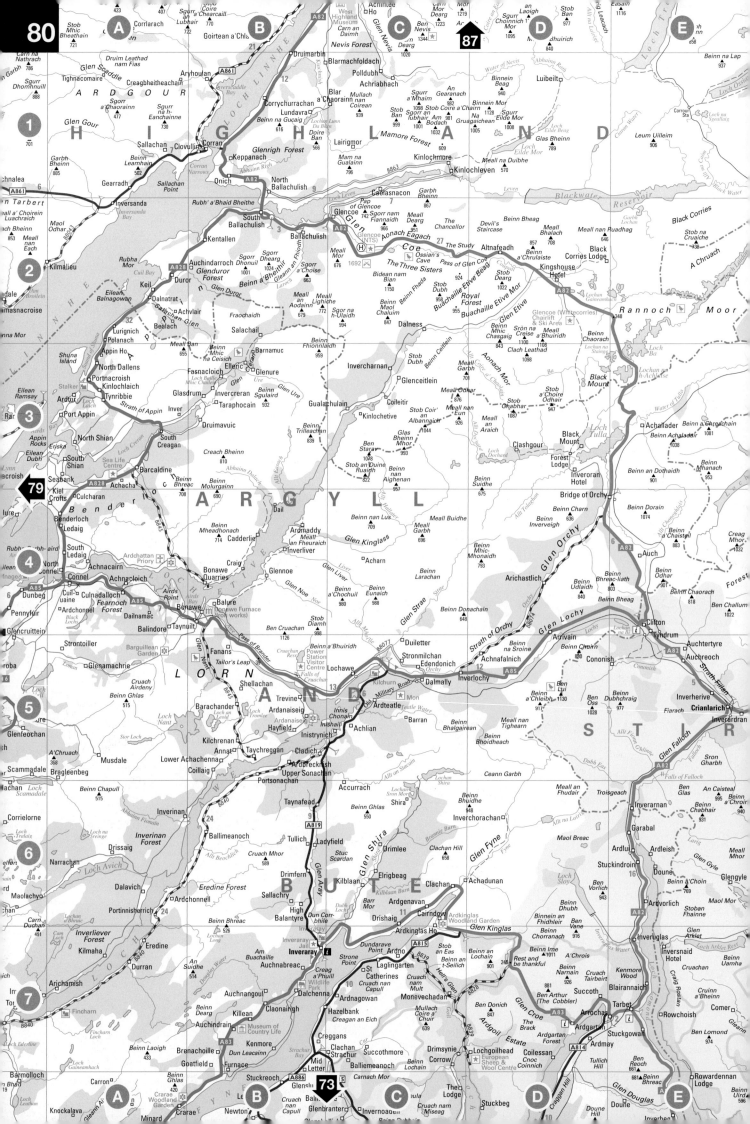

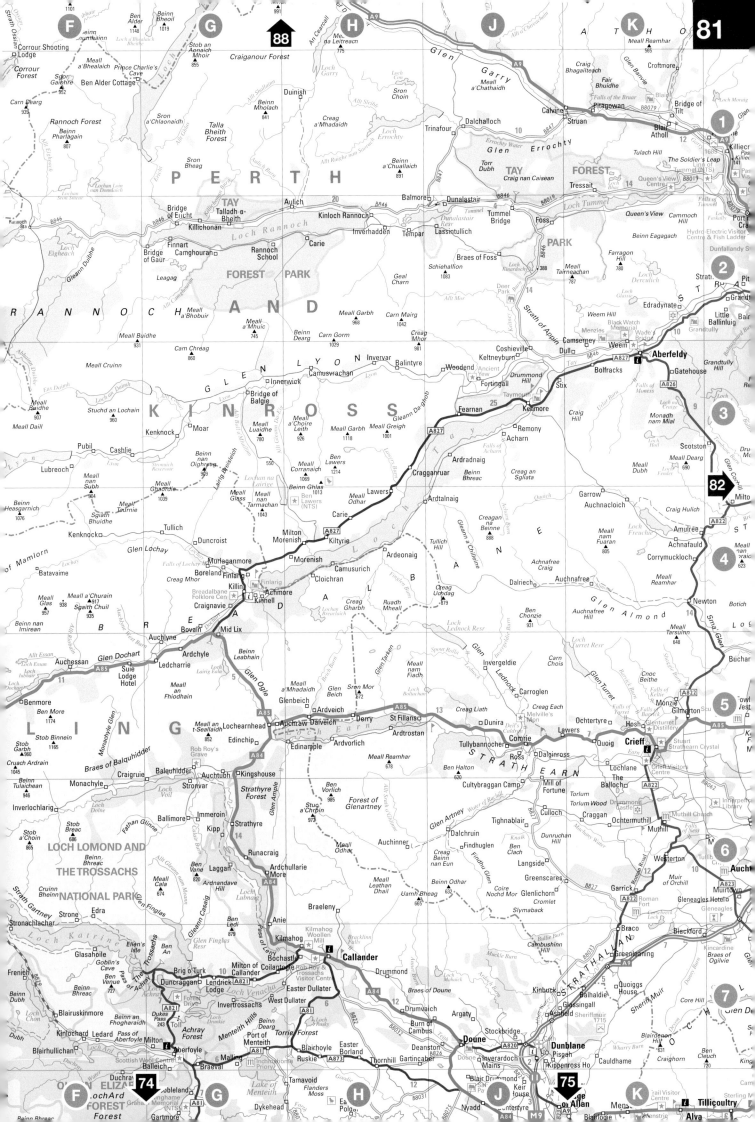

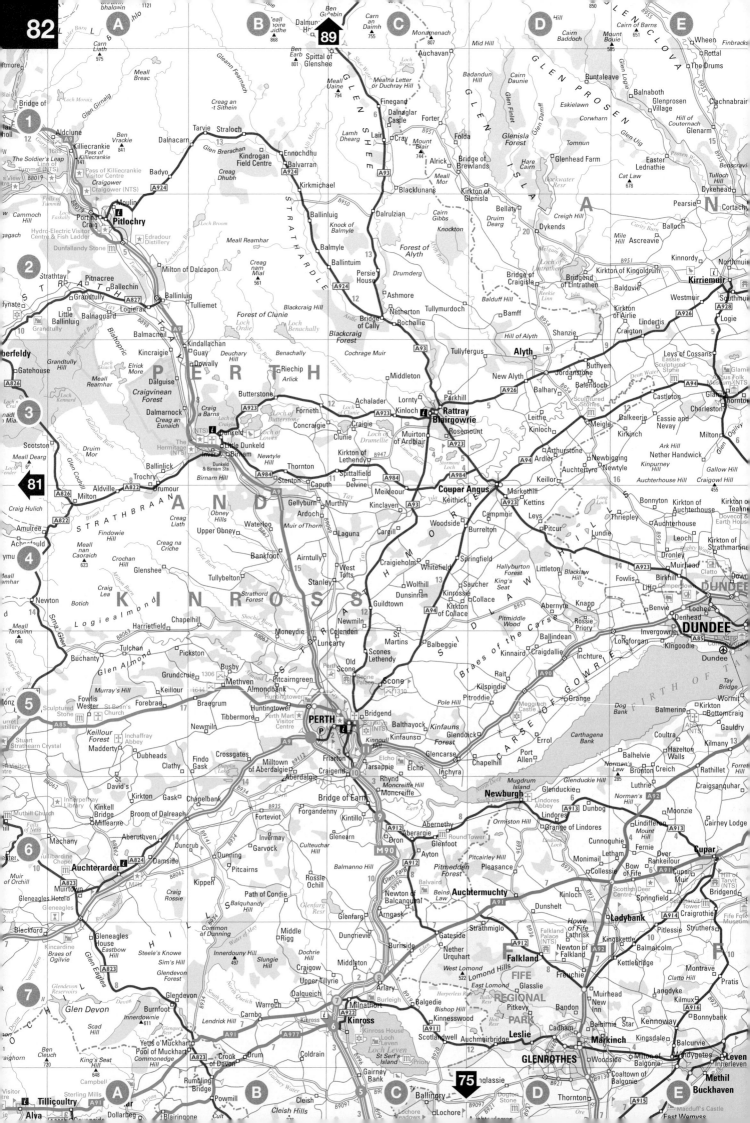

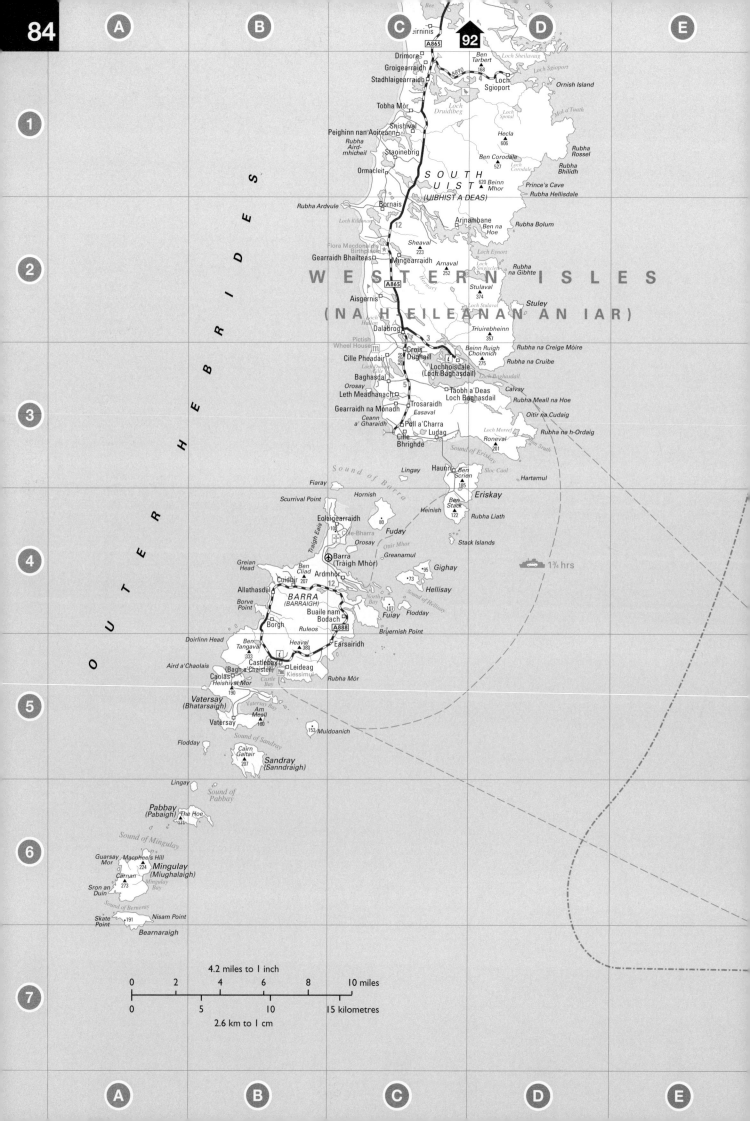

F   G   H   J   K

INNER HEBRIDES

Map labels (Skye area):

Hoe P, Ramasaig, Healabhal Bheag (Macleod's Table South) 488, Orbost, Harlosh, Glen Ose, Beinn na 'Cloiche 232, Am Maol 212, Beinn na 'ine 17, Portree

The Hoe 233, Lorgill, ch nasaig, Balmore, Ose, Oxn, Glennore, Stroc-bheinn 400, Camastiana

Ben Connan 244, Beinn na Boineid 371, Harlosh Point, Bracadale, Ben Duagrich 304, Mugeary

Ben Idrigill 340, Harlosh Island, Dun Beag, A863, Coillore, SKYE, Lower Ollach

MacLeod's Maidens, An Dubh Sgeir, Tarner Island, Ullinish, Struan, Coillore, Upper

Idrigill Point, Wiay, Loch Bracadale, Ardtreck Point, A863, Beinn Totaig, Roineval, Meall an Fhuarain 439, Ben Lee 445, Peinchorran

Oronsay, Portnalong, Fernilea, Rubha nan Clach, Loch Harport, Broc-bheinn, Glen Varragill, Scons

Arnaval 369, Carbost, Drynoch, A863, Glen Drynoch, B8009, Sligachan, Glamaig 775

Gleann Oraid, Talisker, Talisker Bay, Talisker, Stockval 416, Beinn Bhreac 370, HIGHLAND, Beinn Dearg, Garbh-80, Bla Bheinn 92

Biod Mor 383, Eynort, Beinn Bhreac 445, Minginish, Beinn a'Bhraghad 461, Cuillin Hills, Am Basteir 935 965, Sgurr nan Gillean, Harta Corrie, Bruach na Frithe 958, Sgurr a'Mhadaidh 918

Beinn Staic 411, Sgurr Thuilm 879, Sgurr a'Ghreadaidh 973, An Cruachan 435, Sgurr Dearg (Inaccessible Pinnacle) 986, Sgurr na Banachdich 948, Sgurr Mhic Choinnich, Druim Hain, Loch Coruisk, Loch na Creitheach

Glenbrittle, Bualintur, Culnamean, Sgurr Alasdair 993, Sgurr Dubh Mor 944, Loch Scavaig, Loch na Stri, Strea, Camasu

Beinn an Eoin 312, Sgurr nan Eag 924, Gars-bheinn 895, Ki

Rubha Thearna Sgurr, Loch Brittle, Ceann na Beinne, Camasunary

Rubh' an Dunain, Leac nam Faoileann, Beinn Bhreac 141, Loch Scavaig, Elgol

Soay Sound, Soay, Mol-chlach, Camas nan Gall, Prince Charles's Cave, R

CUILLIN SOUND

93

86

Canna / Rum / Eigg area:

CANNA, Camas Tharbernish, Carn a'Ghaill 210, Compass Hill 140, Garrisdale Point, Canna (NTS), A'Chill, Canna Harbour, Rubha Shamhnan Insir

Sron Ruail, Tarbert Bay, Sanday, Sound of Canna, Kilmory

Humla, A'Bhrideanach, Bloodstone Hill 388, Sgaorishal 278, Kilmory, Mullach Mor 304, Rubha na Roinne

Garbh Sgeir, Oigh-sgeir, Sgor Reidh, Orval 571, National Nature Reserve, Kinloch, RUM, Barkeval 591, Bagh na h-Uamha

Harris, An Dornabac 263, Hallival 723, Askival 812

Rubha Sgor an t-Snidhe, Ruinsival 528, Ainshval 781, Sgurr nan Gillean 764

Rubha nam Meirleach, Sound of Rum

Rubha an Fhasaidh, Bay of Laig, Cleadale, An Cruachan 299, Beinn Tighe 315, Laig, EIGG, An Sgurr 393, Kildonnan, Galmisdale

Eilean nan Each, Godag, Rubh' Leam na Laraich 137, Beinn Airein, Port Mor, Muck, Sound of Eigg

Sanna Point, Fascadale, Achateny, Point of Ardnamurchan, Achnaha, Meall nan Con 437, Sanna Bay, irk

Ferry notes:

Oban..............5-7 hours

Oban..............5¼ hours

78

F   G   H   J   K

1   2   3   4   5   6   7

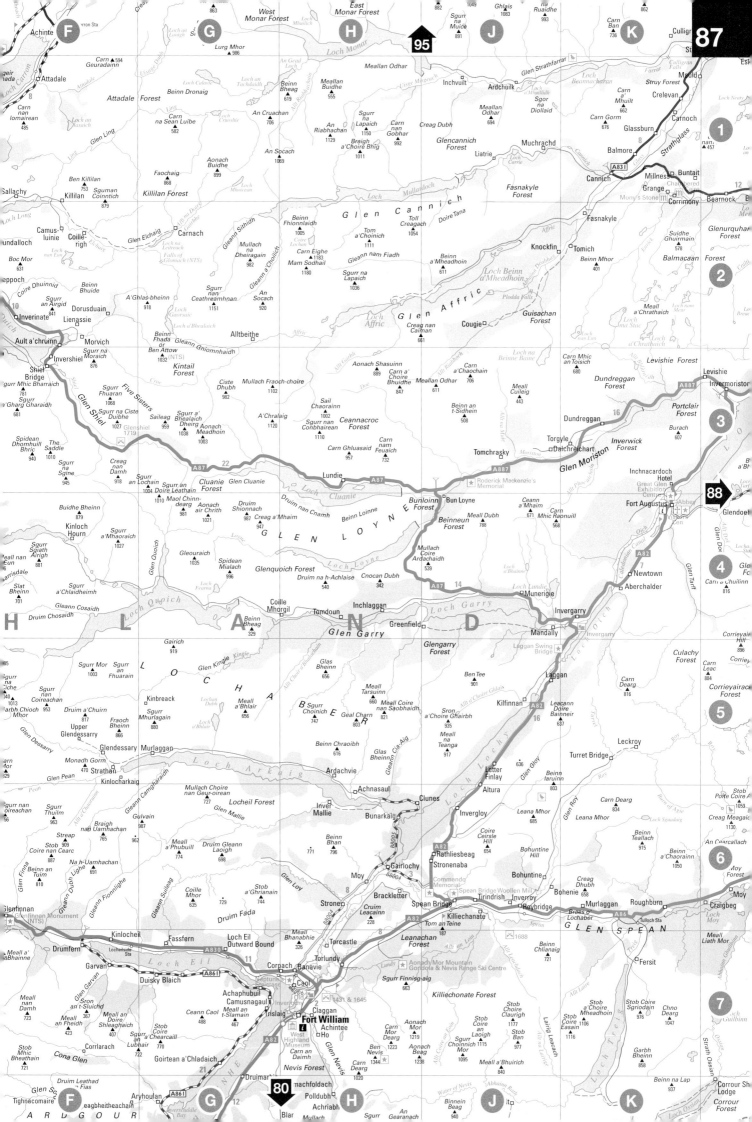

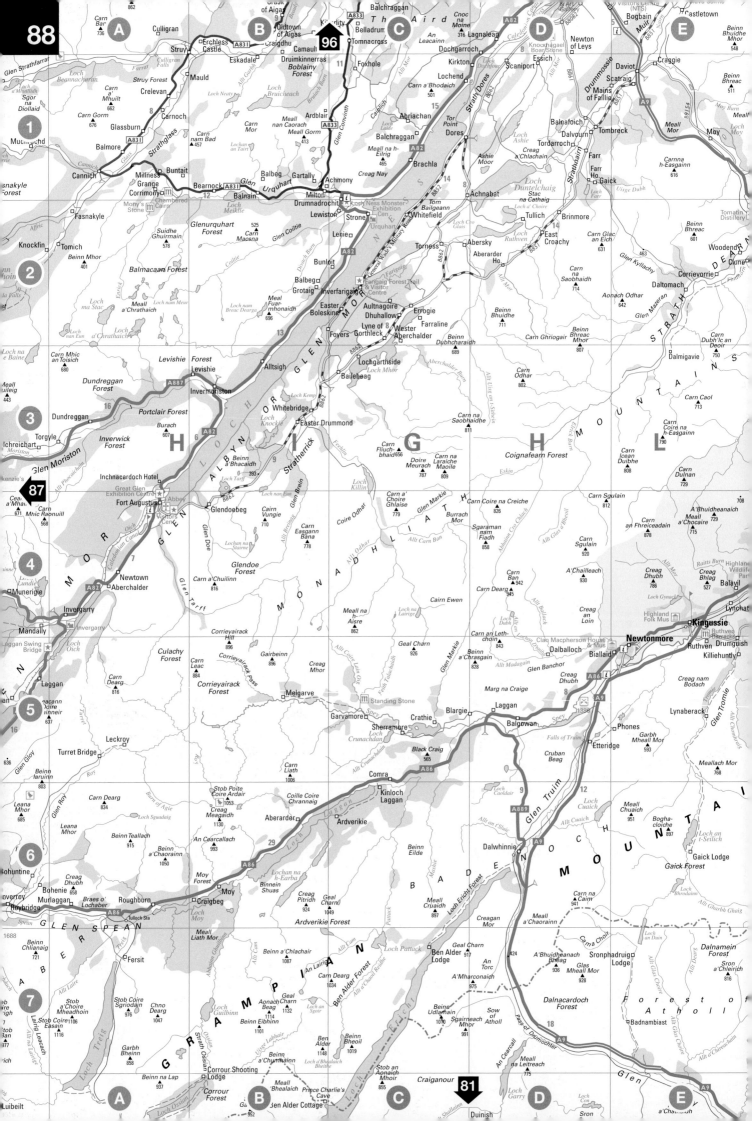

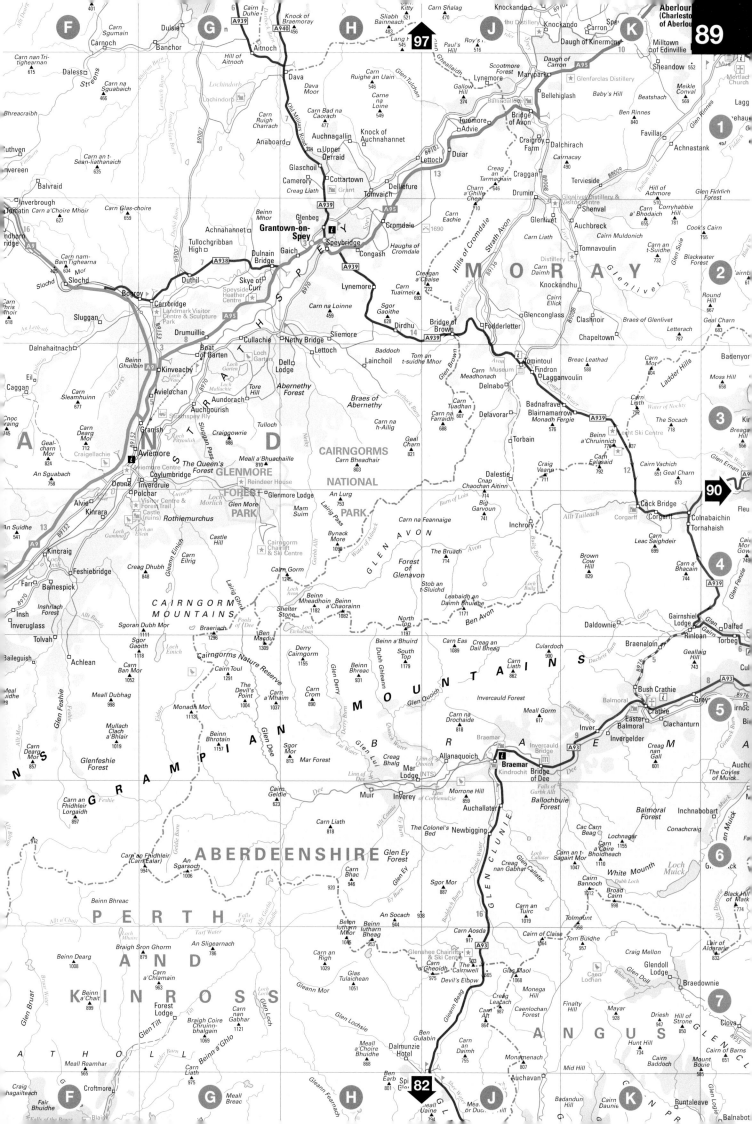

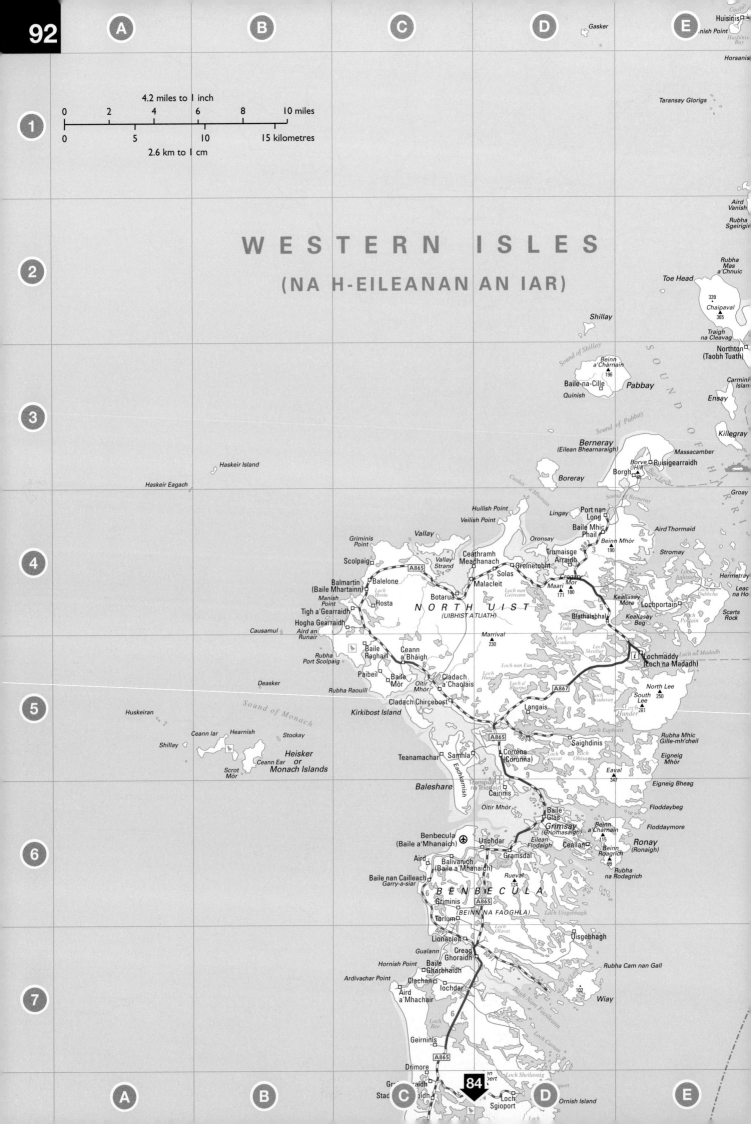

A   B   C   D   E

4.2 miles to 1 inch

0   2   4   6   8   10 miles

0   5   10   15 kilometres

2.6 km to 1 cm

WESTERN ISLES
(NA H-EILEANAN AN IAR)

Huisinis
Hushinish Point
Hushanis Bay
Horsanis

Gasker

Taransay Glorigs

Aird a'Vanish
Rubha Sgeirigin

Shillay

Toe Head

Rubha Mas a'Chnuic

339
Chaipaval
365

Traigh na Cleavag

Northton
(Taobh Tuath)

Carmini Islan

Sound of Shillay

Beinn a'Charnain
196

Baile-na-Cille

Quinish

Pabbay

Ensay

Killegray

Haskeir Island

Sound of Pabbay

Berneray
(Eilean Bhearnaraigh)

Massacamber

Boreray

Borve Hill
85

Ruisigearraidh

Borgh

Groay

Haskeir Eagach

Cuolas a'Mhanain

Sound of Berneray

Huilish Point

Veilish Point

Lingay

Port nan Long

Aird Thormaid

Stromay

Griminis Point

Vallay

Oronsay

Baile Mhic Phail

Beinn Mhor

Scolpaig

Vallay Strand

Ceathramh Meadhanach

Greinetobht

Trumaisge Arraidh

3
190

Loch Aulasay

Hermetray

A865

12

Solas

Crogary Mor

Maari
171 180

Keallasay More

Lochportain

Leac na Ho

Balmartin
(Baile Mhartainn)

Balelone

Malacleit

Keallasay Beg

Scarts Rock

Manish Point

Loch Hosta

Botarua

NORTH UIST
(UIBHIST A TUATH)

Blathaisbhal

Loch Portain

Tigh a'Gearraidh

Hosta

Loch nan Geireann

Hogha Gearraidh

Marrival
230

Loch Scadavay

Loch Skealtar

North Lee

Causamul

Aird an Runair

Baile Raghaill

Ceann a'Bhaigh

Loch Fada

Lochmaddy
(Loch na Madadh)

Loch nan Madadh

Rubha Port Scolpaig

Paibeil

Baile Mor

Oitir Mhor

Cladach a'Chaolais

Loch Huna

Loch an Eun

Loch a'Bharpa

A867

Loch Scadavay

South Lee
250

Deasker

Rubha Raouill

Cladach Chircebost

Langais

281

Rubha Mhic Gille-mh'cheil

Sound of Monach

Kirkibost Island

A865

B894

Saighdinis

Eigneig Mhor

Huskeiran

Ceann Iar

Hearnish

Stockay

Teanamachar

Samhla

Corcena
(Corunna)

Loch Caravat

Loch Obisay

Eaval
347

Eigneig Bheag

Shillay

Ceann Ear

Scrot Mor

Heisker
or
Monach Islands

Baleshare

Eachkamish

9

Floddaybeg

Floddaymore

Teampull na Trionaid

Cairinis

Oitir Mhor

Baile Glas

Grimsay
(Griomasaigh)

Beinn a'Charnain

Ronay
(Ronaigh)

Benbecula
(Baile a'Mhanaich)

Uachdar

Eilean Flodaigh

Ceallan

Beinn Roagrich
99

Aird

Balivanich
(Baile a'Mhanaich)

Gramsdal

115

Rubha na Rodagrich

Baile nan Cailleach

4

Rueval
124

Garry-a-siar

BENBECULA

Griminis

A865

Loch Uisgebhagh

(BEINN NA FAOGHLA)

Torlum

Loch Olavat

Lionacleit

B892

Uisgebhagh

Gualann

Creag Ghoraidh

Rubha Cam nan Gall

Hornish Point

Baile Gharbhaidh

102

Ardivachar Point

Clachan

Iochdar

Bagh Nam Faoileann

Wiay

Aird a'Mhachair

6

Loch Bee

Loch Carnan

Geirninis

A865

Drimore

Loch Sheilavaig

Greadhraidh

Stadh raidh

84

Loch Sgioport

Ornish Island

A   B   C   D   E

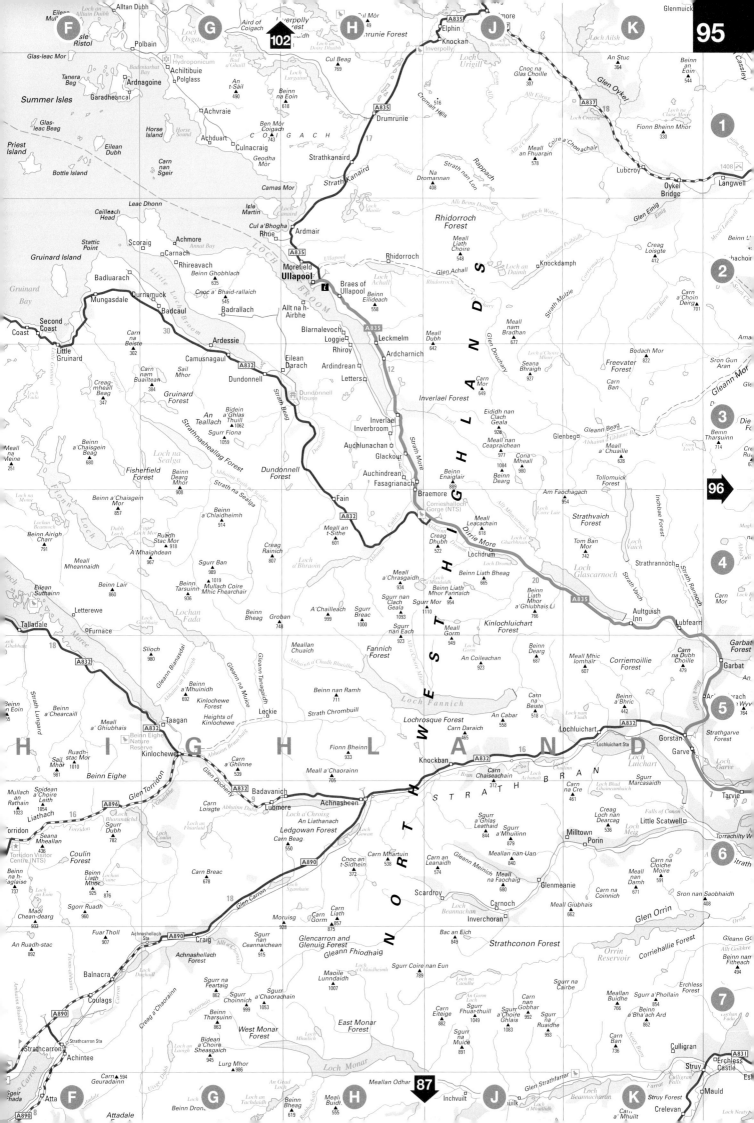

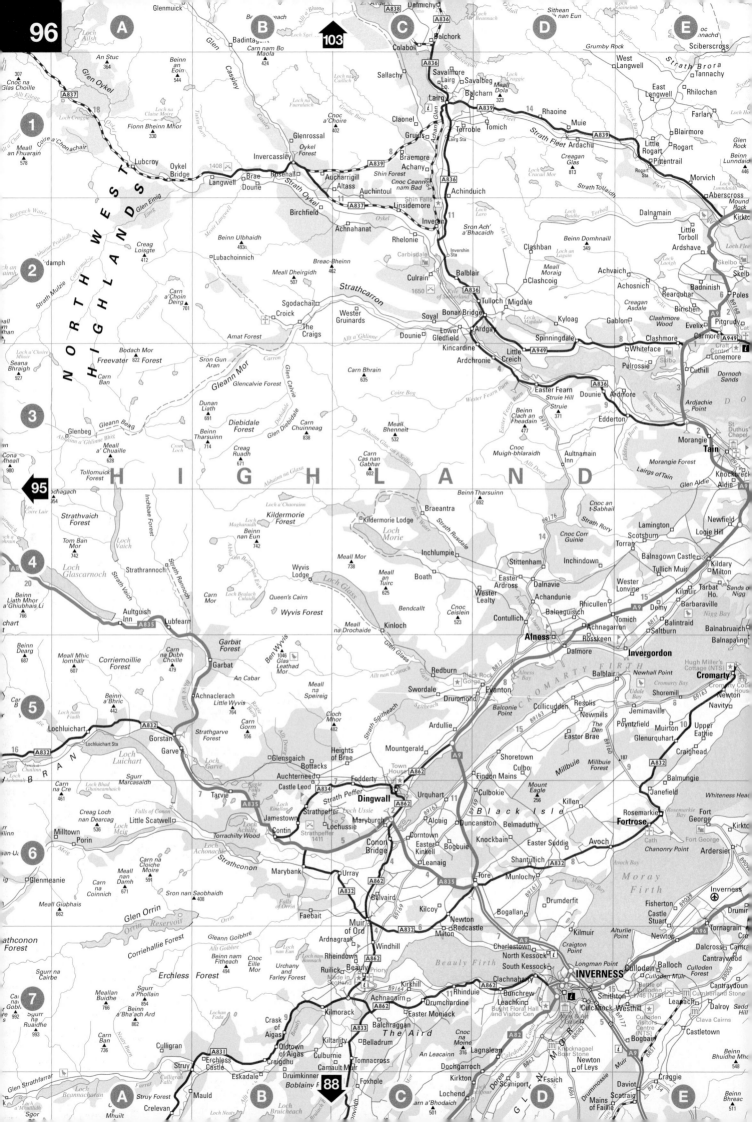

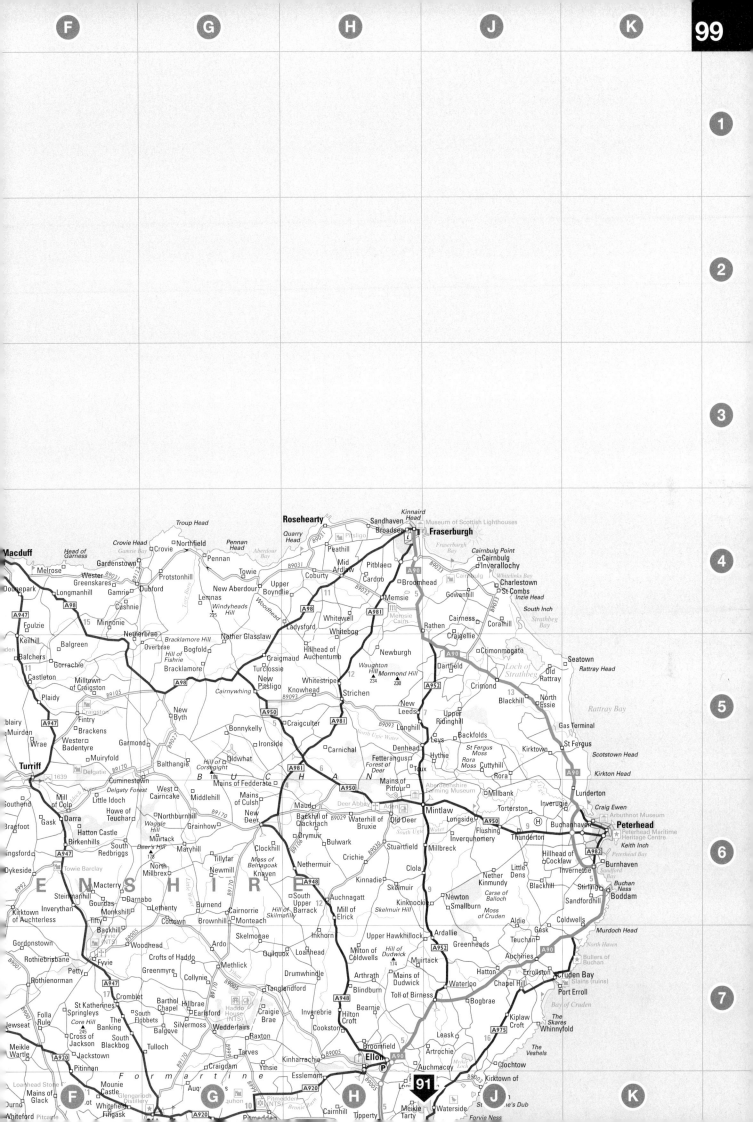

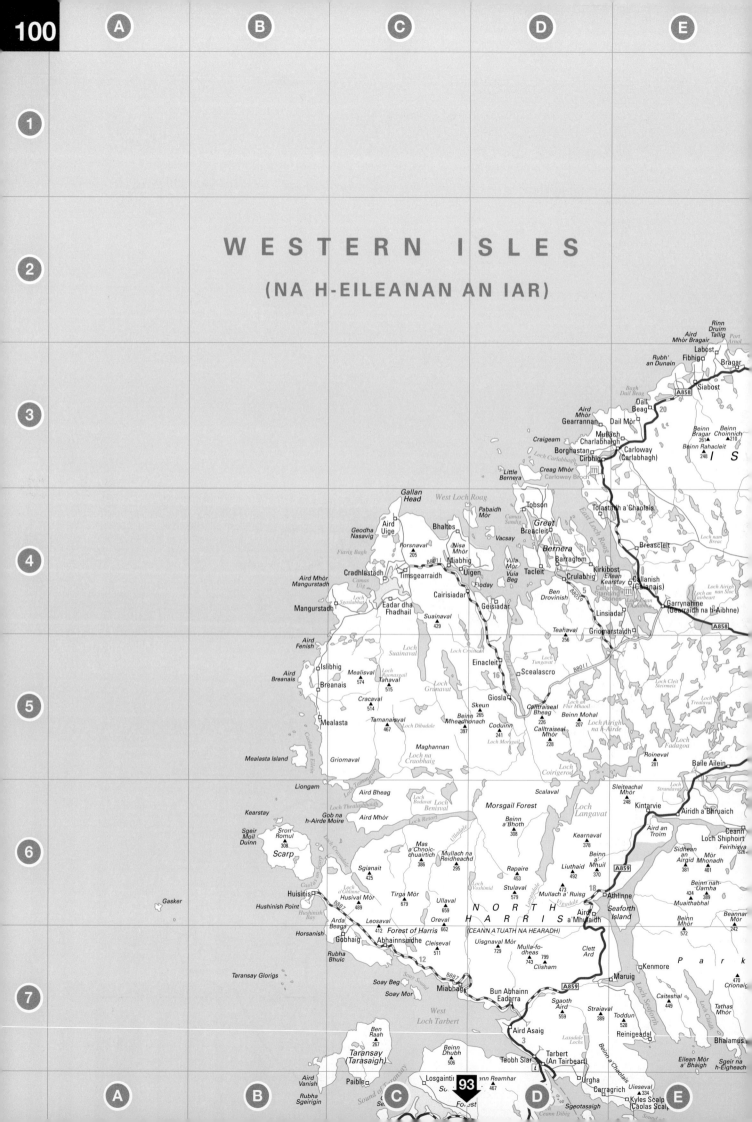

Butt of Lewis
(Rubha Robhanais)

Port
a' Stoth

Teampull Mholuidh

Eoropaidh
Còig Peighinnean

Bad an
Fhithich
Port Nis

Lional
Tabost

Suainebost
Eorodal

Aird Dhail
Port
Skigersta

Cros
Sgiogarstaigh

Dail Bho Dheas
Dail Bho Thuath

Meall Geal

Toa Galson

Gabhsunn Bho
Thuath
Ness

A857
Glen Cross
Port
Alasdair

Gabhsunn Bho Dheas

Cuidhaseadair
Laimhrig

Broch

Mealabost
Roinn a'
Bhuic
Airigh
na Glaice
Cellar Head

Còig Peighinnean
Airighean
Beinn
nan Caorach

Siadar
Iarach
Ben
Dell

Rubha Leathann
Siadar Uarach
Airighean Loch
Breihavat

Baile an Truiseil
Steinacleit Cairn &
Standing Stones

Diaval
Loch Mòr
Sandaval

Gaile
Chraic
A857
Geiraha

Bru
Barvas
(Barabhas)

Loch Mòr
Shanndabhaig

Black
House
Loch Gress

Airtal

Muirneag
248
Tolastadh Ùr

Loch Urrahag
Gleann Mòr Bharabhais
Torray
Tolastadh
Tolsta
Head

Glen Bragar
Gleann Bhruthadail
Port Geiraha

Roishal Mòr
174
Loch
Sandval
Gress
Port nam Bothag

ISLE OF LEWIS
11
Loch an
Tobair

(EILEAN LEODHais)
Loch Mòr
Sandval
12
Gleann
Tholastaidh

Loch na Scravat
Loch
Neigrieach Mòr
Griais
Port Bun a' Ghlinne

Beinn
Mholach
292
Loch
an t-Siurr
Bac
Creag
Fhraoich

Stacashal
216
Col

Loch Ian
Steornig
Breibhig
Rubha Bhataisgeir
Tiumpan Head
(Rubha an t-Siumpain)

Col Sands
Portnaguran
(Port nan Giùran)

A857
Aird Thunga
Sron
Ruadh
Rubha
Deas

Laxdale
Tunga
Loch
a' Tuath
A866
Siulaisiadar

Newmarket
Melbost Sands
10
Seisiadar
Rubha na
Grèine

Stornoway
(Steornabhagh)
Laxdale
(Lacasdal)
East
Roisnish
Garrabost
Eye Peninsula
(An Rubha)

Loch Vatandip
Melbost Pt
Melbost
Aignis
Rubha na
Bearnaich

A858
Sandwick
(Sanndabhaig)
NT Eilean
Cnoc
Pabail
Uarach

Beinn nan
Surrag
Lews
Castle
Stornoway
Harbour
St
Columba's
Church
Suardail
Bagh Phabail

13
223
200
Arnish
Pt.
Branahuie Banks
Pabail
Iarach

Eitshal
Achadh Mòr
Arnish Moor
Ceann na Circ

A859
Rubh
a'Bhaigh
Uaine

Loch Thuha
Bràideu
Loch
Orasay

Un Nisreval
6
B897

Loch
Fada
Liurbost
Grimsiadar
Loch
Grimsiadar

Crosbost
Raerinish Point

12
Tabhaigh
Mhor
Ullapool.............hours 2¾

A859
Ceos
Eilean Chaluim
Chille
Orasaigh

Lacasaigh
Gleann Ghrabhair

Cearsiadar
Gearraidh
Cabharstadh
Torraigh

Tabost
Bhaird

B8060
Marbhig

Malasgair
13

Calbost
Rubha
Iosal

Glen Ouirn
Grabhair

Tom an
Fhuadain
Loch
Odhairn
Kebock
Head

Eisgean
Leumrabhagh
Gob
na Milaid

Loch Shell
Srianach

Eilean
Iubhard

Corlabhadh

Uisenis
371
Mulhagery

Gob
Rubh'Uisenis

Rubha
Bhrollum

Rubh
a'
Bhaird

THE MINCH

SOUND OF SHIANT

Garbh
Eilean
161

102

4.2 miles to 1 inch

| 0 | 2 | 4 | 6 | 8 | 10 miles |

| 0 | 5 | 10 | 15 kilometres |

2.6 km to 1 cm

F G H J K

1 2 3 4 5 6 7

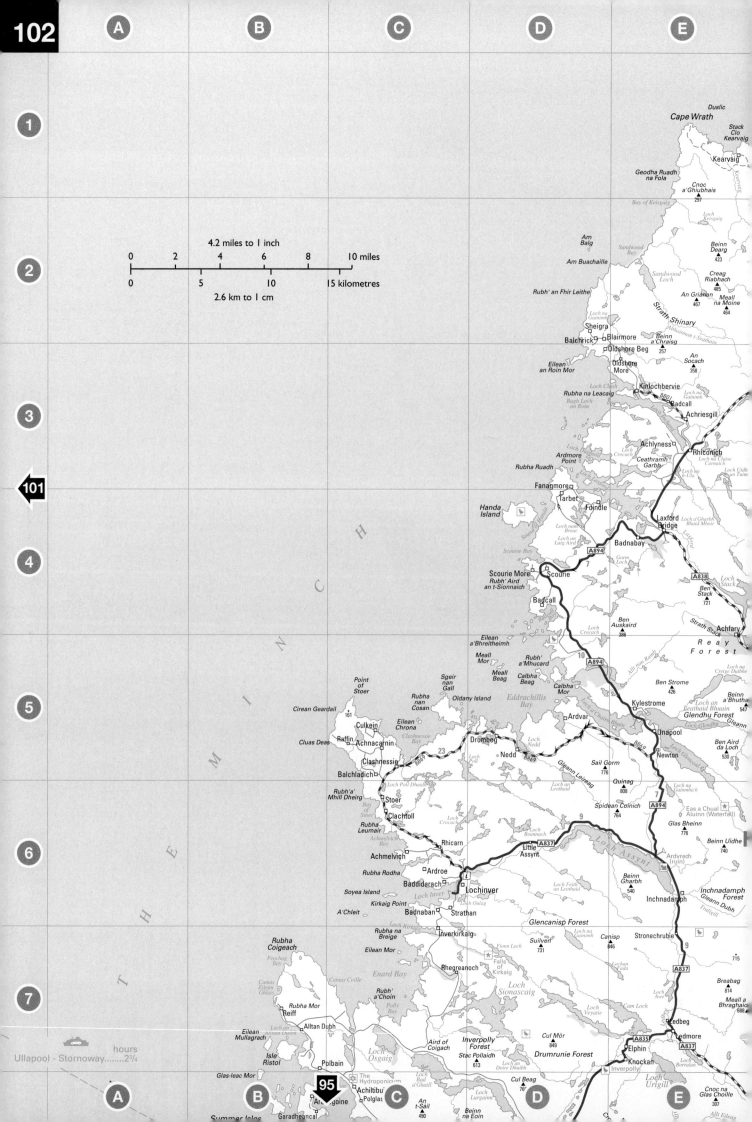

A B C D E

1

2

4.2 miles to 1 inch

0 2 4 6 8 10 miles

0 5 10 15 kilometres

2.6 km to 1 cm

101

3

4

5

6

7

Ullapool - Stornoway........2¾ hours

Cape Wrath
Duslic
Stack Clo Kearvaig
Kearvaig
Geodha Ruadh na Fola
Cnoc a'Ghiubhais 297
Bay of Keisgaig
Loch Keisgaig

Am Balg
Sandwood Bay
Beinn Dearg 423
Creag Riabhach 485
Am Buachaille
Sandwood Loch
An Grianan 467
Meall na Moine 464
Rubh' an Fhir Leithe
Loch na Gainimh
Strath Shinary
Abhainn t-Strathain

Sheigra
Balchrick
Oldshore Beg
Blairmore
Oldshore More
Beinn a'Chraisg 257
An Socach 358

Eilean an Roin Mor
Oldshore More
Kinlochbervie
B801
Badcall
Loch na Gainimh
Achriesgill

Rubha na Leacaig
Bagh Loch an Roin
Achlyness
Ardmore Point
Ceathramh Garbh
Rhiconich
Loch na Claise Carnaich

Rubha Ruadh
Loch Crocach
Loch an h-Ula
Loch Uidh an Tuim

Fanagmore
Tarbet
Foindle
Laxford Bridge

Handa Island
Sound of Handa
Loch nam Breac
Loch a'Gharbh Bhaid Mhoir

Badnabay
A894
Gorm Loch
Ben Stack 721

Scourie More
Scourie
Rubh' Aird an t-Sionnaich
7
Loch Stack
Strath Stack
Achfary

Badcall
Loch Crocach
Ben Auskaird 386
Reay Forest

10
A894
Allt nan Ramh
Loch na Creige Duibhe

Point of Stoer
Rubha nan Cosan
Sgeir nan Gall
Oldany Island
Eddrachillis Bay
Meall Mor
Rubh' a'Mhucard
Calbha Beag
Calbha Mor
Kylestrome
Ben Strome 426
Beinn a'Bhutha 547
Glendhu Forest

Cirean Geardail
161
Eilean Chrona
Clashnessie Bay
Meall Beag
Loch a'Chairn Bhain
Unapool
Ben Aird da Loch 530

Culkein
Achnacarnin
23
Drumbeg
Loch Nedd
Newton
B869

Cluas Deas
Raffin
B869
Nedd
B869
Sail Gorm 776
Gleann Leireag
Quinag 808
7

Clashnessie
Balchladich
Loch Poll Dhaidh
Loch Poll
Loch an Leothaid
Spidean Coinich 764
A894
Eas a Chual Aluinn (Waterfall)

Rubh' a' Mhill Dheirg
Stoer
Bay of Stoer
Loch Crocach
9
Loch na Gainimh
Glas Bheinn 776

Clachtoll
Achmelvich Bay
Rubha Leumair
Little Assynt
A837
Loch Beannach
Loch Assynt
Beinn Uidhe 740

Achmelvich
Rhicarn
Ardvrech (ruin)

Ardroe
Loch Feith an Leothaid
Beinn Gharbh 540
Inchnadamph
Inchnadamph Forest
Gleann Dubh

Rubha Rodha
Baddidarach
Lochinver
Loch Inver
Loch Oalag

Soyea Island
Badnaban
Strathan
Glencanisp Forest
Traligill

A'Chleit
Kirkaig Point
Loch na Gainimh
Stronechrubie
9

Rubha na Breige
Inverkirkaig
Canisp 846
A837
715

Rubha Coigeach
Eilean Mor
Fionn Loch
Suilven 731
Lochan Fada
Breabag 814

Feochag Bay
Rhegreanoch
Falls of Kirkaig
Loch Sionascaig
Cam Loch
Meall a Bhraghaid 688

Camas Eilean Ghlais
Camas Coille
Enard Bay
Rubh' a'Choin
Loch Veyatie
Ledbeg
A835
Ledmore
A837

Rubha Mor
Reiff
Polly Bay
Cul Mor 849
Elphin

Eilean Mullagrach
Alltan Dubh
Aird of Coigach
Inverpolly Forest
Stac Pollaidh 613
Drumrunie Forest
Knockan
Loch Borralan

Isle Ristol
Loch Osgaig
An-t-Sail 490
Cul Beag 76?
Inverpolly
Loch Urigill

Glas-leac Mor
95
The Hydroponicum
Achiltibui
Polglas
Beinn na Eoin
Cnoc na Glas Choille 307

Summer Isles
Ardvoine
Garadheancal
Allt Eileag

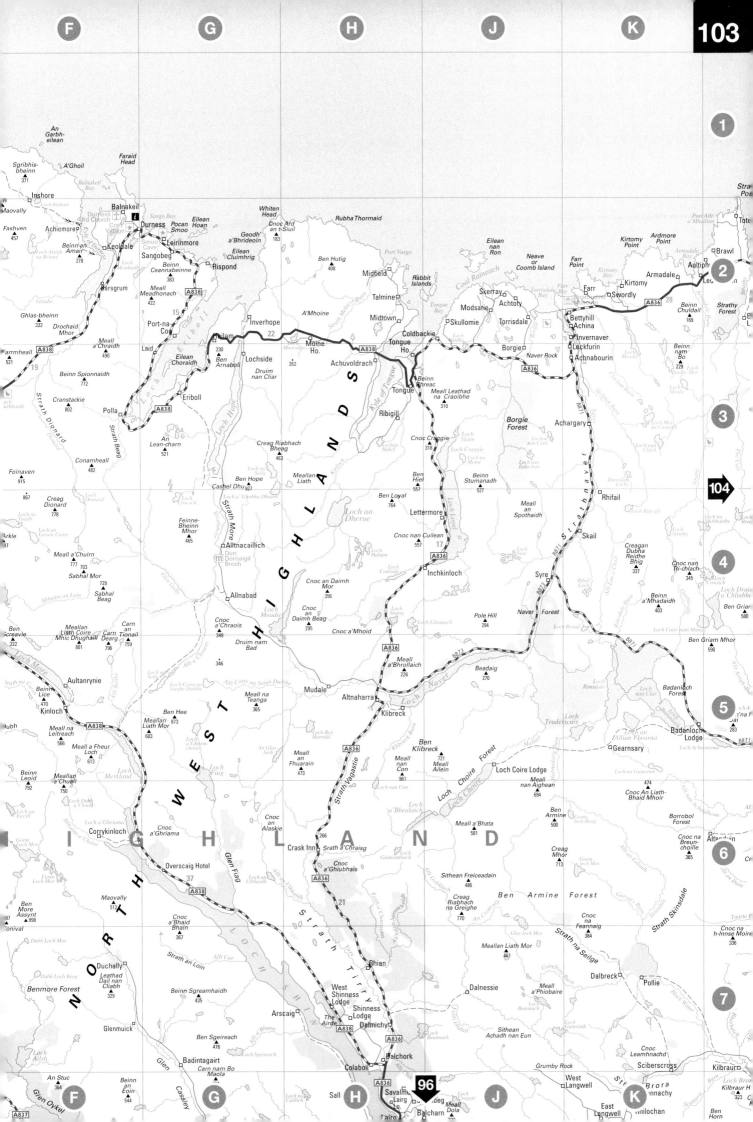

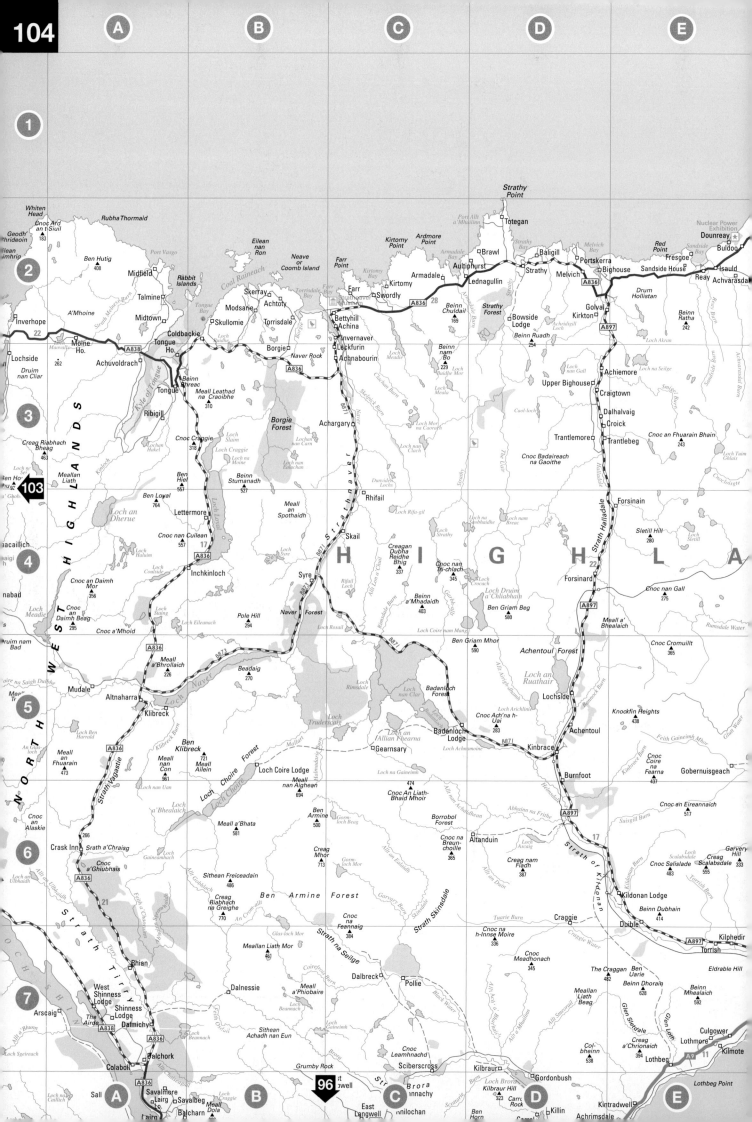

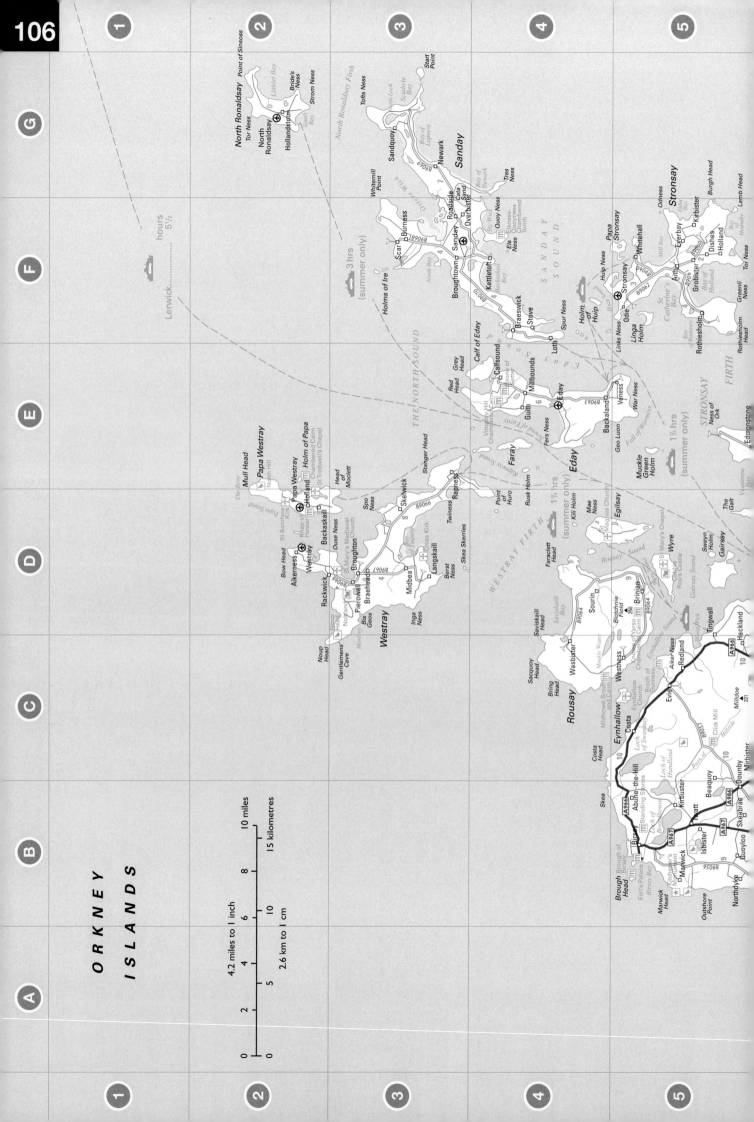

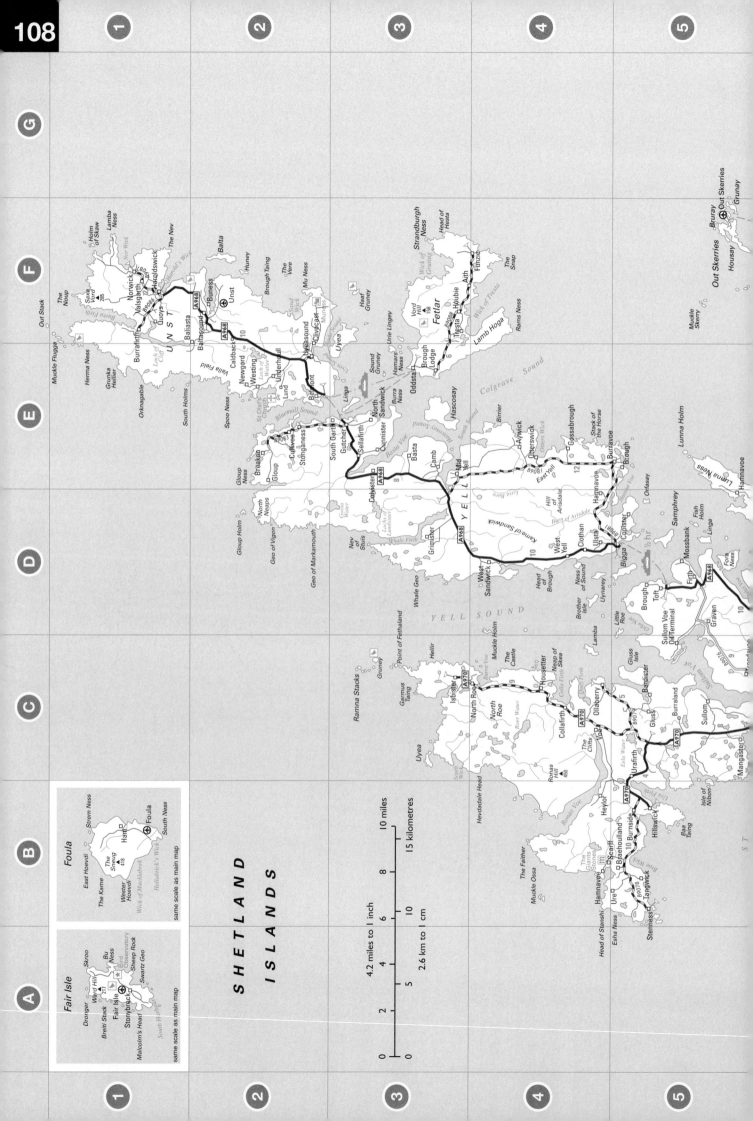

KEY TO MAP SYMBOLS

Motorway — under constr.

Junction number — restricted access

'A'/National primary — dual carriageway

'A'/National secondary — dual carriageway, under constr.

'B'/Regional road — dual carriageway, under constr.

Road distances (in miles)

Railway

Car ferry

Airport

International boundary

National park

Forest park

Urban area

Beach

Canal

15.8 miles to 1 inch

10 km to 1 cm

113

DUBLIN

Mullingar · Trim · Hill of Tara · Rush · Lambay Island · Portrane · Malahide
Athlone · Moate · Kilbeggan · Edenderry · Moyvalley · Dunboyne · Leixlip · Howth · Ireland's Eye
Tullamore · Clara · Clonygowan · Celbridge · Lucan · Newcastle · DUBLIN · Dún Laoghaire
Dublin Bay
Cloghan · Banagher · Kilcormac · Portarlington · Rathangan · Newbridge · Kildare · Naas · Enniskerry · Bray
Birr · Mountmellick · Monasterevan · Kilcullen · Blessington · Greystones
Portlaoise · The Curragh · Dunlavin · Wicklow Mts. National Park · Newtownmountkennedy
Mountrath · Castletown · Stradbally · Athy · Timolin · Baltinglass · Wicklow · Wicklow Head
Roscrea · Abbeyleix · Ballylynan · Castledermot · Rathdrum · Ardmore Point
Moneygall · Rathdowney · Durrow · Graigue · Carlow · Rathvilly · Aughrim · Avoca · Mizen Head
Templemore · Templetuohy · Castlecomer · Tullow · Shillelagh · Inch · Arklow · Kilmichael Point
Thurles · Johnstown · Ballyragget · Leighlinbridge · Ballon · Craanford · Gorey · Courtown
Holycross · Urlingford · Freshford · Whitehall · Muine Bheag · Bunclody · Ballycanew
Kilkenny · Dungarvan · Borris · Ferns · Cahore Point
Killenaule · Callan · Kells · Graiguenamanagh · Enniscorthy · Blackwater
Cashel · Fethard · Knocktopher · Thomastown · Drummin · Clonroche · Castlebridge
Clonmel · Ninemilehouse · Ballyhale · Wexford · Wexford Bay
Carrick-on-Suir · New Ross · Killurin · Taghmon · Rosslare Point
Waterford · Cheekpoint · Wellington Bridge · Killinick · Rosslare Harbour · Greenore Point
Lismore · Tramore · Duncannon · Duncormick · Lady's Island · Carnsore Point
Youghal · Dunmore East · Hook Head · Kilmore Quay · Saltee Islands

Ferry times (hours):
Douglas......2¾–4¾ (summer only)
Holyhead......1¾–3¼
Liverpool......4–9
Mostyn......6–7½
Cherbourg......18 (summer only)
Cherbourg......17½–19
Fishguard......1¾–3½
Pembroke......3¾
Roscoff (summer only)......19
Swansea......10
Roscoff (summer only)......14

Dublin inset

Western Way · National Wax Museum · Dublin Writers Museum · James Joyce Centre
Hugh Lane Gallery · Gate Theatre · PARNELL SQUARE
King's Inns · Rotunda Hospital · St. Mary's Cathedral · Connolly Station · Sheriff St. Lwr.
Cinema · Ilac Shopping Centre · Abbey Theatre · Police Station · Bus Station
Old Jameson Distillery · The Chimney · General Post Office · Hot Press Music Hall of Fame · Custom House
Jervis Shopping Centre · Eden Quay · Custom House Quay
Four Courts · Ormond Quay · Bachelors Wk. · River Liffey · George's Quay · City Quay
Inns Quay · Wellington Quay · Aston Quay · Tara Street Station · Townsend Street
Ushers Quay · Merchants Quay · Essex Quay · Temple Bar · Bank of Ireland · Pearse
Christ Church Cathedral · Dublin's Viking Adventure · Dame Street · College Grn. · Trinity College – Book of Kells & The Dublin Experience
Dvblinia · City Hall · Civic Museum · Suffolk St. · Nassau St. · Pearse Station
Dublin Castle · Police Station · Westbury Mall · Grafton Arcade · Heraldic Museum
St. Patrick's Cathedral · Golden · Gaiety Theatre · Mansion House · National Library · National Gallery
Marsh's Library · Police Station · St. Stephen's Green Shopping Centre · Leinster House · Natural History Museum
Westbury Mall · National Museum · Government Buildings
St. Stephen's Green Park · Newman House Museum

DUBLIN
N
0 · 200 · 400 m
0 · 400 yds

BELFAST inset

University of Ulster · Exchange St. · Dunbar St. · Dunbar Link · Corporation St. · Seacat Terminal · Odyssey Complex

WEST LINK · CARRICK HILL · Little Donegall St. · P.O. · Academy St. · St. Anne's Cathedral · Talbot St. · Hill St. · Tomb St. · G.P.O · Queen's Quay · M3

PETER'S HILL · Library · Library · DONEGALL STREET · ALBERT SQ. · Custom House · Lagan Weir · Lookout

Brown Sq. · NORTH · Union St. · Gresham St. · Royal Ave. · Skipper St. · Clock Tower · Queen's Sq. · QUEEN ELIZABETH BRIDGE · Station St.

Brown St. · Smithfield Market · West St. · Waring St. · Bridge St. · Church St. · Bus Station · DONEGALL QUAY · Queen's Rd.

Millfield Technical College · Castle Court Centre · Rosemary St. · High St. · Victoria St. · ANN ST. · QUEEN'S BRIDGE · BRIDGE END · A2

Francis St. · P.O. · Bank St. · Castle Pl. · Cornmarket · Hipark Centre · Ann Street · OXFORD ST. · River Lagan

DIVIS ST. · John St. · King St. · Castle Street · Castle Lane · Arthur St. · Court House

Old Museum Arts Centre · COLLEGE SQ. N. · Linen Hall Library · Victoria St. · Victoria Square Victoria Centre · Royal Courts of Justice

Technical College · WELLINGTON PL. · DONEGALL SQ. NORTH · CHICHESTER ST. · Callender St. · Gomery St. · Gloucester St.

Royal Belfast Academical Institution · Upper Queen St. · Donegall Sq. West · City Hall · DONEGALL SQ. EAST · MAY STREET · Market · Waterfront Hall · A24

GROSVENOR ROAD · Howard St. · DONEGALL SQ. SOUTH · Joy St. · EAST BRIDGE STREET

Grand Opera House · Glengall St. · Crown Liquor Saloon · Brunswick St. · Franklin Street · Linen Hall Street · Adelaide Street · Alfred Street · Hamilton St. · Central Station

Bus Station · Amelia St. · Group Theatre · Ulster Hall · Clarence Street · Friendly Street

Gt. Victoria Street Station · Gt. Northern Mall · BEDFORD STREET · BBC · Eliza Street · Lwr. Stanfield Street

Hope St. · DUBLIN RD. · BRUCE ST. · Bankmore St. · Raphael St. · Stewart St.

Linfield Rd. · SANDY ROW · GT. VICTORIA ST. · ORMEAU AVENUE · Ormeau Baths Gallery

Coach Park · Rowland Way · Wellwood St. · Ventry St. · Cinema

BELFAST
N
0 — 200 yds
0 — 200 m

Map grid

D · 1 · 2 · 3 · A · B · C · D

A · B · C · 4 · 5 · 6

Tory Is · Tory Sound · Inishbofin · Bloody Foreland · Gweedore · Gortahork · Gola Island · Bunbeg · Gweedore · Owey Island · Rosses Bay · L. Nacung · L. Anure · The Rosses · Burtonport · R259 · N56 · Derryveagh · Aran Island · Dungloe · Slieve Snaght · Crohy Head · Gweebarra Bay · Dawros Head · Loughros More Bay · Ardara · Slievetooey · R250 · Aghla Mountain · Glenties · Blue St · Glen Bay · Glengesh Pass · R263 · Rossan Point · Malin Bay · Malin More · Crownarad · Killybegs · N56 · Donegal · Rathlin O'Birne Island · Slieve League · Fintragh Bay · Doorin Point · Muckross Head · McSwynes Bay · St John's Point · Donegal Bay · Ballyshannon · Mullaghmore Head · Bundoran · Inishmurray · Cliffony · Darty Mts · Truskmore · Glenade Lough · Streedagh Point · Benbulben · Glencar Lough · Roskeeragh Point · Lenadoon Point · Sligo Bay · Aughris Head · Coney I. · Sligo · Manorhamilton · Belha

Stags of Broad Haven · Downpatrick Head · Killala Bay · Benwee Head · Erris Head · Broad Haven · Maumakeogh · Ballycastle · Killala · Bartragh I. · Dromore West · Knockalongy · N59 · Collooney · Belmullet · R314 · R313 · Glenamoy · Owenmore · Easky Lough · Slieve Gamph · N17 · Ballymote · Lough Arrow · Lough Key Forest Park · The Mullet · Carrowmore Lake · Bangor Erris · N59 · Lough Dahybaun · Ballina · Mullany's Cross · Templehouse Lake · Drumkeeran · Inishkea North · Inishkea South · Slieve Car · Nephin Beg · R316 · Nephin · Lough Conn · Tubbercurry · Ballinafad · Boyle · Duvillaun More · Blacksod Bay · Ballycroy · Slieve More · Owenduff · Birreencorragh · Levally Lough · Foxford · N26 · Knock International · Charlestown · Ballaghaderreen · N5 · Frenchpark · R368 · Croaghaun · Doagh · Annagh · Nephin Beg Range · Cushcamcarragh · Lough Feeagh · Swinford · N58 · Bohola · Urlaur Lough · Achill Head · Achill Island · Achill · Mulrany · Beltra Lough · R310 · Knock · Ballyhaunis · Castlerea · Tulsk · Corraun Peninsula · Newport · N59 · Islandeady Lough · Castlebar · Kiltimagh · N83 · N5 · Achillbeg Island · Clew Bay · R311 · Westport · Murrisk · Knock · Ballindine · N60 · R361 · Ballaghaderreen · Clare Island · Croagh Patrick · Claremorris · Roscommon · Glenamaddy · N63 · Louisburgh · Murrisk · Partry · R327 · Ballinrobe · Caher Island · Creganbaun · Benbury · Mweelrea · Bengorm · Aasleagh · Benwee · Kilmaine · N84 · Dunmore · Inishturk · Partry Mts · Lough Mask · Ballygar · Inishbofin · Inishark · Ballynakill Bay · Lough Fee · Devils Mother · Joyce's Country · Cong · Clonbern · N17 · Mount Bellew · Connemara National Park · N59 · Benbaun · Maumturk Mts · Lough Corrib · Headford · R333 · Horseleap · N63 · Omey Island · The Twelve Pins · Recess · Clare · N6 · Clifden · Mannin Bay · Connemara · R336 · Tuam · Ballygar · Slyne Head · R341 · Ballyconneely Bay · Connaght · N84 · Moniva · Mweenish Island · Galway · Gorumna Island · Oranmore · Galway Airport · N18 · Claregalway · Athenry · N6 · Ballin

110 · Galway

21
M1
The North
Luton ✈   13
21

21A
A405
St Albans   3¼
London (North West)
(M1 South)
21A

A405

A1081
St Albans   3
22

A1081

22
A1(M)
A1081
London (North West)
Barnet   3
Hatfield   6
Services
23

A1(M)

SOUTH MIMMS
SERVICES

A41

M1
The North
Luton ✈   13
21

A405
Watford
Harrow (M1)   4¼
21A

23

A1(M)
A1081
Hatfield   6
Barnet   3
London (North West)
Services
23

A1   A1081

A41
Hemel Hempstead   5
Aylesbury   20
20

20

A41

A41
Hemel Hempstead   5
Aylesbury   20
20

A1081
St Albans   3¼
22

A41

A411

A405

A41
Watford   3½
19

19

A404

A404
Rickmansworth   2
Chorleywood   ½
Amersham   7
18

A404
Chorleywood   ½
Amersham   7
18

18

A404

A412
Maple Cross   1
17

A412
Maple Cross   1
Rickmansworth   2
17

17

A405

M40 (East)
Uxbridge   3
London (West)
M40 (West)
Birmingham   100
Oxford   38
16

M40

M40

A40

16

M40 (West)
Birmingham   100
Oxford (A40)   38
M40 (East)
Uxbridge   3
London (West)
16

M4
Heathrow ✈ Terminals
1, 2 & 3   3½
London (West)
Slough   5
The West
15

M4

15

M4

M4
The West
Slough   5
Reading   25
London (West)
Heathrow ✈ Terminals
1, 2 & 3   3½
15

A3113
Heathrow ✈
Terminal 4   3½
& Cargo   3
14

14

A3113
Heathrow ✈
Terminal 4   3½
& Cargo   3
14

A3113

A30
Staines   2
13

13

B376

A308

A30

A30

A308

A30
London (West)
Staines   2
13

M3
Sunbury   6
Southampton   56
Basingstoke   27
12

River Thames

12

M3

M3

M3
Basingstoke   27
Southampton   56
Sunbury   6
12

A317
A320
Chertsey   2
Woking   5
11

A317

11

A3
London (South West)
Guildford   8
Kingston   12
10

A320

A317
A320
Woking   5
Chertsey   2
11

A3

A243
A24
Leatherhead   2
Dorking   6½
9

A244

A243

10

A3
London (South West)
Guildford   8
10

A245

A243

B2122

A24

A243
A24
Leatherhead   2
Dorking   6½
9

9

A24

A217

A217
Sutton   8
Reigate   2
Redhill (A25)   3½
8

A217

8

A217
Reigate   2
Sutton   8
Kingston (A240)   13
8

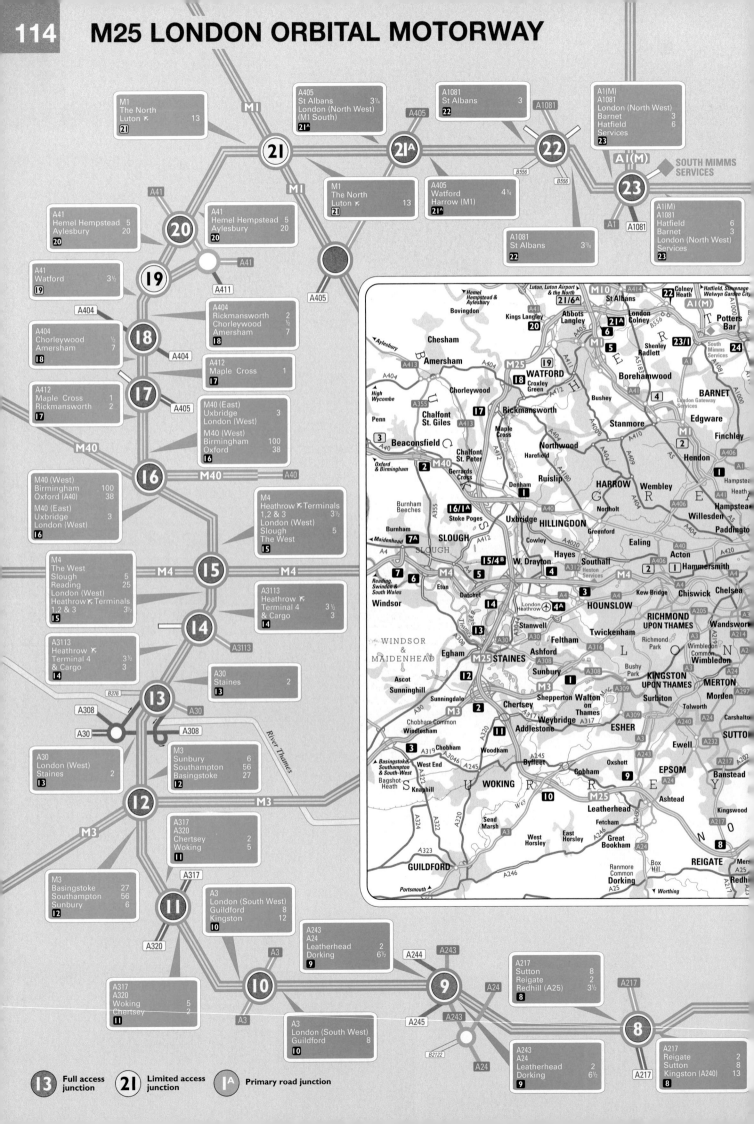

13 Full access junction   **21** Limited access junction   **1A** Primary road junction

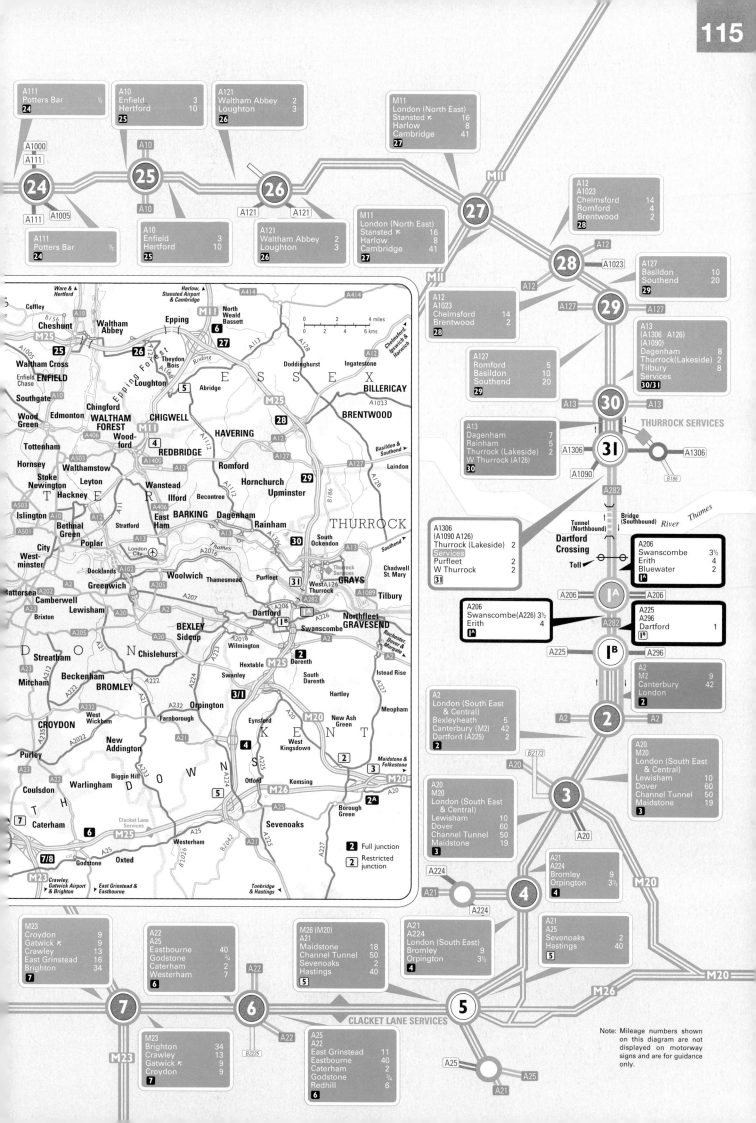

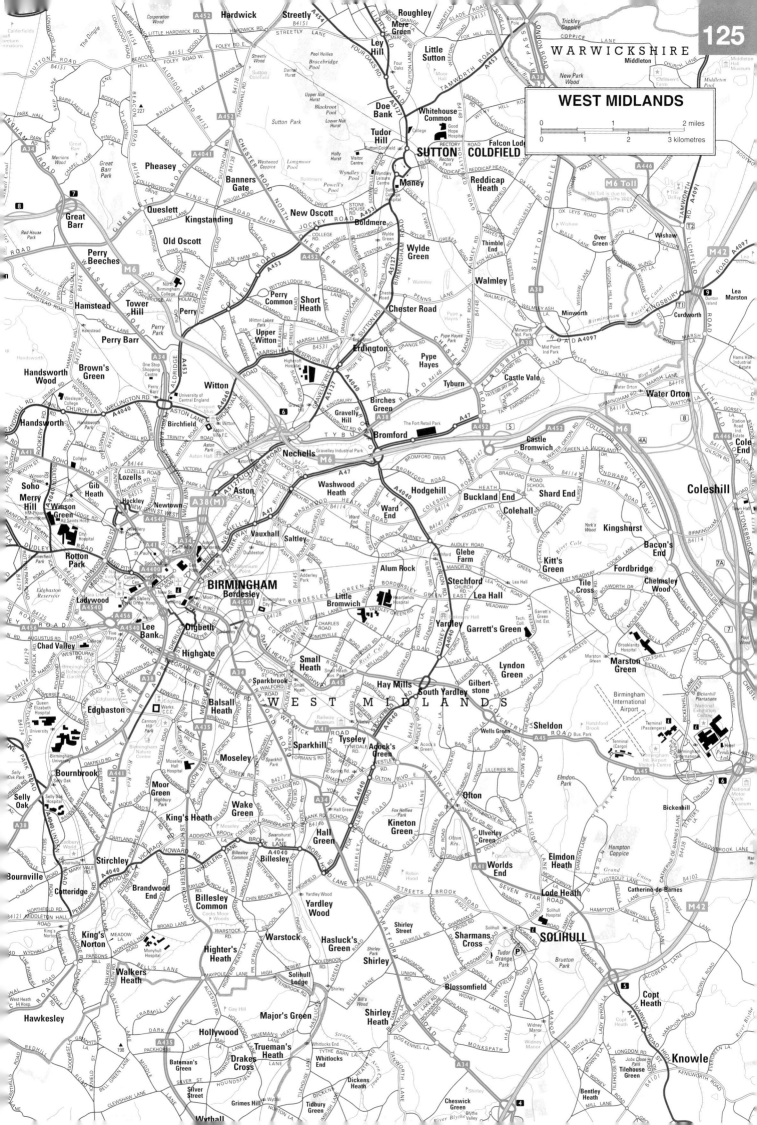

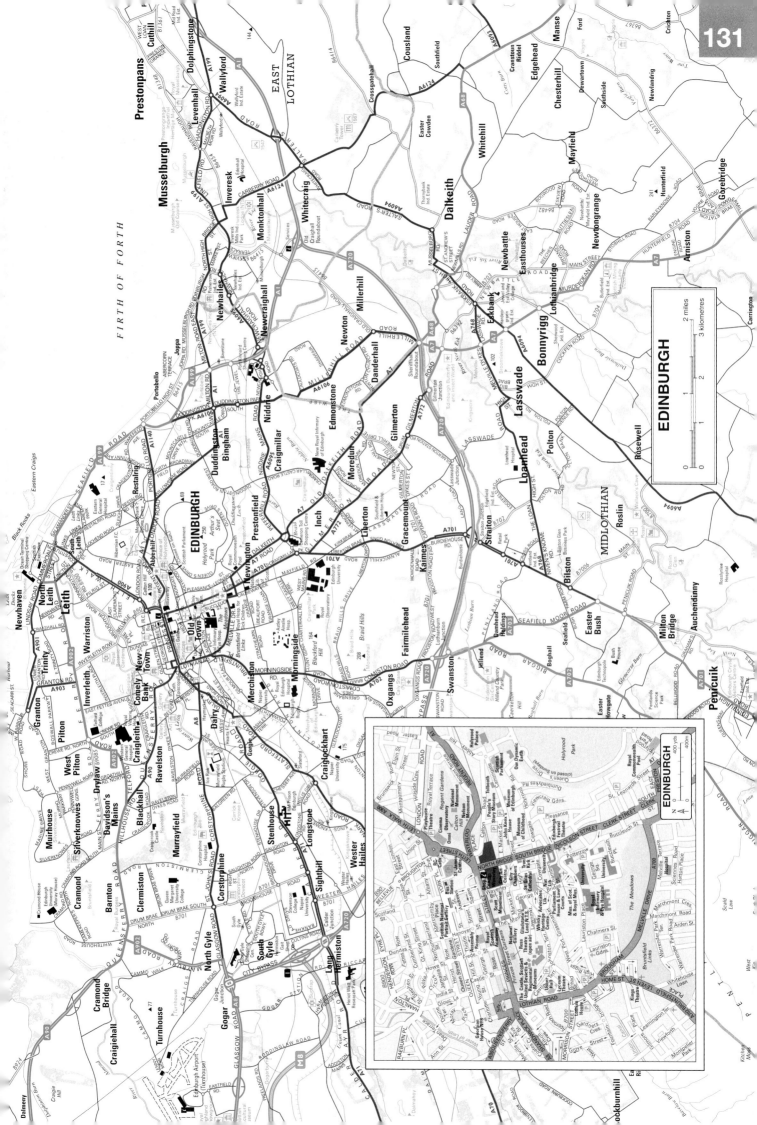

EDINBURGH

INDEX TO PLACE NAMES IN BRITAIN

Use of the Index

In this index place names are followed by a page number and a grid reference. The place can be found by searching that grid square.
Where more than one place has the same name, each can be distinguished by the abbreviated county or unitary authority name shown after the place name.
A list of abbreviations for these names is shown below.

Abbreviations

Aber.	Aberdeenshire
Arg. & B.	Argyll & Bute
B'burn.	Blackburn with Darwen
B. & H.	Brighton & Hove
B. & N.E.Som.	Bath & North East Somerset
B.Gwent	Blaenau Gwent
Beds.	Bedfordshire
Bourne.	Bournemouth
Brack.F.	Bracknell Forest
Bucks.	Buckinghamshire
Caerp.	Caerphilly
Cambs.	Cambridgeshire
Carmar.	Carmarthenshire
Cere.	Ceredigion
Chan.I.	Channel Islands
Ches.	Cheshire
Cornw.	Cornwall
Cumb.	Cumbria
D. & G.	Dumfries & Galloway
Darl.	Darlington
Denb.	Denbighshire
Derbys.	Derbyshire
Dur.	Durham
E.Ayr.	East Ayrshire
E.Dun.	East Dunbartonshire
E.Loth.	East Lothian
E.Renf.	East Renfrewshire
E.Riding	East Riding of Yorkshire
E.Suss.	East Sussex
Edin.	Edinburgh
Falk.	Falkirk
Flints.	Flintshire
Glas.	Glasgow
Glos.	Gloucestershire
Gt.Lon.	Greater London
Gt.Man.	Greater Manchester
Gwyn.	Gwynedd
Hants.	Hampshire
Hart.	Hartlepool
Here.	Herefordshire
Herts.	Hertfordshire
High.	Highland
I.o.A.	Isle of Anglesey
I.o.M.	Isle of Man
I.o.S.	Isles of Scilly
I.o.W.	Isle of Wight
Inclyde	Inverclyde
Lancs.	Lancashire
Leic.	Leicester
Leics.	Leicestershire
Lincs.	Lincolnshire
M.K.	Milton Keynes
M.Tyd.	Merthyr Tydfil
Med.	Medway
Mersey.	Merseyside
Middbro.	Middlesbrough
Midloth.	Midlothian
Mon.	Monmouthshire
N.Ayr.	North Ayrshire
N.E.Lincs.	North East Lincolnshire
N.Lan.	North Lanarkshire
N.Lincs.	North Lincolnshire
N.P.T.	Neath Port Talbot
N.Som.	North Somerset
N.Yorks.	North Yorkshire
Norf.	Norfolk
Northants.	Northamptonshire
Northumb.	Northumberland
Nott.	Nottingham
Notts.	Nottinghamshire
Ork.	Orkney
Oxon.	Oxfordshire
P. & K.	Perth & Kinross
Pembs.	Pembrokeshire
Peter.	Peterborough
Plym.	Plymouth
Ports.	Portsmouth
R. & C.	Redcar & Cleveland
R.C.T.	Rhondda Cynon Taff
Read.	Reading
Renf.	Renfrewshire
Rut.	Rutland
S'end	Southend
S'ham.	Southampton
S.Ayr.	South Ayrshire
S.Glos.	South Gloucestershire
S.Lan.	South Lanarkshire
S.Yorks.	South Yorkshire
Sc.Bord.	Scottish Borders
Shet.	Shetland
Shrop.	Shropshire
Slo.	Slough
Som.	Somerset
Staffs.	Staffordshire
Stir.	Stirling
Stock.	Stockton-on-Tees
Stoke	Stoke-on-Trent
Suff.	Suffolk
Surr.	Surrey
Swan.	Swansea
Swin.	Swindon
T. & W.	Tyne & Wear
Tel. & W.	Telford & Wrekin
Thur.	Thurrock
V. of Glam.	Vale of Glamorgan
W'ham	Wokingham
W. & M.	Windsor & Maidenhead
W.Berks.	West Berkshire
W.Dun.	West Dunbartonshire
W.Isles	Western Isles (Na h-Eileanan an Iar)
W.Loth.	West Lothian
W.Mid.	West Midlands
W.Suss.	West Sussex
W.Yorks.	West Yorkshire
Warks.	Warwickshire
Warr.	Warrington
Wilts.	Wiltshire
Worcs.	Worcestershire
Wrex.	Wrexham

A

Ab Kettleby 42 A3
Abbas Combe 9 G2
Abberley 29 G2
Abberton *Essex* 34 E7
Abberton *Worcs.* 29 J3
Abberwick 71 G2
Abbess Roding 33 J7
Abbey Dore 28 C5
Abbey Hulton 40 B1
Abbey St. Bathans 77 F4
Abbey Village 56 B7
Abbey Wood 23 H4
Abbeycwmhir 27 K1
Abbeystead 55 J4
Abbeytown 60 C1
Abbotrule 70 B2
Abbots Bickington 6 B4
Abbots Bromley 40 C3
Abbots Langley 22 D1
Abbots Leigh 19 J4
Abbots Morton 30 B3
Abbots Ripton 33 F1
Abbot's Salford 30 B3
Abbotsbury 8 E6
Abbotsham 6 C3
Abbotskerswell 5 J4
Abbotsley 33 F3
Abbotts Ann 21 G7
Abbottswood 10 E2
Abdon 38 E7
Aber 17 H1
Aber Bargoed 18 E1
Aber Bowlan 17 K2
Aberaeron 26 D2
Aberaman 18 D1
Aberangell 37 H5
Aberarad 17 G2
Aberarder 88 B6
Aberarder House 88 D2
Aberargie 82 C6
Aberarth 26 D2
Aberavon 18 A3
Aber-banc 17 G1
Aberbeeg 19 F1
Abercanaid 18 D1
Abercarn 19 F2
Abercastle 16 B2
Abercegir 37 H5
Aberchalder 87 K4
Aberchirder 98 E5
Abercorn 75 J3
Abercraf 27 H7
Abercrombie 83 G7
Abercrychan 27 G5
Abercwmboi 18 D1
Abercych 17 F1
Abercynafon 27 K7
Abercynon 18 D2
Aber-Cywarch 37 H4
Aberdalgie 82 B5
Aberdare 18 C1
Aberdaron 36 A3
Aberdaugleddau (Milford Haven) 16 C5
Aberdeen 91 H4
Aberdeen Airport 91 G3
Aberdesach 46 C7
Aberdour 75 K2
Aberdovey (Aberdyfi) 37 F6
Aberduhonw 27 K3
Aberdulais 18 A2
Aberdyfi (Aberdovey) 37 F6
Aberedw 27 K4
Abereiddy 16 B2
Abererch 36 D2
Aberfan 18 D1
Aberfeldy 81 K3
Aberffraw 46 B6
Aberffrwd 27 F1
Aberford 57 K6
Aberfoyle 81 G7
Abergarw 18 C3
Abergavenny (Y Fenni) 28 C7
Abergele 47 H5
Abergiar 17 J1
Abergorlech 17 J2
Abergwaun (Fishguard) 16 C2
Abergwesyn 27 H3
Abergwili 17 H3
Abergwydol 37 G5
Abergwynant 37 F4
Abergwynfi 18 B2
Abergwyngregyn 46 E5
Abergynolwyn 37 F5
Aberhafesp 37 K6
Aberhonddu (Brecon) 27 K6
Aberhosan 37 H6
Aberkenfig 18 B3
Aberlady 76 C2
Aberlemno 83 G2
Aberllefenni 37 G5
Aber-Ilia 27 J7
Aberlour (Charlestown of Aberlour) 97 K7
Abermad 26 E1
Abermaw (Barmouth) 37 F4
Abermeurig 26 E3
Abermule 38 A6
Aber-Naint 38 A3
Abernant *Carmar.* 17 G3
Aber-nant *R.C.T.* 18 D1
Abernethy 82 C6
Abernyte 82 D4
Aberpergwm 18 B1
Aberporth 26 B3
Aberriw (Berriew) 38 A5
Aberscross 96 E1
Abersky 88 C2
Abersoch 36 C3
Abersychan 19 F1
Abertawe (Swansea) 17 K6
Aberteifi (Cardigan) 16 E1
Aberthin 18 D4
Abertillery 19 F1
Abertridwr *Caerp.* 18 E3
Abertridwr *Powys* 37 K4
Abertysswg 18 E1
Aberuthven 82 A6
Aberyscir 27 J6
Aberystwyth 36 E7
Abhainnsuidhe 100 C7
Abingdon 21 H2
Abinger Common 22 E7
Abinger Hammer 22 D7
Abington 68 E1
Abington Pigotts 33 G4
Abingworth 12 E5
Ablington 20 E1
Abney 50 E5
Aboyne 90 D5
Abram 49 F2
Abriachan 88 C1
Abridge 23 H2
Abronhill 75 F3
Abson 19 K4
Abthorpe 31 H4
Abune-the-Hill 106 B5
Aby 53 H5
Acaster Malbis 58 B5
Acaster Selby 58 B5
Accrington 56 C7
Accurrach 80 C6
Acha 78 C2
Achacha 80 A3
Achadacaie 73 G4
Achadh Mòr 101 F5
Achadh-chaorrunn 73 F5
Achadunan 80 C6
Achagavel 79 J2
Achaglass 73 F6
Achahoish 73 F3
Achalader 82 C3
Achallader 80 E3
Achamore 72 D3
Achandunie 96 D4
Achany 96 C1
Achaphubuil 87 G7
Acharacle 79 H1
Achargary 104 C3
Acharn *Arg. & B.* 80 C4
Acharn *P. & K.* 81 J3
Acharonich 79 F4
Acharosson 73 H3
Achateny 79 G1
Achath 91 F3
Achavanich 105 G4
Achduart 95 G1
Achentoul 104 D5
Achfary 102 E4
Achgarve 94 E2
Achiemore *High.* 103 F2
Achiemore *High.* 104 D3
A'Chill 85 H4
Achiltibuie 95 G1
Achina 104 C2
Achindown 97 F7
Achinduich 96 C1
Achingills 105 G2
Achintee 95 F7
Achintee House 87 H7
Achintraid 86 E1
Achlean 89 F5
Achleanan 79 G2
Achleek 79 J2
Achlian 80 C5
Achlyness 102 E3
Achmelvich 102 C6
Achmony 88 B1
Achmore *High.* 86 E1
Achmore *High.* 95 G2
Achmore *Stir.* 81 G4
Achnaba 73 H2
Achnabat 88 C1
Achnabourin 104 C3
Achnacairn 80 A4
Achnacarnin 102 C5
Achnaclerach 96 B5
Achnacloich *Arg. & B.* 80 A4
Achnacloich *High.* 86 B4
Achnaclyth 105 F5
Achnacraig 79 F3
Achnacroish 79 K3
Achnadrish 79 F2
Achnafalnich 80 D5
Achnafauld 81 K4
Achnagairn 96 C7
Achnagarron 96 D4
Achnaha *High.* 79 H3
Achnaha *High.* 79 F1
Achnahanat 96 C2
Achnahannet 89 G2
Achnairn 103 H7
Achnalea 79 K1
Achnamara 73 F2
Achnanellan 79 J1
Achnasaul 87 H6
Achnasheen 95 H6
Achnashelloch 73 G1
Achnastank 89 K1
Achorn 105 G5
Achosnich *High.* 96 E2
Achosnich *High.* 79 F1
Achreamie 105 F2
Achriabhach 80 C1
Achriesgill 102 E3
Achrimsdale 97 G1
Achtoty 103 J2
Achurch 42 D7
Achuvoldrach 103 H3
Achvaich 96 E2
Achvarasdal 104 E2
Achvlair 80 A2
Achvraie 95 G1
Ackergill 105 J3
Acklam *Middbro.* 63 F5
Acklam *N.Yorks.* 58 D3
Ackleton 39 G6
Acklington 71 H3
Ackton 57 K7
Ackworth Moor Top 51 G1
Acle 45 J4
Acock's Green 40 D7
Acol 25 J5
Acomb *Northumb.* 70 E7
Acomb *York* 58 B4
Aconbury 28 E5
Acre 56 C7
Acrefair 38 B1
Acrise Place 15 G3
Acton *Ches.* 49 F7
Acton *Gt.Lon.* 22 E4
Acton *Shrop.* 38 C7
Acton *Suff.* 34 C4
Acton *Worcs.* 29 H2
Acton Beauchamp 29 F3
Acton Bridge 48 E5
Acton Burnell 38 E5
Acton Green 29 F3
Acton Pigott 38 E5
Acton Round 39 F6
Acton Scott 38 D7
Acton Trussell 40 B4
Acton Turville 20 B3
Adamhill 74 C7
Adbaston 39 G3
Adber 8 E2
Adderbury 31 F5
Adderley 39 F2
Adderstone 77 K7
Addiewell 75 H4
Addingham 57 F5
Addington *Bucks.* 31 J6
Addington *Gt.Lon.* 23 G5
Addington *Kent* 23 K6
Addlestone 22 D5
Addlethorpe 53 J6
Adel 57 H6
Adeney 39 F4
Adfa 37 K5
Adforton 28 C1
Adisham 15 H2
Adlestrop 30 D6
Adlingfleet 58 E7
Adlington *Ches.* 49 J4
Adlington *Lancs.* 49 F1
Admaston *Staffs.* 40 C3
Admaston *Tel. & W.* 39 F4
Admington 30 C4
Adsborough 8 B2
Adstock 31 J5
Adstone 31 G3
Adversane 12 D4
Advie 89 J1
Adwalton 57 H7
Adwell 21 K2
Adwick le Street 51 H2
Adwick upon Dearne 51 G2
Ae Village 68 E5
Affleck 91 G2
Affpuddle 9 H5
Afon-wen 47 K5
Afton Bridgend 68 B2
Agglethorpe 57 F1
Aigburth 48 C4
Aignis 101 G4
Aike 59 G5
Aikerness 106 D2
Aikers 107 D8
Aiketgate 61 F2
Aikshaw 60 C2
Aikton 60 D1
Aikwood Tower 69 K1
Ailey 28 C4
Ailsworth 42 E6
Aimster 105 G2
Ainderby Quernhow 57 J1
Ainderby Steeple 62 E7
Aingers Green 35 F7
Ainsdale 48 C1
Ainstable 61 G2
Ainsworth 49 G1
Ainthorpe 63 J6
Aintree 48 C3
Aird 92 C6
Aird a' Mhachair 92 C7
Aird a' Mhulaidh 100 D6
Aird Asaig 100 D7
Aird Dhail 101 G1
Aird Leimhe 93 G3
Aird Mhige 93 G2
Aird Mhighe 93 F3
Aird of Sleat 86 B4
Aird Thunga 101 G4
Aird Uige 100 C4
Airdrie *Fife* 83 G7
Airdrie *N.Lan.* 75 F4
Airidh a' Bhruaich 100 E6
Airieland 65 H5
Airies 66 D7
Airigh-drishaig 86 D1
Airmyn 58 D7
Airntully 82 B4
Airor 86 D4
Airth 75 G2
Airton 56 E4
Airyhassen 64 D6
Aisby *Lincs.* 52 B3
Aisby *Lincs.* 42 D2
Aisgernis 84 C2
Aiskew 57 H1
Aislaby *N.Yorks.* 63 K6
Aislaby *N.Yorks.* 58 D1
Aislaby *Stock.* 63 F5
Aisthorpe 52 C4
Aith *Ork.* 107 B6
Aith *Ork.* 106 F5
Aith *Shet.* 109 C7
Aith *Shet.* 108 F3
Aitnoch 89 G1
Akeld 70 E1
Akeley 31 J5
Akenham 35 F4
Albaston 4 E3
Alberbury 38 C4
Albourne 13 F5
Albrighton *Shrop.* 40 A5
Albrighton *Shrop.* 38 D4
Alburgh 45 G7
Albury *Herts.* 33 H6
Albury *Surr.* 22 D7
Albury Heath 22 D7
Alby Hill 45 F2
Alcaig 96 C6
Alcaston 38 D7
Alcester 30 B3
Alciston 13 J6
Alcombe 7 H1
Alconbury 32 E1
Alconbury Hill 32 E1
Alconbury Weston 32 E1
Aldborough *N.Yorks.* 57 K3
Aldborough *Norf.* 45 F2
Aldbourne 21 F4
Aldbrough 59 J6
Aldbrough St. John 62 C5
Aldburgh 57 H2
Aldbury 32 C7
Aldclune 82 A1
Aldeburgh 35 J3
Aldeby 45 J6
Aldenham 22 E2
Alderbury 10 C2
Alderford 45 F4
Alderholt 10 C3
Alderley 20 A2
Alderley Edge 49 H5
Alderman's Green 41 F7
Aldermaston 21 J5
Aldermaston Soke 21 K5
Aldermaston Wharf 21 K5
Alderminster 30 D4
Alderney Airport 3 J4
Aldersey Green 48 D7
Aldershot 22 B6
Alderton *Glos.* 29 J5
Alderton *Northants.* 31 J4
Alderton *Shrop.* 38 D3
Alderton *Suff.* 35 H4
Alderton *Wilts.* 20 B3
Alderwasley 51 F7
Aldfield 57 H3
Aldford 48 D7
Aldham *Essex* 34 D6
Aldham *Suff.* 34 E4
Aldie *Aber.* 91 J1
Aldie *High.* 96 E3
Aldingbourne 12 C6
Aldingham 55 F2
Aldington *Kent* 15 F4
Aldington *Worcs.* 30 B4
Aldivalloch 90 B2
Aldochlay 74 B1
Aldons 67 F5
Aldreth 33 H1
Aldridge 40 C5
Aldringham 35 J2
Aldro 58 E3
Aldsworth 30 C7
Aldunie 90 B2
Aldville 82 A4
Aldwark *Derbys.* 50 E7
Aldwark *N.Yorks.* 57 K3
Aldwick 12 C7
Aldwincle 42 D7
Aldworth 21 J4
Alexandria 74 B3
Alfardisworthy 6 A4
Alfington 7 K6
Alfold 12 D3
Alfold Crossways 12 D3
Alford *Aber.* 90 D3
Alford *Lincs.* 53 H5
Alford *Som.* 9 F1
Alfreton 51 G7
Alfrick 29 G3
Alfriston 13 J6
Algarkirk 43 F2
Alhampton 9 F1
Alkborough 58 E7
Alkerton 30 E4
Alkham 15 H3
Alkington 38 E2
Alkmonton 40 D2
All Cannings 20 D5
All Saints South Elmham 45 H7
All Stretton 38 D6
Allaleigh 5 J5
Allanaquoich 89 J5
Allancreich 90 D5
Allangillfoot 69 H4
Allanton *D. & G.* 68 E5
Allanton *N.Lan.* 75 G5
Allanton *S.Lan.* 75 F5
Allanton *Sc.Bord.* 77 G5
Allardice 91 G7
Allathasdal 84 B4
Allendale Town 61 K1
Allenheads 61 K2
Allen's Green 33 H7
Allensford 62 B1
Allensmore 28 D5
Allenton 41 F2
Aller 8 C2
Allerby 60 B3
Allerford *Devon* 6 C7
Allerford *Som.* 7 H1
Allerston 58 E1
Allerthorpe 58 D5
Allerton *Mersey.* 48 D4
Allerton *W.Yorks.* 57 G6
Allerton Bywater 57 K7
Allesley 40 E7
Allestree 41 F2
Allexton 42 B5
Allgreave 49 J6
Allhallows 24 E4
Allhallows-on-Sea 24 E4
Alligin Shuas 94 E6
Allimore Green 40 A4
Allington *Lincs.* 42 B1
Allington *Wilts.* 10 D1
Allington *Wilts.* 20 D5
Allithwaite 55 G2
Allnabad 103 G4
Alloa 75 G1
Allonby 60 B2
Alloway 67 H2
Allscot 39 G6
Allt na h-Airbhe 95 H2
Alltachonaich 79 J2
Alltan Dubh 102 B7
Alltbeithe 87 G2
Alltforgan 37 J3
Alltmawr 27 K4
Alltnacaillich 103 G4
Allt-na-subh 87 F2
Alltsigh 88 B3
Alltwalis 17 H2
Alltwen 18 A1
Alltyblaca 17 J1
Almeley 28 C3
Almer 9 J5
Almington 39 F2
Almiston Cross 6 B3
Almondbank 82 B5
Almondbury 50 D1
Almondsbury 19 J3
Alne 57 K3
Alness 96 D5
Alnham 70 E2
Alnmouth 71 H2
Alnwick 71 G2
Alphamstone 34 C5
Alpheton 34 C3
Alphington 7 H6
Alpington 45 G5
Alport 50 E6
Alpraham 48 E7
Alresford 34 E6
Alrewas 40 D4
Alrick 82 C1
Alsager 49 G7
Alsagers Bank 40 A1
Alsop en le Dale 50 D7
Alston *Cumb.* 61 J2
Alston *Devon* 8 C4
Alstone 29 J5
Alstonefield 50 D7
Alswear 7 F3
Altanduin 104 D6
Altarnun 4 C2
Altass 96 C1
Altens 91 H4
Alterwall 105 H2
Altham 56 C6
Althorne 25 F2
Althorpe 52 B2
Alticry 64 C5
Altnafeadh 80 D2
Altnaharra 103 H5
Altofts 57 J7
Alton *Derbys.* 51 F6
Alton *Hants.* 11 J1
Alton *Staffs.* 40 C1
Alton Barnes 20 E5
Alton Pancras 9 F4
Alton Priors 20 E5
Altonside 97 K6
Altrincham 49 G4
Altura 87 J6
Alva 75 G1
Alvanley 48 D5
Alvaston 41 F2
Alvechurch 30 B1
Alvecote 40 E5
Alvediston 9 J2
Alveley 39 G7
Alverdiscott 6 D3
Alverstoke 11 H5
Alverstone 11 G6
Alverton 42 A1
Alves 97 J5
Alvescot 21 F1
Alveston *S.Glos.* 19 K3
Alveston *Warks.* 30 D3
Alvie 89 F4
Alvingham 53 G3
Alvington 19 K1
Alwalton 42 E6
Alweston 9 F3
Alwinton 70 E3
Alwoodley Gates 57 J5
Alyth 82 D3
Amalebra 2 B5
Amber Hill 43 F1
Ambergate 51 F7
Amberley *Glos.* 20 B1
Amberley *W.Suss.* 12 D5
Amble 71 H3
Amblecote 40 A7
Ambleside 60 E6
Ambleston 16 D3
Ambrismore 73 J5
Ambrosden 31 H7
Amcotts 52 B1
Amersham 22 C2
Amesbury 20 E7
Amington 40 E5
Amisfield 69 F5
Amlwch 46 C3
Amlwch Port 46 C3
Ammanford (Rhydaman) 17 K4
Amotherby 58 D2
Ampfield 10 E2
Ampleforth 58 B2
Ampleforth College 58 B2
Ampney Crucis 20 D1
Ampney St. Mary 20 D1
Ampney St. Peter 20 D1
Amport 21 G7
Ampthill 32 D5
Ampton 34 C1
Amroth 16 E5
Amulree 81 K4
An Tairbeart (Tarbert) 100 D7
An T-ób (Leverburgh) 93 F3
Anaboard 89 H1
Anaheilt 79 K1
Ancaster 42 C1
Anchor 38 A7
Ancroft 77 H6
Ancrum 70 B1
Ancton 12 C6
Anderby 53 J5
Anderson 9 H5
Anderton 49 F5
Andover 21 G7
Andover Down 21 G7
Andoversford 30 B6
Andreas 54 D4
Anelog 36 A3
Angarrack 2 C5
Angersleigh 7 K4
Angerton 60 D1
Angle 16 B5
Angler's Retreat 37 G6
Angmering 12 D6
Angram 58 B5
Anie 81 G6
Ankerville 97 F4
Anlaby 59 G7
Anmer 44 B3
Anna Valley 21 G7
Annan 69 G7
Annaside 54 D1
Annat *Arg. & B.* 80 B5
Annat *High.* 94 E6
Annbank 67 J1
Annesley 51 H7
Annesley Woodhouse 51 H7
Annfield Plain 62 C1
Annscroft 38 D5
Ansdell 55 G7
Ansford 9 F1
Ansley 40 E6
Anslow 40 E3
Anslow Gate 40 D3
Anstey *Herts.* 33 H5
Anstey *Leics.* 41 H5
Anstruther 83 G7
Ansty *W.Suss.* 13 F4
Ansty *Warks.* 41 F7
Ansty *Wilts.* 9 J2
Anthill Common 11 H3
Anthorn 60 C1
Antingham 45 G2
Anton's Gowt 43 F1
Antony 4 D5
Antrobus 49 F5
Anvil Corner 6 B5
Anwick 52 E7
Anwoth 65 F5
Aoradh 72 A4
Apethorpe 42 D6
Apley 52 E5
Apperknowle 51 F5
Apperley 29 H6
Appin 80 A3
Appin House 80 A3
Appleby 52 C1
Appleby Magna 41 F4
Appleby Parva 41 F5
Appleby-in-Westmorland 61 H4
Applecross 94 D7
Appledore *Devon* 6 C2
Appledore *Devon* 7 J4
Appledore *Kent* 14 E5
Appledore Heath 14 E4
Appleford 21 J2
Appleshaw 21 G7
Applethwaite 60 D4
Appleton 21 H1
Appleton Roebuck 58 B5
Appleton Thorn 49 F4
Appleton Wiske 62 E6
Appleton-le-Moors 58 D1
Appleton-le-Street 58 D2
Appletreehall 70 A2
Appletreewick 57 F3

Appley 7 J3
Appley Bridge 48 E1
Apse Heath 11 G6
Apsley 22 D1
Apsley End 32 E5
Apuldram 12 B6
Arberth (Narberth) 16 E4
Arbirlot 83 G3
Arborfield 22 A5
Arborfield Cross 22 A5
Arborfield Garrison 22 A5
Arbroath 83 H3
Arbuthnott 91 G7
Archdeacon Newton 62 D5
Archiestown 97 K7
Arclid 49 G6
Ard a' Chapuill 73 J3
Ardacheananbeg 73 J2
Ardacheanranmor 73 J2
Ardachoil 79 J4
Ardachu 96 D1
Ardachvie 87 H5
Ardailly 72 E5
Ardalanish 78 E6
Ardallie 91 J1
Ardanaiseig 80 B5
Ardaneaskan 86 E1
Ardanstur 79 K6
Ardantiobairt 79 H2
Ardantrive 79 K5
Ardarroch 86 E1
Ardbeg Arg. & B. 73 J4
Ardbeg Arg. & B. 72 C6
Ardbeg Arg. & B. 73 J2
Ardblair 88 B1
Ardbrecknish 80 B5
Ardcharnich 95 H3
Ardchiavaig 78 E6
Ardchonnel 80 A4
Ardchonnell 80 A6
Ardchrishnish 79 F5
Ardchronie 96 D3
Ardchuilk 87 J1
Ardchullarie More 81 G6
Ardchyle 81 G5
Arddlin 38 B4
Ardeley 33 G6
Ardelve 86 E2
Arden 74 B2
Ardencaple House 79 J6
Ardens Grafton 30 C3
Ardentallan 79 K5
Ardentinny 73 K2
Ardeonaig 81 H4
Ardersier 96 E6
Ardery 79 J1
Ardessie 95 G3
Ardfad 79 J6
Ardfern 79 K7
Ardfin 72 C4
Ardgartan 80 D7
Ardgay 96 C2
Ardgenavan 80 C6
Ardgowan 74 A3
Ardgowse 90 E3
Ardgye 97 J5
Ardhallow 73 K3
Ardheslaig 94 D6
Ardiecow 98 D4
Ardinamar 79 J6
Ardindrean 95 H3
Ardingly 13 G4
Ardington 21 H3
Ardintoul 86 E2
Ardkinglas House 80 C6
Ardlair 90 D2
Ardlamont 73 H4
Ardleigh 34 E6
Ardleish 80 E6
Ardler 82 D3
Ardley 31 G6
Ardlui 80 E6
Ardlussa 72 E2
Ardmaddy 80 B4
Ardmair 95 H2
Ardmaleish 73 J4
Ardmay 80 D7
Ardmenish 72 D3
Ardmhór 84 C4
Ardminish 72 E6
Ardmolich 86 D7
Ardmore Arg. & B. 72 C6
Ardmore Arg. & B. 73 J4
Ardmore Arg. & B. 74 B3
Ardmore High. 96 E3
Ardnackaig 73 F1
Ardnacross 79 G3
Ardnadam 73 K3
Ardnadrochit 79 J4
Ardnagoine 95 F1
Ardnagowan 80 C7
Ardnagrask 96 C7
Ardnahein 74 A1
Ardnahoe 72 C3
Ardnarff 86 E1
Ardnastang 79 K1
Ardnave 72 A3
Ardno 80 C7
Ardo 91 G1
Ardoch D. & G. 68 D3
Ardoch Moray 97 J6
Ardoch P. & K. 82 B4
Ardochrig 74 E6
Ardoyne 90 E2
Ardpatrick 73 F4
Ardpeaton 74 A2
Ardradnaig 81 J3
Ardrishaig 73 G2
Ardroe 102 C6
Ardrossan 74 A6
Ardscalpsie 73 J5
Ardshave 96 E2
Ardshealach 79 H1
Ardshellach 79 J6
Ardsley 51 F2
Ardslignish 79 G1
Ardtalla 72 C5
Ardtalnaig 81 H4
Ardtaraig 73 J2
Ardteatle 80 C5
Ardtornish 79 J3
Ardtrostan 81 H5
Ardtur 80 A3
Arduaine 79 K7
Ardullie 96 C5
Ardura 79 H4
Ardvar 102 D5
Ardvasar 86 C4
Ardveich 81 H5
Ardverikie 88 C6
Ardvorlich Arg. & B. 80 E6
Ardvorlich P. & K. 81 H5
Ardwall 65 F5
Ardwell D. & G. 64 B6
Ardwell Moray 90 B1
Ardwell S.Ayr. 67 F4

Areley Kings 29 G1
Arford 12 B3
Argaty 81 J7
Argoed 18 E2
Argoed Mill 27 J2
Argrennan 65 H5
Arichamish 80 A7
Arichastlich 80 D4
Arichonan 73 F1
Aridhglas 78 E5
Arienskill 86 D6
Arileod 78 C2
Arinacrinachd 94 D6
Arinafad Beg 73 F2
Arinagour 78 D2
Arinambane 84 C2
Arisaig 86 C6
Arivegaig 79 H1
Arkendale 57 J3
Arkesden 33 H5
Arkholme 55 J2
Arkleby 60 C3
Arkleside 57 F1
Arkleton 69 J4
Arkley 23 F2
Arksey 51 H2
Arkwright 51 G5
Arlary 82 C7
Arlecdon 60 B5
Arlesey 32 E5
Arleston 39 F4
Arley 49 F4
Arlingham 29 G7
Arlington Devon 6 E1
Arlington E.Suss. 13 J6
Arlington Glos. 20 E1
Arlington Beccott 6 E1
Armadale High. 104 C2
Armadale High. 86 C4
Armadale W.Loth. 75 H4
Armathwaite 61 G2
Arminghall 45 G5
Armitage 40 C4
Armscote 30 D4
Armston 42 D7
Armthorpe 51 J2
Arnabost 78 D2
Arncliffe 56 E2
Arncliffe Cote 56 E2
Arncroach 83 G7
Arne 9 J6
Arnesby 41 J6
Arngask 82 C6
Arngibbon 74 E1
Arngomery 74 E1
Arnhall 83 H1
Arnicle 73 F7
Arnipol 86 D6
Arnish 94 C7
Arnol 101 F3
Arnold 41 H1
Arnprior 74 E1
Arnside 55 H2
Arowry 38 D2
Arrad Foot 55 G1
Arradoul 98 C4
Arram 59 G5
Arrat 83 H2
Arrathorne 62 C7
Arreton 11 G6
Arrington 33 G3
Arrivain 80 D4
Arrochar 80 D7
Arrow 30 B3
Arscaig 103 H7
Arthington 57 H5
Arthingworth 42 A7
Arthog 37 F4
Arthrath 91 H1
Arthurstone 82 D3
Artrochie 91 J1
Aruadh 72 A4
Arundel 12 D6
Aryhoulan 80 B1
Asby 60 B4
Ascog 73 K4
Ascot 22 C5
Ascott 30 E5
Ascott-under-Wychwood 30 D7
Ascreavie 82 E2
Asenby 57 J2
Asfordby 42 A4
Asfordby Hill 42 A4
Asgarby Lincs. 53 G6
Asgarby Lincs. 42 E1
Ash Kent 15 H2
Ash Kent 24 C5
Ash Som. 8 D2
Ash Surr. 22 B6
Ash Barton 6 D5
Ash Bullayne 7 F5
Ash Magna 38 E2
Ash Mill 7 F3
Ash Priors 7 K3
Ash Thomas 7 J4
Ash Vale 22 B6
Ashampstead 21 J4
Ashbocking 35 F3
Ashbourne 40 D1
Ashbrittle 7 J3
Ashburnham Place 13 K5
Ashburton 5 H4
Ashbury Devon 6 D6
Ashbury Oxon. 21 F3
Ashby 52 C2
Ashby by Partney 53 H6
Ashby cum Fenby 53 F2
Ashby de la Launde 52 D7
Ashby de la Zouch 41 F4
Ashby Folville 42 A4
Ashby Magna 41 H6
Ashby Parva 41 H7
Ashby Puerorum 53 G5
Ashby St. Ledgers 31 G2
Ashby St. Mary 45 H5
Ashchurch 29 J5
Ashcombe 5 K3
Ashcott 8 D1
Ashdon 33 J4
Ashe 21 J7
Asheldham 25 F1
Ashen 34 B4
Ashenden 14 D4
Ashendon 31 J7
Ashens 73 G3
Ashfield Arg. & B. 73 F2
Ashfield Stir. 81 J7
Ashfield Suff. 35 G2
Ashfield Green 35 G1
Ashfold Crossways 13 F4
Ashford Devon 5 G6
Ashford Devon 6 D2
Ashford Hants. 10 C3
Ashford Kent 15 F3
Ashford Surr. 22 D4
Ashford Bowdler 28 E1

Ashford Carbonel 28 E1
Ashford Hill 21 J5
Ashford in the Water 50 E6
Ashgill 75 F5
Ashiestiel 76 C7
Ashill Devon 7 J4
Ashill Norf. 44 C5
Ashill Som. 8 C3
Ashingdon 24 E2
Ashington Northumb. 71 H5
Ashington Som. 8 E2
Ashington W.Suss. 12 E5
Ashkirk 69 K1
Ashleworth 29 H6
Ashley Cambs. 33 K2
Ashley Ches. 49 G4
Ashley Devon 6 E4
Ashley Glos. 20 C2
Ashley Hants. 10 E1
Ashley Hants. 10 D5
Ashley Kent 15 H3
Ashley Northants. 42 A6
Ashley Staffs. 39 G2
Ashley Wilts. 20 B5
Ashley Green 22 C1
Ashley Heath 10 C4
Ashmanhaugh 45 H3
Ashmansworth 21 H6
Ashmansworthy 6 B4
Ashmore Dorset 9 J3
Ashmore P. & K. 82 C2
Ashorne 30 E3
Ashover 51 F6
Ashow 30 E1
Ashperton 29 F4
Ashprington 5 J5
Ashreigney 6 E4
Ashtead 22 E6
Ashton Ches. 48 E6
Ashton Cornw. 2 C6
Ashton Cornw. 4 D4
Ashton Here. 28 E2
Ashton Northants. 42 D7
Ashton Northants. 31 J4
Ashton Common 20 B6
Ashton Keynes 20 D2
Ashton under Hill 29 J5
Ashton upon Mersey 49 G3
Ashton-in-Makerfield 48 E3
Ashton-under-Lyne 49 J3
Ashurst Hants. 10 E3
Ashurst Kent 13 J3
Ashurst W.Suss. 12 E5
Ashurstwood 13 H3
Ashwater 6 B6
Ashwell Herts. 33 F5
Ashwell Rut. 42 B4
Ashwellthorpe 45 F6
Ashwick 19 K7
Ashwicken 44 B4
Ashybank 70 A2
Askam in Furness 55 F2
Askern 51 H1
Askerswell 8 E5
Askett 22 B1
Askham Cumb. 61 G4
Askham Notts. 51 K5
Askham Bryan 58 B5
Askham Richard 58 B5
Asknish 73 H1
Askrigg 62 A7
Askwith 57 G5
Aslackby 42 D2
Aslacton 45 F6
Aslockton 42 A1
Asloun 90 D3
Aspall 35 F2
Aspatria 60 C2
Aspenden 33 G6
Aspley Guise 32 C5
Aspull 49 F2
Asselby 58 D7
Assington 34 D5
Astbury 49 H6
Astcote 31 H3
Asterby 53 F5
Asterley 38 C5
Asterton 38 C6
Asthall 30 D7
Asthall Leigh 30 E7
Astley Shrop. 38 E4
Astley Warks. 41 F7
Astley Worcs. 29 G2
Astley Abbotts 39 G6
Astley Bridge 49 G1
Astley Cross 29 G2
Astley Green 49 G3
Aston Ches. 39 F1
Aston Ches. 48 E5
Aston Derbys. 50 D4
Aston Flints. 48 C6
Aston Here. 28 D1
Aston Herts. 33 F6
Aston Oxon. 21 G1
Aston S.Yorks. 51 G4
Aston Shrop. 38 E3
Aston Staffs. 39 F5
Aston Tel. & W. 39 F5
Aston W'ham 22 A3
Aston W.Mid. 40 C7
Aston Abbotts 32 B6
Aston Botterell 39 F7
Aston Cantlow 30 C3
Aston Clinton 32 B7
Aston Crews 29 F6
Aston Cross 29 J5
Aston End 33 F6
Aston Eyre 39 F6
Aston Fields 29 J1
Aston Flamville 41 G6
Aston Ingham 29 F6
Aston juxta Mondrum 49 F7
Aston le Walls 31 F3
Aston Magna 30 C5
Aston Munslow 38 E7
Aston on Clun 38 C7
Aston on Trent 41 G3
Aston Rogers 38 C5
Aston Rowant 22 A2
Aston Sandford 22 A1
Aston Somerville 30 B5
Aston Subedge 30 C4
Aston Tirrold 21 J3
Aston Upthorpe 21 J3
Aston-by-Stone 40 B2
Astwick 33 F5
Astwood 32 C4
Astwood Bank 30 B2
Aswarby 42 D1
Aswardby 53 G5
Aswick Grange 43 G4
Atch Lench 30 B3
Atcham 38 E5
Athelhampton 9 G5

Athelney 8 C2
Athelstaneford 76 D3
Atherington 6 D3
Atherstone 41 F6
Atherstone on Stour 30 D3
Atherton 49 F2
Athlinne 100 D6
Atlow 40 E1
Attadale 87 F1
Attenborough 41 H2
Atterby 52 C3
Attleborough Norf. 44 E6
Attleborough Warks. 41 F6
Attlebridge 45 F4
Atwick 59 H4
Atworth 20 B5
Aubourn 52 C6
Auch 80 E4
Auchairne 67 F5
Auchallater 89 J6
Auchameanach 73 G5
Auchamore 98 E6
Auchavan 82 C1
Auchbraad 73 G2
Auchbreck 89 K2
Auchenblae 91 F7
Auchenbothie 74 B3
Auchenbrack 68 C4
Auchenbreck 73 J2
Auchencairn 65 J5
Auchencrow 77 G4
Auchendinny 76 A4
Auchendolly 65 H4
Auchenfoyle 74 B3
Auchengray 75 H5
Auchenhalrig 98 B4
Auchenheath 75 G6
Auchenhessnane 68 D4
Auchenlochan 73 H3
Auchenmalg 64 C5
Auchenrivock 69 J5
Auchentiber 74 B5
Auchenvennal 74 A2
Auchessan 81 F5
Auchgourish 89 G3
Auchinafaud 73 F5
Auchincruive 67 H1
Auchindarrach 73 G2
Auchindarroch 80 B2
Auchindrain 80 B7
Auchindrean 95 H3
Auchininna 98 E6
Auchinleck 74 E3
Auchinloch 74 E3
Auchinner 81 H6
Auchinroath 97 K6
Auchintoul Aber. 90 D3
Auchintoul Aber. 98 E5
Auchintoul High. 96 C1
Auchiries 91 J1
Auchleven 90 E2
Auchlochan 75 G7
Auchlunachan 95 H3
Auchlunies 91 H5
Auchlunkart 98 B6
Auchlyne 81 G5
Auchmacoy 91 H1
Auchmair 90 B2
Auchmantle 64 B4
Auchmithie 83 H3
Auchmuirbridge 82 D7
Auchmull 90 D7
Auchnabony 65 H6
Auchnabreac 80 B7
Auchnacloich 79 J5
Auchnacraig 79 J5
Auchnacree 83 F1
Auchnafree 81 K4
Auchnagallin 89 H1
Auchnagatt 99 H6
Auchnaha 73 H2
Auchnangoul 80 B7
Aucholzie 90 B5
Auchorrie 90 E4
Auchraw 81 G5
Auchreoch 80 E5
Auchronie 90 C6
Auchterarder 82 A6
Auchtercairn 94 E4
Auchterderran 76 A1
Auchterhouse 82 E4
Auchtermuchty 82 D6
Auchterneed 96 B5
Auchtertool 76 A1
Auchtertyre Angus 82 D3
Auchtertyre Moray 97 J6
Auchtertyre Stir. 80 E5
Auchtubh 81 G5
Auckengill 105 J2
Auckley 51 J2
Audenshaw 49 J3
Audlem 39 F1
Audley 49 G7
Audley End 33 J5
Auds 98 E4
Aughton E.Riding 58 D6
Aughton Lancs. 48 C2
Aughton Lancs. 55 J3
Aughton S.Yorks. 51 G4
Aughton Park 48 D2
Auldearn 97 G6
Aulden 28 D3
Auldhame 76 D2
Auldhouse 74 E5
Aulich 81 H2
Ault a' chruinn 87 F2
Ault Hucknall 51 G6
Aultanrynie 103 F5
Aultbea 94 E3
Aultgrishan 94 D3
Aultguish Inn 95 K4
Aultiba 81 F6
Aultiphurst 104 D2
Aultmore 98 C5
Aultnagoire 88 C2
Aultnamain Inn 96 D3
Aultnapaddock 98 B6
Aulton 86 D2
Aundorach 89 G3
Aunk 7 J5
Aunsby 42 D2
Auquhorthies 91 G2
Aust 19 J3
Austerfield 51 J3
Austonley 50 D2
Austrey 40 E5
Austwick 56 C3
Authorpe 53 H4
Authorpe Row 53 J5
Avebury 20 E4
Aveley 23 J3
Avening 20 B2
Averham 51 K7

Aveton Gifford 5 G6
Avielochan 89 G3
Aviemore 89 F3
Avington Hants. 11 G1
Avington W.Berks. 21 G5
Avoch 96 D6
Avon 10 C5
Avon Dassett 31 F3
Avonbridge 75 H3
Avonmouth 19 J4
Avonwick 5 H5
Awbridge 10 E2
Awhirk 64 A5
Awkley 19 J3
Awliscombe 7 K5
Awre 20 A1
Awsworth 41 G1
Axbridge 19 H6
Axford Hants. 21 K7
Axford Wilts. 21 F4
Axminster 8 B5
Axmouth 8 B5
Aycliffe 62 D4
Aydon 71 F7
Aylburton 19 K1
Ayle 61 J2
Aylesbeare 7 J6
Aylesbury 32 B7
Aylesby 53 F2
Aylesford 14 C2
Aylesham 15 H2
Aylestone 41 H5
Aylmerton 45 F2
Aylsham 45 F3
Aylton 29 F5
Aymestrey 28 D2
Aynho 31 G5
Ayot St. Lawrence 32 E7
Ayot St. Peter 33 F7
Ayr 67 H1
Aysgarth 57 F1
Ayshford 7 J4
Ayside 55 G1
Ayston 42 B5
Aythorpe Roding 33 J7
Ayton P. & K. 82 C6
Ayton Sc.Bord. 77 H4
Aywick 108 E4
Azerley 57 H2

B

Babbacombe 5 K4
Babbinswood 38 C2
Babcary 8 E2
Babel 27 H5
Babell 47 K5
Babeny 5 G3
Babraham 33 J4
Babworth 51 J4
Bac 101 G3
Back of Keppoch 86 C6
Backaland 106 E4
Backaskaill 106 D2
Backbarrow 55 G1
Backburn 90 D1
Backfolds 99 J5
Backford 48 C5
Backhill 91 F1
Backhill of Clackriach 99 H6
Backhill of Trustach 90 E5
Backies High. 97 F1
Backies Moray 98 C5
Backlass 105 H3
Backside 90 C1
Backwell 19 H5
Backworth 71 H6
Bacon End 33 J7
Baconsthorpe 45 F2
Bacton Here. 28 C5
Bacton Norf. 45 H2
Bacton Suff. 34 E2
Bacup 56 D7
Badachro 94 D4
Badanloch Lodge 104 C5
Badavanich 95 H6
Badbea 105 F7
Badbury 20 E3
Badby 31 G3
Badcall High. 102 D4
Badcall High. 102 E3
Badcaul 95 G2
Baddeley Green 49 J7
Badden 73 G2
Baddesley Ensor 40 E6
Baddidarach 102 C6
Badenscoth 98 E6
Badenyon 90 B3
Badger 39 G6
Badgerbank 49 H5
Badgers Mount 23 H5
Badgeworth 29 J7
Badgworth 19 G6
Badicaul 86 D2
Badingham 35 H2
Badintagairt 103 G7
Badlesmere 15 F2
Badley 34 E3
Badlipster 105 H4
Badluarach 95 F2
Badminton 20 B3
Badnaban 102 C6
Badnabay 102 E4
Badnafrave 89 K3
Badnagie 105 G5
Badninish 96 E2
Badrallach 95 G2
Badsey 30 B4
Badshot Lea 22 B7
Badsworth 51 G1
Badwell Ash 34 D2
Badyo 82 A1
Bae Cinmel (Kinmel Bay) 47 H4
Bae Colwyn (Colwyn Bay) 47 G5
Bae Penrhyn (Penrhyn Bay) 47 G4
Bag Enderby 53 G5
Bagby 57 K1
Bagendon 20 D1
Baggrave Hall 42 A5
Baggrow 60 C2
Bagh a' Chaisteil (Castlebay) 84 B5
Baghasdal 84 C3
Bagillt 48 B5
Baginton 30 E1
Baglan 18 A2
Bagley 38 D3
Bagnall 49 J7
Bagnor 21 H5
Bagshot Surr. 22 C5
Bagshot Wilts. 21 G5

Bagstone 19 K3
Bagthorpe Norf. 44 B2
Bagthorpe Notts. 51 G7
Baguley 49 H4
Bagworth 41 G5
Bagwyllydiart 28 D6
Baildon 57 G6
Baile a' Mhanaich (Balivanich) 92 C6
Baile Ailein 100 E5
Baile an Truiseil 101 F2
Baile Boidheach 73 F3
Baile Gharbhaidh 92 C7
Baile Glas 92 D6
Baile Mhartainn (Balmartin) 92 C4
Baile Mhic Phail 92 D4
Baile Mòr Arg. & B. 90 D5
Baile Mòr W.Isles 92 C5
Baile nan Cailleach 92 C6
Baile Raghaill 92 C5
Boilebeag 88 C2
Baileguish 89 F5
Baile-na-Cille 92 D3
Bailetown 86 C7
Bailiesward 90 C1
Bainbridge 62 A7
Bainsford 75 G2
Bainshole 90 E1
Bainton E.Riding 59 F4
Bainton Peter. 42 D5
Bairnkine 70 B2
Bakebare 90 B1
Baker Street 24 C3
Baker's End 33 G7
Bakewell 50 E6
Bala 37 J2
Balachuirn 94 B7
Balafark 74 E1
Balaldie 97 F4
Balavil 88 E4
Balbeg High. 88 B1
Balbeg High. 88 B2
Balbeggie 82 C5
Balbirnie 82 D7
Balbithan 91 F3
Balblair High. 96 E5
Balblair High. 96 C2
Balcharn 96 C1
Balcherry 97 F3
Balchers 99 F5
Balchladich 102 C5
Balchraggan High. 96 C7
Balchraggan High. 88 C1
Balchrick 102 D2
Balcombe 13 G3
Balcurvie 82 E7
Baldernock 74 D3
Baldersby 57 J2
Balderstone 56 B6
Balderton 52 B7
Baldhu 2 E4
Baldinnie 83 F6
Baldock 33 F5
Baldovie Angus 82 E2
Baldovie Dundee 83 F4
Baldrine 54 D5
Baldslow 14 C6
Baldwin 54 C5
Baldwinholme 60 E1
Baldwin's Gate 39 G1
Bale 44 E2
Balelone 92 C4
Balemartine 78 A3
Balendoch 82 D3
Balephuil 78 A3
Balerno 75 K4
Balernock 74 A2
Balerominbubh 92 B1
Balerominmore 92 B1
Balevulin 79 F5
Balfield 83 G1
Balfour Aber. 90 D5
Balfour Ork. 107 D6
Balfron 74 D2
Balfron Station 74 D2
Balgedie 82 C7
Balgonar 75 J1
Balgove 91 G1
Balgowan D. & G. 64 B6
Balgowan High. 88 D5
Balgown 93 J5
Balgray 83 F4
Balgreen 99 F5
Balgreggan 64 A5
Balgy 94 E6
Balhaldie 81 K7
Balhalgardy 91 F2
Balhary 82 D3
Balhelvie 82 E5
Balhousie 83 F7
Baliasta 108 F2
Baligill 104 D2
Baligrundle 79 K4
Balindore 80 A4
Balintore 97 F4
Balintraid 96 E4
Balintyre 81 H3
Balivanich (Baile a' Mhanaich) 92 C6
Balkeerie 82 E3
Balkholme 58 D7
Balkissock 67 F5
Ball 38 C3
Ball Haye Green 49 J7
Ball Hill 21 H5
Ballabeg 54 B6
Ballacannell 54 D5
Ballacarnane Beg 54 C5
Ballachulish 80 B2
Balladoole 54 B7
Ballafesson 54 B6
Ballagyr 54 B5
Ballajora 54 D4
Ballakilpheric 54 B6
Ballamodha 54 B6
Ballantrae 66 E5
Ballards Gore 25 F2
Ballasalla I.o.M. 54 B6
Ballasalla I.o.M. 54 C4
Ballater 90 B5
Ballaterach 90 C5
Ballaugh 54 C4
Ballaveare 54 C6
Ballechin 82 A2
Balleich 81 G7
Ballencrieff 76 C3
Ballidon 50 E7
Balliekine 54 D6
Balliemeanoch 80 C7
Balliemore Arg. & B. 73 K1
Balliemore Arg. & B. 79 K5
Ballig 54 B5
Ballimeanoch 80 B6
Ballimore Arg. & B. 73 H2

Ballimore Stir. 81 G6
Ballinaby 72 A4
Ballindean 82 D5
Ballingdon 34 C4
Ballinger Common 22 C1
Ballingham 28 E5
Ballingry 75 K1
Ballinlick 82 A3
Ballinluig P. & K. 82 A2
Ballinluig P. & K. 82 B2
Ballintuim 82 C2
Balloch Angus 82 E2
Balloch High. 96 E7
Balloch N.Lan. 75 F3
Balloch W.Dun. 74 B2
Ballochan 90 D5
Ballochandrain 73 H2
Ballochford 90 B1
Balluchgair 66 B1
Ballochmartin 73 K5
Ballochmorrie 67 G5
Ballochmyle 67 K1
Ballochroy 73 F5
Ballogie 90 D5
Balls Cross 12 C4
Ballyaurgan 73 F3
Ballygown 79 F3
Ballygrant 72 B4
Ballyhaugh 78 C2
Ballymeanoch 73 G1
Ballymichael 73 H7
Balmacara 86 E2
Balmaclellan 65 G3
Balmacneil 82 A2
Balmadies 83 G3
Balmae 65 G6
Balmaha 74 C1
Balmalcolm 82 E7
Balmartin (Baile Mhartainn) 92 C4
Balmeanach Arg. & B. 79 H3
Balmeanach Arg. & B. 79 F4
Balmedie 91 H3
Balmerino 82 E5
Balmerlawn 10 E4
Balminnoch 64 C4
Balmore E.Dun. 74 E3
Balmore High. 87 K1
Balmore High. 93 H7
Balmore P. & K. 81 J2
Balmullo 83 F5
Balmungie 96 E6
Balmyle 82 B2
Balnaboth 82 E1
Balnabruaich 96 E4
Balnacra 95 F7
Balnafoich 88 D1
Balnagall 97 F3
Balnagown Castle 96 E4
Balnaguard 82 A2
Balnaguisich 96 D4
Balnahard Arg. & B. 72 C1
Balnahard Arg. & B. 79 F4
Balnain 88 B1
Balnakeil 103 F2
Balnaknock 93 K5
Balnamoon 83 G1
Balnapaling 96 E5
Balnespick 89 F4
Balquhidder 81 G5
Balsall Common 30 D1
Balscote 30 E4
Balsham 33 J3
Baltasound 108 F2
Balterley 49 G7
Baltersan 64 E4
Balthangie 99 G5
Balthayock 82 C5
Baltonsborough 8 E1
Baluachraig 73 G1
Balulive 72 C4
Balure Arg. & B. 80 B4
Balure Arg. & B. 79 K4
Balvaird 96 C6
Balvarran 82 B1
Balvicar 79 J6
Balvraid High. 86 E3
Balvraid High. 89 F1
Bamber Bridge 55 J7
Bamber's Green 33 J6
Bamburgh 77 K7
Bamff 82 D2
Bamford 50 E4
Bampton Cumb. 61 G5
Bampton Devon 7 H3
Bampton Oxon. 21 G1
Banavie 87 H7
Banbury 31 F4
Bancffosfelen 17 H4
Banchor 97 G7
Banchory 91 F5
Banchory-Devenick 91 H4
Bancyfelin 17 G4
Banc-y-ffordd 17 H2
Bandon 82 D7
Banff 98 E4
Bangor 46 D5
Bangor Teifi 17 G1
Bangor-is-y-coed 38 C1
Banham 44 E7
Bank 10 D4
Bank End 55 F1
Bank Newton 56 E4
Bank Street 29 F2
Bankend D. & G. 69 F7
Bankend S.Lan. 75 G7
Bankfoot 82 B4
Bankhead Aber. 90 E4
Bankhead Aber. 90 E4
Bankhead Aberdeen 91 G3
Bankhead D. & G. 65 H6
Banknock 75 F3
Banks Cumb. 70 A7
Banks Lancs. 55 G7
Bankshill 69 G5
Bannister Green 33 K6
Bannockburn 75 G1
Banstead 23 F6
Bantham 5 G6
Banton 75 F3
Banwell 19 G6
Bapchild 25 F5
Baptiston 74 D2
Bar Hill 33 G2
Barabhas (Barvas) 101 F2
Barachander 80 B5
Barassie 74 B7

Barbaraville 96 E4
Barber Booth 50 D4
Barbon 56 B1
Barbrook 7 F1
Barby 31 G1
Barcaldine 80 A3
Barcaple 65 G5
Barcheston 30 D4
Barcombe 13 H5
Barcombe Cross 13 H5
Barden 62 C7
Bardennoch 67 K4
Bardfield End Green 33 K5
Bardfield Saling 33 K6
Bardister 108 C5
Bardney 52 E6
Bardon Leics. 41 G4
Bardon Moray 97 K6
Bardon Mill 70 C7
Bardsea 55 G2
Bardsey 57 J5
Bardsley 49 J2
Bardwell 34 D1
Barewood 28 C3
Barfad 73 G4
Barford Norf. 45 F5
Barford Warks. 30 D2
Barford St. John 31 F5
Barford St. Martin 10 B1
Barford St. Michael 31 F5
Barfrestone 15 H2
Bargaly 64 E4
Bargany Mains 67 G3
Bargoed 18 E2
Bargrennan 64 D3
Barham Cambs. 32 E1
Barham Kent 15 G2
Barham Suff. 35 F3
Barharrow 65 G5
Barholm 42 D4
Barholm Mains 64 E5
Barkby 41 J5
Barkby Thorpe 41 J5
Barkestone-le-Vale 42 A2
Barkham 22 A5
Barking Gt.Lon. 23 H3
Barking Suff. 34 E3
Barkingside 23 H3
Barkisland 50 C1
Barkston Lincs. 42 C1
Barkston N.Yorks. 57 K6
Barkway 33 G5
Barlae 64 C4
Barlaston 40 A2
Barlavington 12 C5
Barlborough 51 G5
Barlby 58 C6
Barlestone 41 G5
Barley Herts. 33 G5
Barley Lancs. 56 D5
Barleycroft End 33 H6
Barleyhill 62 B1
Barleythorpe 42 B5
Barling 25 F3
Barlings 52 D5
Barlow Derbys. 51 F5
Barlow N.Yorks. 58 C7
Barlow T. & W. 71 G7
Barmby Moor 58 D5
Barmby on the
Marsh 58 C7
Barmer 44 C2
Barmolloch 73 G1
Barmoor Lane End 77 J6
Barmouth
(Abermaw) 37 F4
Barmpton 62 E5
Barmston 59 H4
Barnacabber 73 K2
Barnacarry 73 J1
Barnack 42 D5
Barnacle 41 F7
Barnamuc 80 B3
Barnard Castle 62 B5
Barnard Gate 31 F7
Barnardiston 34 B4
Barnard's Green 29 G4
Barnbarroch
D. & G. 64 D5
Barnbarroch
D. & G. 65 J5
Barnburgh 51 G2
Barnby 45 J6
Barnby Dun 51 J2
Barnby in the
Willows 52 B7
Barnby Moor 51 J4
Barndennoch 68 D5
Barnes 23 F4
Barnet 23 F2
Barnetby le Wold 52 D2
Barney 44 D2
Barnham Suff. 34 C1
Barnham W.Suss. 12 C6
Barnham Broom 44 E5
Barnhead 83 H2
Barnhill 97 J6
Barnhills 66 D6
Barningham Dur. 62 B5
Barningham Suff. 34 D1
Barnoldby le Beck 53 F2
Barnoldswick 56 D5
Barns Green 12 E4
Barnsdale Bar 51 H1
Barnsley Glos. 20 D1
Barnsley S.Yorks. 51 F2
Barnstaple 6 D2
Barnston Essex 33 K7
Barnston Mersey. 48 B4
Barnstone 42 A2
Barnt Green 30 B1
Barnton 49 F5
Barnwell All Saints 42 D7
Barnwell St.
Andrew 42 D7
Barnwood 29 H7
Barr Arg. & B. 72 B4
Barr High. 79 H2
Barr S.Ayr. 67 G4
Barr Hall 34 B5
Barra (Tràigh Mhòr)
Airport 84 C4
Barrackan 79 J7
Barraer 64 D4
Barraglom 100 D4
Barrahormid 73 F2
Barran 80 C5
Barrapoll 78 A3
Barrasford 70 E6
Barravullin 79 K7
Barregarrow 54 C5
Barrhead 74 D5
Barrhill 67 G5
Barrington Cambs. 33 G4
Barrington Som. 8 C3
Barripper 2 D5
Barrisdale 86 E4
Barrmill 74 B5
Barrnacarry 79 K5
Barrock 105 H1
Barrow Lancs. 56 C6
Barrow Rut. 42 B4
Barrow Shrop. 39 F5
Barrow Som. 9 G1
Barrow Suff. 34 B2
Barrow Gurney 19 J5
Barrow Haven 59 G7
Barrow Nook 48 D2
Barrow Street 9 H1
Barrow upon
Humber 59 G7
Barrow upon Soar 41 H4
Barrow upon Trent 41 F3
Barrowby 42 B2
Barrowden 42 C5
Barrowford 56 D6
Barrow-in-Furness 55 F3
Barry Angus 83 G4
Barry V. of Glam. 18 E5
Barsby 42 A4
Barsham 45 H6
Barskimming 67 J1
Barsloisnoch 73 G1
Barston 30 D1
Bartestree 28 E4
Barthol Chapel 91 G1
Barthomley 49 G7
Bartley 10 E3
Bartlow 33 J4
Barton Cambs. 33 H3
Barton Ches. 48 D7
Barton Glos. 30 B6
Barton Lancs. 55 J6
Barton Lancs. 48 C2
Barton N.Yorks. 62 D6
Barton Torbay 5 K4
Barton Warks. 30 C3
Barton Bendish 44 B5
Barton Common 45 H3
Barton End 20 B2
Barton Hartshorn 31 H5
Barton in Fabis 41 H2
Barton in the Beans 41 F5
Barton Mills 34 B1
Barton on Sea 10 D5
Barton St. David 8 E1
Barton Seagrave 32 B1
Barton Stacey 21 H7
Barton Turf 45 H3
Barton-le-Clay 32 D5
Barton-le-Street 58 D2
Barton-le-Willows 58 D3
Barton-on-the-Heath 30 D5
Barton-under-
Needwood 40 D4
Barton-upon-
Humber 59 G7
Barvas (Barabhas) 101 F2
Barway 33 J1
Barwell 41 G6
Barwhinnock 65 G5
Barwick 8 E3
Barwick in Elmet 57 J6
Barwinnock 64 D6
Baschurch 38 D3
Bascote 31 F2
Basford Green 49 J7
Bashall Eaves 56 B5
Bashall Town 56 C5
Bashley 10 D5
Basildon Essex 24 D3
Basildon W.Berks. 21 K4
Basingstoke 21 K6
Baslow 50 E5
Bason Bridge 19 G7
Bassaleg 19 F3
Bassenthwaite 60 D3
Basset's Cross 6 D5
Bassett 11 F3
Bassingbourn 33 G4
Bassingfield 41 J2
Bassingham 52 C6
Bassingthorpe 42 C3
Basta 108 E3
Baston 42 E4
Bastwick 45 J4
Batavaime 81 F4
Batchworth 22 D2
Batchworth Heath 22 D2
Batcombe Dorset 9 F4
Batcombe Som. 9 F1
Bate Heath 49 F5
Bath 20 A5
Bathampton 20 A5
Bathealton 7 J3
Batheaston 20 A5
Bathford 20 A5
Bathgate 75 H4
Bathley 51 K7
Bathpool Cornw. 4 C3
Bathpool Som. 8 B2
Batley 57 H7
Batsford 30 C5
Battersby 63 G6
Battersea 23 F4
Battisborough
Cross 5 G6
Battisford 34 E3
Battisford Tye 34 E3
Battle E.Suss. 14 C6
Battle Powys 27 K5
Battlefield 38 E4
Battlesbridge 24 D2
Battlesden 32 C6
Battleton 7 H3
Battramsley 10 E5
Batt's Corner 22 B7
Bauds of Cullen 98 C4
Baugh 78 B3
Baughton 29 H4
Baughurst 21 J6
Baulds 90 E5
Baulking 21 G2
Baumber 53 F5
Baunton 20 D1
Baveney Wood 29 F1
Baverstock 10 B1
Bawburgh 45 F5
Bawdeswell 44 E3
Bawdrip 8 C1
Bawdsey 35 H4
Bawtry 51 J3
Baxenden 56 C7
Baxterley 40 E6
Baycliff 55 F2
Baydon 21 F4
Bayford Herts. 23 G1
Bayford Som. 9 G2
Bayfordbury 33 G7
Bayham Abbey 13 K3
Bayles 61 J2
Baylham 35 F3
Baynards Green 31 G6
Baysham 28 E6
Bayston Hill 38 D5
Baythorn End 34 B4
Bayton 29 F1
Beach 79 J2
Beachampton 31 J5
Beacharr 72 E6
Beachborough 15 G4
Beachley 19 J2
Beacon 7 K5
Beacon End 34 D6
Beacon Hill 12 B3
Beacon's Bottom 22 A2
Beaconsfield 22 C2
Beadlam 58 C1
Beadnell 71 H1
Beaford 6 D4
Beal N.Yorks. 58 B7
Beal Northumb. 77 J6
Bealach 80 A2
Beambridge 49 F7
Beamhurst 40 C2
Beaminster 8 D4
Beamish 62 D1
Beamsley 57 F4
Bean 23 J4
Beanacre 20 B5
Beanley 71 F2
Beaquoy 106 C5
Beardon 6 D7
Beare Green 22 E7
Bearley 30 C2
Bearnie 91 H1
Bearnock 88 B1
Bearnus 79 F3
Bearpark 62 D2
Bearsbridge 61 J1
Bearsden 74 D3
Bearsted 14 C2
Bearwood 10 B5
Beattock 69 F3
Beauchamp
Roding 23 J1
Beauchief 51 F4
Beaudesert 30 C2
Beaufort 28 A7
Beaulieu 10 E4
Beauly 96 C7
Beaumaris
(Biwmaris) 46 E5
Beaumont Cumb. 60 E1
Beaumont Essex 35 F6
Beausale 30 D1
Beauworth 11 G2
Beaworthy 6 C6
Beazley End 34 B6
Bebington 48 C4
Bebside 71 H5
Beccles 45 J6
Becconsall 55 H7
Beck Foot 61 H7
Beck Hole 63 K6
Beck Row 33 K1
Beck Side 55 F1
Beckbury 39 G5
Beckenham 23 G5
Beckermet 60 B6
Beckfoot Cumb. 60 C6
Beckfoot Cumb. 60 B2
Beckford 29 J5
Beckhampton 20 D5
Beckingham Lincs. 52 B7
Beckingham Notts. 51 K4
Beckington 20 A6
Beckley E.Suss. 14 D5
Beckley Oxon. 31 G7
Beckton 23 H3
Beckwithshaw 57 H4
Becontree 23 H3
Bedale 57 H1
Bedburn 62 C3
Bedchester 9 H3
Beddau 18 D3
Beddgelert 36 E1
Beddingham 13 H6
Beddington 23 G5
Beddington Corner 23 F5
Bedfield 35 G2
Bedford 32 D4
Bedgebury Cross 14 C4
Bedhampton 11 J4
Bedingfield 35 F2
Bedlington 71 H5
Bedlinog 18 D1
Bedminster 19 J4
Bedmond 22 E1
Bednall 40 B4
Bedol 48 B5
Bedrule 70 A2
Bedstone 28 C1
Bedwas 18 E3
Bedwellty 18 E1
Bedworth 41 F7
Beeby 41 J5
Beech Hants. 11 H1
Beech Staffs. 40 A2
Beech Hill 21 K5
Beechamwell 44 B5
Beechingstoke 20 D6
Beedon 21 H4
Beeford 59 H4
Beeley 50 E6
Beelsby 53 F2
Beenham 21 J5
Beer 8 B6
Beer Hackett 8 E3
Beercrocombe 8 C2
Beesands 5 J6
Beesby 53 H4
Beeson 5 J6
Beeston Beds. 32 E4
Beeston Ches. 48 E7
Beeston Norf. 44 D4
Beeston Notts. 41 H2
Beeston W.Yorks. 57 H6
Beeston Regis 45 F1
Beeston
St. Lawrence 45 H3
Beeswing 65 J4
Beetham 55 H2
Beetley 44 D4
Began 19 F3
Begbroke 31 F7
Begelly 16 E5
Beggshill 90 D1
Beguildy 28 A1
Beighton Norf. 45 H5
Beighton S.Yorks. 51 G4
Beith 74 B5
Bekesbourne 15 G2
Belaugh 45 G4
Belbroughton 29 J1
Belchamp Otten 34 C4
Belchamp St. Paul 34 B4
Belchamp Walter 34 C4
Belchford 53 F5
Belford 77 K7
Belgrave 41 H5
Belhaven 76 E3
Belhelvie 91 H3
Belhinnie 90 C2
Bell Bar 23 F1
Bell Busk 56 E4
Bell End 29 J1
Bellabeg 90 B3
Belladrum 96 C7
Bellanoch 73 G1
Bellasize 58 E7
Bellaty 82 D2
Belleau 53 H5
Bellehiglash 89 J1
Bellerby 62 C7
Bellever 5 G3
Belliehill 83 G1
Bellingdon 22 C1
Bellingham 70 D5
Belloch 72 E7
Bellochantuy 72 E7
Bells Yew Green 13 K3
Bellshill N.Lan. 75 F5
Bellshill Northumb. 77 K7
Bellside 75 G5
Bellsquarry 75 J4
Belluton 19 K5
Belmaduthy 96 D6
Belmesthorpe 42 D4
Belmont B'burn. 49 F1
Belmont Gt.Lon. 23 F5
Belmont Shet. 108 E2
Belowda 3 G2
Belper 41 F1
Belper Lane End 41 F1
Belsay 71 G6
Belsford 5 H5
Belstead 35 F4
Belston 67 H1
Belstone 6 E6
Belstone Corner 6 E6
Belsyde 75 H3
Belthorn 56 C7
Beltinge 25 H5
Beltoft 52 B2
Belton Leics. 41 G3
Belton Lincs. 42 C2
Belton N.Lincs. 51 K2
Belton Norf. 45 J5
Belton Rut. 42 B5
Beltring 23 K7
Belvedere 23 H4
Belvoir 42 B2
Bembridge 11 H6
Bemersyde 76 D7
Bempton 59 H2
Ben Alder Cottage 81 F1
Ben Alder Lodge 88 C7
Benacre 45 K7
Benbecula (Baile a'
Mhanaich) Airport 92 C6
Benbuie 68 C4
Benderloch 80 A4
Bendish 32 E6
Benenden 14 D4
Benfield 64 D4
Bengate 45 H3
Bengeo 33 G7
Benholm 83 K1
Beningbrough 58 B4
Benington Herts. 33 F6
Benington Lincs. 43 G1
Benington Sea End 43 H1
Benllech 46 D4
Benmore Arg. & B. 73 K2
Benmore Stir. 81 F5
Bennacott 4 C1
Bennan Cottage 65 G3
Benniworth 53 F4
Benover 14 C3
Benson 21 K2
Benthall Northumb. 71 H1
Benthall Shrop. 39 F5
Bentham 29 J7
Benthoul 91 G4
Bentley E.Riding 59 G6
Bentley Hants. 22 A7
Bentley S.Yorks. 51 H2
Bentley Suff. 35 F5
Bentley Warks. 40 E6
Bentley Heath 30 C1
Benton 6 E2
Benton Square 71 J6
Bentpath 69 J4
Bentworth 21 K7
Benvie 82 E4
Benville Lane 8 E4
Benwick 43 G7
Beoley 30 B2
Bepton 12 B5
Berden 33 H6
Bere Alston 4 E4
Bere Ferrers 4 E4
Bere Regis 9 H5
Berea 16 A3
Berepper 2 D6
Bergh Apton 45 H5
Berinsfield 21 J2
Berkeley 19 K2
Berkhamsted 22 C1
Berkley 20 B7
Berkswell 30 D1
Bermondsey 23 G4
Bernera 86 E2
Berners Roding 24 C1
Bernice 73 K1
Bernisdale 93 K6
Berrick Salome 21 K2
Berriedale 105 G6
Berriew (Aberriw) 38 A5
Berrington
Northumb. 77 J6
Berrington Shrop. 38 E5
Berrow 19 F6
Berrow Green 29 G3
Berry Down Cross 6 D1
Berry Hill Glos. 28 E7
Berry Hill Pembs. 16 D1
Berry Pomeroy 5 J4
Berryhillock 98 D4
Berrynarbor 6 D1
Bersham 38 C1
Berstane 107 D6
Berwick 13 J6
Berwick Bassett 20 D4
Berwick Hill 71 G6
Berwick St. James 10 B1
Berwick St. John 9 J2
Berwick St. Leonard 9 J1
Berwick-upon-
Tweed 77 H5
Bescar 48 C1
Besford Shrop. 38 E3
Besford Worcs. 29 J4
Bessacarr 51 J2
Bessels Leigh 21 H1
Bessingby 59 H3
Bessingham 45 F2
Best Beech Hill 13 K3
Besthorpe Norf. 44 E6
Besthorpe Notts. 52 B6
Beswick 59 G5
Betchworth 23 F6
Bethania Cere. 26 E2
Bethania Gwyn. 37 G1
Bethel Gwyn. 46 D6
Bethel Gwyn. 37 J1
Bethel I.o.A. 46 B5
Bethersden 14 E3
Bethesda Gwyn. 46 E6
Bethesda Pembs. 16 D4
Bethlehem 17 K3
Bethnal Green 23 G3
Betley 39 G1
Betsham 24 C4
Betteshanger 15 J2
Bettiscombe 8 C5
Bettisfield 38 D2
Betton Shrop. 38 C5
Betton Shrop. 39 F2
Bettws 19 F2
Bettws Bledrws 26 E3
Bettws Cedewain 38 A6
Bettws Evan 17 G1
Bettws Gwerfil
Goch 37 K1
Bettws Newydd 19 G1
Bettws-y-crwyn 38 B7
Bettyhill 104 C2
Betws Bridgend 18 C3
Betws Carmar. 17 K4
Betws Disserth 28 A3
Betws Garmon 46 D7
Betws-y-coed 47 F7
Betws-yn-Rhos 47 H5
Beulah Cere. 17 F1
Beulah Powys 27 J3
Bevendean 13 G6
Bevercotes 51 K5
Beverley 59 G6
Beverstone 20 B2
Bevington 19 K2
Bewaldeth 60 D3
Bewcastle 70 A6
Bewdley 29 G1
Bewerley 57 G3
Bewholme 59 H5
Bewley Common 20 C5
Bexhill 14 C7
Bexleyheath 23 H4
Bexwell 44 A5
Beyton 34 D2
Beyton Green 34 D2
Bhalamus 100 E7
Bhaltos 100 C4
Bhatarsaigh
(Vatersay) 84 B5
Biallaid 88 E5
Bibury 20 E1
Bicester 31 G6
Bickenhall 8 B3
Bickenhill 40 D7
Bicker 43 F2
Bickerstaffe 48 D2
Bickerton Ches. 48 E7
Bickerton N.Yorks. 57 K4
Bickford 40 A4
Bickham Bridge 5 H5
Bickham House 7 H7
Bickington Devon 6 D2
Bickington Devon 5 H3
Bickleigh Devon 5 F4
Bickleigh Devon 7 H5
Bickleton 6 D2
Bickley 23 H5
Bickley Moss 38 E1
Bickley Town 38 E1
Bicknacre 24 D1
Bicknoller 7 K2
Bicknor 14 D2
Bickton 10 C3
Bicton Shrop. 38 D4
Bicton Shrop. 38 B7
Bicton Heath 38 D4
Bidborough 23 J7
Biddenden 14 D4
Biddenham 32 D4
Biddestone 20 B4
Biddisham 19 G6
Biddlesden 31 H4
Biddlestone 70 E3
Biddulph 49 H7
Biddulph Moor 49 J7
Bideford 6 C3
Bidford-on-Avon 30 B3
Bidston 48 B3
Bielby 58 D5
Bieldside 91 G4
Bierley I.o.W. 11 G7
Bierley W.Yorks. 57 G6
Bierton 32 B7
Big Sand 94 D4
Bigbury 5 G6
Bigbury-on-Sea 5 G6
Bigby 52 D2
Bigert Mire 60 C7
Biggar Cumb. 54 E3
Biggar S.Lan. 75 J7
Biggin Derbys. 40 E1
Biggin Derbys. 50 D7
Biggin N.Yorks. 58 B6
Biggin Hill 23 H6
Biggin Hill Airport 23 H5
Biggings 109 A6
Biggleswade 32 E4
Bigholms 69 J5
Bighouse 104 D2
Bighton 11 H1
Biglands 60 D1
Bignor 12 C5
Bigrigg 60 B5
Bigton 109 C10
Bilberry 4 A4
Bilborough 41 H1
Bilbrook Som. 7 J1
Bilbrook Staffs. 40 A5
Bilbrough 58 B5
Bilbster 105 H3
Bildershaw 62 C4
Bildeston 34 D4
Billericay 24 C2
Billesdon 42 A5
Billesley 30 C3
Billholm 69 H4
Billingborough 42 E2
Billinge 48 E2
Billingford Norf. 35 F1
Billingford Norf. 44 E3
Billingham 63 F4
Billinghay 52 E7
Billingley 51 G2
Billingshurst 12 D4
Billingsley 39 G7
Billington Beds. 32 C6
Billington Lancs. 56 C6
Billockby 45 J4
Billy Row 62 C3
Bilsborrow 55 J5
Bilsby 53 H5
Bilsdean 77 F3
Bilsham 12 C6
Bilsington 15 F4
Bilsthorpe 51 J6
Bilston Midloth. 76 A4
Bilston W.Mid. 40 B6
Bilstone 41 F5
Bilting 15 F3
Bilton E.Riding 59 H6
Bilton N.Yorks. 57 K4
Bilton N.Yorks. 57 J4
Bilton Northumb. 71 H2
Bilton Warks. 31 F1
Bimbister 107 C6
Binbrook 53 F3
Bincombe 9 F6
Bindal 97 G3
Binegar 19 K7
Bines Green 12 E5
Binfield 22 B4
Binfield Heath 22 A4
Bingfield 70 E6
Bingham 42 A2
Bingham's
Melcombe 9 G4
Bingley 57 G6
Binham 44 D2
Binley Hants. 21 H6
Binley W.Mid. 30 E1
Binniehill 75 G3
Binsoe 57 H2
Binstead 11 G5
Binsted Hants. 22 A7
Binsted W.Suss. 12 C6
Binton 30 C3
Bintree 44 E3
Binweston 38 B5
Birch Essex 34 D7
Birch Gt.Man. 49 H2
Birch Green 34 D7
Birch Heath 48 E6
Birch Vale 50 C4
Bircham Newton 44 B2
Bircham Tofts 44 B2
Birchanger 33 J6
Bircher 28 D2
Birchfield 96 B2
Birchgrove Cardiff 18 E3
Birchgrove Swan. 18 A2
Birchington 25 J5
Birchover 50 E6
Birchwood 49 F3
Bircotes 51 J3
Bird End 40 C6
Birdbrook 34 B4
Birdfield 73 H1
Birdham 12 B7
Birdingbury 31 F2
Birdlip 29 J7
Birdsall 58 E3
Birdsgreen 39 G7
Birdsmoor Gate 8 C4
Birdwell 51 F2
Birdwood 29 G7
Birgham 77 F7
Birichen 96 E2
Birkby 62 E6
Birkdale Mersey. 48 C1
Birkdale N.Yorks. 61 K6
Birkenhead 48 C4
Birkenhills 99 F6
Birkenshaw 57 H7
Birkhall 90 B5
Birkhill Angus 82 E4
Birkhill Sc.Bord. 76 D6
Birkhill Sc.Bord. 69 H2
Birkin 58 B7
Birkwood 75 G7
Birley 28 D3
Birley Carr 51 F3
Birling Kent 24 C5
Birling Northumb. 71 H3
Birling Gap 13 J7
Birlingham 29 J4
Birmingham 40 C7
Birmingham International
Airport 40 D7
Birnam 82 B3
Birsay 106 B5
Birse 90 D5
Birsemore 90 D5
Birstall 41 H5
Birstall Smithies 57 H7
Birstwith 57 H4
Birthorpe 42 E2
Birtley Here. 28 C2
Birtley Northumb. 70 D6
Birtley T. & W. 62 D1
Birts Street 29 G5
Bisbrooke 42 B6
Bish Mill 7 F3
Bisham 22 B3
Bishampton 29 J3
Bishop Auckland 62 D3
Bishop Burton 59 F6
Bishop Middleham 62 E3
Bishop Monkton 57 J3
Bishop Norton 52 C3
Bishop Sutton 19 J6
Bishop Thornton 57 H3
Bishop Wilton 58 D4
Bishopbridge 52 D3
Bishopbriggs 74 E4
Bishopmill 97 K5
Bishops Cannings 20 D5
Bishop's Castle 38 C7
Bishop's Caundle 9 F3
Bishop's Cleeve 29 J6
Bishop's Frome 29 F4
Bishop's Green 33 K7
Bishop's Hull 8 B2
Bishop's Itchington 30 E3
Bishop's Lydeard 7 K3
Bishop's Nympton 7 F3
Bishop's Offley 39 G3
Bishop's Stortford 33 H6
Bishop's Sutton 11 H1
Bishop's Tachbrook 30 E2
Bishop's Tawton 6 D2
Bishop's Waltham 11 G3
Bishop's Wood 40 A5
Bishopsbourne 15 G2
Bishopsteignton 5 K3
Bishopstoke 11 F3
Bishopston 17 J7
Bishopstone
Bucks. 32 B7
Bishopstone
E.Suss. 13 H6
Bishopstone
Here. 28 D4
Bishopstone
Swin. 21 F3
Bishopstone
Wilts. 10 B2
Bishopstrow 20 B7
Bishopswood 8 B3
Bishopsworth 19 J5
Bishopthorpe 58 B5
Bishopton Darl. 62 E4
Bishopton Renf. 74 C3
Bishton 19 G3
Bisley Glos. 20 C1
Bisley Surr. 22 C6
Bispham 55 G5
Bissoe 2 E4
Bisterne 10 C4
Bisterne Close 10 D4
Bitchfield 42 C3
Bittadon 6 D1
Bittaford 5 G5
Bittering 44 D4
Bitterley 28 E1
Bitterne 11 F3
Bitteswell 41 H7
Bitton 19 K5
Biwmaris
(Beaumaris) 46 E5
Bix 22 A3
Bixter 109 C7
Blaby 41 H6
Black Bourton 21 F1
Black Callerton 71 G7
Black Clauchrie 67 G5
Black Corries
Lodge 80 D2
Black Cross 3 G2
Black Dog 7 G5
Black Heddon 71 F6
Black Marsh 38 C6
Black Mount 80 D3
Black Notley 34 B6
Black Pill 17 K6
Black Torrington 6 C5
Blackacre 69 F4
Blackadder 77 G5
Blackawton 5 J5
Blackborough 7 J5
Blackborough End 44 A4
Blackboys 13 J4
Blackbraes Aber. 91 G3
Blackbraes Falk. 75 H3
Blackbrook 39 G2
Blackburn Aber. 91 G3
Blackburn B'burn. 56 B7
Blackburn W.Loth. 75 H4
Blackbushe 22 A6
Blackcastle 97 F6
Blackchambers 91 F3
Blackcraig D. & G. 64 E4
Blackcraig D. & G. 68 C5
Blackden Heath 49 G5
Blackdog 91 H3
Blackdown Devon 5 F3
Blackdown Dorset 8 C4
Blackfield 11 F4
Blackford Aber. 90 E1
Blackford Cumb. 69 J7
Blackford P. & K. 81 K7
Blackford Som. 9 F2
Blackford Som. 19 H7
Blackfordby 41 F4
Blackgang 11 F7
Blackhall 76 A3
Blackhall Colliery 63 F3
Blackhall Rocks 63 F3
Blackham 13 J3
Blackheath Essex 34 D6
Blackheath Gt.Lon. 23 G4
Blackheath Suff. 35 J1
Blackheath Surr. 22 D7
Blackheath W.Mid. 40 B7
Blackhill Aber. 99 J5
Blackhill Aber. 99 J6
Blackhillock 98 C6
Blackhills 97 K6
Blackland 20 D5
Blacklunans 82 C1
Blackmill 18 C3
Blackmoor Hants. 11 J1
Blackmoor Som. 7 K4
Blackmoor Gate 6 E1
Blackmore 24 C1
Blackmore End
Essex 34 B5
Blackmore End
Herts. 32 E7
Blackness Aber. 90 E5
Blackness Falk. 75 J3
Blackness High. 105 H5
Blacknest 22 A7
Blacko 56 D5
Blackpool 55 G6
Blackpool Airport 55 G6
Blackpool Gate 70 A6
Blackridge 75 G4
Blackrock Arg. & B. 72 B4
Blackrock Mon. 28 B7
Blackrod 49 F1
Blackshaw 69 F7
Blackshaw Head 56 E7
Blacksmith's Corner 34 E5
Blackstone 13 F5
Blackthorn 31 H7
Blackthorpe 34 D2
Blacktoft 58 E7
Blacktop 91 G4
Blacktown 19 F3
Blackwater Cornw. 2 E4
Blackwater Hants. 22 B6
Blackwater I.o.W. 11 G6
Blackwater Suff. 35 J1
Blackwaterfoot 66 D1
Blackwell Darl. 62 D5
Blackwell Derbys. 50 D5
Blackwell Derbys. 51 G7
Blackwell Warks. 30 D4
Blackwell Worcs. 29 J1
Blackwells End 29 G6
Blackwood Caerp. 18 E2
Blackwood D. & G. 68 E5
Blackwood S.Lan. 75 F6
Blackwood Hill 49 J7
Blacon 48 C6
Bladbean 15 G3
Blades 62 A7
Bladnoch 64 E5
Bladon 31 F7
Blaen Dyryn 27 J5
Blaenannerch 17 F1
Blaenau
Dolwyddelan 46 E7
Blaenau Ffestiniog 37 F1
Blaenavon 19 F1
Blaenawey 28 B7
Blaencwm 18 C1
Blaenffos 16 E2
Blaengarw 18 C2
Blaengweche 17 K4
Blaengwrach 18 B1
Blaengwynfi 18 B2
Blaenos 27 G5
Blaenpennal 27 F2
Blaenplwyf 26 E1
Blaenporth 17 F1
Blaenrhondda 18 C1
Blaenwaun 17 F3
Blaen-y-coed 17 G3
Blagdon N.Som. 19 H6
Blagdon Torbay 5 J4
Blagdon Hill 8 B3

Place	Page	Grid
Blaich	87	G7
Blaina	19	F1
Blair	74	B6
Blair Atholl	81	K1
Blair Drummond	75	F1
Blairannaich	80	E7
Blairbuie	73	K3
Blairgowrie	82	C3
Blairhall	75	J2
Blairhoyle	81	H1
Blairingone	75	H1
Blairkip	74	D7
Blairlogie	75	G1
Blairmore *Arg. & B.*	73	K2
Blairmore *High.*	96	E1
Blairmore *High.*	102	D2
Blairnairn	74	B2
Blairnamarrow	89	K3
Blairpark	74	A5
Blairquhan	67	H3
Blairquhosh	74	D2
Blair's Ferry	73	H4
Blairshinnoch	98	E4
Blairuskinmore	81	F7
Blairvadach	74	A2
Blairydryne	91	F5
Blairythan Cottage	91	H2
Blaisdon	29	G7
Blake End	33	K6
Blakebrook	29	H1
Blakedown	29	H1
Blakelaw *Sc.Bord.*	77	F7
Blakelaw *T. & W.*	71	H7
Blakemere	28	C4
Blakeney *Glos.*	19	K1
Blakeney *Norf.*	44	E1
Blakenhall *Ches.*	39	G1
Blakenhall *W.Mid.*	40	B6
Blakeshall	40	A7
Blakesley	31	H3
Blanchland	62	A1
Bland Hill	57	H4
Blandford Camp	9	J4
Blandford Forum	9	H4
Blandford St. Mary	9	H4
Blanefield	74	D3
Blankney	52	D6
Blar a' Chaorainn	80	C1
Blargie	88	D5
Blarglas	74	B2
Blarmachfoldach	80	B1
Blarnalevoch	95	H2
Blashford	10	C4
Blaston	42	B6
Blathaisbhal	92	D4
Blatherwycke	42	C6
Blawith	55	F1
Blaxhall	35	H3
Blaxton	51	J2
Blaydon	71	G7
Bleadney	19	H7
Bleadon	19	G6
Bleak Hey Nook	50	C2
Blean	25	H5
Bleasby	42	A1
Bleatarn	61	J5
Blebocraigs	83	F6
Bleddfa	28	B2
Bledington	30	D6
Bledlow	22	A1
Bledlow Ridge	22	A2
Blencarn	61	H3
Blencogo	60	C2
Blencow	61	F3
Blendworth	11	J3
Blennerhasset	60	C2
Blervie Castle	97	H6
Bletchingdon	31	G7
Bletchingley	23	G6
Bletchley *M.K.*	32	B5
Bletchley *Shrop.*	39	F2
Bletherston	16	D3
Bletsoe	32	D3
Blewbury	21	J3
Blickling	45	F3
Blidworth	51	H7
Blindburn *Aber.*	91	H1
Blindburn *Northumb.*	70	D2
Blindcrake	60	C3
Blindley Heath	23	G7
Blisland	4	B3
Bliss Gate	29	G1
Blissford	10	C3
Blisworth	31	J3
Blithbury	40	C3
Blitterlees	60	C1
Blo Norton	34	E1
Blockley	30	C5
Blofield	45	H5
Blore	40	D1
Blossomfield	30	C1
Blount's Green	40	C2
Bloxham	31	F5
Bloxholm	52	D7
Bloxwich	40	B5
Bloxworth	9	H5
Blubberhouses	57	G4
Blue Anchor *Cornw.*	3	G3
Blue Anchor *Som.*	7	J1
Blue Bell Hill	24	D5
Bluewater	23	J4
Blundeston	45	K6
Blunham	32	E3
Blunsdon St. Andrew	20	E2
Bluntisham	33	G1
Blunts	4	D4
Blyborough	52	C3
Blyford	35	J1
Blyhill	40	A4
Blyth *Northumb.*	71	J5
Blyth *Notts.*	51	J4
Blyth Bridge	75	K6
Blythburgh	35	J1
Blythe Bridge	40	B1
Blythe Marsh	40	B1
Blyton	52	B3
Boarhills	83	G6
Boarhunt	11	H4
Boars Hill	21	H1
Boarshead	13	J3
Boarstall	31	H7
Boarzell	14	C5
Boasley Cross	6	D6
Boat o' Brig	98	B5
Boat of Garten	89	G3
Boath	96	C4
Bobbing	24	E5
Bobbington	40	A6
Bobbingworth	23	J1
Bocaddon	4	B5
Bochastle	81	H7
Bockhampton	21	G4
Bocking	34	B6
Bocking Churchstreet	34	B6
Boconnoc	4	B4
Boddam *Aber.*	99	K6
Boddam *Shet.*	109	F9
Boddington	29	H6
Bodedern	46	B4
Bodelwyddan	47	J5
Bodenham *Here.*	28	E3
Bodenham *Wilts.*	10	C2
Bodenham Moor	28	E3
Bodesbeck	69	G3
Bodewryd	46	B3
Bodfari	47	J5
Bodffordd	46	C5
Bodfuan	36	C2
Bodham Street	45	F1
Bodiam	14	C5
Bodicote	31	F5
Bodieve	3	G1
Bodinnick	4	B5
Bodior	46	A5
Bodle Street Green	13	K5
Bodmin	4	A4
Bodney	44	C6
Budorgan	46	B6
Bodsham Green	15	G3
Bodwen	4	A4
Bogallan	96	D6
Bogbain	96	E7
Bogbrae	91	J1
Bogbuie	96	C6
Bogend	74	B7
Bogfern	90	D4
Bogfields	90	D4
Bogfold	99	G5
Boghead *Aber.*	98	E5
Boghead *E.Ayr.*	68	B1
Boghead *S.Lan.*	75	F6
Boghole Farm	97	G6
Bogmoor	98	B4
Bogniebrae	98	D6
Bognor Regis	12	C7
Bograxie	91	F3
Bogroy	89	G2
Bogside	75	H1
Bogston	90	B4
Bogton	98	E5
Bogue	68	B5
Bohenie	87	J6
Bohortha	3	F5
Bohuntine	87	J6
Boirseam	93	F3
Bojewyan	2	A5
Bolam	62	C4
Bolberry	5	G7
Bold Heath	48	E4
Bolderwood	10	D4
Boldon	71	J7
Boldre	10	E5
Boldron	62	B5
Bole	51	K4
Bolehill	50	E7
Boleigh	2	B6
Boleside	76	C7
Bolfracks	81	K3
Bolgoed	17	K5
Bolham	7	J4
Bolham Water	7	K4
Bolingey	2	E3
Bollington	49	J5
Bolney	13	F4
Bolnhurst	32	D3
Bolshan	83	H2
Bolsover	51	G5
Bolsterstone	50	E3
Bolstone	28	E5
Boltby	57	K1
Bolter End	22	A2
Bolton *Cumb.*	61	H4
Bolton *E.Loth.*	76	D3
Bolton *E.Riding*	58	D4
Bolton *Gt.Man.*	49	G2
Bolton *Northumb.*	71	G2
Bolton Abbey	57	F4
Bolton Bridge	57	F4
Bolton by Bowland	56	C5
Bolton Low Houses	60	D2
Bolton Percy	58	B3
Bolton upon Dearne	51	G2
Boltonfellend	69	K7
Boltongate	60	D2
Bolton-le-Sands	55	H3
Bolton-on-Swale	62	D7
Bolventor	4	B3
Bombie	65	H5
Bomere Heath	38	D4
Bonar Bridge	96	D2
Bonawe	80	B4
Bonawe Quarries	80	B4
Bonby	52	D1
Boncath	17	F2
Bonchester Bridge	70	A2
Bonchurch	11	G7
Bondleigh	6	E5
Bonehill	40	D5
Bo'ness	75	H2
Bonhill	74	B3
Boningale	40	A5
Bonjedward	70	B1
Bonkle	75	G5
Bonnington	15	F4
Bonnybank	82	E7
Bonnybridge	75	G2
Bonnykelly	99	G5
Bonnyrigg	76	B4
Bonnyton *Aber.*	90	E1
Bonnyton *Angus*	83	G3
Bonnyton *Angus*	82	E4
Bonsall	50	E7
Bont	28	C7
Bont Dolgadfan	37	H5
Bont Newydd	37	G3
Bontddu	37	F3
Bont-goch (Elerch)	37	F7
Bontnewydd	46	C6
Bontuchel	47	J7
Bonvilston	18	D4
Bon-y-maen	17	K6
Boohay	5	K5
Booker	22	B2
Booley	38	E3
Boor	94	E3
Boosbeck	63	H5
Boot	60	C6
Boothby Graffoe	52	C7
Boothby Pagnell	42	C2
Boothstown	49	G3
Boothtown	57	F7
Boothville	31	J2
Bootle *Cumb.*	54	E1
Bootle *Mersey.*	48	C3
Booton	45	F3
Boquhan	74	D2
Boraston	29	F1
Bordeaux	3	J5
Borden	24	E5
Bordley	56	E3
Bordon	11	J1
Boreham *Essex*	24	D1
Boreham *Wilts.*	20	B7
Boreham Street	13	K5
Borehamwood	22	E2
Boreland *D. & G.*	69	G4
Boreland *Stir.*	81	G4
Boreraig	93	G6
Borgh *W.Isles*	92	B3
Borgh *W.Isles*	84	B4
Borghastan	100	D3
Borgie	103	J3
Borgue *D. & G.*	65	G6
Borgue *High.*	105	G6
Borley	34	C4
Bornais	84	C2
Borness	65	G6
Borough Green	23	K6
Boroughbridge	57	J3
Borras Head	48	C7
Borrowash	41	G2
Borrowby *N.Yorks.*	63	J5
Borrowby *N.Yorks.*	57	K1
Borrowdale	60	D5
Borrowfield	91	G5
Borstal	24	D5
Borth	37	F7
Borthwick	76	B5
Borthwickbrae	69	K2
Borthwickshiels	69	K2
Borth-y-Gest	36	E2
Borve	93	K7
Borwick	55	J2
Bosavern	2	A5
Bosbury	29	F4
Boscastle	4	B1
Boscombe *Bourne.*	10	C5
Boscombe *Wilts.*	10	D1
Boscoppa	4	A5
Bosham	12	B6
Bosherston	16	C6
Bosley	49	J6
Bossall	58	D3
Bossiney	4	A2
Bossingham	15	G3
Bossington *Hants.*	10	E1
Bossington *Som.*	7	G1
Bostock Green	49	F6
Boston	43	G1
Boston Spa	57	K5
Boswinger	3	G4
Botallack	2	A5
Botany Bay	23	F2
Botarua	92	C4
Botcheston	41	G5
Botesdale	34	E1
Bothal	71	H5
Bothamsall	51	J5
Bothel	60	C3
Bothenhampton	8	D5
Bothwell	75	F5
Botley *Bucks.*	22	C1
Botley *Hants.*	11	G3
Botley *Oxon.*	21	H1
Botloe's Green	29	G6
Botolph Claydon	31	J6
Botolphs	12	E6
Bottacks	96	B5
Bottesford *Leics.*	42	B2
Bottesford *N.Lincs.*	52	C2
Bottisham	33	J2
Bottom Head	56	B3
Bottomcraig	82	E5
Botusfleming	4	E4
Botwnnog	36	B2
Bough Beech	23	H7
Boughrood	28	A5
Boughspring	19	J2
Boughton *Norf.*	44	A5
Boughton *Northants.*	31	J2
Boughton *Notts.*	51	J6
Boughton Aluph	15	F3
Boughton Green	14	C2
Boughton Lees	15	F3
Boughton Malherbe	14	D3
Boughton Street	15	F2
Boulby	63	J5
Bouldon	38	E7
Boulmer	71	H2
Boulston	16	C4
Boultenstone Hotel	90	C3
Boultham	52	C6
Bourn	33	G3
Bournbrook	40	C7
Bourne	42	D3
Bourne End *Beds.*	32	C4
Bourne End *Bucks.*	22	B3
Bourne End *Herts.*	22	D1
Bournebridge	23	J2
Bournemouth	10	B5
Bournemouth Airport	10	C5
Bournes Green	20	C1
Bournheath	29	J1
Bournmoor	62	E1
Bournville	40	C7
Bourton *Dorset*	9	G1
Bourton *N.Som.*	19	G5
Bourton *Oxon.*	21	F3
Bourton *Shrop.*	38	E6
Bourton on Dunsmore	31	F1
Bourton-on-the-Hill	30	C5
Bourton-on-the-Water	30	C6
Bousd	78	D1
Boustead Hill	60	D1
Bouth	55	G1
Bouthwaite	57	G2
Bovain	81	G4
Boveney	22	C4
Boveridge	10	B3
Boverton	18	C5
Bovey Tracey	5	J3
Bovingdon	22	D1
Bovinger	23	J1
Bovington Camp	9	H6
Bow *Devon*	7	F5
Bow *Devon*	7	F5
Bow *Ork.*	107	C8
Bow Brickhill	32	C5
Bow Fife	82	E6
Bow Street	37	F7
Bowbank	62	A4
Bowburn	62	E3
Bowcombe	11	F6
Bowd	7	K7
Bowden *Devon*	5	J6
Bowden *Sc.Bord.*	76	D7
Bowden Hill	20	C5
Bowdon	49	G4
Bower	70	C5
Bower Hinton	8	D3
Bowerchalke	10	B2
Bowerhill	20	C5
Bowermadden	105	H2
Bowers Gifford	24	D3
Bowershall	75	J1
Bowertower	105	H2
Bowes	62	A5
Bowgreave	55	H5
Bowland Bridge	55	H1
Bowley	28	E3
Bowlhead Green	12	C3
Bowling	74	C3
Bowling Bank	38	C1
Bowlish	19	K7
Bowmanstead	60	E7
Bowmore	72	B5
Bowness-on-Solway	69	H7
Bowness-on-Windermere	61	F7
Bowsden	77	H6
Bowside Lodge	104	D2
Bowthorpe	45	F5
Bowtrees	75	H2
Box *Glos.*	20	B1
Box *Wilts.*	20	B5
Box End	32	D4
Boxbush	29	G7
Boxford *Suff.*	34	D4
Boxford *W.Berks.*	21	H4
Boxgrove	12	C6
Boxley	14	C2
Boxmoor	22	D1
Boxted *Essex*	34	D5
Boxted *Suff.*	34	C3
Boxted Cross	34	E5
Boxworth	33	G2
Boxworth End	33	G2
Boyden Gate	25	J5
Boydston	74	C7
Boylestone	40	D2
Boyndie	98	E4
Boynton	59	H3
Boysack	83	H3
Boyton *Cornw.*	6	B6
Boyton *Suff.*	35	H4
Boyton *Wilts.*	9	J1
Boyton Cross	24	C1
Bozeat	32	C3
Braaid	54	C6
Braal Castle	105	G2
Brabling Green	35	G3
Brabourne	15	F3
Brabourne Lees	15	F3
Brabster	105	J2
Bracadale	85	J1
Braceborough	42	D4
Bracebridge	52	C6
Bracebridge Heath	52	C6
Braceby	42	D2
Bracewell	56	D5
Brachla	88	C1
Brackenber	61	J4
Brackenfield	51	F7
Brackens	99	F5
Bracklach	90	B2
Bracklamore	99	G5
Brackletter	87	H6
Brackley *Arg. & B.*	73	G2
Brackley *High.*	97	F6
Brackley Northants.	31	G5
Bracknell	22	B5
Braco	81	K7
Bracobrae	98	D5
Bracon Ash	45	F6
Bracora	86	D5
Bracorina	86	D5
Bradbourne	50	E7
Bradbury	62	E4
Bradda	54	B6
Bradden	31	H4
Bradenham	22	B2
Bradenstoke	20	D3
Bradfield *Devon*	7	J5
Bradfield *Essex*	35	F5
Bradfield *Norf.*	45	G2
Bradfield *W.Berks.*	21	K4
Bradfield Combust	34	C3
Bradfield Green	49	F7
Bradfield Heath	35	F6
Bradfield St. Clare	34	D3
Bradfield St. George	34	D3
Bradford *Devon*	6	C5
Bradford Northumb.	77	K7
Bradford *W.Yorks.*	57	G6
Bradford Abbas	8	E3
Bradford Leigh	20	B5
Bradford Peverell	9	F5
Bradford-on-Avon	20	B5
Bradford-on-Tone	7	K3
Brading	11	H6
Bradley *Derbys.*	40	E1
Bradley *Hants.*	21	K7
Bradley *N.E.Lincs.*	53	F2
Bradley or Low Bradley *N.Yorks.*	57	F5
Bradley *Staffs.*	40	A4
Bradley *W.Mid.*	40	B6
Bradley Green	29	J2
Bradley in the Moors	40	C1
Bradley Stoke	19	K3
Bradmore *Notts.*	41	H2
Bradmore *W.Mid.*	40	A6
Bradninch	7	J5
Bradnop	50	C7
Bradpole	8	D5
Bradshaw	49	G1
Bradstone	6	B7
Bradwall Green	49	G6
Bradwell *Derbys.*	50	D4
Bradwell *Essex*	34	C6
Bradwell *M.K.*	32	B5
Bradwell *Norf.*	45	K5
Bradwell Grove	21	F1
Bradwell Waterside	25	F1
Bradwell-on-Sea	25	F1
Bradworthy	6	B4
Brae *D. & G.*	65	J3
Brae *High.*	96	B1
Brae *Shet.*	109	C6
Braeantra	96	C4
Braedownie	89	K7
Braefoot	99	F6
Braegrum	82	B5
Braehead *Glas.*	74	D4
Braehead *Moray*	98	B4
Braehead *Ork.*	107	E7
Braehead *Ork.*	106	D3
Braehead *S.Lan.*	75	G7
Braehead *S.Lan.*	75	H5
Braehead of Lunan	83	H2
Braehoulland	108	B5
Braeleny	81	H6
Braemar	89	J5
Braemore *High.*	96	C1
Braemore *High.*	105	F5
Braemore *High.*	95	H4
Braenaloin	89	K5
Braes of Enzie	98	B5
Braes of Foss	81	J2
Braes of Ullapool	95	H2
Braeside	74	A2
Braeval	81	G7
Brafferton *Darl.*	62	D4
Brafferton *N.Yorks.*	57	K2
Brafield-on-the-Green	32	B3
Bragar	100	E3
Bragbury End	33	F6
Bragleenbeg	80	A5
Braichmelyn	46	E6
Braides	55	H4
Braidley	57	F1
Braidwood	75	G6
Braigo	72	A4
Brailsford	40	E1
Braintree	34	B6
Braiseworth	35	F1
Braishfield	10	E2
Braithwaite *Cumb.*	60	D4
Braithwaite *S.Yorks.*	51	J1
Braithwell	51	H3
Bramber	12	E5
Brambletye	13	H3
Bramcote	41	H2
Bramdean	11	H2
Bramerton	45	G5
Bramfield *Herts.*	33	F7
Bramfield *Suff.*	35	H1
Bramford	35	F4
Bramhall	49	H4
Bramham	57	K5
Bramhope	57	H5
Bramley *Hants.*	21	K6
Bramley *S.Yorks.*	51	G3
Bramley *Surr.*	22	D7
Bramling	15	H2
Brampford Speke	7	H6
Brampton *Cambs.*	33	F1
Brampton *Cumb.*	70	A7
Brampton *Cumb.*	61	H4
Brampton *Derbys.*	51	F5
Brampton *Lincs.*	52	B5
Brampton *Norf.*	45	G3
Brampton *S.Yorks.*	51	G2
Brampton *Suff.*	45	J7
Brampton Abbotts	29	F6
Brampton Ash	42	A7
Brampton Bryan	28	C1
Brampton en le Morthen	51	G4
Bramshall	40	C2
Bramshaw	10	D3
Bramshill	22	A5
Bramshott	12	B3
Bramwell	8	D2
Bran End	33	K6
Branault	79	G1
Brancaster	44	B1
Brancepeth	62	D3
Branchill	97	H6
Brand Green	29	G6
Branderburgh	97	K4
Brandesburton	59	H5
Brandeston	35	G2
Brandis Corner	6	C5
Brandiston	45	F3
Brandon *Dur.*	62	D3
Brandon *Lincs.*	42	C1
Brandon Northumb.	71	F2
Brandon *Suff.*	44	B7
Brandon *Warks.*	31	F1
Brandon Bank	44	A7
Brandon Creek	44	A6
Brandon Parva	44	E5
Brandsby	58	B2
Brandy Wharf	52	D3
Brane	2	A6
Branksome	10	B5
Branksome Park	10	B5
Bransby	52	B5
Branscombe	7	K7
Bransford	29	G3
Bransford Bridge	29	H3
Bransgore	10	C5
Branson's Cross	30	B1
Branston *Leics.*	42	B3
Branston *Lincs.*	52	D6
Branston *Staffs.*	40	E3
Branston Booths	52	D6
Branstone	11	G6
Brant Broughton	52	C7
Brantham	35	F5
Branthwaite *Cumb.*	60	D3
Branthwaite *Cumb.*	60	B4
Brantingham	59	F7
Branton Northumb.	71	F2
Branton *S.Yorks.*	51	J2
Brantwood	60	E7
Branxholm	69	K2
Branxholme	69	K2
Branxton	77	G7
Brassington	50	E7
Brasted	23	H6
Brasted Chart	23	H6
Brathens	90	E5
Bratoft	53	H6
Brattleby	52	C4
Bratton	20	C6
Bratton Clovelly	6	C6
Bratton Fleming	6	E2
Bratton Seymour	9	F2
Braughing	33	G6
Braunston Northants.	31	G2
Braunston Rut.	42	B5
Braunstone	41	H5
Braunton	6	C2
Brawby	58	D2
Brawdy	16	B3
Brawl	104	D2
Brawlbin	105	F3
Bray	22	C4
Bray Shop	4	D3
Bray Wick	22	B4
Braybrooke	42	A7
Brayford	6	E2
Brayshaw	56	C4
Brayton	58	C6
Brazacott	4	C1
Breach	15	G3
Breachwood Green	32	E6
Breacleit	100	D4
Breadsall	41	F2
Breadstone	20	A1
Breage	2	D6
Breakon	108	E2
Bream	19	K1
Breamore	10	C3
Brean	19	F6
Breanais	100	B5
Brearton	57	J3
Breascleit	100	E4
Breaston	41	G2
Brechfa	17	J2
Brechin	83	H1
Brecklate	66	A2
Breckles	44	D6
Brecon (Aberhonddu)	27	K6
Breconside	68	D3
Bredbury	49	J3
Brede	14	D6
Bredenbury	29	F3
Bredfield	35	G3
Bredgar	24	E5
Bredhurst	24	D5
Bredicot	29	J3
Bredon	29	J5
Bredon's Hardwick	29	J5
Bredon's Norton	29	J5
Bredwardine	28	C4
Breedon on the Hill	41	G3
Breibhig	101	G4
Breich	75	H4
Breighton	58	D6
Breinton	28	D4
Bremhill	20	C4
Brenachoille	80	B7
Brenchley	23	K7
Brendon *Devon*	7	F1
Brendon *Devon*	6	B4
Brenkley	71	H6
Brent Eleigh	34	D4
Brent Knoll	19	G6
Brent Pelham	33	H5
Brentford	22	E4
Brentingby	42	A4
Brentwood	23	J2
Brenzett	15	F5
Breoch	65	H5
Brereton	40	C4
Brereton Green	49	G6
Brereton Heath	49	H6
Bressingham	44	E7
Bretabister	109	D7
Bretby	40	E3
Bretford	31	F1
Bretforton	30	B4
Bretherdale Head	61	G6
Bretherton	55	H7
Brettenham *Norf.*	44	D7
Brettenham *Suff.*	34	D3
Bretton	48	C6
Brewood	40	A5
Briach	97	H6
Briantspuddle	9	H5
Bricket Wood	22	E1
Bricklehampton	29	J4
Bride	54	D3
Bridekirk	60	C3
Bridell	16	E1
Bridestones	49	J6
Bridestowe	6	D7
Brideswell	90	D1
Bridford	7	G7
Bridge *Cornw.*	2	D4
Bridge *Kent*	15	G2
Bridge End *Lincs.*	42	E2
Bridge End *Shet.*	109	C9
Bridge Hewick	57	J2
Bridge o' Ess	90	D5
Bridge of Alford	90	D3
Bridge of Allan	75	F1
Bridge of Avon	89	J1
Bridge of Balgie	81	G3
Bridge of Bogendreip	90	E5
Bridge of Brewlands	82	C1
Bridge of Brown	89	J2
Bridge of Cally	82	C2
Bridge of Canny	90	E5
Bridge of Craigisla	82	D2
Bridge of Dee *Aber.*	89	J5
Bridge of Dee *Aber.*	90	E5
Bridge of Dee *D. & G.*	65	H4
Bridge of Don	91	H4
Bridge of Dun	83	H2
Bridge of Dye	90	E6
Bridge of Earn	82	C6
Bridge of Ericht	81	G2
Bridge of Feugh	90	E5
Bridge of Gairn	90	B5
Bridge of Gaur	81	G2
Bridge of Muchalls	91	G5
Bridge of Muick	90	B5
Bridge of Orchy	80	E4
Bridge of Tilt	81	K1
Bridge of Tynet	98	B4
Bridge of Walls	109	B7
Bridge of Weir	74	B4
Bridge Sollers	28	D4
Bridge Street	34	C4
Bridge Trafford	48	D5
Bridgefoot *Cambs.*	33	H4
Bridgefoot *Cumb.*	60	B4
Bridgehampton	8	E2
Bridgemary	11	G4
Bridgemere	39	G1
Bridgend *Aber.*	90	D1
Bridgend *Angus*	83	G1
Bridgend *Arg. & B.*	72	B4
Bridgend *Arg. & B.*	73	G1
Bridgend (Pen-y-bont ar Ogwr) *Bridgend*	18	C3
Bridgend *Cornw.*	4	B5
Bridgend *Cumb.*	61	F5
Bridgend *Fife*	82	E6
Bridgend *Moray*	90	B1
Bridgend *P. & K.*	82	C5
Bridgend *W.Loth.*	75	J3
Bridgend of Lintrathen	82	D2
Bridgerule	6	A5
Bridges	38	C6
Bridgeton	90	D2
Bridgetown *Cornw.*	6	B7
Bridgetown *Som.*	7	H2
Bridgeyate	19	K4
Bridgham	44	D7
Bridgnorth	39	G6
Bridgtown	40	B5
Bridgwater	8	B1
Bridlington	59	H3
Bridport	8	D5
Bridstow	28	E6
Brierfield	56	D6
Brierley *Glos.*	29	F7
Brierley *Here.*	28	D3
Brierley *S.Yorks.*	51	G1
Brierley Hill	40	B7
Brig o'Turk	81	G7
Brigehaugh	90	B1
Brigg	52	D2
Brigham *Cumb.*	60	B3
Brigham *E.Riding*	59	G4
Brighouse	57	G7
Brightstone	11	F6
Brightgate	50	E7
Brighthampton	21	G1
Brightling	13	K4
Brightlingsea	34	E7
Brighton *B. & H.*	13	G6
Brighton *Cornw.*	3	G3
Brightons	75	H3
Brightwalton	21	H4
Brightwell *Oxon.*	21	J2
Brightwell *Suff.*	35	G4
Brightwell Baldwin	21	K2
Brignall	62	B5
Brigsley	53	F2
Brigsteer	55	H1
Brigstock	42	C7
Brill *Bucks.*	31	H7
Brill *Cornw.*	2	E6
Brilley	28	B4
Brilley Mountain	28	B3
Brimfield	28	E2
Brimington	51	G5
Brimington Common	51	G5
Brimley	5	J3
Brimpsfield	29	J7
Brimpton	21	J5
Brimscombe	20	B1
Brimstage	48	C4
Brind	58	D6
Brindister *Shet.*	109	D9
Brindister *Shet.*	109	B7
Brindle	55	J7
Brindley Ford	49	H7
Brineton	40	A4
Bringhurst	42	B6
Brington	32	D1
Brinian	106	D5
Briningham	44	E2
Brinkhill	53	G5
Brinkley	33	K3
Brinklow	31	F1
Brinkworth	20	D3
Brinmore	88	D2
Brinscall	56	B7
Brinsley	41	G1
Brinsop	28	D4
Brinsworth	51	G4
Brinton	44	E2
Brisco	61	F1
Brisley	44	D3
Brislington	19	K4
Bristol	19	J4
Bristol International Airport	19	H5
Briston	44	E2
Britannia	56	D7
Britford	10	C2
Brithdir	37	G4
Brithem Bottom	7	J4
Briton Ferry (Llansawel)	18	A2
Britwell Salome	21	K2
Brixham	5	K5
Brixton	5	F5
Brixton Deverill	9	H1
Brixworth	31	J1
Brize Norton	21	F1
Broad Blunsdon	20	E2
Broad Campden	30	C5
Broad Chalke	10	B2
Broad Green *Beds.*	32	C4
Broad Green *Essex*	34	C6
Broad Green *Worcs.*	29	G3
Broad Haven	16	B4
Broad Hill	33	J1
Broad Hinton	20	E4
Broad Laying	21	H5
Broad Marston	30	C4
Broad Oak *Cumb.*	60	C7
Broad Oak *E.Suss.*	14	D6
Broad Oak *E.Suss.*	13	K4
Broad Oak *Here.*	28	D6
Broad Street	14	D2
Broad Street Green	24	E1
Broad Town	20	D4
Broadbottom	49	J3
Broadbridge	12	B6
Broadbridge Heath	12	E3
Broadclyst	7	H6
Broadford	86	C2
Broadford Bridge	12	D4
Broadgate	54	E1
Broadgroves	33	K7
Broadhaugh	69	K3
Broadheath *Gt.Man.*	49	G4
Broadheath *Worcs.*	29	F2
Broadhembury	7	K5
Broadhempston	5	J4
Broadholme	52	B5
Broadland Row	14	D6
Broadlay	17	G5
Broadley *Lancs.*	49	H1
Broadley *Moray*	98	B4
Broadley Common	23	H1
Broadmayne	9	G6
Broadmeadows	69	K1
Broadmere	21	K7
Broadnymett	7	F5
Broadoak *Carmar.*	17	H3
Broadoak *Dorset*	8	D5
Broadoak *Kent*	25	H5
Broadrashes	98	C5
Broadsea	99	H4
Broadstairs	25	K5
Broadstone *Poole*	10	B5
Broadstone *Shrop.*	38	E7
Broadstreet Common	19	G3
Broadwas	29	G3
Broadwater *Herts.*	33	F6
Broadwater *W.Suss.*	12	E6
Broadway *Carmar.*	17	G5
Broadway *Carmar.*	17	F4
Broadway *Pembs.*	16	B4
Broadway *Som.*	8	C3
Broadway *Suff.*	35	H1
Broadway *Worcs.*	30	B5
Broadwell *Glos.*	30	D6
Broadwell *Glos.*	28	E7
Broadwell *Oxon.*	21	F1
Broadwell *Warks.*	31	F2

Entry	Page	Grid
Broadwell House	62	A1
Broadwey	9	F6
Broadwindsor	8	D4
Broadwood Kelly	6	E5
Broadwoodwidger	6	C7
Brobury	28	C4
Brochel	94	B7
Brochloch	67	K4
Brock	78	B3
Brockbridge	11	H3
Brockdish	35	G1
Brockenhurst	10	E4
Brockfield	58	C4
Brockford Street	35	F2
Brockhall	31	H2
Brockham	22	E7
Brockhampton Glos.	30	B6
Brockhampton Here.	28	E5
Brockholes	50	D1
Brockhurst	13	H3
Brocklebank	60	E2
Brocklesby	52	E2
Brockley N.Som.	19	H5
Brockley Suff.	34	C3
Brockton Shrop.	38	E6
Brockton Shrop.	39	G5
Brockton Shrop.	38	C5
Brockton Shrop.	38	C7
Brockweir	19	J1
Brockwood Park	11	H2
Brockworth	29	H7
Brocton	40	B4
Brodick	73	J7
Brodsworth	51	H2
Brogborough	32	C5
Brogyntyn	38	B2
Broken Cross Ches.	49	H5
Broken Cross Ches.	49	F5
Brokenborough	20	C3
Bromborough	48	C4
Brome	35	F1
Brome Street	35	F1
Bromeswell	35	G3
Bromfield Cumb.	60	D1
Bromfield Shrop.	28	D1
Bromham Beds.	32	D3
Bromham Wilts.	20	C5
Bromley	23	H5
Bromley Green	14	E4
Brompton Med.	24	D5
Brompton N.Yorks.	62	E7
Brompton N.Yorks.	59	F1
Brompton on Swale	62	D6
Brompton Ralph	7	J2
Brompton Regis	7	H2
Bromsash	29	F6
Bromsberrow Heath	29	G5
Bromsgrove	29	J1
Bromstead Heath	40	A4
Bromyard	29	F3
Bromyard Downs	29	F3
Bronaber	37	G2
Brongest	17	G1
Bronington	38	D2
Bronllys	28	A5
Bronnant	27	F2
Bronydd	28	B4
Bron-y-Gaer	17	G4
Brongarth	28	B2
Brook Carmar.	17	F5
Brook Hants.	10	D3
Brook Hants.	10	E2
Brook I.o.W.	10	E6
Brook Kent	15	F3
Brook Surr.	12	C3
Brook Street Essex	23	J2
Brook Street Kent	14	E4
Brook Street Suff.	34	C4
Brook Street W.Suss.	13	G4
Brooke Norf.	45	G6
Brooke Rut.	42	B5
Brookend	19	J2
Brookhouse	55	J3
Brookhouse Green	14	E5
Brookland	14	E5
Brooklands	65	J3
Brookmans Park	23	F1
Brooks	38	A6
Brooks Green	12	E4
Brooksby	41	J4
Brookthorpe	29	H7
Brookwood	22	C6
Broom Beds.	32	E4
Broom Warks.	30	B3
Broom Hill	10	B4
Broom of Dalreach	82	B6
Broomcroft	38	E5
Broome Norf.	45	H6
Broome Shrop.	38	D7
Broome Worcs.	29	J1
Broome Wood	71	G2
Broomedge	49	G4
Broomer's Corner	12	E4
Broomfield Aber.	91	H1
Broomfield Essex	24	D1
Broomfield Kent	25	H5
Broomfield Kent	14	D4
Broomfield Som.	8	B1
Broomfleet	58	D7
Broomhaugh	71	F7
Broomhead	99	H4
Broomhill	71	H3
Broom's Green	29	G5
Brora	97	G1
Broseley	39	F5
Brotherlee	62	A3
Brothertoft	43	F1
Brotherton	57	K7
Brotton	63	H4
Broubster	105	F2
Brough Cumb.	61	J5
Brough Derbys.	50	D4
Brough E.Riding	59	F7
Brough High.	105	H1
Brough Notts.	52	B7
Brough Ork.	107	C6
Brough Shet.	109	E8
Brough Shet.	109	E4
Brough Shet.	108	D5
Brough Shet.	108	E5
Brough Lodge	108	E3
Brough Sowerby	61	J5
Broughall	38	E1
Brougham	61	G4
Broughton Cambs.	33	F1
Broughton Flints.	48	C6
Broughton Hants.	10	E1
Broughton Lancs.	55	J6
Broughton M.K.	32	B4
Broughton N.Lincs.	52	C2
Broughton N.Yorks.	58	D2
Broughton N.Yorks.	56	E4
Broughton Northants.	32	B1
Broughton Ork.	106	D3
Broughton Oxon.	31	F5
Broughton Sc.Bord.	75	K7
Broughton V. of Glam.	18	C4
Broughton Astley	41	H6
Broughton Beck	55	F1
Broughton Gifford	20	B5
Broughton Hackett	29	J3
Broughton in Furness	55	F1
Broughton Mills	60	D7
Broughton Moor	60	B3
Broughton Poggs	21	F1
Broughtown	106	F3
Broughty Ferry	83	F4
Browland	109	B7
Brown Candover	11	G1
Brown Edge Lancs.	48	C1
Brown Edge Staffs.	49	J7
Brown Lees	49	H7
Brownhill	99	G6
Brownhills Fife	83	G6
Brownhills W.Mid.	40	C5
Brownieside	71	G1
Brownlow Heath	49	H6
Brownshill Green	41	F7
Brownston	5	G5
Broxa	63	J3
Broxbourne	23	G1
Broxburn E.Loth.	76	E3
Broxburn W.Loth.	75	J3
Broxholme	52	C5
Broxted	33	J6
Broxton	48	D7
Broxwood	28	C3
Bru	101	F2
Bruachmary	97	F7
Bruan	105	J5
Bruera	48	D6
Bruern	30	D6
Bruichladdich	72	A4
Bruisyard	35	H2
Bruisyard Street	35	H2
Brund	50	D6
Brundall	45	H5
Brundish	35	G2
Brundish Street	35	G1
Bruntingthorpe	41	J7
Bruntland	90	C2
Brunton Fife	82	E5
Brunton Northumb.	71	H1
Brushford Devon	6	E5
Brushford Som.	7	H3
Bruton	9	F1
Bryanston	9	H4
Brydekirk	69	G6
Brymbo	48	B7
Bryn Carmar.	17	J5
Bryn Gt.Man.	48	E2
Bryn N.P.T.	18	B2
Bryn Shrop.	38	B7
Bryn Gates	48	E2
Brynamman	27	G7
Brynberian	16	E2
Bryncae	18	C3
Bryncethin	18	C3
Bryncir	36	D1
Bryn-côch	18	A2
Bryncroes	36	B2
Bryncrug	37	F5
Bryneglwys	38	A1
Brynford	47	K5
Bryngwran	46	B5
Bryngwyn Mon.	19	G1
Bryngwyn Powys	28	A4
Bryn-henllan	16	D2
Brynhoffnant	26	C3
Brynmawr	28	A7
Brynmelyn	28	A1
Brynmenyn	18	C3
Brynna	18	C3
Brynog	26	E3
Brynrefail Gwyn.	46	D6
Brynrefail I.o.A.	46	C4
Brynsadler	18	D3
Brynsiencyn	46	C6
Bryn-teg I.o.A.	46	C4
Brynteg Wrex.	48	C7
Bryn-y-maen	47	G5
Buaile nam Bodach	84	C4
Bualintur	85	K2
Bualnaluib	94	E3
Bubbenhall	30	E1
Bubwith	58	D6
Buccleuch	69	J2
Buchan	65	H4
Buchanan Castle	74	C2
Buchanhaven	99	K6
Buchanty	82	A5
Buchlyvie	74	D1
Buckabank	60	E2
Buckby Wharf	31	H2
Buckden Cambs.	32	E2
Buckden N.Yorks.	56	E2
Buckenham	45	H5
Buckerell	7	K5
Buckfast	5	H4
Buckfastleigh	5	H4
Buckhaven	76	B1
Buckholm	76	C7
Buckhorn Weston	9	G2
Buckhurst Hill	23	H2
Buckie	98	C4
Buckies	105	G2
Buckingham	31	H5
Buckland Bucks.	32	B7
Buckland Devon	5	G6
Buckland Glos.	30	B5
Buckland Herts.	33	G5
Buckland Kent	15	H3
Buckland Oxon.	21	G2
Buckland Surr.	23	F6
Buckland Brewer	6	C3
Buckland Common	22	C1
Buckland Dinham	20	A6
Buckland Filleigh	6	C5
Buckland in the Moor	5	H3
Buckland Monachorum	4	E4
Buckland Newton	9	G4
Buckland St. Mary	8	B3
Buckland-tout-Saints	5	H6
Bucklebury	21	J4
Bucklerheads	83	F4
Bucklers Hard	11	F4
Bucklesham	35	G4
Buckley (Bwcle)	48	B6
Buckman Corner	12	E4
Buckminster	42	B3
Bucknall Lincs.	52	E6
Bucknall Stoke	40	B1
Bucknell Oxon.	31	G6
Bucknell Shrop.	6	B3
Buck's Cross	12	D3
Bucks Green	13	G4
Bucks Hill	22	D1
Bucks Horn Oak	22	B7
Buck's Mills	6	B3
Bucksburn	91	G4
Buckspool	16	C6
Buckton E.Riding	59	H2
Buckton Here.	28	C1
Buckton Northumb.	77	J7
Buckworth	32	E1
Budbrooke	30	D2
Budby	51	J6
Buddon	83	G4
Bude	6	A5
Budlake	7	H5
Budle	77	K7
Budleigh Salterton	7	J7
Budock Water	2	E5
Buerton	39	F1
Bugbrooke	31	H3
Bugle	4	A5
Bugthorpe	58	D4
Buildwas	39	F5
Builth Road	27	K3
Builth Wells	27	K3
Buirgh	93	F2
Bulby	42	D3
Buldoo	104	E2
Bulford	20	E7
Bulford Camp	20	E7
Bulkeley	48	E7
Bulkington Warks.	41	F7
Bulkington Wilts.	20	C6
Bulkworthy	6	B4
Bull Bay	46	C3
Bull Green	14	E4
Bulley	29	G7
Bullington	21	H7
Bullpot Farm	56	B1
Bull's Green	33	F7
Bullwood	73	K3
Bulmer Essex	34	C4
Bulmer N.Yorks.	58	C3
Bulmer Tye	34	C5
Bulphan	24	C3
Bulverhythe	14	C7
Bulwark	99	H6
Bulwell	41	H1
Bulwick	42	C6
Bumble's Green	23	H1
Bun Abhainn Eadarra	100	D7
Bun Loyne	87	J4
Bunacaimb	86	C6
Bunarkaig	87	H6
Bunbury	48	E7
Bunchrew	96	D7
Bundalloch	86	E2
Buness	108	F2
Bunessan	78	E5
Bungay	45	H7
Bunlarie	73	F7
Bunloit	88	C2
Bunnahabhainn	72	C3
Bunny	41	H3
Buntait	87	K1
Buntingford	33	G6
Bunwell	45	F6
Bunwell Street	45	F6
Burbage Derbys.	50	C5
Burbage Leics.	41	G6
Burbage Wilts.	21	F5
Burchett's Green	22	B3
Burcombe	10	B1
Burcot	21	J2
Burcott	32	B6
Burdale	58	E3
Burdocks	12	D4
Bures	34	D5
Bures Green	34	D5
Burford	30	D7
Burgate	34	E1
Burgess Hill	13	G5
Burgh	35	G3
Burgh by Sands	60	E1
Burgh Castle	45	J5
Burgh Heath	23	F6
Burgh le Marsh	53	H6
Burgh next Aylsham	45	G3
Burgh on Bain	53	F4
Burgh St. Margaret	45	J4
Burgh St. Peter	45	J6
Burghclere	21	H5
Burghead	97	J5
Burghfield	21	K5
Burghfield Common	21	K5
Burghfield Hill	21	K5
Burghill	28	D4
Burghwallis	51	H1
Burham	24	D5
Buriton	11	J2
Burland	49	F7
Burlawn	3	G1
Burleigh	22	C5
Burlescombe	7	J4
Burleston	9	G5
Burley Hants.	10	D4
Burley Rut.	42	B4
Burley Gate	28	E4
Burley in Wharfedale	57	G5
Burley Street	10	D4
Burleydam	39	F1
Burlingjobb	28	B3
Burlow	13	J5
Burlton	38	D3
Burmarsh	15	G4
Burmington	30	D5
Burn	58	B7
Burn Farm	90	E7
Burn Naze	55	G5
Burn of Cambus	81	J7
Burnage	49	H3
Burnaston	40	E2
Burnby	58	E5
Burndell	12	C6
Burnend	99	G6
Burneside	61	G7
Burness	106	F3
Burneston	57	J1
Burnett	19	K5
Burnfoot High.	104	D5
Burnfoot P.&K.	82	B7
Burnfoot Sc.Bord.	70	A2
Burnfoot Sc.Bord.	33	K6
Burnham Bucks.	22	C3
Burnham N.Lincs.	52	D1
Burnham Deepdale	44	C1
Burnham Green	33	F7
Burnham Market	44	C1
Burnham Norton	44	C1
Burnham Overy	44	C1
Burnham Thorpe	44	C1
Burnham-on-Crouch	25	F2
Burnham-on-Sea	19	G7
Burnhaven	99	K6
Burnhead D.&G.	67	K5
Burnhead D.&G.	68	D4
Burnhervie	91	F3
Burnhill Green	39	G5
Burnhope	62	C2
Burnhouse	74	B5
Burniston	63	K3
Burnley	56	D6
Burnmouth	77	H4
Burnopfield	62	C1
Burnsall	57	F3
Burnside Aber.	91	F3
Burnside E.Ayr.	67	K2
Burnside Fife	82	C7
Burnside Shet.	108	B5
Burnside W.Loth.	75	J3
Burnside of Duntrune	83	F4
Burnstones	61	H1
Burnswark	69	G6
Burnt Houses	62	C4
Burnt Yates	57	H3
Burntcliff Top	49	J6
Burntisland	76	A2
Burnton E.Ayr.	67	J2
Burnton E.Ayr.	67	J3
Burntwood	40	C4
Burntwood Green	40	C5
Burpham Surr.	22	D6
Burpham W.Suss.	12	D6
Burradon Northumb.	70	E3
Burradon T.&W.	71	H6
Burrafirth	108	F1
Burraland	108	C1
Burras	2	D5
Burravoe Shet.	108	E5
Burravoe Shet.	109	C6
Burrells	61	H5
Burrelton	82	C4
Burridge	11	G3
Burrill	57	H1
Burringham	52	B2
Burrington Devon	6	E4
Burrington Here.	28	D1
Burrington N.Som.	19	H6
Burrough End	33	K3
Burrough Green	33	K3
Burrough on the Hill	42	A4
Burrow Bridge	8	C1
Burrowhill	22	C5
Burry Port	17	H5
Burscough	48	D1
Burscough Bridge	48	E1
Bursea	58	E6
Burshill	59	G5
Bursledon	11	F4
Burslem	40	A1
Burstall	35	F4
Burstock	8	D4
Burston Norf.	45	F7
Burston Staffs.	40	B2
Burstow	23	G3
Burstwick	59	J7
Burtersett	56	D1
Burtle	19	H7
Burton Ches.	48	C5
Burton Ches.	48	E6
Burton Dorset	10	C5
Burton Dorset	9	F5
Burton Lincs.	52	C5
Burton Northumb.	77	K7
Burton Pembs.	16	C5
Burton Som.	7	K1
Burton Wilts.	20	B4
Burton Agnes	59	H3
Burton Bradstock	8	D6
Burton Coggles	42	C3
Burton Fleming	59	G2
Burton Green Warks.	30	D1
Burton Green Wrex.	48	C7
Burton Hastings	41	G6
Burton in Lonsdale	56	B2
Burton Joyce	41	J1
Burton Latimer	32	C1
Burton Lazars	42	A4
Burton Leonard	57	J3
Burton on the Wolds	41	H3
Burton Overy	41	J6
Burton Pedwardine	42	E1
Burton Pidsea	59	J6
Burton Salmon	57	K7
Burton upon Stather	52	B1
Burton upon Trent	40	E3
Burton-in-Kendal	55	J2
Burtonwood	48	E3
Burwardsley	48	E7
Burwarton	39	F7
Burwash	13	K4
Burwash Common	13	K4
Burwash Weald	13	K4
Burwell Cambs.	33	J2
Burwell Lincs.	53	G5
Burwen	46	C3
Burwick Ork.	107	D9
Burwick Shet.	109	C8
Bury Cambs.	43	F7
Bury Gt.Man.	49	H1
Bury Som.	7	H3
Bury W.Suss.	12	D5
Bury Green	33	H6
Bury St. Edmunds	34	C2
Buryas Bridge	2	B6
Burythorpe	58	D3
Busbridge	22	C7
Busby E.Renf.	74	D5
Busby P.&K.	82	B5
Buscot	21	F2
Bush Bank	28	D3
Bush Crathie	89	K5
Bush Green	45	G7
Bushbury	40	B5
Bushby	41	J5
Bushey	22	E2
Bushey Heath	22	E2
Bushley	29	H5
Bushton	20	D4
Bussage	20	B1
Busta	109	C6
Butcher's Cross	13	J4
Butcher's Pasture	33	K6
Butcombe	19	J5
Buthill	97	J5
Butleigh	8	E1
Butleigh Wootton	8	E1
Butler's Cross	22	B1
Butler's Hill	41	H1
Butlers Marston	30	E3
Butley	35	H3
Butsfield	62	C2
Butt Green	49	F7
Butt Lane	49	H7
Butterburn	70	B6
Buttercrambe	58	D4
Butterknowle	62	C4
Butterleigh	7	H5
Butterley	51	G7
Buttermere Cumb.	60	C5
Buttermere Wilts.	21	G5
Butters Green	49	H7
Buttershaw	57	G7
Butterstone	82	B3
Butterton	50	C7
Butterwick Lincs.	43	G1
Butterwick N.Yorks.	59	F2
Butterwick N.Yorks.	58	D2
Buttington	38	B5
Buttonoak	29	G1
Buxhall	34	E3
Buxted	13	H4
Buxton Derbys.	50	C5
Buxton Norf.	45	G3
Buxton Heath	45	F3
Buxworth	50	C4
Bwcle (Buckley)	48	B6
Bwlch	28	A6
Bwlch-clawdd	17	G2
Bwlch-derwin	36	D1
Bwlchgwyn	48	B7
Bwlch-llan	26	E3
Bwlchnewydd	17	G3
Bwlchtocyn	36	C3
Bwlch-y-cibau	38	A4
Bwlch-y-ddar	38	A3
Bwlch-y-ffridd	37	K6
Bwlch-y-groes	17	F2
Bwlch-y-sarnau	27	K1
Byers Green	62	D3
Byfield	31	G3
Byfleet	22	D5
Byford	28	C4
Bygrave	33	F5
Byker	71	H7
Bylane End	4	C5
Bylchau	47	H6
Byley	49	G6
Bynea	17	J6
Byrness	70	C3
Bythorn	32	D1
Byton	28	C2
Byworth	12	C4

C

Entry	Page	Grid
Cabharstadh	101	F5
Cabourne	52	E2
Cabrach Arg.&B.	72	C4
Cabrach Moray	90	B2
Cackle Street	14	D6
Cacrabank	69	J2
Cadboll	97	F4
Cadbury	7	H5
Cadbury Barton	6	E4
Cadbury Heath	19	K4
Cadder	74	E3
Cadderlie	80	B4
Caddington	32	D7
Caddleton	79	J6
Cade Street	13	K4
Cadeby Leics.	41	G5
Cadeby S.Yorks.	51	H2
Cadeleigh	7	H5
Cadgwith	2	E7
Cadham	82	D7
Cadishead	49	G3
Cadle	17	K6
Cadley	21	F5
Cadmore End	22	A2
Cadnam	10	E3
Cadney	52	D2
Cadole	48	B6
Cadover Bridge	5	F4
Cadoxton	18	E5
Cadoxton-Juxta-Neath	18	A2
Cae Ddafydd	37	F1
Caeathro	46	D6
Caehopkin	27	H7
Caen	105	F7
Caenby	52	D4
Caenby Corner	52	C4
Caer Llan	19	H1
Caerau Bridgend	18	B2
Caerau Cardiff	18	E4
Caerdeon	37	F3
Caerdydd (Cardiff)	18	E4
Caerfarchell	16	A3
Caerfyrddin (Carmarthen)	17	H4
Caergeiliog	46	B5
Caergwrle	48	C7
Caergybi (Holyhead)	46	A4
Caerhun	47	F5
Caer-Lan	27	H7
Caerleon	19	G2
Caernarfon	46	C6
Caerphilly	18	E3
Caersws	37	K6
Caerwedros	26	C3
Caerwent	19	H2
Caerwys	47	K5
Caethle Farm	37	F6
Caggan	89	F3
Caio	17	K2
Cairinis	92	D6
Cairisiadar	100	C4
Cairminis	93	F3
Cairnargat	90	C1
Cairnbaan	73	G1
Cairnbeathie	90	D4
Cairnbrogie	91	G2
Cairnbulg	99	J4
Cairncross	77	G4
Cairncurran	74	B4
Cairndoon	64	D7
Cairndow	80	C6
Cairness	99	J4
Cairney Lodge	82	E6
Cairneyhill	75	J2
Cairnhill Aber.	91	H2
Cairnhill Aber.	90	E1
Cairnie Aber.	91	G4
Cairnie Aber.	98	C6
Cairnorrie	99	G6
Cairnryan	64	A4
Cairnsmore	64	E4
Caister-on-Sea	45	K4
Caistor	52	E2
Caistor St. Edmund	45	G5
Caistron	70	E3
Cake Street	44	E6
Calanais (Callanish)	100	E4
Calbost	101	G6
Calbourne	11	F6
Calcot	21	K4
Calcott	25	H5
Caldarvan	74	C2
Caldback	108	F2
Caldbeck	60	E3
Caldbergh	57	F1
Caldecote Cambs.	33	G3
Caldecote Cambs.	42	E7
Caldecote Herts.	33	F5
Caldecote Warks.	41	F6
Caldecott Northants.	32	C2
Caldecott Rut.	42	B6
Calder Bridge	60	B6
Calder Mains	105	F3
Calder Vale	55	J5
Calderbank	75	F4
Calderbrook	49	J1
Caldercruix	75	G4
Calderglen	74	E5
Caldermill	74	E6
Caldhame	83	F3
Caldicot	19	H3
Caldwell Derbys.	40	E4
Caldwell E.Renf.	74	C5
Caldwell N.Yorks.	62	C5
Caldy	48	B4
Caledrhydiau	26	D3
Calfsound	106	E4
Calgary	78	E2
Califer	97	H6
California Falk.	75	G3
California Norf.	45	K4
Calke	41	F3
Callakille	94	C6
Callaly	71	F3
Callander	81	H7
Callanish (Calanais)	100	E4
Callaughton	39	F6
Callerton Lane End	71	G7
Callestick	2	E3
Calligarry	86	C5
Callington	4	D4
Callisterhall	69	H5
Callow	28	D5
Callow End	29	H4
Callow Hill Wilts.	20	D3
Callow Hill Worcs.	29	G1
Callows Grave	28	E2
Calmore	10	E3
Calmsden	20	D1
Calne	20	C4
Calow	51	G5
Calrossie	96	E4
Calshot	11	F4
Calstock	4	E4
Calstone Wellington	20	D5
Calthorpe	45	F2
Calthwaite	61	G2
Calton N.Yorks.	56	E4
Calton Staffs.	50	D7
Calveley	48	E7
Calver	50	E5
Calver Hill	28	C4
Calverhall	39	F2
Calverleigh	7	H4
Calverley	57	H6
Calvert	31	H6
Calverton M.K.	31	J5
Calverton Notts.	41	J1
Calvine	81	K1
Calvo	60	C1
Cam	20	A2
Camasnacroise	79	K2
Camastianavaig	86	B1
Camasunary	86	B3
Camault Muir	96	C7
Camb	108	E3
Camber	14	E6
Camberley	22	B5
Camberwell	23	G4
Camblesforth	58	C7
Cambo	71	F5
Cambois	71	J5
Camborne	2	D4
Cambourne	33	G3
Cambridge Cambs.	33	H3
Cambridge Glos.	20	A1
Cambridge Airport	33	H3
Cambus	75	G1
Cambus o'May	90	C4
Cambusbarron	75	F1
Cambuskenneth	75	G1
Cambuslang	74	E4
Cambusnethan	75	G5
Cameley	19	K6
Camelford	4	B2
Camelon	75	G2
Camelsdale	12	B3
Camer	24	C5
Cameron	74	B2
Camerory	89	H1
Camer's Green	29	G5
Camerton B.&N.E.Som.	19	K6
Camerton Cumb.	60	B3
Camghouran	81	H2
Camis Eskan	74	B2
Cammachmore	91	H5
Cammeringham	52	C4
Campbeltown	66	B2
Campbeltown (Machrihanish) Airport	66	A1
Camperdown	71	H6
Camphouse	79	G1
Campmuir	82	D4
Camps End	33	K4
Camps Heath	45	K6
Campsall	51	H1
Campsey Ash	35	H3
Campton	32	E5
Camptown	70	B2
Camquhart	73	H2
Camrose	16	C3
Camserney	81	K3
Camstraddan House	74	B1
Camus Croise	86	C3
Camus-luinie	87	F2
Camusnagaul High.	87	G7
Camusnagaul High.	95	G3
Camusrich	81	H4
Camusteel	94	D7
Camusterrach	94	D7
Camusurich	81	H4
Camusvrachan	81	H4
Canada	10	D3
Candacraig	90	B5
Candlesby	53	H6
Candy Mill	75	J6
Cane End	21	K4
Canewdon	24	E2
Canford Bottom	10	B4
Canford Cliffs	10	B6
Canford Magna	10	B5
Canisbay	105	J1
Cann	9	H2
Cann Common	9	H2
Cannard's Grave	19	K7
Cannich	87	K1
Cannington	8	B1
Cannock	40	B4
Cannock Wood	40	C4
Canon Bridge	28	D4
Canon Frome	29	F4
Canon Pyon	28	D4
Canonbie	69	J6
Canons Ashby	31	G3
Canon's Town	2	C5
Canterbury Aber.	98	D5
Canterbury Kent	15	G2
Cantley Norf.	45	H5
Cantley S.Yorks.	51	J2
Cantlop	38	E5
Canton	18	E4
Cantray	96	E7
Cantraydoune	96	E7
Cantraywood	96	E7
Cantsfield	56	B2
Canvey Island	24	D3
Canwell Hall	40	D5
Canwick	52	C6
Canworthy Water	4	C1
Caol	87	H7
Caolas Arg.&B.	78	B3
Caolas W.Isles	84	B5
Caolas Scalpaigh (Kyles Scalpay)	93	H2
Caolasnacon	80	C1
Capel Kent	23	K7
Capel Surr.	22	E7
Capel Bangor	37	F7
Capel Betws Lleucu	27	F3
Capel Carmel	36	A3
Capel Coch	46	C4
Capel Curig	47	F7
Capel Cynon	17	G1
Capel Dewi Carmar.	17	H3
Capel Dewi Cere.	37	F7
Capel Dewi Cere.	17	H1
Capel Garmon	47	G7
Capel Gwyn I.o.A.	46	B5
Capel Gwynfe	27	G6
Capel Hendre	17	J4
Capel Isaac	17	J3
Capel Iwan	17	F2
Capel le Ferne	15	H4
Capel Parc	46	C4
Capel St. Andrew	35	H4
Capel St. Mary	34	E5
Capel Seion	27	F1
Capel Tygwydd	17	F1
Capeluchaf	36	D1
Capelulo	47	F5
Capel-y-ffin	28	B5
Capenhurst	48	C5
Capernwray	55	J2
Capheaton	71	F5
Caplaw	74	C5
Cappercleuch	69	H1
Capplegill	69	G3
Capstone	24	D5
Capton	5	J5
Caputh	82	B3
Car Colston	42	A1
Carbellow	68	B1
Carbeth	74	D3
Carbis Bay	2	C5
Carbost High.	93	K7
Carbost High.	85	J1
Carbrain	75	F3
Carbrooke	44	D5
Carburton	51	J5
Carcary	83	H2
Carclew	2	E5
Carco	68	C2
Carcroft	51	H2
Cardenden	76	A1
Cardeston	38	C4
Cardew	60	E2
Cardiff (Caerdydd)	18	E4
Cardiff International Airport	18	D5
Cardigan (Aberteifi)	16	E1
Cardington Beds.	32	D4
Cardington Shrop.	38	E6
Cardinham	4	B4
Cardno	99	H4
Cardoness	65	F5
Cardow	97	J7
Cardrona	76	A7
Cardross	74	B3
Cardurnock	60	C1
Careby	42	D4
Careston	83	G1
Carew	16	D5
Carew Cheriton	16	D5
Carew Newton	16	D5
Carey	28	E5
Carfrae	76	D4
Carfraemill	76	D5
Cargen	65	K3
Cargenbridge	65	K3
Cargill	82	C4
Cargo	60	E1
Cargo Fleet	63	G4
Cargreen	4	E4
Carham	77	F7
Carhampton	7	J1
Carharrack	2	E4
Carie P.&K.	81	H2
Carie P.&K.	81	H4
Carines	2	E3
Carisbrooke	11	F6
Cark	55	G2
Carkeel	4	E4
Carlabhagh (Carloway)	100	E3
Carland Cross	3	F3
Carlby	42	D4
Carlcotes	50	D2
Carleton Cumb.	61	F1
Carleton Cumb.	61	H5
Carleton Lancs.	55	G5
Carleton N.Yorks.	56	E5
Carleton W.Yorks.	57	K7
Carleton Fishery	67	F4
Carleton Forehoe	44	E5
Carleton Rode	45	F6
Carlin How	63	J5
Carlingcott	19	K6
Carlisle	61	F1
Carlops	75	K5

Carloway (Carlabhagh) 100 E3
Carlton Beds. 32 C3
Carlton Cambs. 33 K3
Carlton Leics. 41 F5
Carlton N.Yorks. 58 C7
Carlton N.Yorks. 57 F1
Carlton N.Yorks. 58 C1
Carlton Notts. 41 J1
Carlton S.Yorks. 51 F2
Carlton Stock. 62 E4
Carlton Suff. 35 H2
Carlton W.Yorks. 57 J7
Carlton Colville 45 K6
Carlton Curlieu 41 J6
Carlton Husthwaite 57 K2
Carlton in Lindrick 51 H4
Carlton Miniott 57 J1
Carlton Scroop 42 C1
Carlton-in-Cleveland 63 G6
Carlton-le-Moorland 52 C7
Carlton-on-Trent 52 B6
Carluke 75 G5
Carlyon Bay 4 A5
Carmacoup 68 C1
Carmarthen (Caerfyrddin) 17 H4
Carmel Carmar. 17 J4
Carmel Flints. 47 K5
Carmel Gwyn. 46 C7
Carmel I.o.A. 46 B4
Carmont 91 G6
Carmore 96 E2
Carmunnock 74 E5
Carmyle 74 E4
Carmyllie 83 G3
Carn 72 A5
Carn Brea 2 D4
Carn Dearg 94 D4
Carnaby 59 H3
Carnach High. 87 G2
Carnach High. 95 G2
Carnassarie 79 K7
Carnbee 83 G7
Carnbo 82 B7
Carnduncan 72 A4
Carne 3 G5
Carnforth 55 H2
Carnhell Green 2 D5
Carnichal 99 H5
Carnmore 72 B6
Carno 37 J6
Carnoch High. 87 K1
Carnoch High. 95 J6
Carnoch High. 97 F7
Carnock 75 J2
Carnon Downs 2 E4
Carnousie 98 E5
Carnoustie 83 G4
Carnwath 75 H6
Carnyorth 2 A5
Carperby 62 B7
Carr Shield 61 K2
Carr Vale 51 G5
Carradale 73 G7
Carragrich 93 G2
Carrbridge 89 G2
Carrefour Selous 3 J6
Carreg-lefn 46 B4
Carrick Arg. & B. 73 K1
Carrick Arg. & B. 73 H2
Carrick Fife 83 F5
Carriden 75 J2
Carrine 66 A3
Carrington Gt.Man. 49 G3
Carrington Lincs. 53 G7
Carrington Midloth. 76 B4
Carroch 68 B4
Carrog 38 A1
Carroglen 81 J5
Carrol 97 F1
Carron Arg. & B. 73 H1
Carron Falk. 75 G2
Carron Moray 97 K7
Carron Bridge 75 F2
Carronbridge 68 D4
Carronshore 75 G2
Carrot 83 F3
Carrutherstown 69 G6
Carruthmuir 74 B4
Carrville 62 E2
Carry 73 H4
Carsaig 79 G5
Carscreugh 64 C4
Carse 73 F4
Carse of Ardesier 97 F6
Carsegowan 64 E5
Carseriggan 64 D4
Carsethorn 65 K5
Carsgoe 105 G2
Carshalton 23 F5
Carsington 50 E7
Carsluith 64 E5
Carsphairn 67 K4
Carstairs 75 H6
Carstairs Junction 75 H6
Carswell Marsh 21 G2
Carter's Clay 10 E2
Carterton 21 F1
Carterway Heads 62 B1
Carthew 4 A5
Carthorpe 57 J1
Cartington 71 F3
Cartmel 55 G2
Cartmel Fell 55 H1
Carway 17 H5
Cascob 28 B2
Cashel Farm 74 C1
Cashlie 81 F3
Cashmoor 9 J3
Casnewydd (Newport) 19 G3
Cassencarie 64 E5
Cassington 31 F7
Cassop 62 E3
Castell Gorfod 17 F3
Castell Howell 17 H1
Castell Newydd Emlyn (Newcastle Emlyn) 17 G1
Castellau 18 D3
Castell-Nedd (Neath) 18 A2
Castell-y-bwch 19 F2
Casterton 56 B2
Castle Acre 44 C4
Castle Ashby 32 B3
Castle Bank 40 B3
Castle Bolton 62 A7
Castle Bromwich 40 D7
Castle Bytham 42 C4
Castle Caereinion 38 A5
Castle Camps 33 K4
Castle Carrock 61 G1
Castle Cary 9 F1

Castle Combe 20 B4
Castle Donington 41 G3
Castle Douglas 65 H4
Castle Eaton 20 E2
Castle Eden 63 F3
Castle End 30 D1
Castle Frome 29 F4
Castle Gresley 40 E4
Castle Heaton 77 H6
Castle Hedingham 34 B5
Castle Hill 35 F4
Castle Kennedy 64 B5
Castle Leod 96 B6
Castle Levan 74 A3
Castle Madoc 27 K5
Castle Morris 16 C2
Castle O'er 69 H4
Castle Rising 44 A3
Castle Stuart 96 E6
Castlebay (Bagh a' Chaisteil) 84 B5
Castlebythe 16 D3
Castlecary 75 F3
Castlecraig High. 97 F5
Castlecraig Sc.Bord. 75 K6
Castlefairn 68 C5
Castleford 57 K7
Castlemartin 16 C5
Castlemilk D. & G. 69 G6
Castlemilk Glas. 74 E5
Castlemorton 29 G5
Castleside 62 B2
Castlethorpe 32 B4
Castleton Aber. 82 E3
Castleton Angus 82 E3
Castleton Arg. & B. 73 J7
Castleton Derbys. 50 D4
Castleton Gt.Man. 49 H1
Castleton N.Yorks. 63 H6
Castleton Newport 19 F3
Castleton Sc.Bord. 70 A4
Castletown High. 105 G2
Castletown High. 96 E7
Castletown I.o.M. 54 B7
Castletown T. & W. 62 E1
Castleweary 69 K2
Castlewigg 64 E6
Caston 44 D6
Castor 42 E6
Castramont 64 D4
Cat & Fiddle Inn 50 C5
Catbrain 19 J3
Catchall 2 B6
Catcleugh 70 C3
Catcliffe 51 G4
Catcott 8 C1
Caterham 23 G6
Catesby 31 G3
Catfield 45 H3
Catfirth 109 D7
Catford 23 G4
Catforth 55 H6
Cathedine 28 A6
Catherington 11 H3
Catherton 29 F1
Catlow 56 D6
Catlowdy 69 K6
Catmore 21 H4
Caton Devon 5 H3
Caton Lancs. 55 J3
Cator Court 5 G3
Catrine 67 K1
Catsfield 14 C6
Catshill 29 J1
Cattadale 72 B5
Cattal 57 K4
Cattawade 35 F5
Catterall 55 J5
Catterick 62 D7
Catterick Camp 62 C7
Catterlen 61 F3
Catterline 91 G7
Catterton 58 B5
Catthorpe 31 G1
Cattistock 8 E4
Catton N.Yorks. 57 J2
Catton Norf. 45 G4
Catton Northumb. 61 K1
Catton Hall 40 E4
Catwick 59 H5
Catworth 32 D1
Caudworthy 4 C1
Caulcott 31 G6
Cauldcots 83 H3
Cauldhame Aber. 91 F6
Cauldhame Stir. 74 E1
Cauldhame Stir. 81 K7
Cauldon 40 C1
Caulkerbush 65 K5
Caulside 69 K5
Caundle Marsh 9 F3
Caunsall 40 A7
Caunton 51 K6
Causeway End D. & G. 64 E4
Causeway End Essex 33 K7
Causewayhead Cumb. 60 C1
Causewayhead Stir. 75 G1
Causey Park 71 G4
Causeyend 91 H3
Cautley 61 H7
Cavendish 34 C4
Cavenham 34 B2
Caversfield 31 G6
Caversham 22 A4
Caverswall 40 B1
Cawdor 97 F6
Cawkwell 53 F5
Cawood 58 B6
Cawsand 4 E5
Cawston 45 F3
Cawthorne 50 E2
Cawthorpe 42 D3
Cawton 58 C2
Caxton 33 G3
Caxton Gibbet 33 F3
Caynham 28 E1
Caythorpe Lincs. 42 C1
Caythorpe Notts. 41 J1
Cayton 59 G1
Ceallan 92 D6
Ceann a' Bháigh W.Isles 92 C5
Ceann a' Bháigh W.Isles 93 F3
Ceann Loch Shiphoirt 100 E6
Cearsiadar 101 F5
Ceathramh Meadhanach 92 C4
Cedig 37 J5
Cefn Bychan (Newbridge) 19 F2
Cefn Cantref 27 K6
Cefn Coch 47 K7

Cefn Cribwr 18 B3
Cefn Cross 18 B3
Cefn Einion 38 B7
Cefn Hengoed 18 E2
Cefn-brith 47 H7
Cefn-caer-Ferch 36 D1
Cefn-coch 38 A3
Cefn-coed-y-cymmer 18 D1
Cefn-ddwysarn 37 J2
Cefndeuddwr 37 G3
Cefneithin 17 J4
Cefn-gorwydd 27 J4
Cefn-gwyn 38 A7
Cefn-mawr 38 B1
Cefn-y-bedd 48 C7
Cefn-y-pant 16 E3
Cegidfa (Guilsfield) 38 B4
Ceidio 46 C4
Ceidio Fawr 36 B2
Ceinewydd (New Quay) 26 C3
Ceint 46 C5
Cellan 17 K1
Cellardyke 83 G7
Cellarhead 40 B1
Cemaes 46 B3
Cemmaes 37 H5
Cemmaes Road (Glantwymyn) 37 H5
Cenarth 17 F1
Cennin 36 D1
Ceos 101 F5
Ceres 82 E6
Cerne Abbas 9 F4
Cerney Wick 20 D2
Cerrigceinwen 46 C5
Cerrigydrudion 37 J1
Cessford 70 C1
Chaceley 29 H5
Chacewater 2 E4
Chackmore 31 H5
Chacombe 31 F4
Chad Valley 40 C7
Chadderton 49 J2
Chaddesden 41 F2
Chaddesley Corbett 29 H1
Chaddleworth 21 H4
Chadlington 30 E6
Chadshunt 30 E3
Chadwell 42 A3
Chadwell St. Mary 24 C4
Chadwick End 30 D1
Chaffcombe 8 C3
Chafford Hundred 24 C4
Chagford 7 F7
Chailey 13 G5
Chainhurst 14 C3
Chalbury Common 10 B4
Chaldon 23 G6
Chaldon Herring or East Chaldon 9 G6
Chale 11 F7
Chale Green 11 F7
Chalfont Common 22 D2
Chalfont St. Giles 22 C2
Chalfont St. Peter 22 D2
Chalford 20 B1
Chalgrove 21 K2
Chalk 24 C4
Challaborough 5 G6
Challoch 64 D4
Challock 15 F2
Chalmington 8 E4
Chalton Beds. 32 D6
Chalton Hants. 11 J3
Chalvington 13 J6
Champany 75 J3
Chandler's Cross 22 D2
Chandler's Ford 11 F2
Channerwick 109 D10
Chantry Som. 20 A7
Chantry Suff. 35 F4
Chapel 76 A1
Chapel Allerton Som. 19 H6
Chapel Allerton W.Yorks. 57 J6
Chapel Amble 3 G1
Chapel Brampton 31 J2
Chapel Chorlton 40 A2
Chapel Cross 13 K4
Chapel End 41 F6
Chapel Fields 30 E1
Chapel Haddlesey 58 B7
Chapel Hill Aber. 91 J1
Chapel Hill Lincs. 53 F7
Chapel Hill Mon. 19 J1
Chapel Lawn 28 C1
Chapel of Garioch 91 F2
Chapel Rossan 64 B6
Chapel Row 21 J5
Chapel St. Leonards 53 J5
Chapel Stile 60 E6
Chapel Town 3 F3
Chapelbank 82 B6
Chapeldonan 67 F3
Chapel-en-le-Frith 50 C4
Chapelgate 43 H3
Chapelhall 75 F4
Chapelhill High. 97 F4
Chapelhill P. & K. 82 D5
Chapelhill P. & K. 82 B4
Chapelknowe 69 J6
Chapel-le-Dale 56 C2
Chapelton Aber. 91 G6
Chapelton Angus 83 H3
Chapelton S.Lan. 74 E6
Chapeltown B'burn. 49 G1
Chapeltown Cumb. 69 K6
Chapeltown Moray 89 K2
Chapeltown S.Yorks. 51 F3
Chapmans Well 6 B6
Chapmanslade 20 B7
Chapmore End 33 G7
Chappel 34 C6
Chard 8 C4
Chard Junction 8 C4
Chardstock 8 C4
Charfield 20 A2
Charing 14 E3
Charing Heath 14 E3
Charingworth 30 D5
Charlbury 30 E7
Charlcombe 20 A5
Charlcutt 20 C4
Charlecote 30 D3
Charles 6 E2
Charles Tye 34 E3
Charlesfield 70 A1
Charleshill 22 B7
Charleston 82 E3
Charlestown Aber. 99 J4

Charlestown Aberdeen 91 H4
Charlestown Cornw. 4 A5
Charlestown Dorset 9 F7
Charlestown Fife 75 J2
Charlestown High. 94 E4
Charlestown High. 96 D7
Charlestown of Aberlour (Aberlour) 97 K7
Charlesworth 50 C3
Charleton 8 B1
Charlinch 8 B1
Charlton Gt.Lon. 23 H4
Charlton Hants. 21 G7
Charlton Herts. 32 E6
Charlton Northants. 31 G5
Charlton Northumb. 70 D5
Charlton Oxon. 21 H3
Charlton Som. 19 K6
Charlton Wilts. 9 J1
Charlton Wilts. 20 C3
Charlton Wilts. 20 E6
Charlton Worcs. 30 B4
Charlton Abbots 30 B6
Charlton Adam 8 E2
Charlton Horethorne 9 F2
Charlton Kings 29 J6
Charlton Mackrell 8 E2
Charlton Marshall 9 H4
Charlton Musgrove 9 G2
Charlton-All-Saints 10 C2
Charlton-on-Otmoor 31 G7
Charltons 63 H5
Charlwood 23 F7
Charminster 9 F5
Charmouth 8 C5
Charndon 31 H6
Charney Bassett 21 G2
Charnock Richard 48 E1
Charsfield 35 G3
Chart Corner 14 C3
Chart Sutton 14 D3
Charter Alley 21 K6
Charterhouse 19 H6
Charterville Allotments 30 E7
Chartham 15 G2
Chartham Hatch 15 F2
Chartridge 22 C1
Charwelton 31 G3
Chase End Street 29 G5
Chase Terrace 40 C4
Chasetown 40 C5
Chastleton 30 D6
Chasty 6 B5
Chatburn 56 C5
Chatcull 39 G2
Chatham 24 D5
Chathill 71 G1
Chattenden 24 D4
Chatteris 43 G7
Chattisham 34 E4
Chatto 70 C2
Chatton 71 F1
Chawleigh 7 F4
Chawley 21 H1
Chawston 32 E3
Chawton 11 J1
Cheadle Gt.Man. 49 H4
Cheadle Staffs. 40 C1
Cheadle Hulme 49 H4
Cheam 23 F5
Cheapside 22 C5
Chearsley 22 A1
Chebsey 40 A3
Checkendon 21 K3
Checkley Ches. 39 G1
Checkley Here. 28 E5
Checkley Staffs. 40 C2
Chedburgh 34 B3
Cheddar 19 H6
Cheddington 32 C7
Cheddleton 49 J7
Cheddon Fitzpaine 8 B2
Chedglow 20 C2
Chedgrave 45 H6
Chedington 8 D4
Chediston 35 H1
Chedworth 30 B7
Chedzoy 8 C1
Cheeklaw 77 F5
Cheesden 49 H1
Cheeseman's Green 15 F4
Cheetham Hill 49 H2
Cheldon 7 F4
Chelford 49 H5
Chellaston 41 F2
Chelmarsh 39 G7
Chelmondiston 35 G5
Chelmorton 50 D6
Chelmsford 24 D1
Chelsea 23 F4
Chelsfield 23 H5
Chelsham 23 G5
Chelsworth 34 D4
Cheltenham 29 J6
Chelveston 32 C2
Chelvey 19 H5
Chelwood 19 K5
Chelwood Gate 13 H4
Chelworth 20 C2
Cheney Longville 38 D7
Chenies 22 D2
Chepstow 19 J2
Cherhill 20 D4
Cherington Glos. 20 C2
Cherington Warks. 30 D5
Cheriton Devon 7 F1
Cheriton Hants. 11 G2
Cheriton Kent 15 H4
Cheriton Pembs. 16 C6
Cheriton Swan. 17 H6
Cheriton Bishop 7 F6
Cheriton Cross 7 F6
Cheriton Fitzpaine 7 G4
Cherrington 39 F4
Cherry Burton 59 F5
Cherry Hinton 33 H3
Cherry Willingham 52 D5
Chertsey 22 D5
Cheselbourne 9 G5
Chesham 22 C1
Chesham Bois 22 C2
Cheshunt 23 G1
Cheslyn Hay 40 B5
Chessington 22 E5
Chester 48 D6
Chesterblade 19 K7
Chesterfield Derbys. 51 F5
Chesterfield Staffs. 40 D5
Chester-le-Street 62 D1
Chesters Sc.Bord. 70 B1
Chesters Sc.Bord. 70 B1
Chesterton Cambs. 33 H2

Chesterton Cambs. 42 E6
Chesterton Oxon. 31 G6
Chesterton Shrop. 39 G6
Chesterton Staffs. 40 A1
Chesterton Green 30 E3
Chestfield 25 H5
Cheswardine 39 G3
Cheswick 77 J6
Chetnole 9 F4
Chettiscombe 7 H4
Chettisham 43 J7
Chettle 9 J3
Chetton 39 F6
Chetwode 31 H6
Chetwynd Aston 39 G4
Cheveley 33 K2
Chevening 23 H6
Cheverell's Green 32 D7
Chevington 34 B3
Chevington Drift 71 H4
Chevithorne 7 H4
Chew Magna 19 J5
Chew Stoke 19 J5
Chewton Keynsham 19 K5
Chewton Mendip 19 J6
Chicheley 32 C4
Chichester 12 B6
Chickerell 9 F6
Chickering 35 G1
Chicklade 9 J1
Chickney 33 J6
Chicksands 32 E5
Chidden 11 H3
Chiddingfold 12 C3
Chiddingly 13 J5
Chiddingstone 23 H7
Chiddingstone Causeway 23 J7
Chiddingstone Hoath 23 H7
Chideock 8 D5
Chidham 11 J4
Chieveley 21 H4
Chignall St. James 24 C1
Chignall Smealy 33 K7
Chigwell 23 H2
Chigwell Row 23 H2
Chilbolton 21 G7
Chilcomb 11 G2
Chilcombe 8 E5
Chilcompton 19 K6
Chilcote 40 E4
Child Okeford 9 H3
Childer Thornton 48 C5
Childerditch 24 C3
Childrey 21 G3
Child's Ercall 39 F3
Childswickham 30 B5
Childwall 48 D4
Childwick Green 32 E7
Chilfrome 8 E5
Chilgrove 12 B5
Chilham 15 F2
Chillaton 6 C7
Chillenden 15 H2
Chillerton 11 F6
Chillesford 35 H3
Chillingham 71 F1
Chillington Devon 5 H6
Chillington Som. 8 C3
Chilmark 9 J1
Chilson 30 E7
Chilsworthy Cornw. 4 E3
Chilsworthy Devon 6 B5
Chilthorne Domer 8 E3
Chilton Bucks. 31 H7
Chilton Dur. 62 D3
Chilton Oxon. 21 H3
Chilton Candover 11 G1
Chilton Cantelo 8 E2
Chilton Foliat 21 G4
Chilton Polden 8 C1
Chilton Street 34 B4
Chilton Trinity 8 B1
Chilvers Coton 41 F6
Chilworth Hants. 11 F3
Chilworth Surr. 22 D7
Chimney 21 G1
Chineham 21 K6
Chingford 8 B3
Chinley 50 C4
Chinley Head 50 C4
Chinnor 22 A1
Chipchase Castle 70 D6
Chipley Park 7 K3
Chipnall 39 G2
Chippenham Cambs. 33 K2
Chippenham Wilts. 20 C4
Chipperfield 22 D1
Chipping Herts. 33 G5
Chipping Lancs. 56 B5
Chipping Campden 30 C5
Chipping Hill 34 C7
Chipping Norton 30 E6
Chipping Ongar 23 J1
Chipping Sodbury 20 A3
Chipping Warden 31 F4
Chipstable 7 J3
Chipstead Kent 23 H6
Chipstead Surr. 23 F6
Chirbury 38 B6
Chirk 38 B2
Chirmorrie 64 C3
Chirnside 77 G5
Chirnsidebridge 77 G5
Chirton 20 D6
Chisbury 21 F5
Chiscan 66 A2
Chiselborough 8 D3
Chiseldon 20 E3
Chislehampton 21 J2
Chislehurst 23 H4
Chislet 25 J5
Chiswell Green 22 E1
Chiswick 23 F4
Chisworth 49 J3
Chithurst 12 B4
Chittering 33 H1
Chitterne 20 C7
Chittlehamholt 6 E3
Chittlehampton 6 E3
Chittoe 20 C5
Chivelstone 5 H7
Chobham 22 C5
Choicelee 77 F5
Cholderton 21 F7
Cholesbury 22 C1
Chollerford 70 E6
Chollerton 70 E6
Cholsey 21 J3
Cholstrey 28 D3
Cholwell B. & N.E.Som. 19 K6
Cholwell Devon 6 C7
Chop Gate 63 G6
Choppell 62 C1
Chorley Ches. 48 E7
Chorley Lancs. 48 E1

Chorley Shrop. 39 F7
Chorley Staffs. 40 C4
Chorleywood 22 D2
Chorlton 49 G7
Chorlton Lane 38 D1
Chorlton-cum-Hardy 49 H3
Chowley 48 D7
Chrishall 33 H5
Chrishall Grange 33 H4
Chrisswell 74 A3
Christchurch Cambs. 43 H6
Christchurch Dorset 10 C5
Christchurch Glos. 28 E7
Christchurch Newport 19 G3
Christian Malford 20 C4
Christleton 48 D6
Christmas Common 22 A2
Christon 19 G6
Christon Bank 71 H1
Christow 7 G7
Chryston 74 E3
Chudleigh 5 J3
Chudleigh Knighton 5 J3
Chulmleigh 6 E4
Chunal 50 C3
Church 56 C7
Church Aston 39 G4
Church Brampton 31 J2
Church Broughton 40 E2
Church Common 35 H3
Church Crookham 22 B6
Church Eaton 40 A4
Church End Beds. 32 E5
Church End Beds. 32 C6
Church End Beds. 32 C6
Church End Cambs. 43 G5
Church End Cambs. 33 H3
Church End Cambs. 33 G1
Church End E.Riding 59 G4
Church End Essex 33 J4
Church End Essex 34 B6
Church End Hants. 21 K6
Church End Herts. 32 E7
Church End Lincs. 43 F2
Church End Lincs. 53 H3
Church End Warks. 40 E6
Church End Wilts. 20 D4
Church Enstone 30 E6
Church Fenton 58 B6
Church Green 7 K6
Church Gresley 40 E4
Church Hanborough 31 F7
Church Houses 63 H7
Church Knowle 9 J6
Church Langley 23 H1
Church Langton 42 A6
Church Lawford 31 F1
Church Lawton 49 H7
Church Leigh 40 C2
Church Lench 30 B3
Church Minshull 49 F6
Church Norton 12 B7
Church Preen 38 E6
Church Pulverbatch 38 D5
Church Stoke 38 B6
Church Stowe 31 H3
Church Street 24 D4
Church Stretton 38 D6
Church Village 18 D3
Church Warsop 51 H6
Churcham 29 G7
Churchdown 29 H6
Churchend Essex 25 G2
Churchend Essex 33 K6
Churchend S.Glos. 20 A2
Churchgate 23 G1
Churchgate Street 23 H1
Churchill N.Som. 19 H6
Churchill Oxon. 30 D6
Churchill Worcs. 29 J3
Churchill Worcs. 29 H1
Churchingford 8 B3
Churchover 41 H7
Churchstanton 7 K4
Churchstow 5 H6
Churchthorpe 53 G3
Churchtown Devon 6 E1
Churchtown I.o.M. 54 D1
Churchtown Lancs. 55 H5
Churchtown Mersey. 48 C1
Churnsike Lodge 70 B6
Churston Ferrers 5 K5
Churt 12 B3
Churton 48 D7
Churwell 57 H7
Chute Cadley 21 G6
Chute Standen 21 G6
Chwilog 36 D2
Chwitffordd (Whitford) 47 K5
Chyandour 2 B5
Cilan Uchaf 36 C3
Cilcain 47 K6
Cilcennin 26 E2
Cilfrew 18 A1
Cilfynydd 18 D2
Cilgerran 16 E1
Cilgwyn Carmar. 27 G6
Cilgwyn Pembs. 16 D2
Ciliau-Aeron 26 E3
Cille Bhrighde 84 C3
Cille Pheadair 84 C3
Cilmery 27 K3
Cilrhedyn 17 F2
Cilrhedyn Bridge 16 D2
Cilsan 17 J3
Ciltalgarth 37 H1
Cilwendeg 17 F2
Cilybebyll 18 A1
Cilycwm 27 G4
Cinderford 29 F7
Cippyn 16 E1
Cirbhig 100 D3
Cirencester 20 D1
City 23 G3
City Airport 23 H3
City Dulas 46 C4
Clabach 78 C2
Clachaig 73 K2
Clachan Arg. & B. 80 C6
Clachan Arg. & B. 79 K3
Clachan Arg. & B. 73 F5
Clachan High. 86 B1
Clachan W.Isles 92 C7
Clachan of Campsie 74 E3
Clachan of Glendaruel 73 J2
Clachan Strachur 80 C7
Clachandhu 79 F4
Clachaneasy 64 D3
Clachanmore 64 A6
Clachan-Seil 79 J6

Clachanturn 89 K5
Clachbreck 73 F3
Clachnabrain 82 E1
Clachnaharry 96 D7
Clachtoll 102 C6
Clackmannan 75 H1
Clacton-on-Sea 35 F7
Cladach a' Chaolais 92 C5
Cladach Chircebost 92 C5
Cladich 80 B5
Claggan High. 87 H7
Claggan High. 79 J3
Claigan 93 H6
Claines 29 H3
Clandown 19 K6
Clanfield Hants. 11 H3
Clanfield Oxon. 21 F1
Clannaborough Barton 7 F5
Clanville 21 G7
Claonaig 73 G5
Claonairigh 80 B7
Claonel 96 C1
Clap Gate 57 J5
Clapgate 10 B4
Clapham Beds. 32 D3
Clapham Gt.Lon. 23 F4
Clapham N.Yorks. 56 C3
Clapham W.Suss. 12 D6
Clapham Hill 25 H5
Clappers 77 H5
Clappersgate 60 E6
Clapton 8 D4
Clapton-in-Gordano 19 H4
Clapton-on-the-Hill 30 C7
Clapworthy 6 E3
Clarach 37 F7
Clarbeston 16 D3
Clarbeston Road 16 D3
Clarborough 51 K4
Clardon 105 G2
Clare 34 B4
Clarebrand 65 H4
Clarencefield 69 F7
Clareton 57 J4
Clarilaw 70 A2
Clarkston 74 D5
Clashban 96 D2
Clashcoig 96 D2
Clashgour 80 D3
Clashindarroch 90 C1
Clashmore 96 E2
Clashnessie 102 C5
Clashnoir 89 K2
Clathy 82 A5
Clatt 90 D2
Clatter 37 J6
Clatterford End 23 J1
Clatterin Bridge 90 E7
Clatteringshaws 65 F3
Clatworthy 7 J2
Claughton Lancs. 55 J3
Claughton Lancs. 55 J5
Claverdon 30 C2
Claverham 19 H5
Clavering 33 H5
Claverley 39 G6
Claverton 20 A5
Clawdd-newydd 47 J7
Clawfin 67 K3
Clawthorpe 55 J2
Clawton 6 B6
Claxby Lincs. 53 H5
Claxby Lincs. 52 E3
Claxby Pluckacre 53 G6
Claxton N.Yorks. 58 C3
Claxton Norf. 45 H5
Clay Common 45 J7
Clay Coton 31 G1
Clay Cross 51 F6
Clay of Allan 97 F4
Claybrooke Magna 41 G7
Claybrooke Parva 41 G7
Claydene 23 H7
Claydon Oxon. 31 F3
Claydon Suff. 35 F4
Claygate Kent 14 C3
Claygate Surr. 22 E5
Claygate Cross 23 K6
Clayhanger Devon 7 J3
Clayhanger W.Mid. 40 C5
Clayhidon 7 K4
Clayock 105 G3
Claypole 42 B1
Claythorpe 53 H5
Clayton S.Yorks. 51 G2
Clayton Staffs. 40 A1
Clayton W.Suss. 13 G5
Clayton W.Yorks. 57 G6
Clayton West 50 E1
Clayton-le-Moors 56 C6
Clayton-le-Woods 55 J7
Clayworth 51 K4
Cleadale 85 K6
Cleadon 71 J7
Clearbrook 5 F4
Clearwell 19 J1
Cleasby 62 D5
Cleat 107 D9
Cleatlam 62 C5
Cleatop 56 D3
Cleator 60 B5
Cleator Moor 60 B5
Cleckheaton 57 G7
Clee St. Margaret 38 E7
Cleedownton 38 E7
Cleehill 28 E1
Cleethorpes 53 G2
Cleeton St. Mary 29 F1
Cleeve N.Som. 19 H5
Cleeve Oxon. 21 K3
Cleeve Hill 29 J6
Cleeve Prior 30 B4
Cleghorn 75 H6
Clehonger 28 D5
Cleigh 79 K5
Cleish 75 J1
Cleland 75 G5
Clench Common 20 E5
Clenchwarton 43 J3
Clent 29 J1
Cleobury Mortimer 29 F1
Cleobury North 39 F7
Clephanton 97 F6
Clerklands 70 A1
Clestrain 107 C7
Cleuch Head 70 A2
Cleughbrae 69 F6
Clevancy 20 D4
Clevedon 19 H4
Cleveland Tontine 63 F7
Cleveleys 55 G5
Clevelode 29 H4
Cleverton 20 C3
Clewer 19 H6
Clewer Village 22 C4

Cley next the Sea 44 E1
Cliburn 61 G4
Cliddesden 21 K7
Cliff Carmar. 17 G5
Cliff High. 79 H1
Cliff End 14 D6
Cliffe Med. 24 D4
Cliffe N.Yorks. 58 C6
Cliffe Woods 24 D4
Clifford Here. 28 B4
Clifford W.Yorks. 57 K5
Clifford Chambers 30 C3
Clifford's Mesne 29 G6
Cliffs End 25 K5
Clifton Beds. 32 E5
Clifton Bristol 19 J4
Clifton Cumb. 61 G4
Clifton Derbys. 40 D1
Clifton Lancs. 55 H6
Clifton Northumb. 71 H5
Clifton Nott. 41 H2
Clifton Oxon. 31 F5
Clifton Stir. 80 E4
Clifton Worcs. 29 H4
Clifton Campville 40 E4
Clifton Hampden 21 J2
Clifton Reynes 32 C3
Clifton upon Dunsmore 31 G1
Clifton upon Teme 29 G2
Cliftonville 25 K4
Climping 12 D6
Climpy 75 H5
Clint 57 H4
Clint Green 44 E4
Clinterty 91 G3
Clintmains 76 E7
Clippesby 45 J4
Clipsham 42 C4
Clipston Northants. 42 A7
Clipston Notts. 41 J2
Clipstone 51 H6
Clitheroe 56 C5
Clive 38 E3
Clivocast 108 F2
Clocaenog 47 J7
Clochan 98 C4
Clochtow 91 J1
Clock Face 48 E3
Clockhill 99 G6
Cloddach 97 J6
Clodock 28 C6
Cloford 20 A7
Cloichran 81 H4
Clola 99 J6
Clonrae 68 D4
Clophill 32 D5
Clopton 32 D1
Clopton Green 34 B3
Close Clark 54 B6
Closeburn 68 D4
Closworth 8 E3
Clothall 33 F5
Clothan 108 D4
Clotton 48 E6
Clough Cumb. 61 J7
Clough Gt.Man. 49 J1
Clough Foot 56 E7
Cloughton 63 K3
Cloughton Newlands 63 K3
Clounlaid 79 J2
Clousta 109 C7
Clouston 107 C6
Clova Aber. 90 C2
Clova Angus 90 B7
Clove Lodge 62 A5
Clovelly 6 B3
Clovelly Cross 6 B3
Clovenfords 76 C7
Clovenstone 91 F3
Cloverhill 91 H3
Cloves 97 J5
Clovullin 80 B1
Clowne 51 G5
Clows Top 29 G1
Cloyntie 67 H3
Cluanach 72 B5
Clubworthy 4 C1
Cluer 93 G2
Clun 38 B7
Clunas 97 F7
Clunbury 38 C7
Clune High. 88 E2
Clune Moray 98 D4
Clunes 87 H6
Clungunford 28 C1
Clunie Aber. 98 E5
Clunie P. & K. 82 C3
Clunton 38 C7
Cluny 76 A1
Clutton B. & N.E.Som. 19 K6
Clutton Ches. 48 D7
Clwt-y-bont 46 D6
Clydach Mon. 28 B7
Clydach Swan. 17 K5
Clydach Vale 18 C2
Clydebank 74 D4
Clydey 17 F2
Clyffe Pypard 20 D4
Clynder 74 A2
Clynderwen 16 E4
Clynelish 97 F1
Clynfyw 17 F2
Clynnog-fawr 36 D1
Clyro 28 B4
Clyst Honiton 7 H6
Clyst Hydon 7 J5
Clyst St. George 7 H7
Clyst St. Lawrence 7 J5
Clyst St. Mary 7 H6
Cnewr 27 H6
Cnoc 101 G4
Cnwch Coch 27 F1
Coachford 98 C6
Coad's Green 4 C3
Coal Aston 51 F5
Coalbrookdale 39 F5
Coalbrookvale 18 E1
Coalburn 75 G7
Coalburns 71 G7
Coalcleugh 61 K2
Coaley 20 A1
Coalpit Heath 19 K3
Coalpit Hill 49 H7
Coalport 39 G5
Coalsnaughton 75 H1
Coaltown of Balgonie 76 B1
Coaltown of Wemyss 76 B1
Coalville 41 G4
Coast 95 F2
Coat 8 D2
Coatbridge 75 F4
Coate Swin. 20 E3
Coate Wilts. 20 D5
Coates Cambs. 43 G6
Coates Glos. 20 C1
Coates Lincs. 52 C4
Coates W.Suss. 12 C5
Coatham 63 G4
Coatham Mundeville 62 D4
Cobairdy 98 D6
Cobbaton 6 E3
Coberley 29 J7
Cobham Kent 24 C5
Cobham Surr. 22 E6
Cobleland 74 D1
Cobler's Green 33 K7
Cobnash 28 D2
Coburty 99 H4
Cochno 74 C3
Cock Alley 51 G6
Cock Bridge 89 K4
Cock Clarks 24 E1
Cockayne 63 H7
Cockayne Hatley 33 F4
Cockburnspath 77 F3
Cockenzie & Port Seton 76 C3
Cockerham 55 H4
Cockermouth 60 C3
Cockernhoe 32 E6
Cockett 17 K6
Cockfield Dur. 62 C4
Cockfield Suff. 34 D3
Cockfosters 23 F2
Cocking 12 B5
Cockington 5 J4
Cocklake 19 H7
Cockley Beck 60 D6
Cockley Cley 44 B5
Cockpole Green 22 A3
Cockshutt 38 D3
Cockthorpe 44 D1
Cockwood 7 H7
Codda 4 B3
Coddenham 35 F3
Coddington Ches. 48 D7
Coddington Here. 29 G4
Coddington Notts. 52 B7
Codford St. Mary 9 J1
Codford St. Peter 20 C7
Codicote 33 F7
Codmore Hill 12 D5
Codnor 41 G1
Codrington 20 A4
Codsall 40 A5
Codsall Wood 40 A5
Coed Morgan 28 C7
Coed Ystumgwern 36 E3
Coedcae 19 F1
Coedely 18 D3
Coedkernew 19 F3
Coedpoeth 48 B7
Coed-y-paen 19 G2
Coed-yr-ynys 28 A6
Coelbren 27 H7
Coffinswell 5 J4
Cofton Hackett 30 B1
Cogan 18 E4
Cogenhoe 32 B2
Coggeshall 34 C6
Coggeshall Hamlet 34 C6
Coggins Mill 13 J4
Cóig Peighinnean W.Isles 101 F2
Cóig Peighinnean W.Isles 101 H1
Coilantogle 81 G7
Coileitir 80 C3
Coilessan 80 D7
Coillaig 80 B5
Coille Mhorgil 87 H4
Coille-righ 87 F2
Coillore 85 J1
Coity 18 C3
Col 101 G3
Colaboll 103 H7
Colan 3 F2
Colaton Raleigh 7 J7
Colbost 93 H7
Colbury 10 E3
Colby Cumb. 61 H4
Colby I.o.M. 54 B6
Colby Norf. 45 G2
Colchester 34 D6
Colcot 18 E5
Cold Ash 21 J5
Cold Ashby 31 H1
Cold Ashton 20 A4
Cold Aston 30 C6
Cold Blow 16 E4
Cold Brayfield 32 C3
Cold Chapel 68 E1
Cold Hanworth 52 D4
Cold Hesledon 63 F2
Cold Higham 31 H3
Cold Kirby 58 B1
Cold Newton 42 A5
Cold Norton 24 E1
Cold Overton 42 B5
Coldbackie 103 J2
Coldblow 23 J4
Coldean 13 G6
Coldeast 5 J3
Colden Common 11 F2
Coldfair Green 35 J2
Coldham 43 H5
Coldharbour 22 E7
Coldingham 77 G4
Coldrain 82 B7
Coldred 15 H3
Coldrey 22 A7
Coldridge 6 E5
Coldrife 71 F4
Coldstream 77 G7
Coldwaltham 12 D5
Coldwells 99 K6
Cole 9 F1
Cole Green 33 F7
Colebatch 38 C7
Colebrook 7 J5
Colebrooke 7 F5
Coleby Lincs. 52 C6
Coleby N.Lincs. 52 C1
Coleford Devon 7 F5
Coleford Glos. 28 E7
Coleford Som. 19 K7
Colehill 10 B4
Coleman's Hatch 13 H3
Colemere 38 D2
Colemore 11 J1
Colenden 82 C5
Coleorton 41 G4
Colerne 20 B4
Cole's Cross 5 H6
Colesbourne 30 B7
Colesden 32 E3
Coleshill Bucks. 22 C2
Coleshill Oxon. 21 F2
Coleshill Warks. 40 E7
Colestocks 7 J5
Colfin 64 A5
Colgate 13 F3
Colgrain 74 B2
Colinsburgh 83 F7
Colinton 76 A4
Colintraive 73 J3
Colkirk 44 D3
Collace 82 D4
Collafirth Shet. 109 D6
Collafirth Shet. 108 C4
Collamoor Head 4 B1
Collaton St. Mary 5 J4
Collessie 82 D6
Colleton Mills 6 E4
Collett's Green 29 H3
Collier Row 23 J2
Collier Street 14 C3
Collier's End 33 G6
Colliery Row 62 E1
Collieston 91 J2
Collin 69 F6
Collingbourne Ducis 21 F6
Collingbourne Kingston 21 F6
Collingham Notts. 52 B6
Collingham W.Yorks. 57 J5
Collington 29 F2
Collingtree 31 J3
Collins Green 48 E3
Colliston 83 H3
Colliton 7 J5
Collmuir 90 D4
Collycroft 41 F7
Collynie 91 G1
Collyweston 42 D5
Colmonell 67 F5
Colmworth 32 E3
Coln Rogers 20 D1
Coln St. Aldwyns 20 E1
Coln St. Dennis 30 B7
Colnabaichin 89 K4
Colnbrook 22 D4
Colne Cambs. 33 G1
Colne Lancs. 56 D5
Colne Engaine 34 C5
Colney 45 F5
Colney Heath 23 F1
Colney Street 22 E1
Colonsay 72 B1
Colpy 90 E1
Colquhar 76 B6
Colsterdale 57 G1
Colsterworth 42 C3
Colston Bassett 42 A2
Coltfield 97 J5
Coltishall 45 G4
Colton Cumb. 55 G1
Colton N.Yorks. 58 B5
Colton Norf. 45 F4
Colton Staffs. 40 C3
Colva 28 B3
Colvend 65 J5
Colvister 108 E3
Colwall Green 29 G4
Colwall Stone 29 G4
Colwell 70 E6
Colwich 40 C3
Colwick 41 J1
Colwinston 18 C4
Colworth 12 C6
Colwyn Bay (Bae Colwyn) 47 G5
Colyford 8 B5
Colyton 8 B5
Combe Here. 28 C2
Combe Oxon. 31 F7
Combe W.Berks. 21 G5
Combe Cross 5 H3
Combe Down 20 A5
Combe Florey 7 K2
Combe Hay 20 A5
Combe Martin 6 D1
Combe Raleigh 7 K5
Combe St. Nicholas 8 B3
Combeinteignhead 5 K3
Comberbach 49 F5
Comberford 40 D5
Comberton Cambs. 33 G3
Comberton Here. 28 D2
Combpyne 8 B5
Combrook 30 E3
Combs Derbys. 50 C5
Combs Suff. 34 E3
Combs Ford 34 E3
Combwich 19 F7
Comer 80 E7
Comers 90 E4
Commercial End 33 J2
Commins Coch 37 H5
Common Edge 55 G6
Common Moor 4 C4
Common Side 51 F5
Commondale 63 H5
Commonside 40 E1
Compstall 49 J3
Compton Devon 5 J4
Compton Hants. 11 F2
Compton Surr. 22 C7
Compton W.Berks. 21 J4
Compton W.Suss. 11 J3
Compton Abbas 9 H3
Compton Abdale 30 B7
Compton Bassett 20 D4
Compton Beauchamp 21 F3
Compton Bishop 19 G6
Compton Chamberlayne 10 B2
Compton Dando 19 K5
Compton Dundon 8 D1
Compton Martin 19 J6
Compton Pauncefoot 9 F2
Compton Valence 8 E5
Comra 88 C5
Comrie 81 J5
Conchra Arg. & B. 73 J2
Conchra High. 86 E2
Concraigie 82 C3
Conder Green 55 H4
Conderton 29 J5
Condicote 30 C6
Condorrat 75 F3
Condover 38 D5
Coney Weston 34 D1
Coneyhurst 12 E4
Coneysthorpe 58 D2
Coneythorpe 57 J4
Conford 12 B3
Congash 89 H2
Congdon's Shop 4 C3
Congerstone 41 F5
Congham 44 B3
Congleton 49 H6
Congresbury 19 H5
Conicavel 97 G6
Coningsby 53 F7
Conington Cambs. 42 E7
Conington Cambs. 33 G2
Conisbrough 51 H3
Conisby 72 A4
Conisholme 53 H3
Coniston Cumb. 60 E7
Coniston E.Riding 59 H6
Coniston Cold 56 E4
Conistone 56 E3
Conland 98 E6
Connah's Quay 48 B6
Connel 80 A4
Connel Park 68 B2
Connor Downs 2 C5
Conon Bridge 96 C6
Cononish 80 E5
Cononley 56 E5
Cononsyth 83 G3
Consall 40 B1
Consett 62 C1
Constable Burton 62 C7
Constantine 2 E6
Contin 96 B6
Contlaw 91 G4
Contullich 96 D4
Conwy 47 F5
Conyer 25 F5
Cooden 14 C7
Coodham 74 B7
Cookbury 6 C5
Cookham 22 B3
Cookham Dean 22 B3
Cookham Rise 22 B3
Cookhill 30 B3
Cookley Suff. 35 H1
Cookley Worcs. 40 A7
Cookley Green 21 K3
Cookney 91 G5
Cooksbridge 13 H5
Cookshill 40 B1
Cooksmill Green 24 C1
Cookston 91 H1
Coolham 12 E4
Cooling 24 D4
Coombe Cornw. 3 G3
Coombe Cornw. 6 A4
Coombe Cornw. 2 D4
Coombe Devon 5 H6
Coombe Devon 7 G7
Coombe Bissett 10 C2
Coombe Hill 29 H6
Coombe Keynes 9 H6
Coombes 12 E6
Coombes Moor 28 C2
Cooper's Corner E.Suss. 14 C5
Cooper's Corner Kent 23 H7
Cooper's Hill 22 C4
Coopersale Common 23 H1
Cootham 12 D5
Cop Street 15 H2
Copdock 35 F4
Copford Green 34 D6
Copgrove 57 J3
Copister 108 D5
Cople 32 E4
Copley 62 B4
Coplow Dale 50 D5
Copmanthorpe 58 B5
Coppathorne 6 A5
Coppenhall 40 B4
Coppenhall Moss 49 G7
Coppingford 32 E1
Coppleridge 9 H2
Copplestone 7 F5
Coppull 48 E1
Coppull Moor 48 E1
Copsale 12 E4
Copster Green 56 B6
Copston Magna 41 G7
Copt Heath 30 C1
Copt Hewick 57 J2
Copt Oak 41 G4
Copthorne 13 G3
Copy Lake 6 E4
Copythorne 10 E3
Coralhill 99 J4
Corbiegoe 105 J4
Corbridge 70 E7
Corby 42 B7
Corby Glen 42 D3
Cordach 90 E5
Coreley 29 F1
Corfcott Green 6 B6
Corfe 8 B3
Corfe Castle 9 J6
Corfe Mullen 9 J5
Corfton 38 D7
Corgarff 89 K4
Corhampton 11 H2
Corley 40 E7
Corley Ash 40 E7
Corley Moor 40 E7
Cornabus 72 B6
Corney 60 C7
Cornforth 62 E3
Cornhill 98 D5
Cornhill on Tweed 77 G7
Cornholme 56 E7
Cornish Hall End 33 K5
Cornquoy 107 E7
Cornriggs 61 K2
Cornsay 62 C2
Cornsay Colliery 62 C2
Corntown High. 96 C6
Corntown V. of Glam. 18 C4
Cornwell 30 D6
Cornwood 5 G5
Cornworthy 5 J5
Corpach 87 H7
Corpusty 45 F3
Corrachree 90 C4
Corran Arg. & B. 74 A1
Corran High. 86 E4
Corran High. 80 B1
Corranbuie 73 G4
Corranmore 79 J7
Corrany 54 D5
Corrie 73 J6
Corrie Common 69 H5
Corriechrevie 73 F5
Corriecravie 66 D1
Corriedoo 68 B5
Corrielorne 79 K6
Corrievorrie 88 E2
Corrimony 87 K1
Corringham Lincs. 52 B3
Corringham Thur. 24 D3
Corris 37 G5
Corris Uchaf 37 G5
Corrlarach 87 F7
Corrour Shooting Lodge 81 F1
Corrow 80 C7
Corry 86 C2
Corrychurrachan 80 B1
Corrykinloch 103 F6
Corrylach 66 B1
Corrymuckloch 81 K4
Corsback 105 H2
Corscombe 8 E4
Corse Aber. 98 E6
Corse Glos. 29 G6
Corse Lawn 29 H5
Corse of Kinnoir 98 D6
Corsebank 68 D2
Corsehill 69 G5
Corsewall 64 A4
Corsham 20 B4
Corsindae 90 E4
Corsley 20 B7
Corsley Heath 20 B7
Corsock 65 H3
Corston B. & N.E.Som. 19 K5
Corston Wilts. 20 C3
Corstorphine 75 K3
Cortachy 82 E2
Corton Suff. 45 K6
Corton Wilts. 20 C7
Corton Denham 9 F2
Corúna (Corunna) 92 D5
Corunna (Corúna) 92 D5
Corwar House 67 G5
Corwen 37 K1
Coryton Devon 6 C7
Coryton Thur. 24 D3
Cosby 41 H6
Coseley 40 B6
Cosford 39 G5
Cosgrove 31 J4
Cosham 11 H4
Cosheston 16 D5
Coshieville 81 J3
Cossall 41 G1
Cossington Leics. 41 J4
Cossington Som. 19 G7
Costa 106 C5
Costessey 45 F4
Costock 41 H3
Coston Leics. 42 B3
Coston Norf. 44 E5
Cote Oxon. 21 G1
Cote Som. 19 G7
Cotebrook 48 E6
Cotehill 61 F1
Cotes Cumb. 55 H1
Cotes Leics. 41 H3
Cotes Staffs. 40 A2
Cotesbach 41 H7
Cotgrave 41 J2
Cothall 91 G3
Cotham 42 A1
Cothelstone 7 K2
Cothercott 38 D5
Cotheridge 29 G3
Cotherstone 62 B5
Cothill 21 H2
Cotleigh 8 B4
Coton Cambs. 33 H3
Coton Northants. 31 H1
Coton Staffs. 40 B2
Coton Staffs. 40 D5
Coton Clanford 40 A3
Coton in the Clay 40 D3
Coton in the Elms 40 E4
Cott 5 H4
Cottam E.Riding 59 F3
Cottam Lancs. 55 H6
Cottam Notts. 52 B4
Cottartown 89 H1
Cottenham 33 H2
Cotterdale 61 K7
Cottered 33 G6
Cotteridge 40 C7
Cotterstock 42 D6
Cottesbrooke 31 J1
Cottesmore 42 C4
Cottingham E.Riding 59 G6
Cottingham Northants. 42 B6
Cottisford 31 G5
Cotton 34 E2
Cotton End 32 D4
Cottown Aber. 90 D2
Cottown Aber. 99 G6
Cottown Aber. 91 F3
Cotwalton 40 B2
Couch's Mill 4 B5
Coughton Here. 28 E6
Coughton Warks. 30 B2
Cougie 87 J2
Coulaghailtro 73 F4
Coulags 95 F7
Coulby Newham 63 G5
Coull 90 D4
Coulport 74 A2
Coulsdon 23 G6
Coulston 20 C6
Coulter 75 J7
Coultershaw Bridge 12 C5
Coultings 19 F7
Coulton 58 C2
Coultra 82 E5
Cound 38 E5
Coundon 62 D3
Coundon Grange 62 D4
Countersett 56 E1
Countess 20 E7
Countess Wear 7 H6
Countesthorpe 41 H6
Countisbury 7 F1
County Oak 13 F3
Coupar Angus 82 D3
Coupland Cumb. 61 J5
Coupland Northumb. 77 H7
Cour 73 G6
Court Barton 7 G6
Court Henry 17 J3
Court House Green 41 F7
Court-at-Street 15 F4
Courteenhall 31 J3
Courtsend 25 G2
Courtway 8 B1
Cousland 76 B4
Cousley Wood 13 K3
Coustonn 73 J3
Cove Arg. & B. 74 A2
Cove Devon 7 H4
Cove Hants. 22 B6
Cove High. 94 E2
Cove Sc.Bord. 77 F3
Cove Bay 91 H4
Covehithe 45 K7
Coven 40 B5
Coveney 43 H7
Covenham St. Bartholomew 53 G3
Covenham St. Mary 53 G3
Coventry 30 E1
Coverack 2 E7
Coverham 57 F1
Covesea 97 J4
Covington Cambs. 32 D1
Covington S.Lan. 75 H7
Cowan Bridge 56 B2
Cowbeech 13 K5
Cowbit 43 F4
Cowbridge 18 D4
Cowden 23 H7
Cowden Pound 23 H7
Cowdenbeath 75 K1
Cowes 11 F5
Cowesby 63 F7
Cowfold 13 F4
Cowgill 56 C1
Cowie Aber. 91 G6
Cowie Stir. 75 G2
Cowlam Manor 59 F3
Cowley Devon 7 H6
Cowley Glos. 29 J7
Cowley Gt.Lon. 22 D3
Cowley Oxon. 21 J1
Cowling N.Yorks. 56 E5
Cowling N.Yorks. 57 H1
Cowlinge 34 B3
Cowmes 50 D1
Cowpen 71 H5
Cowpen Bewley 63 F4
Cowplain 11 H3
Cowshill 61 K2
Cowthorpe 57 K4
Cox Common 45 H7
Coxbank 39 F1
Coxbench 41 F1
Coxheath 14 C2
Coxhoe 62 E3
Coxley 19 J7
Coxtie Green 23 J2
Coxwold 58 B2
Coychurch 18 C4
Coylet 73 K2
Coylton 67 J2
Coylumbridge 89 G3
Coynach 90 C4
Coynachie 90 C1
Coytrahen 18 B3
Crabbet Park 13 G3
Crabbs Cross 30 B2
Crabtree Plym. 5 F5
Crabtree W.Suss. 13 F4
Crackaig 72 D4
Crackenthorpe 61 H4
Crackington 4 B1
Crackington Haven 4 B1
Crackleybank 39 G4
Crackpot 62 A7
Cracoe 56 E3
Craddock 7 J4
Cradhlastadh 100 C4
Cradley Here. 29 G4
Cradley W.Mid. 40 B7
Crafthole 4 D5
Cragg 57 F7
Craggan Moray 89 J1
Craggan P. & K. 81 K6
Cragganruar 81 H3
Craggie High. 88 E1
Craggie High. 104 D6
Craghead 62 D1
Craibstone Aberdeen 91 G3
Craibstone Moray 98 C5
Craichie 83 F3
Craig Arg. & B. 80 B4
Craig Arg. & B. 79 G5
Craig D. & G. 65 G4
Craig High. 94 D5
Craig High. 95 G7
Craig S.Ayr. 67 H3
Craigans 73 H1
Craigbeg 88 B6
Craig-cefn-parc 17 K5
Craigcleuch 69 J5
Craigculter 99 H5
Craigdallie 82 D5
Craigdam 91 G1
Craigdarroch D. & G. 68 C4
Craigdarroch E.Ayr. 68 B3
Craigdhu D. & G. 64 D6
Craigdhu High. 96 B7
Craigearn 91 F3
Craigellachie 97 K7
Craigellie 99 J4
Craigencallie 65 F3
Craigend Moray 97 J6
Craigend P. & K. 82 C5
Craigendive 73 J2
Craigendoran 74 B2
Craigengillan 67 J3
Craigenputtock 68 C5
Craigens 72 A4
Craigglas 73 G2
Craighall 83 F6
Craighat 74 C2
Craighead Fife 83 H7
Craighead High. 96 E5
Craighlaw 64 D4
Craighouse 72 D4
Craigie Aber. 91 H3
Craigie P. & K. 82 C3
Craigie S.Ayr. 74 C7
Craigie Brae 91 G1
Craigieburn 69 G3
Craigieholm 82 C4
Craiglockhart 76 A3
Craiglug 91 G5
Craigmaud 99 G5
Craigmillar 76 A3
Craigmore 73 K4
Craigmyle House 90 E4
Craignafeoch 73 H3
Craignant 38 B2
Craignavie 81 G4
Craigneil 67 F5
Craignure 79 J4
Craigo 83 H1
Craigoch 67 H3
Craigow 82 B7
Craigrothie 82 E6
Craigroy 97 J6
Craigroy Farm 89 J1
Craigruie 81 G5
Craigsanquhar 82 E6
Craigton Aberdeen 91 G4
Craigton Angus 83 G4
Craigton Angus 82 E2
Craigton Stir. 74 E2
Craigtown 104 D3
Craig-y-nos 27 H7
Craik Aber. 90 C2
Craik Sc.Bord. 69 J3
Crail 83 H7
Crailing 70 B1
Crailinghall 70 B1
Crakehill 57 K2
Crambe 58 D3
Cramlington 71 H6
Cramond 75 K3
Cranage 49 G6
Cranberry 40 A2
Cranborne 10 B3
Cranbourne 22 C4
Cranbrook 14 C4
Cranbrook Common 14 C4
Cranfield 32 C4
Cranford Devon 6 B3
Cranford Gt.Lon. 22 E4
Cranford St. Andrew 32 C1
Cranford St. John 32 C1
Cranham Glos. 29 H7
Cranham Gt.Lon. 23 J3
Crank 48 E2
Cranleigh 12 D3
Cranmer Green 34 E1
Cranmore I.o.W. 11 F5
Cranmore Som. 19 K7
Cranna 98 E5
Crannach 98 C5
Cranoe 42 A6
Cransford 35 H2
Cranshaws 76 E4
Cranstal 54 D3
Crantock 2 E2
Cranwell 42 D1
Cranwich 44 B6
Cranworth 44 D5
Craobh Haven 79 J7
Crapstone 5 F4
Crarae 73 H1
Crask Inn 103 H6
Crask of Aigas 96 B7
Craskins 90 D4
Craster 71 H1
Craswall 28 B5
Cratfield 35 H1
Crathes 91 F5
Crathie Aber. 89 K5
Crathie High. 88 C5
Crathorne 63 F6
Craven Arms 38 D7
Craw 73 G6
Crawcrook 71 G7
Crawford Lancs. 48 D2
Crawford S.Lan. 68 E1
Crawfordjohn 68 D1
Crawfordton 68 C4
Crawick 68 C2
Crawley Hants. 11 F1
Crawley Oxon. 30 E7
Crawley W.Suss. 13 F3
Crawley Down 13 G3
Crawleyside 62 A2
Crawshawbooth 56 D7
Crawton 91 G7
Crawyn 54 C4
Cray N.Yorks. 56 E2
Cray P. & K. 82 C1
Cray Powys 27 H6
Crayford 23 J4
Crayke 58 B2
Crays Hill 24 D2
Cray's Pond 21 K3
Crazies Hill 22 A3
Creacombe 7 G4
Creag Ghoraidh 92 D7
Creagbheitheachain 80 A1
Creaton 31 J1
Creca 69 H6
Credenhill 28 D4
Crediton 7 G5
Creech Heathfield 8 B2
Creech St. Michael 8 B2
Creed 3 G4
Creedy Park 7 G5
Creekmouth 23 H3
Creeting St. Mary 34 E3
Creeton 42 D3
Creetown 64 E5
Creggans 80 B7
Cregneash 54 A7
Cregrina 28 A3
Creich 82 E5
Creigiau 18 D3
Crelevan 87 K1
Cremyll 4 E5
Cressage 38 E5
Cresselly 16 D5
Cressing 34 B6
Cresswell Northumb. 71 H4
Cresswell Staffs. 40 B2
Cresswell Quay 16 D5
Creswell 51 H5
Cretingham 35 G3
Cretshengan 73 F4
Crewe Ches. 49 G7
Crewe Ches. 48 D7
Crewgreen 38 C4
Crewkerne 8 D4
Crewton 41 F2
Crianlarich 80 E5
Cribbs Causeway 19 J3
Cribyn 26 E3
Criccieth 36 D2
Crich 51 F7
Crich Carr 51 F7
Crichie 99 H6
Crichton 76 B4
Crick Mon. 19 H3
Crick Northants. 31 G1
Crickadarn 27 K4
Cricket Malherbie 8 C3
Cricket St. Thomas 8 C4
Crickheath 38 B3
Crickhowell 28 B7
Cricklade 20 D2
Cridling Stubbs 58 B7
Crieff 81 K5
Criggion 38 B4
Crigglestone 51 F1
Crimdon Park 63 F3
Crimond 99 J5
Crimonmogate 99 J5
Crimplesham 44 A5
Crinan 73 F1
Cringleford 45 F5
Cringletie 76 A6
Crinow 16 E4
Cripplesease 2 B5
Cripp's Corner 14 C5
Crix 34 B7
Croalchapel 68 E4
Croasdale 60 B5
Crock Street 8 C3
Crockenhill 23 J5
Crockernwell 7 F6
Crockerton 20 B7
Crocketford or Ninemile Bar 65 J3
Crockey Hill 58 C5
Crockham Hill 23 H6
Crockhurst Street 23 K7

Crockleford Heath 34 E6
Croes Hywel 28 C7
Croes y pant 19 G1
Croesau Bach 38 B3
Croeserw 18 B2
Croesgoch 16 B3
Croes-lan 17 G1
Croesor 37 F1
Croespenmaen 18 E2
Croesyceiliog Carmar. 17 H4
Croesyceiliog Torfaen 19 G2
Croes-y-mwyalch 19 G2
Croft Leics. 41 H6
Croft Lincs. 53 J6
Croft Warr. 49 F3
Crofthead 69 J6
Croftmore 81 K1
Crofton W.Yorks. 51 F1
Crofton Wilts. 21 F5
Croft-on-Tees 62 D5
Crofts 65 H3
Crofts of Benachielt 105 C5
Crofts of Buinach 97 J6
Crofts of Haddo 91 G1
Crofty 17 J6
Crogen 37 K2
Croggan 79 J5
Croglin 61 G2
Croick High. 96 B2
Croick High. 104 D3
Croig 79 F2
Crois Dughaill 84 C3
Croit e Caley 54 B6
Cromarty 96 E5
Crombie Mill 83 G3
Cromblet 91 F1
Cromdale 89 H2
Cromer Herts. 33 F6
Cromer Norf. 45 G1
Cromer Hyde 33 F7
Cromford 50 E7
Cromhall 19 K2
Cromhall Common 19 K3
Crompton Fold 49 J2
Cromwell 52 B6
Cronberry 68 B1
Crondall 22 A7
Cronk-y-Voddy 54 C5
Cronton 48 D4
Crook Cumb. 61 F7
Crook Dur. 62 C3
Crook of Devon 82 B7
Crookedholm 74 C7
Crookham Northumb. 77 H7
Crookham W.Berks. 21 J5
Crookham Village 22 A6
Crooklands 55 J1
Cropredy 31 F4
Cropston 41 H4
Cropthorne 29 J4
Cropton 58 D1
Cropwell Bishop 41 J2
Cropwell Butler 41 J2
Cros 101 G1
Crosbie 74 A6
Crosbost 101 F5
Crosby Cumb. 60 B3
Crosby I.o.M. 54 C6
Crosby Mersey. 48 C3
Crosby N.Lincs. 52 B1
Crosby Court 62 E7
Crosby Garrett 61 J6
Crosby Ravensworth 61 H5
Croscombe 19 J7
Cross 19 H6
Cross Ash 28 D7
Cross Foxes Inn 37 G4
Cross Gates 57 J6
Cross Green Devon 6 B7
Cross Green Suff. 34 D3
Cross Green Suff. 34 C3
Cross Hands Carmar. 17 J4
Cross Hands Pembs. 16 D4
Cross Hill 41 G1
Cross Hills 57 F5
Cross Houses 38 E5
Cross in Hand 13 J4
Cross Inn Cere. 26 C3
Cross Inn Cere. 26 E2
Cross Inn R.C.T. 18 D3
Cross Keys 20 B4
Cross Lane Head 39 G6
Cross Lanes Cornw. 2 E4
Cross Lanes N.Yorks. 58 B3
Cross Lanes Wrex. 38 C1
Cross o' the Hands 40 E1
Cross of Jackson 91 F1
Cross Street 35 F1
Crossaig 73 G5
Crossapol 78 C2
Crossapoll 78 A3
Cross-at-Hand 14 C3
Crossbush 12 D6
Crosscanonby 60 B3
Crossdale Street 45 G2
Crossens 55 G7
Crossford D. & G. 68 D5
Crossford Fife 75 J2
Crossford S.Lan. 75 G6
Crossgate 43 F3
Crossgatehall 76 B4
Crossgates Fife 75 K2
Crossgates P. & K. 82 B5
Crossgates Powys 27 K2
Crossgill 55 J3
Crosshands 74 C7
Crosshill Fife 75 K1
Crosshill S.Ayr. 67 H3
Crosshouse 74 B7
Crosskeys 19 F2
Crosskirk 105 F1
Crosslanes Cornw. 2 D6
Crosslanes Shrop. 38 C4
Crosslee Renf. 74 C4
Crosslee Sc.Bord. 69 J2
Crosslet 74 C3
Crossmichael 65 H4
Crossmoor 55 H6
Crossroads Aber. 91 F5
Crossroads E.Ayr. 74 C7
Crossway Mon. 28 D7
Crossway Powys 27 K3
Crossway Green 29 H2
Crossways Dorset 9 G6
Crossways Glos. 28 E7
Crosswell 16 E2
Crosthwaite 61 F7
Croston 48 D1
Crostwick 45 G4
Crostwight 45 H2
Crouch 23 K6
Crouch Hill 9 G3
Croughton 31 G5
Crovie 99 G4
Crow 10 C4
Crow Hill 29 F6
Crowan 2 D5
Crowborough 13 J3
Crowcombe 7 K2
Crowdecote 50 D6
Crowdhill 11 F2
Crowfield Northants. 31 H4
Crowfield Suff. 35 F3
Crowhurst E.Suss. 14 C6
Crowhurst Surr. 23 G7
Crowhurst Lane End 23 G7
Crowland Lincs. 43 F4
Crowland Suff. 34 E1
Crowlas 2 C5
Crowle N.Lincs. 51 K1
Crowle Worcs. 29 J3
Crowle Green 29 J3
Crowmarsh Gifford 21 K3
Crownhill 4 E5
Crownthorpe 44 E5
Crowntown 2 D5
Crows-an-wra 2 A6
Crowthorne 22 B5
Crowton 48 E5
Croxall 40 D4
Croxdale 62 D3
Croxden 40 C2
Croxley Green 22 D2
Croxton Cambs. 33 F3
Croxton N.Lincs. 52 E1
Croxton Norf. 44 C7
Croxton Staffs. 39 G2
Croxton Green 48 E7
Croxton Kerrial 42 B3
Croxtonbank 39 G2
Croy High. 96 E7
Croy N.Lan. 75 F3
Croyde 6 C2
Croydon Cambs. 33 G4
Croydon Gt.Lon. 23 G5
Cruach 72 B5
Cruchie 98 D6
Cruckmeole 38 D5
Cruckton 38 D4
Cruden Bay 91 J1
Crudgington 39 F4
Crudwell 20 C2
Crug 28 A1
Crugmeer 3 G1
Crugybar 17 K2
Crulabhig 100 D4
Crumlin 19 F2
Crundale Kent 15 F3
Crundale Pembs. 16 C4
Crutherland 74 E5
Cruwys Morchard 7 G4
Crux Easton 21 H6
Crwbin 17 H4
Cryers Hill 22 B2
Crymlyn 46 E5
Crymych 16 E2
Crynant 18 A1
Crystal Palace 23 G4
Cuaig 94 D6
Cubbington 30 E2
Cubert 2 E3
Cublington 32 B6
Cuckfield 13 G4
Cucklington 9 G2
Cuckney 51 H5
Cuckoo's Nest 48 C6
Cuddesdon 21 J1
Cuddington Bucks. 31 J7
Cuddington Ches. 49 F5
Cuddington Heath 38 D1
Cuddy Hill 55 H6
Cudham 23 H6
Cudlipptown 5 F3
Cudworth S.Yorks. 51 F2
Cudworth Som. 8 C3
Cuffley 23 G1
Cuidhaseadair 101 H2
Cuidhir 84 B4
Cuidhtinis 93 F3
Cuidrach 93 J6
Cuilmuich 73 K1
Cuil-uaine 80 A4
Culag 74 B1
Culbo 96 D5
Culbokie 96 D6
Culbone 7 G1
Culburnie 96 B7
Culcabock 96 D7
Culcharan 80 A4
Culcharry 97 F6
Culcheth 49 F3
Culdrain 90 D1
Culduie 94 D7
Culford 34 C2
Culgaith 61 H4
Culgower 104 E7
Culham 21 J2
Culindrach 73 H5
Culkein 102 C5
Culkerton 20 C2
Cullachie 89 G2
Cullen 98 D4
Cullercoats 71 J6
Cullicudden 96 D5
Culligran 95 K7
Cullingworth 57 F6
Cullipool 79 J6
Cullivoe 108 E2
Culloch 81 J6
Culloden 96 E7
Cullompton 7 J5
Culmaily 97 F2
Culmalzie 64 D5
Culmington 38 D7
Culmstock 7 J4
Culnacraig 95 G1
Culnadalloch 80 A4
Culnaknock 94 B5
Culnamean 85 K2
Culpho 35 G4
Culquhirk 64 E5
Culrain 96 C2
Culross 75 H2
Culroy 67 H2
Culsh 90 B5
Culshabbin 64 D5
Culswick 109 B8
Culter Allers Farm 75 J7
Cultercullen 91 H2
Cults Aber. 90 D1
Cults Aberdeen 91 G4
Cults D. & G. 64 E6
Cultybraggan Camp 81 J6
Culverhouse Cross 18 E4
Culverstone Green 24 C5
Culverthorpe 42 D1
Culvie 98 D5
Culworth 31 G4
Cumberhead 75 F7
Cumbernauld 75 F3
Cumberworth 53 J5
Cuminestown 99 G5
Cumloden 64 E4
Cummersdale 60 E1
Cummertrees 69 G7
Cummingstown 97 J5
Cumnock 67 K1
Cumnor 21 H1
Cumrew 61 G1
Cumrue 69 F5
Cumstoun 65 G5
Cumwhinton 61 F1
Cumwhitton 61 G1
Cundall 57 K2
Cunninghamhead 74 B6
Cunnister 108 E3
Cunnoquhie 82 E6
Cupar 82 E6
Cupar Muir 82 E6
Curbar 50 E5
Curbridge Hants. 11 G3
Curbridge Oxon. 21 G1
Curdridge 11 G3
Curdworth 40 D6
Curland 8 B3
Curload 8 C2
Curridge 21 H4
Currie 75 K4
Curry Mallet 8 C2
Curry Rivel 8 C2
Curteis' Corner 14 D4
Curtisden Green 14 C3
Cury 2 D6
Cushnie 99 F4
Cushuish 7 K2
Cusop 28 B4
Cutcloy 64 E7
Cutcombe 7 H2
Cuthill 96 E3
Cutiau 37 F4
Cutnall Green 29 H2
Cutsdean 30 B5
Cutthorpe 51 F5
Cutts 109 D9
Cuttyhill 99 J5
Cuxham 21 K2
Cuxton 24 D5
Cuxwold 52 E2
Cwm B.Gwent 18 E1
Cwm Denb. 47 J5
Cwm Ffrwd-oer 19 F1
Cwm Gwaun 16 D2
Cwm Irfon 27 H4
Cwmafan 18 A2
Cwmaman 18 D2
Cwmann 17 J1
Cwmbach Carmar. 17 F3
Cwmbach Powys 28 A5
Cwmbach Powys 27 K3
Cwmbach R.C.T. 18 D1
Cwmbelan 37 J7
Cwmbrân 19 F2
Cwmbrwyno 37 G7
Cwmcarn 19 F2
Cwmcarvan 19 H1
Cwm-Cewydd 37 H4
Cwmcoy 17 F1
Cwmdare 18 C1
Cwmdu Carmar. 17 K2
Cwmdu Powys 28 A6
Cwmduad 17 G2
Cwmfelin Boeth 16 E4
Cwmfelin Mynach 17 F3
Cwmfelinfach 18 E2
Cwmffrwd 17 H4
Cwmgiedd 27 G7
Cwmgors 27 G7
Cwmgwrach 18 B1
Cwmisfael 17 H4
Cwm-Llinau 37 H5
Cwmllyfri 17 G4
Cwmllynfell 27 G7
Cwm-Morgan 17 F2
Cwm-parc 18 C2
Cwmpengraig 17 G2
Cwmsychbant 17 H1
Cwmsymlog 37 F7
Cwmtillery 19 F1
Cwm-twrch Isaf 27 G7
Cwm-y-glo 46 D6
Cwmyoy 28 C6
Cwm-yr-Eglwys 16 D1
Cwmystwyth 27 G1
Cwrt 37 F5
Cwrt-newydd 17 H1
Cwrt-y-gollen 28 B7
Cydweli (Kidwelly) 17 H5
Cyffylliog 47 J7
Cyfronydd 38 A5
Cymmer N.P.T. 18 B2
Cymmer R.C.T. 18 D2
Cynghordy 27 H5
Cynheidre 17 H5
Cynwyd 37 K1
Cynwyl Elfed 17 G3

D

Dabton 68 D4
Daccombe 5 K4
Dacre Cumb. 61 F4
Dacre N.Yorks. 57 G3
Dacre Banks 57 G3
Daddry Shield 61 K3
Dadford 31 H5
Dadlington 41 G6
Dafen 17 J5
Daffy Green 44 D5
Dagenham 23 H3
Daggons 10 C3
Daglingworth 20 C1
Dagnall 32 C7
Dail 80 B4
Dail Beag 100 E3
Dail Bho Dheas 101 G1
Dail Bho Thuath 101 G1
Dail Mòr 100 E3
Dailly 67 G3
Dailnamac 80 A4
Dairsie or Osnaburgh 83 F6
Dalabrog 84 C2
Dalavich 80 A6
Dalballoch 88 D5
Dalbeattie 65 J4
Dalblair 68 B2
Dalbog 90 D7
Dalbreck 104 C7
Dalbury 40 E2
Dalby 54 B6
Dalcairnie 67 J3
Dalchalloch 81 J1
Dalchalm 97 G1
Dalchenna 80 B7
Dalchirach 89 J1
Dalchork 103 H7
Dalchreichart 87 J3
Dalchruin 81 J6
Dalcross 96 E7
Dalderby 53 F6
Daldownie 89 K4
Dale Derbys. 41 G2
Dale Pembs. 16 B5
Dale Head 61 F5
Dale of Walls 109 A7
Dale Park 12 C6
Dalehouse 63 J5
Dalelia 79 J1
Daless 89 F1
Dalestie 89 J3
Dalfad 90 B4
Dalganachan 105 F4
Dalgarven 74 A6
Dalgety Bay 75 K2
Dalgig 67 K2
Dalginross 81 J5
Dalgonar 68 C3
Dalguise 82 A3
Dalhalvaig 104 D3
Dalham 34 B2
Daligan 74 B2
Dalivaddy 66 A2
Daljarrock 67 F5
Dalkeith 76 B4
Dallas 97 J6
Dallaschyle 97 F7
Dallash 64 E4
Dallinghoo 35 G3
Dallington E.Suss. 13 K5
Dallington Northants. 31 J2
Dalmadilly 91 F3
Dalmally 80 C5
Dalmarnock 82 A3
Dalmary 74 D1
Dalmellington 67 J3
Dalmeny 75 K3
Dalmichy 103 H7
Dalmigavie 88 E3
Dalmore 96 D5
Dalmunzie Hotel 89 H7
Dalnabreck 79 J1
Dalnacarn 82 B1
Dalnaglar Castle 82 C1
Dalnaha 79 H5
Dalnahaitnach 89 F3
Dalnamain 96 E2
Dalnatrat 80 A2
Dalnavie 96 D4
Dalness 80 C2
Dalnessie 103 J7
Dalnigap 64 B3
Dalqueich 82 B7
Dalreoch 67 F5
Dalriech 81 J4
Dalroy 96 E7
Dalrulzian 82 C2
Dalry 74 A6
Dalrymple 67 H2
Dalserf 75 F5
Dalshangan 67 K5
Dalskairth 65 K3
Dalston 60 E1
Dalswinton 68 E5
Daltomach 88 E2
Dalton D. & G. 69 G6
Dalton Lancs. 48 D2
Dalton N.Yorks. 57 K2
Dalton N.Yorks. 62 C6
Dalton Northumb. 71 G6
Dalton Northumb. 62 A1
Dalton S.Yorks. 51 G3
Dalton Piercy 63 F3
Dalton-in-Furness 55 F2
Dalton-le-Dale 63 F2
Dalton-on-Tees 62 D6
Daltote 73 F2
Daltra 97 G7
Dalveich 81 H5
Dalvennan 67 H2
Dalvourn 88 D1
Dalwhinnie 88 D6
Dalwood 8 B4
Damerham 10 C3
Damgate 45 J5
Damnaglaur 64 B7
Damside 82 A6
Danbury 24 D1
Danby 63 J6
Danby Wiske 62 E7
Dandaleith 97 K7
Danderhall 76 B4
Dane End 33 G6
Dane Hills 41 H5
Danebridge 49 J6
Danehill 13 H4
Danesmoor 51 G6
Danestone 91 H3
Danskine 76 D4
Darby Green 22 B5
Darenth 23 J4
Daresbury 48 E4
Darfield 51 G2
Dargate 25 G5
Dargues 70 D4
Darite 4 C4
Darlaston 40 B6
Darley 57 H4
Darley Dale 50 E6
Darlingscott 30 D4
Darlington 62 D5
Darliston 38 E2
Darlton 51 K5
Darnabo 99 F6
Darnall 51 F4
Darnconner 67 K1
Darnford 91 F5
Darngarroch 65 G4
Darnick 76 D7
Darowen 37 H5
Darra 99 F6
Darras Hall 71 G6
Darrington 51 G1
Darsham 35 J2
Dartfield 99 J5
Dartford 23 J4
Dartington 5 H4
Dartmeet 5 G3
Dartmouth 5 J5
Darton 51 F2
Darvel 74 D7
Darvell 14 C5
Darwen 56 B7
Datchet 22 C4
Datchworth 33 F7
Datchworth Green 33 F7
Daubhill 49 G2
Daugh of Kinermony 97 K7
Dauntsey 20 C3
Dava 89 H1
Davaar 66 B2
Davan 90 C4
Davenham 49 F5
Daventry 31 G2
Davidstow 4 B2
Davington 69 H3
Daviot Aber. 91 F2
Daviot High. 88 E1
Davoch of Grange 98 C5
Dawley 39 F5
Dawlish 5 K3
Dawn 47 G5
Daws Heath 24 E3
Dawsmere 43 H2
Daylesford 30 D6
Ddôl 47 K5
Deadwaters 75 F6
Deal 15 J2
Deal Hall 25 G2
Dean Cumb. 60 B4
Dean Devon 5 H4
Dean Dorset 9 J3
Dean Hants. 11 G3
Dean Oxon. 30 E6
Dean Som. 19 K7
Dean Bank 62 D3
Dean Prior 5 H4
Dean Row 49 H4
Dean Street 14 C2
Deanburnhaugh 69 J2
Deane 21 J7
Deanland 9 J3
Deanscales 60 B4
Deanshanger 31 J4
Deanston 81 J7
Dearham 60 B3
Debach 35 G3
Debate 69 H5
Debden 33 J5
Debden Green 33 J5
Debenham 35 F2
Dechmont 75 J3
Deddington 31 F5
Dedham 34 E5
Deecastle 90 C5
Deene 42 C6
Deenethorpe 42 C6
Deepcar 50 E3
Deepcut 22 C6
Deepdale Cumb. 56 C1
Deepdale N.Yorks. 56 D2
Deeping Gate 42 E5
Deeping St. James 42 E5
Deeping St. Nicholas 43 F4
Deerhill 98 C5
Deerhurst 29 H6
Defford 29 J4
Defynnog 27 J6
Deganwy 47 F5
Degnish 79 J6
Deighton N.Yorks. 62 E6
Deighton York 58 C5
Deiniolen 46 D6
Delabole 4 A2
Delamere 48 E6
Delavorar 89 J3
Delfrigs 91 H2
Dell Lodge 89 H3
Delliefure 89 H1
Delnabo 89 J3
Delny 96 E4
Delph 49 J2
Delphorrie 90 C3
Delves 62 C2
Delvine 82 C3
Dembleby 42 D2
Denaby 51 G3
Denaby Main 51 G3
Denbigh (Dinbych) 47 J6
Denbury 5 J4
Denby 41 F1
Denby Dale 50 E2
Denchworth 21 G2
Dendron 55 F2
Denend 90 D1
Denford 32 C1
Dengie 25 F1
Denham Bucks. 22 D3
Denham Suff. 35 F1
Denham Suff. 34 B2
Denham Green 22 D3
Denhead Aber. 91 F3
Denhead Aber. 99 H5
Denhead Dundee 82 E4
Denhead Fife 83 F6
Denhead of Arbirlot 83 G3
Denholm 70 A2
Denholme 57 F6
Denholme Clough 57 F6
Denio 36 C2
Denmead 11 H3
Denmill 91 G3
Denmoss 98 E6
Dennington 35 G2
Denny 75 G2
Dennyloanhead 75 G2
Denshaw 49 J1
Denside 91 G5
Densole 15 H3
Denston 34 B3
Denstone 40 C1
Dent 56 C1
Denton Cambs. 42 E7
Denton Darl. 62 D5
Denton E.Suss. 13 H6
Denton Gt.Man. 49 J3
Denton Kent 15 H3
Denton Lincs. 42 B2
Denton N.Yorks. 57 G5
Denton Norf. 45 G7
Denton Northants. 32 B3
Denton Oxon. 21 J1
Denver 44 A5
Denvilles 11 J4
Denwick 71 H2
Deopham 44 E5
Deopham Green 44 E6
Depden 34 B3
Deptford Gt.Lon. 23 G4
Deptford Wilts. 10 B1
Derby 41 F2
Derbyhaven 54 B7
Dereham (East Dereham) 44 D4
Dererach 79 G5
Deri 18 E1
Derringstone 15 G3
Derrington 40 A3
Derry 81 H5
Derry Hill 20 C4
Derrythorpe 52 B2
Dersingham 44 A2
Dervaig 79 F2
Derwen 47 J7
Derwenlas 37 G6
Derwydd 17 K4
Derybruich 73 H3
Desborough 42 B7
Desford 41 G5
Detchant 77 J7
Detling 14 C2
Deuddwr 38 B4
Deunant 47 H6
Deuxhill 39 F7
Devauden 19 H2
Devil's Bridge (Pontarfynach) 27 G1
Devizes 20 D5
Devonport 4 E5
Devonside 75 H1
Devoran 2 E5
Dewar 76 B6
Dewlish 9 G5
Dewsall Court 28 D5
Dewsbury 57 H7
Dhiseig 79 F4
Dhoon 54 D5
Dhoor 54 D4
Dhowin 54 D3
Dhuhallow 88 C2
Dial Post 12 E5
Dibden 11 F4
Dibden Purlieu 11 F4
Dickleburgh 45 F7
Didbrook 30 B5
Didcot 21 J3
Diddington 32 E2
Diddlebury 38 E7
Didley 28 D5
Didling 12 B5
Didmarton 20 B3
Didsbury 49 H3
Didworthy 5 G4
Digby 52 D7
Digg 93 K5
Diggle 50 C2
Digmoor 48 D2
Digswell 33 F7
Dihewyd 26 D3
Dildawn 65 H5
Dilham 45 H3
Dilhorne 40 B1
Dilston 70 E7
Dilton Marsh 20 B6
Dilwyn 28 D3
Dilwyn Common 28 D3
Dinas Carmar. 17 F2
Dinas Gwyn. 46 C7
Dinas Gwyn. 36 B2
Dinas Cross 16 D2
Dinas Dinlle 46 C7
Dinas Powys 18 E4
Dinas-Mawddwy 37 H4
Dinbych (Denbigh) 47 J6
Dinbych-y-Pysgod (Tenby) 16 E5
Dinder 19 J7
Dinedor 28 E5
Dingestow 28 D7
Dingley 42 A7
Dingwall 96 C6
Dinlabyre 70 A4
Dinnet 90 C5
Dinnington S.Yorks. 51 H4
Dinnington Som. 8 D3
Dinnington T. & W. 71 H6
Dinorwig 46 D6
Dinton Bucks. 31 J7
Dinton Wilts. 10 B1
Dinvin 64 A5
Dinwoodie Mains 69 G4
Dinworthy 6 B4
Dippen 73 F7
Dippenhall 22 B7
Dippin 66 E1
Dipple Moray 98 B5
Dipple S.Ayr. 67 G3
Diptford 5 H5
Dipton 62 C1
Dirdhu 89 H2
Dirleton 76 D2
Discoed 28 B2
Diseworth 41 G3
Dishes 106 F5
Dishforth 57 J2
Disley 49 J4
Diss 45 F7
Disserth 27 K3
Distington 60 B4
Ditcheat 9 F1
Ditchingham 45 H6
Ditchley 30 E6
Ditchling 13 G5
Ditteridge 20 B5
Dittisham 5 J5
Ditton Halton 48 D4
Ditton Kent 14 C2
Ditton Green 33 K3
Ditton Priors 39 F7
Dixton Glos. 29 J5
Dixton Mon. 28 E7
Dobcross 49 J2
Dobwalls 4 C4
Doc Penfro (Pembroke Dock) 16 C5
Doccombe 7 F7
Dochgarroch 96 D7
Dockenfield 22 B7
Docking 44 B2
Docklow 28 E3
Dockray 60 E4
Doddinghurst 23 J2
Doddington Cambs. 43 G6
Doddington Kent 14 E2
Doddington Lincs. 52 C5
Doddington Northumb. 77 H7
Doddington Shrop. 29 F1
Doddiscombsleigh 7 G7
Dodford Northants. 31 H2
Dodford Worcs. 29 J1
Dodington S.Glos. 20 A3
Dodington Som. 7 K1
Dodington Ash 20 A4
Dodleston 48 C6
Dodworth 51 F2
Doe Lea 51 G6
Dog Village 7 H6
Dogdyke 53 F7
Dogmersfield 22 A6
Dol Fawr 37 H5
Dolanog 37 K4
Dolau 28 A2
Dolbenmaen 36 E1
Dolfach 27 J1
Dolfor 38 A7
Dolgarreg 27 G5
Dolgarrog 47 F6
Dolgellau 37 G4
Dolgoch 37 F5
Dol-gran 17 H2
Doll 97 F1
Dollar 75 H1
Dollarbeg 75 H1
Dolleycanney 28 A4
Dolphinholme 55 J4
Dolphinton 75 K6
Dolton 6 D4
Dolwen Conwy 47 G5
Dolwen Powys 37 J5
Dolwyddelan 47 F7
Dolybont 37 F7
Dolyhir 28 B3
Dolywern 38 B2
Domgay 38 B4
Doncaster 51 H2
Donhead St. Andrew 9 J2
Donhead St. Mary 9 J2
Donibristle 75 K2
Doniford 7 J1
Donington 43 F2
Donington le Heath 41 G4
Donington on Bain 53 F4
Donisthorpe 41 F4
Donkey Town 22 C5
Donnington Glos. 30 C6
Donnington Here. 29 G5
Donnington Shrop. 38 E5
Donnington Tel. & W. 39 G4
Donnington W.Berks. 21 H5
Donnington W.Suss. 12 B6
Donyatt 8 C3
Dorchester Dorset 9 F5
Dorchester Oxon. 21 J2
Dordon 40 E5
Dore 51 F4
Dores 88 C1
Dorket Head 41 H1
Dorking 22 E7
Dormans Park 23 G7
Dormansland 23 H7
Dormanstown 63 G4
Dormington 28 E4
Dorney 22 C4
Dornie 86 E2
Dornoch 96 E3
Dornock 69 H7
Dorrery 105 F3
Dorridge 30 C1
Dorrington Lincs. 52 D7
Dorrington Shrop. 38 D5
Dorsell 90 D3
Dorsington 30 C3
Dorstone 28 C4
Dorton 31 H7
Dorusduain 87 F2
Dosthill 40 E5
Dotland 62 A1
Dottery 8 D5
Doublebois 4 B4
Dougalston 74 D3
Dougarie 73 G7
Doughton 20 B2
Douglas I.o.M. 54 C6
Douglas S.Lan. 75 G7
Douglas & Angus 83 F4
Douglas Hall 65 J5
Douglas Water 75 G7
Douglastown 83 F3
Doulting 19 K7
Dounby 106 B5
Doune Arg. & B. 74 B1
Doune Arg. & B. 80 E6
Doune High. 89 F3
Doune High. 96 B1
Doune Stir. 81 J7
Dounepark 99 F4
Douneside 90 C4
Dounie High. 96 D3
Dounie High. 96 C2
Dounreay 104 E2
Dousland 5 F4
Dovaston 38 C3
Dove Holes 50 C5
Dovenby 60 B3
Dover 15 J3
Dovercourt 35 G6
Doverdale 29 H2
Doveridge 40 D2
Doversgreen 23 F7
Dowally 82 B3
Dowdeswell 30 B6
Dowhill 67 G3
Dowland 6 D4
Dowlands 8 B5
Dowlish Wake 8 C3
Down Ampney 20 E2
Down End 19 G7
Down Hatherley 29 H6
Down St. Mary 7 F5
Down Thomas 5 F6
Downderry 4 D5
Downe 23 H5
Downend I.o.W. 11 G6
Downend S.Glos. 19 K4
Downend W.Berks. 21 H4
Downfield 82 E4
Downfields 33 J1
Downgate 4 D3
Downham Essex 24 D2
Downham Lancs. 56 C5
Downham Northumb. 77 G7
Downham Market 44 A5
Downhead Cornw. 4 C2
Downhead Som. 19 K7
Downholland Cross 48 C2
Downholme 62 C7
Downies 91 H5
Downing 47 K5
Downley 22 B2
Downside N.Som. 19 H5
Downside Som. 19 K7
Downside Surr. 22 E6
Downton Devon 6 D7
Downton Devon 5 J5
Downton Hants. 10 D5
Downton Wilts. 10 C2
Downton on the Rock 28 D1
Dowsby 42 E2
Dowthwaitehead 60 E4
Doynton 20 A4
Draethen 19 F3
Draffan 75 F6
Drakeland Corner 5 F5
Drakes Broughton 29 J4
Drakes Cross 30 B1
Draughton N.Yorks. 57 F4
Draughton Northants. 31 J1
Drax 58 C7
Draycote 31 F1
Draycott Derbys. 41 G2
Draycott Glos. 30 C5

Draycott Som. 19 H6
Draycott Worcs. 29 H4
Draycott in the Clay 40 D3
Draycott in the Moors 40 B2
Drayton Leics. 42 B6
Drayton Lincs. 43 F2
Drayton Norf. 45 F4
Drayton Oxon. 31 F4
Drayton Oxon. 21 H2
Drayton Ports. 11 H4
Drayton Som. 8 D2
Drayton Worcs. 29 J1
Drayton Bassett 40 D5
Drayton Beauchamp 32 C7
Drayton Parslow 32 B6
Drayton St. Leonard 21 J2
Drebley 57 F4
Dreemskerry 54 D4
Dreenhill 16 C4
Drefach Carmar. 17 G2
Drefach Carmar. 17 J4
Dre-fach Cere. 17 J1
Dreghorn 74 B7
Drellingore 15 H3
Drem 76 D3
Drewsteignton 7
Driby 53 G5
Driffield E.Riding 59 G4
Driffield Glos. 20 D2
Drigg 60 B7
Drighlington 57 H7
Drimfern 80 B6
Drimlee 80 C6
Drimnin 79 G2
Drimore 84 C1
Drimpton 8 D4
Drimsynie 80 C7
Drimvore 73 G1
Drinan 86 B3
Drinkstone 34 D2
Drinkstone Green 34 D3
Drishaig 80 C6
Drissaig 80 A6
Droiton 40 C3
Droitwich 29 H2
Dron 82 C6
Dronfield 51 F5
Dronfield Woodhouse 51 F5
Drongan 67 J2
Dronley 82 E4
Dropmore 22 C3
Droxford 11 H3
Droylsden 49 J3
Druid 37 K1
Druidston 16 B4
Druimarbin 80 B1
Druimavuic 80 B3
Druimdrishaig 73 F3
Druimindarroch 86 C6
Druimkinnerras 96 B7
Drum Arg. & B. 73 H3
Drum P. & K. 82 B7
Drumachloy 73 J4
Drumbeg 102 D5
Drumblade 98 D6
Drumblair 98 E6
Drumbuie D. & G. 68 C2
Drumbuie High. 86 D1
Drumburgh 74 D3
Drumchapel 74 D3
Drumchardine 96 C7
Drumchork 94 E3
Drumclog 74 E7
Drumdelgie 98 C6
Drumderfit 96 D6
Drumeldrie 83 F7
Drumelzier 75 K7
Drumfearn 86 C3
Drumfern 87 F7
Drumgarve 66 B3
Drumgley 83 F3
Drumguish 88 E5
Drumhead 90 E5
Drumin 89 J1
Drumine 96 E6
Drumjohn 67 K4
Drumlamford House 64 C3
Drumlasie 90 E4
Drumlemble 66 A2
Drumlithie 91 F6
Drummond High. 96 D5
Drummond Stir. 81 H7
Drummore 64 B7
Drummuir Castle 98 B6
Drumnadrochit 98 C1
Drumnagorrach 98 D5
Drumnatorran 79 K1
Drumoak 91 F5
Drumore 66 B1
Drumour 82 A3
Drumrash 65 G3
Drumrunie 95 H1
Drums 91 H2
Drumsturdy 83 F4
Drumuie 93 K7
Drumuillie 89 G2
Drumvaich 81 H7
Drumwhindle 91 H1
Drumwhirn 68 C5
Drunkendub 83 H3
Drury 48 B6
Drws-y-nant 37 H3
Dry Doddington 42 B1
Dry Drayton 33 G2
Dry Harbour 94 C6
Dry Sandford 21 H2
Dry Street 24 C3
Drybeck 61 H5
Drybridge Moray 98 C4
Drybridge N.Ayr. 74 B7
Drybrook 29 F7
Dryburgh 76 D7
Dryhope 69 H1
Drymen 74 C2
Drymuir 99 H6
Drynoch 85 K1
Dryslwyn 17 J3
Dryton 38 E5
Duachy 79 K5
Dubford 99 F4
Dubhchladach 73 G4
Dubheads 82 A5
Dubton 83 G2
Duchal 74 B4
Duchally 103 F7
Duchray 74 C1
Duck End 33 K6
Duckington 48 D7
Ducklington 21 G1
Duck's Cross 32 E3
Duddenhoe End 33 H5

Duddingston 76 A3
Duddington 42 C5
Duddleswell 13 H4
Duddo 77 H6
Duddon 48 E6
Duddon Bridge 54 E1
Dudleston Heath 38 C2
Dudley T. & W. 71 H6
Dudley W.Mid. 40 B6
Dudley Hill 57 G6
Dudley Port 40 B6
Duffield 41 F1
Duffryn 18 B2
Dufftown 98 B6
Duffus 97 J5
Dufton 61 H4
Duggleby 58 E3
Duiar 89 J1
Duible 104 E6
Duiletter 80 C5
Duinish 81 H1
Duirinish 86 D1
Duisdealmor 86 D3
Duisky 87 G7
Dukestown 28 A7
Dukinfield 49 J3
Dulas 46 C4
Dulax 90 B3
Dulcote 19 J7
Dulford 7 J5
Dull 81 K3
Dullatur 75 F3
Dullingham 33 K3
Dulnain Bridge 89 G2
Duloe Beds. 32 E2
Duloe Cornw. 4 C5
Dulsie 97 G3
Dulverton 7 H3
Dulwich 23 G4
Dumbarton 74 C3
Dumbleton 30 B5
Dumcrieff 69 G3
Dumeath 90 C1
Dumfin 74 B2
Dumfries 65 K3
Dumgoyne 74 D2
Dummer 21 J7
Dun 83 H2
Dunach 79 K5
Dunalastair 81 J2
Dunan Arg. & B. 73 K3
Dunan High. 86 B2
Dunans 73 J1
Dunball 19 G7
Dunbar 76 E3
Dunbeath 105 G6
Dunbeg 79 K4
Dunblane 81 J7
Dunbog 82 D6
Duncanston Aber. 90 D2
Duncanston High. 96 C6
Dunchideock 7 G7
Dunchurch 31 F1
Duncote 31 H3
Duncow 68 E5
Duncraggan 81 G7
Duncrievie 82 C7
Duncroist 81 G4
Duncrub 82 B6
Duncryne 74 C2
Duncton 12 C5
Dundee 83 F4
Dundee Airport 82 E5
Dundon 8 D1
Dundonald 74 B7
Dundonnell 95 G3
Dundraw 60 D2
Dundreggan 87 K3
Dundrennan 65 H6
Dundry 19 J5
Dunearn 76 A2
Dunecht 91 F4
Dunfermline 75 J2
Dunfield 20 E2
Dunford Bridge 50 D2
Dungavel 74 E7
Dunham 52 B5
Dunham Town 49 G4
Dunham-on-the-Hill 48 D5
Dunhampton 29 H2
Dunholme 52 D5
Dunino 83 G6
Dunipace 75 G2
Dunira 81 J5
Dunkeld 82 B3
Dunkerton 20 A6
Dunkeswell 7 K5
Dunkeswick 57 J5
Dunkirk 15 F2
Dunk's Green 23 K6
Dunlappie 83 G1
Dunley 29 G2
Dunlop 74 C6
Dunloskin 73 K3
Dunmere 4 A4
Dunmore Arg. & B. 73 F4
Dunmore Falk. 75 G2
Dunn 105 G3
Dunnabie 69 H5
Dunnet 105 H1
Dunnichen 83 G3
Dunnington E.Riding 59 H4
Dunnington Warks. 30 B3
Dunnington York 58 C4
Dunnockshaw 56 D7
Dunoon 73 K3
Dunragit 64 B5
Dunrostan 73 F2
Duns 77 F5
Duns Tew 31 F6
Dunsby 42 E3
Dunscore 68 D5
Dunscroft 51 J2
Dunsdale 63 H5
Dunsden Green 22 A4
Dunsfold 12 D3
Dunsford 7 G7
Dunshelt 82 D6
Dunsinnan 82 C4
Dunsland Cross 6 C5
Dunsley 63 K5
Dunsmore 22 B1
Dunsop Bridge 56 B4
Dunstable 32 D6
Dunstall 40 D3
Dunstall Green 34 B2
Dunstan 71 H1
Dunster 7 H1
Dunston Lincs. 52 D6
Dunston Norf. 45 G5
Dunston T. & W. 71 H7
Dunstone Devon 5 H6

Dunstone Devon 5 H3
Dunstone Devon 5 F5
Dunsville 51 J2
Dunswell 59 G6
Dunsyre 75 J6
Dunterton 4 D3
Duntisbourne Abbots 20 C1
Duntisbourne Leer 20 C1
Duntisbourne Rouse 20 C1
Duntish 9 F4
Duntocher 74 C3
Dunton Beds. 33 F4
Dunton Bucks. 32 B6
Dunton Norf. 44 C2
Dunton Bassett 41 H6
Dunton Green 23 J6
Dunton Waylets 24 C3
Duntulm 93 K4
Dunure 67 G2
Dunure Mains 67 G2
Dunvant 17 J6
Dunvegan 93 H7
Dunwich 35 J1
Dura 83 F6
Durdar 61 F1
Durgates 13 K3
Durham 62 D2
Durinemast 79 H2
Durisdeer 68 D3
Durleigh 8 B1
Durley Hants. 11 G3
Durley Wilts. 21 F5
Durnamuck 95 G2
Durness 103 F2
Durno 91 F7
Duror 80 A2
Durran Arg. & B. 80 A7
Durran High. 105 G2
Durrington W.Suss. 12 E6
Durrington Wilts. 20 E7
Dursley 20 A2
Durston 8 B2
Durweston 9 H4
Dury 109 D6
Duston 31 J2
Duthil 89 G2
Dutlas 28 B1
Duton Hill 33 K6
Dutton 48 E5
Duxford 33 H4
Dwygyfylchi 47 F5
Dwyran 46 C6
Dyce 91 G3
Dyfatty 17 H5
Dyffryn Bridgend 18 B2
Dyffryn (Valley) I.o.A. 46 A5
Dyffryn Pembs. 16 C2
Dyffryn Ardudwy 36 E3
Dyffryn Castell 37 G7
Dyffryn Ceidrych 27 G6
Dyffryn Cellwen 27 H7
Dyke Devon 6 B3
Dyke Lincs. 42 E3
Dyke Moray 97 G6
Dykehead Angus 82 E1
Dykehead N.Lan. 75 G5
Dykehead Stir. 74 D1
Dykelands 83 J1
Dykends 82 D2
Dykeside 99 F6
Dylife 37 H6
Dymchurch 15 F5
Dymock 29 G5
Dyrham 20 A4
Dysart 76 B1
Dyserth 47 J5

E

Eadar dha Fhadhail 100 C4
Eagland Hill 55 H5
Eagle 52 B6
Eaglescliffe 63 F5
Eaglesfield Cumb. 60 B4
Eaglesfield D. & G. 69 H6
Eaglesham 74 D5
Eaglethorpe 42 D6
Eagley 49 G1
Eairy 54 C6
Eakley 32 B3
Eakring 51 J6
Ealand 51 K1
Ealing 22 E3
Eamont Bridge 61 G4
Earby 56 E5
Earcroft 56 B7
Eardington 39 G6
Eardisland 28 D3
Eardisley 28 C4
Eardiston Shrop. 38 C3
Eardiston Worcs. 29 F2
Earith 33 G1
Earl Shilton 41 G6
Earl Soham 35 G2
Earl Sterndale 50 C6
Earl Stonham 35 F3
Earle 70 E1
Earlestown 48 E3
Earley 22 A4
Earlham 45 F5
Earlish 93 J5
Earls Barton 32 B2
Earls Colne 34 C6
Earl's Common 29 J3
Earl's Croome 29 H4
Earl's Green 34 E2
Earlsdon 30 E1
Earlsferry 83 F7
Earlsford 91 G1
Earlston 76 D7
Earlswood Mon. 19 H2
Earlswood Warks. 30 C1
Earnley 12 B7
Earsairidh 84 C5
Earsdon 71 J6
Earsdon Moor 71 G4
Earsham 45 H7
Earswick 58 C4
Eartham 12 C6
Earthcott Green 19 K3
Easby 63 K5
Easdale 79 J6
Easebourne 12 B4
Easenhall 31 F1
Eashing 22 C7
Easington Bucks. 21 K1
Easington Dur. 62 E2
Easington E.Riding 53 H1
Easington Northumb. 77 K7
Easington Oxon. 21 K2
Easington R. & C. 63 J5
Easington Colliery 63 F2

Easington Lane 62 E2
Easingwold 58 B3
Easole Street 15 H2
Eassie & Nevay 82 E3
East Aberthaw 18 D5
East Allington 5 H6
East Anstey 7 G3
East Appleton 62 D7
East Ardsley 57 J7
East Ashey 11 G6
East Ashling 12 B6
East Auchronie 91 G4
East Ayton 59 F1
East Barkwith 52 E4
East Barming 14 C2
East Barnby 63 K5
East Barnet 23 F2
East Barsham 44 D2
East Beckham 45 F2
East Bedfont 22 D4
East Bergholt 34 E5
East Bilney 44 D4
East Blatchington 13 H7
East Boldon 71 J7
East Boldre 10 E4
East Bolton 71 G2
East Bradenham 44 D5
East Brent 19 G6
East Bridge 35 J2
East Bridgford 41 J1
East Brora 97 F1
East Buckland 6 E2
East Budleigh 7 J7
East Burnham 22 C3
East Burra 109 C7
East Burton 9 H6
East Cairnbeg 91 F7
East Calder 75 J4
East Carleton 45 F5
East Carlton 42 B7
East Chaldon or Chaldon Herring 9 G6
East Challow 21 G3
East Charleton 5 H6
East Chelborough 8 E4
East Chiltington 13 G5
East Chinnock 8 D3
East Chisenbury 20 E6
East Clandon 22 D6
East Claydon 31 J6
East Clyth 105 H5
East Coker 8 E3
East Cornworthy 5 J5
East Cottingwith 58 D5
East Cowes 11 G5
East Cowick 58 C7
East Cowton 62 E6
East Cranmore 19 K7
East Creech 9 J6
East Croachy 88 D2
East Darlochan 66 A1
East Davoch 90 C4
East Dean E.Suss. 13 J7
East Dean Hants. 10 D2
East Dean W.Suss. 12 C5
East Dereham (Dereham) 44 D4
East Down 6 E1
East Drayton 51 K5
East End Hants. 21 H5
East End Hants. 10 E5
East End Herts. 33 H6
East End Kent 14 D4
East End N.Som. 19 H4
East End Oxon. 30 E7
East End Poole 9 J5
East End Suff. 35 F5
East Farleigh 14 C2
East Farndon 42 A7
East Ferry 52 B3
East Fortune 76 D3
East Garston 21 G4
East Ginge 21 H3
East Goscote 41 J4
East Grafton 21 F5
East Grimstead 10 D2
East Grinstead 13 G3
East Guldeford 14 E5
East Haddon 31 H2
East Hagbourne 21 J3
East Halton 52 E1
East Ham 23 H3
East Hanney 21 H2
East Hanningfield 24 D1
East Hardwick 51 G1
East Harling 44 D7
East Harlsey 63 F7
East Harptree 19 J6
East Hartford 71 H6
East Harting 11 J3
East Hatch 9 J2
East Hatley 33 F3
East Hauxwell 62 C7
East Haven 83 G4
East Heckington 42 E1
East Hedleyhope 62 C2
East Helmsdale 105 F7
East Hendred 21 H3
East Heslerton 59 F2
East Hoathly 13 J5
East Horndon 24 C3
East Horrington 19 J7
East Horsley 22 D6
East Horton 77 J7
East Huntspill 19 G7
East Hyde 32 E7
East Ilsley 21 H3
East Keal 53 G6
East Kennett 20 E5
East Keswick 57 J5
East Kilbride 74 E5
East Kirkby 53 G6
East Knapton 58 E2
East Knighton 9 H6
East Knoyle 9 H1
East Lambrook 8 D3
East Langdon 15 J3
East Langton 42 A6
East Langwell 96 E1
East Lavant 12 B6
East Lavington 12 C5
East Layton 62 C5
East Leake 41 H3
East Learmouth 77 G7
East Learney 90 E4
East Leigh 7 F5
East Lexham 44 C4
East Lilburn 71 F1
East Linton 76 D3
East Liss 11 J2
East Looe 4 C5
East Lound 51 K3
East Lulworth 9 H6
East Lutton 59 F3
East Lydford 8 E1
East Mains 91 F5
East Malling 14 C2
East March 83 F4
East Marden 12 B5
East Markham 51 K5

East Marton 56 E4
East Meon 11 H2
East Mere 7 H4
East Mersea 34 E7
East Mey 105 J1
East Midlands Airport 41 G3
East Molesey 22 E5
East Morden 9 J5
East Morton 57 F5
East Ness 58 C2
East Norton 42 A5
East Oakley 21 J7
East Ogwell 5 J3
East Orchard 9 H3
East Ord 77 H5
East Panson 6 B6
East Peckham 23 K7
East Pennard 8 E1
East Portlemouth 5 H7
East Prawle 5 H7
East Preston 12 D6
East Putford 6 B4
East Quantoxhead 7 K1
East Rainton 62 E2
East Ravendale 53 F3
East Raynham 44 C3
East Rigton 57 J5
East Rolstone 19 G5
East Rounton 63 F6
East Rudham 44 C3
East Runton 45 F1
East Ruston 45 H3
East Saltoun 76 C4
East Shefford 21 G4
East Sleekburn 71 H5
East Somerton 45 J4
East Stockwith 51 K3
East Stoke Dorset 9 H6
East Stoke Notts. 42 A1
East Stour 9 G2
East Stourmouth 25 J5
East Stratton 11 G1
East Studdal 15 J3
East Suisnish 86 B1
East Taphouse 4 B4
East Thirston 71 G4
East Tilbury 24 C4
East Tisted 11 J1
East Torrington 52 E4
East Tuddenham 44 E4
East Tytherley 10 D2
East Tytherton 20 C4
East Village 7 G5
East Wall 38 E6
East Walton 44 B4
East Wellow 10 E2
East Wemyss 76 B1
East Whitburn 75 H4
East Wickham 23 H4
East Williamston 16 D5
East Winch 44 A4
East Wittering 11 J5
East Witton 57 G1
East Woodhay 21 H5
East Worldham 11 J1
East Worlington 7 F4
East Youlstone 6 A4
Eastbourne Darl. 62 E5
Eastbourne E.Suss. 13 K7
Eastburn Herts. 22 E2
Eastburn W.Berks. 21 G4
Eastby 57 F4
Eastchurch 25 F4
Eastcombe Glos. 20 B1
Eastcombe Som. 7 K2
Eastcote Gt.Lon. 22 E3
Eastcote Northants. 31 H3
Eastcote W.Mid. 30 C1
Eastcott Cornw. 6 A4
Eastcott Wilts. 20 D6
Eastcourt Wilts. 20 C2
Eastend 30 E6
Easter Ardross 96 D4
Easter Balmoral 89 K5
Easter Boleskine 88 C2
Easter Borland 81 H7
Easter Brae 96 D5
Easter Buckieburn 75 F2
Easter Compton 19 J3
Easter Drummond 88 B3
Easter Dullater 81 G7
Easter Ellister 72 A5
Easter Fearn 96 D3
Easter Galcantray 97 F7
Easter Howlaws 77 F6
Easter Kinkell 96 C6
Easter Lednathie 82 E1
Easter Moniack 96 C7
Easter Ord 91 G4
Easter Poldar 74 E1
Easter Quarff 109 D9
Easter Skeld 109 C8
Easter Suddie 96 D6
Easter Tulloch 91 F7
Easter Whyntie 98 E4
Eastergate 12 C6
Easterhouse 74 E4
Easterton 20 D6
Eastertown 19 G6
Eastfield N.Lan. 75 G4
Eastfield N.Yorks. 59 G1
Eastfield Hall 71 H3
Eastgate Dur. 62 A3
Eastgate Lincs. 42 E4
Eastgate Norf. 45 F3
Eastham 48 C4
Easthampstead 22 B5
Eastheath 22 B5
Easthope 38 E6
Easthorpe Essex 34 D6
Easthorpe Leics. 42 B2
Easthorpe Notts. 51 K7
Easthouses 76 B4
Eastington Devon 7 F5
Eastington Glos. 20 C1
Eastington Glos. 20 A1
Eastleach Martin 21 F1
Eastleach Turville 21 F1
Eastleigh Devon 6 C3
Eastleigh Hants. 11 F3
Eastling 14 E2
Eastney 11 H5
Eastnor 29 G5
Eastoft 52 B1
Eastoke 11 J5
Easton Cambs. 32 E1
Easton Cumb. 69 K6
Easton Cumb. 60 D1
Easton Devon 7 F7
Easton Dorset 9 F7
Easton Hants. 11 G1
Easton I.o.W. 10 E6
Easton Lincs. 42 C3
Easton Norf. 45 F4
Easton Som. 19 J7

Easton Suff. 35 G3
Easton Wilts. 20 B4
Easton Grey 20 B3
Easton Maudit 32 B3
Easton Royal 21 F5
Easton-in-Gordano 19 J4
Easton-on-the-Hill 42 D5
Eastriggs 69 H7
Eastrington 58 D6
Eastry 15 H2
Eastside 107 D8
East-the-Water 6 C3
Eastville 53 H7
Eastwell 42 A3
Eastwick 33 H7
Eastwood Notts. 41 G1
Eastwood S'end 24 E3
Eastwood W.Yorks. 56 E7
Eathorpe 30 E2
Eaton Ches. 49 H6
Eaton Ches. 48 E6
Eaton Leics. 42 A3
Eaton Norf. 45 G5
Eaton Notts. 51 K5
Eaton Oxon. 21 H1
Eaton Shrop. 38 E6
Eaton Shrop. 38 C7
Eaton Bishop 28 D5
Eaton Bray 32 C6
Eaton Constantine 38 E5
Eaton Ford 32 E3
Eaton Green 32 C6
Eaton Hall 48 D6
Eaton Hastings 21 F2
Eaton Socon 32 E3
Eaton upon Tern 39 F3
Eavestone 57 H3
Ebberston 59 F1
Ebbesborne Wake 9 J2
Ebbw Vale 18 E1
Ebchester 62 C1
Ebford 7 H7
Ebrington 30 C4
Ecchinswell 21 J6
Ecclaw 77 F4
Ecclefechan 69 G6
Eccles Gt.Man. 49 G3
Eccles Kent 24 D5
Eccles Sc.Bord. 77 F6
Eccles Road 44 E6
Ecclesfield 51 F3
Ecclesgreig 83 J1
Eccleshall 40 A3
Eccleshall 77 J3
Ecclesmachan 75 J3
Eccleston Ches. 48 D6
Eccleston Lancs. 48 E1
Eccleston Mersey. 48 D3
Eccup 57 H5
Echt 91 F4
Eckford 70 C1
Eckington Derbys. 51 G5
Eckington Worcs. 29 J4
Ecton Northants. 32 B2
Ecton Staffs. 50 C7
Edale 50 D4
Edburton 13 F5
Edderside 60 C2
Edderton 96 E3
Eddington 21 G5
Eddleston 76 A6
Eddlewood 75 F5
Eden Park 23 G5
Edenbridge 23 H7
Edendonich 80 C5
Edenfield 49 H1
Edenhall 61 G3
Edenham 42 D3
Edensor 50 E6
Edentaggart 74 B1
Edenthorpe 51 J2
Edern 36 B2
Edgarley 8 E1
Edgbaston 40 C7
Edgcott 31 H6
Edgcumbe 2 E6
Edge Glos. 20 B1
Edge Shrop. 38 C5
Edge End 28 E7
Edgebolton 38 E3
Edgefield 45 F2
Edgeley 38 E1
Edgeworth 20 C1
Edgmond 39 G3
Edgmond Marsh 39 G3
Edgton 38 C7
Edgware 23 F2
Edgworth 49 G1
Edial 40 C5
Edinample 81 H5
Edinbanchory 90 C3
Edinbane 93 J6
Edinbarnet 74 D3
Edinburgh 76 A3
Edinburgh Airport 75 K3
Edinchip 81 G5
Edingale 40 E4
Edingley 51 J7
Edingthorpe 45 H2
Edington Som. 8 C1
Edington Wilts. 20 C6
Edintore 98 C6
Edinvale 97 J6
Edistone 6 A3
Edith Weston 42 C5
Edithmead 19 G7
Edlaston 40 D1
Edlesborough 32 C7
Edlingham 71 G3
Edlington 53 F5
Edmondsham 10 B3
Edmondsley 62 D2
Edmondthorpe 42 B4
Edmonston 106 C5
Edmonstone 106 C5
Edmonton 23 G2
Edmundbyers 62 B2
Ednam 77 F7
Ednaston 40 E1
Edney Common 24 C1
Edra 81 G6
Edradynate 81 K2
Edrom 77 G5
Edstaston 38 E2
Edstone 30 C2
Edvin Loach 29 F3
Edwalton 41 H2
Edwardstone 34 D4
Edwinsford 17 K2
Edwinstowe 51 J6
Edworth 33 F4
Edwyn Ralph 29 F3
Edzell 83 H1
Efail Isaf 18 D3
Efailnewydd 36 C2
Efailwen 16 E3

Effingham 22 E6
Effirth 109 C7
Efford 7 G5
Egbury 21 H6
Egdean 12 C4
Egerton Gt.Man. 49 G1
Egerton Kent 14 E3
Egerton Forstal 14 D3
Egerton Green 48 E7
Eggborough 58 B7
Eggbuckland 5 F5
Eggerness 64 E6
Eggesford Barton 6 E4
Eggington 32 C6
Egginton 40 E3
Egglescliffe 63 F5
Eggleston 62 B4
Egham 22 D4
Egleton 42 B5
Eglingham 71 G2
Egloshayle 4 A3
Egloskerry 4 C2
Eglwys Cross 38 D1
Eglwys Fach 37 F6
Eglwysbach 47 G5
Eglwys-Brewis 18 D5
Eglwyswrw 16 E2
Egmanton 51 K6
Egmere 44 D2
Egremont 60 B5
Egton 63 K6
Egton Bridge 63 K6
Egypt 21 H7
Eight Ash Green 34 D6
Eignaig 79 J3
Eil 89 F3
Eilanreach 86 E3
Eilean Darach 95 H3
Eilean Iarmain (Isleornsay) 86 C3
Einacleit 100 D5
Eisgean 101 F6
Eisingrug 37 F2
Eisteddfa Gurig 37 G7
Elan Village 27 J2
Elberton 19 J3
Elburton 5 F5
Elcho 82 C5
Elcombe 20 E3
Eldernell 43 G6
Eldersfield 29 G5
Elderslie 74 C4
Eldrick 67 G5
Eldroth 56 C3
Eldwick 57 G5
Elerch (Bont-goch) 37 F7
Elford Northumb. 77 K7
Elford Staffs. 40 D4
Elgin 97 K5
Elgol 86 B3
Elham 15 G3
Elie 83 F7
Elilaw 70 E3
Elim 46 B4
Eling 10 E3
Eliock 68 D3
Elishader 94 B5
Elishaw 70 D4
Elkesley 51 J5
Elkstone 29 J7
Elland 57 G7
Ellary 73 F3
Ellastone 40 D1
Ellemford 77 F4
Ellenborough 60 B3
Ellenhall 40 A3
Ellen's Green 12 D3
Ellerbeck 63 F7
Ellerby 63 J5
Ellerdine Heath 39 F3
Elleric 80 B3
Ellerker 59 F7
Ellerton E.Riding 58 D5
Ellerton N.Yorks. 62 D7
Ellerton Shrop. 39 G3
Ellesborough 22 B1
Ellesmere 38 C2
Ellesmere Port 48 C5
Ellingham Hants. 10 C4
Ellingham Norf. 45 H6
Ellingham Northumb. 71 G1
Ellingstring 57 G1
Ellington Cambs. 32 E1
Ellington Northumb. 71 H4
Ellisfield 21 K7
Ellistown 41 G4
Ellon 91 H1
Ellonby 61 F3
Ellough 45 J7
Elloughton 59 F7
Ellwood 19 J1
Elm 43 H5
Elm Park 23 J3
Elmbridge 29 J2
Elmdon Essex 33 H5
Elmdon W.Mid. 40 D7
Elmdon Heath 40 D7
Elmesthorpe 41 G6
Elmhurst 40 D4
Elmley Castle 29 J4
Elmley Lovett 29 H2
Elmore 29 G7
Elmore Back 29 G7
Elmscott 6 A3
Elmsett 34 E4
Elmstead Market 34 E6
Elmstone 25 J5
Elmstone Hardwicke 29 J6
Elmswell E.Riding 59 F4
Elmswell Suff. 34 D2
Elmton 51 H5
Elphin 102 E7
Elphinstone 76 B3
Elrick Aber. 91 G4
Elrick Moray 90 D6
Elrig 64 D6
Elrigbeag 80 C6
Elsdon 70 E4
Elsecar 51 F2
Elsenham 33 J6
Elsfield 21 J1
Elsham 52 D1
Elsing 44 E4
Elslack 56 E5
Elson 38 C2
Elsrickle 75 J6
Elstead 22 C7
Elsted 12 B5
Elsthorpe 42 D3
Elston Lancs. 55 J6
Elston Notts. 42 A1
Elstone 6 E4
Elstow 32 D4
Elstree 22 E2
Elstronwick 59 J6
Elswick 55 H6

Name	Page	Grid
Elsworth	33	G2
Elterwater	60	E6
Eltham	23	H4
Eltisley	33	F3
Elton *Cambs.*	42	D6
Elton *Ches.*	48	D5
Elton *Derbys.*	50	E6
Elton *Glos.*	29	G7
Elton *Here.*	28	D1
Elton *Notts.*	42	A2
Elton *Stock.*	63	F5
Elvanfoot	68	E2
Elvaston	41	G2
Elveden	34	C1
Elvingston	76	C3
Elvington *Kent*	15	H2
Elvington *York*	58	D5
Elwick *Hart.*	63	F3
Elwick *Northumb.*	77	K7
Elworth	49	G6
Elworthy	7	J2
Ely *Cambs.*	33	J1
Ely *Cardiff*	18	E4
Emberton	32	B4
Embleton *Cumb.*	60	C3
Embleton *Northumb.*	71	H1
Embo	97	F2
Embo Street	97	F2
Emborough	19	K6
Embsay	57	F4
Emery Down	10	D4
Emley	50	E1
Emmer Green	22	A4
Emmington	22	A1
Emneth	43	H5
Emneth Hungate	43	J5
Empingham	42	C5
Empshott	11	J1
Emsworth	11	J4
Enborne	21	H5
Enchmarsh	38	E6
Enderby	41	H6
Endmoor	55	J1
Endon	49	J7
Enfield	23	G2
Enford	20	E6
Engine Common	19	K3
Englefield	21	K4
Englefield Green	22	C4
Englesea-brook	49	G7
English Bicknor	28	E7
English Frankton	38	D3
Englishcombe	20	A5
Enham Alamein	21	G7
Enmore	8	B1
Ennerdale Bridge	60	B5
Ennochdhu	82	B1
Ensay	78	E3
Ensdon	38	D4
Ensis	6	D3
Enstone	30	E6
Enterkinfoot	68	D3
Enterpen	63	F6
Enville	40	A7
Eolaigearraidh	84	C4
Eorabus	78	E5
Eorodal	101	H1
Eoropaidh	101	H1
Epperstone	41	J1
Epping	23	H1
Epping Green *Essex*	23	H1
Epping Green *Herts.*	23	F1
Epping Upland	23	H1
Eppleby	62	C5
Eppleworth	59	G6
Epsom	23	F5
Epwell	30	E4
Epworth	51	K2
Erbistock	38	C1
Erbusaig	86	D2
Erchless Castle	96	B7
Erdington	40	D6
Eredine	80	A7
Eriboll	103	G3
Ericstane	69	F2
Eridge Green	13	J3
Eriff	67	K3
Erines	73	G3
Eriswell	34	B1
Erith	23	J4
Erlestoke	20	C6
Ermington	5	G5
Erpingham	45	F2
Errogie	88	C2
Errol	82	D5
Errollston	91	J1
Erskine	74	C3
Ervie	64	A4
Erwarton	35	G5
Erwood	27	K4
Eryholme	62	E6
Eryrys	48	B7
Escart	73	G4
Escart Farm	73	G5
Escomb	62	C4
Escrick	58	C5
Esgair	17	G3
Esgairgeiliog	37	G5
Esh	62	C2
Esh Winning	62	C2
Esher	22	E5
Eshott	71	H4
Eshton	56	E4
Eskadale	88	B1
Eskbank	76	B4
Eskdale Green	60	C6
Eskdalemuir	69	H4
Eskham	53	G3
Esknish	72	B4
Espley Hall	71	G4
Esprick	55	H6
Essendine	42	D4
Essendon	23	F1
Essich	88	D1
Essington	40	B5
Esslemont	91	H2
Eston	63	G5
Etal	77	H7
Etchilhampton	20	D5
Etchingham	14	C5
Etchinghill *Kent*	15	G3
Etchinghill *Staffs.*	40	C4
Ethie Mains	83	H3
Eton	22	C4
Eton Wick	22	C4
Etteridge	88	D5
Ettington	30	D4
Etton *E.Riding*	59	F5
Etton *Peter.*	42	E5
Ettrick	69	H2
Ettrickbridge	69	J1
Ettrickhill	69	H2
Etwall	40	E2
Eurach	79	K7
Euston	34	C1
Euxton	48	E1
Evanton	96	D5
Evedon	42	D1
Evelix	96	E2
Evenjobb	28	B2
Evenley	31	G5
Evenlode	30	D6
Evenwood	62	C4
Everbay	106	F5
Evercreech	9	F1
Everdon	31	G3
Everingham	58	E5
Everleigh	21	F6
Everley *High.*	105	J2
Everley *N.Yorks.*	59	F1
Eversholt	32	C5
Evershot	8	E4
Eversley	22	A5
Eversley Cross	22	A5
Everthorpe	59	F6
Everton *Beds.*	33	F3
Everton *Hants.*	10	D5
Everton *Notts.*	51	J3
Evertown	69	J6
Evesbatch	29	F4
Evesham	30	B4
Evie	106	C5
Evington	41	J5
Ewart Newtown	77	H7
Ewden Village	50	E3
Ewell	23	F5
Ewell Minnis	15	H3
Ewelme	21	K2
Ewen	20	D2
Ewenny	18	C4
Ewerby	42	E1
Ewerby Thorpe	42	E1
Ewhurst *E.Sus.*	14	C5
Ewhurst *Surr.*	22	D7
Ewhurst Green	12	D3
Ewloe	48	B6
Ewood	56	B7
Eworthy	6	C6
Ewshot	22	B7
Ewyas Harold	28	C6
Exbourne	6	E5
Exbury	11	F4
Exebridge	7	H3
Exelby	57	H1
Exeter	7	H6
Exeter Airport	7	H6
Exford	7	G2
Exfords Green	38	D5
Exhall *Warks.*	30	C3
Exhall *Warks.*	41	F7
Exlade Street	21	K3
Exminster	7	H7
Exmouth	7	J7
Exnaboe	109	F9
Exning	33	K2
Exton *Devon*	7	H7
Exton *Hants.*	11	H2
Exton *Rut.*	42	C4
Exton *Som.*	7	H2
Exwick	7	H6
Eyam	50	E5
Eydon	31	G3
Eye *Here.*	28	D2
Eye *Peter.*	43	F5
Eye *Suff.*	35	F1
Eye Green	43	F5
Eyemouth	77	H4
Eyeworth	33	F4
Eyhorne Street	14	D2
Eyke	35	H3
Eynesbury	32	E3
Eynort	85	J2
Eynsford	23	J5
Eynsham	21	H1
Eype	8	D5
Eyre	93	K6
Eythorne	15	H3
Eyton *Here.*	28	D2
Eyton *Shrop.*	38	C7
Eyton *Wrex.*	38	C1
Eyton upon the Weald Moors	39	F4
Eywood	28	C3

F

Name	Page	Grid
Faccombe	21	G6
Faceby	63	F6
Fachwen	46	D6
Faddiley	48	E7
Fadmoor	58	C1
Faebait	96	B6
Faifley	74	D3
Fail	67	J1
Failand	19	J4
Failford	67	J1
Failsworth	49	H2
Fain	95	H4
Fair Oak *Hants.*	11	F3
Fair Oak *Hants.*	21	J5
Fairbourne	37	F4
Fairburn	57	K7
Fairfield *Derbys.*	50	C5
Fairfield *Worcs.*	29	J1
Fairford	20	E1
Fairgirth	65	J5
Fairholm	75	F5
Fairley	91	G4
Fairlie	74	A5
Fairlight	14	D6
Fairlight Cove	14	D6
Fairmile	7	J6
Fairmilehead	76	A4
Fairnington	70	B1
Fairoak	39	G2
Fairseat	24	C5
Fairstead *Essex*	34	B7
Fairstead *Norf.*	45	G3
Fairwarp	13	H4
Fairy Cross	6	C3
Fairyhill	17	H6
Fakenham	44	D3
Fala	76	C4
Fala Dam	76	C4
Falahill	76	B5
Faldingworth	52	D4
Falfield *Fife*	83	F7
Falfield *S.Glos.*	19	K2
Falkenham	35	G5
Falkirk	75	G3
Falkland	82	D7
Falla	70	C2
Fallgate	51	F6
Fallin	75	G1
Falmer	13	G6
Falsgrave	59	G1
Falstone	70	C5
Fanagmore	102	D3
Fanans	80	B5
Fancott	32	D6
Fangdale Beck	63	G7
Fangfoss	58	D4
Fanmore	79	F3
Fans	76	E6
Far Cotton	31	J3
Far Forest	29	G1
Far Gearstones	56	C1
Farcet	43	F6
Farden	28	E1
Fareham	11	G4
Farewell	40	C4
Farforth	53	G5
Faringdon	21	F2
Farington	55	J7
Farlam	61	G1
Farlary	96	E1
Farleigh *N.Som.*	19	H5
Farleigh *Surr.*	23	G5
Farleigh Hungerford	20	A6
Farleigh Wallop	21	K7
Farlesthorpe	53	H5
Farleton	55	J1
Farley *Shrop.*	38	C5
Farley *Staffs.*	40	C1
Farley *Wilts.*	10	D2
Farley Green	22	D7
Farley Hill	22	A5
Farleys End	29	G7
Farlington	58	C3
Farlow	39	F7
Farmborough	19	K5
Farmcote	30	B6
Farmington	30	C7
Farmoor	21	H1
Farmtown	98	D5
Farnborough *Gt.Lon.*	23	H5
Farnborough *Hants.*	22	B6
Farnborough *W.Berks.*	21	H3
Farnborough *Warks.*	31	F3
Farnborough Green	22	B6
Farncombe	22	C7
Farndish	32	C2
Farndon *Ches.*	48	D7
Farndon *Notts.*	51	K7
Farnell	83	H2
Farnham *Dorset*	9	J3
Farnham *Essex*	33	H6
Farnham *N.Yorks.*	57	J3
Farnham *Suff.*	35	H2
Farnham *Surr.*	22	B7
Farnham Common	22	C3
Farnham Green	33	H6
Farnham Royal	22	C3
Farningham	23	J5
Farnley	57	H5
Farnley Tyas	50	D1
Farnsfield	51	J7
Farnworth *Gt.Man.*	49	G2
Farnworth *Halton*	48	E4
Farr *High.*	104	C2
Farr *High.*	88	D1
Farr *High.*	89	F4
Farr House	88	D1
Farraline	88	C2
Farringdon	7	J6
Farrington Gurney	19	K6
Farsley	57	H6
Farthinghoe	31	G5
Farthingloe	15	H3
Farthingstone	31	H3
Farway	7	K6
Fasag	94	E6
Fasagrianach	95	H3
Fascadale	86	B7
Faslane	74	A2
Fasnacloich	80	B3
Fasnakyle	87	K2
Fassfern	87	G7
Fatfield	62	E1
Fattahead	98	E5
Faugh	61	G1
Fauldhouse	75	H4
Faulkbourne	34	B7
Faulkland	20	A6
Fauls	38	E2
Faversham	25	G5
Favillar	89	K1
Fawdington	57	K2
Fawdon	71	H7
Fawfieldhead	50	C6
Fawkham Green	23	J5
Fawler	30	E7
Fawley *Bucks.*	22	A3
Fawley *Hants.*	11	F4
Fawley *W.Berks.*	21	G3
Fawley Chapel	28	E6
Fawsyde	91	G7
Faxfleet	58	E7
Faxton	31	J1
Faygate	13	F3
Fazeley	40	E5
Fearby	57	G1
Fearn	97	F4
Fearnan	81	J3
Fearnbeg	94	D6
Fearnhead	49	F3
Fearnmore	94	D5
Fearnoch *Arg. & B.*	73	J3
Fearnoch *Arg. & B.*	73	H3
Featherstone *Staffs.*	40	B5
Featherstone *W.Yorks.*	51	G1
Featherstone Castle	70	B7
Feckenham	30	B2
Feering	34	C6
Feetham	62	A1
Feith-hill	98	E6
Feizor	56	C3
Felbridge	13	G3
Felbrigg	45	G2
Felcourt	23	G7
Felden	22	D1
Felindre *Carmar.*	27	G6
Felindre *Carmar.*	17	G2
Felindre *Carmar.*	17	G2
Felindre *Powys*	38	A7
Felindre *Swan.*	17	K5
Felinfach	27	K5
Felinfoel	17	J5
Felingwmuchaf	17	H3
Felixkirk	57	K1
Felixstowe	35	H5
Felixstowe Ferry	35	H5
Felkington	77	H6
Felldownhead	6	B7
Felling	71	H7
Fellonmore	79	H5
Felmersham	32	C3
Felmingham	45	G3
Felpham	12	C7
Felsham	34	D3
Felsted	33	K6
Feltham	22	E4
Felthorpe	45	F4
Felton *Here.*	28	E4
Felton *N.Som.*	19	J5
Felton *Northumb.*	71	G3
Felton Butler	38	C4
Feltwell	44	B7
Fen Ditton	33	H3
Fen Drayton	33	G2
Fen End	30	D1
Fen Street	34	D1
Fence	56	D6
Fence Houses	62	E1
Fencott	31	G7
Fendike Corner	53	H6
Fenhouses	43	F1
Feniscowles	56	B7
Feniton	7	K6
Fenny Bentley	50	D7
Fenny Bridges	7	K6
Fenny Compton	31	F3
Fenny Drayton	41	F6
Fenny Stratford	32	B5
Fenrother	71	G4
Fenstanton	33	G2
Fenton *Cambs.*	33	G1
Fenton *Lincs.*	52	B5
Fenton *Lincs.*	52	B7
Fenton *Northumb.*	77	H7
Fenton *Stoke*	40	A1
Fenwick *E.Ayr.*	74	C6
Fenwick *Northumb.*	71	F6
Fenwick *Northumb.*	77	J6
Fenwick *S.Yorks.*	51	H1
Feochaig	66	B2
Feock	3	F5
Feolin	72	D4
Feolin Ferry	72	C4
Feorlan	66	A3
Feorlin	73	H1
Feriniquarrie	93	G6
Fern	83	F1
Ferndale	18	C2
Ferndown	10	B4
Ferness	97	G7
Fernham	21	F2
Fernhill Heath	29	H3
Fernhurst	12	B4
Fernie	82	E6
Ferniea	85	J1
Fernilee	50	C5
Fernybank	90	D7
Ferrensby	57	J3
Ferring	12	D6
Ferrybridge	57	K7
Ferryden	83	J2
Ferryhill	62	D3
Ferryside	17	G4
Fersfield	44	E7
Fersit	87	K7
Ferwig	16	E1
Feshiebridge	89	F4
Fetcham	22	E6
Fetterangus	99	H5
Fettercairn	90	E7
Fetternear House	91	F3
Feus of Caldhame	83	H1
Fewcott	31	G6
Fewston	57	G4
Ffairfach	17	K3
Ffair-Rhos	27	G2
Ffarmers	17	K1
Ffawyddog	28	B7
Ffestiniog	37	G1
Ffordd-las	47	K6
Fforest	17	J5
Fforest-fach	17	K6
Ffostrasol	17	G1
Ffos-y-ffin	26	D2
Ffridd Uchaf	46	D7
Ffrith	48	B7
Ffrwdgrech	27	K6
Ffynnon Taf (Taff's Well)	18	E3
Ffynnon-ddrain	17	H3
Ffynnongroyw	47	K4
Fibhig	100	E3
Fichlie	90	C3
Fidden	78	E5
Fiddington *Glos.*	29	J5
Fiddington *Som.*	19	F7
Fiddler's Green	28	E5
Fiddlers Hamlet	23	H1
Field	40	C2
Field Broughton	55	G1
Field Dalling	44	E2
Field Head	41	G5
Fife Keith	98	C5
Fifehead Magdalen	9	G2
Fifehead Neville	9	G3
Fifield *Oxon.*	30	D7
Fifield *W. & M.*	22	C4
Fifield Bavant	10	B2
Figheldean	20	E7
Filby	45	J4
Filey	59	H2
Filgrave	32	B4
Filkins	21	F1
Filleigh *Devon*	6	E3
Filleigh *Devon*	7	F4
Fillingham	52	C4
Fillongley	40	E7
Filmore Hill	11	H2
Filton	19	J4
Fimber	59	F3
Finavon	83	F2
Fincham	44	A5
Finchampstead	22	A5
Finchdean	11	J3
Finchingfield	33	K5
Finchley	23	F2
Findern	41	F2
Findhorn	97	H5
Findhorn Bridge	89	F2
Findhuglen	81	J6
Findo Gask	82	B5
Findochty	98	C4
Findon *Aber.*	91	H5
Findon *W.Sus.*	12	E6
Findon Mains	96	C5
Findrassie	97	J5
Findron	89	J3
Finedon	32	C1
Fingal Street	35	G2
Fingask	91	F3
Fingerpost	29	G1
Fingest	22	A2
Finghall	57	G1
Fingland *Cumb.*	60	D1
Fingland *D. & G.*	68	C3
Fingland *D. & G.*	68	C2
Finglesham	15	J2
Fingringhoe	34	E6
Finlarig	81	G4
Finmere	31	H5
Finnart *Arg. & B.*	74	A1
Finnart *P. & K.*	81	G2
Finningham	34	E2
Finningley	51	J3
Finnygaud	98	E5
Finsbury	23	G3
Finstall	29	J1
Finsthwaite	55	G1
Finstock	30	E7
Finstown	107	C6
Fintry *Aber.*	99	F5
Fintry *Stir.*	74	E2
Finzean	90	D5
Fionnphort	78	E5
Fir Tree	62	C3
Fir Vale	51	F4
Firbank	61	H7
Firbeck	51	H4
Firgrove	49	J1
Firs Road	10	D1
Firsby	53	H6
Firth	108	D5
Fishbourne *I.o.W.*	11	G5
Fishbourne *W.Suss.*	12	B6
Fishburn	62	E3
Fisherford	90	E1
Fisher's Pond	11	F2
Fisher's Row	55	H5
Fisherstreet	12	C3
Fisherton *High.*	96	E6
Fisherton *S.Ayr.*	67	G2
Fisherton de la Mere	10	B1
Fishguard (Abergwaun)	16	C2
Fishlake	51	J1
Fishleigh Barton	6	D3
Fishnish	79	H3
Fishpond Bottom	8	C5
Fishponds	19	K4
Fishpool	49	G1
Fishtoft	43	G1
Fishtoft Drove	43	G1
Fishtown of Usan	83	J2
Fishwick *Lancs.*	55	J6
Fishwick *Sc.Bord.*	77	H5
Fiskerton *Lincs.*	52	D5
Fiskerton *Notts.*	51	K7
Fittleton	20	E6
Fittleworth	12	D5
Fitton End	43	H4
Fitz	38	D4
Fitzhead	7	K3
Fitzwilliam	51	G1
Fiunary	79	H3
Five Ash Down	13	H4
Five Ashes	13	J4
Five Bridges	29	F4
Five Oak Green	23	K7
Five Oaks *Chan.I.*	3	K7
Five Oaks *W.Suss.*	12	D4
Five Roads	17	H5
Five Turnings	28	B1
Five Wents	14	D2
Fivehead	8	C2
Fivelanes	4	C2
Flackwell Heath	22	B3
Fladbury	29	J4
Fladdabister	109	D9
Flagg	50	D6
Flamborough	59	J2
Flamstead	32	D7
Flamstead End	23	G1
Flansham	12	C6
Flasby	56	E4
Flash	50	C6
Flashader	93	J6
Flask Inn	63	J2
Flaunden	22	D1
Flawborough	42	A1
Flawith	57	K3
Flax Bourton	19	J5
Flaxby	57	J4
Flaxley	29	F7
Flaxpool	7	K2
Flaxton	58	C3
Fleckney	41	J6
Flecknoe	31	G2
Fleet *Hants.*	22	B6
Fleet *Lincs.*	43	G3
Fleet Hargate	43	G3
Fleetwood	55	G5
Flemingston	18	D5
Flemington	74	E5
Flempton	34	C2
Fleoideabhagh	93	F3
Fletchertown	60	D2
Fletching	13	H4
Fleuchats	90	B4
Fleur-de-lis	18	E2
Flexbury	6	A5
Flexford	22	C6
Flimby	60	B3
Flimwell	14	C4
Flint (Y Fflint)	48	B5
Flint Cross	33	H4
Flint Mountain	48	B5
Flintham	42	A1
Flinton	59	J6
Flishinghurst	14	C4
Flitcham	44	B3
Flitton	32	D5
Flitwick	32	D5
Flixborough	52	B1
Flixton *Gt.Man.*	49	G3
Flixton *N.Yorks.*	59	G2
Flixton *Suff.*	45	H7
Flockton	50	E1
Flockton Green	50	E1
Flodden	77	H7
Flodigarry	93	K4
Flookburgh	55	G2
Floors	98	C5
Flordon	45	F6
Flore	31	H2
Flotterton	71	F3
Flowton	34	E4
Flushing *Aber.*	99	J6
Flushing *Cornw.*	3	F5
Flushing *Cornw.*	3	F5
Flyford Flavell	29	J3
Fobbing	24	D3
Fochabers	98	B5
Fochriw	18	E1
Fockerby	52	B1
Fodderletter	89	J2
Foddery	96	C6
Foel	37	J4
Foggathorpe	58	D6
Fogo	77	F6
Fogorig	77	F6
Foindle	102	D4
Folda	82	C1
Fole	40	C2
Foleshill	41	F7
Folke	9	F3
Folkestone	15	H4
Folkingham	42	D2
Folkington	13	J6
Folksworth	42	E7
Folkton	59	G2
Folla Rule	91	F1
Follifoot	57	J4
Folly *Dorset*	9	G4
Folly *Pembs.*	16	C3
Folly Gate	6	D6
Fonthill Bishop	9	J1
Fonthill Gifford	9	J1
Fontmell Magna	9	H3
Fontwell	12	C6
Foolow	50	D5
Foots Cray	23	H4
Forbestown	90	B3
Force Forge	60	E7
Forcett	62	C5
Forches Cross	7	F5
Ford *Arg. & B.*	79	K7
Ford *Bucks.*	22	A1
Ford *Devon*	5	G5
Ford *Devon*	6	C3
Ford *Devon*	5	H6
Ford *Glos.*	30	B6
Ford *Mersey.*	48	C2
Ford *Midloth.*	76	B4
Ford *Northumb.*	77	H7
Ford *Pembs.*	16	C3
Ford *Shrop.*	38	D4
Ford *Som.*	7	J3
Ford *W.Suss.*	12	C6
Ford *Wilts.*	20	B4
Ford End	33	K7
Ford Street	7	K4
Fordcombe	23	J7
Fordell	75	K2
Forden	38	B5
Forder Green	5	H4
Fordham *Cambs.*	33	K1
Fordham *Essex*	34	D6
Fordham *Norf.*	44	A6
Fordham Abbey	33	K2
Fordingbridge	10	C3
Fordon	59	G2
Fordoun	91	F7
Fordstreet	34	D6
Fordwells	30	E7
Fordwich	15	G2
Fordyce	98	D4
Forebrae	82	A5
Foreland	72	A4
Forest Gate	23	H3
Forest Green	22	E7
Forest Hall *Cumb.*	61	G6
Forest Hall *T. & W.*	71	H7
Forest Head	61	G1
Forest Hill	21	J1
Forest Lodge *Arg. & B.*	80	D3
Forest Lodge *P. & K.*	89	G7
Forest Mill	75	H1
Forest Row	13	H3
Forest Town	51	H6
Forestburn Gate	71	F4
Forest-in-Teesdale	61	K3
Forestside	11	J3
Forfar	83	F2
Forgandenny	82	B6
Forgie	98	B5
Formby	48	B2
Forncett End	45	F6
Forncett St. Mary	45	F6
Forncett St. Peter	45	F6
Forneth	82	B3
Fornham All Saints	34	C2
Fornham St. Martin	34	C2
Fornighty	97	G6
Forres	97	H6
Forrest	75	G4
Forrest Lodge	67	K5
Forsbrook	40	B1
Forse	105	H5
Forsie	105	F2
Forsinain	104	E4
Forsinard	104	D4
Forston	9	F5
Fort Augustus	87	K4
Fort George	96	E6
Fort William	87	H7
Forter	82	C1
Forteviot	82	B6
Forth	75	H5
Forthampton	29	H5
Fortingall	81	J3
Forton *Hants.*	21	H7
Forton *Lancs.*	55	H4
Forton *Shrop.*	38	D4
Forton *Som.*	8	C4
Forton *Staffs.*	39	G3
Fortrie	98	E6
Fortrose	96	E6
Fortuneswell	9	F7
Forty Green	22	C2
Forty Hill	23	G2
Forward Green	34	E3
Fosbury	21	G6
Foscot	30	D6
Fosdyke	43	G2
Foss	81	J2
Foss Cross	20	D1
Fossdale	61	K7
Fossebridge	30	B7
Foster Street	23	H1
Foster's Booth	31	H3
Foston *Derbys.*	40	D2
Foston *Lincs.*	42	B1
Foston *N.Yorks.*	58	C3
Foston on the Wolds	59	H4
Fotherby	53	G3
Fotheringhay	42	D6
Foubister	107	E7
Foul Mile	13	K5
Foulbog	69	H3
Foulden *Norf.*	44	B6
Foulden *Sc.Bord.*	77	H5
Foulridge	56	D5
Foulsham	44	E3
Foulzie	99	F4
Fountainhall	76	C6
Four Ashes *Staffs.*	40	B5
Four Ashes *Suff.*	34	D1
Four Crosses *Denb.*	37	K1
Four Crosses *Powys*	38	B4
Four Crosses *Powys*	37	K5
Four Crosses *Staffs.*	40	B5
Four Elms	23	H7
Four Forks	8	B1
Four Gotes	43	H4
Four Lanes	2	D5
Four Marks	11	H1
Four Mile Bridge	46	A5
Four Oaks *E.Suss.*	14	D5
Four Oaks *W.Mid.*	40	E7
Four Oaks *W.Mid.*	40	D5
Four Roads	17	H5
Four Throws	14	C5
Fourlane Ends	51	F7
Fourlanes End	49	H7
Fourpenny	96	E2
Fourstones	70	D7
Fovant	10	B2
Foveran House	91	H2
Fowey	4	B5
Fowlis	82	E4
Fowlis Wester	82	A5
Fowlmere	33	H4
Fownhope	28	E5
Fox Lane	22	B6
Fox Street	34	E6
Foxcote	30	B7
Foxdale	54	B6
Foxearth	34	C4
Foxfield	55	F1
Foxham	20	C4
Foxhole *Cornw.*	3	G3
Foxhole *High.*	88	C1
Foxholes	59	G2
Foxhunt Green	13	J5
Foxley *Here.*	28	D4
Foxley *Norf.*	44	E3
Foxley *Northants.*	31	H3
Foxley *Wilts.*	20	B3
Foxt	40	C1
Foxton *Cambs.*	33	H4
Foxton *Dur.*	62	E4
Foxton *Leics.*	42	A6
Foxup	56	D2
Foxwist Green	49	F6
Foy	28	E6
Foyers	88	B2
Frachadil	78	E2
Fradley	40	D4
Fradswell	40	B2
Fraisthorpe	59	H3
Framfield	13	H4
Framingham Earl	45	G5
Framingham Pigot	45	G5
Framlingham	35	G2
Frampton *Dorset*	9	F5
Frampton *Lincs.*	43	G2
Frampton Cotterell	19	K3
Frampton Mansell	20	C1
Frampton on Severn	20	A1
Frampton West End	43	G1
Framsden	35	G3
Framwellgate Moor	62	D2
Franche	29	H1
Frankby	48	B4
Frankley	40	B7
Frankton	31	F1
Frant	13	J3
Fraserburgh	99	H4
Frating	34	E6
Fratton	11	H4
Freathy	4	D5
Freckenham	33	K1
Freckleton	55	H7
Freeby	42	B3
Freefolk	21	H7
Freeland	31	F7
Freemantle	11	F3
Freester	109	D7
Freethorpe	45	J5
Freethorpe Common	45	J5
Freiston	43	G1
Freiston Shore	43	G1
Fremington *Devon*	6	D2
Fremington *N.Yorks.*	62	B7
Frenchay	19	K4
Frenchbeer	6	E7
Frendraught	98	E6
Frenich	81	F7
Frensham	22	B7
Fresgoe	104	E2
Freshfield	48	B2
Freshford	20	A5
Freshwater	10	E6
Freshwater East	16	D6
Fressingfield	35	G1
Freston	35	F5
Freswick	105	J2
Frettenham	45	G4
Freuchie	82	D7
Freystrop Cross	16	C4
Friars Carse	68	E5
Friar's Gate	13	H3
Friarton	82	C5
Friday Bridge	43	H5
Friday Street *E.Suss.*	13	K6
Friday Street *Surr.*	22	E7
Fridaythorpe	58	E4
Friern Barnet	23	F2
Friesthorpe	52	D4
Frieston	42	C1
Frieth	22	A2
Frilford	21	H2
Frilsham	21	J4
Frimley	22	B6
Frimley Green	22	B6
Frindsbury	24	D5
Fring	44	B2
Fringford	31	H6
Frinsted	14	E2
Frinton-on-Sea	35	G7
Friockheim	83	G3
Friog	37	F4
Frisby on the Wreake	41	J4
Friskney	53	H7
Friskney Eaudyke	53	H7
Friston *E.Suss.*	13	J7
Friston *Suff.*	35	J2
Fritchley	51	F7
Frith	14	E2
Frith Bank	43	G1
Frith Common	29	F2
Fritham	10	D3
Frithelstock	6	C4
Frithelstock Stone	6	C4
Frithville	53	G7
Frittenden	14	D3
Fritton *Norf.*	45	G6
Fritton *Norf.*	45	J5
Fritwell	31	G6
Frizington	60	B5
Frocester	20	A1
Frochas	38	B5
Frodesley	38	E5
Frodsham	48	E5
Frog End	33	H3
Frog Pool	29	G2
Froggatt	50	E5
Froghall	40	C1
Frogham	10	C3

Frogmore Devon 5 H6
Frogmore Hants. 22 B6
Frogmore Herts. 22 E1
Frolesworth 41 H6
Frome 20 A7
Frome Market 20 B6
Frome St. Quentin 8 E4
Fromes Hill 29 F4
Fron Gwyn. 36 C2
Fron Powys 38 B5
Fron Powys 27 K2
Froncysyllte 38 B1
Fron-goch 37 J2
Frostenden 45 J7
Frosterley 62 B3
Froxfield 21 F5
Froxfield Green 11 J2
Fryerning 24 C1
Fryton 58 C2
Fugglestone
  St. Peter 10 C1
Fulbeck 52 C7
Fulbourn 33 J3
Fulbrook 30 D7
Fulford Som. 8 B2
Fulford Staffs. 40 B2
Fulford York 58 C5
Fulham 23 F4
Fulking 13 F5
Full Sutton 58 D4
Fuller Street 34 B7
Fuller's Moor 48 D7
Fullerton 10 E1
Fulletby 53 F5
Fullwood 74 C6
Fulmer 22 C3
Fulmodeston 44 D2
Fulnetby 52 D5
Fulready 30 D4
Fulstow 53 G3
Fulwell Oxon. 30 E6
Fulwell T. & W. 62 E1
Fulwood Lancs. 55 J6
Fulwood S.Yorks. 51 F4
Fundenhall 45 F6
Funtington 12 B6
Funtley 11 G4
Funzie 108 F4
Furley 8 B4
Furnace Arg. & B. 80 B7
Furnace Cere. 37 F6
Furnace High. 95 F4
Furness Vale 50 C4
Furneux Pelham 33 H6
Furze Platt 22 B3
Furzehill 7 F1
Fyfett 8 B3
Fyfield Essex 23 J1
Fyfield Glos. 21 F1
Fyfield Hants. 21 F7
Fyfield Oxon. 21 H2
Fyfield Wilts. 20 E5
Fylingthorpe 63 J2
Fyvie 91 F1

G

Gabhsann Bho
  Dheas 101 G2
Gabhsann Bho
  Thuath 101 G2
Gablon 96 E2
Gabroc Hill 74 C5
Gaddesby 41 J5
Gaddesden Row 32 D7
Gaer Newport 19 F3
Gaer Powys 28 A6
Gaerllwyd 19 H2
Gaerwen 46 C5
Gagingwell 31 F6
Gaich 89 H2
Gaick 88 D1
Gaick Lodge 88 E6
Gailey 40 B4
Gainford 62 C5
Gainsborough 52 B3
Gairloch 94 E4
Gairlochy 87 H6
Gairney Bank 75 K1
Gairnshiel Lodge 89 K4
Gaitsgill 60 E2
Galabank 76 C6
Galashiels 76 C7
Galdenoch 64 B4
Galgate 55 H4
Galhampton 9 F2
Gallanach 79 K5
Gallantry Bank 48 E7
Gallatown 76 A1
Gallchoille 73 F2
Gallery 83 H1
Galley Common 41 F6
Galleyend 24 D1
Galleywood 24 D1
Gallowfauld 83 F3
Gallowstree
  Common 21 K4
Gallowstree Elm 40 A7
Gallt Melyd
  (Meliden) 47 J4
Galltair 86 E3
Galmisdale 85 K6
Galmpton Devon 5 G6
Galmpton Torbay 5 J5
Galphay 57 H2
Galston 74 D7
Galtrigill 93 G6
Gamble's Green 34 B7
Gamblesby 61 H3
Gamelsby 60 D1
Gamlingay 33 F3
Gammaton Moor 6 C3
Gammersgill 57 F1
Gamrie 99 F4
Gamston Notts. 51 K5
Gamston Notts. 41 J2
Ganarew 28 E7
Ganllwyd 37 G3
Gannochy 90 E7
Ganstead 59 H6
Ganthorpe 58 C2
Ganton 59 F2
Gaodhail 79 H4
Gara Bridge 5 H5
Garabal 80 E6
Garadheancal 95 F1
Garbat 96 B5
Garbhallt 73 J1
Garboldisham 44 E7
Garden 74 D1
Garden City 48 C6
Gardenstown 99 G4
Garderhouse 109 C8
Gardham 59 F5
Gare Hill 20 A7

Garelochhead 74 A1
Garford 21 H2
Garforth 57 K6
Gargrave 56 E4
Gargunnock 75 F1
Gariob 73 F2
Garlies Castle 64 E4
Garlieston 64 E6
Garlogie 91 F4
Garmond 99 G5
Garmony 79 H3
Garmouth 98 B4
Garnant 17 K4
Garndolbenmaen 36 D1
Garneddwen 37 G5
Garnett Bridge 61 G7
Garnfadryn 36 B2
Garnswllt 17 K5
Garrabost 101 H4
Garrachra 73 J2
Garralburn 98 C5
Garras 2 D6
Garreg 37 F1
Garreg Bank 38 B4
Garrick 81 K6
Garrigill 61 J2
Garroch 67 K5
Garrochty 73 J5
Garros 94 B5
Garrow 81 K4
Garryhorn 67 K4
Garrynahine (Gearraidh
  na h-Aibhne) 100 E4
Garsdale Head 61 J7
Garsdon 20 C3
Garshall Green 40 B2
Garsington 21 J1
Garstang 55 H5
Garston 48 D4
Garswood 48 E3
Gartachoil 74 D1
Gartally 88 B1
Gartavaich 73 G5
Gartbreck 72 A5
Gartcosh 74 E4
Garth Bridgend 18 B2
Garth Gwyn. 46 D5
Garth I.o.M. 54 C6
Garth Powys 27 J4
Garth Shet. 109 B7
Garth Wrex. 38 B1
Garthbrengy 27 K5
Gartheli 26 E3
Garthmyl 38 A6
Garthorpe Leics. 42 B3
Garthorpe N.Lincs. 52 B1
Garths 61 G7
Garthynty 27 G4
Gartincaber 81 H7
Gartly 90 D1
Gartmore 74 D1
Gartnagrenach 73 F5
Gartnatra 73 B5
Gartness 74 D2
Gartocharn 74 C2
Garton 59 J6
Garton-on-
  the-Wolds 59 F3
Garvald 76 D3
Garvamore 88 C5
Garvan 87 F7
Garvard 72 B1
Garve 95 K5
Garveld 66 A3
Garvestone 44 E5
Garvie 73 J2
Garvock Aber. 91 F7
Garvock Inclyde 74 A3
Garvock P. & K. 82 B6
Garwald 69 H3
Garwaldwaterfoot 69 H3
Garway 28 D6
Garway Hill 28 D6
Gask Aber. 99 J6
Gask Aber. 99 F6
Gask P. & K. 82 A6
Gaskan 86 E7
Gass 67 J3
Gastard 20 B5
Gasthorpe 44 D7
Gatcombe 11 F6
Gate Burton 52 B4
Gate Helmsley 58 C4
Gate House 72 D3
Gateacre 48 D4
Gatebeck 55 J1
Gateford 51 H4
Gateforth 58 B7
Gatehead 74 B7
Gatehouse 81 K3
Gatehouse of Fleet 65 G5
Gatelawbridge 68 E4
Gateley 44 D3
Gatenby 57 J1
Gateshaw 70 C1
Gateshead 71 H7
Gatesheath 48 D6
Gateside Aber. 90 E3
Gateside Angus 83 F3
Gateside Fife 82 C7
Gateside N.Ayr. 74 B5
Gateslack 68 D3
Gathurst 48 E2
Gatley 49 H4
Gattonside 76 D7
Gatwick Airport 23 F7
Gaufron 27 J2
Gaulby 41 J5
Gauldry 82 E5
Gaunt's Common 10 B4
Gautby 52 E5
Gavinton 77 F5
Gawber 51 F2
Gawcott 31 H5
Gawsworth 49 H6
Gawthrop 56 B1
Gawthwaite 55 F1
Gay Street 12 D4
Gaydon 30 E3
Gayhurst 32 B4
Gayles 62 C6
Gayton Mersey. 48 B4
Gayton Norf. 44 B4
Gayton Northants. 31 J3
Gayton Staffs. 40 B3
Gayton le Marsh 53 H4
Gayton le Wold 53 F4
Gayton Thorpe 44 B4
Gaywood 44 A3
Gazeley 34 B2
Geanies House 97 F4
Gearach 72 A5
Gearnsary 104 C5
Gearradh 80 A1
Gearraidh Bhailteas 84 C2
Gearraidh Bhaird 101 F5
Gearraidh na h-Aibhne
  (Garrynahine) 100 E4

Gearraidh na
  Monadh 84 C3
Gearrannan 100 D3
Geary 93 H5
Gedding 34 D3
Geddington 42 B7
Gedgrave Hall 35 J4
Gedling 41 J1
Gedney 43 H3
Gedney Broadgate 43 H3
Gedney Drove End 43 H3
Gedney Dyke 43 H3
Gedney Hill 43 G4
Gee Cross 49 J3
Geirninis 92 C7
Geisiadar 100 D4
Geldeston 45 H6
Gell Conwy 47 G6
Gell Gwyn. 36 D2
Gelli Gynan 47 K7
Gelligaer 18 E2
Gellilydan 37 F2
Gellioedd 37 J1
Gelly 16 D4
Gellyburn 82 B4
Gellywen 17 F3
Gelston 65 H5
Gembling 59 H4
Gemmil 79 J7
Genoch 64 B5
Genoch Square 64 B5
Gentleshaw 40 C4
George Green 22 D3
George Nympton 7 F3
Georgeham 6 C2
Georgetown 74 C4
Gerlan 46 E6
Germansweek 6 C6
Germoe 2 C6
Gerrans 3 F5
Gerrards Cross 22 C3
Gerston 105 G3
Gestingthorpe 34 C5
Geuffordd 38 B4
Geufron 37 H7
Gibbshill 65 H3
Gibraltar 53 J7
Gidea Park 23 J3
Gidleigh 6 E7
Giffnock 74 D5
Gifford 76 D4
Giffordland 74 A6
Giggleswick 56 D3
Gilberdyke 58 E7
Gilchriston 76 C4
Gilcrux 60 C3
Gildersome 57 H7
Gildingwells 51 H4
Gileston 18 D5
Gilfach 18 E2
Gilfach Goch 18 C3
Gilfachrheda 26 D3
Gilgarran 60 B4
Gillamoor 63 H7
Gillen 93 H5
Gilling East 58 C1
Gilling West 62 C6
Gillingham Dorset 9 H1
Gillingham Med. 24 D5
Gillingham Norf. 45 J6
Gillivoan 105 G5
Gillock 105 H3
Gillow Heath 49 H7
Gills 105 J1
Gill's Green 14 C4
Gilmanscleuch 69 J1
Gilmerton Edin. 76 A4
Gilmerton P. & K. 81 K5
Gilmilnscroft 67 K1
Gilmonby 62 A5
Gilmorton 41 H7
Gilsland 70 B7
Gilsland Spa 70 B7
Gilston 76 C5
Gilston Park 33 H7
Gilwern 28 B7
Gimingham 45 G2
Giosla 100 D5
Gipping 34 E2
Gipsey Bridge 43 F1
Girlsta 109 D7
Girsby 62 E6
Girtford 32 E4
Girthon 65 G5
Girton Cambs. 33 H2
Girton Notts. 52 B6
Girvan 67 F4
Gisburn 56 D5
Gisleham 45 K7
Gislingham 34 E1
Gissing 45 F7
Gittisham 7 K6
Givons Grove 22 E6
Glackour 95 H3
Gladestry 28 B3
Gladsmuir 76 C3
Glaic 73 J3
Glais 18 A1
Glaisdale 63 J6
Glaister 73 H7
Glame 94 B7
Glamis 82 E3
Glan Conwy 47 G7
Glan Honddu 27 K5
Glanaber Terrace 37 G1
Glanadda 46 D5
Glanaman 17 K4
Glanbran 27 G5
Glanderston 90 D1
Glandford 44 E1
Glandwr B.Gwent 19 F1
Glandwr Pembs. 16 E3
Glan-Dwyfach 36 D1
Glangrwyne 28 B7
Glanllynfi 18 B2
Glanmule 38 A6
Glanrhyd 16 E1
Glanton 71 F2
Glantwymyn
  (Cemmaes Road) 37 H5
Glanvilles Wootton 9 F4
Glan-y-don 47 K5
Glan-y-llyn 18 E3
Glan-yr-afon
  Gwyn. 37 J1
Glan-yr-afon
  Gwyn. 37 K1
Glapthorn 42 D7
Glapwell 51 G6
Glasahoile 81 F7
Glaschoil 89 H1
Glascoed 19 G1
Glascorrie 90 B5
Glascote 40 E5
Glascwm 28 A3

Glasdrum 80 B3
Glasfryn 47 H7
Glasgow 74 D4
Glasgow Airport 74 C4
Glasgow Prestwick
  International
  Airport 67 H1
Glashmore 91 F4
Glasinfryn 46 D6
Glasnacardoch 86 C5
Glasnakille 86 B3
Glaspant 17 F2
Glaspwll 37 G6
Glassburn 87 K1
Glassel 90 E5
Glassenbury 14 C4
Glasserton 64 E7
Glassford 75 F6
Glasshouse Hill 29 G6
Glasshouses 57 G3
Glassingall 81 J7
Glasslie 82 D7
Glasson Cumb. 69 H7
Glasson Lancs. 55 H4
Glassonby 61 G3
Glasterlaw 83 G2
Glaston 42 B5
Glastonbury 8 D1
Glatton 42 E7
Glazebury 49 F3
Glazeley 39 G7
Gleadless 51 F4
Gleadsmoss 49 H6
Gleann Ghrabhair 101 F5
Gleann
  Tholastaidh 101 H3
Gleaston 55 F2
Glecknabae 73 J4
Gledhow 57 J6
Gledrid 38 B2
Glemsford 34 C4
Glen D. & G. 65 J3
Glen D. & G. 65 F5
Glen Auldyn 54 D4
Glen Parva 41 H6
Glen Trool Lodge 67 J5
Glen Vine 54 C6
Glenae 68 E5
Glenaladale 86 E7
Glenald 74 A1
Glenamachrie 80 A5
Glenapp Castle 66 E5
Glenarm 82 E1
Glenbarr 72 E7
Glenbatrick 72 D3
Glenbeg High. 79 G1
Glenbeg High. 89 H2
Glenbeich 81 H5
Glenbervie Aber. 91 F6
Glenbervie Falk. 75 G2
Glenboig 75 F4
Glenborrodale 79 H1
Glenbranter 73 K1
Glenbreck 69 F1
Glenbrittle 85 K2
Glenbuck 68 C1
Glenbyre 79 G5
Glencaple 65 K4
Glencarse 82 C5
Glencat 90 D5
Glenceitlein 80 C3
Glencloy 73 J7
Glencoe 80 C2
Glenconglass 89 J2
Glencraig 75 K1
Glencripesdale 79 H2
Glencrosh 68 C5
Glencruittein 79 K5
Glencuie 90 C3
Glendearg D. & G. 69 H3
Glendearg
  Sc.Bord. 76 D7
Glendessary 87 F5
Glendevon 82 A7
Glendoebeg 88 B3
Glendoick 82 D5
Glendoll Lodge 82 E1
Glendoune 67 F4
Glendrissaig 67 F4
Glenduckie 82 D6
Glenduisk 67 G5
Glendye Lodge 90 E6
Gleneagles Hotel 82 A6
Gleneagles House 82 A7
Glenearn 82 C6
Glenegedale 72 B5
Glenelg 86 E3
Glenfarg 82 C6
Glenfeochan 79 K5
Glenfield 41 H5
Glenfinnan 87 F6
Glenfoot 82 C6
Glengalmadale 79 K2
Glengap 65 G5
Glengarnock 74 B5
Glengarrisdale 72 E1
Glengennet 67 G4
Glengolly 105 G2
Glengorm Castle 79 F2
Glengrasco 93 K7
Glengyle 80 E6
Glenhead 68 D5
Glenhead Farm 82 D1
Glenhurich 79 K1
Glenkerry 69 H2
Glenkiln 73 J7
Glenkin 73 K3
Glenkindie 90 C3
Glenlair 65 H3
Glenlatterach 97 K6
Glenlean 73 J2
Glenlee Angus 90 C6
Glenlee D. & G. 68 B5
Glenlichorn 81 K6
Glenlivet 89 J2
Glenlochar 65 H4
Glenluce 64 B5
Glenmallan 74 A1
Glenmanna 68 C3
Glenmavis 75 F4
Glenmaye 54 B6
Glenmeanie 95 J6
Glenmore
  Arg. & B. 73 J4
Glenmore High. 93 K7
Glenmore Lodge 89 G4
Glenmoy 82 E1
Glenmuick 103 F7
Glennoe 80 B4
Glenochar 68 E2
Glenogil 82 E1
Glenprosen Village 82 E1
Glenquiech 82 E1
Glenramskill 66 B2
Glenrazie 64 D4
Glenridding 60 E5
Glenrisdell 73 G5
Glenrossal 96 B1
Glenrothes 82 D7

Glensanda 79 K3
Glensaugh 90 E7
Glensgaich 96 B5
Glenshalg 90 D4
Glenshellish 73 K1
Glensluain 73 J1
Glentaggart 68 D1
Glentham 52 D3
Glenton 90 E2
Glentress 76 A7
Glentrool 64 D3
Glentruan 54 D3
Glentworth 52 C4
Glenuachdarach 93 K6
Glenuig 86 C7
Glenure 80 B3
Glenurquhart 96 E5
Glenwhilly 64 B3
Glespin 68 D1
Gletness 109 D7
Glewstone 28 E6
Glinton 42 E5
Glooston 42 A6
Glororum 77 K7
Glossop 50 C3
Gloster Hill 71 H3
Gloucester 29 H7
Gloup 108 E2
Gloweth 2 E4
Glusburn 57 F5
Gluss 108 C5
Glympton 31 F6
Glyn 47 F7
Glyn Ceiriog 38 B2
Glynarthen 17 G1
Glyncoch 18 D2
Glyncorrwg 18 B2
Glyn-Cywarch 37 F2
Glynde 13 H6
Glyndebourne 13 H5
Glyndyfrdwy 38 A1
Glynneath 18 B1
Glynogwr 18 C3
Glyntaff 18 D3
Glynteg 17 G2
Gnosall 40 A3
Gnosall Heath 40 A4
Goadby 42 A6
Goadby Marwood 42 A3
Goatacre 20 D4
Goatfield 80 B7
Goathill 9 F3
Goathland 63 K6
Goathurst 8 B1
Gobernuisgeach 104 E5
Gobhaig 100 C7
Gobowen 38 B2
Godalming 22 C7
Godford Cross 7 K5
Godmanchester 33 F2
Godmanstone 9 F5
Godmersham 15 F2
Godolphin Cross 2 D5
Godor 38 B4
Godre'r-graig 18 A1
Godshill Hants. 10 C3
Godshill I.o.W. 11 G6
Godstone 23 G6
Goetre 19 G1
Goff's Oak 23 G1
Gogar 75 K3
Gogarth 47 F4
Goginan 37 F7
Goirtean
  a' Chladaich 87 G7
Goirtein 73 H2
Golan 36 E1
Golant 4 B5
Golberdon 4 D3
Golborne 49 F3
Golcar 50 D1
Gold Hill 43 J6
Goldcliff 19 G3
Golden Cross 13 J5
Golden Green 23 K7
Golden Grove 17 J4
Golden Pot 22 A7
Golden Valley 29 J6
Goldenhill 49 H7
Golders Green 23 F3
Goldhanger 24 E1
Goldielea 65 K3
Golding 38 E5
Goldington 32 D3
Goldsborough
  N.Yorks. 63 K5
Goldsborough
  N.Yorks. 57 J4
Goldsithney 2 C5
Goldthorpe 51 G2
Goldworthy 6 B3
Gollanfield 97 F6
Golspie 97 F2
Golval 104 D2
Gomeldon 10 C1
Gomersal 57 H7
Gometra House 78 E3
Gomshall 22 D7
Gonachan Cottage 74 E2
Gonalston 41 J1
Gonfirth 109 C6
Good Easter 33 K7
Gooderstone 44 B5
Goodleigh 6 E2
Goodmanham 58 E5
Goodnestone Kent 15 H2
Goodnestone Kent 25 G5
Goodrich 28 E7
Goodrington 5 J5
Goodwick (Wdig) 16 C2
Goodworth
  Clatford 21 G7
Goodyers End 41 F7
Goole 58 D7
Goonbell 2 E4
Goonhavern 2 E3
Goose Green 23 K6
Gooseham 6 A4
Goosewell 5 F5
Goosey 21 G2
Goosnargh 55 J6
Goostrey 49 G5
Gorcott Hill 30 B2
Gordon 76 E6
Gordonbush 97 F1
Gordonstoun 97 J5
Gordonstown
  Aber. 98 D5
Gordonstown
  Aber. 91 F1
Gore Cross 20 D6
Gore Street 25 J5
Gorebridge 76 B4
Gorefield 43 H4
Gorey 3 K7
Goring 21 K3
Goring-by-Sea 12 E6
Gorleston on Sea 45 K5

Gorllwyn 17 G2
Gornalwood 40 B6
Gorrachie 99 F5
Gorran Churchtown 3 G4
Gorran Haven 4 A6
Gors 27 F1
Gorsedd 47 K5
Gorseinon 17 J6
Gorseness 107 D6
Gorsgoch 26 D3
Gorslas 17 J4
Gorsley 29 F6
Gorsley Common 29 F6
Gorstan 95 K5
Gorstanvorran 86 E7
Gorsten 79 J4
Gortenbuie 79 G4
Gortenorn 79 H1
Gorton Arg. & B. 78 C2
Gorton Gt.Man. 49 H3
Gosbeck 35 F3
Gosberton 43 F2
Goseley Dale 41 F3
Gosfield 34 B6
Gosforth Cumb. 60 B6
Gosforth T. & W. 71 H7
Gosmore 32 E6
Gospel End 40 B6
Gosport 11 H5
Gossabrough 108 E4
Gossops Green 13 F3
Goswick 77 J6
Gotham 41 H2
Gotherington 29 J6
Gott 109 D8
Goudhurst 14 C4
Goulceby 53 F5
Gourdas 99 F6
Gourdon 91 G7
Gourock 74 A3
Govan 74 D4
Goveton 5 H6
Govilon 28 B7
Gowanhill 99 J4
Gowdall 58 C7
Gowerton 17 J6
Gowkhall 75 J2
Gowthorpe 58 D4
Goxhill E.Riding 59 H5
Goxhill N.Lincs. 59 H7
Goytre 18 A3
Grabhair 101 F6
Gradbach 49 J6
Grade 2 E7
Graffham 12 C5
Grafham Cambs. 32 E2
Grafham Surr. 22 D7
Grafton Here. 28 D5
Grafton N.Yorks. 57 K3
Grafton Oxon. 21 F1
Grafton Shrop. 38 D4
Grafton Worcs. 29 E2
Grafton Flyford 29 J3
Grafton Regis 31 J4
Grafton
  Underwood 32 C1
Grafty Green 14 D3
Graianrhyd 48 B7
Graig Conwy 47 G5
Graig Denb. 47 J5
Graig Penllyn 18 C4
Graig-fechan 47 K7
Grain 24 E4
Grainel 72 A4
Grainhow 99 G6
Grainsby 53 F3
Grainthorpe 53 G3
Graiselound 51 K3
Grampound 3 G4
Grampound Road 3 G3
Gramsdal 92 D6
Granborough 31 J6
Granby 42 A2
Grandborough 31 F2
Grandtully 82 A2
Grange Cumb. 60 D5
Grange High. 87 K1
Grange Med. 24 D5
Grange N.Yorks. 63 G7
Grange P. & K. 82 D5
Grange Crossroads 98 C5
Grange Hall 97 H5
Grange Hill 23 H2
Grange Moor 50 E1
Grange of Lindores 82 D6
Grange Villa 62 D1
Grangemill 50 E7
Grangemouth 75 H2
Grangemuir 83 G7
Grange-over-Sands 55 H2
Grangeston 67 G4
Grangetown
  Cardiff 18 E4
Grangetown
  R. & C. 63 G4
Granish 89 G3
Gransmoor 59 H4
Granston 16 B2
Grantchester 33 H3
Grantham 42 C2
Grantley 57 H2
Grantlodge 91 F3
Granton House 69 F3
Grantown-on-Spey 89 H2
Grantshouse 77 G4
Grappenhall 49 F4
Grasby 52 D2
Grasmere 60 E6
Grasscroft 49 J2
Grassendale 48 C4
Grassholme 62 A4
Grassington 57 F3
Grassmoor 51 G6
Grassthorpe 51 K6
Grateley 21 F7
Gratwich 40 C2
Graveley Cambs. 33 F2
Graveley Herts. 33 F6
Gravelly Hill 40 D6
Gravels 38 C5
Graven 108 D5
Graveney 25 G5
Gravesend 24 C4
Grayingham 52 C3
Grayrigg 61 G7
Grays 24 C4
Grayshott 12 B3
Grayswood 12 C3
Graythorp 63 G4
Grazeley 22 A5
Greasbrough 51 G3
Greasby 48 B4
Great Abington 33 J4
Great Addington 32 C1
Great Alne 30 C3
Great Altcar 48 C2
Great Amwell 33 G7
Great Asby 61 H5
Great Ashfield 34 D2
Great Ayton 63 G5

Great Baddow 24 D1
Great Bardfield 33 K5
Great Barford 32 E3
Great Barr 40 C6
Great Barrington 30 D7
Great Barrow 48 D6
Great Barton 34 C2
Great Barugh 58 D2
Great Bavington 70 E5
Great Bealings 35 G4
Great Bedwyn 21 F5
Great Bentley 35 F6
Great Billing 32 B2
Great Bircham 44 B2
Great Blakenham 35 F3
Great Bolas 39 F3
Great Bookham 22 E6
Great Bourton 31 F4
Great Bowden 42 A7
Great Bradley 33 K3
Great Braxted 34 C7
Great Bricett 34 E3
Great Brickhill 32 C5
Great Bridgeford 40 A3
Great Brington 31 H2
Great Bromley 34 E6
Great Broughton
  Cumb. 60 B3
Great Broughton
  N.Yorks. 63 G6
Great Budworth 49 F5
Great Burdon 62 E5
Great Burstead 24 C2
Great Busby 63 G6
Great Canfield 33 J7
Great Canney 24 E1
Great Carlton 53 H4
Great Casterton 42 D5
Great Chart 14 E3
Great Chatwell 39 G4
Great Chesterford 33 J4
Great Cheverell 20 C6
Great Chishill 33 H5
Great Clacton 35 F7
Great Clifton 60 B4
Great Coates 53 F2
Great Comberton 29 J4
Great Corby 61 F1
Great Cornard 34 C4
Great Cowden 59 J5
Great Coxwell 21 F2
Great Crakehall 62 D7
Great Cransley 32 B1
Great Cressingham 44 C5
Great Crosby 48 C2
Great Cubley 40 D2
Great Dalby 42 A4
Great Doddington 32 B2
Great Dunham 44 C4
Great Dunmow 33 K6
Great Durnford 10 C1
Great Easton
  Essex 33 K6
Great Easton
  Leics. 42 B6
Great Eccleston 55 H5
Great Edstone 58 D1
Great Ellingham 44 E6
Great Elm 20 A7
Great Eversden 33 G3
Great Fencote 62 D7
Great Finborough 34 E3
Great Fransham 44 C4
Great Gaddesden 32 D7
Great Gidding 42 E7
Great Givendale 58 E4
Great Glemham 35 H2
Great Glen 41 J6
Great Gonerby 42 B2
Great Gransden 33 F3
Great Green Norf. 45 G6
Great Green Suff. 34 D2
Great Habton 58 D2
Great Hale 42 E1
Great Hallingbury 33 J7
Great Harrowden 32 B1
Great Harwood 56 C6
Great Haseley 21 K1
Great Hatfield 59 H5
Great Haywood 40 C3
Great Heath 41 F7
Great Heck 58 B7
Great Henny 34 C5
Great Hinton 20 C6
Great Hockham 44 D6
Great Holland 35 G7
Great Horkesley 34 D5
Great Hormead 33 H5
Great Horwood 31 J5
Great Houghton
  Northants. 31 J3
Great Houghton
  S.Yorks. 51 G2
Great Hucklow 50 D5
Great Kelk 59 H4
Great Kimble 22 B1
Great Kingshill 22 B2
Great Langton 62 D7
Great Leighs 34 B7
Great Limber 52 E2
Great Linford 32 B4
Great Livermere 34 C1
Great Longstone 50 E5
Great Lumley 62 D2
Great Lyth 38 D5
Great Malvern 29 G4
Great Maplestead 34 C5
Great Marton 55 G6
Great Massingham 44 B3
Great Melton 45 F5
Great Milton 21 K1
Great Missenden 22 B1
Great Mitton 56 C6
Great Mongeham 15 J2
Great Moulton 45 F6
Great Munden 33 G6
Great Musgrave 61 J5
Great Ness 38 C4
Great Notley 34 B6
Great Oak 28 C7
Great Oakley
  Essex 35 F6
Great Oakley
  Northants. 42 B7
Great Offley 32 E6
Great Ormside 61 J5
Great Orton 60 E1
Great Ouseburn 57 K3
Great Oxendon 42 A7
Great Oxney Green 24 C1
Great Palgrave 44 C4
Great Parndon 23 H1
Great Paxton 33 F2
Great Plumpton 55 G6
Great Plumstead 45 G5
Great Ponton 42 C2
Great Preston 57 K7
Great Raveley 43 F7
Great Rissington 30 C7

Great Rollright 30 E5
Great Ryburgh 44 D3
Great Ryle 71 F2
Great Ryton 38 D5
Great Saling 33 K6
Great Salkeld 61 G3
Great Sampford 33 K5
Great Sankey 48 E4
Great Saxham 34 B2
Great Shefford 21 G4
Great Shelford 33 H3
Great Smeaton 62 E6
Great Snoring 44 D2
Great Somerford 20 C3
Great Stainton 62 E4
Great Stambridge 24 E2
Great Staughton 32 E2
Great Steeping 53 H6
Great Stonar 15 J2
Great Strickland 61 G4
Great Stukeley 33 F1
Great Sturton 53 F5
Great Sutton _Ches._ 48 C5
Great Sutton _Shrop._ 38 E7
Great Swinburne 70 E6
Great Tew 30 E6
Great Tey 34 C6
Great Thurlow 33 K4
Great Torrington 6 D4
Great Tosson 71 F3
Great Totham _Essex_ 34 C7
Great Totham _Essex_ 34 C7
Great Urswick 55 F2
Great Wakering 25 F3
Great Waldingfield 34 D4
Great Walsingham 44 D2
Great Waltham 33 K7
Great Warley 23 J5
Great Washbourne 29 J5
Great Welnetham 34 C3
Great Wenham 34 E5
Great Whittington 71 F6
Great Wigborough 34 D7
Great Wilbraham 33 J3
Great Wishford 10 B1
Great Witcombe 29 J7
Great Witley 29 G2
Great Wolford 30 D5
Great Wratting 33 K4
Great Wymondley 33 F6
Great Wyrley 40 B5
Great Wytheford 38 E4
Great Yarmouth 45 K5
Great Yeldham 34 B5
Greatford 42 D4
Greatgate 40 C1
Greatham _Hants._ 11 J1
Greatham _Hart._ 62 E4
Greatham _W.Suss._ 12 D5
Greatstone-on-Sea 15 F5
Greatworth 31 G4
Green End _Beds._ 32 E3
Green End _Herts._ 33 G6
Green Hammerton 57 K4
Green Ore 19 J6
Green Street 22 E2
Green Street Green _Gt.Lon._ 23 H5
Green Street Green _Kent_ 23 J4
Green Tye 33 H7
Greenburn 83 F4
Greencroft 62 C2
Greendams 90 E5
Greendykes 71 F1
Greenfield _Beds._ 32 D5
Greenfield (Maes-Glas) _Flints._ 47 K5
Greenfield _Gt.Man._ 50 C2
Greenfield _High._ 87 J4
Greenfield _Oxon._ 22 A2
Greenford 22 E3
Greengairs 75 F3
Greenhalgh 55 H6
Greenhall _Som._ 7 J3
Greenham _W.Berks._ 21 H5
Greenhaugh 70 C5
Greenhead 70 B7
Greenheads 91 J1
Greenhill _Gt.Lon._ 22 E3
Greenhill _High._ 96 D3
Greenhill _S.Yorks._ 51 F4
Greenhithe 23 J4
Greenholm 74 D7
Greenholme 61 G6
Greenhow Hill 57 G3
Greenigo 107 D7
Greenland 105 H2
Greenlands 22 A3
Greenlaw _Aber._ 98 E5
Greenlaw _Sc.Bord._ 77 F6
Greenloaning 81 K7
Greenmount 49 G1
Greenmyre 91 G1
Greenock 74 A3
Greenodd 55 G1
Greens Norton 31 H3
Greenscares 81 J6
Greenside 71 F7
Greenstead Green 34 C6
Greensted 23 J1
Greenway _Pembs._ 16 D2
Greenway _Som._ 8 B2
Greenwich _Gt.Lon._ 23 G4
Greenwich _Gt.Lon._ 23 G4
Greet 30 B5
Greete 28 E1
Greetham _Lincs._ 53 G5
Greetham _Rut._ 42 C4
Greetland 57 F7
Greinetobht 92 D4
Greinton 8 D1
Grenaby 54 B6
Grendon _Northants._ 32 B2
Grendon _Warks._ 40 E6
Grendon Common 40 E6
Grendon Green 28 E3
Grendon Underwood 31 H6
Grenoside 51 F3
Greosabhagh 93 G2
Gresford 48 C7
Gresham 45 F2
Greshornish 93 J6
Gressenhall 44 D4
Gressingham 55 J2
Greta Bridge 62 B5
Gretna 69 J7
Gretna Green 69 J7
Gretton _Glos._ 30 B5
Gretton _Northants._ 42 C6
Gretton _Shrop._ 38 E6

Grewelthorpe 57 H2
Greygarth 57 G2
Greylake 8 C1
Greys Green 22 A3
Greysouthen 60 B4
Greystoke 61 F3
Greystone _Aber._ 89 K5
Greystone _Angus_ 83 G3
Greystone _Lancs._ 56 D5
Greywell 22 A6
Griais 101 G3
Gribthorpe 58 D6
Gribton 68 E5
Griff 41 F7
Griffithstown 19 F2
Grigadale 79 F1
Grigghall 61 F7
Grimeford Village 49 F1
Grimethorpe 51 G2
Griminis 92 C6
Grimister 108 D3
Grimley 29 H2
Grimmet 67 H2
Grimness 107 D8
Grimoldby 53 G4
Grimpo 38 C3
Grimsargh 55 J6
Grimsbury 31 F4
Grimsby 53 F2
Grimscote 31 H3
Grimscott 6 A5
Grimshader 101 G5
Grimsthorpe 42 D3
Grimston _Leics._ 41 J3
Grimston _Norf._ 44 B3
Grimstone 9 F5
Grindale 59 H2
Grindiscol 109 D9
Grindle 39 G5
Grindleford 50 E5
Grindleton 56 C5
Grindley 40 C3
Grindlow 50 D5
Grindon _Northumb._ 77 H6
Grindon _Staffs._ 50 C7
Gringley on the Hill 51 K3
Grinsdale 60 E1
Grinshill 38 E3
Grinton 62 B7
Griomarstaidh 100 E4
Grishipoll 78 C2
Gristhorpe 59 G1
Griston 44 D6
Gritley 107 E7
Grittenham 20 D3
Grittleton 20 B3
Grizebeck 55 F1
Grizedale 60 E7
Grobister 106 F5
Groby 41 H5
Groes 47 J6
Groes-faen 18 D3
Groesffordd 36 B2
Groesffordd Marli 47 J5
Groeslon 46 C7
Groes-lwyd 38 B4
Grogport 73 G6
Groigearraidh 84 C1
Gromford 35 H3
Gronant 47 J4
Groombridge 13 J3
Grosmont _Mon._ 28 D6
Grosmont _N.Yorks._ 63 K6
Grotaig 88 B2
Groton 34 D4
Groundistone Heights 69 K2
Grouville 3 K7
Grove _Dorset_ 9 F7
Grove _Kent_ 25 J5
Grove _Notts._ 51 K5
Grove _Oxon._ 21 H2
Grove Park 23 H4
Grovesend 17 J5
Gruids 96 C1
Gruinart Flats 72 A4
Gruline 79 G4
Grundcruie 82 B5
Grundisburgh 35 G3
Gruting 109 B8
Grutness 109 G10
Gualachulain 80 C3
Guardbridge 83 F6
Guarlford 29 H4
Guay 82 B3
Gubbergill 60 B7
Guernsey Airport 3 H5
Guestling Green 14 D6
Guestling Thorn 14 D6
Guestwick 44 E3
Guide Post 71 H5
Guilden Morden 33 F4
Guilden Sutton 48 D6
Guildford 22 C7
Guildtown 82 C4
Guilsborough 31 H1
Guilsfield (Cegidfa) 38 B4
Guisborough 63 H5
Guiseley 57 G5
Guist 44 D3
Guith 106 E4
Guiting Power 30 B6
Gulberwick 109 D9
Gullane 76 C2
Gulval 2 B5
Gulworthy 4 E3
Gumfreston 16 E5
Gumley 41 J7
Gunby _E.Riding_ 58 D6
Gunby _Lincs._ 42 C3
Gundleton 11 H1
Gunn 6 E2
Gunnerside 62 A7
Gunnerton 70 E6
Gunness 52 B1
Gunnislake 4 E3
Gunnista 109 D8
Gunter's Bridge 12 C4
Gunthorpe _Norf._ 44 E2
Gunthorpe _Notts._ 41 J1
Gunville 11 F6
Gunwalloe 2 D6
Gurnard 11 F5
Gurney Slade 19 K7
Gurnos 18 A1
Gussage All Saints 10 B3
Gussage St. Michael 9 J3
Guston 15 J3
Gutcher 108 E3
Guthrie 83 G2
Guyhirn 43 G5
Guynd 83 G3
Guy's Head 43 H3
Guy's Marsh 9 H2
Guyzance 71 H3
Gwaelod-y-garth 18 E3
Gwaenysgor 47 J4

Gwaithla 28 B3
Gwalchmai 46 B5
Gwaun-Cae-Gurwen 27 G7
Gwaynynog 47 J6
Gwbert 16 E1
Gweek 2 E6
Gwehelog 19 G1
Gwenddwr 27 K4
Gwennap 2 E4
Gwenter 2 E7
Gwernaffield 48 B6
Gwernesney 19 H1
Gwernogle 17 J2
Gwernymynydd 48 B6
Gwersyllt 48 C7
Gwespyr 47 K4
Gwinear 2 C5
Gwithian 2 C4
Gwyddelwern 37 K1
Gwyddgrug 17 H2
Gwystre 27 K2
Gwytherin 47 G6
Gyfelia 38 C1
Gyffin 47 F5
Gyre 107 C7
Gyrn Goch 36 D1

H

Habberley 38 C5
Habrough 52 E1
Haccombe 5 J3
Hacconby 42 E3
Haceby 42 D2
Hacheston 35 H3
Hackenthorpe 51 G4
Hackford 44 E5
Hackforth 62 D7
Hackland 106 C5
Hackleton 32 B3
Hacklinge 15 J2
Hackness _N.Yorks._ 63 J3
Hackness _Ork._ 107 C8
Hackney 23 G3
Hackthorn 52 C4
Hackthorpe 61 G4
Hadden 77 F7
Haddenham _Bucks._ 22 A1
Haddenham _Cambs._ 33 H1
Haddington _E.Loth._ 76 D3
Haddington _Lincs._ 52 C6
Haddiscoe 45 J6
Haddon 42 E6
Hademore 40 D5
Hadfield 50 C3
Hadham Cross 33 H7
Hadham Ford 33 H6
Hadley 39 F4
Hadley End 40 D3
Hadley Wood 23 F2
Hadlow 23 K7
Hadlow Down 13 J4
Hadnall 38 E3
Hadstock 33 J4
Hadzor 29 J2
Haffenden Quarter 14 D3
Hafod-Dinbych 47 G7
Hafodunos 47 G6
Haggate 56 D6
Haggbeck 69 K6
Haggs 75 F3
Hagley _Here._ 28 E4
Hagley _Worcs._ 40 B7
Hagnaby 53 G6
Hagworthingham 53 G6
Haigh 49 F2
Haighton Green 55 J6
Hail Weston 32 E2
Haile 60 B6
Hailes 30 B5
Hailey _Herts._ 33 G7
Hailey _Oxon._ 21 K3
Hailey _Oxon._ 30 E7
Hailsham 13 J6
Haimer 105 G2
Hainault 23 H2
Hainford 45 G4
Hainton 52 E4
Haisthorpe 59 H3
Halam 51 J7
Halbeath 75 K2
Halberton 7 J4
Halcro 105 H2
Hale _Gt.Man._ 49 G4
Hale _Hants._ 10 C3
Hale _Surr._ 22 B7
Hale Bank 48 D4
Hale Street 23 K7
Halebarns 49 G4
Hales _Norf._ 45 H6
Hales _Staffs._ 39 G2
Hales Place 15 G2
Halesowen 40 B7
Halesworth 35 H1
Halewood 48 D4
Half Way Inn 7 J6
Halford _Shrop._ 38 D7
Halford _Warks._ 30 D4
Halfpenny Green 40 A6
Halfway _Carmar._ 17 K2
Halfway _Powys_ 27 H5
Halfway _S.Yorks._ 51 G4
Halfway _W.Berks._ 21 H5
Halfway House 38 C4
Halfway Houses 25 F4
Halghton Mill 38 D1
Halifax 57 F7
Halistra 93 H6
Halkirk 105 G3
Halkyn 48 B5
Hall 74 C5
Hall Dunnerdale 60 D7
Hall Green 40 D7
Hall of the Forest 38 B7
Halland 13 J5
Hallaton 42 A6
Hallatrow 19 K6
Hallbankgate 61 G1
Hallen 19 J4
Hallin 93 H6
Halling 24 D5
Hallington _Lincs._ 53 G4
Hallington _Northumb._ 70 E6
Halloughton 51 J7
Hallow 29 H3
Hallow Heath 29 H3
Hallrule 70 A2
Halls 76 E3
Hall's Green 33 F6
Hall's Tenement 61 G1
Hallsands 5 J7

Hallworthy 4 B2
Halmer End 39 G1
Halmore 19 K1
Halmyre Mains 75 K6
Halnaker 12 C6
Halsall 48 C1
Halse _Northants._ 31 G4
Halse _Som._ 7 K3
Halsetown 2 C5
Halsham 59 J7
Halsinger 6 D2
Halstead _Essex_ 34 C5
Halstead _Kent_ 23 H5
Halstead _Leics._ 42 A5
Halstock 8 E4
Haltham 53 F6
Haltoft End 43 G1
Halton _Bucks._ 32 B7
Halton _Halton_ 48 E4
Halton _Lancs._ 55 J3
Halton _Northumb._ 71 F7
Halton _Wrex._ 38 C2
Halton East 57 F4
Halton Gill 56 D2
Halton Holegate 53 H6
Halton Lea Gate 61 H1
Halton West 56 D4
Haltwhistle 70 C7
Halvergate 45 J5
Halwell 5 H5
Halwill 6 C6
Halwill Junction 6 C6
Ham _Glos._ 19 K2
Ham _Gt.Lon._ 22 E4
Ham _High._ 105 H1
Ham _Kent_ 15 J2
Ham _Shet._ 108 B1
Ham _Som._ 8 B2
Ham _Wilts._ 21 G5
Ham Green _N.Som._ 19 J4
Ham Green _Worcs._ 30 B2
Ham Hill 24 C5
Ham Street 8 E1
Hambleden 22 A3
Hambledon _Hants._ 11 H3
Hambledon _Surr._ 12 C3
Hamble-le-Rice 11 F4
Hambleton _Lancs._ 55 G5
Hambleton _N.Yorks._ 58 B6
Hambleton Moss Side 55 G5
Hambridge 8 C2
Hambrook _S.Glos._ 19 K4
Hambrook _W.Suss._ 11 J4
Hameringham 53 G6
Hamerton 32 E1
Hamilton 75 F5
Hamlet 7 K6
Hammer 12 B3
Hammerpot 12 D6
Hammersmith 23 F4
Hammerwich 40 C5
Hammerwood 13 H3
Hammond Street 23 G1
Hamnavoe _Shet._ 109 C9
Hamnavoe _Shet._ 108 D4
Hamnavoe _Shet._ 108 B4
Hamnavoe _Shet._ 108 D5
Hampden Park 13 K6
Hampnett 30 C7
Hampole 51 H2
Hampreston 10 B5
Hampstead 23 F3
Hampstead Norreys 21 J4
Hampsthwaite 57 H4
Hampton _Gt.Lon._ 22 E5
Hampton _Shrop._ 39 G7
Hampton _Worcs._ 30 B4
Hampton Bishop 28 E5
Hampton Heath 38 D1
Hampton in Arden 40 E7
Hampton Lovett 29 H2
Hampton Lucy 30 D3
Hampton on the Hill 30 D2
Hampton Poyle 31 G7
Hamptworth 10 D2
Hamsey 13 H5
Hamstall Ridware 40 D4
Hamstead _I.o.W._ 11 F5
Hamstead _W.Mid._ 40 C6
Hamstead Marshall 21 H5
Hamsterley _Dur._ 62 B2
Hamsterley _Dur._ 62 C1
Hamstreet 15 F4
Hamworthy 9 J5
Hanbury _Staffs._ 40 D3
Hanbury _Worcs._ 29 J2
Hanbury Woodend 40 D3
Hanchurch 40 A1
Handbridge 48 D6
Handcross 13 F4
Handforth 49 H4
Handley 48 D7
Handsacre 40 C4
Handsworth _S.Yorks._ 51 G4
Handsworth _W.Mid._ 40 C6
Handy Cross 22 B2
Hanford 40 A1
Hanging Bridge 40 D1
Hanging Langford 10 B1
Hangingshaw 69 G5
Hangleton 13 F6
Hanham 19 K4
Hankelow 39 F1
Hankerton 20 C2
Hankham 13 K6
Hanley 40 A1
Hanley Castle 29 H4
Hanley Child 29 F2
Hanley Swan 29 H4
Hanley William 29 F2
Hanlith 56 E3
Hanmer 38 D2
Hannah 53 H5
Hannington _Hants._ 21 J6
Hannington _Northants._ 32 B1
Hannington _Swin._ 20 E2
Hannington Wick 20 E2
Hanslope 32 B4
Hanthorpe 42 D3
Hanwell _Gt.Lon._ 22 E4
Hanwell _Oxon._ 31 F4
Hanwood 38 D5
Hanworth _Gt.Lon._ 22 E4
Hanworth _Norf._ 45 F2
Happendon 75 G7
Happisburgh 45 H2
Happisburgh Common 45 H3
Hapsford 48 D5
Hapton _Lancs._ 56 C6
Hapton _Norf._ 45 F6
Harberton 5 H5

Harbertonford 5 H5
Harbledown 15 G2
Harborne 40 C7
Harborough Magna 31 F1
Harbottle 70 E3
Harbourneford 5 H4
Harbridge 10 C3
Harburn 75 J4
Harbury 30 E3
Harby _Leics._ 42 A2
Harby _Notts._ 52 B5
Harcombe 7 K6
Harden 57 F6
Hardenhuish 20 C4
Hardgate 91 F4
Hardham 12 D5
Hardingham 44 E5
Hardings Wood 49 H7
Hardingstone 31 J3
Hardington 20 A6
Hardington Mandeville 8 E3
Hardington Marsh 8 E4
Hardley 11 F4
Hardley Street 45 H5
Hardmead 32 C4
Hardraw 61 K7
Hardstoft 51 G6
Hardway _Hants._ 11 H4
Hardway _Som._ 9 G1
Hardwick _Bucks._ 32 B7
Hardwick _Cambs._ 33 G3
Hardwick _Norf._ 45 G6
Hardwick _Northants._ 32 B2
Hardwick _Oxon._ 21 G1
Hardwick _Oxon._ 31 G6
Hardwick Village 51 J5
Hardwicke _Glos._ 29 J6
Hardwicke _Glos._ 29 G7
Hardwicke _Here._ 28 B4
Hardy's Green 34 D7
Hare Green 34 E6
Hare Hatch 22 B4
Hare Street _Herts._ 33 G6
Hare Street _Herts._ 33 G6
Hareby 53 G6
Hareden 56 B4
Harefield 22 D2
Harehills 57 J6
Harelaw 75 H6
Haresceugh 61 H2
Harescombe 29 H7
Haresfield 29 H7
Hareshaw 74 E6
Harewood 57 J5
Harewood End 28 E6
Harford 5 G5
Hargate 45 F6
Hargatewall 50 D5
Hargrave _Ches._ 48 D6
Hargrave _Northants._ 32 D1
Hargrave _Suff._ 34 B3
Harker 69 J7
Harkstead 35 F5
Harlaston 40 E4
Harlaxton 42 B2
Harle Syke 56 D6
Harlech 36 E2
Harlesden 23 F3
Harleston _Norf._ 45 G7
Harleston _Suff._ 34 E3
Harlestone 31 J2
Harley 38 E5
Harleyholm 75 H7
Harlington 32 D5
Harlosh 93 H7
Harlow 33 H7
Harlow Hill 71 F7
Harlthorpe 58 D6
Harlton 33 G3
Harman's Cross 9 J6
Harmby 62 C7
Harmer Green 33 F7
Harmer Hill 38 D3
Harmondsworth 22 D4
Harmston 52 C6
Harnham 10 C2
Harnhill 20 D1
Harold Hill 23 J2
Harold Wood 23 J2
Haroldston West 16 B4
Haroldswick 108 F1
Harome 58 C1
Harpenden 32 E7
Harpford 7 J6
Harpham 59 G3
Harpley _Norf._ 44 B3
Harpley _Worcs._ 29 F2
Harpole 31 H2
Harprigg 56 B1
Harpsdale 105 G3
Harpsden 22 A3
Harpswell 52 C3
Harpur Hill 50 C5
Harpurhey 49 H2
Harrapool 86 C2
Harrietfield 82 A4
Harrietsham 14 D2
Harrington _Lincs._ 53 G5
Harrington _Northants._ 31 J1
Harringworth 42 C6
Harris 85 J5
Harriseahead 49 H7
Harrogate 57 J4
Harrold 32 C3
Harrow _Gt.Lon._ 22 E3
Harrow _High._ 105 H1
Harrow on the Hill 22 E3
Harrow Weald 22 E2
Harrowbarrow 4 E3
Harrowden 32 D4
Harston _Cambs._ 33 H3
Harston _Leics._ 42 B2
Hart 63 F3
Hartburn _Northumb._ 71 F5
Hartburn _Stock._ 63 F5
Hartest 34 C3
Hartfield _E.Suss._ 13 H3
Hartford _Cambs._ 33 F1
Hartford _Ches._ 49 F5
Hartford End 33 K7
Hartfordbridge 22 A6
Hartforth 62 C6
Harthill _Ches._ 48 E7
Harthill _N.Lan._ 75 H4
Harthill _S.Yorks._ 51 G4
Hartington 50 D6
Hartland 6 A3
Hartland Quay 6 A3
Hartlebury 29 H1
Hartlepool 63 G3
Hartley _Cumb._ 61 J6
Hartley _Kent_ 24 C5
Hartley _Kent_ 14 C4
Hartley _Northumb._ 71 J6
Hartley Wespall 22 M4

Hartley Wintney 22 A6
Hartlip 24 E5
Harton _N.Yorks._ 58 D3
Harton _Shrop._ 38 D7
Harton _T. & W._ 71 J7
Hartpury 29 G6
Hartrigge 70 B1
Hartshill 41 F6
Hartshorne 41 F3
Hartsop 61 F5
Hartwell _Bucks._ 32 B7
Hartwell _E.Suss._ 13 H3
Hartwell _Northants._ 31 J4
Hartwood 75 G5
Harvel 24 C5
Harvington _Worcs._ 30 B4
Harvington _Worcs._ 29 H1
Harwell _Notts._ 51 J3
Harwell _Oxon._ 21 H3
Harwich 35 G5
Harwood _Dur._ 61 K3
Harwood _Gt.Man._ 49 G1
Harwood Dale 63 J3
Harwood on Teviot 69 K3
Harworth 51 J3
Hasbury 40 B7
Hascombe 12 C3
Haselbech 31 J1
Haselbury Plucknett 8 D3
Haseley 30 D2
Haselor 30 C3
Hasfield 29 H6
Hasguard 16 B5
Haskayne 48 C2
Hasketon 35 G3
Hasland 51 F6
Haslemere 12 C3
Haslingden 56 C7
Haslingden Grane 56 C7
Haslingfield 33 H3
Haslington 49 G7
Hassall 49 G7
Hassall Green 49 G7
Hassall Street 15 F3
Hassendean 70 A1
Hassingham 45 H5
Hassocks 13 F5
Hassop 50 E5
Haster 105 J3
Hastigrow 105 H2
Hastingleigh 15 F3
Hastings 14 D7
Hastingwood 23 H1
Hastoe 22 C1
Haswell 62 E2
Hatch _Beds._ 32 E4
Hatch _Hants._ 21 K6
Hatch Beauchamp 8 B2
Hatch End 22 E2
Hatch Green 8 B3
Hatching Green 32 E7
Hatchmere 48 E5
Hatcliffe 53 F2
Hatfield _Here._ 28 E3
Hatfield _Herts._ 23 F1
Hatfield _S.Yorks._ 51 J2
Hatfield Broad Oak 33 J7
Hatfield Heath 33 J7
Hatfield Hyde 33 F7
Hatfield Peverel 34 B7
Hatfield Woodhouse 51 J2
Hatford 21 G2
Hatherden 21 G6
Hatherleigh 6 D5
Hathern 41 G3
Hatherop 20 E1
Hathersage 50 E4
Hatherton _Ches._ 39 F1
Hatherton _Staffs._ 40 B4
Hatley St. George 33 F3
Hatt 4 D4
Hattingley 11 H1
Hatton _Aber._ 91 J1
Hatton _Derbys._ 40 E3
Hatton _Gt.Lon._ 22 E4
Hatton _Lincs._ 52 E5
Hatton _Shrop._ 38 D6
Hatton _Warks._ 30 D2
Hatton _Warr._ 48 E4
Hatton Castle 99 F6
Hatton Heath 48 D6
Hatton of Fintray 91 G3
Hattoncrook 91 G2
Haugh Head 71 F1
Haugh of Glass 90 C1
Haugh of Urr 65 J4
Haugham 53 G4
Haughhead 74 E3
Haughley 34 E2
Haughley Green 34 E2
Haughley New Street 34 E2
Haughs 98 D6
Haughton _Notts._ 51 J5
Haughton _Shrop._ 39 F6
Haughton _Shrop._ 38 D4
Haughton _Shrop._ 38 E4
Haughton _Staffs._ 40 A3
Haughton Green 49 J3
Haughton le Skerne 62 E5
Haultwick 33 G6
Haunn 84 C3
Haunton 40 E4
Hauxley 71 H3
Hauxton 33 H3
Havant 11 J4
Haven 28 D3
Haven Side 59 K7
Havenstreet 11 G5
Haverfordwest (Hwlffordd) 16 C4
Haverhill 33 K4
Haverigg 54 E2
Havering-atte-Bower 23 J2
Haversham 32 B4
Haverthwaite 55 G1
Haverton Hill 63 F4
Hawarden 48 C6
Hawbridge 29 J4
Hawbush Green 34 B7
Hawcoat 55 F2
Hawen 26 C4
Hawes 56 D1
Hawford 29 H2
Hawick 70 A2
Hawkchurch 8 C4
Hawkedon 34 B3
Hawkenbury 14 D3
Hawkeridge 20 B6
Hawkerland 7 J7
Hawkes End 41 F7
Hawkesbury 20 A3
Hawkesbury Upton 20 A3
Hawkhill 71 H2

Hawkhurst 14 C4
Hawkinge 15 H3
Hawkley 11 J2
Hawkridge 7 G2
Hawkshead 60 E7
Hawksland 75 G7
Hawkswick 56 E2
Hawksworth _Notts._ 42 A1
Hawksworth _W.Yorks._ 57 G5
Hawkwell _Essex_ 24 E2
Hawkwell _Northumb._ 71 F6
Hawley _Hants._ 22 B6
Hawley _Kent_ 23 J4
Hawling 30 B6
Hawnby 63 G7
Haworth 57 F6
Hawstead 34 C3
Hawthorn _Dur._ 63 F2
Hawthorn _Wilts._ 20 B5
Hawthorn Hill _Brack.F._ 22 B4
Hawthorn Hill _Lincs._ 53 F7
Hawthorpe 42 D3
Hawton 51 K7
Haxby 58 C4
Haxey 51 K3
Haxted 23 H7
Hay Mills 40 D7
Hay Street 33 G6
Haydock 48 E3
Haydon 9 F3
Haydon Bridge 70 D7
Haydon Wick 20 E3
Haye 4 D4
Hayes _Gt.Lon._ 22 D3
Hayes _Gt.Lon._ 23 H5
Hayfield _Arg. & B._ 80 B5
Hayfield _Derbys._ 50 C4
Hayfield _High._ 105 G2
Hayhillock 83 G3
Haylands 11 G5
Hayle 2 C5
Haynes 32 E4
Haynes Church End 32 D4
Hay-on-Wye 28 B4
Hayscastle 16 B3
Hayscastle Cross 16 C3
Hayton _Cumb._ 61 G1
Hayton _Cumb._ 60 C2
Hayton _E.Riding_ 58 E5
Hayton _Notts._ 51 K4
Hayton's Bent 38 E7
Haytor Vale 5 H3
Haywards Heath 13 G4
Haywood Oaks 51 J7
Hazel End 33 H6
Hazel Grove 49 J4
Hazelbank _Arg. & B._ 80 B7
Hazelbank _S.Lan._ 75 G6
Hazelbury Bryan 9 G4
Hazeleigh 24 E1
Hazeley 22 A6
Hazelside 68 D1
Hazelslade 40 C4
Hazelton Walls 82 E5
Hazelwood _Derbys._ 41 F1
Hazelwood _Gt.Lon._ 23 H5
Hazlehead 65 H6
Hazlemere 22 B2
Hazlerigg 71 H6
Hazleton 30 B7
Heacham 44 A2
Head Bridge 6 E4
Headbourne Worthy 11 F1
Headcorn 14 D3
Headington 21 J1
Headlam 62 C5
Headless Cross 30 B2
Headley _Hants._ 12 B3
Headley _Hants._ 21 J5
Headley _Surr._ 23 F6
Headley Down 12 B3
Headon 51 K5
Heads Nook 61 F1
Heage 51 F7
Healaugh _N.Yorks._ 62 B7
Healaugh _N.Yorks._ 58 B5
Heald Green 49 H4
Heale _Lancs._ 49 H1
Healey _Lancs._ 49 H1
Healey _N.Yorks._ 57 G1
Healey _Northumb._ 62 B1
Healeyfield 62 B2
Healing 53 F1
Heamoor 2 B5
Heanish 78 B3
Heanor 41 G1
Heanton Punchardon 6 D2
Heanton Satchville 6 D4
Heapey 56 B7
Heapham 52 B4
Hearthstone 51 F7
Heasley Mill 7 F2
Heast 86 C3
Heath 51 G6
Heath & Reach 32 C6
Heath End _Hants._ 21 J5
Heath End _Surr._ 22 B7
Heath Hayes 40 C4
Heath Hill 39 G4
Heath House 19 H7
Heath Town 40 B6
Heathcot 91 G4
Heathcote _Derbys._ 50 D6
Heathcote _Shrop._ 39 F3
Heather 41 F4
Heathfield _Devon_ 5 J3
Heathfield _E.Suss._ 13 J4
Heathfield _Som._ 7 K3
Heathrow Airport 22 D4
Heathton 40 A6
Heatley 49 G4
Heaton _Lancs._ 55 H3
Heaton _Staffs._ 49 J6
Heaton _T. & W._ 71 H7
Heaton Moor 49 H3
Heaverham 23 J6
Heaviley 49 J4
Hebburn 71 J7
Hebden 57 F3
Hebden Bridge 56 E7
Hebden Green 49 F6
Hebing End 33 G6
Hebron _Carmar._ 16 E3
Hebron _Northumb._ 71 G5
Heck 69 F5
Heckfield 22 A5

Heckfield Green 35 F1
Heckfordbridge 34 D6
Heckingham 45 H6
Heckington 42 E1
Heckmondwike 57 H7
Heddington 20 C5
Heddle 107 C6
Heddon-on-the-Wall 71 G7
Hedenham 45 H6
Hedge End 11 F3
Hedgerley 22 C3
Hedging 8 B2
Hedley on the Hill 62 B1
Hednesford 40 C4
Hedon 59 H7
Hedsor 22 C3
Heeley 51 F4
Heglibister 109 C7
Heighington *Darl.* 62 D4
Heighington *Lincs.* 52 D6
Heights of Brae 96 C5
Heilam 103 G2
Heithat 69 G5
Heiton 77 F7
Hele *Devon* 6 D1
Hele *Devon* 7 H5
Hele Bridge 6 D5
Hele Lane 7 F4
Helebridge 6 A5
Helensburgh 74 A2
Helford 2 E6
Helhoughton 44 C3
Helions Bumpstead 33 K4
Helland 4 A3
Hellandbridge 4 A3
Hellesdon 45 F4
Hellidon 31 G3
Hellifield 56 D4
Hellingly 13 J5
Hellington 45 H5
Hellister 109 C8
Helmdon 31 G4
Helmingham 35 F3
Helmsdale 105 F7
Helmshore 56 C7
Helmsley 58 C1
Helperby 57 K2
Helperthorpe 59 F2
Helpringham 42 E1
Helpston 42 E5
Helsby 48 D5
Helston 2 D6
Helstone 4 A2
Helton 61 G4
Helwith Bridge 56 D3
Hemblington 45 H4
Hemborough Post 5 J5
Hemel Hempstead 22 D1
Hemingbrough 58 C6
Hemingby 53 F5
Hemingford Abbots 33 F1
Hemingford Grey 33 F1
Hemingstone 35 F3
Hemington *Leics.* 41 G3
Hemington *Northants.* 42 D7
Hemington *Som.* 20 A6
Hemley 35 G4
Hemlington 63 F5
Hempholme 59 G5
Hempnall 45 G6
Hempnall Green 45 G6
Hempriggs 97 J5
Hempriggs House 105 J4
Hempstead *Essex* 33 K5
Hempstead *Norf.* 45 J3
Hempstead *Norf.* 45 F2
Hempsted 29 H7
Hempton *Norf.* 44 D3
Hempton *Oxon.* 31 F5
Hemsby 45 J4
Hemswell 52 C3
Hemsworth 51 G1
Hemyock 7 K4
Henbury *Bristol* 19 J4
Henbury *Ches.* 49 H5
Henderland 65 J3
Hendersyde Park 77 F7
Hendon *Gt.Lon.* 23 F3
Hendon *T. & W.* 62 E1
Hendy 17 J5
Heneglwys 46 C5
Henfield 13 F5
Henford 6 B6
Henghurst 14 E4
Hengoed *Caerp.* 18 E2
Hengoed *Powys* 28 B3
Hengoed *Shrop.* 38 B2
Hengrave 34 C2
Henham 33 J6
Heniarth 38 A5
Henlade 8 B2
Henley *Shrop.* 28 E1
Henley *Som.* 8 D1
Henley *Suff.* 35 F3
Henley *W.Suss.* 12 B4
Henley Corner 8 D1
Henley Park 22 C6
Henley-in-Arden 30 C2
Henley-on-Thames 22 A3
Henley's Down 14 C6
Henllan *Carmar.* 17 G2
Henllan *Denb.* 47 J6
Henllan Amgoed 16 E3
Henllys 19 F2
Henlow 32 E5
Hennock 7 G7
Henny Street 34 C5
Henryd 47 F5
Henry's Moat 16 D3
Hensall 58 B7
Henshaw 70 C7
Hensingham 60 A5
Henstead 45 J7
Hensting 11 F2
Henstridge 9 G3
Henstridge Ash 9 G2
Henstridge Marsh 9 G2
Henton *Oxon.* 22 A1
Henton *Som.* 19 H7
Henwick 29 H3
Henwood 4 C3
Heogan 109 D8
Heol Senni 27 J6
Heol-ddu 17 J4
Heol-y-Cyw 18 C3
Hepburn 71 F1
Hepple 70 E3
Hepscott 71 H5
Heptonstall 56 E7
Hepworth *Suff.* 34 D1
Hepworth *W.Yorks.* 50 D2
Herbrandston 16 B5
Herdicott 6 B6
Hereford 28 E4
Heriot 76 B5
Hermiston 75 K3
Hermitage *D. & G.* 65 J4
Hermitage *Dorset* 9 F4
Hermitage *Sc.Bord.* 70 A4
Hermitage *W.Berks.* 21 J4
Hermitage *W.Suss.* 11 J4
Hermon *Carmar.* 17 G2
Hermon *I.o.A.* 46 B6
Hermon *Pembs.* 17 F2
Herne 25 H5
Herne Bay 25 H5
Herne Common 25 H5
Herner 6 D3
Hernhill 25 G5
Herodsfoot 4 C4
Herongate 24 C2
Heron's Ghyll 13 H4
Heronsgate 22 D2
Herriard 21 K7
Herringfleet 45 J6
Herring's Green 32 D4
Herringswell 34 B2
Herrington 62 E1
Hersden 25 H5
Hersham *Cornw.* 6 A5
Hersham *Surr.* 22 E5
Herstmonceux 13 K5
Herston *Dorset* 10 B7
Herston *Ork.* 107 D8
Hertford 33 G7
Hertford Heath 33 G7
Hertingfordbury 33 G7
Hesket Newmarket 60 E3
Hesketh Bank 55 H7
Hesketh Lane 56 B5
Heskin Green 48 E1
Hesleden 63 F3
Hesleyside 70 D5
Heslington 58 C4
Hessay 58 B4
Hessenford 4 D5
Hessett 34 D2
Hessle 59 G7
Hest Bank 55 H3
Heston 22 E4
Heswall 48 B4
Hethe 31 G6
Hetherington 70 D6
Hethersett 45 F5
Hethersgill 69 K7
Hethpool 70 D1
Hett 62 D3
Hetton 56 E4
Hetton-le-Hole 62 E2
Heugh 71 F6
Heugh-head *Aber.* 90 B3
Heugh-head *Aber.* 90 D5
Heveningham 35 H1
Hever 23 H7
Heversham 55 H1
Hevingham 45 F3
Hewas Water 3 G4
Hewell Grange 30 B2
Hewell Lane 30 B2
Hewelsfield 19 J1
Hewelsfield Common 19 J1
Hewish *N.Som.* 19 G5
Hewish *Som.* 8 D4
Hewton 6 D6
Hexham 70 E7
Hextable 23 J4
Hexton 32 E5
Hexworthy 5 G3
Heybridge *Essex* 24 C2
Heybridge *Essex* 24 E1
Heybridge Basin 24 E1
Heybrook Bay 5 F6
Heydon *Cambs.* 33 H4
Heydon *Norf.* 45 F3
Heydour 42 D2
Heylipoll 78 A3
Heylor 108 B4
Heysham 55 H3
Heyshaw 57 G3
Heyshott 12 B5
Heyside 49 J2
Heytesbury 20 C7
Heythrop 30 E6
Heywood *Gt.Man.* 49 H1
Heywood *Wilts.* 20 B6
Hibaldstow 52 C2
Hickleton 51 G2
Hickling *Norf.* 45 J3
Hickling *Notts.* 41 J3
Hickling Green 45 J3
Hickling Heath 45 J3
Hickstead 13 F4
Hidcote Boyce 30 C4
High Ackworth 51 G1
High Balantyre 80 B6
High Beach 23 H2
High Bentham 56 B3
High Bickington 6 D3
High Birkwith 56 D2
High Blantyre 74 E5
High Bonnybridge 75 G3
High Borgue 65 G5
High Bradfield 50 E3
High Bray 6 E2
High Brooms 23 J7
High Bullen 6 D3
High Burton 57 H1
High Buston 71 H3
High Callerton 71 G6
High Catton 58 D4
High Cogges 21 G1
High Coniscliffe 62 D5
High Cross *Hants.* 11 J2
High Cross *Herts.* 33 G7
High Cross Bank 40 E4
High Easter 33 K7
High Ellington 57 G1
High Entercommon 62 E6
High Ercall 38 E4
High Etherley 62 C4
High Garrett 34 B6
High Gate 56 E7
High Grange 62 C3
High Green *Norf.* 45 F5
High Green *S.Yorks.* 51 F3
High Green *Worcs.* 29 H4
High Halden 14 D4
High Halstow 24 D4
High Ham 8 D1
High Harrington 60 B4
High Harrogate 57 J4
High Hatton 39 F3
High Hawsker 63 J2
High Heath 39 F3
High Hesket 61 F2
High Hoyland 50 E2
High Hunsley 59 F6
High Hurstwood 13 H4
High Hutton 58 D3
High Ireby 60 D3
High Kilburn 58 B1
High Lane *Derbys.* 41 G1
High Lane *Worcs.* 29 F2
High Laver 23 J1
High Legh 49 G4
High Leven 63 F5
High Littleton 19 K6
High Lorton 60 C4
High Melton 51 H2
High Newton 55 H1
High Newton by-the-Sea 71 H1
High Nibthwaite 60 D7
High Offley 39 G3
High Ongar 23 J1
High Onn 40 A4
High Risby 52 C1
High Roding 33 K7
High Salvington 12 E6
High Shaw 61 K7
High Spen 71 G7
High Street *Cornw.* 3 G3
High Street *Kent* 14 C4
High Street *Suff.* 35 J3
High Street Green 34 E3
High Toynton 53 F6
High Trewhitt 71 F3
High Wollaston 19 J2
High Wray 60 E7
High Wych 33 H7
High Wycombe 22 B2
Higham *Derbys.* 51 F7
Higham *Kent* 24 D4
Higham *Lancs.* 56 D6
Higham *Suff.* 34 B2
Higham *Suff.* 34 E5
Higham Dykes 71 G6
Higham Ferrers 32 C2
Higham Gobion 32 E5
Higham on the Hill 41 F6
Higham Wood 23 K7
Highampton 6 C5
Highbridge 19 G7
Highbrook 13 G3
Highburton 50 D1
Highbury 19 K7
Highbury Vale 41 H1
Highclere 21 H5
Highcliffe 10 D5
Higher Ansty 9 G4
Higher Ashton 7 G7
Higher Ballam 55 G6
Higher Blackley 49 H2
Higher Brixham 5 K5
Higher Cheriton 7 J5
Higher Gabwell 5 K4
Higher Green 49 G3
Higher Kingcombe 8 E5
Higher Tale 7 J5
Higher Thrushgill 56 B3
Higher Town 2 C1
Higher Walreddon 4 E3
Higher Walton *Lancs.* 55 J7
Higher Walton *Warr.* 48 E4
Higher Whatcombe 9 H4
Higher Whitley 49 F4
Higher Wych 38 D1
Highfield *E.Riding* 58 D6
Highfield *N.Ayr.* 74 B5
Highfield *T. & W.* 62 C1
Highfields 33 G3
Highgreen Manor 70 D4
Highlane *Ches.* 49 H6
Highlane *Derbys.* 51 G4
Highlaws 60 C2
Highleadon 29 G6
Highleigh 12 B7
Highley 39 G7
Highmead 17 J1
Highmoor Cross 21 K3
Highmoor Hill 19 H3
Highnam 29 G7
Highstead 25 J5
Highsted 25 F5
Highstreet Green 34 B5
Hightae 69 F6
Hightown *Ches.* 49 H6
Hightown *Mersey.* 48 B2
Highway 20 D4
Highweek 5 J3
Highworth 21 F2
Hilborough 44 C5
Hilcott 20 E6
Hilden Park 23 J7
Hildenborough 23 J7
Hildersham 33 J4
Hilderstone 40 B2
Hilderthorpe 59 H3
Hilfield 9 F4
Hilgay 44 A6
Hill 19 K2
Hill Brow 11 J2
Hill Chorlton 39 G2
Hill Dyke 43 G1
Hill End *Dur.* 62 B3
Hill End *Fife* 75 J1
Hill End *N.Yorks.* 57 F4
Hill Head 11 G4
Hill of Beath 75 K1
Hill of Fearn 97 F4
Hill Ridware 40 C4
Hill Top *Hants.* 11 F4
Hill Top *W.Yorks.* 51 F1
Hill View 9 J5
Hillam 58 B7
Hillbeck 61 J5
Hillberry 54 C5
Hillborough 25 J5
Hillbrae *Aber.* 98 E6
Hillbrae *Aber.* 91 F2
Hillbrae *Aber.* 91 G1
Hillend *Aber.* 98 C6
Hillend *Fife* 75 K2
Hillend *Midloth.* 76 A4
Hillesden 31 H6
Hillesley 20 A3
Hillfarrance 7 K3
Hillhead 5 K5
Hillhead of Auchentumb 99 H5
Hillhead of Cocklaw 99 J6
Hilliard's Cross 40 D4
Hilliclay 105 G2
Hillingdon 22 D3
Hillington 44 B3
Hillmorton 31 G1
Hillockhead *Aber.* 90 B4
Hillockhead *Aber.* 90 C3
Hillowton 65 H4
Hillpound 11 G3
Hills Town 51 G6
Hillsford Bridge 7 F1
Hillside *Aber.* 91 H5
Hillside *Angus* 83 J1
Hillside *Moray* 97 J5
Hillside *Shet.* 109 D6
Hillswick 108 B5
Hillway 11 H6
Hillwell 109 F9
Hilmarton 20 D4
Hilperton 20 B6
Hilsea 11 H4
Hilton *Cambs.* 33 F2
Hilton *Cumb.* 61 J4
Hilton *Derbys.* 40 E2
Hilton *Dorset* 9 G4
Hilton *Dur.* 62 C4
Hilton *High.* 97 G3
Hilton *Shrop.* 39 G6
Hilton *Stock.* 63 F5
Hilton Croft 91 H1
Hilton of Cadboll 97 F4
Hilton of Delnies 97 F6
Himbleton 29 J3
Himley 40 A6
Hincaster 55 J1
Hinckley 41 G6
Hinderclay 34 E1
Hinderwell 63 J5
Hindford 38 C2
Hindhead 12 B3
Hindley 49 F2
Hindley Green 49 F2
Hindlip 29 H3
Hindolveston 44 E3
Hindon 9 J1
Hindringham 44 D2
Hingham 44 E5
Hinstock 39 F3
Hintlesham 34 E4
Hinton *Hants.* 10 D5
Hinton *Here.* 28 C5
Hinton *Northants.* 31 G3
Hinton *S.Glos.* 20 A4
Hinton *Shrop.* 38 D5
Hinton Admiral 10 D5
Hinton Ampner 11 G2
Hinton Blewett 19 J6
Hinton Charterhouse 20 A6
Hinton Martell 10 B4
Hinton on the Green 30 B4
Hinton Parva 21 F3
Hinton St. George 8 D3
Hinton St. Mary 9 G3
Hinton Waldrist 21 G2
Hinton-in-the-Hedges 31 G5
Hints *Shrop.* 29 F1
Hints *Staffs.* 40 D5
Hinwick 32 C2
Hinxhill 15 F3
Hinxton 33 H4
Hinxworth 33 F4
Hipperholme 57 G7
Hirn 91 F4
Hirnant 37 K3
Hirst 71 H5
Hirst Courtney 58 C7
Hirwaen 47 K6
Hirwaun 18 C1
Hiscott 6 D3
Histon 33 H2
Hitcham *Bucks.* 22 C3
Hitcham *Suff.* 34 D3
Hitchin 32 E6
Hither Green 23 G4
Hittisleigh 7 F6
Hixon 40 C3
Hoaden 25 J5
Hoaldalbert 28 C6
Hoar Cross 40 D3
Hoarwithy 28 E6
Hoath 25 H5
Hobarris 28 C1
Hobbister 107 C7
Hobbs Lots Bridge 43 G5
Hobkirk 70 A2
Hobland Hall 45 K5
Hobson 62 C1
Hoby 41 J4
Hockering 44 E4
Hockerton 51 K7
Hockley 24 E2
Hockley Heath 30 C1
Hockliffe 32 C6
Hockwold cum Wilton 44 B7
Hockworthy 7 J4
Hoddesdon 23 G1
Hoddlesden 56 C7
Hodgeston 16 D6
Hodnet 39 F3
Hodthorpe 51 H5
Hoe 44 D4
Hoe Gate 11 H3
Hoff 61 H5
Hoffleet Stow 43 F2
Hoggeston 32 B6
Hoggie 98 D4
Hogha Gearraidh 92 C4
Hoghton 56 B7
Hognaston 50 E7
Hogsthorpe 53 J5
Holbeach 43 G3
Holbeach Bank 43 G3
Holbeach Clough 43 G3
Holbeach Drove 43 G4
Holbeach Hurn 43 G3
Holbeach St. Johns 43 G4
Holbeach St. Marks 43 G2
Holbeach St. Matthew 43 H2
Holbeck 51 H5
Holberrow Green 30 B3
Holbeton 5 G5
Holborough 24 D5
Holbrook *Derbys.* 41 F1
Holbrook *Suff.* 35 F5
Holburn 77 J7
Holbury 11 F4
Holcombe *Devon* 5 K3
Holcombe *Som.* 19 K7
Holcombe Rogus 7 J4
Holcot 31 J2
Holden 56 C5
Holdenby 31 H2
Holdenhurst 10 C5
Holdgate 38 E7
Holdingham 42 D1
Holditch 8 C4
Hole Park 14 D4
Hole Street 12 E5
Hole-in-the-Wall 29 F6
Holford 7 K1
Holker 55 G2
Holkham 44 C1
Hollacombe *Devon* 6 B5
Hollacombe *Devon* 6 E4
Holland *Ork.* 106 D2
Holland *Ork.* 106 F5
Holland *Surr.* 23 H6
Holland-on-Sea 35 F7
Hollandstoun 106 G2
Hollee 69 H7
Hollesley 35 H4
Hollingbourne 14 D2
Hollingbury 13 G6
Hollington *Derbys.* 40 E2
Hollington *E.Suss.* 14 C6
Hollington *Staffs.* 40 C2
Hollingworth 50 C3
Hollins 49 H2
Hollins Green 49 F3
Hollinsclough 50 C6
Hollinswood 39 G5
Hollinwood 38 E2
Holloway 51 F7
Hollowell 31 H1
Holly End 43 J5
Holly Green 29 H4
Hollybush *Caerp.* 18 E1
Hollybush *E.Ayr.* 67 H2
Hollybush *Worcs.* 29 G5
Hollym 59 K7
Holm 69 H4
Holm of Drumlanrig 68 D4
Holmbury St. Mary 22 E7
Holmbush *Cornw.* 4 A5
Holmbush *W.Suss.* 13 F3
Holme *Cambs.* 42 E7
Holme *Cumb.* 55 J2
Holme *Notts.* 52 B7
Holme *W.Yorks.* 50 D2
Holme Chapel 56 D7
Holme Hale 44 C5
Holme Lacy 28 E5
Holme Marsh 28 C3
Holme next the Sea 44 B1
Holme on the Wolds 59 F5
Holme Pierrepont 41 J2
Holmebridge 9 H6
Holme-on-Spalding-Moor 58 E6
Holmer 28 E4
Holmer Green 22 C2
Holmes Chapel 49 G6
Holme's Hill 13 J5
Holmesfield 51 F5
Holmeswood 48 D1
Holmewood 51 G6
Holmfield 57 F7
Holmfirth 50 D2
Holmhead *D. & G.* 68 C5
Holmhead *E.Ayr.* 67 K1
Holmpton 59 K7
Holmrook 60 B6
Holmsgarth 109 D8
Holmside 62 D2
Holmston 67 H1
Holmwrangle 61 G2
Holne 5 H4
Holnest 9 F4
Holsworthy 6 B5
Holsworthy Beacon 6 B5
Holt *Dorset* 10 B4
Holt *Norf.* 44 E2
Holt *Wilts.* 20 B5
Holt *Worcs.* 29 H2
Holt *Wrex.* 48 D7
Holt End *Hants.* 11 H1
Holt End *Worcs.* 30 B2
Holt Fleet 29 H2
Holt Heath *Dorset* 10 B4
Holt Heath *Worcs.* 29 H2
Holtby 58 C4
Holton *Oxon.* 21 K1
Holton *Som.* 9 F2
Holton *Suff.* 35 H1
Holton cum Beckering 52 E4
Holton Heath 9 J5
Holton le Clay 53 F2
Holton le Moor 52 D3
Holton St. Mary 34 E5
Holtspur 22 C2
Holtye Common 13 H3
Holwell *Dorset* 9 G3
Holwell *Herts.* 32 E5
Holwell *Leics.* 42 A3
Holwell *Oxon.* 21 F1
Holwell *Som.* 20 A7
Holwick 62 A4
Holworth 9 G6
Holy Cross 29 J1
Holy Island 77 K6
Holybourne 22 A7
Holyhead (Caergybi) 46 A4
Holymoorside 51 F6
Holyport 22 B4
Holystone 70 E3
Holytown 75 F4
Holywell *Cambs.* 33 G1
Holywell *Cornw.* 2 E3
Holywell *Dorset* 8 E4
Holywell *E.Suss.* 13 J7
Holywell (Treffynnon) *Flints.* 47 K5
Holywell Green 50 C1
Holywell Lake 7 K3
Holywell Row 34 B1
Holywood 68 E5
Hom Green 28 E6
Homer 39 F5
Homersfield 45 G7
Homington 10 C2
Honey Hill 25 H5
Honey Tye 34 D5
Honeyborough 16 C5
Honeybourne 30 C4
Honeychurch 6 E5
Honiley 30 D1
Honing 45 H3
Honingham 45 F4
Honington *Lincs.* 42 C1
Honington *Suff.* 34 D1
Honington *Warks.* 30 D4
Honiton 7 K5
Honley 50 D1
Hoo *Med.* 24 D4
Hoo *Suff.* 35 G3
Hooe *E.Suss.* 13 K6
Hooe *Plym.* 5 F5
Hooe Common 13 K5
Hook *E.Riding* 58 D7
Hook *Gt.Lon.* 22 E5
Hook *Hants.* 22 A6
Hook *Pembs.* 16 C4
Hook *Wilts.* 20 D3
Hook Green *Kent* 13 K3
Hook Green *Kent* 24 C5
Hook Green *Kent* 24 C4
Hook Norton 30 E5
Hook-a-Gate 38 D5
Hooke 8 E4
Hookgate 39 G2
Hookway 7 G6
Hookwood 23 F7
Hoole 48 D6
Hooley 23 F6
Hooton 48 C5
Hooton Levitt 51 H3
Hooton Pagnell 51 G2
Hooton Roberts 51 G3
Hopcrofts Holt 31 F6
Hope *Derbys.* 50 D4
Hope *Devon* 5 G7
Hope *Flints.* 48 C7
Hope *Powys* 38 B5
Hope *Shrop.* 38 C5
Hope Bagot 28 E1
Hope Bowdler 38 D6
Hope End Green 33 J7
Hope Mansell 29 F7
Hope under Dinmore 28 E3
Hopehouse 69 H2
Hopeman 97 J5
Hope's Green 24 D3
Hopesay 38 C7
Hopkinstown 18 D2
Hopton *Derbys.* 50 E7
Hopton *Norf.* 45 K5
Hopton *Shrop.* 38 E3
Hopton *Staffs.* 40 B3
Hopton *Suff.* 34 D1
Hopton Cangeford 38 E7
Hopton Castle 28 C1
Hopton Wafers 29 F1
Hoptonheath 28 C1
Hopwas 40 D5
Hopwood 30 B1
Horam 13 J5
Horbling 42 E2
Horbury 50 E1
Horden 63 F2
Horderley 38 D7
Hordle 10 D5
Hordley 38 C2
Horeb *Carmar.* 17 H5
Horeb *Cere.* 17 G1
Horfield 19 J4
Horham 35 G1
Horkesley Heath 34 D6
Horkstow 52 C1
Horley *Oxon.* 31 F4
Horley *Surr.* 23 F7
Horn Hill 22 D2
Hornblotton Green 8 E1
Hornby *Lancs.* 55 J3
Hornby *N.Yorks.* 62 D7
Hornby *N.Yorks.* 62 E6
Horncastle 53 F6
Hornchurch 23 J3
Horncliffe 77 H5
Horndean *Hants.* 11 J3
Horndean *Sc.Bord.* 77 G6
Horndon 6 D7
Horndon on the Hill 24 C3
Horne 23 G7
Horniehaugh 83 F1
Horning 45 H4
Horninghold 42 B6
Horninglow 40 E3
Horningsea 33 H2
Horningsham 20 B7
Horningtoft 44 D3
Horningtops 4 C4
Horns Cross *Devon* 6 B3
Horns Cross *E.Suss.* 14 D5
Hornsby 61 G2
Hornsby Gate 61 G1
Hornsea 59 J5
Hornsey 23 G3
Hornton 30 E4
Horrabridge 5 F4
Horridge 5 H3
Horringer 34 C2
Horse Bridge 49 J7
Horsebridge *Devon* 4 E3
Horsebridge *Hants.* 10 E1
Horsebrook 40 A4
Horsehay 39 F5
Horseheath 33 K4
Horsehouse 57 F1
Horsell 22 C6
Horseman's Green 38 D1
Horseway 43 H7
Horsey 45 J3
Horsford 45 F4
Horsforth 57 H6
Horsham *W.Suss.* 12 E3
Horsham *Worcs.* 29 G3
Horsham St. Faith 45 G4
Horsington *Lincs.* 52 E6
Horsington *Som.* 9 F2
Horsley *Derbys.* 41 F1
Horsley *Glos.* 20 B2
Horsley *Northumb.* 71 F7
Horsley *Northumb.* 70 D4
Horsley Cross 35 F6
Horsley Woodhouse 41 F1
Horsleycross Street 35 F6
Horsmonden 14 C3
Horspath 21 J1
Horstead 45 G4
Horsted Keynes 13 G4
Horton *Bucks.* 32 C7
Horton *Dorset* 10 B4
Horton *Lancs.* 56 D4
Horton *Northants.* 32 B3
Horton *S.Glos.* 20 A3
Horton *Som.* 8 C3
Horton *Staffs.* 49 J7
Horton *Swan.* 17 H7
Horton *W. & M.* 22 D4
Horton *Wilts.* 20 D5
Horton Cross 8 C3
Horton Grange 71 G6
Horton Green 38 D1
Horton Heath 11 F3
Horton in Ribblesdale 56 D2
Horton Inn 10 B4
Horton Kirby 23 J5
Horton-cum-Studley 31 G7
Horwich 49 F1
Horwich End 50 C4
Horwood 6 D3
Hose 42 A3
Hoses 60 D7
Hosh 81 K5
Hosta 92 C4
Hoswick 109 D10
Hotham 58 E6
Hothfield 14 E3
Hoton 41 H3
Houbie 108 F3
Hough 49 G7
Hough Green 48 D4
Hougham 42 B1
Hough-on-the-Hill 42 C1
Houghton *Cambs.* 33 F1
Houghton *Cumb.* 61 F1
Houghton *Devon* 5 G6
Houghton *Hants.* 10 E1
Houghton *Pembs.* 16 C5
Houghton *W.Suss.* 12 D5
Houghton Bank 62 D4
Houghton Conquest 32 D4
Houghton le Spring 62 E2
Houghton on the Hill 41 J5
Houghton Regis 32 D6
Houghton St. Giles 44 D2
Houghton-le-Side 62 D4
Houlsyke 63 J6
Hound 11 F4
Hound Green 22 A6
Houndslow 76 E6
Houndwood 77 G4
Hounsdown 10 E3
Hounslow 22 E4
Hounslow Green 33 K7
Househill 97 F6
Housetter 108 C4
Houston 74 C4
Houstry 105 G5
Houstry of Dunn 105 H3
Houton 107 C7
Hove 13 F6
Hoveringham 41 J1
Hoveton 45 H4
Hovingham 58 C2
How 61 G1
How Caple 29 F5
How End 32 D4
How Man 60 A5
Howden 58 D7
Howden-le-Wear 62 C3
Howe *Cumb.* 55 H1
Howe *High.* 105 J2
Howe *N.Yorks.* 57 J1
Howe *Norf.* 45 G5
Howe Green 24 D1
Howe of Teuchar 99 F6
Howe Street *Essex* 33 K7
Howe Street *Essex* 33 K5
Howell 42 E1
Howey 27 K3
Howgate 76 A5
Howgill 57 F4
Howick 71 H2
Howle 39 F3
Howlett End 33 J5
Howley 8 B4
Hownam 70 C2
Hownam Mains 70 C1
Howpasley 69 J3
Howsham *N.Lincs.* 52 D2
Howsham *N.Yorks.* 58 D3
Howtel 77 G7
Howton 28 D6
Howwood 74 C4
Hoxa 107 D8
Hoxne 35 F1
Hoy 105 H2
Hoylake 48 B4
Hoyland 51 F2
Hoyland Swaine 50 E2
Hubberholme 56 E2
Hubbert's Bridge 43 F1
Huby *N.Yorks.* 58 B3
Huby *N.Yorks.* 57 H5
Hucclecote 29 H7
Hucking 14 D2
Hucknall 41 H1
Huddersfield 50 D1
Huddington 29 J3
Hudscott 6 E3
Hudswell 62 C6
Huggate 58 E4
Hugglescote 41 G4
Hugh Town 2 C1
Hughenden Valley 22 B2
Hughley 38 E6
Hugmore 48 C7
Huish *Devon* 6 D4
Huish *Wilts.* 20 E5
Huish Champflower 7 J3
Huish Episcopi 8 D2
Huisinis 100 B6
Hulcott 32 B7
Hull 59 H7
Hulland 40 E1
Hullavington 20 B3
Hullbridge 24 E2
Hulme End 50 D7
Hulme Walfield 49 H6
Hulver Street 45 J7
Humber 28 E3
Humberside International Airport 52 E2
Humberston 53 G2
Humberstone 41 J5
Humbie 76 C4
Humbleton *E.Riding* 59 J6
Humbleton *Northumb.* 70 E1
Humby 42 D2
Hume 77 F6
Humehall 77 F6
Humshaugh 70 E6
Huna 105 J1
Huncoat 56 C6
Huncote 41 H6
Hundalee 70 B2
Hunderthwaite 62 A4
Hundleby 53 G6
Hundleton 16 C5
Hundon 34 B4
Hundred Acres 11 G3
Hundred End 55 H7
Hundred House 28 A3
Hungarton 41 J5
Hungerford *Hants.* 10 C3
Hungerford *W.Berks.* 21 G5
Hungerford Newtown 21 G4
Hunglader 93 J4
Hunmanby 59 H2
Hunningham 30 E2
Hunny Hill 11 F6
Hunsdon 33 H7
Hunsingore 57 K4
Hunsonby 61 G3
Hunspow 105 H1
Hunstanton 44 A1
Hunstanworth 62 A2
Hunston *Suff.* 34 D2
Hunston *W.Suss.* 12 B6
Hunstrete 19 K5
Hunt End 30 B2

Place	Pg	Ref
Hunt House	63	K7
Huntercombe End	21	K3
Hunters Forstal	25	H5
Hunter's Inn	6	E1
Hunter's Quay	73	K3
Hunterston	73	K5
Huntford	70	B3
Huntingdon	33	F1
Huntingfield	35	H1
Huntingford	9	H1
Huntington *Here.*	28	B3
Huntington *Staffs.*	40	B4
Huntington *York*	58	C4
Huntingtower	82	B5
Huntley	29	G7
Huntly	98	D6
Huntlywood	76	E6
Hunton *Hants.*	11	F1
Hunton *Kent*	14	C3
Hunton *N.Yorks.*	62	C7
Hunton Bridge	22	D1
Hunt's Cross	48	D4
Huntsham	7	J3
Huntshaw Cross	6	D3
Huntspill	19	G7
Huntworth	8	C1
Hunwick	62	C3
Hunworth	44	E2
Hurdsfield	49	J5
Hurley *W. & M.*	22	B3
Hurley *Warks.*	40	E6
Hurley Bottom	22	B3
Hurlford	74	C7
Hurliness	107	B9
Hurn	10	C5
Hursley	11	F2
Hurst *Gt.Man.*	49	J2
Hurst *N.Yorks.*	62	B6
Hurst *W'ham*	22	A4
Hurst Green *E.Suss.*	14	C5
Hurst Green *Lancs.*	56	B6
Hurst Green *Surr.*	23	G6
Hurstbourne Priors	21	H7
Hurstbourne Tarrant	21	G6
Hurstpierpoint	13	F5
Hurstway Common	28	B4
Hurstwood	56	D6
Hurtmore	22	C7
Hurworth-on-Tees	62	E5
Hury	62	A4
Husabost	93	H6
Husbands Bosworth	41	J7
Husborne Crawley	32	C5
Husthwaite	58	B2
Huthwaite	51	G7
Huttoft	53	J5
Hutton *Cumb.*	61	F4
Hutton *Essex*	24	C2
Hutton *Lancs.*	55	H7
Hutton *N.Som.*	19	G6
Hutton *Sc.Bord.*	77	H5
Hutton Bonville	62	E6
Hutton Buscel	59	F1
Hutton Conyers	57	J2
Hutton Cranswick	59	G4
Hutton End	61	F3
Hutton Henry	63	F3
Hutton Magna	62	C5
Hutton Roof *Cumb.*	55	J2
Hutton Roof *Cumb.*	60	E3
Hutton Rudby	63	F6
Hutton Sessay	57	K2
Hutton Wandesley	58	B4
Hutton-le-Hole	63	J7
Huxley	48	E6
Huxter *Shet.*	109	C7
Huxter *Shet.*	109	E6
Huyton	48	D3
Hwlffordd (Haverfordwest)	16	C4
Hycemoor	54	D1
Hyde *Gt.Man.*	49	J3
Hyde Heath	22	C1
Hyde Lea	40	B4
Hydestile	22	C7
Hyndford Bridge	75	H6
Hyndlee	70	A3
Hynish	78	A4
Hyssington	38	C6
Hythe *Hants.*	11	F4
Hythe *Kent*	15	G4
Hythe End	22	D4
Hythie	99	J5
Hyton	54	D1

I

Place	Pg	Ref
Ianstown	98	C4
Ibberton	9	G4
Ible	50	E7
Ibsley	10	C4
Ibstock	41	G4
Ibstone	22	A2
Ibthorpe	21	G6
Ibworth	21	J6
Icelton	19	G5
Ickburgh	44	C6
Ickenham	22	D3
Ickford	21	K1
Ickham	15	H2
Icklesham	14	D6
Ickleton	33	H1
Icklingham	34	B1
Ickwell Green	32	E4
Icomb	30	D6
Idbury	30	D6
Iddesleigh	6	D5
Ide	7	H6
Ide Hill	23	H6
Ideford	5	J3
Iden	14	E5
Iden Green *Kent*	14	C4
Iden Green *Kent*	14	D4
Idlicote	30	D4
Idmiston	10	C1
Idridgehay	40	E1
Idrigil	93	J5
Idvies	83	G3
Iffley	21	J1
Ifield or Singlewell *Kent*	24	C4
Ifield *W.Suss.*	13	F3
Ifieldwood	13	F3
Ifold	12	D3
Iford	13	H6
Ifton Heath	38	C2
Ightfield	38	E2
Ightham	23	J6
Iken	35	J3
Ilam	50	D7
Ilchester	8	E2
Ilderton	71	F1
Ilford	23	H3
Ilfracombe	6	D1
Ilkeston	41	G1
Ilketshall St. Andrew	45	H7
Ilketshall St. Lawrence	45	H7
Ilketshall St. Margaret	45	H7
Ilkley	57	G5
Illey	40	B7
Illington	44	D7
Illingworth	57	F7
Illogan	2	D4
Illston on the Hill	42	A6
Ilmer	22	A1
Ilmington	30	D4
Ilminster	8	C3
Ilsington	5	H3
Ilston	17	J6
Ilton *N.Yorks.*	57	G2
Ilton *Som.*	8	C3
Imachar	73	G6
Immeroin	81	G6
Immingham	52	E1
Immingham Dock	52	F1
Impington	33	H2
Ince	48	D5
Ince Blundell	48	C2
Ince-in-Makerfield	48	E2
Inch of Arnhall	90	E7
Inchbare	83	H1
Inchberry	98	B5
Inchbraoch	83	J2
Inchgrundle	90	D7
Inchindown	96	D4
Inchinnan	74	C4
Inchkinloch	103	J4
Inchlaggan	87	H4
Inchlumpie	96	C4
Inchmarlo	90	E5
Inchnabobart	90	B6
Inchnacardoch Hotel	87	K3
Inchnadamph	102	E6
Inchock	83	H3
Inchrory	89	J4
Inchture	82	D5
Inchvuilt	87	J1
Inchyra	82	C6
Indian Queens	3	G3
Inerval	72	B6
Ingatestone	24	C1
Ingbirchworth	50	E2
Ingerthorpe	57	H3
Ingestre	40	B3
Ingham *Lincs.*	52	C4
Ingham *Norf.*	45	H3
Ingham *Suff.*	34	C1
Ingleby *Derbys.*	41	F3
Ingleby *Lincs.*	52	B5
Ingleby Arncliffe	63	F6
Ingleby Barwick	63	F5
Ingleby Cross	63	F6
Ingleby Greenhow	63	G6
Inglesbatch	19	K5
Inglesham	21	F2
Ingleton *Dur.*	62	C4
Ingleton *N.Yorks.*	56	B2
Inglewhite	55	J5
Ingmire Hall	61	H7
Ingoe	71	F6
Ingoldisthorpe	44	A2
Ingoldmells	53	J6
Ingoldsby	42	D2
Ingon	30	D3
Ingram	71	F2
Ingrave	24	C2
Ingrow	57	F6
Ings	61	F7
Ingst	19	J3
Ingworth	45	F3
Inistrynich	80	C5
Injebreck	54	C5
Inkberrow	30	B3
Inkhorn	91	H1
Inkpen	21	G5
Inkstack	105	H1
Innellan	73	K4
Innergellie	83	G7
Innerleithen	76	B7
Innerleven	82	E7
Innermessan	64	A4
Innerwick *E.Loth.*	77	F3
Innerwick *P. & K.*	81	G3
Inninbeg	79	J3
Innsworth	29	H6
Insch	90	E2
Insh	89	F4
Inshore	103	F2
Inskip	55	H6
Instow	6	C2
Intake	51	F4
Intwood	45	F5
Inver *Aber.*	89	K5
Inver *Arg. & B.*	80	A3
Inver *High.*	97	F3
Inver *High.*	105	G5
Inver Mallie	87	H6
Inverailort	86	D6
Inverallan	89	G2
Inverallochy	99	J4
Inveran	96	C2
Inveraray	80	B7
Inverardoch Mains	81	J7
Inverardran	80	E5
Inverarish	86	B1
Inverarity	83	F3
Inverarnan	80	E6
Inverasdale	94	E3
Inverbain	94	D6
Inverbeg	74	B1
Inverbervie	91	G7
Inverbroom	95	H3
Inverbrough	89	F2
Invercassley	96	B1
Inverchaolain	73	J3
Invercharnan	80	C3
Inverchoran	95	J6
Invercreran	80	B3
Inverdruie	89	G3
Inverebrie	91	H1
Invereen	89	F1
Inveresk	76	B3
Inverey	89	H6
Inverfarigaig	88	C2
Invergarry	87	K4
Invergelder	89	K5
Invergeldie	81	J5
Invergloy	87	J6
Invergordon	96	E5
Invergowrie	82	E4
Inverguseran	86	D4
Inverhadden	81	H2
Inverharroch	90	B1
Inverherive	80	E5
Inverhope	103	G2
Inverie	86	D4
Inverinan	80	A6
Inverinate	87	F2
Inverkeilor	83	H3
Inverkeithing	75	K2
Inverkeithny	98	E6
Inverkip	73	K3
Inverkirkaig	102	C7
Inverlael	95	H3
Inverlauren	74	B2
Inverliever	79	K7
Inverliver	80	B4
Inverlochlarig	81	F6
Inverlochy	80	C5
Inverlussa	72	E2
Invermay	82	B6
Invermoriston	88	B3
Invernaver	104	C2
Inverneil	73	G2
Inverness	96	D7
Inverness Airport	96	E6
Invernettie	99	K6
Invernoaden	73	K1
Inveroran Hotel	80	D3
Inverquharity	83	F2
Inverquhomery	99	J6
Inverroy	87	J6
Inversanda	80	A2
Invershiel	87	F3
Invershin	96	C2
Inversnaid Hotel	80	E7
Invertrossachs	81	G7
Inverugie	99	K6
Inveruglas	80	E7
Inveruglass	89	F4
Inverurie	91	F2
Invervar	81	H3
Invervegain	73	J3
Invery House	90	E5
Inverythan	99	F6
Inwardleigh	6	D6
Inworth	34	C7
Iochdar	92	C7
Iping	12	B4
Ipplepen	5	J4
Ipsden	21	K3
Ipstones	50	C7
Ipswich	35	F4
Irby	48	B4
Irby in the Marsh	53	H6
Irby upon Humber	52	E2
Irchester	32	C2
Ireby *Cumb.*	60	D3
Ireby *Lancs.*	56	B2
Ireland *Ork.*	107	C7
Ireland *Shet.*	109	C10
Ireleth	55	F2
Ireshopeburn	61	K3
Irlam	49	G3
Irnham	42	D3
Iron Acton	19	K3
Iron Cross	30	B3
Ironbridge	39	F5
Ironside	99	G5
Ironville	51	G7
Irstead	45	H3
Irthington	69	K7
Irthlingborough	32	C1
Irton	59	G1
Irvine	74	B7
Isauld	104	E2
Isbister *Ork.*	107	C6
Isbister *Ork.*	106	B5
Isbister *Shet.*	109	E6
Isbister *Shet.*	108	C3
Isfield	13	H5
Isham	32	B1
Ishriff	79	H4
Islay Airport	72	B5
Islay House	72	B4
Isle Abbotts	8	C2
Isle Brewers	8	C2
Isle of Man Airport	54	B7
Isle of Whithorn	64	B7
Isleham	33	K1
Isleornsay (Eilean Iarmain)	86	C3
Islesburgh	109	C6
Isleworth	22	E4
Isley Walton	41	G3
Islibhig	100	B5
Islip *Northants.*	32	C1
Islip *Oxon.*	31	G7
Isombridge	39	F4
Istead Rise	24	C5
Itchen	11	F3
Itchen Abbas	11	G1
Itchen Stoke	11	G1
Itchingfield	12	E4
Itchington	19	K3
Itteringham	45	F2
Itton	6	E6
Itton Common	19	H2
Ivegill	61	F2
Ivelet	62	A7
Iver	22	D3
Iver Heath	22	D3
Iveston	62	C1
Ivinghoe	32	C7
Ivinghoe Aston	32	C7
Ivington	28	D3
Ivington Green	28	D3
Ivy Hatch	23	J6
Ivy Todd	44	C5
Ivybridge	5	G5
Ivychurch	15	F5
Iwade	25	F5
Iwerne Courtney (Shroton)	9	H3
Iwerne Minster	9	H3
Ixworth	34	D1
Ixworth Thorpe	34	D1

J

Place	Pg	Ref
Jack Hill	57	G4
Jackstown	91	F1
Jackton	74	D5
Jacobstow	4	B1
Jacobstowe	6	D5
Jameston	16	D6
Jamestown *D. & G.*	69	J4
Jamestown *High.*	96	B6
Jamestown *W.Dun.*	74	B2
Janefield	96	E6
Janetstown	105	F2
Jarrow	71	J7
Jarvis Brook	13	J4
Jasper's Green	34	B6
Jawcraig	75	G3
Jayes Park	22	E7
Jaywick	35	F7
Jedburgh	70	B1
Jeffreyston	16	D5
Jemimaville	96	E5
Jersay	75	G4
Jersey Airport	3	J5
Jerviswood	75	G6
Jesmond	71	H7
Jevington	13	J6
Jodrell Bank	49	G5
John o' Groats	105	J1
Johnby	61	F3
John's Cross	14	C5
Johnshaven	83	J1
Johnston	16	C4
Johnston Mains	83	J1
Johnstone	74	C4
Johnstone Castle	74	C4
Johnstonebridge	69	F4
Johnstown *Carmar.*	17	G4
Johnstown *Wrex.*	38	C1
Joppa *Edin.*	76	B3
Joppa *S.Ayr.*	67	J2
Jordans	22	C2
Jordanston	16	C2
Jordanstone	82	D3
Jump	51	F2
Juniper Green	75	K4
Jura House	72	C4
Jurby East	54	C4
Jurby West	54	C4

K

Place	Pg	Ref
Kaber	61	J5
Kaimes	76	A4
Kames *Arg. & B.*	73	H3
Kames *Arg. & B.*	79	K6
Kames *E.Ayr.*	68	B1
Kea	3	F4
Keadby	52	B1
Keal Cotes	53	G6
Kearsley	49	G2
Kearstwick	56	B2
Kearton	62	B7
Kearvaig	102	E1
Keasden	56	C3
Kebholes	98	E5
Keckwick	48	E4
Keddington	53	G4
Kedington	34	B4
Kedleston	41	F1
Keelby	52	E2
Keele	40	A1
Keeley Green	32	D4
Keeres Green	33	J7
Keeston	16	C4
Keevil	20	C6
Kegworth	41	G3
Kehelland	2	D4
Keig	90	E3
Keighley	57	F5
Keil *Arg. & B.*	66	A3
Keil *High.*	80	A2
Keilhill	99	F5
Keillmore	72	E2
Keillor	82	D3
Keillour	82	A5
Keills	72	D4
Keils	72	D4
Keinton Mandeville	8	E1
Keir House	75	F1
Keir Mill	68	D4
Keisby	42	D3
Keisley	61	J4
Keiss	105	J2
Keith	98	C5
Keithick	82	D4
Keithmore	90	B1
Keithock	83	H1
Kelbrook	56	E5
Kelby	42	D1
Keld *Cumb.*	61	H5
Keld *N.Yorks.*	61	K6
Keldholme	58	D1
Keldy Castle	63	J7
Kelfield *E.Riding*	58	B2
Kelfield *N.Lincs.*	52	B2
Kelham	51	K7
Kellacott	6	C7
Kellan	79	G3
Kellas *Angus*	83	F4
Kellas *Moray*	97	J6
Kellaton	5	J7
Kelleth	61	H6
Kellethorpe	59	G4
Kelling	44	E1
Kellington	58	B7
Kelloe	62	E3
Kelloholm	68	C3
Kelly *Cornw.*	4	A3
Kelly *Devon*	6	B7
Kelly Bray	4	D3
Kelmarsh	31	J1
Kelmscott	21	F2
Kelsale	35	H2
Kelsall	48	E6
Kelsay	72	A2
Kelshall	33	G5
Kelsick	60	C1
Kelso	77	F7
Kelstedge	51	F6
Kelstern	53	F3
Kelston	19	K5
Keltneyburn	81	J3
Kelton	65	K3
Kelton Hill or Rhonehouse	65	H5
Kelty	75	K1
Kelvedon	34	C7
Kelvedon Hatch	23	J2
Kelynack	2	A5
Kemback	83	F6
Kemberton	39	G5
Kemble	20	C2
Kemerton	29	J5
Kemeys Commander	19	G1
Kemeys Inferior	19	G2
Kemnay	91	F3
Kemp Town	13	G6
Kempley	29	F6
Kempley Green	29	F6
Kempsey	29	H4
Kempsford	20	E2
Kempshott	21	K7
Kempston	32	D4
Kempston Church End	32	D4
Kempston Hardwick	32	D4
Kempton	38	C7
Kemsing	23	J6
Kemsley	25	F5
Kenardington	14	E4
Kenchester	28	D4
Kencott	21	F1
Kendal	61	G7
Kenderchurch	28	D6
Kenfig	18	B3
Kenfig Hill	18	B3
Kenilworth	30	D1
Kenknock *P. & K.*	81	G3
Kenknock *Stir.*	81	F4
Kenley *Gt.Lon.*	23	G6
Kenley *Shrop.*	38	E5
Kenmore *Arg. & B.*	80	B7
Kenmore *High.*	94	D6
Kenmore *P. & K.*	81	J3
Kenmore *W.Isles*	100	E7
Kenn *Devon*	7	H7
Kenn *N.Som.*	19	H5
Kennacraig	73	G4
Kennards House	4	C2
Kennavay	93	H2
Kennerleigh	7	G5
Kennerty	90	E5
Kennet	75	H1
Kennethmont	90	D2
Kennett	33	K2
Kennford	7	H7
Kenninghall	44	E7
Kennington *Kent*	15	F3
Kennington *Oxon.*	21	J1
Kennoway	82	E7
Kennyhill	33	K1
Kennythorpe	58	D3
Kensaleyre	93	K6
Kensington	23	F3
Kensworth	32	D7
Kensworth Common	32	D7
Kent Street *E.Suss.*	14	C6
Kent Street *Kent*	23	K6
Kentchurch	28	D6
Kentford	34	B2
Kentisbeare	7	J5
Kentisbury	6	E1
Kentisbury Ford	6	E1
Kentmere	61	F6
Kenton *Devon*	7	H7
Kenton *Suff.*	35	F2
Kenton *T. & W.*	71	H7
Kentra	79	H1
Kents Bank	55	H2
Kent's Green	29	G6
Kent's Oak	10	E2
Kenwick	38	D2
Kenwyn	3	F4
Kenyon	49	F3
Keoldale	103	F2
Keppanach	80	B1
Keppoch *Arg. & B.*	74	B3
Keppoch *High.*	86	E2
Keprigan	66	A2
Kepwick	63	F7
Keresley	41	F7
Kerne Bridge	28	E7
Kerridge	49	J5
Kerris	2	B6
Kerry	38	A7
Kerrycroy	73	K4
Kerry's Gate	28	C5
Kerrysdale	94	E4
Kersall	51	K6
Kersey	34	E4
Kershopefoot	69	K5
Kerswell	7	J5
Kerswell Green	29	H4
Kesgrave	35	G4
Kessingland	45	K7
Kessingland Beach	45	K7
Kestle Mill	3	F3
Keston	23	H5
Keswick *Cumb.*	60	D4
Keswick *Norf.*	45	G5
Keswick *Norf.*	45	H2
Ketsby	53	G5
Kettering	32	B1
Ketteringham	45	F5
Kettins	82	D4
Kettlebaston	34	D4
Kettlebridge	82	E7
Kettlebrook	40	E5
Kettleburgh	35	G3
Kettleholm	69	G6
Kettleness	63	K5
Kettleshulme	49	J5
Kettlesing	57	H4
Kettlesing Bottom	57	H4
Kettlestone	44	D2
Kettlethorpe	52	B5
Kettletoft	106	F4
Kettlewell	56	E2
Ketton	42	C5
Kew	22	E4
Kewstoke	19	G5
Kexbrough	51	F2
Kexby *Lincs.*	52	B4
Kexby *York*	58	D4
Key Green	49	H6
Keyham	41	J5
Keyhaven	10	E5
Keyingham	59	J7
Keymer	13	G5
Keynsham	19	K5
Key's Toft	53	H7
Keysoe	32	D2
Keysoe Row	32	D2
Keyston	32	D1
Keyworth	41	J2
Kibblesworth	62	D1
Kibworth Beauchamp	41	J6
Kibworth Harcourt	41	J6
Kidbrooke	23	H4
Kiddal Lane End	57	J6
Kiddemore Green	40	A5
Kidderminster	29	H1
Kiddington	31	F6
Kidlington	31	F7
Kidmore End	21	K4
Kidsdale	64	E7
Kidsgrove	49	H7
Kidstones	56	E1
Kidwelly (Cydweli)	17	H5
Kiel Crofts	80	A4
Kielder	70	B4
Kilbarchan	74	C4
Kilbeg	86	C4
Kilberry	73	F4
Kilbirnie	74	B5
Kilblaan	80	C6
Kilbraur	104	D7
Kilbrennan	79	F3
Kilbride *Arg. & B.*	79	K5
Kilbride *Arg. & B.*	73	J3
Kilbride *High.*	86	B2
Kilbride Farm	73	H4
Kilbridemore	73	J1
Kilburn *Derbys.*	41	F1
Kilburn *N.Yorks.*	58	B2
Kilby	41	J6
Kilchattan	73	K5
Kilchenzie	66	A1
Kilcheran	79	K4
Kilchiaran	72	A5
Kilchoan *Arg. & B.*	79	J6
Kilchoan *High.*	79	F1
Kilchoman	72	A4
Kilchrenan	80	B5
Kilchrist	66	A2
Kilconquhar	83	F7
Kilcot	29	F6
Kilcoy	96	C6
Kilcreggan	74	A2
Kildale	63	H6
Kildary	96	E4
Kildavie	66	B2
Kildermorie Lodge	96	C4
Kildonan	66	E1
Kildonan Lodge	104	E6
Kildonnan	85	K6
Kildrochet House	64	A5
Kildrummy	90	C3
Kildwick	57	F5
Kilfinan	73	H3
Kilfinnan	87	J5
Kilgetty	16	E5
Kilgwrrwg Common	19	H2
Kilham *E.Riding*	59	G3
Kilham *Northumb.*	77	G7
Kilkenneth	78	A3
Kilkenny	30	B7
Kilkerran *Arg. & B.*	66	B2
Kilkerran *S.Ayr.*	67	H3
Kilkhampton	6	A4
Killamarsh	51	G4
Killay	17	K6
Killbeg	79	H3
Killean *Arg. & B.*	72	E6
Killean *Arg. & B.*	80	B7
Killearn	74	D2
Killellan	66	A2
Killen	96	D6
Killerby	62	C4
Killichonan	81	G2
Killiechanate	87	J6
Killiechronan	79	G3
Killiecrankie	82	A1
Killiehuntly	88	E5
Killiemor	79	F4
Killilan	87	F1
Killimster	105	J3
Killin *High.*	97	F1
Killin *Stir.*	81	G4
Killinallan	72	B3
Killinghall	57	H4
Killington	56	B1
Killingworth	71	H6
Killochyett	76	C6
Killocraw	66	A1
Killunaig	79	F5
Killundine	79	G3
Kilmacolm	74	B4
Kilmaha	80	A7
Kilmahog	81	H7
Kilmalieu	79	K2
Kilmaluag	93	K4
Kilmany	82	E5
Kilmarie	86	B3
Kilmarnock	74	C7
Kilmartin	73	G1
Kilmaurs	74	C6
Kilmelford	79	K6
Kilmersdon	19	K6
Kilmeston	11	G2
Kilmichael	66	A1
Kilmichael Glassary	73	G1
Kilmichael of Inverlussa	73	F2
Kilmington *Devon*	8	B5
Kilmington *Wilts.*	9	G1
Kilmington Street	9	G1
Kilmorack	96	B7
Kilmore *Arg. & B.*	79	K5
Kilmore *High.*	86	C4
Kilmory *Arg. & B.*	73	F3
Kilmory *High.*	85	J4
Kilmote	104	E7
Kilmuir *High.*	93	J4
Kilmuir *High.*	96	D7
Kilmuir *High.*	96	E4
Kilmuir *High.*	93	J4
Kilmun	73	K2
Kilmux	82	E7
Kiln Green	22	B4
Kiln Pit Hill	62	B1
Kilnave	72	A3
Kilncadzow	75	G6
Kilndown	14	C4
Kilnhurst	51	G3
Kilninian	79	F3
Kilninver	79	K5
Kilnsea	53	H1
Kilnsey	56	E3
Kilnwick	59	G5
Kiloran	72	B1
Kilpatrick	66	D1
Kilpeck	28	D5
Kilphedir	104	E7
Kilpin	58	D7
Kilrenny	83	G7
Kilsby	31	G1
Kilspindie	82	D5
Kilstay	64	B7
Kilsyth	75	F3
Kiltarlity	96	C7
Kilton *R. & C.*	63	H5
Kilton *Som.*	7	K1
Kiltyrie	81	H4
Kilvaxter	93	J5
Kilve	7	K1
Kilverstone	44	C7
Kilvington	42	B1
Kilwinning	74	B6
Kimberley *Norf.*	44	E5
Kimberley *Notts.*	41	H1
Kimble Wick	22	B1
Kimblesworth	62	D2
Kimbolton *Cambs.*	32	E2
Kimbolton *Here.*	28	E2
Kimcote	41	H7
Kimmeridge	9	J7
Kimmerston	77	H7
Kimpton *Hants.*	21	F7
Kimpton *Herts.*	32	E7
Kinaldy	83	G7
Kinblethmont	83	H3
Kinbrace	104	D5
Kinbreack	87	G5
Kinbuck	81	J7
Kincaldrum	83	F3
Kincaple	83	F6
Kincardine *Fife*	75	H2
Kincardine O'Neil	90	D5
Kinclaven	82	C4
Kincorth	91	H4
Kincraig *Aber.*	91	H2
Kincraig *High.*	89	F4
Kincraigie	82	A3
Kindallachan	82	A2
Kindrogan Field Centre	82	B1
Kinellar	91	G3
Kineton *Glos.*	30	B6
Kineton *Warks.*	30	E3
Kineton Green	40	D7
Kinfauns	82	C5
King Sterndale	50	C5
Kingarth	73	J5
Kingcoed	19	H1
Kingerby	52	D3
Kingham	30	D6
Kingholm Quay	65	K3
Kinghorn	76	A2
Kinglassie	76	A1
Kingoodie	82	E5
King's Bromley	40	D4
Kings Caple	28	E6
King's Cliffe	42	D6
King's Coughton	30	B3
King's Green	29	G5
King's Heath	40	C7
Kings Hill *Kent*	23	K6
King's Hill *W.Mid.*	40	B6
Kings Langley	22	D1
King's Lynn	44	A3
Kings Meaburn	61	H4
King's Mills	3	H5
King's Muir	76	A7
King's Newton	41	F3
King's Norton *Leics.*	41	J5
King's Norton *W.Mid.*	30	B1
King's Nympton	6	E4
King's Pyon	28	D3
Kings Ripton	33	F1
King's Somborne	10	E1
King's Stag	9	G3
King's Stanley	20	B1
King's Sutton	31	F5
King's Walden	32	E6
Kings Worthy	11	F1
Kingsand	4	E5
Kingsbarns	83	G6
Kingsbridge *Devon*	5	H6
Kingsbridge *Som.*	7	H2
Kingsburgh	93	J6
Kingsbury *Gt.Lon.*	22	E3
Kingsbury *Warks.*	40	E6
Kingsbury Episcopi	8	D2
Kingscavil	75	J3
Kingsclere	21	J6
Kingscote	20	B2
Kingscott	6	D4
Kingscross	66	E1
Kingsdale	82	E7
Kingsdon	8	E2
Kingsdown	15	J3
Kingseat	75	K1
Kingsey	22	A1
Kingsfold *Pembs.*	16	C6
Kingsfold *W.Suss.*	12	E3
Kingsford *Aber.*	99	F6
Kingsford *Aberdeen*	91	G4
Kingsford *E.Ayr.*	74	C6
Kingsford *Worcs.*	40	A7
Kingsforth	52	D1
Kingsgate	25	K4
Kingsheanton	6	D2
Kingshouse	81	G6
Kingshouse Hotel	80	D2
Kingskerswell	5	J4
Kingskettle	82	E7
Kingsland *Here.*	28	D2
Kingsland *I.o.A.*	46	A4
Kingsley *Ches.*	48	E5
Kingsley *Hants.*	11	J1
Kingsley *Staffs.*	40	C1
Kingsley Green	12	B3
Kingsmuir	83	F3
Kingsnorth	15	F4
Kingsnorth Power Station	24	E4
Kingstanding	40	C6
Kingsteignton	5	J3
Kingsteps	97	G6
Kingsthorne	28	D5
Kingsthorpe	31	J2
Kingston *Cambs.*	33	G3
Kingston *Devon*	5	G6
Kingston *Dorset*	9	G4
Kingston *Dorset*	9	J7
Kingston *E.Loth.*	76	D2
Kingston *Hants.*	10	C4
Kingston *I.o.W.*	11	F6
Kingston *Kent*	15	G2
Kingston *Moray*	98	B4
Kingston *W.Suss.*	12	D6
Kingston Bagpuize	21	H2
Kingston Blount	22	A2
Kingston by Sea	13	F6
Kingston Deverill	9	H1
Kingston Lisle	21	G3
Kingston near Lewes	13	G6
Kingston on Soar	41	H3
Kingston Russell	8	E5
Kingston St. Mary	8	B2
Kingston Seymour	19	G5
Kingston Upon Hull	59	H7
Kingston upon Thames	22	E5
Kingston Warren	21	G3
Kingstone *Here.*	28	D5
Kingstone *Som.*	8	C3
Kingstone *Staffs.*	40	C3
Kingswear	5	J5
Kingswells	91	G4
Kingswinford	40	A7
Kingswood *Bucks.*	31	H7
Kingswood *Glos.*	20	A2
Kingswood *Here.*	28	B3
Kingswood *Kent*	14	D2
Kingswood *Powys*	38	B5
Kingswood *S.Glos.*	19	K4
Kingswood *Surr.*	23	F6
Kingswood *Warks.*	30	C1
Kingthorpe	52	E5
Kington *Here.*	28	B3
Kington *Worcs.*	29	J3
Kington Langley	20	C4
Kington Magna	9	G2
Kington St. Michael	20	B4
Kingussie	88	E4

Kingweston 8 E1
Kinharrachie 91 H1
Kinharvie 65 K4
Kinkell 74 E3
Kinkell Bridge 82 A6
Kinknockie 99 J6
Kinlet 39 G7
Kinloch *Fife* 82 D6
Kinloch *High.* 103 F5
Kinloch *High.* 79 H2
Kinloch *High.* 85 K5
Kinloch *High.* 80 D6
Kinloch *P. & K.* 82 D3
Kinloch *P. & K.* 82 C3
Kinloch Hourn 87 F4
Kinloch Laggan 88 C6
Kinloch Rannoch 81 H2
Kinlochan 79 K1
Kinlochard 81 F7
Kinlocharkaig 87 F5
Kinlochbeoraid 86 E6
Kinlochbervie 102 E3
Kinlocheil 87 F7
Kinlochetive 80 C3
Kinlochewe 95 G5
Kinlochlaich 80 A3
Kinlochleven 80 C1
Kinlochmoidart 86 D7
Kinlochmorar 86 E5
Kinlochmore 80 C1
Kinlochspelve 79 H5
Kinloss 97 H5
Kinmel Bay
 (Bae Cinmel) 47 H4
Kinmuck 91 G3
Kinnadie 99 H6
Kinnaird 82 D5
Kinneff 91 G7
Kinnelhead 69 F3
Kinnell *Angus* 83 H2
Kinnell *Stir.* 81 G4
Kinnerley 38 C3
Kinnersley *Here.* 28 C4
Kinnersley *Worcs.* 29 H4
Kinnerton 28 B2
Kinnesswood 82 C7
Kinnettles 83 F3
Kinninvie 62 B4
Kinnordy 82 E2
Kinoulton 41 J2
Kinrara 89 F4
Kinross 82 C7
Kinrossie 82 C4
Kinsbourne Green 32 E7
Kinsham 28 C2
Kinsley 51 G1
Kinson 10 B5
Kintarvie 100 E6
Kintbury 21 G5
Kintessack 97 G5
Kintillo 82 C6
Kintocher 90 D4
Kinton *Here.* 28 D1
Kinton *Shrop.* 38 C4
Kintore 91 F3
Kintour 72 C5
Kintra *Arg. & B.* 72 B6
Kintra *Arg. & B.* 78 E5
Kintradwell 97 G1
Kintraw 79 K7
Kinuachdrachd 73 F1
Kinveachy 89 G3
Kinver 40 A7
Kiplaw Croft 91 J1
Kiplin 62 D7
Kiplingcotes 59 F5
Kipp 81 G6
Kippax 57 K6
Kippen *P. & K.* 82 B6
Kippen *Stir.* 74 E1
Kippenross House 81 J7
Kippford or Scaur 65 J5
Kipping's Cross 23 K7
Kirbister *Ork.* 107 C7
Kirbister *Ork.* 106 F5
Kirbuster 106 B5
Kirby Bedon 45 G5
Kirby Cane 45 H6
Kirby Corner 30 D1
Kirby Cross 35 G7
Kirby Grindalythe 59 F3
Kirby Hill *N.Yorks.* 62 C6
Kirby Hill *N.Yorks.* 57 J3
Kirby Knowle 57 K1
Kirby le Soken 35 G6
Kirby Misperton 58 D2
Kirby Muxloe 41 H5
Kirby Row 45 H6
Kirby Sigston 57 F7
Kirby Underdale 58 E4
Kirby Wiske 57 J1
Kirdford 12 D4
Kirk 105 H3
Kirk Bramwith 51 J1
Kirk Deighton 57 J4
Kirk Ella 59 G7
Kirk Hallam 41 G1
Kirk Hammerton 57 K4
Kirk Ireton 50 E7
Kirk Langley 40 E2
Kirk Merrington 62 D3
Kirk Michael 54 C4
Kirk of Shotts 75 G4
Kirk Sandall 51 J2
Kirk Smeaton 51 H1
Kirk Yetholm 70 D1
Kirkabister 109 D9
Kirkandrews 65 G6
Kirkandrews-
 upon-Eden 60 E1
Kirkbampton 60 E1
Kirkbean 65 K5
Kirkbride 60 D1
Kirkbridge 62 D7
Kirkbuddo 83 G3
Kirkburn *E.Riding* 59 F4
Kirkburn *Sc.Bord.* 76 A7
Kirkburton 50 D1
Kirkby *Lincs.* 52 D3
Kirkby *Mersey.* 48 D3
Kirkby *N.Yorks.* 63 G6
Kirkby Bellars 42 A4
Kirkby Fleetham 62 D7
Kirkby Green 42 D7
Kirkby in Ashfield 51 G7
Kirkby la Thorpe 42 D1
Kirkby Lonsdale 56 B2
Kirkby Malham 56 D3
Kirkby Mallory 41 G5
Kirkby Malzeard 57 H2
Kirkby Mills 58 D1
Kirkby on Bain 53 F6
Kirkby Overblow 57 J5
Kirkby Stephen 61 J6
Kirkby Thore 61 H4
Kirkby Underwood 42 D3

Kirkby Wharfe 58 B5
Kirkbymoorside 58 C1
Kirkcaldy 76 A1
Kirkcambeck 70 A7
Kirkcolm 64 A4
Kirkconnel 68 C2
Kirkconnell 65 K4
Kirkcowan 64 D4
Kirkcudbright 65 G5
Kirkdale House 65 F5
Kirkdean 75 K6
Kirkfieldbank 75 G6
Kirkgunzeon 65 J4
Kirkham *Lancs.* 55 H6
Kirkham *N.Yorks.* 58 D3
Kirkhamgate 57 H7
Kirkharle 71 F5
Kirkhaugh 61 H2
Kirkheaton
 Northumb. 71 F6
Kirkheaton
 W.Yorks. 50 D1
Kirkhill *Angus* 83 H1
Kirkhill *High.* 96 C7
Kirkhill *Moray* 98 B5
Kirkhope 69 J1
Kirkibost *High.* 86 B3
Kirkibost *W.Isles* 100 D4
Kirkinch 82 E3
Kirkinner 64 E5
Kirkintilloch 74 E3
Kirkland *Cumb.* 61 H3
Kirkland *Cumb.* 60 B5
Kirkland *D. & G.* 68 D4
Kirkland *D. & G.* 68 C2
Kirkland *D. & G.* 69 F5
Kirkland of
 Longcastle 64 D6
Kirkleatham 63 G4
Kirklevington 63 F5
Kirkley 45 K6
Kirklington
 N.Yorks. 57 J1
Kirklington *Notts.* 51 J7
Kirklinton 69 K7
Kirkliston 75 K3
Kirkmaiden 64 B7
Kirkmichael *P. & K.* 82 B1
Kirkmichael *S.Ayr.* 67 H3
Kirkmuirhill 75 F6
Kirknewton
 Northumb. 70 E1
Kirknewton
 W.Loth. 75 K4
Kirkney 90 D1
Kirkoswald *Cumb.* 61 G2
Kirkoswald *S.Ayr.* 67 G3
Kirkpatrick Durham 65 H3
Kirkpatrick-Fleming 69 H6
Kirksanton 54 E1
Kirkstall 57 H6
Kirkstead 52 E6
Kirkstile *Aber.* 90 D1
Kirkstile *D. & G.* 69 J4
Kirkton *Aber.* 90 E2
Kirkton *Aber.* 98 E5
Kirkton *Aber.* 90 E3
Kirkton *Angus* 83 F3
Kirkton *Arg. & B.* 79 J7
Kirkton *D. & G.* 68 E5
Kirkton *Fife* 82 E5
Kirkton *High.* 88 D1
Kirkton *High.* 96 E2
Kirkton *High.* 104 D2
Kirkton *High.* 86 E2
Kirkton *P. & K.* 82 A6
Kirkton *Sc.Bord.* 70 A2
Kirkton Manor 76 A7
Kirkton of Airlie 82 E2
Kirkton of
 Auchterhouse 82 E4
Kirkton of Barevan 97 F7
Kirkton of Bourtie 91 G2
Kirkton of Collace 82 C4
Kirkton of Craig 83 J2
Kirkton of
 Culsalmond 90 E1
Kirkton of Durris 91 F5
Kirkton of
 Glenbuchat 90 B3
Kirkton of Glenisla 82 D1
Kirkton of
 Kingoldrum 82 E2
Kirkton of
 Lethendy 82 C3
Kirkton of Logie
 Buchan 91 H2
Kirkton of
 Maryculter 91 G5
Kirkton of Menmuir 83 G1
Kirkton of Monikie 83 G4
Kirkton of Rayne 90 E1
Kirkton of Skene 91 G4
Kirkton of
 Strathmartine 82 E4
Kirkton of Tealing 83 F4
Kirktonhill 83 H1
Kirktown 99 J5
Kirktown of Alvah 98 E4
Kirktown of
 Auchterless 99 F6
Kirktown of
 Deskford 98 D4
Kirktown of
 Fetteresso 91 G6
Kirktown of Slains 91 J2
Kirkwall 107 D6
Kirkwall Airport 107 D7
Kirkwhelpington 70 E5
Kirmington 52 E1
Kirmond le Mire 52 E3
Kirn 73 K3
Kirriemuir 82 E2
Kirstead Green 45 G6
Kirtlebridge 69 H6
Kirtling 33 K3
Kirtling Green 33 K3
Kirtlington 31 F7
Kirtomy 104 C2
Kirton *Lincs.* 43 G2
Kirton *Notts.* 51 J6
Kirton *Suff.* 35 G5
Kirton End 43 F1
Kirton Holme 43 F1
Kirton in Lindsey 52 C3
Kiscadale 66 E1
Kislingbury 31 H3
Kismeldon Bridge 6 B4
Kites Hardwick 31 F2
Kitley 5 F5
Kittisford 7 J3
Kitwood 11 H1
Kiveton Park 51 G4
Klibreck 103 H5
Knabbygates 98 D5
Knaith 52 B4
Knap Corner 9 H2

Knaphill 22 C6
Knapp *P. & K.* 82 D4
Knapp *Som.* 8 B2
Knapton *Norf.* 45 H2
Knapton *York* 58 B4
Knapton Green 28 D3
Knapwell 33 G2
Knaresborough 57 J4
Knarsdale 61 H1
Knaven 99 G6
Knayton 57 K1
Knebworth 33 F7
Knedlington 58 D7
Kneesall 51 K6
Kneesworth 33 G4
Kneeton 42 A1
Knelston 17 H7
Knettishall 34 D1
Knightacott 6 E2
Knightcote 31 F3
Knighton *Devon* 5 F6
Knighton *Leic.* 41 J5
Knighton *Powys* 28 B1
Knighton *Som.* 7 K1
Knighton *Staffs.* 39 G3
Knighton *Staffs.* 39 G2
Knighton *Wilts.* 21 F4
Knightwick 29 G3
Knill 28 B2
Knipoch 79 K5
Knipton 42 B2
Knitsley 62 C2
Kniveton 50 E7
Knock *Arg. & B.* 79 G4
Knock *Cumb.* 61 H4
Knock *Moray* 98 D5
Knock of
 Auchnahannet 89 H1
Knockalava 73 H1
Knockally 105 G6
Knockaloe Moar 54 B5
Knockan 102 E7
Knockandhu 89 K2
Knockando 97 J7
Knockbain 96 D6
Knockban 95 J5
Knockbreck 96 E3
Knockbrex 65 F6
Knockdamph 95 J2
Knockdee 105 G2
Knockdow 73 K3
Knockdown 20 B3
Knockenkelly 66 E1
Knockentiber 74 C7
Knockfin 87 J2
Knockgray 67 K4
Knockholt 23 H6
Knockholt Pound 23 H6
Knockin 38 C3
Knocklearn 65 H3
Knocknaha 66 A2
Knocknain 66 D7
Knocknalling 67 K5
Knockrome 72 D3
Knocksharry 54 B5
Knockville 64 D3
Knockvologan 78 E6
Knodishall 35 J2
Knolls Green 49 H5
Knolton 38 C2
Knook 20 C7
Knossington 42 B5
Knott End-on-Sea 55 G5
Knotting 32 D2
Knotting Green 32 D2
Knottingley 58 B7
Knotty Ash 48 D3
Knotty Green 22 C2
Knowbury 28 E1
Knowe 64 D3
Knowes of Elrick 98 E5
Knowesgate 70 E5
Knoweside 67 G2
Knowetownhead 70 A2
Knowhead 99 H5
Knowl Green 34 B4
Knowl Hill 22 B4
Knowl Wall 40 A2
Knowle *Bristol* 19 K4
Knowle *Devon* 7 F5
Knowle *Devon* 6 C2
Knowle *Devon* 7 J7
Knowle *Shrop.* 28 E1
Knowle *W.Mid.* 30 C1
Knowle Green 56 B6
Knowle Hall 19 G7
Knowlton *Dorset* 10 B3
Knowlton *Kent* 15 H2
Knowsley 48 D3
Knowstone 7 G3
Knucklas 28 B1
Knutsford 49 G5
Knypersley 49 H7
Kuggar 2 E7
Kyle of Lochalsh 86 D2
Kyleakin 86 D2
Kylerhea 86 D2
Kyles Scalpay (Caolas
 Scalpaigh) 93 H2
Kylesbeg 86 C7
Kylesknoydart 86 E5
Kylesmorar 86 E5
Kylestrome 102 E5
Kyloag 96 D2
Kynnersley 39 F4
Kyre Park 29 F2

L

Labost 100 E3
Lacasaigh 101 F5
Lacasdal
 (Laxdale) 101 G4
Laceby 53 F2
Lacey Green 22 B1
Lach Dennis 49 G5
Lackford 34 B1
Lacock 20 C5
Ladbroke 31 F3
Laddingford 23 K7
Lade Bank 53 G7
Ladock 3 F3
Lady Hall 54 E1
Ladybank 82 D6
Ladycross 6 B7
Ladyfield 80 B6
Ladykirk 77 G6
Lady's Green 34 B3
Ladysford 99 H4
Laga 79 H1
Lagalochan 79 K6
Lagavulin 72 C6
Lagg *Arg. & B.* 72 D3
Lagg *Arg. & B.* 66 D1
Lagg *S.Ayr.* 67 G3
Laggan *Arg. & B.* 72 A5
Laggan *High.* 87 J5
Laggan *High.* 88 D5

Laggan *Moray* 90 B1
Laggan *Stir.* 79 J3
Lagganulva 79 F3
Lagganvoulin 89 J3
Laglingarten 80 C7
Lagnalean 96 D7
Lagrae 68 C2
Laguna 82 C4
Laid 103 G3
Laide 94 E2
Laig 85 K6
Laight 68 B2
Lainchoil 89 H3
Laindon 24 C3
Lair 82 C1
Lairg 96 C1
Lairg Lodge 96 C1
Lairigmor 80 C1
Laithers 98 E6
Laithes 61 F3
Lake 10 C1
Lakenham 45 G5
Lakenheath 44 B7
Lakeside *Cumb.* 55 G1
Lakeside *Thur.* 23 J4
Laleham 22 D5
Laleston 18 B4
Lamancha 76 A5
Lamarsh 34 C5
Lamas 45 G3
Lamb Corner 34 E5
Lamberhurst 13 K3
Lamberhurst
 Quarter 13 K3
Lamberton 77 H5
Lambeth 23 G4
Lambfell Moar 54 B5
Lambley
 Northumb. 61 H1
Lambley *Notts.* 41 J1
Lamborough 21 G4
Lambourn 21 G4
Lambourne End 23 H2
Lambs Green 13 F3
Lambston 16 C4
Lamellion 4 C4
Lamerton 4 E3
Lamesley 62 D1
Lamington *High.* 96 E4
Lamington *S.Lan.* 75 H7
Lamlash 73 J7
Lamloch 67 K4
Lamonby 61 F3
Lamorran 3 F4
Lampert 70 B6
Lampeter 17 J1
Lampeter Velfrey 16 E4
Lamphey 16 D5
Lamplugh 60 B4
Lamport 31 J1
Lamyatt 9 F1
Lana 6 B6
Lanark 75 G6
Lancaster 55 H3
Lanchester 62 C2
Lancing 12 E6
Landbeach 33 H2
Landcross 6 C3
Landerberry 91 F4
Landewednack 2 E7
Landford 10 D3
Landimore 17 H6
Landkey 6 D2
Landore 17 K6
Landrake 4 D4
Landscove 5 H4
Landshipping 16 D4
Landulph 4 E4
Landwade 33 K2
Landywood 40 B5
Lane End *Bucks.* 22 B2
Lane End *Cumb.* 60 C7
Lane End *Derbys.* 51 G6
Lane End *Dorset* 9 H5
Lane End *Kent* 23 J4
Lane Green 40 A5
Lane Head *Dur.* 62 C5
Lane Head
 Gt.Man. 49 F3
Lane Head
 W.Yorks. 50 D2
Laneast 4 C2
Lane-end 4 A5
Laneham 52 B5
Lanehead 70 D5
Laneshawbridge 56 D5
Langais 92 D5
Langamull 78 E2
Langar 42 A2
Langbank 74 B3
Langbar 57 F4
Langcliffe 56 D3
Langdale End 63 J3
Langdon 6 B7
Langdon Beck 61 K3
Langdon Hills 24 C3
Langdon House 5 K3
Langdyke 82 E7
Langenhoe 34 E7
Langford *Beds.* 32 E4
Langford *Devon* 7 J5
Langford *Essex* 24 E1
Langford *Notts.* 52 B7
Langford *Oxon.* 21 F1
Langford Budville 7 K3
Langham *Essex* 34 E5
Langham *Norf.* 44 E1
Langham *Rut.* 42 B4
Langham *Suff.* 34 E2
Langham Moor 34 E5
Langho 56 B6
Langholm 69 J5
Langlands 65 G5
Langlee 70 E2
Langleeford 70 E2
Langley *Ches.* 49 J5
Langley *Derbys.* 41 G1
Langley *Essex* 33 H5
Langley *Hants.* 11 F4
Langley *Herts.* 33 F6
Langley *Kent* 14 D2
Langley *Slo.* 22 D4
Langley *W.Suss.* 12 B4
Langley *Warks.* 30 C2
Langley Burrell 20 C4
Langley Green 40 E2
Langley Heath 14 D2
Langley Marsh 7 J3
Langley Mill 41 G1
Langley Moor 62 D2
Langley Park 62 D2
Langley Street 45 H5
Langney 13 K6
Langold 51 H4
Langore 4 C2
Langport 8 D2
Langrick 43 F1

Langridge
 B. & N.E.Som. 20 A5
Langridge *Devon* 6 D3
Langridgeford 6 D3
Langrigg 60 C2
Langrish 11 J2
Langriville 43 F1
Langsett 50 E2
Langshaw 76 D7
Langshawburn 69 H3
Langside 81 J6
Langskaill 106 D3
Langstone 11 J4
Langthorne 62 D7
Langthorpe 57 J3
Langthwaite 62 B6
Langtoft *E.Riding* 59 G3
Langtoft *Lincs.* 42 E4
Langton *Dur.* 62 C5
Langton *Lincs.* 53 G5
Langton *Lincs.* 53 F6
Langton *N.Yorks.* 58 D3
Langton by
 Wragby 52 E5
Langton Green 13 J3
Langton Herring 9 F6
Langton Long
 Blandford 9 J4
Langton Matravers 10 B7
Langtree 6 C4
Langwathby 61 G3
Langwell 96 B1
Langwell House 105 G6
Langworth 52 D5
Lanivet 4 A4
Lanlivery 4 A5
Lanner 2 E4
Lanreath 4 B5
Lansallos 4 B5
Lansdown 20 A5
Lanteglos 4 A2
Lanton *Northumb.* 77 H7
Lanton *Sc.Bord.* 70 B1
Lapford 7 F5
Laphroaig 72 B6
Lapley 40 A4
Lapworth 30 C1
Larach na Gaibhre 73 F4
Larachbeg 79 H3
Larbert 75 G2
Larden Green 48 E7
Larg 64 D3
Largie 90 E1
Largiemore 73 H2
Largoward 83 F7
Largs 74 A5
Largue 98 E6
Largybaan 66 A2
Largybeg 66 E1
Largymore 66 E1
Lark Hall 33 J3
Larkhall 75 F5
Larkhill 20 E7
Larling 44 D7
Larriston 70 A4
Lartington 62 B5
Lary 90 B4
Lasborough 20 B2
Lasham 21 K7
Lashenden 14 D3
Lassington 29 G6
Lassodie 75 K1
Lassintullich 81 J2
Lastingham 63 J7
Latchford 49 F4
Latchingdon 24 E1
Latchley 4 E3
Lately Common 49 F3
Lathallan Mill 83 F7
Lathbury 32 B4
Latheron 105 G5
Latheronwheel 105 G5
Lathockar 83 F6
Lathones 83 F7
Lathrisk 82 D7
Latimer 22 D2
Latteridge 19 K3
Lattiford 9 F2
Latton 20 D2
Lauchentyre 65 F5
Lauchintilly 91 F3
Lauder 76 D6
Laugharne 17 G4
Laughterton 52 B5
Laughton *E.Suss.* 13 J5
Laughton *Leics.* 41 J7
Laughton *Lincs.* 42 D2
Laughton *Lincs.* 52 B3
Laughton en le
 Morthen 51 H4
Launcells 6 A5
Launcells Cross 6 A5
Launceston 6 B7
Launde Abbey 42 B5
Launton 31 H6
Laurencekirk 91 F7
Laurieston *D. & G.* 65 G4
Laurieston *Falk.* 75 H3
Lavendon 32 C3
Lavenham 34 D4
Laverhay 69 G4
Lavernock 18 E5
Laversdale 69 K7
Laverstock 10 C1
Laverstoke 21 H7
Laverton *Glos.* 30 B5
Laverton *N.Yorks.* 57 H2
Laverton *Som.* 20 A6
Lavister 48 C7
Law 75 G5
Lawers *P. & K.* 81 J5
Lawers *P. & K.* 81 H4
Lawford 34 E5
Lawhitton 6 B7
Lawkland 56 C3
Lawley 39 F5
Lawnhead 40 A3
Lawrenny 16 D5
Laws 83 F4
Lawshall 34 C3
Lawton 28 D3
Laxay 101 F5
Laxdale
 (Lacasdal) 101 G4
Laxey 54 D5
Laxfield 35 G1
Laxfirth *Shet.* 109 D7
Laxfirth *Shet.* 109 D8
Laxford Bridge 102 E4
Laxo 109 D6
Laxton *E.Riding* 58 D7
Laxton *Northants.* 42 C6
Laxton *Notts.* 51 K6
Laycock 57 F5
Layer Breton 34 D7
Layer de la Haye 34 D7
Layer Marney 34 D7
Layham 34 E4
Laytham 58 D6
Lazenby 63 G4
Lazonby 61 G3

Lazonby 61 G3
Lea *Derbys.* 51 F7
Lea *Here.* 29 F6
Lea *Lincs.* 52 B4
Lea *Shrop.* 38 C7
Lea *Shrop.* 38 D5
Lea *Wilts.* 20 C3
Lea Marston 40 E6
Lea Town 55 H6
Lea Yeat 56 C1
Leac a' Li 93 G2
Leachd 73 J1
Leachkin 96 D7
Leadburn 76 A5
Leaden Roding 33 J7
Leadenham 52 C7
Leadgate *Cumb.* 61 H2
Leadgate *Dur.* 62 C1
Leadgate *T. & W.* 62 C1
Leadhills 68 D2
Leafield 30 E7
Leagrave 32 D6
Leake Common
 Side 53 G7
Leake Hurn's End 43 H1
Lealands 13 J5
Lealholm 63 J6
Lealt *Arg. & B.* 72 E1
Lealt *High.* 94 B5
Leamington
 Hastings 31 F2
Leamington Spa 30 E2
Leanach *Arg. & B.* 73 J1
Leanach *High.* 96 E7
Leanaig 96 C6
Leanoch 97 J6
Leargybreck 72 D3
Leasgill 55 H1
Leasingham 42 D1
Leask 91 J1
Leatherhead 22 E6
Leathley 57 H5
Leaton 38 D4
Leaveland 15 F2
Leavenheath 34 D5
Leavening 58 D3
Leaves Green 23 H5
Lebberston 59 G1
Lechlade 21 F2
Leck 56 B2
Leckford 21 H7
Leckfurin 104 C3
Leckgruinart 72 A4
Leckhampstead
 Bucks. 31 J5
Leckhampstead
 W.Berks. 21 H4
Leckhampton 29 J7
Leckie *High.* 95 G5
Leckie *Stir.* 74 E1
Leckmelm 95 H2
Leckroy 87 K5
Leckuary 73 G1
Leckwith 18 E4
Leconfield 59 G5
Ledaig 80 A4
Ledard 81 F7
Ledbeg 102 E7
Ledburn 32 B6
Ledbury 29 G5
Ledcharrie 81 G5
Ledgemoor 28 D3
Ledicot 28 D2
Ledmore *Arg. & B.* 79 G3
Ledmore *High.* 102 E7
Lednagullin 104 C2
Ledsham *Ches.* 48 C5
Ledsham *W.Yorks.* 57 K7
Ledston 57 K7
Ledwell 31 F6
Lee *Arg. & B.* 79 F5
Lee *Devon* 6 C1
Lee *Hants.* 10 E3
Lee *Lancs.* 55 J4
Lee *Shrop.* 38 D2
Lee Brockhurst 38 E3
Lee Clump 22 C1
Lee Mill Bridge 5 F5
Lee Moor 5 F4
Leebotten 109 D10
Leebotwood 38 D6
Leece 55 F3
Leeds *Kent* 14 D2
Leeds *W.Yorks.* 57 H6
Leeds Bradford
 International
 Airport 57 H5
Leedstown 2 D5
Leegomery 39 F4
Leek 49 J7
Leek Wootton 30 D2
Leeming *N.Yorks.* 57 H1
Leeming *W.Yorks.* 57 F6
Leeming Bar 62 D7
Lee-on-the-Solent 11 G4
Lees *Derbys.* 40 E2
Lees *Gt.Man.* 49 J2
Leeswood 48 B7
Legars 77 F6
Legbourne 53 G4
Legerwood 76 D6
Legsby 52 E4
Leicester 41 H5
Leideag 84 B5
Leigh *Dorset* 9 F4
Leigh *Glos.* 29 H6
Leigh *Gt.Man.* 49 F2
Leigh *Kent* 23 J7
Leigh *Shrop.* 38 C5
Leigh *Surr.* 23 F7
Leigh *Wilts.* 20 D2
Leigh *Worcs.* 29 G3
Leigh Beck 24 E3
Leigh Common 9 G2
Leigh Delamere 20 B4
Leigh Green 14 E4
Leigh Sinton 29 G3
Leigh upon Mendip 19 K7
Leigh Woods 19 J4
Leigh-on-Sea 24 E3
Leighterton 20 B2
Leighton *N.Yorks.* 57 G2
Leighton *Powys* 38 B5
Leighton *Shrop.* 39 F5
Leighton *Som.* 20 A7
Leighton
 Bromswold 32 E1
Leighton Buzzard 32 C6
Leinthall Earls 28 D2
Leinthall Starkes 28 D2
Leintwardine 28 D1
Leire 41 H7
Leirinmore 103 G2
Leiston 35 J2
Leitfie 82 D3
Leith 76 A3
Leitholm 77 F6
Lelant 2 C5
Lelley 59 J6

Lem Hill 29 G1
Lemington 71 G7
Lemnas 99 G4
Lempitlaw 77 F7
Lemsford 33 F7
Lenchwick 30 B4
Lendalfoot 67 F5
Lendrick Lodge 81 G7
Lenham 14 D2
Lenham Heath 14 E3
Lenie 88 C2
Lenimore 73 G6
Lennel 77 G6
Lennox Plunton 65 G5
Lennoxtown 74 E3
Lenton 42 D2
Lenwade 45 F4
Lenzie 74 E3
Leoch 82 E4
Leochel-Cushnie 90 D3
Leominster 28 D3
Leonard Stanley 20 B1
Leorin 72 B6
Lepe 11 F5
Lephinchapel 73 H1
Lephinmore 73 H1
Leppington 58 D3
Lepton 50 E1
Lerags 79 K5
Lerryn 4 B5
Lerwick 109 D8
Lesbury 71 H2
Leschangie 91 F3
Lescrow 4 B5
Leslie *Aber.* 90 D2
Leslie *Fife* 82 D7
Lesmahagow 75 G7
Lesnewth 4 B1
Lessendrum 98 D6
Lessingham 45 H3
Lessonhall 60 D1
Leswalt 64 A4
Letchmore Heath 22 E2
Letchworth Garden
 City 33 F5
Letcombe Bassett 21 G3
Letcombe Regis 21 G3
Leth Meadhanach 84 C3
Letham *Angus* 83 G3
Letham *Fife* 82 E6
Lethanhill 67 J2
Lethenty 99 G6
Letheringham 35 G3
Letheringsett 44 E2
Lettaford 7 F7
Letter Finlay 87 J5
Letterewe 95 F4
Letterfearn 86 E2
Lettermorar 86 D6
Lettermore
 Arg. & B. 79 G3
Letters 95 H3
Lettershaws 68 D1
Letterston 16 C3
Lettoch *High.* 89 H3
Lettoch *High.* 89 H1
Letton *Here.* 28 C4
Letton *Here.* 28 C1
Letty Green 33 F7
Letwell 51 H4
Leuchars 83 F5
Leumrabhagh 101 F6
Levedale 40 A4
Leven *E.Riding* 59 H5
Leven *Fife* 82 E7
Levencorroch 66 E1
Levenhall 76 B3
Levens 55 H1
Levenshulme 49 H3
Levenwick 109 D10
Leverburgh
 (An T-òb) 93 F3
Leverington 43 H4
Leverstock Green 22 D1
Leverton Outgate 43 H1
Levington 35 G5
Levisham 63 K7
Levishie 88 B3
Lew 21 G1
Lewannick 4 C2
Lewdown 6 C7
Lewes 13 H5
Leweston 16 C3
Lewisham 23 G4
Lewiston 88 C2
Lewknor 22 A2
Leworthy 6 E2
Lewtrenchard 6 C7
Ley *Aber.* 90 D3
Ley *Cornw.* 4 B4
Ley Green 32 E6
Leybourne 23 K6
Leyburn 62 C7
Leycett 39 G1
Leyland 55 J7
Leylodge 91 F3
Leys *Aber.* 90 C4
Leys *P. & K.* 82 D4
Leys of Cossans 82 E3
Leysdown-on-Sea 25 G4
Leysmill 83 H3
Leysters 28 E2
Leyton 23 G3
Lezant 4 D3
Lhanbryde 97 K5
Liatrie 87 J1
Libanus 27 J6
Libberton 75 H6
Liceasto 93 G2
Lichfield 40 D5
Lickey 29 J1
Lickey End 29 J1
Lickfold 12 C4
Liddel 107 D9
Liddesdale 79 J2
Liddington 21 F3
Lidgate *Derbys.* 51 F5
Lidgate *Suff.* 34 B3
Lidlington 32 C5
Lidsing 24 D5
Lidstone 30 E6
Lienassie 87 F2
Lieurary 105 F2
Liff 82 E4
Lifton 6 B7
Liftondown 6 B7
Lighthorne 30 E3
Lightwater 22 C5
Lightwood 40 B1
Lightwood Green
 Ches. 39 F1
Lightwood Green
 Wrex. 38 C1
Lilbourne 31 G1
Lilburn Tower 71 F1

Lilleshall 39 G4
Lilley *Herts.* 32 E6
Lilley *W.Berks.* 21 H4
Lilliesleaf 70 A1
Lillingstone Dayrell 31 J5
Lillingstone Lovell 31 J4
Lillington 9 F3
Lilliput 10 B5
Lilstock 7 K1
Limbrick 49 F1
Limbury 32 D6
Limefield 49 H1
Limehillock 98 D5
Limekilnburn 75 F5
Limekilns 75 J2
Limerigg 75 G3
Limerstone 11 F6
Limington 8 E2
Limpenhoe 45 H5
Limpley Stoke 20 A5
Limpsfield 23 H6
Linbriggs 70 D3
Linby 51 H7
Linchmere 12 B3
Lincoln 52 C5
Lincomb 29 H2
Lincombe 5 H5
Lindal in Furness 55 F2
Lindale 55 H1
Lindean 76 C7
Lindertis 82 E2
Lindfield 13 G4
Lindford 12 B3
Lindifferon 82 E6
Lindley 50 D1
Lindores 82 D6
Lindridge 29 F2
Lindsaig 73 H3
Lindsell 33 K6
Lindsey 34 D4
Linford *Hants.* 10 C4
Linford *Thur.* 24 C4
Lingague 54 B6
Lingdale 63 H5
Lingen 28 C2
Lingfield 23 G7
Lingwood 45 H5
Linhead 98 E5
Linhope 69 K3
Linicro 93 J5
Linkenholt 21 G6
Linkhill 14 D5
Linkinhorne 4 D3
Linklater 107 D9
Linksness *Ork.* 107 B7
Linksness *Ork.* 107 E6
Linktown 76 A1
Linley 38 C6
Linley Green 29 F3
Linlithgow 75 H3
Linlithgow Bridge 75 H3
Linn of Muick Cottage 90 B6
Linnels 70 E7
Linney 16 B6
Linshiels 70 D3
Linsiadar 100 E4
Linsidemore 96 C2
Linslade 32 C6
Linstead Parva 35 H1
Linstock 61 F1
Linthwaite 50 D1
Lintlaw 77 G5
Lintmill 98 D4
Linton *Cambs.* 33 J4
Linton *Derbys.* 40 E4
Linton *Here.* 29 F6
Linton *Kent* 14 C3
Linton *N.Yorks.* 56 E3
Linton *Sc.Bord.* 70 C1
Linton *W.Yorks.* 57 J5
Linton-on-Ouse 57 K3
Lintzford 62 C1
Linwood *Hants.* 10 C4
Linwood *Lincs.* 52 E4
Linwood *Renf.* 74 C4
Lionacleit 92 C7
Lional 101 H1
Liphook 12 B3
Liscombe 7 G2
Liskeard 4 C4
L'Islet 3 J5
Liss 11 J2
Liss Forest 11 J2
Lissett 59 H4
Lissington 52 E4
Liston 34 C4
Lisvane 18 E3
Liswerry 19 G3
Litcham 44 C4
Litchborough 31 H3
Litchfield 21 H6
Litherland 48 C3
Litlington *Cambs.* 33 G4
Litlington *E.Suss.* 13 J6
Little Abington 33 J4
Little Addington 32 C1
Little Alne 30 C2
Little Amwell 33 G7
Little Assynt 102 D6
Little Aston 40 C6
Little Atherfield 11 F7
Little Ayton 63 G5
Little Baddow 24 D1
Little Badminton 20 A3
Little Ballinluig 82 A2
Little Bampton 60 D1
Little Bardfield 33 K5
Little Barford 32 E3
Little Barningham 45 F2
Little Barrington 30 D7
Little Barugh 58 D2
Little Bealings 35 G4
Little Bedwyn 21 F5
Little Bentley 35 F6
Little Berkhamsted 23 F1
Little Billing 32 B2
Little Birch 28 E5
Little Bispham 55 G5
Little Blakenham 35 F4
Little Bollington 49 G4
Little Bookham 22 E6
Little Bowden 42 A7
Little Bradley 33 K3
Little Brampton 38 C7
Little Braxted 34 C7
Little Brechin 83 G1
Little Brickhill 32 C5
Little Bridgeford 40 A3
Little Brington 31 H2
Little Bromley 34 E6
Little Broughton 60 B3
Little Budworth 48 E6
Little Burstead 24 C2
Little Burton 59 H5
Little Bytham 42 D4
Little Carlton *Lincs.* 53 H4
Little Carlton *Notts.* 51 K7
Little Casterton 42 D5
Little Catwick 59 H5
Little Cawthorpe 53 G4
Little Chalfont 22 C2
Little Chart 14 E3
Little Chesterford 33 J4
Little Cheverell 20 C6
Little Chishill 33 H5
Little Clacton 35 F7
Little Clifton 60 B4
Little Comberton 29 J4
Little Common 14 C7
Little Compton 30 D5
Little Corby 61 F1
Little Cowarne 29 F3
Little Coxwell 21 F2
Little Crakehall 62 D7
Little Creich 96 D3
Little Cressingham 44 C6
Little Crosby 48 C2
Little Cubley 40 D2
Little Dalby 42 A4
Little Dens 99 J6
Little Dewchurch 28 E5
Little Downham 43 J7
Little Driffield 59 G4
Little Dunham 44 C4
Little Dunkeld 82 B3
Little Dunmow 33 K6
Little Easton 33 K6
Little Eaton 41 F1
Little Ellingham 44 E6
Little End 23 J1
Little Eversden 33 G3
Little Fakenham 34 D1
Little Faringdon 21 F1
Little Fencote 62 D7
Little Fenton 58 B6
Little Finborough 34 E3
Little Fransham 44 C4
Little Gaddesden 32 C7
Little Garway 28 D6
Little Gidding 42 E7
Little Glemham 35 H3
Little Glenshee 82 A4
Little Gorsley 29 F6
Little Gransden 33 F3
Little Green 34 E1
Little Grimsby 53 G3
Little Gruinard 95 F3
Little Habton 58 D2
Little Hadham 33 H6
Little Hale 42 E1
Little Hallingbury 33 H7
Little Hampden 22 B1
Little Harrowden 32 B1
Little Haseley 21 K1
Little Hautbois 45 G3
Little Haven 16 B4
Little Hay 40 D5
Little Hayfield 50 C4
Little Haywood 40 C3
Little Heath 41 F7
Little Hereford 28 E2
Little Holtby 62 D7
Little Horkesley 34 D5
Little Hormead 33 H6
Little Horsted 13 H5
Little Horwood 31 J5
Little Houghton 32 B3
Little Hucklow 50 D5
Little Hulton 49 G2
Little Hungerford 21 J4
Little Idoch 99 F6
Little Kimble 22 B1
Little Kineton 30 E3
Little Kingshill 22 B2
Little Langford 10 B1
Little Laver 23 J1
Little Lawford 31 F1
Little Leigh 49 F5
Little Leighs 34 B7
Little Lever 49 G2
Little Ley 90 E3
Little Linford 32 B4
Little London *E.Suss.* 13 J5
Little London *Hants.* 21 G6
Little London *Hants.* 21 K6
Little London *I.o.M.* 54 C5
Little London *Lincs.* 43 H3
Little London *Lincs.* 43 F3
Little London *Lincs.* 53 G5
Little London *Norf.* 43 J3
Little London *Norf.* 44 B6
Little Longstone 50 D5
Little Malvern 29 G4
Little Maplestead 34 C5
Little Marcle 29 F5
Little Marlow 22 B3
Little Massingham 44 B3
Little Melton 45 F5
Little Mill 19 G1
Little Milton 21 K1
Little Missenden 22 C2
Little Musgrave 61 J5
Little Ness 38 D4
Little Neston 48 B5
Little Newcastle 16 C3
Little Newsham 62 C5
Little Oakley *Essex* 35 G6
Little Oakley *Northants.* 42 B7
Little Orton 60 E1
Little Ouseburn 57 K3
Little Parndon 23 H1
Little Paxton 32 E2
Little Petherick 3 G1
Little Plumstead 45 H4
Little Ponton 42 C2
Little Raveley 33 F1
Little Ribston 57 J4
Little Rissington 30 C6
Little Rogart 96 E1
Little Ryburgh 44 D3
Little Ryle 71 F2
Little Salkeld 61 G3
Little Sampford 33 K5
Little Saxham 34 B2
Little Scatwell 95 K6
Little Shelford 33 H3
Little Smeaton 51 H1
Little Snoring 44 D2
Little Sodbury 20 A3
Little Somborne 10 E1
Little Somerford 20 C3
Little Stainton 62 E4
Little Stanney 48 D5
Little Staughton 32 E2
Little Steeping 53 H6
Little Stonham 35 F3
Little Stretton *Leics.* 41 J6
Little Stretton *Shrop.* 38 D6
Little Strickland 61 G4
Little Stukeley 33 F1
Little Sutton 48 C5
Little Swinburne 70 E6
Little Tew 30 E6
Little Tey 34 C6
Little Thetford 33 J1
Little Thirkleby 57 K2
Little Thorpe 63 F2
Little Thurlow 33 K3
Little Thurrock 24 C4
Little Torboll 96 E2
Little Torrington 6 C4
Little Totham 34 C7
Little Town 60 D5
Little Urswick 55 F2
Little Wakering 25 F3
Little Walden 33 J4
Little Waldingfield 34 D4
Little Walsingham 44 D2
Little Waltham 34 B7
Little Warley 24 C2
Little Weighton 59 F6
Little Welland 29 H5
Little Welnetham 34 C3
Little Wenham 34 E5
Little Wenlock 39 F5
Little Whittingham Green 35 G1
Little Whittington 70 E7
Little Wilbraham 33 J3
Little Witcombe 29 J7
Little Witley 29 G2
Little Wittenham 21 J2
Little Wolford 30 D5
Little Wratting 33 K4
Little Wymondley 33 F6
Little Wyrley 40 C5
Little Yeldham 34 B5
Littlebeck 63 K6
Littleborough *Gt.Man.* 49 J1
Littleborough *Notts.* 52 B4
Littlebourne 15 G2
Littlebredy 8 E6
Littlebury 33 J5
Littlebury Green 33 H5
Littledean 29 F7
Littleferry 97 F2
Littleham *Devon* 6 C3
Littleham *Devon* 7 J7
Littlehampton 12 D6
Littlehempston 5 J4
Littlehoughton 71 H2
Littlemill *E.Ayr.* 67 J2
Littlemill *High.* 97 G6
Littlemore 21 J1
Littleover 41 F2
Littleport 43 J7
Littlestone-on-Sea 15 F5
Littlethorpe 57 J3
Littleton *Ches.* 48 D6
Littleton *Hants.* 11 F1
Littleton *P. & K.* 82 D4
Littleton *Som.* 8 D1
Littleton *Surr.* 22 D5
Littleton Drew 20 B3
Littleton Panell 20 C6
Littleton-on-Severn 19 J3
Littletown 62 E2
Littlewick Green 22 B4
Littleworth *Oxon.* 21 G2
Littleworth *Staffs.* 40 C4
Littleworth *Worcs.* 29 H3
Littley Green 33 K7
Litton *Derbys.* 50 D5
Litton *N.Yorks.* 56 E2
Litton *Som.* 19 J6
Litton Cheney 8 E5
Liurbost 101 F5
Liverpool 48 C3
Liverpool John Lennon Airport 48 D4
Liversedge 57 G7
Liverton *Devon* 5 J3
Liverton *R. & C.* 63 J5
Liverton Street 14 D3
Livingston 75 J4
Livingston Village 75 J4
Lixwm 47 K5
Lizard 2 D7
Llaingoch 46 A4
Llaithddu 37 K7
Llan 37 H5
Llanaber 37 F4
Llanaelhaearn 36 C1
Llanaeron 26 D2
Llanafan 27 F1
Llanafan-fawr 27 J3
Llanafan-fechan 27 J3
Llanallgo 46 C4
Llanarmon 36 D2
Llanarmon Dyffryn Ceiriog 38 A2
Llanarmon-yn-Ial 47 K7
Llanarth *Cere.* 26 D3
Llanarth *Mon.* 28 C7
Llanarthney 17 J3
Llanasa 47 K4
Llanbabo 46 B4
Llanbadarn Fawr 36 E7
Llanbadarn Fynydd 27 K1
Llanbadarn-y-garreg 28 A4
Llanbadoc 19 G1
Llanbadrig 46 B3
Llanbeder 19 G2
Llanbedr *Gwyn.* 36 E3
Llanbedr *Powys* 28 B6
Llanbedr *Powys* 28 A4
Llanbedr-Dyffryn-Clwyd 47 K7
Llanbedrgoch 46 D4
Llanbedrog 36 C2
Llanbedr-y-cennin 47 F6
Llanberis 46 D6
Llanbethery 18 D5
Llanbister 28 A1
Llanblethian 18 C4
Llanboidy 17 F3
Llanbradach 18 E2
Llanbrynmair 37 H5
Llancarfan 18 D4
Llancayo 19 G1
Llancynfelyn 37 F6
Llan-dafal 18 E1
Llandaff 18 E4
Llandaff North 18 E4
Llandanwg 36 E3
Llandawke 17 F4
Llanddaniel Fab 46 C5
Llanddarog 17 J4
Llanddeiniol 26 E1
Llanddeiniolen 46 D6
Llandderfel 37 J2
Llanddeusant *Carmar.* 27 G6
Llanddeusant *I.o.A.* 46 B4
Llanddew 27 K5
Llanddewi 17 H7
Llanddewi Rhydderch 28 C7
Llanddewi Skirrid 28 C7
Llanddewi Velfrey 16 E4
Llanddewi Ystradenni 28 A2
Llanddewi-Brefi 27 F3
Llanddewi'r Cwm 27 K4
Llanddoged 47 G6
Llanddona 46 D5
Llanddowror 17 F4
Llanddulas 47 H5
Llanddwywe 36 E3
Llanddyfnan 46 D5
Llandefaelog 17 H4
Llandefaelog Fach 27 K5
Llandefaelog-tre'r-graig 28 A6
Llandefalle 28 A5
Llandegfan 46 D5
Llandegla 47 K7
Llandegley 28 A2
Llandegveth 19 G2
Llandegwning 36 B2
Llandeilo 17 K3
Llandeilo Abercywyn 17 G4
Llandeilo Graban 27 K4
Llandeilo'r-Fan 27 H5
Llandeloy 16 B3
Llandenny 19 H1
Llandevenny 19 H3
Llandinabo 28 E6
Llandinam 37 K7
Llandissilio 16 E3
Llandogo 19 J1
Llandough *V. of Glam.* 18 E4
Llandough *V. of Glam.* 18 C4
Llandovery 27 G5
Llandow 18 C4
Llandre *Carmar.* 17 K1
Llandre *Carmar.* 16 E3
Llandre *Cere.* 37 F7
Llandrillo 37 K2
Llandrillo-yn-Rhôs 47 G4
Llandrindod Wells 27 K2
Llandrinio 38 B4
Llandudno 47 F4
Llandudno Junction 47 F5
Llandwrog 46 C7
Llandybie 17 K4
Llandyfriog 17 G1
Llandyfrydog 46 C4
Llandygai 46 D5
Llandygwydd 17 F1
Llandyrnog 47 K6
Llandyry 17 H5
Llandysilio 38 B4
Llandyssil 38 A6
Llandysul 17 H1
Llanedeyrn 19 F3
Llanegryn 37 F5
Llanegwad 17 J3
Llaneilian 46 C3
Llanelian-yn-Rhôs 47 G5
Llanelidan 47 K7
Llanelieu 28 A5
Llanellen 28 C7
Llanelli 17 J5
Llanelltyd 37 G4
Llanelly 28 B7
Llanelly Hill 28 B7
Llanelwedd 27 K3
Llanelwy (St. Asaph) 47 J5
Llanenddwyn 36 E3
Llanengan 36 B3
Llanerch-y-medd 46 C4
Llanerfyl 37 K5
Llanfachraeth 46 B4
Llanfachreth 37 G3
Llanfaelog 46 B5
Llanfaelrhys 36 B3
Llan-faes *I.o.A.* 46 E5
Llanfaes *Powys* 27 K6
Llanfaethlu 46 B4
Llanfaglan 46 C6
Llanfair 36 E3
Llanfair Caereinion 38 A5
Llanfair Clydogau 27 F3
Llanfair Dyffryn Clwyd 47 K7
Llanfair Talhaiarn 47 H5
Llanfair Waterdine 28 B1
Llanfairfechan 46 E5
Llanfair-Nant-Gwyn 16 E2
Llanfair-Orllwyn 17 G1
Llanfairpwllgwyngyll 46 D5
Llanfairynghornwy 46 B3
Llanfair-yn-neubwll 46 B5
Llanfallteg 16 E4
Llanfallteg West 16 E4
Llanfaredd 27 K3
Llanfarian 26 E1
Llanfechain 38 A3
Llanfechell 46 B3
Llanfendigaid 36 E5
Llanferres 47 K6
Llanfflewyn 46 B4
Llanfigael 46 B4
Llanfihangel ar-arth 17 H2
Llanfihangel Crucorney 28 C6
Llanfihangel Glyn Myfyr 37 J1
Llanfihangel Nant Bran 27 J5
Llanfihangel Rhydithon 28 A2
Llanfihangel Rogiet 19 H3
Llanfihangel uwch-gwili 17 H3
Llanfihangel-nant-Melan 28 A3
Llanfihangel-Tal-y-llyn 28 A6
Llanfihangel-y-Creuddyn 27 F1
Llanfihangel-yng-Ngwynfa 37 K4
Llanfihangel-y-pennant *Gwyn.* 36 E1
Llanfihangel-y-pennant *Gwyn.* 37 F5
Llanfilo 28 A5
Llanfoist 28 B7
Llanfor 37 J2
Llanfrechfa 19 G2
Llanfrothen 37 F1
Llanfrynach 27 K6
Llanfwrog *Denb.* 47 K7
Llanfwrog *I.o.A.* 46 B4
Llanfyllin 38 A4
Llanfynydd *Carmar.* 17 J3
Llanfynydd *Flints.* 48 B7
Llanfyrnach 17 F2
Llangadfan 37 K4
Llangadog 27 G6
Llangadwaladr *I.o.A.* 46 B6
Llangadwaladr *Powys* 38 A2
Llangaffo 46 C6
Llangain 17 G4
Llangammarch Wells 27 J4
Llangan 18 C4
Llangarron 28 E6
Llangasty-Talyllyn 28 A6
Llangathen 17 J3
Llangattock 28 B7
Llangattock Lingoed 28 C6
Llangattock-Vibon-Avel 28 D7
Llangedwyn 38 A3
Llangefni 46 C5
Llangeinor 18 C3
Llangeitho 27 F3
Llangeler 17 G2
Llangelynin 36 E5
Llangendeirne 17 H4
Llangennech 17 J5
Llangennith 17 H6
Llangenny 28 B7
Llangernyw 47 G6
Llangian 36 B3
Llangiwg 18 A1
Llanglydwen 16 E3
Llangoed 46 E5
Llangoedmor 16 E1
Llangollen 38 B1
Llangolman 16 E3
Llangorse 28 A6
Llangorwen 37 F7
Llangovan 19 H1
Llangower 37 J2
Llangrannog 26 C3
Llangristiolus 46 C5
Llangrove 28 E7
Llangua 28 C6
Llangunllo 28 B1
Llangunnor 17 H3
Llangurig 27 J1
Llangwm *Conwy* 37 J1
Llangwm *Mon.* 19 H1
Llangwm *Pembs.* 16 C5
Llangwnnadl 36 B2
Llangwyfan 47 K6
Llangwyllog 46 C5
Llangwyryfon 26 E1
Llangybi *Cere.* 27 F3
Llangybi *Gwyn.* 36 D1
Llangybi *Mon.* 19 G2
Llangyfelach 17 K6
Llangynhafal 47 K6
Llangynidr 28 A7
Llangyniew 38 A5
Llangynin 17 F4
Llangynog *Carmar.* 17 G4
Llangynog *Powys* 37 K3
Llangynwyd 18 B3
Llanhamlach 27 K6
Llanharan 18 D3
Llanharry 18 D3
Llanhennock 19 G2
Llanhilleth 19 F1
Llanidloes 37 J7
Llaniestyn 36 B2
Llanigon 28 B5
Llanilar 27 F1
Llanilid 18 C3
Llanishen *Cardiff* 18 E3
Llanishen *Mon.* 19 H1
Llanllawddog 17 H3
Llanllechid 46 E6
Llanlleonfel 27 J4
Llanllugan 37 K5
Llanllwch 17 G4
Llanllwchaiarn 38 A6
Llanllwni 17 H1
Llanllyfni 46 C7
Llanllywel 19 G2
Llanmadoc 17 H6
Llanmaes 18 C5
Llanmartin 19 G3
Llanmerewig 38 A6
Llanmihangel 18 C4
Llanmiloe 17 F5
Llanmorlais 17 J6
Llannefydd 47 H5
Llannerch 47 J5
Llannerch-y-Môr 47 K5
Llannon 17 J5
Llannor 36 C2
Llanon 26 E2
Llanover 19 G1
Llanpumsaint 17 H3
Llanreithan 16 B3
Llanrhaeadr 47 J6
Llanrhaeadr-ym-Mochnant 38 A3
Llanrhian 16 B2
Llanrhidian 17 J6
Llanrhos 47 F4
Llanrhyddlad 46 B4
Llanrhystud 26 E2
Llanrothal 28 D7
Llanrug 46 D6
Llanrumney 19 F3
Llanrwst 47 F6
Llansadurnen 17 F4
Llansadwrn *Carmar.* 17 K2
Llansadwrn *I.o.A.* 46 D5
Llansaint 17 G5
Llansamlet 17 K6
Llansanffraid Glan Conwy 47 G5
Llansannan 47 H6
Llansannor 18 C4
Llansantffraed 28 A6
Llansantffraed-Cwmdeuddwr 27 J2
Llansantffraed-in-Elvel 27 K3
Llansantffraid 26 E2
Llansantffraid-ym-Mechain 38 B3
Llansawel *Carmar.* 17 K2
Llansawel (Briton Ferry) *N.P.T.* 18 A2
Llansilin 38 B3
Llansoy 19 H1
Llanspyddid 27 K6
Llanstadwell 16 C5
Llansteffan 17 G4
Llanstephan 28 A4
Llantarnam 19 G2
Llanteg 16 E4
Llanthony 28 B6
Llantilio Crossenny 28 C7
Llantilio Pertholey 28 C7
Llantood 16 E1
Llantrisant *Mon.* 19 G2
Llantrisant *R.C.T.* 18 D3
Llantrithyd 18 D4
Llantwit Fardre 18 D3
Llantwit Major 18 C5
Llantysilio 38 A1
Llanuwchllyn 37 H2
Llanvaches 19 H2
Llanvair-Discoed 19 H2
Llanvapley 28 C7
Llanvetherine 28 C7
Llanveynoe 28 C5
Llanvihangel Gobion 19 G1
Llanvihangel-Ystern-Llewern 28 D7
Llanwarne 28 E6
Llanwddyn 37 K4
Llanwenog 17 H1
Llanwern 19 G3
Llanwinio 17 F3
Llanwnda *Gwyn.* 46 C7
Llanwnda *Pembs.* 16 C2
Llanwnen 17 J1
Llanwnog 37 K6
Llanwonno 18 D2
Llanwrda 27 G5
Llanwrin 37 G5
Llanwrthwl 27 J2
Llanwrtyd 27 H4
Llanwrtyd Wells 27 H4
Llanwyddelan 37 K5
Llanyblodwel 38 B3
Llanybri 17 G4
Llanybydder 17 J1
Llanycefn 16 E3
Llanychaer Bridge 16 C2
Llanycil 37 J2
Llanycrwys 17 K1
Llanymawddwy 37 J4
Llanymynech 38 B3
Llanynghenedl 46 B4
Llanynys 47 K6
Llan-y-pwll 48 C7
Llanyre 27 K2
Llanystumdwy 36 D2
Llanywern 28 A6
Llawhaden 16 D4
Llawnt 38 B2
Llawr-y-dref 36 B3
Llawryglyn 37 J6
Llay 48 C7
Llechcynfarwy 46 B4
Llechfaen 27 K6
Llechryd *Caerp.* 18 E1
Llechryd *Cere.* 17 F1
Llechrydau 38 B2
Lledrod *Cere.* 27 F1
Lledrod *Powys* 38 B2
Llethr 16 B3
Llidiadnenog 17 J2
Llidiardau 37 H2
Llithfaen 36 C1
Lloc 47 K5
Llong 48 B6
Llowes 28 A4
Lloyney 28 B1
Llwydcoed 18 C1
Llwydiarth 37 K4
Llwyn 38 B7
Llwyncelyn 26 D3
Llwyndafydd 26 C3
Llwynderw 38 B5
Llwyndyrys 36 C1
Llwyngwril 36 E5
Llwynhendy 17 J6
Llwyn-Madoc 27 J3
Llwynmawr 38 B2
Llwyn-onn 26 D3
Llwyn-y-brain *Carmar.* 17 F4
Llwyn-y-brain *Carmar.* 27 G5
Llwynypia 18 C2
Llynclys 38 B3
Llynfaes 46 C5
Llysfaen 47 G5
Llyswen 28 A5
Llysworney 18 C4
Llys-y-fran 16 D3
Llywel 27 H5
Loandhu 97 F4
Loanhead *Aber.* 91 H1
Loanhead *Midloth.* 76 A4
Loans 74 B7
Loch Baghasdail (Lochboisdale) 84 C3
Loch Coire Lodge 103 J5
Loch Eil Outward Bound 87 G7
Loch Head *D. & G.* 64 D6
Loch Head *D. & G.* 67 J4
Loch na Madadh (Lochmaddy) 92 E5
Loch Sgioport 84 D1
Lochailort 86 D6
Lochaline 79 H3
Lochans 64 A5
Locharbriggs 68 E5
Lochawe 80 C5
Lochboisdale (Loch Baghasdail) 84 C3
Lochbuie 79 H5
Lochcarron 86 E1
Lochdhu Hotel 105 F4
Lochdon 79 J4
Lochdrum 95 J4
Lochearnhead 81 G5
Lochee 82 E4
Lochend *High.* 105 H2
Lochend *High.* 88 C1
Lochfoot 65 K3
Lochgair 73 H1
Lochgarthside 88 C3
Lochgelly 75 K1
Lochgilphead 73 G2
Lochgoilhead 80 D7
Lochgoin 74 D6
Lochhill *E.Ayr.* 68 B2
Lochhill *Moray* 97 K5
Lochinch Castle 64 B4
Lochinver 102 C6
Lochlair 83 G3
Lochlane 81 K5
Lochlea 67 J1
Lochluichart 95 K5
Lochmaben 69 F5
Lochmaddy (Loch na Madadh) 92 E5
Lochore 75 K1
Lochportain 92 E4
Lochranza 73 H6
Lochside *Aber.* 83 J1
Lochside *High.* 103 G3
Lochside *High.* 104 D5
Lochside *High.* 105 H2
Lochslin 97 F3
Lochton 67 G5
Lochty 83 G7
Lochuisge 79 J2
Lochurr 68 C5
Lochussie 96 B6
Lochwinnoch 74 B5
Lockengate 4 A4
Lockerbie 69 G5
Lockeridge 20 E5
Lockerley 10 D2
Locking 19 G6
Lockington *E.Riding* 59 G5
Lockington *Leics.* 41 G3
Lockleywood 39 F3
Locks Heath 11 G4
Locksbottom 23 H5
Lockton 63 K7
Loddington *Leics.* 42 A5
Loddington *Northants.* 32 B1
Loddiswell 5 H6
Loddon 45 H6
Lode 33 J2
Loders 8 D5
Lodsworth 12 C4
Lofthouse *N.Yorks.* 57 F2
Lofthouse *W.Yorks.* 57 J7
Loftus 63 J5
Logan *D. & G.* 64 A6
Logan *E.Ayr.* 67 K1
Loganlea 75 H4
Loggerheads 39 G2
Loggie 95 H2
Logie *Angus* 83 H1
Logie *Angus* 82 E2
Logie *Fife* 83 F5
Logie *Moray* 97 H6
Logie Coldstone 90 C4
Logie Hill 96 E4
Logie Newton 90 E1
Logie Pert 83 H1
Logierait 82 A2
Login 16 E3
Lolworth 33 G2
Lonbain 94 C6
Londesborough 58 E5
London 23 G3
London Beach 14 D4
London Biggin Hill Airport 23 H5
London City Airport 23 H3
London Colney 22 E1
London Gatwick Airport 23 F7
London Heathrow Airport 22 D4
London Luton Airport 32 E6
London Southend Airport 24 E3
London Stansted Airport 33 J6
Londonderry 57 H1
Londonthorpe 42 C2
Londubh 94 E3
Lonemore 96 E3
Long Ashton 19 J4
Long Bennington 42 B1
Long Bredy 8 E5
Long Buckby 31 H2
Long Clawson 42 A3
Long Common 11 G3
Long Compton *Staffs.* 40 A3
Long Compton *Warks.* 30 D5
Long Crendon 21 K1
Long Crichel 9 J3
Long Ditton 22 E5
Long Downs 2 E5
Long Drax 58 C7
Long Duckmanton 51 G5
Long Eaton 41 G2
Long Gill 56 C4
Long Hanborough 31 F7
Long Itchington 31 F2
Long Lawford 31 F1
Long Load 8 D2
Long Marston *Herts.* 32 B7
Long Marston *N.Yorks.* 58 B4
Long Marston *Warks.* 30 C4
Long Marton 61 H4
Long Melford 34 C4
Long Newnton 20 C2
Long Preston 56 D4
Long Riston 59 H5
Long Stratton 45 F6
Long Street 31 J4
Long Sutton *Hants.* 22 A7
Long Sutton *Lincs.* 43 H3
Long Sutton *Som.* 8 D2
Long Thurlow 34 E2
Long Waste 39 F4
Long Whatton 41 G3
Long Wittenham 21 J2
Longbenton 71 H7
Longborough 30 C6
Longbridge *W.Mid.* 30 B1
Longbridge *Warks.* 30 D2
Longbridge Deverill 20 B7
Longburgh 60 E1
Longburton 9 F3
Longcliffe 50 E7
Longcot 21 F2
Longcroft 75 F3
Longcross *Devon* 4 E3
Longcross *Surr.* 22 C5
Longden 38 D5

Place	Page	Grid
Longdon *Staffs.*	40	C4
Longdon *Worcs.*	29	H5
Longdon upon Tern	39	F4
Longdown	7	G6
Longdrum	91	H3
Longfield	24	C5
Longfield Hill	24	C5
Longfleet	9	H6
Longford *Derbys.*	40	E2
Longford *Gt.Lon.*	22	D4
Longford *Shrop.*	39	F2
Longford *Tel. & W.*	39	G4
Longford *W.Mid.*	41	F7
Longforgan	82	E5
Longformacus	76	E5
Longframlington	71	G3
Longham *Dorset*	10	B5
Longham *Norf.*	44	D4
Longhill	99	H5
Longhirst	71	H5
Longhope *Glos.*	29	F7
Longhope *Ork.*	107	C8
Longhorsley	71	G4
Longhoughton	71	H2
Longlands *Aber.*	90	C2
Longlands *Cumb.*	60	D3
Longlane *Derbys.*	40	E2
Longlane *W.Berks.*	21	J4
Longley Green	29	G3
Longmanhill	99	F4
Longmoor Camp	11	J1
Longmorn	97	K6
Longnewton *Sc.Bord.*	70	A1
Longnewton *Stock.*	62	E5
Longney	29	G7
Longnor *Shrop.*	38	D5
Longnor *Staffs.*	50	C6
Longparish	21	H7
Longridge *Lancs.*	56	B6
Longridge *W.Loth.*	75	H4
Longridge Towers	77	H5
Longriggend	75	G3
Longrock	2	B5
Longsdon	49	J7
Longside	99	J6
Longslow	39	F2
Longstanton	33	G2
Longstock	10	E1
Longstowe	33	G3
Longstreet	20	E6
Longthorpe	42	E6
Longton *Lancs.*	55	H7
Longton *Stoke*	40	B1
Longtown *Cumb.*	69	J7
Longtown *Here.*	28	C6
Longville in the Dale	38	E6
Longwell Green	19	K4
Longwick	22	A1
Longwitton	71	F5
Longworth	21	G2
Longyester	76	D4
Lonmore	93	H7
Looe	4	C5
Loose	14	C2
Loosegate	43	G3
Loosley Row	22	B1
Lopcombe Corner	10	D1
Lopen	8	D3
Loppington	38	D3
Lorbottle	71	F3
Lorbottle Hall	71	F3
Lorgill	93	G7
Lorn	74	B2
Lornty	82	C3
Loscoe	41	G1
Losgaintir	93	F2
Lossiemouth	97	K4
Lossit	72	A2
Lostock Gralam	49	F5
Lostock Green	49	F5
Lostock Junction	49	F2
Lostwithiel	4	B5
Loth	106	F4
Lothbeg	104	E7
Lothersdale	56	E5
Lothmore	104	E7
Loudwater	22	C2
Loughborough	41	H4
Loughor	17	J6
Loughton *Essex*	23	H2
Loughton *M.K.*	32	B5
Loughton *Shrop.*	39	F7
Lound *Lincs.*	42	D4
Lound *Notts.*	51	J4
Lound *Suff.*	45	K6
Lount	41	F4
Lour	83	F3
Louth	53	G4
Love Clough	56	D7
Lovedean	11	H3
Lover	10	D2
Loversall	51	H3
Loves Green	24	C1
Loveston	16	D5
Lovington	8	E1
Low	55	H1
Low Ballevain	66	A1
Low Barlay	65	F5
Low Bentham	56	B3
Low Bolton	62	B7
Low Bradfield	50	E3
Low Bradley or Bradley	57	F5
Low Braithwaite	61	F2
Low Brunton	70	E6
Low Burnham	51	K2
Low Burton	57	H1
Low Catton	58	D4
Low Coniscliffe	62	D5
Low Craighead	67	G3
Low Crosby	61	F1
Low Dinsdale	62	E5
Low Eggborough	58	B7
Low Entercommon	62	E6
Low Etherley	62	C4
Low Gate	70	E7
Low Habberley	29	H1
Low Ham	8	D2
Low Hawsker	63	J2
Low Haygarth	61	H7
Low Hesket	60	F2
Low Hesleyhurst	71	F4
Low Hutton	58	D3
Low Laithe	57	G3
Low Leighton	50	C4
Low Marishes	58	E2
Low Mill	63	H7
Low Moor	56	C5
Low Newton-by-the-Sea	71	H1
Low Risby	52	C1
Low Row *Cumb.*	70	A7
Low Row *N.Yorks.*	62	A7
Low Santon	52	C1
Low Stillaig	73	H4
Low Street	45	H3
Low Torry	75	J2
Low Toynton	53	F5
Low Waters	75	F5
Low Wood	55	G1
Low Worsall	62	E5
Lowdham	41	J1
Lower Achachanna	80	B5
Lower Aisholt	7	K2
Lower Apperley	29	H6
Lower Ashton	7	G7
Lower Assendon	22	A3
Lower Auchalick	73	H3
Lower Barewood	28	C3
Lower Beeding	13	F4
Lower Benefield	42	C7
Lower Berry Hill	28	E7
Lower Bockhampton	9	G5
Lower Boddington	31	F3
Lower Boscaswell	2	A5
Lower Bourne	22	B7
Lower Brailes	30	E5
Lower Breakish	86	C2
Lower Broadheath	29	H3
Lower Broughton	49	H3
Lower Brynamman	27	G7
Lower Bullingham	28	E5
Lower Burgate	10	C3
Lower Caldecote	32	E4
Lower Cam	8	D1
Lower Camster	105	H4
Lower Chapel	27	K5
Lower Chute	21	G6
Lower Crossings	50	C4
Lower Darwen	56	B7
Lower Dean	32	D2
Lower Diabaig	94	D5
Lower Dicker	13	J5
Lower Dinchope	38	D7
Lower Down	38	C7
Lower Drift	2	B6
Lower Dunsforth	57	K3
Lower Earley	22	A4
Lower Egleton	29	F4
Lower End	32	B2
Lower Everleigh	20	E6
Lower Failand	19	J4
Lower Farringdon	11	J1
Lower Freystrop	16	C4
Lower Froyle	22	A7
Lower Gabwell	5	K4
Lower Gledfield	96	C2
Lower Godney	19	H7
Lower Green *Kent*	23	K7
Lower Green *Norf.*	44	D2
Lower Green *Staffs.*	40	B5
Lower Green Bank	55	J4
Lower Halstow	24	E5
Lower Hardres	15	G2
Lower Hawthwaite	55	F1
Lower Hayton	38	E7
Lower Hergest	28	B3
Lower Heyford	31	F6
Lower Higham	24	D4
Lower Holbrook	35	F5
Lower Hordley	38	C3
Lower Horsebridge	13	J5
Lower Kilchattan	72	B1
Lower Killeyan	72	A6
Lower Kingcombe	8	E5
Lower Kinnerton	48	C6
Lower Langford	19	H5
Lower Largo	83	F7
Lower Lemington	30	D5
Lower Lovacott	6	D3
Lower Lydbrook	28	E7
Lower Lye	28	D2
Lower Machen	19	F3
Lower Maes-coed	28	C5
Lower Moor	29	J4
Lower Nazeing	23	G1
Lower Oakfield	75	K1
Lower Oddington	30	D6
Lower Ollach	86	B1
Lower Penarth	18	E4
Lower Penn	40	A6
Lower Pennington	10	E5
Lower Peover	49	G5
Lower Quinton	30	C4
Lower Seagry	20	C3
Lower Shelton	32	C4
Lower Shiplake	22	A4
Lower Shuckburgh	31	F2
Lower Slaughter	30	C6
Lower Stanton St. Quintin	20	C3
Lower Stoke	24	E4
Lower Stondon	32	E5
Lower Street	14	C6
Lower Sundon	32	D6
Lower Swanwick	11	F4
Lower Swell	30	C6
Lower Tean	40	C2
Lower Thurlton	45	J6
Lower Thurnham	55	H4
Lower Town *I.o.S.*	2	C1
Lower Town *Pembs.*	16	C2
Lower Tysoe	30	E4
Lower Upham	11	G3
Lower Vexford	7	K2
Lower Wallop	38	C5
Lower Walton	49	F4
Lower Weare	19	H6
Lower Welson	28	B3
Lower Whitley	49	F5
Lower Wield	21	K7
Lower (Nether) Winchendon	31	J7
Lower Withington	49	H6
Lower Woodend	22	B3
Lower Woodford	10	C1
Lower Wraxall	8	E4
Lower Wyche	29	G4
Lowesby	42	A5
Lowestoft	45	K6
Lowestoft End	45	K6
Loweswater	60	C4
Lowfield Heath	23	F7
Lowgill *Cumb.*	61	H7
Lowgill *Lancs.*	56	B3
Lowick *Cumb.*	55	F1
Lowick *Northants.*	42	C7
Lowick *Northumb.*	77	J7
Lownie Moor	83	F3
Lowsonford	30	C2
Lowther	61	G4
Lowther Castle	61	G4
Lowthorpe	59	G4
Lowton	49	F3
Lowton Common	49	F3
Loxbeare	7	H4
Loxhill	12	D3
Loxhore	6	E2
Loxley	30	D3
Loxton	19	G6
Loxwood	12	D3
Lubachoan	96	B2
Lubcroy	95	K1
Lubenham	42	A7
Lubfearn	95	K4
Lubmore	95	G6
Lubreoch	81	F3
Luccombe	7	H1
Luccombe Village	11	G7
Lucker	77	K7
Luckett	4	D3
Luckington	20	B3
Lucklawhill	83	F5
Luckwell Bridge	7	H2
Lucton	28	D2
Ludag	84	C3
Ludborough	53	F3
Ludchurch	16	E4
Luddenden	57	F7
Luddenden Foot	57	F7
Luddenham Court	25	F5
Luddesdown	24	C5
Luddington *N.Lincs.*	52	B1
Luddington *Warks.*	30	C3
Luddington in the Brook	42	E7
Ludford *Lincs.*	53	F4
Ludford Magna	53	F4
Ludford Parva	52	E4
Ludgershall *Bucks.*	31	H7
Ludgershall *Wilts.*	21	F6
Ludgvan	2	B5
Ludham	45	H4
Ludlow	28	E1
Ludney	53	G3
Ludstock	29	F5
Ludwell	9	J2
Ludworth	62	E2
Luffincott	6	B6
Luffness	76	C2
Lugar	67	K1
Luggiebank	75	F3
Lugton	74	C5
Lugwardine	28	E4
Luib	86	B2
Luibeilt	80	D1
Lulham	28	D4
Lullington *Derbys.*	40	E4
Lullington *Som.*	20	A6
Lulsgate Bottom	19	J5
Lulsley	29	G3
Lulworth Camp	9	H6
Lumb	57	F7
Lumbutts	56	E7
Lumby	57	K6
Lumphanan	90	D4
Lumphinnans	75	K1
Lumsdaine	77	G4
Lumsden	90	C2
Lunan	83	H2
Lunanhead	83	F2
Luncarty	82	B5
Lund *E.Riding*	59	F5
Lund *N.Yorks.*	58	C6
Lund *Shet.*	108	E2
Lundavra	80	B1
Lunderton	99	K6
Lundie *Angus*	82	D4
Lundie *High.*	87	H3
Lundin Links	83	F7
Lunga	79	J7
Lunna	109	D6
Lunning	109	E6
Lunsford's Cross	14	C6
Lunt	48	C2
Luntley	28	C3
Luppitt	7	K5
Lupton	55	J1
Lurgashall	12	C4
Lurgnich	80	A2
Lusby	53	G6
Luss	74	B1
Lussagiven	72	E2
Lusta	93	H6
Lustleigh	7	F7
Luston	28	D2
Luthermuir	83	H1
Luthrie	82	E6
Luton *Devon*	7	J5
Luton *Devon*	5	K3
Luton *Luton*	32	D6
Luton *Med.*	24	D5
Luton Airport	32	E6
Lutterworth	41	H7
Lutton *Devon*	5	F5
Lutton *Lincs.*	43	H3
Lutton *Northants.*	42	E7
Luxborough	7	H2
Luxulyan	4	A5
Lybster *High.*	105	F2
Lybster *High.*	105	H5
Lydacott	6	C5
Lydbury North	38	C7
Lydcott	6	E2
Lydd	15	F5
Lydd Airport	15	F5
Lydden	15	H3
Lyddington	42	B6
Lydd-on-Sea	15	F5
Lydeard St. Lawrence	7	K2
Lydford	6	D7
Lydford-on-Fosse	8	E1
Lydgate	56	E7
Lydham	38	C6
Lydiard Millicent	20	D3
Lydiate	48	C2
Lydlinch	9	G3
Lydney	19	K1
Lydstep	16	D6
Lye	40	B7
Lye Green	22	C1
Lyford	21	G2
Lymbridge Green	15	G3
Lyme Regis	8	C5
Lymekilns	74	E5
Lyminge	15	G3
Lymington	10	E5
Lyminster	12	D6
Lymm	49	F4
Lymore	10	E5
Lympne	15	G4
Lympsham	19	G6
Lympstone	7	H7
Lynaberack	88	E5
Lynchat	88	E4
Lyndhurst	10	E4
Lyndon	42	C5
Lyne *Aber.*	91	F4
Lyne *Sc.Bord.*	76	A6
Lyne *Surr.*	22	D5
Lyne of Gorthleck	88	C2
Lyne of Skene	91	F3
Lyne Station	76	A7
Lyneal	38	D2
Lynedale House	93	J6
Lynegar	105	H3
Lyneham *Oxon.*	30	D6
Lyneham *Wilts.*	20	D4
Lyneholmeford	70	A6
Lynemore *High.*	89	H2
Lynemore *Moray*	89	J1
Lynemouth	71	H4
Lyness	107	C8
Lynford	44	C6
Lyng *Norf.*	44	E4
Lyng *Som.*	8	C2
Lynmouth	7	F1
Lynsted	25	F5
Lynton	7	F1
Lyon's Gate	9	F4
Lyonshall	28	C3
Lyrabus	72	A4
Lytchett Matravers	9	J5
Lytchett Minster	9	J5
Lyth	105	H2
Lytham	55	G7
Lytham St. Anne's	55	G7
Lythe	63	K5
Lythe Hill	12	C3
Lythes	107	D9
Lythmore	105	F2

M

Place	Page	Grid
Mabe Burnthouse	2	E5
Mabie	65	K3
Mablethorpe	53	J4
Macclesfield	49	J5
Macclesfield Forest	49	J5
Macduff	99	F4
Machan	75	F5
Machany	82	A6
Macharioch	66	B3
Machen	19	F3
Machrie *Arg. & B.*	72	A4
Machrie *Arg. & B.*	72	B6
Machrie *N.Ayr.*	73	H7
Machrihanish	66	A2
Machrins	72	B1
Machynlleth	37	G5
McInroy's Point	74	A3
Mackworth	41	F2
Macmerry	76	C3
Macterry	99	F6
Madderty	82	A5
Maddiston	75	H3
Madehurst	12	C5
Madeley *Staffs.*	39	G1
Madeley *Tel. & W.*	39	G5
Madeley Heath	39	G1
Madford	7	K4
Madingley	33	G3
Madjeston	9	H2
Madley	28	D5
Madresfield	29	H4
Madron	2	B5
Maen Porth	2	E6
Maenaddwyn	46	C4
Maenclochog	16	D3
Maendy	18	D4
Maentwrog	37	F1
Maer	39	G2
Maerdy *Carmar.*	17	K3
Maerdy *Carmar.*	17	K3
Maerdy *Conwy*	37	K1
Maerdy *Mon.*	19	G1
Maerdy *R.C.T.*	18	C2
Maesbrook	38	B3
Maesbury Marsh	38	C3
Maes-Glas (Greenfield) *Flints.*	47	K5
Maes-glas *Newport*	19	F3
Maesgwynne	17	F3
Maeshafn	48	B6
Maesllyn	17	G1
Maesmynis	27	K4
Maesteg	18	B2
Maes-Treylow	28	B2
Maesybont	17	J4
Maesycrugiau	17	H1
Maesycwmmer	18	E2
Magdalen Laver	23	J1
Magham Down	13	K5
Maghull	48	C2
Magor	19	H3
Maiden Bradley	9	G1
Maiden Law	62	C2
Maiden Newton	8	E5
Maiden Wells	16	C5
Maidencombe	5	K4
Maidenhead	22	B3
Maidens	67	G3
Maiden's Green	22	B4
Maidensgrove	22	A3
Maidenwell *Cornw.*	4	B3
Maidenwell *Lincs.*	53	G5
Maidford	31	H3
Maids' Moreton	31	J5
Maidstone	14	C2
Maidwell	31	J1
Mail	109	D10
Mains of Ardestie	83	G4
Mains of Balgavies	83	G2
Mains of Ballindarg	83	F2
Mains of Burgie	97	H6
Mains of Culsh	99	G6
Mains of Dillavaird	91	F6
Mains of Drum	91	G4
Mains of Dudwick	91	H1
Mains of Faillie	88	E1
Mains of Fedderate	99	G6
Mains of Glack	91	F2
Mains of Glassaugh	98	D4
Mains of Glenbuchat	90	B3
Mains of Linton	91	F4
Mains of Melgund	83	G2
Mains of Pitfour	99	H6
Mains of Pittrichie	91	G2
Mains of Sluie	97	H6
Mains of Tannachy	98	B4
Mains of Thornton	90	E7
Mains of Tig	67	F5
Mains of Watten	105	H3
Mainsriddle	65	K5
Mainstone	38	B7
Maisemore	29	H6
Makendon	70	D3
Makerstoun	76	D7
Malacleit	92	C4
Malborough	5	H7
Malden Rushett	22	E5
Maldon	24	E1
Malham	56	E3
Maligar	93	K5
Mallaig	86	C5
Mallaigmore	86	D5
Mallaigvaig	86	C5
Malleny Mills	75	K4
Malletsheugh	74	D5
Malling	81	G7
Malltraeth	46	C6
Mallwyd	37	H4
Malmesbury	20	C3
Malmsmead	7	F1
Malpas *Ches.*	38	D1
Malpas *Cornw.*	3	F4
Malpas *Newport*	19	G2
Maltby *S.Yorks.*	51	H3
Maltby *Stock.*	63	F5
Maltby le Marsh	53	H4
Maltman's Hill	14	E3
Malton	58	D2
Malvern Link	29	G4
Malvern Wells	29	G4
Mambeg	74	A2
Mamble	29	F1
Mamhead	7	H7
Mamhilad	19	G1
Manaccan	2	E6
Manafon	38	A5
Manais	93	G3
Manaton	7	F7
Manby	53	G4
Mancetter	41	F6
Manchester	49	H3
Manchester Airport	49	H4
Mancot Royal	48	C6
Mandally	87	J4
Manea	43	H7
Maneight	67	K3
Manfield	62	D5
Mangaster	108	C5
Mangotsfield	19	K4
Mangurstadh	100	C4
Mankinholes	56	E7
Manley	48	E5
Manmoel	18	E1
Mannal	78	A3
Manningford Abbots	20	E6
Manningford Bohune	20	E6
Manningford Bruce	20	E6
Mannings Heath	13	F4
Mannington	10	B4
Manningtree	35	F5
Mannofield	91	H4
Manorbier	16	D6
Manordeifi	17	F1
Manordeilo	17	K3
Manorowen	16	C2
Mansell Gamage	28	C4
Mansell Lacy	28	D4
Mansergh	56	B1
Mansfield	51	H6
Mansfield Woodhouse	51	H6
Mansriggs	55	F1
Manston *Dorset*	9	H3
Manston *Kent*	25	K5
Manswood	9	J4
Manthorpe *Lincs.*	42	D4
Manthorpe *Lincs.*	42	C2
Manton *N.Lincs.*	52	C2
Manton *Rut.*	42	B5
Manton *Wilts.*	20	E5
Manuden	33	H6
Maolachy	79	K6
Maperton	9	F2
Maple Cross	22	D2
Maplebeck	51	K6
Mapledurham	21	K4
Mapledurwell	21	K6
Maplehurst	12	E4
Mapleton	40	D1
Mapperley	41	G1
Mapperton	8	E5
Mappleborough Green	30	B2
Mappleton	59	J5
Mapplewell	51	F2
Mappowder	9	G4
Mar Lodge	89	H5
Marazion	2	C5
Marbhig	101	G6
Marbury	38	E1
March	43	H6
Marcham	21	H2
Marchamley	38	E3
Marchington	40	D2
Marchington Woodlands	40	D3
Marchwiel	38	C1
Marchwood	10	E3
Marcross	18	C5
Marcus	83	G2
Marden *Here.*	28	E4
Marden *Kent*	14	C3
Marden *T. & W.*	71	J6
Marden *Wilts.*	20	D6
Marden Beech	14	C3
Marden Thorn	14	C3
Mardy	28	C7
Mare Green	8	C2
Marefield	42	A5
Mareham le Fen	53	F6
Mareham on the Hill	53	F6
Maresfield	13	H4
Marfleet	59	H7
Marford	48	C7
Margam	18	A3
Margaret Marsh	9	H3
Margaret Roding	33	J7
Margaretting	24	C1
Margate	25	K4
Margnaheglish	73	J7
Margrie	65	J3
Margrove Park	63	H5
Marham	44	B5
Marhamchurch	6	A5
Marholm	42	E5
Marian Cwm	47	J5
Marian-Glas	46	D4
Mariansleigh	7	F3
Marishader	93	K5
Maristow House	4	E4
Mark	19	G7
Mark Causeway	19	G7
Mark Cross	13	J3
Markbeech	23	H3
Markby	53	H5
Markdhu	64	B3
Market Bosworth	41	G5
Market Deeping	42	E4
Market Drayton	39	F2
Market Harborough	42	A7
Market Lavington	20	D6
Market Overton	42	B4
Market Rasen	52	E4
Market Stainton	53	F5
Market Street	51	H6
Market Warsop	51	H6
Market Weighton	58	E5
Market Weston	34	D1
Markethill	82	D4
Markfield	41	G4
Markham	18	E1
Markham Moor	51	K5
Markinch	82	D7
Markington	57	H3
Marks Gate	23	H3
Marks Tey	34	D6
Marksbury	19	K5
Markwell	4	D5
Markyate	32	D7
Marlborough	20	E5
Marldon	5	J4
Marlesford	35	H3
Marley Green	38	E1
Marley Hill	62	D1
Marlingford	45	F5
Marloes	16	A5
Marlow	22	B3
Marlpit Hill	23	H7
Marlpool	41	G1
Marnhull	9	G3
Marnoch	98	D5
Marple	49	J4
Marr	51	H2
Marrel	105	F7
Marrister	109	E6
Marros	17	F5
Marsden *T. & W.*	71	K7
Marsden *W.Yorks.*	50	C1
Marsett	56	E1
Marsh	8	B3
Marsh Baldon	21	J2
Marsh Benham	21	H5
Marsh Chapel	53	G3
Marsh Gibbon	31	H6
Marsh Green *Devon*	7	J6
Marsh Green *Kent*	23	H7
Marsh Green *Tel. & W.*	39	F4
Marsh Lane	51	G5
Marsh Street	7	H1
Marshall's Heath	32	E7
Marshalsea	8	C4
Marsham	45	F3
Marshaw	55	J4
Marshborough	15	H2
Marshbrook	38	D7
Marshfield *Newport*	19	F3
Marshfield *S.Glos.*	20	A4
Marshgate	4	B1
Marshside	48	C1
Marshwood	8	C4
Marske	62	C6
Marske-by-the-Sea	63	H4
Marston *Ches.*	49	F5
Marston *Here.*	28	C3
Marston *Lincs.*	42	B1
Marston *Oxon.*	21	J1
Marston *Staffs.*	40	B3
Marston *Staffs.*	40	A4
Marston *Warks.*	40	E6
Marston *Wilts.*	20	C6
Marston Green	40	D7
Marston Magna	8	E2
Marston Meysey	20	E2
Marston Montgomery	40	D2
Marston Moretaine	32	C4
Marston on Dove	40	E3
Marston St. Lawrence	31	G4
Marston Stannett	28	E3
Marston Trussell	41	J7
Marstow	28	E7
Marsworth	32	C7
Marten	21	F5
Marthall	49	H5
Martham	45	J4
Martin *Hants.*	10	B3
Martin *Lincs.*	52	E6
Martin Drove End	10	B2
Martin Hussingtree	29	H2
Martinhoe	6	E1
Martinscroft	49	F4
Martinstown	9	F6
Martlesham	35	G4
Martlesham Heath	35	G4
Martletwy	16	D4
Martley	29	G2
Martock	8	D2
Marton *Ches.*	49	H6
Marton *Cumb.*	55	F2
Marton *E.Riding*	59	H6
Marton *Lincs.*	52	B4
Marton *Middbro.*	63	G5
Marton *N.Yorks.*	57	K3
Marton *N.Yorks.*	58	D2
Marton *Shrop.*	38	B5
Marton *Warks.*	31	F2
Marton Abbey	57	J2
Marton-le-Moor	57	J2
Martyr Worthy	11	G1
Martyr's Green	22	D6
Maruig	100	E7
Marwick	106	B5
Marwood	6	D2
Mary Tavy	6	D7
Marybank	96	B6
Maryburgh	96	C6
Maryfield	109	D8
Marygold	77	G5
Maryhill *Aber.*	99	G6
Maryhill *Glas.*	74	D4
Marykirk	83	H1
Marylebone *Gt.Lon.*	23	F3
Marylebone *Gt.Man.*	48	E2
Marypark	89	K1
Maryport *Cumb.*	60	B3
Maryport *D. & G.*	64	B7
Marystow	6	C7
Maryton	83	H2
Marywell *Aber.*	91	H5
Marywell *Aber.*	91	H2
Marywell *Angus*	83	H3
Masham	57	H1
Mashbury	33	K7
Mastrick	91	G4
Matching	33	J7
Matching Green	33	J7
Matching Tye	33	J7
Matfen	71	F6
Matfield	23	K7
Mathern	19	J2
Mathon	29	G4
Mathry	16	B2
Matlaske	45	F2
Matlock	51	F6
Matlock Bank	50	E6
Matlock Bath	50	E7
Matson	29	H7
Matterdale End	60	E4
Mattersey	51	J4
Mattingley	22	A6
Mattishall	44	E4
Mattishall Burgh	44	E4
Maud	99	H6
Maufant	3	K7
Maugersbury	30	C6
Maughold	54	D4
Mauld	87	K1
Maulden	32	D5
Maulds Meaburn	61	H5
Maunby	57	J1
Maund Bryan	28	E3
Maundown	7	J3
Mautby	45	J4
Mavesyn Ridware	40	C4
Mavis Enderby	53	G6
Maw Green	40	C6
Mawbray	60	B2
Mawdesley	48	D1
Mawdlam	18	B3
Mawgan	2	E6
Mawla	2	D4
Mawnan	2	E6
Mawnan Smith	2	E6
Mawsley	32	B1
Maxey	42	E5
Maxstoke	40	E7
Maxton *Kent*	15	H3
Maxton *Sc.Bord.*	70	B1
Maxwellheugh	77	F7
Maxwelltown	65	K3
Maxworthy	4	C1
Maybole	67	H3
Mayen	98	D6
Mayfield *E.Suss.*	13	J4
Mayfield *Midloth.*	76	B4
Mayfield *Staffs.*	40	D1
Mayford	22	C6
Mayland	25	F1
Maylandsea	25	F1
Maynard's Green	13	J5
Maypole *I.o.S.*	2	C1
Maypole *Kent*	25	H5
Maypole *Mon.*	28	D7
Maypole Green	45	J6
Maywick	109	C10
Meabhag	100	E7
Mead End	10	B2
Meadle	22	B1
Meadow Hall	51	F3
Meadowmill	76	C3
Meadowtown	38	C5
Meal Bank	61	G7
Mealabost	101	G2
Mealasta	100	B5
Meals	53	H3
Mealsgate	60	D2
Meanley	56	C5
Mearbeck	56	D3
Meare	19	H7
Mears Ashby	32	B2
Measham	41	F4
Meathop	55	H1
Meavy	5	F4
Medbourne	42	B6
Meddon	6	A4
Meden Vale	51	H6
Medmenham	22	B3
Medomsley	62	C1
Medstead	11	H1
Meer End	30	D1
Meerbrook	49	J6
Meesden	33	H5
Meeth	6	D5
Meggethead	69	G1
Meidrim	17	F3
Meifod *Denb.*	47	J7
Meifod *Powys*	38	A4
Meigle	82	D3
Meikle Earnock	75	F5
Meikle Grenach	73	J4
Meikle Kilmory	73	J4
Meikle Rahane	74	A2
Meikle Strath	90	E7
Meikle Tarty	91	H2
Meikle Wartle	91	F1
Meiklour	82	C4
Meinciau	17	H4
Meir	40	B1
Meirheath	40	B1
Melbost	101	G4
Melbourn	33	G4
Melbourne *Derbys.*	41	F3
Melbourne *E.Riding*	58	D5
Melbury	6	B4
Melbury Abbas	9	H3
Melbury Bubb	8	E4
Melbury Osmond	8	E4
Melbury Sampford	8	E4
Melby	109	A7
Melchbourne	32	D2
Melchet Court	10	D2
Melcombe Bingham	9	G4
Melcombe Regis	9	F6
Meldon *Devon*	6	D6
Meldon *Northumb.*	71	G5
Meldreth	33	G4
Melfort	79	K6
Melgarve	88	B5
Melgum	90	C4
Meliden (Gallt Melyd)	47	J4
Melincourt	18	B1
Melincryddan	18	A2
Melin-y-coed	47	G6
Melin-y-ddol	37	K5
Melin-y-grug	37	K5
Melin-y-Wig	37	K1
Melkinthorpe	61	H4
Melkridge	70	C7
Melksham	20	C5
Melksham Forest	20	C5
Melldalloch	73	H3
Melling *Lancs.*	55	J2
Melling *Mersey.*	48	C2
Melling Mount	48	D2
Mellis	34	E1
Mellon Charles	94	E2
Mellon Udrigle	94	E2
Mellor *Gt.Man.*	49	J4
Mellor *Lancs.*	56	B6
Mellor Brook	56	B6
Mells	20	A7
Melmerby *Cumb.*	61	H3

Melmerby *N.Yorks.* 57 F1
Melmerby *N.Yorks.* 57 J2
Melplash 8 D5
Melrose *Aber.* 99 F4
Melrose *Sc.Bord.* 76 D7
Melsetter 107 B9
Melsonby 62 C6
Meltham 50 C1
Melton 35 G3
Melton Constable 44 E2
Melton Mowbray 42 A4
Melton Ross 52 D1
Meltonby 58 D4
Melvaig 94 D3
Melverley 38 C4
Melverley Green 38 C4
Melvich 104 D2
Membury 8 B4
Memsie 99 H4
Memus 83 F2
Menabilly 4 A5
Menai Bridge (Porthaethwy) 46 D5
Mendham 45 G7
Mendlesham 35 F2
Mendlesham Green 34 E2
Menethorpe 58 D3
Menheniot 4 C4
Menie House 91 H2
Mennock 68 D3
Menston 57 G5
Menstrie 75 G1
Mentmore 32 C7
Meoble 86 D6
Meole Brace 38 D4
Meon 11 G4
Meonstoke 11 H3
Meopham 24 C5
Meopham Green 24 C5
Mepal 43 H7
Meppershall 32 E5
Merbach 28 C4
Mercaston 40 E1
Mere *Ches.* 49 G4
Mere *Wilts.* 9 H1
Mere Brow 48 D1
Mere Green 40 D6
Mereworth 23 K6
Mergie 91 F6
Meriden 40 E7
Merkland 65 H3
Merley 10 B5
Merlin's Bridge 16 C4
Merridge 8 B1
Merrifield 5 J6
Merrington 38 D3
Merrion 16 C6
Merriott 8 D3
Merrivale 5 F3
Merrow 22 D6
Merry Hill *Herts.* 22 E2
Merry Hill *W.Mid.* 40 B7
Merrymeet 4 C4
Mersham 15 F4
Merstham 23 F6
Merston 12 B6
Merstone 11 G6
Merther 3 F4
Merthyr 17 G3
Merthyr Cynog 27 J5
Merthyr Dyfan 18 E5
Merthyr Mawr 18 B4
Merthyr Tydfil 18 D1
Merthyr Vale 18 D2
Merton *Devon* 6 D4
Merton *Norf.* 44 C6
Merton *Oxon.* 31 G7
Mertyn 47 K5
Mervinslaw 70 B2
Meshaw 7 F4
Messing 34 C7
Messingham 52 B2
Metfield 45 G7
Metheringham 52 D6
Methil 76 B1
Methlem 36 A2
Methley 57 J7
Methlick 91 G1
Methven 82 B5
Methwold 44 B6
Methwold Hythe 44 B6
MetroCentre 71 H7
Mettingham 45 H6
Metton 45 F2
Mevagissey 4 A6
Mexborough 51 G3
Mey 105 H1
Meysey Hampton 20 E1
Miabhag 100 C7
Miabhig 100 C4
Mial 94 D4
Michaelchurch 28 E6
Michaelchurch Escley 28 C5
Michaelchurch-on-Arrow 28 B3
Michaelston-le-Pit 18 E4
Michaelston-y-Fedw 19 F3
Michaelstow 4 A3
Micheldever 11 G1
Michelmersh 10 E2
Mickfield 35 F2
Mickle Trafford 48 D6
Mickleby 63 K5
Mickleham 22 E6
Micklehurst 49 J2
Mickleover 41 F2
Micklethwaite 60 D1
Mickleton *Dur.* 62 A4
Mickleton *Glos.* 30 C4
Mickletown 57 J7
Mickley 57 H2
Mickley Square 71 F7
Mid Ardlaw 99 H4
Mid Beltie 90 E4
Mid Cairncross 90 D7
Mid Calder 75 J4
Mid Clyth 105 H5
Mid Lavant 12 B6
Mid Letter 80 B7
Mid Lix 81 G5
Mid Mossdale 61 K7
Mid Sannox 73 J6
Mid Yell 108 E3
Midbea 106 D3
Middle Assendon 22 A3
Middle Aston 31 F6
Middle Barton 31 F6
Middle Claydon 31 J6
Middle Drums 83 G2
Middle Handley 51 G5
Middle Harling 44 D7
Middle Kames 73 H2
Middle Littleton 30 B4
Middle Maes-coed 28 C5
Middle Mill 16 B3
Middle Rasen 52 D4
Middle Rigg 82 B7
Middle Salter 56 B3
Middle Town 2 C1
Middle Tysoe 30 E4
Middle Wallop 10 D1
Middle Winterslow 10 D1
Middle Woodford 10 C1
Middlebie 69 H6
Middleham 57 G1
Middlehill *Aber.* 99 G6
Middlehill *Cornw.* 4 C4
Middlehope 38 D7
Middlemarsh 9 F4
Middlesbrough 63 F4
Middleshaw 55 J1
Middlesmoor 57 F2
Middlestone Moor 62 D3
Middlestown 50 E1
Middleton *Aber.* 91 C3
Middleton *Angus* 83 G3
Middleton *Cumb.* 56 B1
Middleton *Derbys.* 50 E7
Middleton *Derbys.* 50 D6
Middleton *Essex* 34 C4
Middleton *Gt.Man.* 49 H2
Middleton *Hants.* 21 H7
Middleton *Lancs.* 55 H4
Middleton *Midloth.* 76 B5
Middleton *N.Yorks.* 58 D1
Middleton *Norf.* 44 A4
Middleton *Northants.* 42 B7
Middleton *Northumb.* 71 F5
Middleton *Northumb.* 77 J7
Middleton *P.& K.* 82 C7
Middleton *P.& K.* 82 C3
Middleton *Shrop.* 38 B6
Middleton *Shrop.* 28 E1
Middleton *Shrop.* 38 C3
Middleton *Suff.* 35 J2
Middleton *Swan.* 17 H7
Middleton *W.Yorks.* 57 G5
Middleton *W.Yorks.* 57 H7
Middleton *Warks.* 40 D6
Middleton Bank Top 71 F5
Middleton Cheney 31 F4
Middleton Green 40 B2
Middleton Hall 70 E1
Middleton of Potterton 91 H3
Middleton on the Hill 28 E2
Middleton One Row 62 E5
Middleton Park 91 H3
Middleton Priors 39 F7
Middleton Quernhow 57 J2
Middleton St. George 62 E5
Middleton Scriven 39 F7
Middleton Stoney 31 G6
Middleton Tyas 62 D6
Middleton-in-Teesdale 62 A4
Middleton-on-Leven 63 F5
Middleton-on-Sea 12 C7
Middleton-on-the-Wolds 59 F5
Middletown *Cumb.* 60 A6
Middletown *Powys* 38 C4
Middlewich 49 G6
Middlewood 49 J4
Middlewood Green 34 E2
Middleyard 74 D7
Middlezoy 8 C1
Middridge 62 D4
Midfield 103 H2
Midford 20 A5
Midge Hall 55 J7
Midgeholme 61 H1
Midgham 21 J5
Midgley *W.Yorks.* 50 E1
Midgley *W.Yorks.* 57 F7
Midhopestones 50 E3
Midhurst 12 B4
Midlem 70 A1
Midpark 73 J5
Midsomer Norton 19 K6
Midtown *High.* 103 H2
Midtown *High.* 94 E3
Midtown of Barras 91 G6
Midville 53 G7
Migdale 96 D2
Migvie 90 C4
Milarrochy 74 C1
Milber 5 J3
Milbethill 98 E5
Milborne Port 9 F3
Milborne St. Andrew 9 H5
Milborne Wick 9 F2
Milbourne 71 G6
Milburn 61 H4
Milbury Heath 19 K2
Milcombe 31 F5
Milden 34 D4
Mildenhall *Suff.* 34 B1
Mildenhall *Wilts.* 21 F4
Mile Elm 20 C5
Mile End *Essex* 34 D6
Mile End *Glos.* 28 E7
Milebrook 28 C1
Milebush 14 C3
Mileham 44 D4
Milesmark 75 J2
Milfield 77 H7
Milford *Derbys.* 41 F1
Milford *Devon* 6 A3
Milford *Shrop.* 38 D3
Milford *Staffs.* 40 B3
Milford *Surr.* 22 C7
Milford Haven (Aberdaugleddau) 16 C5
Milford on Sea 10 D5
Milkwall 19 J1
Mill Bank 57 F7
Mill End *Bucks.* 22 A3
Mill End *Herts.* 33 G5
Mill End Green 33 K6
Mill Green *Essex* 24 C1
Mill Green *Shrop.* 39 F3
Mill Hill 23 F2
Mill Houses 56 B3
Mill Lane 22 A6
Mill of Camsail 74 A2
Mill of Colp 99 F6
Mill of Elrick 99 H6
Mill of Fortune 81 J5
Mill of Kingoodie 91 G2
Mill of Monquich 91 G5
Mill of Uras 91 G7
Mill Street 44 E4
Milland 12 B4
Millbank 99 J6
Millbeck 60 D4
Millbounds 106 E4
Millbreck 99 J6
Millbridge 22 B7
Millbrook *Beds.* 32 D5
Millbrook *Cornw.* 4 E5
Millbrook *S'ham.* 10 E3
Millburn *Aber.* 90 D2
Millburn *Aber.* 90 E1
Millcombe 5 J6
Millcorner 14 D5
Millden 91 H3
Milldens 83 G2
Millearne 82 A6
Millenheath 38 E2
Millerhill 76 B4
Miller's Dale 50 D5
Millholme 61 G7
Millhouse *Arg. & B.* 73 H3
Millhouse *Cumb.* 60 E3
Millhousebridge 69 G5
Millikenpark 74 C4
Millington 58 E4
Millmeece 40 A2
Millness 87 K1
Millom 54 E1
Millport 73 K5
Millthrop 61 H7
Milltimber 91 G4
Milltown *Aber.* 90 C3
Milltown *D.& G.* 69 J6
Milltown *Derbys.* 51 F6
Milltown *Devon* 6 D2
Milltown *High.* 97 G7
Milltown *High.* 95 K6
Milltown of Aberdalgie 82 B5
Milltown of Auchindoun 98 B6
Milltown of Craigston 99 F5
Milltown of Edinvillie 97 K7
Milltown of Rothiemay 98 D6
Milltown of Towie 90 C3
Milnathort 82 C7
Milngavie 74 D3
Milnrow 49 J1
Milnsbridge 50 D1
Milnthorpe 55 H1
Milovaig 93 G6
Milrig 74 D7
Milson 29 F1
Milstead 14 E2
Milston 20 E7
Milton *Angus* 82 E3
Milton *Cambs.* 33 H2
Milton *Cumb.* 70 A7
Milton *D.& G.* 68 D5
Milton *D.& G.* 65 J3
Milton *Derbys.* 41 F3
Milton *High.* 96 E4
Milton *High.* 97 G6
Milton *High.* 94 D7
Milton *High.* 96 C7
Milton *High.* 105 J3
Milton *High.* 88 B1
Milton *Moray* 98 D4
Milton *N.Som.* 19 G5
Milton *Newport* 19 G3
Milton *Notts.* 51 K5
Milton *Oxon.* 31 F5
Milton *Oxon.* 21 H2
Milton *P.& K.* 82 A4
Milton *Pembs.* 16 D5
Milton *Stir.* 81 G7
Milton *Stir.* 74 C1
Milton *Stoke* 49 J7
Milton *W.Dun.* 74 C3
Milton Abbas 9 H4
Milton Abbot 4 E3
Milton Bridge 76 A4
Milton Bryan 32 C5
Milton Clevedon 9 F1
Milton Combe 4 E4
Milton Damerel 6 B4
Milton Ernest 32 D3
Milton Green 48 D7
Milton Hill 21 H2
Milton Keynes 32 B5
Milton Keynes Village 32 B5
Milton Lilbourne 20 E5
Milton Lockhart 75 G6
Milton Malsor 31 J3
Milton Morenish 81 H4
Milton of Auchinhove 90 D4
Milton of Balgonie 82 E7
Milton of Cairnborrow 98 C6
Milton of Callander 81 G7
Milton of Campfield 90 E4
Milton of Campsie 74 E3
Milton of Coldwells 91 H1
Milton of Cullerlie 91 F4
Milton of Cushnie 90 D3
Milton of Dalcapon 82 A2
Milton of Inveramsay 91 F2
Milton of Noth 90 D2
Milton of Tullich 90 B5
Milton on Stour 9 G2
Milton Regis 24 E5
Miltonduff 97 J5
Miltonhill 97 H5
Miltonise 64 B3
Milton-under-Wychwood 30 D7
Milverton 7 K3
Milwich 40 B2
Minard 73 H1
Minard Castle 73 H1
Minchington 9 J3
Minchinhampton 20 B1
Mindrum 77 G7
Minehead 7 H1
Minera 48 B7
Minety 20 D2
Minffordd *Gwyn.* 37 G4
Minffordd *Gwyn.* 36 E2
Mingearraidh 84 C2
Miningsby 53 G6
Minions 4 C3
Minishant 67 H2
Minley Manor 22 B6
Minllyn 37 H4
Minnes 91 H2
Minnigaff 64 E4
Minnonie 99 F4
Minskip 57 J3
Minstead 10 D3
Minster *Kent* 25 F4
Minster *Kent* 25 K5
Minster Lovell 30 E7
Minsterley 38 C5
Minsterworth 29 G7
Minterne Magna 9 F4
Minting 52 E5
Mintlaw 99 J6
Minto 70 A1
Minton 38 D6
Minwear 16 D4
Minworth 40 D6
Miodar 78 B3
Mirbister 106 C5
Mireland 105 J2
Mirfield 57 G7
Miserden 20 C1
Miskin *R.C.T.* 18 D3
Miskin *R.C.T.* 18 D2
Misson 51 J3
Misterton *Leics.* 41 H7
Misterton *Notts.* 51 K3
Misterton *Som.* 8 D4
Mitcham 23 F5
Mitchel Troy 28 D7
Mitcheldean 29 F7
Mitchell 3 F3
Mitchelland 61 F7
Mitcheltroy Common 19 H1
Mitford 71 G5
Mithian 2 E3
Mitton 40 A4
Mixbury 31 H5
Moar 81 G3
Moat 69 K6
Mobberley 49 G5
Moccas 28 C4
Mochdre *Conwy* 47 G5
Mochdre *Powys* 37 K7
Mochrum 64 D6
Mockbeggar 14 C3
Mockerkin 60 B4
Modbury 5 G5
Moddershall 40 B2
Modsarie 103 J2
Moelfre *I.o.A.* 46 D4
Moelfre *Powys* 38 A3
Moffat 69 F3
Mogerhanger 32 E4
Moin'a'choire 72 B4
Moine House 103 H2
Moira 41 F4
Molash 15 F2
Mol-chlach 85 K3
Mold (Yr Wyddgrug) 48 B6
Molehill Green 33 J6
Molescroft 59 G5
Molesworth 32 D1
Mollance 65 H4
Molland 7 G3
Mollington *Ches.* 48 C5
Mollington *Oxon.* 31 F4
Mollinsburn 75 F3
Monachty 26 E2
Monachyle 81 F6
Moncreiffe 82 C6
Monevechadan 80 C7
Monewden 35 G3
Moneydie 82 B5
Moniaive 68 C4
Monifieth 83 F4
Monikie 83 F4
Monimail 82 D6
Monington 16 E1
Monk Fryston 58 B7
Monk Sherborne 21 K6
Monk Soham 35 G2
Monk Street 33 K6
Monken Hadley 23 F2
Monkhill 60 E1
Monkhopton 39 F6
Monkland 28 D3
Monkleigh 6 C3
Monknash 18 C4
Monkokehampton 6 D5
Monks Eleigh 34 D4
Monk's Gate 13 F4
Monks' Heath 49 H5
Monks Kirby 41 G7
Monks Risborough 22 B1
Monkseaton 71 J6
Monkshill 99 F6
Monksilver 7 J2
Monkstadt 93 J5
Monkswood 19 G1
Monkton *Devon* 7 K5
Monkton *Kent* 25 J5
Monkton *S.Ayr.* 67 H1
Monkton *T.& W.* 71 J7
Monkton Combe 20 A5
Monkton Deverill 9 H1
Monkton Farleigh 20 A5
Monkton Heathfield 8 B2
Monkton Up Wimborne 10 B3
Monkwearmouth 62 E1
Monkwood 11 H1
Monmore Green 40 B6
Monmouth (Trefynwy) 28 E7
Monnington on Wye 28 C4
Monreith 64 D6
Montacute 8 D3
Monteach 99 G6
Montford 38 D4
Montford Bridge 38 D4
Montgarrie 90 D3
Montgomery (Trefaldwyn) 38 B6
Montgreenan 74 B6
Montrave 82 E7
Montrose 83 J2
Monxton 21 G7
Monyash 50 D6
Monymusk 90 E3
Monzie 81 K5
Moodiesburn 74 E3
Moonzie 82 E6
Moor Allerton 57 J6
Moor Cock 56 B3
Moor Crichel 9 J4
Moor End *Cumb.* 55 J2
Moor End *E.Riding* 58 E6
Moor Monkton 58 B4
Moor Nook 56 B6
Moor Row 60 B5
Moor Side 53 F7
Moorby 53 F6
Moorcot 28 C3
Moordown 10 B5
Moore 48 E4
Moorends 51 J1
Moorgreen 41 G1
Moorhall 51 F5
Moorhampton 28 C4
Moorhouse *Cumb.* 60 E1
Moorhouse *Notts.* 51 K6
Moorland or Northmoor Green 8 C1
Moorlinch 8 C1
Moorsholm 63 H5
Moorside 49 J2
Moortown *I.o.W.* 11 F6
Moortown *Lincs.* 52 D3
Morangie 96 E3
Morar 86 C5
Morborne 42 E6
Morchard Bishop 7 F5
Morcombelake 8 C5
Morcott 42 C6
Morda 38 B3
Morden *Dorset* 9 J5
Morden *Gt.Lon.* 23 F5
Mordiford 28 E5
Mordington Holdings 77 H5
Mordon 62 E4
More 38 C6
Morebath 7 H3
Morebattle 70 C1
Morecambe 55 H3
Morefield 95 H2
Moreleigh 5 H5
Morenish 81 H4
Moresby 60 A4
Morestead 11 G2
Moreton *Dorset* 9 H6
Moreton *Essex* 23 J1
Moreton *Here.* 28 E2
Moreton *Mersey.* 48 B4
Moreton *Oxon.* 21 K1
Moreton Corbet 38 E3
Moreton Jeffries 29 F4
Moreton Morrell 30 E3
Moreton on Lugg 28 E4
Moreton Pinkney 31 G4
Moreton Say 39 F2
Moreton Valence 20 A1
Moretonhampstead 7 F7
Moreton-in-Marsh 30 D5
Morfa Bychan 36 E2
Morfa Glas 18 B1
Morfa Nefyn 36 B1
Morgan's Vale 10 C2
Mork 19 J1
Morland 61 G4
Morley *Derbys.* 41 F1
Morley *Dur.* 62 C4
Morley *W.Yorks.* 57 H7
Morley Green 49 H4
Morley St. Botolph 44 E5
Morningside *Edin.* 76 A3
Morningside *N.Lan.* 75 G5
Morningthorpe 45 G6
Morpeth 71 G5
Morphie 83 J1
Morrey 40 D4
Morriston *S.Ayr.* 67 G3
Morriston *Swan.* 17 K6
Morroch 86 C6
Morston 44 E1
Mortehoe 6 C1
Mortimer 21 K5
Mortimer West End 21 K5
Mortimer's Cross 28 D2
Mortlake 23 F4
Morton *Derbys.* 51 G6
Morton *Lincs.* 42 E3
Morton *Lincs.* 52 B3
Morton *Notts.* 51 K7
Morton *S.Glos.* 19 K2
Morton *Shrop.* 38 B3
Morton Bagot 30 C2
Morton on the Hill 45 F4
Morton-on-Swale 62 E7
Morvah 2 A5
Morval 4 C5
Morvich *High.* 87 F2
Morvich *High.* 96 E1
Morvil 16 D2
Morville 39 F6
Morwellham 4 E4
Morwenstow 6 A4
Morwick Hall 71 H3
Mosborough 51 G4
Moscow 74 C6
Mosedale 60 E3
Moselden Height 50 C1
Moseley *W.Mid.* 40 C7
Moseley *Worcs.* 29 H3
Moss *Arg. & B.* 78 A3
Moss *S.Yorks.* 51 H1
Moss *Wrex.* 48 C7
Moss Bank 48 E3
Moss Nook 49 H4
Moss of Barmuckity 97 K5
Moss Side 55 G6
Mossat 90 C3
Mossbank 108 D5
Mossblown 67 J1
Mossburnford 70 B2
Mossdale 65 G3
Mossend 75 F4
Mossgiel 67 J1
Mosshead 90 D1
Mosside of Ballinshoe 83 F2
Mossley 49 J2
Mossley Hill 48 C4
Mosspaul Hotel 69 K4
Moss-side *High.* 97 F6
Moss-side *Moray* 98 D5
Mosstodloch 98 B4
Mosston 83 G3
Mosterton 8 D4
Mostyn 47 K4
Motcombe 9 H2
Motherby 61 F4
Motherwell 75 F5
Mottingham 23 H4
Mottisfont 10 E2
Mottistone 11 F6
Mottram in Longdendale 49 J3
Mottram St. Andrew 49 H5
Mouldsworth 48 E5
Moulin 82 A2
Moulsecoomb 13 G6
Moulsford 21 J3
Moulsham 24 D1
Moulsoe 32 C4
Moulton *Ches.* 49 F6
Moulton *Lincs.* 43 G3
Moulton *N.Yorks.* 62 D6
Moulton *Northants.* 31 J2
Moulton *Suff.* 33 K2
Moulton Chapel 43 F4
Moulton St. Mary 45 H5
Moulton Seas End 43 G3
Mounie Castle 91 F2
Mount *Cornw.* 2 E3
Mount *Cornw.* 4 B4
Mount *High.* 97 G7
Mount Bures 34 D5
Mount Hawke 2 E4
Mount Manisty 48 C5
Mount Oliphant 67 H2
Mount Pleasant *Derbys.* 41 F1
Mount Pleasant *Suff.* 35 J1
Mount Tabor 57 F7
Mountain Ash 18 D2
Mountain Cross 75 K6
Mountain Water 16 C3
Mountbenger 69 J1
Mountblairy 98 E5
Mountfield 14 C5
Mountgerald 96 C5
Mountjoy 3 F2
Mountnessing 24 C2
Mounton 19 J2
Mountsorrel 41 H4
Mousehole 2 B6
Mouswald 69 F6
Mow Cop 49 H7
Mowden 62 D5
Mowhaugh 70 D1
Mowsley 41 J7
Mowtie 91 G6
Moxley 40 B6
Moy *High.* 87 H6
Moy *High.* 88 B6
Moy *High.* 88 E1
Moy House 97 H5
Moyles Court 10 C4
Moylgrove 16 E1
Muasdale 72 E6
Much Birch 28 E5
Much Cowarne 29 F4
Much Dewchurch 28 D5
Much Hadham 33 H7
Much Hoole 55 H7
Much Marcle 29 F5
Much Wenlock 39 F5
Muchalls 91 G5
Muchelney 8 D2
Muchlarnick 4 C5
Muchra 69 H2
Muchrachd 87 J1
Mucking 24 C3
Mucklestone 39 G2
Muckleton 38 E3
Muckletown 90 D2
Muckton 53 G4
Mudale 103 H5
Muddiford 6 D2
Muddles Green 13 J5
Muddleswood 13 F5
Mudeford 10 C5
Mudford 8 E3
Mudgley 19 H7
Mugeary 85 K1
Mugginton 40 E1
Muggleswick 62 B1
Muie 96 D1
Muir 89 H6
Muir of Fowlis 90 D3
Muir of Lochs 98 B4
Muir of Ord 96 C6
Muirden 99 F5
Muirdrum 83 G4
Muirhead *Aber.* 90 D3
Muirhead *Angus* 82 E4
Muirhead *Fife* 82 D7
Muirhead *Moray* 97 H5
Muirhead *N.Lan.* 74 E4
Muirhouses 75 J2
Muirkirk 68 B1
Muirmill 75 F2
Muirtack *Aber.* 91 H1
Muirtack *Aber.* 99 G6
Muirton 96 E5
Muirton of Ardblair 82 C3
Muirton of Ballochy 83 H1
Muirtown 82 A6
Muiryfold 99 F5
Muker 62 A7
Mulbarton 45 F5
Mulben 98 B5
Mulhagery 101 F7
Mullach Charlabhaigh 100 E3
Mullacott Cross 6 D1
Mullion 2 D7
Mumby 53 J5
Munderfield Row 29 F3
Munderfield Stocks 29 F3
Mundesley 45 H2
Mundford 44 B6
Mundham 45 H6
Mundon 24 E1
Mundurno 91 H3
Munerigie 87 J4
Mungasdale 95 F2
Mungoswells 76 C3
Mungrisdale 60 E3
Munlochy 96 D6
Munnoch 74 A6
Munsley 29 F4
Munslow 38 E7
Murchington 6 E7
Murcott 31 G7
Murdostoun 75 G5
Murkle 105 G2
Murlaganmore 81 G4
Murlaggan *High.* 87 G5
Murlaggan *High.* 87 K6
Murra 107 B7
Murroes 83 F4
Murrow 43 G5
Mursley 32 B6
Murston 25 F5
Murthill 83 F2
Murthly 82 B4
Murton *Cumb.* 61 J4
Murton *Dur.* 62 E2
Murton *Northumb.* 77 H6
Murton *York* 58 C4
Musbury 8 B5
Muscoates 58 C1
Musdale 80 A5
Musselburgh 76 B3
Muston *Leics.* 42 B2
Muston *N.Yorks.* 59 H2
Mustow Green 29 H1
Mutford 45 J7
Muthill 81 K6
Mutterton 7 J5
Mybster 105 G3
Myddfai 27 G5
Myddle 38 D3
Myddlewood 38 D3
Mydroilyn 26 D3
Mylor 3 F5
Mylor Bridge 3 F5
Mynachlog-ddu 16 E2
Myndtown 38 C7
Mynydd Llandygai 46 E6
Mynydd-bach 19 H2
Mynytho 36 C2
Myrebird 91 F5
Mytchett 22 B6
Mytholm 56 E7
Mytholmroyd 57 F7
Myton-on-Swale 57 K3

N

Naast 94 E3
Naburn 58 B5
Nackington 15 G2
Nacton 35 G4
Nafferton 59 G4
Nailbridge 29 F7
Nailsea 19 H4
Nailstone 41 G5
Nailsworth 20 B2
Nairn 97 F6
Nancegollan 2 D5
Nancledra 2 B5
Nanhoron 36 B2
Nannau 37 G3
Nannerch 47 K6
Nanpantan 41 H4
Nanpean 3 G3
Nanstallon 4 A4
Nant Peris 46 E7
Nant-ddu 27 K7
Nanternis 26 C3
Nantgaredig 17 H3
Nantgarw 18 E3
Nant-glas 27 J2
Nantglyn 47 J6
Nantlle 46 D7
Nantmawr 38 B3
Nantmel 27 K2
Nantmor 37 F1
Nantwich 49 F7
Nantycaws 17 H4
Nant-y-derry 19 G1
Nant-y-dugoed 37 J4
Nantyffyllon 18 B2
Nantyglo 18 E1
Nant-y-groes 27 K2
Nant-y-moel 18 C2
Nant-y-Pandy 46 E5
Naphill 22 B2
Nappa 56 D4
Napton on the Hill 31 F2
Narberth (Arberth) 16 E4
Narborough *Leics.* 41 H6
Narborough *Norf.* 44 B4
Narrachan 80 A6
Nasareth 46 C7
Naseby 31 H1
Nash *Bucks.* 31 J5
Nash *Here.* 28 C2
Nash *Newport* 19 G3
Nash *Shrop.* 28 E1
Nash *V. of Glam.* 18 C4
Nash Lee 22 B1
Nassington 42 D6
Nasty 33 G6
Nateby *Cumb.* 61 J6
Nateby *Lancs.* 55 H5
Nately Scures 22 A6
Natland 55 J1
Naughton 34 E4
Naunton *Glos.* 30 C6
Naunton *Worcs.* 29 H5
Naunton Beauchamp 29 J3
Navenby 52 C7
Navestock 23 J2
Navestock Side 23 J2
Navidale 105 F7
Navity 96 E5
Nawton 58 C1
Nayland 34 D5
Nazeing 23 H1
Neacroft 10 C5
Neal's Green 41 F7
Neap 109 E7
Near Cotton 40 C1
Near Sawrey 60 E7
Neasham 62 E5
Neath (Castell-Nedd) 18 A2
Neatham 22 A7
Neatishead 45 H3
Nebo *Cere.* 26 E2
Nebo *Conwy* 47 G7
Nebo *Gwyn.* 46 C7
Nebo *I.o.A.* 46 C3
Necton 44 C5
Nedd 102 D5
Nedderton 71 H5
Nedging Tye 34 E4
Needham 45 G7
Needham Market 34 E3
Needingworth 33 G1
Neen Savage 29 F1
Neen Sollars 29 F1
Neenton 39 F7
Nefyn 36 C1
Neilston 74 C5
Nelson *Caerp.* 18 E2
Nelson *Lancs.* 56 D6
Nelson Village 71 H6
Nemphlar 75 G6
Nempnett Thrubwell 19 J5
Nenthall 61 J2
Nenthead 61 J2
Nenthorn 76 E7
Nerabus 72 A5
Nercwys 48 B6
Neriby 72 B4
Nerston 74 E5
Nesbit 77 H7
Ness 48 C5
Ness of Tenston 107 B6
Nesscliffe 38 C4
Neston *Ches.* 48 B5
Neston *Wilts.* 20 B5
Nether Alderley 49 H5
Nether Auchendrane 67 H2
Nether Barr 64 E4
Nether Blainslie 76 D6
Nether Broughton 41 J3
Nether Burrow 56 B2
Nether Cerne 9 F5

Nether Compton 8 E3
Nether Crimond 91 G2
Nether Dalgliesh 69 H3
Nether Dallachy 98 B4
Nether End 50 E5
Nether Exe 7 H6
Nether Glasslaw 99 G5
Nether Handwick 82 E3
Nether Haugh 51 G3
Nether Headon 51 K5
Nether Heselden 56 D2
Nether Heyford 31 H3
Nether Kellet 55 J3
Nether Kinmundy 99 J6
Nether Langwith 51 H5
Nether Lenshie 98 E6
Nether Moor 51 F6
Nether Padley 50 E5
Nether Pitforthie 91 G7
Nether Poppleton 58 B4
Nether Silton 63 F7
Nether Stowey 7 K2
Nether Urquhart 82 C7
Nether Wallop 10 E1
Nether Wasdale 60 C6
Nether Wellwood 68 B1
Nether Whitacre 40 E6
Nether (Lower) Winchendon 31 J7
Nether Worton 31 F5
Netheravon 20 E7
Netherbrae 99 F5
Netherbrough 107 C6
Netherburn 75 G6
Netherbury 8 D5
Netherby Cumb. 69 K6
Netherby N.Yorks. 57 J5
Nethercott 31 F6
Netherend 19 J2
Netherfield E.Suss. 14 C6
Netherfield Notts. 41 J1
Netherfield S.Lan. 75 F6
Netherhall 74 A4
Netherhampton 10 C1
Netherley 91 G5
Nethermill 69 F5
Nethermuir 99 H6
Netherseal 40 E4
Nethershield 67 K1
Netherstreet 20 C5
Netherthird D. & G. 65 H5
Netherthird E.Ayr. 67 K2
Netherthong 50 D2
Netherthorpe 51 H4
Netherton Angus 83 G2
Netherton Ches. 48 E5
Netherton Devon 5 J3
Netherton Mersey. 48 C2
Netherton Northum. 70 E3
Netherton Oxon. 21 H2
Netherton P. & K. 82 C2
Netherton S.Lan. 75 H5
Netherton W.Mid. 40 B7
Netherton W.Yorks. 50 E1
Netherton W.Yorks. 50 D1
Netherton Worcs. 29 J4
Nethertown Cumb. 60 A6
Nethertown Ork. 105 J1
Netherwitton 71 G5
Netherwood D. & G. 65 K3
Netherwood E.Ayr. 68 B1
Nethy Bridge 89 H2
Netley Abbey 11 F4
Netley Marsh 10 E3
Nettlebed 22 A3
Nettlebridge 19 K7
Nettlecombe Dorset 8 E5
Nettlecombe Som. 7 J2
Nettleden 22 D1
Nettleham 52 D5
Nettlestead Kent 23 K6
Nettlestead Suff. 34 E4
Nettlestead Green 23 K6
Nettlestone 11 H5
Nettleton Lincs. 52 E2
Nettleton Wilts. 20 B4
Netton Devon 5 F6
Netton Wilts. 10 C1
Neuadd Cere. 26 D3
Neuadd I.o.A. 46 B3
Neuadd Powys 27 J4
Nevendon 24 D2
Nevern 16 D2
Nevill Holt 42 B6
New Aberdour 99 G4
New Addington 23 G5
New Alresford 11 G1
New Alyth 82 D3
New Arley 40 E6
New Ash Green 24 C5
New Barn 24 C5
New Barnet 23 F2
New Belses 70 A1
New Bewick 71 F1
New Bolingbroke 53 G7
New Bradwell 32 B4
New Bridge 65 K3
New Brighton Hants. 11 J4
New Brighton Mersey. 48 C3
New Brinsley 51 G7
New Broughton 48 C7
New Buckenham 44 E6
New Byth 99 G5
New Cheriton 11 G2
New Costessey 45 F5
New Cross 27 F1
New Cumnock 68 B2
New Deer 99 G6
New Duston 31 J2
New Earswick 58 C4
New Edlington 51 H3
New Elgin 97 K5
New Eltham 23 H4
New End 30 B2
New England 42 E5
New Farnley 57 H6
New Ferry 48 C4
New Fryston 57 K7
New Galloway 65 G3
New Gilston 83 F7
New Grimsby 2 B1
New Hartley 71 J6

New Haw 22 D5
New Hedges 16 E5
New Holland 59 G7
New Houghton Derbys. 51 H6
New Houghton Norf. 44 B3
New Houses 56 D2
New Hutton 61 G4
New Hythe 14 C2
New Inn Carmar. 17 H2
New Inn Fife 82 D7
New Inn Mon. 19 H1
New Inn Torfaen 19 F2
New Invention Shrop. 28 B1
New Invention W.Mid. 40 B5
New Lanark 75 G6
New Lane 48 D1
New Leake 53 H7
New Leeds 99 H5
New Leslie 90 D2
New Longton 55 J7
New Luce 64 B4
New Mains 75 G7
New Mains of Ury 91 G6
New Malden 23 F5
New Marske 63 H4
New Marton 38 C2
New Mill Cornw. 2 B5
New Mill Herts. 32 C7
New Mill W.Yorks. 50 D2
New Mill End 32 E7
New Mills Cornw. 3 F3
New Mills Derbys. 49 J4
New Mills Mon. 19 J1
New Mills Powys 37 K5
New Milton 10 D5
New Mistley 35 F5
New Moat 16 D3
New Orleans 66 B2
New Park 4 B2
New Pitsligo 99 G5
New Polzeath 3 G1
New Quay (Ceinewydd) 26 C3
New Rackheath 45 G4
New Radnor 28 B2
New Rent 61 F3
New Romney 15 F5
New Rossington 51 J3
New Row 56 B6
New Sawley 41 G2
New Silksworth 62 E1
New Town E.Loth. 76 C3
New Town E.Suss. 13 H4
New Town Glos. 30 B6
New Tredegar 18 E1
New Tupton 51 F6
New Ulva 73 F2
New Walsoken 43 H5
New Waltham 53 F2
New Winton 76 C3
New Yatt 31 F7
New York Lincs. 53 F7
New York T. & W. 71 J6
Newark Ork. 106 G3
Newark Peter. 43 F5
Newark-on-Trent 52 B7
Newarthill 75 F5
Newbarn 15 G3
Newbarns 55 F2
Newbiggin Cumb. 61 F4
Newbiggin Cumb. 61 H4
Newbiggin Cumb. 61 G2
Newbiggin Cumb. 55 F3
Newbiggin Dur. 62 A4
Newbiggin N.Yorks. 57 F1
Newbiggin N.Yorks. 62 A7
Newbiggin Northumb. 70 E7
Newbiggin-by-the-Sea 71 J5
Newbigging Aber. 91 G5
Newbigging Aber. 89 J6
Newbigging Angus 83 F4
Newbigging Angus 83 F4
Newbigging Angus 82 D3
Newbigging S.Lan. 75 J6
Newbiggin-on-Lune 61 J4
Newbold Derbys. 51 F5
Newbold Leics. 41 G4
Newbold on Avon 31 F1
Newbold on Stour 30 D3
Newbold Pacey 30 D3
Newbold Verdon 41 Gb
Newborough I.o.A. 46 C6
Newborough Peter. 43 F5
Newborough Staffs. 40 D3
Newbottle 31 G5
Newbourne 35 G4
Newbridge (Cefn Bychan) Caerp. 19 F2
Newbridge Cornw. 2 B5
Newbridge Cornw. 4 D4
Newbridge Edin. 75 K3
Newbridge Hants. 10 E3
Newbridge I.o.W. 11 F6
Newbridge Oxon. 21 H1
Newbridge Pembs. 16 C2
Newbridge Wrex. 38 B1
Newbridge Green 29 H5
Newbridge-on-Usk 19 G2
Newbrough 70 D7
Newburgh Aber. 99 H5
Newburgh Aber. 91 H2
Newburgh Fife 82 D6
Newburgh Lancs. 48 D1
Newburgh Sc.Bord. 69 J2
Newburn 71 G7
Newbury 21 H5
Newby Cumb. 61 G4
Newby Lancs. 56 D5
Newby N.Yorks. 63 G5
Newby N.Yorks. 56 D2
Newby Bridge 55 G1
Newby East 61 F1
Newby West 60 E1
Newby Wiske 57 J1
Newcastle Bridgend 18 C4
Newcastle Mon. 28 D7
Newcastle Shrop. 38 B7

Newcastle Emlyn (Castell Newydd Emlyn) 17 G1
Newcastle International Airport 71 G6
Newcastle upon Tyne 71 H7
Newcastleton 69 K5
Newcastle-under-Lyme 40 A1
Newchapel Pembs. 17 F2
Newchapel Stoke 49 H7
Newchapel Surr. 23 G7
Newchurch Carmar. 17 G3
Newchurch I.o.W. 11 G6
Newchurch Kent 15 F4
Newchurch Lancs. 56 D7
Newchurch Lancs. 56 D6
Newchurch Mon. 19 H2
Newchurch Powys 28 B3
Newcott 8 B4
Newcraighall 76 B3
Newdigate 22 E7
Newell Green 22 B4
Newenden 14 D5
Newent 29 G6
Newerne 19 K1
Newfield Dur. 62 D3
Newfield Dur. 62 D1
Newfield High. 96 E4
Newgale 16 B3
Newgate 44 E1
Newgate Street 23 G1
Newgord 108 E2
Newhall Ches. 39 F1
Newhall Derbys. 40 E3
Newham 71 G1
Newham Hall 71 G1
Newhaven 13 H6
Newhey 49 J1
Newholm 63 K5
Newhouse 75 F4
Newick 13 H4
Newingreen 15 G4
Newington Kent 15 G4
Newington Kent 24 E5
Newington Oxon. 21 K2
Newington Bagpath 20 B2
Newland Glos. 19 J1
Newland N.Yorks. 58 C7
Newland Worcs. 29 G4
Newlandrig 76 B4
Newlands Northumb. 62 B1
Newlands Sc.Bord. 70 A4
Newland's Corner 22 D7
Newlands of Geise 105 F2
Newlyn 2 B6
Newlyn East 3 F3
Newmachar 91 G3
Newmains 75 G5
Newmarket Suff. 33 K2
Newmarket W.Isles 101 G4
Newmill Aber. 91 F6
Newmill Aber. 99 G6
Newmill Aber. 91 G2
Newmill Moray 98 C5
Newmill Sc.Bord. 69 K2
Newmill of Inshewan 83 F1
Newmills 96 D5
Newmiln P. & K. 82 C4
Newmiln P. & K. 82 B5
Newmilns 74 D7
Newnham Glos. 29 F7
Newnham Hants. 22 A6
Newnham Herts. 33 F5
Newnham Kent 14 E2
Newnham Northants. 31 G3
Newnham Worcs. 29 F2
Newnham Paddox 41 G7
Newnoth 90 D1
Newport Cornw. 6 B7
Newport Devon 6 D2
Newport E.Riding 58 E6
Newport Essex 33 J5
Newport Glos. 19 K2
Newport High. 105 G6
Newport I.o.W. 11 G6
Newport (Casnewydd) Newport 19 G3
Newport Norf. 45 K4
Newport Pembs. 16 D2
Newport Tel. & W. 39 G4
Newport Pagnell 32 B4
Newport-on-Tay 83 F5
Newpound Common 12 D4
Newquay 3 F2
Newquay Cornwall Airport 3 F2
Newseat 91 F1
Newsham Lancs. 55 J6
Newsham N.Yorks. 62 C5
Newsham N.Yorks. 57 J1
Newsham Northumb. 71 H6
Newsholme E.Riding 58 D7
Newsholme Lancs. 56 D4
Newstead Northumb. 71 G1
Newstead Notts. 51 H7
Newstead Sc.Bord. 76 D7
Newthorpe N.Yorks. 57 K6
Newton Aber. 98 C6
Newton Aber. 91 J6
Newton Arg. & B. 73 J1
Newton Bridgend 18 B4
Newton Cambs. 43 H4
Newton Cambs. 33 H4
Newton Ches. 48 D7
Newton Ches. 48 D5
Newton Cumb. 55 F2
Newton D. & G. 69 G4
Newton Gt.Man. 49 J3
Newton Here. 28 C2
Newton High. 105 J4
Newton High. 96 E7
Newton High. 105 H3
Newton High. 96 C6
Newton High. 96 E5
Newton Lancs. 56 B4
Newton Lancs. 55 J2
Newton Lincs. 42 D2
Newton Moray 98 B4
Newton N.Ayr. 73 H5
Newton Norf. 44 C4
Newton Northant. 42 B7
Newton Notts. 41 J1
Newton P. & K. 81 K4

Newton Pembs. 16 C3
Newton Pembs. 16 C5
Newton S.Lan. 75 H7
Newton Sc.Bord. 70 A1
Newton Staffs. 40 C3
Newton Suff. 34 D4
Newton Swan. 17 K7
Newton W.Loth. 75 J3
Newton W.Yorks. 57 K7
Newton Warks. 31 G1
Newton Wilts. 10 D2
Newton Abbot 5 J3
Newton Arlosh 60 C1
Newton Aycliffe 62 D4
Newton Bewley 63 F4
Newton Blossomville 32 C3
Newton Bromswold 32 D2
Newton Burgoland 41 F5
Newton by Toft 52 D4
Newton Ferrers 5 F6
Newton Flotman 45 G6
Newton Harcourt 41 J6
Newton Kyme 57 K5
Newton Longville 32 B5
Newton Mearns 74 D5
Newton Morrell 62 D6
Newton Mountain 16 C5
Newton Mulgrave 63 J5
Newton of Affleck 83 F4
Newton of Ardtoe 86 C7
Newton of Balcanquhal 82 C6
Newton of Dalvey 97 H6
Newton of Falkland 82 D7
Newton of Leys 96 D7
Newton on Trent 52 B5
Newton Poppleford 7 J7
Newton Purcell 31 H5
Newton Regis 40 E5
Newton Reigny 61 F3
Newton St. Cyres 7 G6
Newton St. Faith 45 G4
Newton St. Loe 20 A5
Newton St. Petrock 6 C4
Newton Solney 40 E3
Newton Stacey 21 H7
Newton Stewart 64 E4
Newton Tony 21 F7
Newton Tracey 6 D3
Newton under Roseberry 63 G5
Newton upon Derwent 58 D5
Newton Valence 11 J1
Newtonairds 68 D5
Newtongrange 76 B4
Newtonhill 91 H5
Newton-le-Willows Mersey. 48 E3
Newton-le-Willows N.Yorks. 57 H1
Newtonmill 83 H1
Newtonmore 88 E5
Newton-on-Ouse 58 B3
Newton-on-Rawcliffe 63 K7
Newton-on-the-Moor 71 G3
Newtown B.Gwent 28 A7
Newtown Bucks. 22 C1
Newtown Ches. 48 D7
Newtown Cumb. 70 A7
Newtown Derbys. 49 J4
Newtown Hants. 11 H3
Newtown Hants. 21 H5
Newtown Hants. 10 D3
Newtown Hants. 10 E2
Newtown Hants. 11 G3
Newtown Here. 29 G5
Newtown Here. 29 F4
Newtown High. 87 K4
Newtown I.o.M. 54 C6
Newtown I.o.W. 11 F5
Newtown Northumb. 71 F3
Newtown Northumb. 71 F1
Newtown Poole 10 B5
Newtown (Y Drenewydd) Powys 38 A6
Newtown Shrop. 38 D2
Newtown Staffs. 49 J6
Newtown Staffs. 50 C6
Newtown Wilts. 9 J2
Newtown in St. Martin 2 E6
Newtown Linford 41 H4
Newtown St. Boswells 76 D7
Newtown Unthank 41 G5
Newtyle 82 D3
Neyland 16 C5
Nibley Glos. 19 K1
Nibley S.Glos. 19 K3
Nicholashayne 7 K4
Nicholaston 17 J7
Nidd 57 J3
Niddrie 76 A3
Nigg Aberdeen 91 H4
Nigg High. 97 F4
Nightcott 7 G3
Nilig 47 J7
Nimlet 20 A4
Nine Ashes 23 J1
Nine Elms 20 E3
Nine Mile Burn 75 K5
Ninebanks 61 J1
Ninemile Bar or Crocketford 65 J3
Ninfield 14 C6
Ningwood 11 F6
Nisbet 70 B1
Niton 11 G7
Nitshill 74 D4
Nizels 23 J6
No Man's Heath Ches. 38 E1
No Man's Heath Warks. 40 E5
Noak Hill 23 J2
Noblehill 65 K3
Nobottle 31 H2
Nocton 52 D6
Noddsdale 74 A4
Noke 31 G7
Nolton 16 B4
Nomansland Devon 7 G4
Nomansland Wilts. 10 D3
Noneley 38 D3
Nonington 15 H2
Nook Cumb. 69 K6
Nook Cumb. 55 J1
Noonsbrough 109 B7
Noranside 83 F1

Norbiton 22 E5
Norbreck 55 G5
Norbury Ches. 38 E1
Norbury Derbys. 40 D1
Norbury Shrop. 38 C6
Norbury Staffs. 39 G3
Norchard 29 H2
Nordelph 43 J5
Norden 9 J6
Nordley 39 F6
Norham 77 H6
Norland Town 57 F7
Norley 48 E5
Norleywood 10 E5
Norman Cross 42 E6
Normanby N.Lincs. 52 B1
Normanby N.Yorks. 58 D1
Normanby R. & C. 63 G5
Normanby by Stow 52 B4
Normanby le Wold 52 E3
Normanby-by-Spital 52 D4
Normandy 22 C6
Norman's Ruh 79 F3
Norman's Bay 13 K6
Norman's Green 7 J5
Normanton Derby 41 F2
Normanton Leics. 42 B1
Normanton Lincs. 42 C1
Normanton Notts. 51 K7
Normanton Rut. 42 C5
Normanton W.Yorks. 57 J7
Normanton le Heath 41 F4
Normanton on Soar 41 H3
Normanton on Trent 51 K6
Normanton-on-the-Wolds 41 J2
Normoss 55 G6
Norrington Common 20 B5
Norris Hill 41 F4
North Anston 51 H4
North Ascot 22 C5
North Aston 31 F6
North Baddesley 10 E2
North Ballachulish 80 B1
North Balloch 67 H4
North Barrow 9 F2
North Barsham 44 D2
North Benfleet 24 D3
North Bersted 12 C6
North Berwick 76 D2
North Boarhunt 11 H3
North Bogbain 98 B5
North Bovey 7 F7
North Bradley 20 B6
North Brentor 6 C7
North Brewham 9 G1
North Buckland 6 C1
North Burlingham 45 H4
North Cadbury 9 F2
North Cairn 66 D6
North Camp 22 B6
North Carlton Lincs. 52 C5
North Carlton Notts. 51 H4
North Cave 58 E6
North Cerney 20 D1
North Chailey 13 G4
North Charford 10 C3
North Charlton 71 G1
North Cheriton 9 F2
North Cliffe 58 E6
North Clifton 52 B5
North Cockerington 53 G3
North Coker 8 E3
North Connel 80 A4
North Cornelly 18 B3
North Cotes 53 G2
North Cove 45 J7
North Cowton 62 D6
North Crawley 32 C4
North Creake 44 C2
North Curry 8 C2
North Dallens 80 A3
North Dalton 59 F4
North Dawn 107 D7
North Deighton 57 J4
North Duffield 58 C6
North Elkington 53 F3
North Elmham 44 D3
North Elmsall 51 G1
North End Bucks. 32 B6
North End Essex 33 K7
North End Hants. 21 H5
North End N.Som. 19 H5
North End Norf. 44 E6
North End Northumb. 71 G3
North End Ports. 11 H4
North End W.Suss. 12 E5
North Erradale 94 D3
North Essie 99 J5
North Ferriby 59 F7
North Frodingham 59 H4
North Gorley 10 C3
North Green 45 G7
North Grimston 58 E3
North Hayling 11 J4
North Hazelrigg 77 F7
North Heasley 7 F2
North Heath 12 D4
North Hill 4 C3
North Hinksey 21 H1
North Holmwood 22 E7
North Huish 5 H5
North Hykeham 52 C6
North Johnston 16 C4
North Kelsey 52 D2
North Kessock 96 D7
North Killingholme 52 E1
North Kilvington 57 K1
North Kilworth 41 J7
North Kyme 52 E7
North Lancing 12 E6
North Lee 30 C7
North Leigh 30 E7
North Leverton with Habblesthorpe 51 K4
North Littleton 30 B4
North Lopham 44 E7
North Luffenham 42 C5
North Marden 12 B5
North Marston 31 J6
North Middleton 76 B5
North Millbrex 99 G6
North Molton 7 F3
North Moreton 21 J3

North Mundham 12 B6
North Muskham 51 K7
North Newbald 59 F5
North Newington 31 F5
North Newton 20 E6
North Nibley 20 A2
North Oakley 21 J6
North Ockendon 23 J3
North Ormesby 63 G4
North Ormsby 53 F3
North Otterington 62 E7
North Owersby 52 D3
North Perrott 8 D4
North Petherton 8 B1
North Petherwin 4 C2
North Pickenham 44 C5
North Piddle 29 J3
North Poorton 8 E5
North Queensferry 75 K2
North Radworthy 7 F2
North Rauceby 42 D1
North Reston 53 G4
North Rigton 57 H5
North Rode 49 H6
North Roe 108 C4
North Runcton 44 A4
North Sandwick 108 E3
North Scale 54 E3
North Scarle 52 B6
North Seaton 71 H5
North Shian 80 A3
North Shields 71 J7
North Shoebury 25 F3
North Side 43 F6
North Skelton 63 H5
North Somercotes 53 H3
North Stainley 57 H2
North Stainmore 61 K5
North Stifford 24 C3
North Stoke B. & N.E.Som. 19 K5
North Stoke Oxon. 21 K3
North Stoke W.Suss. 12 D5
North Stoneham 11 F3
North Street Hants. 11 H1
North Street Kent 15 F2
North Street W.Berks. 21 K4
North Sunderland 77 K4
North Tamerton 6 B6
North Tarbothill 91 H3
North Tawton 6 E5
North Third 75 F2
North Thoresby 53 F3
North Tidworth 21 F7
North Togston 71 H3
North Town Devon 6 D5
North Town Hants. 22 B6
North Tuddenham 44 E4
North Walsham 45 G2
North Waltham 21 J7
North Warnborough 22 A6
North Watten 105 H3
North Weald Bassett 23 H1
North Wheatley 51 K4
North Whilborough 5 J4
North Wick 19 J5
North Widcombe 19 J6
North Willingham 52 E4
North Wingfield 51 G6
North Witham 42 C3
North Wootton Dorset 9 F3
North Wootton Norf. 44 A3
North Wootton Som. 19 J7
North Wraxall 20 B4
North Wroughton 20 E3
North Yardhope 70 E3
Northacre 44 D6
Northall Green 44 E4
Northallerton 62 E7
Northam Devon 6 C3
Northam S'ham. 11 F3
Northampton 31 J2
Northaw 23 F1
Northay 8 B3
Northborough 42 E5
Northbourne 15 J2
Northbrook 31 F6
Northburnhill 99 G6
Northchapel 12 C4
Northchurch 22 C1
Northcote Manor 6 E4
Northcott 6 B6
Northdyke 106 B5
Northend B. & N.E.Som. 20 A5
Northend Bucks. 22 A2
Northend Warks. 30 E3
Northfield Aber. 99 G4
Northfield Aberdeen 91 G4
Northfield High. 105 J4
Northfield Sc.Bord. 77 H4
Northfield W.Mid. 30 B1
Northfleet 24 C4
Northhouse 69 K3
Northiam 14 D5
Northill 32 E4
Northington 11 G1
Northlands 53 G7
Northleach 30 C7
Northleigh Devon 7 K6
Northleigh Devon 6 E2
Northlew 6 D6
Northmoor 21 H1
Northmoor Green or Moorland 8 C1
Northmuir 82 E2
Northney 11 J4
Northolt 22 E3
Northop 48 B6
Northop Hall 48 B6
Northorpe Lincs. 43 F2
Northorpe Lincs. 52 B3
Northorpe Lincs. 42 D4
Northover 8 D2
Northowram 57 G7
Northpunds 109 D10
Northrepps 45 G2
Northton (Taobh Tuath) 92 E3
Northway 29 J5
Northwich 49 F5
Northwick 19 J3
Northwold 44 B6
Northwood Gt.Lon. 22 D2
Northwood I.o.W. 11 F5
Northwood Shrop. 38 D2

Northwood Green 29 G7
Norton Glos. 29 H6
Norton Halton 48 E4
Norton Herts. 33 F5
Norton I.o.W. 10 E6
Norton N.Yorks. 58 D2
Norton Northants. 31 H2
Norton Notts. 51 H5
Norton Powys 28 C2
Norton S.Yorks. 51 H1
Norton S.Yorks. 51 F4
Norton Shrop. 38 E5
Norton Shrop. 39 G5
Norton Stock. 63 F4
Norton Suff. 34 D2
Norton W.Mid. 40 A7
Norton W.Suss. 12 C6
Norton W.Suss. 12 B7
Norton Wilts. 20 B3
Norton Worcs. 29 H3
Norton Worcs. 30 B4
Norton Bavant 20 C7
Norton Bridge 40 A2
Norton Canes 40 C5
Norton Canon 28 C4
Norton Disney 52 B7
Norton Ferris 9 G1
Norton Fitzwarren 7 K3
Norton Green 10 E6
Norton Hawkfield 19 J5
Norton Heath 24 C1
Norton in Hales 39 F2
Norton in the Moors 49 H7
Norton Lindsey 30 D2
Norton Malreward 19 J5
Norton Mandeville 23 J1
Norton St. Philip 20 A6
Norton sub Hamdon 8 D3
Norton Subcourse 45 J6
Norton Wood 28 C4
Norton-Juxta-Twycross 41 F5
Norton-le-Clay 57 J2
Norwell 51 K6
Norwell Woodhouse 51 K6
Norwich 45 G5
Norwich Airport 45 G4
Norwick 108 F1
Norwood Green 23 F7
Norwood Hill 23 F7
Noseley 42 A6
Noss Mayo 5 F6
Nosterfield 57 H1
Nostie 86 E2
Notgrove 30 C6
Nottage 18 B4
Nottingham High. 105 H3
Nottingham Nott. 41 H1
Notton S.Yorks. 51 F1
Notton Wilts. 20 C5
Nounsley 34 B1
Noutard's Green 29 G2
Nowton 34 C2
Nox 38 D4
Noyadd Trefawr 17 F1
Nuffield 21 K3
Nun Monkton 58 B4
Nunburnholme 58 E5
Nuneaton 41 F6
Nuneham Courtenay 21 J2
Nunney 20 A7
Nunnington 58 C2
Nunnington Park 7 J3
Nunthorpe 63 G5
Nunton 10 C2
Nunwick N.Yorks. 57 J2
Nunwick Northumb. 70 D6
Nup End Bucks. 32 B7
Nup End Glos. 29 H6
Nursling 10 E3
Nursted 11 J2
Nurton 40 A6
Nutbourne W.Suss. 12 D5
Nutbourne W.Suss. 11 J4
Nutfield 23 G6
Nuthall 41 H1
Nuthampstead 33 H5
Nuthurst W.Suss. 12 E4
Nuthurst Warks. 30 C1
Nutley E.Suss. 13 H4
Nutley Hants. 21 K7
Nutwell 51 J2
Nyadd 75 F1
Nybster 105 J2
Nyetimber 12 B7
Nyewood 11 J2
Nymet Rowland 7 F5
Nymet Tracey 7 F5
Nympsfield 20 B1
Nynehead 7 K3
Nythe 8 D1
Nyton 12 C6

O
Oad Street 24 E5
Oadby 41 J5
Oak Cross 6 D6
Oakamoor 40 C1
Oakbank Arg. & B. 79 J4
Oakbank W.Loth. 75 J4
Oakdale 18 E2
Oake 7 K3
Oaken 40 A5
Oakenclough 55 J5
Oakengates 39 F4
Oakenhead 97 K5
Oakenshaw Dur. 62 D3
Oakenshaw W.Yorks. 57 G7
Oakford Cere. 26 D3
Oakford Devon 7 H3
Oakfordbridge 7 H3
Oakgrove 49 J6
Oakham 42 B5
Oakhanger 11 J1
Oakhill 19 K7
Oakington 33 H2
Oaklands Conwy 47 G7
Oaklands Herts. 33 F7
Oakle Street 29 G7
Oakley Beds. 32 D3
Oakley Bucks. 31 H7
Oakley Fife 75 J2
Oakley Hants. 21 J6
Oakley Suff. 35 F1
Oakley Green 22 C4
Oakley Park 37 J7
Oakridge Lynch 20 C1
Oaks 38 D5
Oaksey 20 C2

Oakshaw Ford 70 A6
Oakthorpe 41 F4
Oaktree Hill 62 E7
Oakwoodhill 12 E3
Oakworth 57 F6
Oalinlongart 73 K2
Oare *Kent* 25 G5
Oare *Som.* 7 G1
Oare *Wilts.* 20 E5
Oasby 42 D2
Oatfield 66 A2
Oathlaw 83 F2
Oban 79 K5
Obley 28 C1
Oborne 9 F3
Occlestone Green 49 F6
Occold 35 F1
Occumster 105 H5
Ochiltree 67 K1
Ochr-y-Mynydd 18 D1
Ochtermuthill 81 K6
Ochtertyre *P. & K.* 81 K5
Ochtertyre *Stir.* 75 F1
Ockbrook 41 G2
Ockham 22 D6
Ockle 86 B7
Ockley 12 E3
Ocle Pychard 28 E4
Octon 59 G3
Odcombe 8 E3
Odd Down 20 A5
Oddingley 29 J3
Oddington 31 G7
Oddsta 108 E3
Odell 32 C3
Odie 106 F5
Odiham 22 A6
Odstock 10 C2
Odstone 41 F5
Offchurch 30 E2
Offenham 30 B4
Offerton 49 J4
Offham *E.Suss.* 13 H5
Offham *Kent* 23 K6
Offord Cluny 33 F2
Offord D'Arcy 33 F2
Offton 34 E4
Offwell 7 K6
Ogbourne Maizey 20 E4
Ogbourne
St. Andrew 20 E4
Ogbourne
St. George 20 E4
Ogden 57 F6
Ogil 83 F1
Ogle 71 G6
Ogmore 18 B4
Ogmore Vale 18 C2
Ogmore-by-Sea 18 B4
Oil Terminal 107 C8
Okeford Fitzpaine 9 H3
Okehampton 6 D6
Okehampton Camp 6 D6
Okraquoy 109 D9
Old 31 J1
Old Aberdeen 91 H4
Old Alresford 11 G1
Old Arley 40 E6
Old Basford 41 H1
Old Basing 21 K6
Old Belses 70 A1
Old Bewick 71 F1
Old Bolingbroke 53 G6
Old Brampton 51 F5
Old Bridge of Urr 65 H4
Old Buckenham 44 E6
Old Burghclere 21 H6
Old Byland 58 B1
Old Cleeve 7 J1
Old Clipstone 51 J6
Old Colwyn 47 G5
Old Craig 91 H2
Old Craighall 76 B3
Old Crombie 98 D5
Old Dailly 67 G4
Old Dalby 41 J3
Old Deer 99 H6
Old Ellerby 59 H6
Old Felixstowe 35 H5
Old Fletton 42 E6
Old Glossop 50 C3
Old Goginan 37 F7
Old Goole 58 D7
Old Gore 29 F6
Old Grimsby 2 B1
Old Hall 53 F1
Old Heath 34 E6
Old Hill 40 B7
Old Hutton 55 J1
Old Kea 3 F4
Old Kilpatrick 74 C3
Old Kinnernie 91 F4
Old Knebworth 33 F6
Old Leake 53 H7
Old Leslie 90 D2
Old Malton 58 D2
Old Micklefield 57 K6
Old Milverton 30 D2
Old Montsale 25 G2
Old Netley 11 F3
Old Newton 34 E2
Old Philpstoun 75 J3
Old Poltalloch 79 K7
Old Radnor 28 B3
Old Rattray 99 J5
Old Rayne 90 E2
Old Romney 15 F5
Old Scone 82 C5
Old Shields 75 G3
Old Sodbury 20 A3
Old Somerby 42 C2
Old Stratford 31 J4
Old Sunderlandwick 59 G4
Old Swarland 71 G3
Old Swinford 40 B7
Old Town *Cumb.* 55 J1
Old Town *I.o.S.* 2 C1
Old Town
Northumb. 70 D4
Old Tupton 51 F6
Old Warden 32 E4
Old Weston 32 E1
Old Windsor 22 C4
Old Wives Lees 15 F2
Old Woking 22 D6
Old Wolverton 32 B4
Old Woods 38 D3
Oldberrow 30 C2
Oldborough 7 F5
Oldbury *Kent* 23 J6
Oldbury *Shrop.* 39 G6
Oldbury *W.Mid.* 40 B6
Oldbury *Warks.* 41 F6
Oldbury Naite 19 K2
Oldbury on the Hill 20 B3
Oldbury-on-Severn 19 K2
Oldcastle 28 C6
Oldcastle Heath 38 D1
Oldcotes 51 H4
Oldfield *W.Yorks.* 57 F6
Oldfield *Worcs.* 29 H2
Oldford 20 A6
Oldhall *Aber.* 90 C5
Oldhall *High.* 105 H3
Oldham 49 J2
Oldhamstocks 77 F3
Oldhurst 33 F1
Oldland 19 K4
Oldmeldrum 91 G2
Oldmill 90 D4
Oldpark 39 F5
Oldridge 7 G6
Oldshore Beg 102 D3
Oldshore More 102 E3
Oldstead 58 B1
Oldtown of Aigas 96 B7
Oldtown of Ord 98 E5
Oldwalls 17 H6
Oldways End 7 G3
Oldwhat 99 G5
Olgrinmore 105 F3
Oliver 69 G1
Oliver's Battery 11 F2
Ollaberry 108 C4
Ollerton *Ches.* 49 G5
Ollerton *Notts.* 51 J6
Ollerton *Shrop.* 39 F3
Olmstead Green 33 K4
Olney 32 B3
Olrig House 105 G2
Olton 40 D7
Olveston 19 J3
Ombersley 29 H2
Ompton 51 J6
Onchan 54 C6
Onecote 50 C7
Ongar Hill 43 J3
Ongar Street 28 C2
Onibury 28 D1
Onich 80 B1
Onllwyn 27 H7
Onneley 39 G1
Onslow Village 22 C7
Opinan *High.* 94 E2
Opinan *High.* 94 D4
Orange Lane 77 F6
Orbliston 98 B5
Orbost 93 H7
Orby 53 H6
Orcadia 73 K4
Orchard 73 K2
Orchard Portman 8 B2
Orchard Wyndham 7 J2
Orcheston 20 D7
Orcop 28 D6
Orcop Hill 28 D6
Ord 86 C3
Ordhead 90 E3
Ordie 90 C4
Ordiequish 98 B5
Ordsall 51 K5
Ore 14 D6
Oreham Common 13 F5
Oreston 5 F5
Oreton 39 F7
Orford *Suff.* 35 J4
Orford *Warr.* 49 F3
Orgreave 40 D4
Orleton *Here.* 28 D2
Orleton *Worcs.* 29 F2
Orleton Common 28 D2
Orlingbury 32 B1
Ormacleit 84 C1
Ormesby 63 G5
Ormesby
St. Margaret 45 J4
Ormesby
St. Michael 45 J4
Ormiscaig 94 E2
Ormiston 76 C4
Ormsaigmore 79 F1
Ormsdale 73 J2
Ormskirk 48 D2
Ormwe 105 G2
Orphir 107 C7
Orpington 23 H5
Orrell 48 E2
Orrisdale 54 C4
Orrok House 91 H3
Orroland 65 H6
Orsett 24 C3
Orslow 40 A4
Orston 42 A1
Orton *Cumb.* 61 H6
Orton *Northants.* 32 B1
Orton Longueville 42 E6
Orton Waterville 42 E6
Orton-on-the-Hill 41 F5
Orwell 33 G4
Osbaldeston 56 B6
Osbaldwick 58 C4
Osbaston *Leics.* 41 G5
Osbaston
Tel. & W. 38 E4
Osborne 11 G5
Osbournby 42 D2
Oscroft 48 E6
Ose 93 J7
Osgathorpe 41 G4
Osgodby *Lincs.* 52 D3
Osgodby *N.Yorks.* 58 C6
Osgodby *N.Yorks.* 59 G1
Oskaig 86 B1
Osmaston *Derby* 41 F2
Osmaston *Derbys.* 40 D1
Osmington 9 G6
Osmington Mills 9 G6
Osmotherley 63 F7
Osnaburgh or
Dairsie 83 F6
Osney 21 J1
Ospringe 15 F2
Ossett 57 H7
Ossington 51 K6
Ostend 25 F2
Osterley 22 E4
Oswaldkirk 58 C2
Oswaldtwistle 56 C7
Oswestry 38 B3
Otford 23 J6
Otham 14 C2
Othery 8 C1
Otley *Suff.* 35 G3
Otley *W.Yorks.* 57 H5
Otter 73 H3
Otter Ferry 73 H2
Otterbourne 11 F2
Otterburn
N.Yorks. 56 D4
Otterburn
Northumb. 70 D4
Otterburn Camp 70 D4
Otterden Place 14 E2
Otterham 4 B1
Otterhampton 19 F7
Ottershaw 22 D5
Otterswick 108 E4
Otterton 7 J7
Ottery St. Mary 7 J6
Ottinge 15 G3
Ottringham 59 J7
Oughterby 60 D1
Oughtershaw 56 D1
Oughtibridge 51 F3
Oulston 58 B2
Oulton *Cumb.* 60 D1
Oulton *Norf.* 45 F3
Oulton *Staffs.* 40 B2
Oulton *Suff.* 45 K6
Oulton *W.Yorks.* 57 J7
Oulton Broad 45 K6
Oulton Street 45 F3
Oundle 42 D7
Ousby 61 H3
Ousdale 105 F6
Ousden 34 B3
Ousefleet 58 E7
Ouston *Dur.* 62 D1
Ouston *Northumb.* 71 F6
Out Newton 59 K7
Out Rawcliffe 55 H5
Outertown 107 B6
Outgate 60 E7
Outhgill 61 J6
Outlands 39 G3
Outlane 50 C1
Outwell 43 J5
Outwood *Surr.* 23 G7
Outwood *W.Yorks.* 57 J7
Ovenden 57 F7
Over *Cambs.* 33 G2
Over *Ches.* 49 F6
Over *S.Glos.* 19 J3
Over Compton 8 E3
Over End 50 E5
Over Haddon 50 E6
Over Kellet 55 J2
Over Kiddington 31 F6
Over Norton 30 E6
Over Peover 49 G5
Over Rankeilour 82 E6
Over Silton 63 F7
Over Stowey 7 K2
Over Stratton 8 D3
Over Tabley 49 G4
Over Wallop 10 D1
Over Whitacre 40 E6
Over (Upper)
Winchendon 31 J7
Over Worton 31 F6
Overbister 106 F3
Overbrae 99 G5
Overbury 29 J5
Overcombe 9 F6
Overleigh 8 D1
Overpool 48 C5
Overscaig Hotel 103 G6
Overseal 40 E4
Oversland 15 F2
Oversley Green 30 B3
Overstone 32 B2
Overstrand 45 G1
Overton *Aber.* 91 F3
Overton *Aberdeen* 91 G3
Overton *Hants.* 21 J7
Overton *Lancs.* 55 H4
Overton *N.Yorks.* 58 B4
Overton *Shrop.* 28 E1
Overton *Swan.* 17 H7
Overton *Wrex.* 38 C1
Overtown 75 G5
Overy Staithe 44 C1
Oving *Bucks.* 31 J6
Oving *W.Suss.* 12 C6
Ovingdean 13 G6
Ovingham 71 F7
Ovington *Dur.* 62 C5
Ovington *Essex* 34 B4
Ovington *Hants.* 11 G1
Ovington *Norf.* 44 D5
Ovington
Northumb. 71 F7
Ower 10 E3
Owermoigne 9 G6
Owlswick 22 A1
Owmby 52 D2
Owmby-by-Spital 52 D4
Owslebury 11 G2
Owston 42 A5
Owston Ferry 52 B2
Owstwick 59 J6
Owthorpe 41 J2
Oxborough 44 B5
Oxcliffe Hill 55 H3
Oxcombe 53 G5
Oxen End 33 K6
Oxen Park 55 G1
Oxenholme 61 G7
Oxenhope 57 F6
Oxenton 29 J5
Oxenwood 21 G6
Oxford 21 J1
Oxhill 30 E4
Oxley 40 B5
Oxley Green 34 D7
Oxley's Green 13 K4
Oxnam 70 B2
Oxnead 45 G3
Oxnop Ghyll 62 A7
Oxshott 22 E5
Oxspring 50 E2
Oxted 23 G6
Oxton *Mersey.* 48 C4
Oxton *Notts.* 51 J7
Oxton *Sc.Bord.* 76 C5
Oxwich 17 J7
Oxwich Green 17 J7
Oxwick 44 D3
Oykel Bridge 95 K1
Oyne 90 E2
Ozleworth 20 A2

P

Pabail Iarach 101 H4
Pabail Uarach 101 H4
Packington 41 F4
Padanaram 83 F2
Padbury 31 J5
Paddington 23 F3
Paddlesworth 15 G3
Paddock Wood 23 K7
Paddockhaugh 97 K6
Paddockhole 69 H5
Paddolgreen 38 E2
Padeswood 48 B6
Padiham 56 C6
Padside 57 G4
Padstow 3 G1
Padworth 21 K5
Pagham 12 B7
Paglesham
Churchend 25 F2
Paglesham
Eastend 25 F2
Paibeil 92 C5
Paible 93 F2
Paignton 5 J4
Pailton 41 G7
Painscastle 28 A4
Painshawfield 71 F7
Painswick 20 B1
Paisley 74 C4
Pakefield 45 K6
Pakenham 34 D2
Pale 37 J2
Palestine 21 F7
Paley Street 22 B4
Palgowan 67 H5
Palgrave 35 F1
Pallinsburn House 77 G7
Palmerscross 97 K5
Palmerstown 18 E5
Palnackie 65 J5
Palnure 64 E4
Palterton 51 G6
Pamber End 21 K6
Pamber Green 21 K6
Pamber Heath 21 K5
Pamington 29 J5
Pamphill 9 J4
Pampisford 33 H4
Pan 107 C8
Panborough 19 H7
Panbride 83 G4
Pancrasweek 6 A5
Pandy *Gwyn.* 37 F5
Pandy *Mon.* 28 C6
Pandy *Powys* 37 J5
Pandy *Wrex.* 38 A2
Pandy Tudur 47 G6
Panfield 34 B6
Pangbourne 21 K4
Pannal 57 J4
Panpunton 28 B1
Pant *Shrop.* 38 B3
Pant *Wrex.* 38 B1
Pant Glas 36 D1
Pant Gwyn 37 H3
Pant Mawr 37 H7
Pantasaph 47 K5
Pantglas 37 G6
Pantgwyn 17 F1
Pant-lasau 17 K5
Panton 52 E5
Pant-pastynog 47 J6
Pantperthog 37 G5
Pant-y-dwr 27 J1
Pantyffordd 48 B7
Pant-y-ffridd 38 A5
Pantyffynnon 17 K4
Panxworth 45 H4
Papcastle 60 C3
Papple 76 D3
Papplewick 51 H7
Papworth Everard 33 F2
Papworth
St. Agnes 33 F2
Par 4 A5
Parbold 48 D1
Parbrook 8 E1
Parc 37 H2
Parcllyn 26 B3
Parcrhydderch 27 F3
Parc-Seymour 19 H2
Pardshaw 60 B4
Parham 35 H2
Parish Holm 68 C1
Park 98 D5
Park Corner 21 K3
Park End 70 D6
Park Gate 11 G4
Park Lane 38 D2
Park Street 22 E1
Parkend *Cumb.* 60 D3
Parkend *Glos.* 19 K1
Parkeston 35 G5
Parkford 83 F2
Parkgate *Ches.* 48 B5
Parkgate *D. & G.* 69 F5
Parkgate *S.Yorks.* 51 G3
Parkgate *Surr.* 23 F7
Parkham 6 B3
Parkham Ash 6 B3
Parkhill *Angus* 83 H3
Parkhill *P. & K.* 82 C3
Parkhouse 19 J1
Parkhurst 11 F5
Parkmill 17 J7
Parkmore 98 B6
Parkneuk 91 F7
Parkstone 10 B5
Parley Cross 10 B5
Parracombe 6 E1
Parrog 16 D2
Parson Drove 43 G5
Parsonby 60 C3
Partick 74 D4
Partington 49 G3
Partney 53 H6
Parton *Cumb.* 60 A4
Parton *D. & G.* 65 G3
Partridge Green 12 E5
Parwich 50 D7
Passenham 31 J5
Passfield 12 B3
Passingford
Bridge 23 H2
Paston 45 H2
Patcham 13 G6
Patching 12 D6
Patchole 6 E1
Patchway 19 J3
Pateley Bridge 57 G3
Path of Condie 82 B6
Pathe 8 C1
Pathfinder Village 7 G6
Pathhead *Aber.* 83 J1
Pathhead *E.Ayr.* 68 B2
Pathhead *Fife* 76 A1
Pathhead *Midloth.* 76 B4
Patmore Heath 33 H6
Patna 67 J2
Patney 20 D6
Patrick 54 B5
Patrick Brompton 62 D7
Patrington 59 K7
Patrishow 28 B6
Patrixbourne 15 G2
Patterdale 60 E5
Pattingham 40 A6
Pattishall 31 H3
Pattiswick 34 C6
Paul 2 B6
Paulerspury 31 J4
Paull 59 H7
Paulton 19 K6
Pauperhaugh 71 G4
Pavenham 32 C3
Pawlett 19 F7
Pawston 77 G7
Paxford 30 C5
Paxhill Park 13 G4
Paxton 77 H5
Payhembury 7 J5
Paynes Hall 33 G7
Paythorne 56 D4
Peacehaven 13 H6
Peacemarsh 9 H2
Peachley 29 H3
Peak Dale 50 C5
Peak Forest 50 D5
Peakirk 42 E5
Pean Hill 25 H5
Pearsie 82 E2
Pease Pottage 13 F3
Peasedown
St. John 20 A6
Peasemore 21 H4
Peasenhall 35 H2
Peaslake 22 D7
Peasmarsh 14 D5
Peaston 76 C4
Peastonbank 76 C4
Peat Inn 83 F7
Peathill 99 H4
Peatling Magna 41 H6
Peatling Parva 41 H7
Peaton 38 E7
Pebble Coombe 23 F6
Pebmarsh 34 C5
Pebworth 30 C4
Pecket Well 56 E7
Peckforton 48 E7
Peckleton 41 G5
Pedmore 40 B7
Pedwell 8 D1
Peebles 76 A6
Peel 54 B5
Pegswood 71 H5
Peighinn nan
Aoireann 84 C1
Peinchorran 86 B1
Peinlich 93 K6
Pelaw 71 H7
Pelcomb Bridge 16 C4
Pelcomb Cross 16 C4
Peldon 34 D7
Pelsall 40 C5
Pelton 62 D1
Pelutho 60 C2
Pelynt 4 C5
Pembrey 17 H5
Pembridge 28 C3
Pembroke (Penfro) 16 C5
Pembroke Dock
(Doc Penfro) 16 C5
Pembury 23 K7
Penallt 28 E7
Penally 16 E6
Penalt 28 E6
Penare 3 G4
Penarth 18 E4
Pen-bont
Rhydybeddau 37 F7
Penboyr 17 G2
Penbryn 26 B3
Pencader 17 H2
Pencaenewydd 36 D1
Pencaitland 76 C4
Pencarreg 17 J1
Pencelli 27 K6
Pen-clawdd 17 J6
Pencoed 18 C3
Pencombe 28 E3
Pencoyd 28 E6
Pencraig *Here.* 28 E6
Pencraig *Powys* 37 K3
Pendeen 2 A5
Penderyn 18 C1
Pendine 17 F5
Pendlebury 49 G2
Pendleton 56 C6
Pendock 29 G5
Pendoggett 4 A3
Pendomer 8 E3
Pendoylan 18 D4
Penegoes 37 G5
Pen-ffordd 16 D3
Penfro (Pembroke) 16 C5
Pengam 18 E2
Penge 23 G4
Pengenffordd 28 A5
Pengorffwysfa 46 C3
Pengover Green 4 C4
Pen-groes-oped 19 G1
Pengwern 47 J5
Penhale 2 D7
Penhallow 2 E3
Penhalvean 2 E5
Penhow 19 H2
Penhurst 13 K5
Peniarth 37 F5
Penicuik 76 A4
Penifiler 93 K7
Peninver 66 B1
Penisa'r Waun 46 D6
Penisarcwn 37 K4
Penistone 50 E2
Penjerrick 2 E5
Penketh 48 E4
Penkill 67 G4
Penkridge 40 B4
Penley 38 D2
Penllech 36 B2
Penllergaer 17 K6
Pen-llyn *I.o.A.* 46 B4
Penllyn
V. of Glam. 18 C4
Penmachno 47 F7
Penmaen 17 J7
Penmaenmawr 47 F5
Penmaenpool 37 F4
Penmark 18 D5
Penmon 46 E4
Penmorfa 36 E1
Penmynydd 46 D5
Penn *Bucks.* 22 C2
Penn *W.Mid.* 40 A6
Penn Street 22 C2
Pennal 37 F5
Pennan 99 G4
Pennance 2 E4
Pennant *Cere.* 26 E2
Pennant *Powys* 37 H6
Pennant Melangell 37 K3
Pennard 17 J7
Pennerley 38 C6
Penninghame 64 D4
Pennington 55 F2
Pennsylvania 20 A4
Penny Bridge 55 G1
Pennyfuir 79 K4
Pennyghael 79 G5
Pennyglen 67 G2
Pennygown 79 H3
Pennymoor 7 G4
Penparc *Cere.* 17 F1
Penparc *Pembs.* 16 B2
Penparcau 36 E7
Penperlleni 19 G1
Penpillick 4 A5
Penpol 3 F5
Penpoll 4 B5
Penpont *D. & G.* 68 D4
Penpont *Powys* 27 J6
Penprysg 18 C3
Penrherber 17 F2
Penrhiwceiber 18 D2
Penrhiwgoch 17 J4
Penrhiw-llan 17 G1
Penrhiw-pal 17 G1
Penrhos *Gwyn.* 36 C2
Penrhos *I.o.A.* 46 A4
Penrhos *Mon.* 28 D7
Penrhos *Powys* 27 H7
Penrhos-garnedd 46 D5
Penrhyn Bay
(Bae Penrhyn) 47 G4
Penrhyn-coch 37 F7
Penrhyndeudraeth 37 F2
Penrhyn-side 47 G4
Penrhys 18 D2
Penrice 17 H7
Penrith 61 G3
Penrose 3 F1
Penruddock 61 F4
Penryn 2 E5
Pensarn *Carmar.* 17 H4
Pensarn *Conwy* 47 H5
Pen-sarn *Gwyn.* 36 E3
Pen-sarn *Gwyn.* 36 D1
Pensax 29 G2
Pensby 48 B4
Penselwood 9 G1
Pensford 19 K5
Pensham 29 J4
Penshaw 62 E1
Penshurst 23 J7
Pensilva 4 C4
Pensnett 40 B7
Pentewan 4 A6
Pentir 46 D6
Pentire 2 E2
Pentireglaze 3 G1
Pentlepoir 16 E5
Pentlow 34 C4
Pentney 44 B4
Penton Mewsey 21 G7
Pentraeth 46 D5
Pentre *Powys* 37 K3
Pentre *Powys* 37 K7
Pentre *Powys* 28 B2
Pentre *Powys* 38 B6
Pentre *R.C.T.* 18 C2
Pentre *Shrop.* 38 C4
Pentre *Wrex.* 38 B1
Pentre Berw 46 C5
Pentre Galar 16 E2
Pentre Gwenlais 17 K4
Pentre Gwynfryn 36 E3
Pentre Halkyn 48 B5
Pentre Isaf 47 G6
Pentre Llanrhaeadr 47 J6
Pentre Maelor 38 C1
Pentre Saron 47 J6
Pentrebach *M.Tyd.* 18 D1
Pentre-bach
Powys 27 J5
Pentrebach *Swan.* 17 K5
Pentre-bont 47 F7
Pentre-bwlch 38 A1
Pentrecagal 17 G1
Pentre-celyn
Denb. 47 K7
Pentre-celyn
Powys 37 H5
Pentre-chwyth 17 K6
Pentreclwydau 18 B1
Pentre-cwrt 17 G2
Pentre-Dolau-
Honddu 27 J4
Pentredwr *Denb.* 38 A1
Pentre-dwr *Swan.* 17 K6
Pentrefelin *Carmar.* 17 J3
Pentrefelin *Cere.* 17 K1
Pentrefelin *Conwy* 47 G5
Pentrefelin *Gwyn.* 36 E2
Pentrefelin *Powys* 38 A3
Pentrefoelas 47 G7
Pentregat 26 C3
Pentreheyling 38 B6
Pentre-Llwyn-
Llwyd 27 J3
Pentre-llyn-cymmer 47 H7
Pentre-piod 37 H2
Pentre-Poeth 19 F3
Pentre'r beirdd 38 A4
Pentre'r-felin 27 J5
Pentre-tafarn-y-
fedw 47 G6
Pentre-ty-gwyn 27 H5
Pentrich 51 F7
Pentridge 10 B3
Pentwyn *Cardiff* 19 F3
Pen-twyn *Mon.* 19 J1
Pentyrch 18 E3
Penuwch 26 E2
Penwithick 4 A5
Penwortham 55 J7
Penwyllt 27 H7
Pen-y-banc 17 K3
Pen-y-bont
Carmar. 27 G5
Pen-y-bont *Powys* 37 K4
Pen-y-bont *Powys* 38 B3
Penybont *Powys* 28 A2
Pen-y-bont ar Ogwr
(Bridgend) 18 C4
Penybontfawr 37 K3
Penybryn *Caerp.* 18 E2
Pen-y-bryn *Gwyn.* 37 F4
Pen-y-cae *Powys* 27 H7
Penycae *Wrex.* 38 B1
Pen-y-cae-mawr 19 H2
Pen-y-cefn 47 K5
Pen-y-clawdd 19 H1
Pen-y-coedcae 18 D3
Penycwm 16 B3
Pen-y-fai 18 B3
Penyffordd 48 C6
Pen-y-garn 17 J2
Penygarnedd 38 A3
Pen-y-garreg 27 K4
Penygraig 18 C2
Penygroes *Carmar.* 17 J4
Penygroes *Gwyn.* 46 C7
Pen-y-Gwryd Hotel 46 E7
Pen-y-Park 28 B4
Pen-yr-hoel 28 D7
Pen-y-sarn 46 C3
Pen-y-stryt 47 K7
Penywaun 18 C1
Penzance 2 B5
Penzance Heliport 2 B5
Peopleton 29 J3
Peover Heath 49 G5
Peper Harow 22 C7
Peplow 39 F3
Perceton 74 B6
Percie 90 D5
Perham Down 21 F7
Perivale 22 E3
Perkhill 90 D4
Perkins Beach 38 C5
Perlethorpe 51 J5
Perranarworthal 2 E5
Perranporth 2 E3
Perranuthnoe 2 C6
Perranzabuloe 2 E3
Perry Barr 40 C6
Perry Green 33 H7
Perry Street 24 C4
Pershall 40 A3
Pershore 29 J4
Persie House 82 C2
Pert 83 H1
Pertenhall 32 D2
Perth 82 C5
Perthy 38 C2
Perton 40 A6
Peter Tavy 5 F3
Peterborough 42 E6
Peterburn 94 D3
Peterchurch 28 C5
Peterculter 91 G4
Peterhead 99 K6
Peterlee 63 F2
Peter's Green 32 E7
Peters Marland 6 C4
Petersfield 11 J2
Peterstone
Wentlooge 19 F3
Peterston-super-Ely 18 D4
Peterstow 28 E6
Petham 15 G2
Petrockstow 6 D5
Pett 14 D6
Pettaugh 35 F3
Pettinain 75 H6
Pettistree 35 G3
Petton *Devon* 7 J3
Petton *Shrop.* 38 D3
Petty 91 F1
Pettycur 76 A2
Pettymuick 91 H2
Petworth 12 C4
Pevensey 13 K6
Pevensey Bay 13 K6
Pewsey 20 E5
Phesdo 90 E7
Philham 6 A3
Philiphaugh 69 K1
Phillack 2 C5
Philleigh 3 F5
Philpstoun 75 J3
Phoenix Green 22 A6
Phones 88 E5
Phorp 97 H6
Pibsbury 8 D2
Pica 60 B4
Piccadilly Corner 45 G7
Piccotts End 22 D1
Pickerells 23 J1
Pickering 58 E1
Picket Piece 21 G7
Picket Post 10 C4
Pickford Green 40 E7
Pickhill 57 J1
Picklescott 38 D6
Pickletillem 83 F5
Pickmere 49 F5
Pickstock 39 G3
Pickston 82 A5
Pickwell *Devon* 6 C1
Pickwell *Leics.* 42 A4
Pickworth *Lincs.* 42 D2
Pickworth *Rut.* 42 C4
Picton *Ches.* 48 D5
Picton *N.Yorks.* 63 F6
Piddinghoe 13 H6
Piddington
Northants. 32 B3
Piddington *Oxon.* 31 H7
Piddlehinton 9 G5
Piddletrenthide 9 G5
Pidley 33 G1
Piercebridge 62 D5
Pierowall 106 D3
Pigdon 71 G5
Pikehall 50 D7
Pilgrims Hatch 23 J2
Pilham 52 B3
Pill 19 J4
Pillaton 4 D4
Pillerton Hersey 30 D4
Pillerton Priors 30 D4
Pilleth 28 B2
Pilley *Glos.* 29 J7
Pilley *Hants.* 10 E5
Pilley *S.Yorks.* 51 F2
Pilling 55 H5
Pilling Lane 55 G5
Pillowell 19 K1
Pilning 19 J3
Pilsbury 50 D6
Pilsdon 8 D5
Pilsgate 42 D5
Pilsley *Derbys.* 51 G6
Pilsley *Derbys.* 50 E5
Piltdown 13 H4
Pilton *Devon* 6 D2
Pilton *Northants.* 42 D7
Pilton *Rut.* 42 C5
Pilton *Som.* 19 J7
Pimperne 9 J4
Pinchbeck 43 F3
Pinchbeck Bars 43 F3
Pinchbeck West 43 F3
Pinchinthorpe 63 G5
Pinfold 48 C1
Pinhay 8 C5
Pinhoe 7 H6
Pinkneys Green 22 B3
Pinley Green 30 D2
Pinminnoch 67 F4
Pinmore 67 G4
Pinn 7 K7
Pinner 22 E3
Pinner Green 22 E2
Pinvin 29 J4
Pinwherry 67 F5
Pinxton 51 G7
Pipe & Lyde 28 E4
Pipe Gate 39 G1
Pipe Ridware 40 C4
Piperhall 73 J5
Piperhill 97 F6
Pipers Pool 4 C2
Pipewell 42 B7
Pippacott 6 D2
Pipton 28 A5
Pirbright 22 C6
Pirnmill 73 G6
Pirton *Herts.* 32 E5
Pirton *Worcs.* 29 H4
Pisgah 81 J7
Pishill 22 A3
Pistyll 36 C1

Place	Page	Grid
Pitagowan	81	K1
Pitblae	99	H4
Pitcairngreen	82	B5
Pitcairns	82	B6
Pitcaple	91	F2
Pitch Green	22	A1
Pitch Place	22	C6
Pitchcombe	20	B1
Pitchcott	31	J7
Pitchford	38	E5
Pitcombe	9	F1
Pitcot	18	B4
Pitcox	76	E3
Pitcur	82	D4
Pitfichie	90	E3
Pitgrudy	96	E2
Pitinnan	91	F1
Pitkennedy	83	G2
Pitkevy	82	D7
Pitlessie	82	E7
Pitlochry	82	A2
Pitmedden	91	G2
Pitminster	8	B3
Pitmuies	83	G3
Pitmunie	90	E3
Pitnacree	82	A2
Pitney	8	D2
Pitroddie	82	D5
Pitscottie	83	F6
Pitsea	24	D3
Pitsford	31	J2
Pitsford Hill	7	J2
Pitstone	32	C7
Pitstone Green	32	C7
Pitt *Devon*	7	J4
Pitt *Hants.*	11	F2
Pittendreich	97	J5
Pittentrail	96	E1
Pittenweem	83	G7
Pittington	62	E2
Pittodrie House	90	E2
Pitton	10	D1
Pity Me	62	D2
Pityme	3	G1
Pixey Green	35	G1
Place Newton	58	E2
Plaidy	99	F5
Plains	75	F4
Plaish	38	E6
Plaistow	12	D3
Plaitford	10	D3
Plas	17	H3
Plas Gogerddan	37	F7
Plas Gwynant	46	E2
Plas Isaf	37	K1
Plas Llwyd	47	H5
Plas Llwyngwern	37	G5
Plas Llysyn	37	J6
Plas Nantyr	38	A2
Plasisaf	47	H6
Plas-rhiw-Saeson	37	J5
Plastow Green	21	J5
Plas-yn-Cefn	47	J5
Platt	23	K6
Platt Bridge	49	F2
Platt Lane	38	E2
Plawsworth	62	D2
Plaxtol	23	K6
Play Hatch	22	A4
Playden	14	E5
Playford	35	G4
Playing Place	3	F4
Plealey	38	D5
Plean	75	G2
Pleasance	82	D6
Pleasington	56	B7
Pleasley	51	H6
Plenmeller	70	C7
Pleshey	33	K7
Plockton	86	E1
Ploughfield	28	C4
Plowden	38	C7
Ploxgreen	38	C5
Pluckley	14	E3
Pluckley Thorne	14	E3
Plumbland	60	C3
Plumley	49	G5
Plumpton *Cumb.*	61	F3
Plumpton *E.Suss.*	13	G5
Plumpton End	31	J4
Plumpton Green	13	G5
Plumpton Head	61	G3
Plumstead *Gt.Lon.*	23	H4
Plumstead *Norf.*	45	F2
Plumtree	41	J2
Plungar	42	A2
Plush	9	G4
Plwmp	26	C3
Plym Bridge	5	F5
Plymouth	4	E5
Plymouth City Airport	5	F4
Plympton	5	F5
Plymstock	5	F5
Plymtree	7	J5
Pockley	58	C1
Pocklington	58	E5
Pocombe Bridge	7	G6
Pode Hole	43	F3
Podimore	8	E2
Podington	32	C2
Podmore	39	G2
Poffley End	30	E7
Pointon	42	E2
Pokesdown	10	C5
Polanach	80	A2
Polapit Tamar	6	B7
Polbae	64	C3
Polbain	102	B7
Polbathic	4	D5
Polbeth	75	J4
Polchar	89	F4
Poldean	69	G4
Pole Moor	50	C1
Polebrook	42	D7
Polegate	13	J6
Poles	96	E2
Polesworth	40	E5
Polglass	95	G1
Polgooth	3	G3
Polgown	68	C3
Poling	12	D6
Poling Corner	12	D6
Polkerris	4	A5
Poll a' Charra	84	C3
Polla	103	F3
Polldubh	80	C1
Pollie	104	C7
Pollington	51	J1
Polloch	79	J1
Pollokshaws	74	D4
Polmassick	3	G4
Polmont	75	H3
Polnoon	74	D5
Polperro	4	C5
Polruan	4	B5
Polsham	19	J7
Polstead	34	D5
Poltalloch	73	G1
Poltimore	7	H6
Polton	76	A4
Polwarth	77	F5
Polyphant	4	C1
Polzeath	3	G1
Pond Street	33	H5
Ponders End	23	G2
Pondersbridge	43	F6
Ponsanooth	2	E5
Ponsonby	60	B6
Ponsworthy	5	H3
Pont Aber	27	G6
Pont Aberglaslyn	46	E1
Pont Ceri	17	F1
Pont Crugnant	37	H6
Pont Cyfyng	47	F7
Pont Dolgarrog	47	F6
Pont Nedd Fechan	18	C1
Pont Pen-y-benglog	46	E6
Pont Rhyd-sarn	37	H3
Pont Rhyd-y-cyff	18	B3
Pont Walby	18	B1
Pont yr Alwen	47	H7
Pontamman	17	K4
Pontantwn	17	H4
Pontardawe	18	A1
Pontarddulais	17	J5
Pontarfynach (Devil's Bridge)	27	G1
Pontargothi	17	J3
Pontarsais	17	H3
Pontblyddyn	48	B6
Pontbren Llwyd	18	C1
Pontefract	57	K7
Ponteland	71	G6
Ponterwyd	37	G7
Pontesbury	38	D5
Pontesford	38	D5
Pontfadog	38	B2
Pontfaen *Pembs.*	16	D2
Pont-faen *Powys*	27	J5
Pont-Henri	17	H5
Ponthir	19	G2
Ponthirwaun	17	F1
Pontllanfraith	18	E2
Pontlliw	17	K5
Pontllyfni	46	C7
Pontlottyn	18	E1
Pontnewydd	19	F2
Pontnewynydd	19	F1
Pontrhydfendigaid	27	G2
Pontrhydyfen	18	A2
Pont-rhyd-y-groes	27	G1
Pontrhydyrun	19	F2
Pontrilas	28	C6
Pontrobert	38	A4
Pont-rug	46	D6
Ponts Green	13	K5
Pontshaen	17	H1
Pontshill	29	F6
Pontsticill	27	K7
Pontwelly	17	H2
Pontyates	17	H4
Pontyberem	17	J4
Pontybodkin	48	B7
Pontyclun	18	D3
Pontycymer	18	C2
Pontygwaith	18	D2
Pontymister	19	F3
Pont-y-pant	47	F7
Pontypool	19	F1
Pontypridd	18	D3
Pontywaun	19	F2
Pooksgreen	10	E3
Pool *Cornw.*	2	D4
Pool *W.Yorks.*	57	H5
Pool Bank	55	H1
Pool of Muckhart	82	B7
Pool Quay	38	B4
Pool Street	34	B5
Poole	10	B5
Poole Keynes	20	C2
Poolewe	94	E3
Pooley Bridge	61	F4
Poolhill	29	G6
Pope Hill	16	C4
Popeswood	22	B5
Popham	21	J7
Poplar	23	G3
Porchfield	11	F5
Porin	95	K6
Poringland	45	G5
Porkellis	2	D5
Porlock	7	G1
Porlock Weir	7	G1
Port Allen	82	D5
Port Appin	80	A3
Port Askaig	72	C4
Port Bannatyne	73	J4
Port Carlisle	69	H7
Port Charlotte	72	A5
Port Clarence	63	G4
Port Driseach	73	H3
Port e Vullen	54	D4
Port Ellen	72	B6
Port Elphinstone	91	F3
Port Erin	54	B7
Port Erroll	91	J1
Port Eynon	17	H7
Port Glasgow	74	B3
Port Henderson	94	D4
Port Isaac	4	A2
Port Logan	64	A6
Port Mòr	85	K7
Port Mulgrave	63	J5
Port na Craig	82	A2
Port nan Giùran (Portnaguran)	101	H4
Port nan Long	92	D4
Port Nis	101	H1
Port o' Warren	65	J4
Port of Menteith	81	G7
Port Penrhyn	46	D5
Port Quin	3	G1
Port Ramsay	79	K3
Port St. Mary	54	B7
Port Solent	11	H4
Port Sunlight	48	C4
Port Talbot	18	A3
Port Wemyss	72	A2
Port William	64	D6
Portachoillan	73	F5
Portavadie	73	H4
Portbury	19	H4
Portchester	11	H4
Portencross	73	K6
Portesham	9	F6
Portessie	98	C4
Portfield	83	J5
Portfield Gate	16	C4
Portgate	6	C7
Portgordon	98	B4
Portgower	105	F7
Porth *Cornw.*	3	F2
Porth *R.C.T.*	18	D2
Porth Colmon	36	A2
Porth Mellin	2	D7
Porth Navas	2	E6
Porthaethwy (Menai Bridge)	46	D5
Porthallow *Cornw.*	2	E6
Porthallow *Cornw.*	4	C5
Porthcawl	18	B4
Porthcothan	3	F1
Porthcurno	2	A6
Porthgain	16	B2
Porthkerry	18	D5
Porthleven	2	D6
Porthmadog	36	E2
Porthmeor	2	B5
Portholland	3	G4
Porthoustock	3	F6
Porthpean	4	A5
Porthtowan	2	D4
Porthyrhyd *Carmar.*	27	G5
Porthyrhyd *Carmar.*	17	J4
Porth-y-waen	38	B3
Portincaple	74	A1
Portington	58	D6
Portinnisherrich	80	A6
Portinscale	60	D4
Portishead	19	H4
Portknockie	98	C4
Portlethen	91	H5
Portlethen Village	91	H5
Portloe	3	G5
Portmahomack	97	G3
Portmeirion	36	E2
Portmellon	4	A6
Portmore	11	F5
Port-na-Con	103	G2
Portnacroish	80	A3
Portnaguran (Port nan Giùran)	101	H4
Portnahaven	72	A2
Portnalong	85	J1
Portnaluchaig	86	C6
Portobello	76	B3
Porton	10	C1
Portpatrick	64	A5
Portreath	2	D4
Portree	93	K7
Portscatho	3	F5
Portsea	11	H4
Portskerra	104	D2
Portskewett	19	J3
Portslade	13	F6
Portslade-by-Sea	13	F6
Portslogan	64	A5
Portsmouth	11	H5
Portsonachan	80	B5
Portsoy	98	D4
Portswood	11	F3
Portuairk	79	F1
Portway *Here.*	28	C4
Portway *Worcs.*	30	B1
Portwrinkle	4	D5
Portyerrock	64	E7
Poslingford	34	B4
Postbridge	5	G3
Postcombe	22	A2
Postling	15	G4
Postwick	45	G5
Potarch	90	E5
Potsgrove	32	C6
Pott Row	44	B3
Pott Shrigley	49	J5
Potten End	22	D1
Potter Heigham	45	J3
Potter Street	23	H1
Potterhanworth	52	D6
Potterhanworth Booths	52	D6
Potterne	20	C6
Potterne Wick	20	C6
Potters Bar	23	F1
Potter's Cross	40	A7
Potters Crouch	22	E1
Potterspury	31	J4
Potterton	91	H3
Potto	63	F6
Potton	33	F4
Poughill *Cornw.*	6	A5
Poughill *Devon*	7	G5
Poulner	10	C4
Poulshot	20	C6
Poulton	20	E1
Poulton-le-Fylde	55	G6
Pound Bank	29	G1
Pound Green	13	J4
Pound Hill	13	F3
Poundffald	17	J6
Poundgate	13	H4
Poundland	67	F5
Poundon	31	H6
Poundsbridge	23	J7
Poundsgate	5	H3
Poundstock	4	C1
Povey Cross	23	F7
Pow Green	29	G4
Powburn	71	F2
Powderham	7	H7
Powerstock	8	E5
Powfoot	69	G7
Powick	29	H3
Powler's Piece	6	B4
Powmill	75	J1
Poxwell	9	G6
Poyle	22	D4
Poynings	13	F5
Poyntington	9	F2
Poynton *Ches.*	49	J4
Poynton *Tel. & W.*	38	E4
Poynton Green	38	E4
Poyntzfield	96	E5
Poys Street	35	H1
Poyston Cross	16	C4
Poystreet Green	34	D3
Praa Sands	2	C6
Pratis	82	E7
Pratt's Bottom	23	H5
Praze-an-Beeble	2	D5
Prednannack Wollas	2	D7
Prees	38	E2
Prees Green	38	E2
Prees Higher Heath	38	E2
Preesall	55	G5
Preesgweene	38	B2
Prenbrigog	48	B6
Prendergast	16	C4
Prendwick	71	F2
Pren-gwyn	17	H1
Prenteg	36	E1
Prenton	48	C4
Prescot	48	D3
Prescott	38	D3
Presley	97	H6
Pressen	77	G7
Prestatyn	47	J4
Prestbury *Ches.*	49	H5
Prestbury *Glos.*	29	J6
Presteigne	28	C2
Presthope	38	E6
Prestleigh	19	K7
Prestolee	49	G2
Preston *B. & H.*	13	G6
Preston *Devon*	5	J3
Preston *Dorset*	9	G6
Preston *E.Loth.*	76	D3
Preston *E.Riding*	59	H6
Preston *Glos.*	29	F5
Preston *Glos.*	20	D1
Preston *Herts.*	32	E6
Preston *Kent*	25	G5
Preston *Kent*	25	J5
Preston *Lancs.*	55	J7
Preston *Northumb.*	71	G1
Preston *Rut.*	42	B5
Preston *Sc.Bord.*	77	F5
Preston *Suff.*	34	D3
Preston *T. & W.*	71	J7
Preston *Wilts.*	20	D4
Preston Bagot	30	C2
Preston Bissett	31	H6
Preston Brockhurst	38	E3
Preston Brook	48	E4
Preston Candover	21	K7
Preston Capes	31	G3
Preston Deanery	31	J3
Preston Gubbals	38	D4
Preston on Stour	30	D3
Preston on the Hill	48	E4
Preston on Wye	28	C4
Preston Plucknett	8	E3
Preston upon the Weald Moors	39	F4
Preston Wynne	28	E4
Prestonpans	76	B3
Preston-under-Scar	62	B7
Prestwich	49	H2
Prestwick *Northumb.*	71	G6
Prestwick *S.Ayr.*	67	H1
Prestwick International Airport	67	H1
Prestwold	41	H3
Prestwood	22	B1
Price Town	18	C2
Prickwillow	43	J7
Priddy	19	J6
Priest Hill	56	B6
Priest Hutton	55	J2
Priestland	74	D7
Priestweston	38	B6
Primethorpe	41	H6
Primrose Green	44	E4
Princes End	40	B6
Princes Gate	16	E4
Princes Risborough	22	B1
Princethorpe	31	F1
Princetown *Caerp.*	28	A7
Princetown *Devon*	5	F3
Prior Muir	83	G6
Prior's Frome	28	E5
Priors Hardwick	31	F3
Priors Marston	31	F3
Priory Wood	28	B4
Priston	19	K5
Prittlewell	24	E3
Privett	11	H2
Prixford	6	D2
Proaig	72	C5
Probus	3	F4
Protstonhill	99	G4
Prudhoe	71	G7
Pubil	81	F3
Publow	19	K5
Puckeridge	33	G6
Puckington	8	C3
Pucklechurch	19	K4
Puddinglake	49	G6
Puddington *Ches.*	48	C5
Puddington *Devon*	7	G4
Puddlebrook	29	F7
Puddledock	44	E6
Puddletown	9	G5
Pudleston	28	E3
Pudsey	57	H6
Pulborough	12	D5
Puldagon	105	J4
Puleston	39	G3
Pulford	48	C7
Pulham	9	G4
Pulham Market	45	F7
Pulham St. Mary	45	G7
Pulloxhill	32	D5
Pulrossie	96	E3
Pulverbatch	38	D5
Pumpherston	75	J4
Pumsaint	17	K1
Puncheston	16	D3
Puncknowle	8	E6
Punnett's Town	13	K4
Purbrook	11	H4
Purfleet	23	J4
Puriton	19	G7
Purleigh	24	E1
Purley	23	G5
Purley on Thames	21	K4
Purlogue	28	B1
Purls Bridge	43	H7
Purlpit	20	B5
Purse Caundle	9	F3
Purslow	38	C7
Purston Jaglin	51	G1
Purton *Glos.*	19	K1
Purton *Wilts.*	20	D3
Purton Green	34	B3
Purton Stoke	20	D2
Purves Hall	77	F6
Pury End	31	J4
Pusey	21	G2
Putley	29	F5
Putloe	20	A1
Putney	23	F4
Putsborough	6	C1
Puttenham *Herts.*	32	B7
Puttenham *Surr.*	22	C7
Puttock End	34	C4
Putts Corner	7	K6
Puxton	19	H5
Pwll	17	H5
Pwll Trap	17	F4
Pwllcrochan	16	C5
Pwlldefaid	36	A3
Pwllgloyw	27	K5
Pwllheli	36	C2
Pwllmeyric	19	J2
Pwll-y-glaw	18	A2
Pye Corner *Herts.*	33	H7
Pye Corner *Newport*	19	G3
Pye Green	40	B4
Pyecombe	13	F5
Pyle *Bridgend*	18	B3
Pyle *I.o.W.*	11	F7
Pylle	9	F1
Pymore	43	H7
Pyrford	22	D6
Pyrton	21	K2
Pytchley	32	B1
Pyworthy	6	B5

Q

Place	Page	Grid
Quabbs	38	B7
Quadring	43	F2
Quadring Eaudike	43	F2
Quainton	31	J7
Quarley	21	F7
Quarmby	50	D1
Quarndon	41	F1
Quarr Hill	11	G5
Quarrier's Village	74	B4
Quarrington	42	D1
Quarrington Hill	62	E3
Quarry Bank	40	B7
Quarrybank	48	E6
Quarrywood	97	J5
Quarter	75	F5
Quatford	39	G6
Quatt	39	G7
Quebec	62	C2
Quedgeley	29	H7
Queen Adelaide	43	J7
Queen Camel	8	E2
Queen Charlton	19	K5
Queen Street	23	K7
Queenborough	25	F4
Queen's Head	38	C3
Queensbury	57	G6
Queensferry	48	C6
Queenzieburn	74	E3
Quemerford	20	D4
Quendale	109	F9
Quendon	33	J5
Queniborough	41	J4
Quenington	20	E1
Quernmore	55	J3
Queslett	40	C6
Quethiock	4	D4
Quholm	107	B6
Quidenham	44	E7
Quidhampton *Hants.*	21	J6
Quidhampton *Wilts.*	10	C1
Quilquox	91	H1
Quina Brook	38	E2
Quindry	107	D8
Quine's Hill	54	C6
Quinhill	73	F5
Quinton *Northants.*	31	J3
Quinton *W.Mid.*	40	B7
Quintrell Downs	3	F2
Quoditch	6	C6
Quoig	81	K5
Quoisley	38	E1
Quorn	41	H4
Quothquan	75	H7
Quoyloo	106	B5
Quoys	108	F1
Quoys of Reiss	105	J3

R

Place	Page	Grid
Raby	48	C5
Rachan	75	K7
Rachub	46	E6
Rackenford	7	G4
Rackham	12	D5
Rackheath	45	G4
Racks	69	F6
Rackwick *Ork.*	107	B8
Rackwick *Ork.*	106	D2
Radbourne	40	E2
Radcliffe *Gt.Man.*	49	G2
Radcliffe *Northumb.*	71	H3
Radcliffe on Trent	41	J2
Radclive	31	H5
Radcot	21	F2
Radford *Oxon.*	31	F6
Radford *W.Mid.*	41	F7
Radford Semele	30	E2
Radipole	9	F6
Radlett	22	E1
Radley	21	J2
Radstock	19	K6
Radstone	31	G4
Radway	30	E4
Radway Green	49	G7
Radwell *Beds.*	32	D3
Radwell *Herts.*	33	F5
Radwinter	33	K5
Radyr	18	E3
Raechester	70	E5
Raemoir House	90	E5
Raffin	102	C5
Rafford	97	H6
Ragdale	41	J4
Raglan	19	H1
Ragnall	52	B5
Rahoy	79	H2
Rainford	48	D2
Rainham *Gt.Lon.*	23	J3
Rainham *Med.*	24	E5
Rainhill	48	D3
Rainhill Stoops	48	E3
Rainow	49	J5
Rainton	57	J2
Rainworth	51	H7
Raisbeck	61	H6
Raise	61	J2
Rait	82	D5
Raithby *Lincs.*	53	G5
Raithby *Lincs.*	53	G4
Rake	12	B4
Raleigh's Cross	7	J2
Ram	17	J1
Ram Lane	14	E3
Ramasaig	93	G7
Rame *Cornw.*	2	E5
Rame *Cornw.*	4	E6
Rampisham	8	E4
Rampside	55	F3
Rampton *Cambs.*	33	H2
Rampton *Notts.*	52	B5
Ramsbottom	49	G1
Ramsbury	21	F4
Ramscraigs	105	G6
Ramsdean	11	J3
Ramsdell	21	J6
Ramsden	30	E7
Ramsden Bellhouse	24	D2
Ramsden Heath	24	D2
Ramsey *Cambs.*	43	F7
Ramsey *Essex*	35	G5
Ramsey *I.o.M.*	54	D4
Ramsey Forty Foot	43	G7
Ramsey Heights	43	F7
Ramsey Island	25	F1
Ramsey Mereside	43	F7
Ramsey St. Mary's	43	F7
Ramsgate	25	K5
Ramsgate Street	44	E2
Ramsgill	57	G2
Ramsholt	35	H4
Ramshorn	40	C1
Ramsnest Common	12	C3
Ranachan	79	J3
Ranby *Lincs.*	53	F5
Ranby *Notts.*	51	J4
Rand	52	E5
Randwick	20	B1
Rangemore	40	D3
Rangeworthy	19	K3
Rankinston	67	J2
Ranmore Common	22	E6
Rannoch School	81	G2
Ranochan	86	E6
Ranskill	51	J4
Ranton	40	A3
Ranworth	45	H4
Rapness	106	E3
Rascarrel	65	J6
Raskelf	57	K2
Rassau	28	A7
Rastrick	57	G7
Ratagan	87	F3
Ratby	41	H5
Ratcliffe Culey	41	F6
Ratcliffe on Soar	41	G3
Ratcliffe on the Wreake	41	J4
Ratford Bridge	16	C4
Rathen	99	J4
Rathillet	82	E5
Rathliesbeag	87	J6
Rathmell	56	D3
Ratho	75	K3
Ratho Station	75	K3
Rathven	98	C4
Ratley	30	E4
Ratlinghope	38	D6
Rattar	105	H1
Ratten Row	55	H5
Rattery	5	H4
Rattlesden	34	D3
Rattray	82	C3
Raughton Head	60	E2
Raunds	32	C1
Ravenfield	51	G3
Ravenglass	60	B7
Raveningham	45	H6
Ravenscar	63	J2
Ravensdale	54	C4
Ravensden	32	D3
Ravenshaw	56	E5
Ravenshayes	7	H5
Ravenshead	51	H7
Ravensmoor	49	F7
Ravensthorpe *Northants.*	31	H1
Ravensthorpe *W.Yorks.*	50	E1
Ravenstone *Leics.*	41	G4
Ravenstone *M.K.*	32	B4
Ravenstonedale	61	J6
Ravenstruther	75	H6
Ravensworth	62	C6
Raw	63	J2
Rawcliffe *E.Riding*	58	C7
Rawcliffe *York*	58	B4
Rawcliffe Bridge	58	C7
Rawdon	57	H6
Rawmarsh	51	G3
Rawreth	24	D2
Rawridge	7	K5
Rawtenstall	56	D7
Rawyards	75	F4
Raxton	91	G1
Raydon	34	E5
Raylees	70	E4
Rayleigh	24	E2
Raymond's Hill	8	C5
Rayne	34	B6
Reach	33	J2
Read	56	C6
Reading	22	A4
Reading Street	14	E4
Reagill	61	H5
Rearquhar	96	E2
Rearsby	41	J4
Rease Heath	49	F7
Reaster	105	H2
Reaveley	71	F2
Reawick	109	C8
Reay	104	E2
Reculver	25	J5
Red Dial	60	D2
Red Hill *Hants.*	11	J3
Red Hill *Warks.*	30	C3
Red Lodge	33	K1
Red Oaks Hill	33	J5
Red Point	94	D5
Red Post *Cornw.*	6	A5
Red Post *Devon*	5	J4
Red Rock	48	E2
Red Roses	17	F4
Red Row	71	H4
Red Street	49	H7
Red Wharf Bay	46	D4
Redberth	16	D5
Redbourn	32	E7
Redbourne	52	C2
Redbrook	19	J1
Redbrook Street	14	E4
Redburn *High.*	96	C5
Redburn *High.*	97	G7
Redcar	63	H4
Redcastle *Angus*	83	H2
Redcastle *High.*	96	C7
Redcliff Bay	19	H4
Redcloak	91	G6
Reddish	49	H3
Redditch	30	B2
Rede	34	C3
Redenhall	45	G7
Redesmouth	70	D5
Redford *Aber.*	83	J1
Redford *Angus*	83	G3
Redford *Dur.*	62	B3
Redford *W.Suss.*	12	B4
Redgrave	34	E1
Redheugh	83	F1
Redhill *Aber.*	90	E1
Redhill *Aber.*	91	F4
Redhill *Moray*	98	D6
Redhill *N.Som.*	19	J5
Redhill *Notts.*	41	H1
Redhill *Tel. & W.*	39	G4
Redhill Aerodrome & Heliport	23	F7
Redhouse *Aber.*	90	D2
Redhouse *Arg. & B.*	73	G4
Redhouses	72	B4
Redisham	45	J7
Redland *Bristol*	19	J4
Redland *Ork.*	106	C5
Redlingfield	35	F1
Redlynch *Som.*	9	F1
Redlynch *Wilts.*	10	D2
Redmarley D'Abitot	29	G5
Redmarshall	62	E4
Redmile	42	B2
Redmire	62	B7
Redmoor	4	A4
Rednal *Shrop.*	38	C3
Rednal *W.Mid.*	30	B1
Redpath	76	D7
Redruth	2	D4
Redscarhead	76	A6
Redshaw	68	D1
Redstone Bank	16	E4
Redwick *Newport*	19	H3
Redwick *S.Glos.*	19	J3
Redworth	62	D4
Reed	33	G5
Reedham	45	J5
Reedness	58	C7
Reepham *Lincs.*	52	D5
Reepham *Norf.*	45	F3
Reeth	62	B7
Regaby	54	D4
Regil	19	J5
Regoul	97	F6
Reiff	102	B7
Reigate	23	F6
Reighton	59	H2
Reinigeadal	100	E7
Reisgill	105	H5
Reiss	105	J3
Rejerrah	2	E3
Relubbus	2	C5
Relugas	97	G7
Remenham	22	A3
Remenham Hill	22	A3
Remony	81	J3
Rempstone	41	H3
Rendcomb	30	B7
Rendham	35	H2
Rendlesham	35	H3
Renfrew	74	D4
Renhold	32	D3
Renishaw	51	G5
Rennington	71	H2
Renton	74	B3
Renwick	61	G2
Repps	45	J4
Repton	41	F3
Rescobie	83	G2
Resipole	79	J1
Resolis	96	D5
Resolven	18	B1
Resourie	86	E7
Reston	77	G4
Reswallie	83	G2
Retew	3	G3
Retford	51	K4
Rettendon	24	D2
Rettendon Place	24	D2
Retyn	3	F3
Revesby	53	F6
Rew	5	H3
Rewe	7	H6
Reydon	35	J1
Reymerston	44	E5
Reynalton	16	D5
Reynoldston	17	H7
Rezare	4	D3
Rhandirmwyn	27	G4
Rhaoine	96	D1
Rhayader	27	J2
Rhedyn	36	B2
Rhegreanoch	102	C7
Rheindown	96	C7
Rhelonie	96	C2
Rhemore	79	G2
Rhes-y-cae	47	K6
Rhewl *Denb.*	38	A1
Rhewl *Denb.*	47	K6
Rhewl *Shrop.*	38	C2
Rhian	103	H7
Rhicarn	102	C6
Rhiconich	102	E3
Rhicullen	96	D4
Rhidorroch	95	H2
Rhifail	104	C4
Rhigos	18	C1
Rhilochan	96	E1
Rhinduie	96	C7
Rhiroy	95	G2
Rhiw	36	B3
Rhiwargor	37	J3
Rhiwbryfdir	37	F1
Rhiwderin	19	F3
Rhiwlas *Gwyn.*	46	D6
Rhiwlas *Gwyn.*	37	J2
Rhiwlas *Powys*	38	B2
Rhodes Minnis	15	G3
Rhodesia	51	H5
Rhodiad-y-Brenin	16	A3
Rhodmad	26	E1
Rhonadale	73	F7
Rhonehouse or Kelton Hill	65	H5
Rhoose	18	D5
Rhos *Carmar.*	17	G2
Rhos *N.P.T.*	18	A1
Rhos-berse	48	B7
Rhoscolyn	46	A5
Rhoscrowther	16	C5
Rhos-ddu	48	C7
Rhosesmor	48	B6
Rhos-fawr	36	C2
Rhosgadfan	46	D7
Rhosgoch *I.o.A.*	46	C4
Rhosgoch *Powys*	28	A4
Rhos-hill	16	E1
Rhoshirwaun	36	A3
Rhoslan	36	E1
Rhoslefain	36	E5
Rhosllanerchrugog	38	B1
Rhosmaen	17	K3
Rhosmeirch	46	C5
Rhosneigr	46	B5
Rhosnesni	48	C7
Rhôs-on-Sea	47	G4
Rhossili	17	G7
Rhosson	16	A3
Rhostryfan	46	C7
Rhostyllen	38	C1
Rhos-y-bol	46	C4
Rhos-y-brwyner	48	B7
Rhos-y-gwaliau	37	J3
Rhos-y-llan	36	B2
Rhos-y-mawn	47	G6
Rhos-y-Meirch	28	B2
Rhu	74	A2
Rhuallt	47	J5
Rhubodach	73	J3
Rhuddlan	47	J5
Rhue	95	G2

Rhulen 28 A4
Rhumach 86 C6
Rhunahaorine 73 F6
Rhuthun (Ruthin) 47 K7
Rhyd Gwyn. 37 F1
Rhyd Powys 37 J5
Rhydaman (Ammanford) 17 K4
Rhydargaeau 17 H3
Rhydcymerau 17 J2
Rhydd 29 H4
Rhyd-Ddu 46 D7
Rhydding 18 A2
Rhydlanfair 47 G7
Rhydlewis 17 G1
Rhydlios 36 A2
Rhydlydan Conwy 47 G7
Rhydlydan Powys 37 K6
Rhydolion 36 B3
Rhydowen 17 H1
Rhyd-rosser 26 E2
Rhydspence 28 B4
Rhydtalog 48 B7
Rhyd-uchaf 37 J2
Rhyd-wen 37 J3
Rhyd-wyn 46 B4
Rhyd-y-clafdy 36 C2
Rhydycroesau 38 B2
Rhydyfelin Cere. 26 E1
Rhydyfelin R.C.T. 18 D3
Rhyd-y-foel 47 H5
Rhyd-y-fro 18 A1
Rhydymain 37 G3
Rhyd-y-meirch 19 G1
Rhydymwyn 48 B6
Rhyd-yr-onnen 37 F5
Rhydywrach 16 E4
Rhyl 47 J4
Rhymney 18 E1
Rhyn 38 C2
Rhynd 82 C5
Rhynie Aber. 90 C2
Rhynie High. 97 F4
Ribbesford 29 G1
Ribbleton 55 J6
Ribchester 56 B6
Ribigill 103 H3
Riby 52 E2
Riccall 58 C6
Riccarton 74 C7
Richard's Castle 28 D2
Richings Park 22 D4
Richmond Gt.Lon. 22 E4
Richmond N.Yorks. 62 C6
Rickarton 91 G6
Rickford 19 H6
Rickinghall 34 E1
Rickling 33 H5
Rickling Green 33 J6
Rickmansworth 22 D2
Riddell 70 A1
Riddings 51 G7
Riddlecombe 6 E4
Riddlesden 57 F5
Ridge Dorset 9 J6
Ridge Herts. 23 F1
Ridge Wilts. 9 J1
Ridge Green 23 G7
Ridge Lane 40 E6
Ridgebourne 27 K2
Ridgeway 51 G4
Ridgeway Cross 29 G4
Ridgewell 34 B4
Ridgewood 13 H4
Ridgmont 32 C5
Riding Mill 71 F7
Ridley 24 C5
Ridleywood 48 C7
Ridlington Norf. 45 H2
Ridlington Rut. 42 B5
Ridsdale 70 E5
Riechip 82 B3
Rievaulx 58 B1
Rigg D. & G. 69 H7
Rigg High. 94 B6
Riggend 75 F4
Rigmaden Park 56 B1
Rigsby 53 H5
Rigside 75 G7
Rileyhill 40 D4
Rillaton 4 C3
Rillington 58 E2
Rimington 56 D5
Rimpton 9 F2
Rimswell 59 K7
Rinaston 16 C3
Ringford 65 G5
Ringland 45 F4
Ringles Cross 13 H4
Ringmer 13 H5
Ringmore 5 G6
Ringorm 97 K5
Ring's End 43 G5
Ringsfield 45 J7
Ringsfield Corner 45 J7
Ringshall Herts. 32 C7
Ringshall Suff. 34 E3
Ringshall Stocks 34 E3
Ringstead Norf. 44 B1
Ringstead Northants. 32 C1
Ringwood 10 C4
Ringwould 15 J3
Rinloan 89 K4
Rinmore 90 C3
Rinnigill 107 C8
Rinsey 2 C6
Ripe 13 J6
Ripley Derbys. 51 G7
Ripley Hants. 10 C5
Ripley N.Yorks. 57 H3
Ripley Surr. 22 D6
Riplingham 59 F6
Ripon 57 J2
Rippingale 42 E3
Ripple Kent 15 J2
Ripple Worcs. 29 H5
Ripponden 50 C1
Risabus 72 B6
Risbury 28 E3
Risby 34 B2
Risca 19 F2
Rise 59 H5
Risegate 43 F2
Riseley Beds. 32 D2
Riseley W'ham 22 A5
Rishangles 35 F2
Rishton 56 C6
Rishworth 50 C1
Risley Derbys. 41 G2
Risley Warr. 49 F3
Risplith 57 H3
Rispond 103 G2
Rivar 21 G5
Rivenhall 34 C7

Rivenhall End 34 C7
River 12 C4
River Bank 33 J2
River Bridge 19 G7
Riverford Bridge 5 H4
Riverhead 23 J6
Rivington 49 F1
Roa Island 55 F3
Roade 31 J3
Roadhead 70 A6
Roadside High. 105 G2
Roadside Ork. 106 F3
Roadside of Kinneff 91 G7
Roadwater 7 J2
Roag 93 H7
Roath 19 F4
Roberton S.Lan. 68 E1
Roberton Sc.Bord. 69 K2
Robertsbridge 14 C5
Robertstown 97 K7
Roberttown 57 H7
Robeston Cross 16 B5
Robeston Wathen 16 D4
Robin Hood Derbys. 50 E5
Robin Hood W.Yorks. 57 J7
Robin Hood's Bay 63 J2
Robins 12 B4
Roborough Devon 6 D4
Roborough Plym. 5 F4
Roby 48 D3
Roby Mill 48 E2
Rocester 40 D2
Roch 16 B3
Rochallie 82 C2
Rochdale 56 D1
Roche 3 G2
Rochester Med. 24 D5
Rochester Northumb. 70 D4
Rochford Essex 24 E2
Rochford Worcs. 29 F2
Rock Caerp. 18 E2
Rock Cornw. 3 G1
Rock Northumb. 71 H1
Rock Worcs. 29 G1
Rock Ferry 48 C4
Rockbeare 7 J6
Rockbourne 10 C3
Rockcliffe Cumb. 69 J7
Rockcliffe D. & G. 65 J5
Rockfield Arg. & B. 73 G5
Rockfield High. 97 G3
Rockfield Mon. 28 D7
Rockhampton 19 K2
Rockhead 4 A2
Rockingham 42 B6
Rockland All Saints 44 D6
Rockland St. Mary 45 H5
Rockland St. Peter 44 D6
Rockley 20 E4
Rockside 72 A4
Rockwell End 22 A3
Rockwell Green 7 K4
Rodborough 20 B1
Rodbourne 20 C3
Rodbridge Corner 34 C4
Rodd 28 C2
Roddam 71 F1
Rodden 9 F6
Rode 20 B6
Rode Heath 49 H5
Rodeheath 49 H6
Rodel (Roghadal) 93 F3
Roden 38 E4
Rodhuish 7 J2
Rodington 38 E4
Rodley 29 G7
Rodmarton 20 C2
Rodmell 13 H6
Rodmersham 25 F5
Rodney Stoke 19 H6
Rodsley 40 E1
Rodway 19 F7
Roe Green 33 G5
Roecliffe 57 J3
Roehampton 23 F4
Roesound 109 C6
Roffey 12 E3
Rogart 96 E1
Rogate 12 B4
Rogerstone 19 F3
Roghadal (Rodel) 93 F3
Rogiet 19 H3
Roker 63 F1
Rollesby 45 J4
Rolleston Leics. 42 A5
Rolleston Notts. 51 K7
Rolleston Staffs. 40 E3
Rolstone 20 D7
Rolston 59 J5
Rolvenden 14 D4
Rolvenden Layne 14 D4
Romaldkirk 62 A4
Romanby 62 E7
Romannobridge 75 K6
Romansleigh 7 F3
Romford Dorset 10 B4
Romford Gt.Lon. 23 J3
Romiley 49 J3
Romney Street 23 J5
Romsey 10 E2
Romsley Shrop. 39 G7
Romsley Worcs. 29 J7
Ronachan 73 F5
Ronague 54 B6
Ronnachmore 72 B5
Rookhope 62 A2
Rookley 11 G6
Rooks Bridge 19 G6
Rookwith 57 H1
Roos 59 J6
Roosecote 55 F3
Rootpark 75 H5
Ropley 11 H1
Ropley Dean 11 H1
Ropley Soke 11 H1
Ropsley 42 C2
Rora 99 J5
Rorandle 90 E3
Rorrington 38 B5
Rosarie 98 B5
Rose 2 E3
Rose Ash 7 F3
Rose Green 34 C6
Roseacre 55 H6
Rosebank 75 G6
Rosebrough 71 G1
Rosebush 16 D3
Rosedale Abbey 63 J7

Roseden 71 F1
Rosehall 96 B1
Rosehearty 99 H4
Rosehill Aber. 90 D5
Rosehill Shrop. 39 F2
Roseisle 97 J5
Rosemarket 16 C5
Rosemarkie 96 E6
Rosemary Lane 7 K4
Rosemount P. & K. 82 C3
Rosemount S.Ayr. 67 H1
Rosepool 16 B4
Rosewarne 2 D5
Rosewell 76 A4
Roseworthy 2 D5
Rosgill 61 G5
Roshven 86 D7
Roskhill 93 H7
Rosley 60 E2
Roslin 76 A4
Rosliston 40 E4
Rosneath 74 A2
Ross D. & G. 65 G6
Ross Northumb. 77 K7
Ross P. & K. 81 J5
Ross Priory 74 C2
Rossdhu House 74 B2
Rossett 48 C7
Rossie Farm School 83 H2
Rossie Ochill 82 B6
Rossie Priory 82 D4
Rossington 51 J3
Rosskeen 96 D5
Ross-on-Wye 29 F6
Roster 105 H5
Rostherne 49 G4
Rosthwaite Cumb. 60 D5
Rosthwaite Cumb. 55 F1
Roston 40 D1
Rosyth 75 K2
Rothbury 71 F3
Rotherby 41 J4
Rotherfield 13 J4
Rotherfield Greys 22 A3
Rotherfield Peppard 22 A3
Rotherham 51 G3
Rothersthorpe 31 J3
Rotherwick 22 A6
Rothes 97 K7
Rothesay 73 J4
Rothiebrisbane 91 F1
Rothienorman 91 F1
Rothiesholm 106 F5
Rothley Leics. 41 H4
Rothley Northumb. 71 F5
Rothwell Lincs. 52 E3
Rothwell Northants. 42 B7
Rothwell W.Yorks. 57 J7
Rotsea 59 G4
Rottal 82 E1
Rottingdean 13 G6
Rottington 60 A5
Roud 11 G6
Roudham 44 D7
Rough Close 40 B2
Rough Common 15 G2
Rougham Norf. 44 C3
Rougham Suff. 34 D2
Rougham Green 34 D2
Roughburn 87 K6
Roughlee 56 D5
Roughley 40 D6
Roughton Lincs. 53 F6
Roughton Norf. 45 G2
Roughton Shrop. 39 G6
Roundhay 57 J6
Roundstreet Common 12 D4
Roundway 20 D5
Rous Lench 30 B3
Rousdon 8 B5
Rousham 31 F6
Rousham Gap 31 F6
Routenburn 74 A4
Routh 59 G5
Row Cornw. 4 A3
Row Cumb. 55 H1
Row Cumb. 61 H3
Row Heath 35 F7
Row Town 22 D5
Rowanburn 69 K6
Rowardennan Lodge 74 B1
Rowberrow 19 H6
Rowchoish 80 E7
Rowde 20 C5
Rowen 47 F5
Rowfoot 70 B7
Rowhedge 34 E6
Rowhook 12 E3
Rowington 30 D1
Rowington Green 30 D1
Rowland 50 E5
Rowland's Castle 11 J3
Rowlands Gill 62 C1
Rowledge 22 B7
Rowley Devon 7 F4
Rowley Dur. 62 B2
Rowley E.Riding 59 F6
Rowley Shrop. 38 C5
Rowley Regis 40 B7
Rowlstone 28 C6
Rowly 22 D7
Rowner 11 G4
Rowney Green 30 B1
Rownhams 10 E3
Rowrah 60 B5
Rowsham 32 B7
Rowsley 50 E6
Rowstock 21 H3
Rowston 52 D7
Rowthorne 51 G6
Rowton Ches. 48 D6
Rowton Shrop. 38 C4
Rowton Tel. & W. 39 F4
Roxburgh 76 E7
Roxby N.Lincs. 52 C1
Roxby N.Yorks. 63 J5
Roxton 32 E3
Roxwell 24 C1
Royal British Legion Village 14 C2
Royal Leamington Spa 30 E2
Royal Tunbridge Wells 13 J3
Roybridge 87 J6
Roydon Essex 33 H7
Roydon Norf. 44 E7

Roydon Norf. 44 B3
Roydon Hamlet 23 H1
Royston Herts. 33 G4
Royston S.Yorks. 51 F1
Royton 49 J2
Ruabon 38 C1
Ruaig 78 B3
Ruan Lanihorne 3 F4
Ruan Major 2 D7
Ruan Minor 2 E7
Ruanaich 78 D5
Ruardean 29 F7
Ruardean Woodside 29 F7
Rubery 29 J1
Ruckcroft 61 G2
Ruckinge 15 F4
Ruckland 53 G5
Ruckley 38 E5
Rudbaxton 16 C3
Rudby 63 F6
Rudchester 71 G7
Ruddington 41 H2
Ruddlemoor 4 A5
Rudford 29 G6
Rudge 20 B6
Rudgeway 19 K3
Rudgwick 12 D3
Rudhall 29 F6
Rudheath 49 F5
Rudley Green 24 E1
Rudry 18 E3
Rudston 59 G3
Rudyard 49 J7
Rufford 48 D1
Rufforth 58 B4
Ruffside 62 A1
Rugby 31 G1
Rugeley 40 C4
Ruilick 96 C7
Ruishton 8 B2
Ruisigearraidh 92 E3
Ruislip 22 D3
Rumbling Bridge 75 J1
Rumburgh 45 H7
Rumford 3 F1
Rumney 19 F4
Rumwell 7 K3
Runacraig 81 G6
Runcorn 48 E4
Runcton 12 B6
Runcton Holme 44 A5
Rundlestone 5 F3
Runfold 22 B7
Runhall 44 E5
Runham 45 J4
Runnington 7 K3
Runsell Green 24 D1
Runswick Bay 63 K5
Runtaleave 82 D1
Runwell 24 D2
Ruscombe 22 A4
Rush Green 23 J3
Rushall Here. 29 F5
Rushall Norf. 45 F7
Rushall W.Mid. 40 C5
Rushall Wilts. 20 E6
Rushbrooke 34 C2
Rushbury 38 E6
Rushden Herts. 33 G5
Rushden Northants. 32 C2
Rushford 44 D7
Rushlake Green 13 K5
Rushmere 45 J7
Rushmere St. Andrew 35 F4
Rushmoor Surr. 22 B7
Rushmoor Tel. & W. 39 F4
Rushock 29 H1
Rusholme 49 H3
Rushton Ches. 48 E6
Rushton Northants. 42 B7
Rushton Spencer 49 J6
Rushwick 29 H3
Rushyford 62 D4
Ruskie 81 H7
Ruskington 52 D7
Rusko 65 F5
Rusland 55 G1
Rusper 13 F3
Ruspidge 29 F7
Russel 94 E7
Russel Green 34 D5
Russell's Water 22 A3
Rusthall 23 J7
Rustington 12 D6
Ruston 59 F1
Ruston Parva 59 G3
Ruswarp 63 K6
Rutherend 74 E5
Rutherford 70 B1
Rutherglen 74 E4
Ruthernbridge 4 A4
Ruthin (Rhuthun) 47 K7
Ruthrieston 91 H4
Ruthven Aber. 98 D6
Ruthven Angus 82 D3
Ruthven High. 89 F1
Ruthven High. 88 E5
Ruthvoes 3 G2
Ruthwaite 60 D3
Ruthwell 69 F7
Ruyton-XI-Towns 38 C3
Ryal 71 F6
Ryal Fold 56 B7
Ryall 8 D5
Ryarsh 23 K6
Rydal 60 E6
Ryde 11 G5
Rydon 6 B5
Rye 14 E5
Rye Foreign 14 D5
Rye Harbour 14 E6
Rye Park 23 G1
Ryhall 42 D4
Ryhill 51 F1
Ryhope 63 F1
Ryland 52 D4
Rylstone 56 E4
Ryme Intrinseca 8 E3
Ryther 58 B6
Ryton Glos. 29 G5
Ryton N.Yorks. 58 D2
Ryton Shrop. 39 G5
Ryton T. & W. 71 G7
Ryton-on-Dunsmore 30 E1

S

Sabden 56 C6
Sackers Green 34 D5
Sacombe 33 G7
Sacriston 62 D2
Sadberge 62 E5

Saddell 73 F7
Saddington 41 J6
Saddle Bow 44 A4
Sadgill 61 F6
Saffron Walden 33 J5
Sageston 16 D5
Saham Toney 44 C5
Saighdinis 92 D5
Saighton 48 D6
St. Abbs 77 H4
St. Agnes 2 E3
St. Albans 22 E1
St. Allen 3 F3
St. Andrews 83 G6
St. Andrews Major 18 E4
St. Anne 3 K4
St. Anne's 55 G7
St. Ann's 69 F4
St. Ann's Chapel Cornw. 4 E3
St. Ann's Chapel Devon 5 G6
St. Anthony Cornw. 2 E6
St. Anthony Cornw. 3 F5
St. Arvans 19 J2
St. Asaph (Llanelwy) 47 J5
St. Athan 18 D5
St. Aubin 3 J7
St. Audries 7 K1
St. Austell 4 A5
St. Bees 60 A5
St. Blazey 4 A5
St. Blazey Gate 4 A5
St. Boswells 76 D7
St. Brelade 3 J7
St. Breock 3 G1
St. Breward 4 A3
St. Briavels 19 J1
St. Brides 16 B4
St. Brides Major 18 B4
St. Brides Netherwent 19 H3
St. Brides Wentloge 19 F3
St. Bride's-super-Ely 18 D4
St. Budeaux 4 E5
St. Buryan 2 B6
St. Catherine 20 A4
St. Catherines 80 C7
St. Clears 17 F4
St. Cleer 4 C4
St. Clement 3 F4
St. Clether 4 C2
St. Columb Major 3 G2
St. Columb Minor 3 F2
St. Columb Road 3 G3
St. Combs 99 J4
St. Cross South Elmham 45 G7
St. Cyrus 83 J1
St. Davids Fife 75 K2
St. David's P. & K. 82 A5
St. David's (Tyddewi) Pembs. 16 A3
St. Day 2 E4
St. Decumans 7 J1
St. Dennis 3 G3
St. Dogmaels 16 E1
St. Dogwells 16 C3
St. Dominick 4 E4
St. Donats 18 C5
St. Edith's Marsh 20 C5
St. Endellion 3 G1
St. Enoder 3 F3
St. Erme 3 F4
St. Erney 4 C5
St. Erth 2 C5
St. Erth Praze 2 C5
St. Ervan 3 F1
St. Eval 3 F2
St. Ewe 3 G4
St. Fagans 18 E4
St. Fergus 99 K5
St. Fillans 81 H5
St. Florence 16 D5
St. Gennys 4 B1
St. George 47 H5
St. Georges N.Som. 19 G5
St. George's V. of Glam. 18 D4
St. Germans 4 D5
St. Giles in the Wood 6 D3
St. Giles on the Heath 6 B6
St. Harmon 27 J1
St. Helen Auckland 62 C4
St. Helena 45 F4
St. Helen's E.Suss. 14 D6
St. Helens I.o.W. 11 H6
St. Helens Mersey. 48 E3
St. Helier 3 J7
St. Hilary Cornw. 2 C5
St. Hilary V. of Glam. 18 D4
St. Hill 13 G3
St. Illtyd 19 F1
St. Ippollitts 33 F6
St. Ishmael 17 K3
St. Ishmael's 16 B5
St. Issey 3 G1
St. Ive 4 D4
St. Ives Cambs. 33 G1
St. Ives Cornw. 2 C4
St. Ives Dorset 10 C4
St. James South Elmham 45 H7
St. John Chan.I. 3 J6
St. John Cornw. 4 E5
St. John's I.o.M. 54 B5
St. John's Surr. 22 C6
St. John's Worcs. 29 H3
St. John's Chapel Devon 6 D3
St. John's Chapel Dur. 61 K3
St. John's Fen End 43 J4
St. Johns Hall 62 B3
St. John's Highway 43 J4
St. John's Kirk 75 H7
St. John's Town of Dalry 68 B5
St. Judes 54 C4
St. Just 2 A5
St. Just in Roseland 3 F5
St. Katherines 91 F1
St. Keverne 2 E6
St. Kew 4 A3
St. Kew Highway 4 A3
St. Keyne 4 C4
St. Lawrence Cornw. 4 A4
St. Lawrence Essex 25 F1

St. Lawrence I.o.W. 11 G7
St. Leonards Bucks. 22 C1
St. Leonards Dorset 10 C4
St. Leonards E.Suss. 14 D7
St. Leonard's Grange 11 F5
St. Leonard's Street 23 K6
St. Levan 2 A6
St. Lythans 18 E4
St. Mabyn 4 A3
St. Margaret South Elmham 45 H7
St. Margarets Here. 28 C5
St. Margarets Herts. 33 G7
St. Margaret's at Cliffe 15 J3
St. Margaret's Hope 107 D8
St. Mark's 54 C6
St. Martin Chan.I. 3 J5
St. Martin Chan.I. 3 K7
St. Martin Cornw. 2 E6
St. Martins P. & K. 82 C4
St. Martin's Shrop. 38 C2
St. Mary Bourne 21 H6
St. Mary Church 18 D4
St. Mary Cray 23 H5
St. Mary in the Marsh 15 F5
St. Marychurch 5 K4
St. Mary's 107 D7
St. Mary's Airport 2 C1
St. Mary's Bay 15 F5
St. Mary's Croft 64 A4
St. Mary's Grove 19 H5
St. Mary's Hoo 24 D4
St. Mawes 3 F5
St. Mawgan 3 F2
St. Mellion 4 D4
St. Mellons 19 F3
St. Merryn 3 F1
St. Mewan 3 G3
St. Michael Caerhays 3 G4
St. Michael Penkevil 3 F4
St. Michael South Elmham 45 H7
St. Michaels Kent 14 D4
St. Michaels Worcs. 28 E2
St. Michael's on Wyre 55 H5
St. Minver 3 G1
St. Monans 83 G7
St. Neot 4 B4
St. Neots 32 E3
St. Nicholas Pembs. 16 B2
St. Nicholas V. of Glam. 18 D4
St. Nicholas at Wade 25 J5
St. Ninians 75 F1
St. Osyth 35 F7
St. Ouen 3 J6
St. Owen's Cross 28 E6
St. Paul's Cray 23 H5
St. Paul's Walden 32 E6
St. Peter 3 J7
St. Peter Port 3 J5
St. Peter's 25 K5
St. Petrox 16 C6
St. Pinnock 4 C4
St. Quivox 67 H1
St. Sampson 3 J5
St. Saviour 3 J7
St. Stephen 3 G3
St. Stephens Cornw. 4 E5
St. Stephens Cornw. 6 B7
St. Stephens Herts. 22 E1
St. Teath 4 A2
St. Tudy 4 A3
St. Twynnells 16 C6
St. Veep 4 B5
St. Vigeans 83 H3
St. Wenn 3 G2
St. Weonards 28 D6
Saintbury 30 C4
Salachail 80 B2
Salcombe 5 H7
Salcombe Regis 7 K7
Salcott 34 D7
Sale 49 G3
Sale Green 29 J3
Saleby 53 H5
Salehurst 14 C5
Salem Carmar. 17 K3
Salem Cere. 37 F7
Salem Gwyn. 46 D7
Salen Arg. & B. 79 G3
Salen High. 79 H1
Salesbury 56 B6
Salford Beds. 32 C5
Salford Gt.Man. 49 H3
Salford Oxon. 30 D6
Salford Priors 30 B3
Salfords 23 F7
Salhouse 45 H4
Saline 75 J1
Salisbury 10 C1
Salkeld Dykes 61 G3
Sall 45 F3
Sallachan 80 A1
Sallachy High. 96 C1
Sallachy High. 87 F1
Salmonby 53 G5
Salmond's Muir 83 G4
Salperton 30 B6
Salph End 32 D3
Salsburgh 75 G4
Salt 40 B3
Salt Hill 22 C4
Saltaire 57 G6
Saltash 4 E5
Saltburn 96 E4
Saltburn-by-the-Sea 63 H4
Saltby 42 B3
Saltcoats 74 A6
Saltcotes 55 G7
Saltdean 13 G6
Salterforth 56 D5
Saltergate 63 K7
Salterhill 97 K5

Salterswall 49 F6
Saltfleet 53 H3
Saltfleetby All Saints 53 H3
Saltfleetby St. Clements 53 H3
Saltfleetby St. Peter 53 H4
Saltford 19 K5
Salthaugh Grange 59 J7
Salthouse 44 E1
Saltley 40 C7
Saltmarshe 58 D7
Saltney 48 C6
Salton 58 D1
Saltwick 71 G5
Saltwood 15 G4
Salvington 12 E6
Salwarpe 29 H2
Salwayash 8 D5
Sambourne 30 B2
Sambrook 39 G3
Samhla 92 C5
Samlesbury 55 J6
Samlesbury Bottoms 56 B7
Sampford Arundel 7 K4
Sampford Brett 7 J1
Sampford Courtenay 6 E5
Sampford Peverell 7 J4
Sampford Spiney 5 F3
Samuelston 76 C3
Sanaigmore 72 A4
Sancreed 2 B6
Sancton 59 F6
Sand 109 C8
Sand Hole 58 E6
Sand Hutton 58 C4
Sand Side 55 F1
Sandaig Arg. & B. 78 A3
Sandaig High. 86 D4
Sandaig High. 86 D3
Sandbach 49 G6
Sandbank 73 K2
Sandbanks 10 B6
Sandend 98 D4
Sanderstead 23 G5
Sandford Cumb. 61 J5
Sandford Devon 7 G5
Sandford Dorset 9 J5
Sandford I.o.W. 11 G6
Sandford N.Som. 19 H6
Sandford S.Lan. 75 F6
Sandford St. Martin 31 F6
Sandfordhill 99 K6
Sandford-on-Thames 21 J1
Sandgarth 107 E6
Sandgate 15 H4
Sandgreen 65 F5
Sandhaven 99 H4
Sandhead 64 A5
Sandhills Dorset 9 F3
Sandhills Surr. 12 C3
Sandhoe 70 E7
Sandholme E.Riding 58 E6
Sandholme Lincs. 43 G2
Sandhurst Brack.F. 22 B5
Sandhurst Glos. 29 H6
Sandhurst Kent 14 C5
Sandhutton 57 J1
Sandiacre 41 G2
Sandilands 53 J4
Sandiway 49 F5
Sandleheath 10 C3
Sandleigh 21 H1
Sandling 14 C2
Sandness 109 B7
Sandon Essex 24 D1
Sandon Herts. 33 G5
Sandon Staffs. 40 B3
Sandown 11 G6
Sandplace 4 C5
Sandquoy 106 G3
Sandridge Herts. 32 E7
Sandridge Wilts. 20 C5
Sandringham 44 A3
Sandrocks 13 G4
Sandsend 63 K5
Sandside House 104 E2
Sandsound 109 C8
Sandtoft 51 K2
Sanduck 7 F7
Sandway 14 D2
Sandwich 15 J2
Sandwick Cumb. 61 F5
Sandwick Shet. 109 D10
Sandwick (Sanndabhaig) W.Isles 101 G4
Sandwith 60 A5
Sandy 32 E4
Sandy Haven 16 B5
Sandy Lane W.Yorks. 57 G6
Sandy Lane Wilts. 20 C5
Sandycroft 48 C6
Sandygate Devon 5 J3
Sandygate I.o.M. 54 C4
Sandylands 55 H3
Sandyway 28 D6
Sangobeg 103 G2
Sanna 79 F1
Sannaig 72 D4
Sanndabhaig (Sandwick) 101 G4
Sanquhar 68 C3
Santon Bridge 60 C6
Santon Downham 44 C7
Sapcote 41 G6
Sapey Common 29 G2
Sapiston 34 D1
Sapperton Glos. 20 C1
Sapperton Lincs. 42 D2
Saracen's Head 43 G3
Sarclet 105 J4
Sardis 16 C5
Sarisbury 11 G4
Sarn Bridgend 18 C3
Sarn Powys 38 B6
Sarn Bach 36 C3
Sarn Meyllteyrn 36 B2
Sarnau Carmar. 17 G4
Sarnau Cere. 26 C3
Sarnau Gwyn. 37 J2
Sarnau Powys 38 B4
Sarnesfield 28 C3
Saron Carmar. 17 K4
Saron Carmar. 17 J2
Saron Gwyn. 46 D6
Sarratt 22 D2
Sarre 25 J5
Sarsden 30 D6

Place	Page	Grid
Sarsgrum	103	F2
Sartfield	54	C4
Satley	62	C2
Satterleigh	6	E3
Satterthwaite	60	E7
Sauchen	90	E3
Saucher	82	C4
Sauchie	75	G1
Sauchieburn	83	H1
Sauchrie	67	H2
Saughall	48	C6
Saughall Massie	48	B4
Saughtree	70	A4
Saul	20	A1
Saundby	51	K4
Saunderton	22	A1
Saunton	6	C2
Sausthorpe	53	G6
Savalbeg	96	C1
Savalmore	96	C1
Sawbridgeworth	33	H7
Sawdon	59	F1
Sawley Derbys.	41	F1
Sawley Lancs.	56	C5
Sawley N.Yorks.	57	H3
Sawston	33	H4
Sawtry	42	E7
Saxby Leics.	42	B4
Saxby Lincs.	52	C1
Saxby All Saints	52	C1
Saxelbye	42	A3
Saxilby	52	B5
Saxlingham	44	E2
Saxlingham Green	45	G6
Saxlingham Nethergate	45	G6
Saxlingham Thorpe	45	G6
Saxmundham	35	H2
Saxon Street	33	K3
Saxondale	41	J2
Saxtead Green	35	G2
Saxtead Little Green	35	G2
Saxthorpe	45	F2
Saxton	57	K6
Sayers Common	13	F5
Scackleton	58	C2
Scadabhagh	93	G2
Scaftworth	51	J3
Scagglethorpe	58	E2
Scalasaig	72	B1
Scalby E.Riding	58	E5
Scalby N.Yorks.	59	G1
Scaldwell	31	J1
Scale Houses	61	G2
Scaleby	69	K7
Scalebyhill	69	K7
Scales Cumb.	60	E4
Scales Cumb.	55	F2
Scalford	42	A3
Scaling	63	J5
Scallasaig	86	E3
Scallastle	79	J4
Scalloway	109	C9
Scamblesby	53	F5
Scammadale	79	K5
Scamodale	86	E7
Scampston	58	E2
Scampton	52	C5
Scaniport	88	D1
Scapa	107	D7
Scar	106	F3
Scarborough	59	G1
Scarcewater	3	G3
Scarcliffe	51	G6
Scarcroft	57	J5
Scardroy	95	J6
Scarff	108	B4
Scarfskerry	105	H1
Scargill	62	B5
Scarinish	78	B3
Scarisbrick	48	C1
Scarning	44	D4
Scarrington	42	A1
Scarth Hill	48	D2
Scartho	53	F2
Scaur D. & G.	65	J3
Scaur or Kippford D. & G.	65	J5
Scawby	52	C2
Scawton	58	B1
Scayne's Hill	13	G4
Scealascro	100	D5
Scethrog	28	A6
Schaw	67	J1
Scholar Green	49	H7
Scholes W.Yorks.	57	J6
Scholes W.Yorks.	50	F7
Sciberscross	104	C7
Scleddau	16	C2
Sco Ruston	45	G3
Scofton	51	J4
Scole	35	F1
Scolpaig	92	C4
Scone	82	C5
Scones Lethendy	82	C5
Sconser	86	B1
Scoor	79	F6
Scopwick	52	D7
Scoraig	95	G2
Scorborough	59	G5
Scorrier	2	E4
Scorriton	5	H4
Scorton Lancs.	55	J5
Scorton N.Yorks.	62	D6
Scotby	61	F1
Scotch Corner	62	D6
Scotforth	55	H4
Scothern	52	D5
Scotland Gate	71	H5
Scotlandwell	82	C7
Scotnish	73	F2
Scots' Gap	71	F5
Scotsburn	96	E4
Scotston Aber.	91	F7
Scotston P. & K.	82	A3
Scotstown	79	K1
Scotter	52	B2
Scotterthorpe	52	B2
Scottlethorpe	42	D3
Scotton Lincs.	52	B3
Scotton N.Yorks.	62	C6
Scotton N.Yorks.	57	J4
Scottow	45	G3
Scoulton	44	D5
Scourie	102	D4
Scourie More	102	D4
Scousburgh	109	F9
Scrabster	105	F1
Scrainwood	70	E3
Scrane End	43	G1
Scraptoft	41	J5
Scratby	45	K4
Scrayingham	58	D3
Scredington	42	D1
Scremby	53	H6
Scremerston	77	J6
Screveton	42	A1
Scriven	57	J4
Scrooby	51	J3
Scropton	40	D2
Scrub Hill	53	F7
Scruton	62	D7
Sculthorpe	44	C2
Scunthorpe	52	B1
Scurlage	17	H7
Sea Palling	45	J3
Seabank	80	A3
Seaborough	8	D4
Seacombe	48	B3
Seacroft Lincs.	53	J6
Seacroft W.Yorks.	57	J6
Seafield Arg. & B.	73	F2
Seafield S.Ayr.	67	H1
Seafield W.Loth.	75	J4
Seaford	13	H7
Seaforth	48	C3
Seagrave	41	J4
Seaham	63	F2
Seahouses	77	K4
Seal	23	J6
Sealand	48	C6
Seale	22	B7
Seamer N.Yorks.	63	F5
Seamer N.Yorks.	59	G1
Seamill	74	A6
Searby	52	D2
Seasalter	25	G5
Seascale	60	B6
Seathwaite Cumb.	60	D7
Seathwaite Cumb.	60	D5
Seatoller	60	D5
Seaton Cornw.	4	D5
Seaton Cumb.	60	B3
Seaton Devon	8	B5
Seaton Dur.	63	F2
Seaton E.Riding	59	H5
Seaton Northumb.	71	J6
Seaton Rut.	42	C6
Seaton Burn	71	H6
Seaton Carew	63	G3
Seaton Delaval	71	J6
Seaton Junction	8	B5
Seaton Ross	58	D5
Seaton Sluice	71	J6
Seatown Aber.	99	K5
Seatown Dorset	8	D5
Seatown Moray	98	C4
Seatown Moray	98	D4
Seave Green	63	G6
Seaview	11	H5
Seaville	60	C1
Seavington St. Mary	8	D3
Seavington St. Michael	8	D3
Sebastopol	19	F2
Sebergham	60	E2
Seckington	40	E5
Second Coast	95	F2
Sedbergh	61	H7
Sedbury	19	J2
Sedbusk	61	K7
Sedgeberrow	30	B5
Sedgebrook	42	B2
Sedgefield	62	E4
Sedgeford	44	B2
Sedgehill	9	H2
Sedgley	40	B6
Sedgwick	55	J1
Sedlescombe	14	C6
Sedlescombe Street	14	C6
Seend	20	C5
Seend Cleeve	20	C5
Seer Green	22	C2
Seething	45	H6
Sefton	48	C2
Seghill	71	H6
Seifton	38	D7
Seighford	40	A3
Seilebost	93	F2
Seion	46	D6
Seisdon	40	A6
Seisiadar	101	H4
Selattyn	38	B2
Selborne	11	J1
Selby	58	C6
Selham	12	C4
Selkirk	69	K1
Sellack	28	E6
Sellafield	60	B6
Sellafirth	108	E3
Sellindge	15	F4
Selling	15	F2
Sells Green	20	C5
Selly Oak	40	C7
Selmeston	13	J6
Selsdon	23	G5
Selsey	12	B7
Selsfield Common	13	G3
Selside	56	C2
Selstead	15	H3
Selston	51	G7
Selworthy	7	H1
Semblister	109	C7
Semer	34	D4
Semington	20	B5
Semley	9	H2
Send	22	D6
Send Marsh	22	D6
Senghenydd	18	E2
Sennen	2	A6
Sennen Cove	2	A6
Sennybridge	27	J6
Senwick	65	G6
Sequer's Bridge	5	G5
Sessay	57	K2
Setchey	44	A4
Setley	10	E4
Setter Shet.	109	E8
Setter Shet.	109	C7
Settiscarth	107	C6
Settle	56	D3
Settrington	58	E2
Seven Bridges	20	E2
Seven Kings	23	H3
Seven Sisters	18	B1
Seven Springs	29	J7
Sevenhampton Glos.	30	B6
Sevenhampton Swin.	21	F2
Sevenoaks	23	J6
Sevenoaks Weald	23	J6
Severn Beach	19	J3
Severn Stoke	29	H4
Sevington	15	F3
Sewards End	33	J5
Sewardstone	23	G2
Sewerby	59	J3
Seworgan	2	E5
Sewstern	42	B3
Sexhow	63	F6
Sgarasta Mhòr	93	F2
Sgiogarstaigh	101	H1
Sgodachail	96	B2
Shabbington	21	K1
Shackerley	40	A5
Shackerstone	41	F5
Shackleford	22	C7
Shadfen	71	H5
Shadforth	62	E2
Shadingfield	45	J7
Shadoxhurst	14	E4
Shadwell	44	D7
Shaftesbury	9	H2
Shafton	51	F1
Shalbourne	21	G5
Shalcombe	11	F6
Shalden	21	K7
Shaldon	5	K3
Shalfleet	11	F6
Shalford Essex	34	B6
Shalford Surr.	22	D7
Shalford Green	34	B6
Shallowford	7	F1
Shalmsford Street	15	F2
Shalmstry	105	G2
Shalstone	31	H5
Shalunt	73	J3
Shambellie	65	K4
Shamley Green	22	D7
Shandon	74	A2
Shandwick	97	F4
Shangton	42	A6
Shankend	70	A3
Shankhouse	71	H6
Shanklin	11	G6
Shannochie	66	D1
Shantron	74	B2
Shantullich	96	D6
Shanzie	82	D2
Shap	61	G5
Shapwick Dorset	9	J4
Shapwick Som.	8	D1
Shardlow	41	G2
Shareshill	40	B5
Sharlston	51	F1
Sharnbrook	32	D3
Sharnford	41	G6
Sharoe Green	55	J6
Sharow	57	J2
Sharpenhoe	32	D5
Sharperton	70	E3
Sharpham House	5	J5
Sharpness	19	K1
Sharpthorne	13	G3
Sharrington	44	E2
Shatterford	39	G7
Shaugh Prior	5	F4
Shavington	49	F7
Shaw Gt.Man.	49	J2
Shaw Swin.	20	E3
Shaw W.Berks.	21	H5
Shaw Wilts.	20	B5
Shaw Mills	57	H3
Shawbury	38	E3
Shawclough	49	H1
Shawell	41	H7
Shawford	11	F2
Shawforth	56	D7
Shawhead	65	J3
Shawtonhill	74	E6
Sheanachie	66	B2
Sheandow	89	K1
Shear Cross	20	B7
Shearington	69	F7
Shearsby	41	J6
Shebbear	6	C5
Shebdon	39	G3
Shebster	105	F2
Shedfield	11	G3
Sheen	50	D6
Sheepscombe	29	H7
Sheepstor	5	F4
Sheepwash Devon	6	C5
Sheepwash Northumb.	71	H5
Sheepway	19	H4
Sheepy Magna	41	F5
Sheepy Parva	41	F5
Sheering	33	J7
Sheerness	25	F4
Sheet	11	J2
Sheffield	51	F4
Sheffield Bottom	21	K5
Sheffield City Airport	51	G4
Sheffield Green	13	H4
Shefford	32	E5
Shefford Woodlands	21	G4
Sheigra	102	D2
Sheinton	39	F5
Shelderton	28	D1
Sheldon Derbys.	50	D6
Sheldon Devon	7	K5
Sheldon W.Mid.	40	D7
Sheldwich	15	F2
Shelf	57	G7
Shelfanger	45	F7
Shelfield	40	C5
Shelford	41	J1
Shellachan Arg. & B.	79	K4
Shellachan Arg. & B.	80	B5
Shellbrook Hill	38	C1
Shelley Essex	23	J1
Shelley Suff.	34	E5
Shelley W.Yorks.	50	E1
Shellingford	21	G2
Shellow Bowells	24	C1
Shelsley Beauchamp	29	G2
Shelsley Walsh	29	G2
Shelton Beds.	32	D2
Shelton Norf.	45	G6
Shelton Notts.	42	A1
Shelton Shrop.	38	D4
Shelton Green	45	G6
Shelve	38	C6
Shelwick	28	E4
Shenfield	24	C2
Shenington	30	E4
Shenley	22	E1
Shenley Brook End	32	B5
Shenley Church End	32	B5
Shenleybury	22	E1
Shenmore	28	C5
Shennanton	64	D4
Shenstone Staffs.	40	D5
Shenstone Worcs.	29	H1
Shenstone Woodend	40	D5
Shenton	41	F5
Shenval	89	K2
Shepeau Stow	43	G4
Shephall	33	F6
Shepherd's Green	22	A3
Shepherdswell (Sibertswold)	15	H3
Shepley	50	D2
Sheppardstown	105	H5
Shepperdine	19	K2
Shepperton	22	D5
Shepreth	33	G4
Shepshed	41	G4
Shepton Beauchamp	8	D3
Shepton Mallet	19	K7
Shepton Montague	9	F1
Shepway	14	C2
Sheraton	63	F3
Sherborne Dorset	9	F3
Sherborne Glos.	30	C7
Sherborne St. John	21	K6
Sherbourne	30	D2
Sherburn Dur.	62	E2
Sherburn N.Yorks.	59	F2
Sherburn in Elmet	57	K6
Shere	22	D7
Shereford	44	C3
Sherfield English	10	D2
Sherfield on Loddon	21	K6
Sherford	5	H6
Sheriff Hutton	58	C3
Sheriffhales	39	G4
Sheringham	45	F1
Sherington	32	B4
Shernborne	44	B2
Sherramore	88	C5
Sherrington	9	J1
Sherston	20	B3
Sherwood Green	6	D3
Shettleston	74	E4
Shevington	48	E2
Shevington Moor	48	E1
Sheviock	4	D5
Shiel Bridge	87	F3
Shieldaig High.	94	E6
Shieldaig High.	94	E4
Shieldhill	75	G3
Shielfoot	86	C7
Shielhill	83	F2
Shiels	90	E4
Shifford	21	G1
Shifnal	39	G5
Shilbottle	71	G3
Shildon	62	D4
Shillingford Devon	7	H3
Shillingford Oxon.	21	J2
Shillingford St. George	7	H7
Shillingstone	9	H3
Shillington	32	E5
Shillmoor	70	D3
Shilstone	6	D5
Shilton Oxon.	21	F1
Shilton Warks.	41	G7
Shimpling Norf.	45	F7
Shimpling Suff.	34	C3
Shimpling Street	34	C3
Shincliffe	62	D2
Shiney Row	62	E1
Shinfield	22	A5
Shingay	33	G4
Shingle Street	35	H4
Shinner's Bridge	5	H4
Shinness Lodge	103	H7
Shipbourne	23	J6
Shipdham	44	D5
Shipham	19	H6
Shiphay	5	J4
Shiplake	22	A4
Shipley Northumb.	71	G2
Shipley Shrop.	40	A6
Shipley W.Suss.	12	E4
Shipley W.Yorks.	57	G6
Shipley Bridge Devon	5	G4
Shipley Bridge Surr.	23	G7
Shipmeadow	45	H6
Shippon	21	H2
Shipston on Stour	30	D4
Shipton Glos.	30	B7
Shipton N.Yorks.	58	B4
Shipton Shrop.	38	E6
Shipton Bellinger	21	F7
Shipton Gorge	8	D5
Shipton Green	12	B7
Shipton Moyne	20	B3
Shipton-on-Cherwell	31	F7
Shiptonthorpe	58	E5
Shipton-under-Wychwood	30	D7
Shira	80	C6
Shirburn	21	K2
Shirdley Hill	48	C1
Shire Oak	40	C5
Shirebrook	51	H6
Shirehampton	19	J4
Shiremoor	71	J6
Shirenewton	19	H2
Shireoaks	51	H4
Shirl Heath	28	D3
Shirland	51	G7
Shirley Derbys.	40	E1
Shirley Gt.Lon.	23	G5
Shirley Hants.	10	C5
Shirley S'ham.	11	F3
Shirley W.Mid.	30	C1
Shirrell Heath	11	G3
Shirwell	6	D2
Shirwell Cross	6	D2
Shiskine	66	D1
Shobdon	28	C2
Shobrooke	7	G5
Shocklach	38	D1
Shoeburyness	25	F3
Sholden	15	J2
Sholing	11	F3
Shoot Hill	38	D4
Shooter's Hill	23	H4
Shop Cornw.	3	F1
Shop Cornw.	6	A4
Shop Corner	35	G5
Shoreditch	23	G3
Shoreham	23	J5
Shoreham-by-Sea	13	F6
Shoremill	96	E5
Shoresdean	77	H6
Shoreswood	77	H6
Shoretown	96	D5
Shorncote	20	D2
Shorne	24	C4
Shorne Ridgeway	24	C4
Short Cross	38	B5
Short Green	44	E7
Short Heath Derbys.	41	F4
Short Heath W.Mid.	40	C6
Shortacombe	6	D7
Shortgate	13	H5
Shortgrove	33	J5
Shortlanesend	3	F4
Shorwell	11	F6
Shoscombe	20	A6
Shotesham	45	G6
Shotgate	24	D2
Shotley	35	G5
Shotley Bridge	62	B1
Shotley Gate	35	G5
Shotleyfield	62	B1
Shottenden	15	F2
Shottermill	12	B3
Shottery	30	C3
Shotteswell	31	F4
Shottisham	35	H4
Shottle	51	F7
Shottlegate	41	F1
Shotton Dur.	63	F3
Shotton Flints.	48	C6
Shotton Northumb.	77	G7
Shotton Colliery	62	E2
Shotts	75	G4
Shotwick	48	C5
Shoughlaige-e-Caine	54	C5
Shouldham	44	A5
Shouldham Thorpe	44	A5
Shoulton	29	H3
Shover's Green	13	K3
Shrawardine	38	C4
Shrawley	29	H2
Shrewley	30	D2
Shrewsbury	38	D4
Shrewton	20	D7
Shripney	12	C6
Shrivenham	21	F3
Shropham	44	D6
Shroton (Iwerne Courtney)	9	H3
Shrub End	34	D6
Shucknall	28	E4
Shudy Camps	33	K4
Shurdington	29	J7
Shurlock Row	22	B4
Shurrery	105	F3
Shurrery Lodge	105	F3
Shurton	7	K1
Shustoke	40	E6
Shut Heath	40	A3
Shute	8	B5
Shutford	30	E4
Shuthonger	29	H5
Shutlanger	31	J3
Shuttington	40	E5
Shuttlewood	51	G5
Shuttleworth	49	H1
Siabost	100	E3
Siadar larach	101	F2
Siadar Uarach	101	F2
Sibbaldbie	69	G5
Sibbertoft	41	J7
Sibdon Carwood	38	D7
Sibertswold (Shepherdswell)	15	H3
Sibford Ferris	30	E5
Sibford Gower	30	E5
Sible Hedingham	34	B5
Sibsey	53	G7
Sibson Cambs.	42	D6
Sibson Leics.	41	F5
Sibster	105	J3
Sibthorpe	42	A1
Sibton	35	H2
Sicklesmere	34	C3
Sicklinghall	57	J5
Sidbury Devon	7	K6
Sidbury Shrop.	39	F7
Sidcot	19	H6
Sidcup	23	H4
Siddington Ches.	49	H5
Siddington Glos.	20	D2
Sidemoor	29	J1
Sidestrand	45	G2
Sidford	7	K6
Sidlesham	12	B7
Sidley	14	C7
Sidlow	23	F7
Sidmouth	7	K7
Sigford	5	H3
Sigglesthorne	59	H5
Sigingstone	18	C4
Silchester	21	K5
Sileby	41	J4
Silecroft	54	E1
Silfield	45	F6
Silian	26	E3
Silk Willoughby	42	D1
Silkstone	50	E2
Silkstone Common	50	E2
Silksworth	62	E1
Silloth	60	C1
Sills	70	D3
Sillyearn	98	D5
Silpho	63	J3
Silsden	57	F5
Silsoe	32	D5
Silver End	34	C7
Silver Hill	14	C5
Silverburn	76	A4
Silvercraigs	73	G2
Silverdale Lancs.	55	H2
Silverdale Staffs.	40	A1
Silverhill	14	D6
Silverley's Green	35	G1
Silvermoss	91	G1
Silverstone	31	H4
Silverton	7	H5
Silvington	29	F1
Silwick	109	B8
Simonburn	70	D6
Simonsbath	7	F2
Simonstone	56	C6
Simprim	77	G6
Simpson	32	B5
Sinclair's Hill	77	G5
Sinclairston	67	J2
Sinderby	57	J1
Sinderhope	61	K1
Sindlesham	22	A5
Singdean	70	A3
Singleton Lancs.	55	G6
Singleton W.Suss.	12	B5
Singlewell or Ifield	24	C4
Sinnahard	90	C3
Sinnington	58	D1
Sinton Green	29	H2
Sipson	22	D4
Sirhowy	28	A7
Sisland	45	H6
Sissinghurst	14	C4
Siston	19	K4
Sithney	2	D6
Sittingbourne	25	F5
Siulaisiadar	101	H4
Six Ashes	39	G7
Six Mile Bottom	33	J3
Sixhills	52	E4
Sixmile Cottages	15	G3
Sixpenny Handley	9	J3
Sizewell	35	J2
Skail	104	C4
Skaill Ork.	107	B6
Skaill Ork.	107	E7
Skares Aber.	90	E1
Skares Aber.	67	K2
Skarpigarth	109	A7
Skateraw	77	F3
Skaw	109	E6
Skeabost	93	K7
Skeabrae	106	B5
Skeeby	62	C6
Skeffington	42	A5
Skeffling	53	G1
Skegby	51	H6
Skegness	53	J6
Skelberry	109	F9
Skelbo	96	E2
Skeldon	67	H2
Skeldyke	43	G2
Skellingthorpe	52	C5
Skellister	109	D7
Skellow	51	H1
Skelmanthorpe	50	E1
Skelmersdale	48	D2
Skelmonae	91	G1
Skelmorlie	73	K4
Skelmuir	99	H6
Skelpick	104	C3
Skelton Cumb.	61	F3
Skelton E.Riding	58	D7
Skelton N.Yorks.	62	B6
Skelton N.Yorks.	57	J3
Skelton R. & C.	63	H5
Skelton York	58	B4
Skelton Green	63	H5
Skelwick	106	D3
Skelwith Bridge	60	E6
Skendleby	53	H6
Skenfrith	28	D6
Skerne	59	G4
Skeroblingarry	66	B1
Skerray	103	J2
Skerton	55	H3
Sketty	17	K6
Skewen	18	A2
Skewsby	58	C2
Skeyton	45	G3
Skidbrooke	53	H3
Skidby	59	G6
Skilgate	7	H3
Skillington	42	C3
Skinburness	60	C1
Skinflats	75	H2
Skinidin	93	H7
Skinnet	105	G2
Skinningrove	63	J4
Skipness	73	H5
Skipsea	59	H4
Skipton	56	E4
Skipton-on-Swale	57	J2
Skipwith	58	C6
Skirbeck	43	G1
Skirlaugh	59	H6
Skirling	75	J7
Skirmett	22	A3
Skirpenbeck	58	D4
Skirwith Cumb.	61	H3
Skirwith N.Yorks.	56	C2
Skirza	105	J2
Skulamus	86	C2
Skullomie	103	J2
Skye of Curr	89	G2
Slack	90	C1
Slackhall	50	C4
Slackhead	98	C4
Slad	20	B1
Slade	6	D1
Slade Green	23	J4
Slaggyford	61	H1
Slaidburn	56	C4
Slains Park	91	G7
Slaithwaite	50	C1
Slaley	62	A1
Slamannan	75	G3
Slapton Bucks.	32	C6
Slapton Devon	5	J6
Slapton Northants.	31	H4
Slate Haugh	98	C4
Slatenber	56	C2
Slattadale	94	E4
Slattocks	49	H2
Slaugham	13	F4
Slaughden	35	J3
Slaughterford	20	B4
Slawston	42	A6
Sleaford Hants.	12	B3
Sleaford Lincs.	42	D1
Sleagill	61	G4
Sleap	38	D3
Sledge Green	29	H5
Sledmere	59	F3
Sleights	63	K6
Slepe	9	J5
Slickly	105	H2
Sliddery	66	D1
Sliemore	89	H3
Sligachan	85	K2
Slimbridge	20	A1
Slindon Staffs.	40	A2
Slindon W.Suss.	12	C6
Slinfold	12	E3
Slingsby	58	C2
Slioch	90	D1
Slip End Beds.	32	D7
Slip End Herts.	33	F5
Slipton	32	C1
Slochd	89	F3
Slockavullin	73	G1
Slogarie	65	G4
Sloley	45	G3
Sloothby	53	H5
Slough	22	C4
Sluggan	89	F3
Slyne	55	H3
Smailholm	76	E7
Small Dole	13	F5
Small Hythe	14	D5
Smallbridge	49	J1
Smallburgh	45	H3
Smallburn Aber.	99	J6
Smallburn E.Ayr.	68	B1
Smalley	41	G1
Smallfield	23	G7
Smallridge	8	B4
Smallthorne	49	H7
Smallworth	44	E7
Smannell	21	G7
Smardale	61	J6
Smarden	14	D3
Smaull	72	A4
Smeale Farm	54	D3
Smeatharpe	7	K4
Smeeth	15	F4
Smeeton Westerby	41	J6
Smelthouses	57	G3
Smerral	105	G5
Smethwick	40	C7
Smirisary	86	C7
Smisby	41	F4
Smith End Green	29	G3
Smithfield	69	K7
Smithincott	7	J4
Smith's Green	33	J6
Smithton	96	E7
Smithy Green	49	G5
Smug Oak	22	E1
Smyrton	67	F5
Smythe's Green	34	D7
Snailbeach	38	C5
Snailwell	33	K2
Snainton	59	F1
Snaith	58	C7
Snape N.Yorks.	57	H1
Snape Suff.	35	H3
Snape Green	48	C1
Snarestone	41	F5
Snarford	52	D4
Snargate	14	E5
Snave	15	F4
Sneachill	29	J3
Snead	38	C6
Sneaton	63	K6
Sneatonthorpe	63	J2
Snelland	52	D4
Snellings	60	A6
Snelston	40	D1
Snetterton	44	D6
Snettisham	44	A2
Snibston	41	G4
Snishival	84	C1
Snitter	71	F3
Snitterby	52	C3
Snitterfield	30	D3
Snitton	28	E1
Snodhill	28	C4
Snodland	24	D5
Snowshill	30	B5
Soar Carmar.	17	K3
Soar Devon	5	H7
Soberton	11	H3
Soberton Heath	11	H3
Sockburn	62	E6
Sodylt Bank	38	C2
Soham	33	J1
Solas	92	D4
Soldon Cross	6	B4
Soldridge	11	H1
Sole Street Kent	15	F3
Sole Street Kent	24	C5
Solihull	30	C1
Solihull Lodge	30	B1
Sollers Dilwyn	28	D3
Sollers Hope	29	F5
Sollom	48	D1
Solsgirth	75	H1
Solva	16	A3
Solwaybank	69	J6
Somerby	42	A4
Somercotes	51	G7
Somerford Keynes	20	D2
Somerley	12	B7
Somerleyton	45	J6
Somersal Herbert	40	D2
Somersby	53	G5
Somersham Cambs.	33	G1
Somersham Suff.	34	E4
Somerton Oxon.	31	F6
Somerton Som.	8	D2
Somerton Suff.	34	C3
Sompting	12	E6
Sonning	22	A4
Sonning Common	22	A3
Sonning Eye	22	A4
Sopley	10	C5
Sopworth	20	B3
Sorbie	64	E6
Sordale	105	G2
Sorisdale	78	D1
Sorn	67	K1
Sornhill	74	D7
Soroba	79	K5
Sortat	105	H2
Sotby	53	F5
Sots Hole	52	E6
Sotterly	45	J7
Soudley	39	G3
Soughton	48	B6
Soulbury	32	B6
Soulby	61	J5
Souldern	31	G5
Souldrop	32	C2
Sound Ches.	39	F1
Sound Shet.	109	D8
Sound Shet.	109	C7
Soundwell	19	K4
Sourhope	70	D1
Sourin	106	D4
Sourton	6	D7
Soutergate	55	F1
South Acre	44	C4
South Allington	5	H7
South Alloa	75	G1
South Ambersham	12	C4
South Anston	51	H4
South Ascot	22	C5
South Ballachulish	80	B2
South Balloch	67	H4
South Bank	63	G4
South Barrow	9	F2
South Beddington	23	F5
South Bellsdyke	75	H2
South Benfleet	24	D3
South Bersted	12	C7
South Blackbog	91	F1
South Bowood	8	D5
South Brent	5	G4
South Brewham	9	G1
South Broomhill	71	H4
South Burlingham	45	H5
South Cadbury	9	F2
South Cairn	66	D7
South Carlton	52	C5
South Cave	59	F6
South Cerney	20	D2
South Chard	8	C4
South Charlton	71	G1
South Cheriton	9	F2
South Cliffe	58	E6
South Clifton	52	B5
South Cockerington	53	G4
South Common	13	G5

South Cornelly 18 B4
South Corrygills 73 J7
South Cove 45 J7
South Creagan 80 A3
South Creake 44 C2
South Croxton 41 J4
South Dalton 59 F5
South Darenth 23 J5
South Duffield 58 C6
South Elkington 53 F4
South Elmsall 51 G1
South End *Bucks.* 32 B6
South End *Cumb.* 55 F3
South End *N.Lincs.* 52 E1
South Erradale 94 D4
South Fambridge 24 E2
South Fawley 21 G3
South Ferriby 59 F7
South Flobbets 91 F1
South Garth 108 E3
South Godstone 23 G7
South Gorley 10 C3
South Green *Essex* 24 C2
South Green *Norf.* 44 E4
South Hall 73 J3
South Hanningfield 24 D2
South Harting 11 J3
South Hayling 11 J5
South Hazelrigg 77 J7
South Heath 22 C1
South Heighton 13 H6
South Hetton 62 E2
South Hiendley 51 F1
South Hill 4 D3
South Hinksey 21 J1
South Hole 6 A4
South Holmwood 22 E7
South Hornchurch 23 J3
South Hourat 74 A5
South Huish 5 G6
South Hykeham 52 C6
South Hylton 62 E1
South Kelsey 52 D3
South Kessock 96 D7
South Killingholme 52 E1
South Kilvington 57 K1
South Kilworth 41 J7
South Kirkby 51 G1
South Kirkton 91 F4
South Kyme 42 E1
South Lancing 12 E6
South Ledaig 80 A4
South Leigh 21 G1
South Leverton 51 K4
South Littleton 30 B4
South Lopham 44 E7
South Luffenham 42 C5
South Malling 13 H5
South Marston 20 E3
South Milford 57 K6
South Milton 5 H6
South Mimms 23 F1
South Molton 7 F3
South Moor 62 C1
South Moreton 21 J3
South Mundham 12 B6
South Muskham 51 K7
South Newbald 59 F6
South Newington 31 F5
South Newton 10 B1
South Normanton 51 G7
South Norwood 23 G5
South Nutfield 23 G7
South Ockendon 23 J3
South Ormsby 53 G5
South Otterington 57 J1
South Oxhey 22 E2
South Park 23 F7
South Perrott 8 D4
South Petherton 8 D3
South Petherwin 6 B7
South Pickenham 44 C5
South Pool 5 H6
South Queensferry 75 K3
South Radworthy 7 F2
South Rauceby 42 D1
South Raynham 44 C3
South Redbriggs 99 F6
South Reston 53 H4
South Runcton 44 A5
South Scarle 52 B6
South Shian 80 A3
South Shields 71 J7
South Somercotes 53 H3
South Stainley 57 J3
South Stoke *Oxon.* 21 K3
South Stoke *W.Suss.* 12 D6
South Street *E.Suss.* 13 G5
South Street *Kent* 24 C5
South Tawton 6 E6
South Thoresby 53 H5
South Tidworth 21 F7
South Town 11 H1
South Upper Barrack 99 H6
South Walsham 45 H4
South Warnborough 22 A7
South Weald 23 J2
South Weston 22 A2
South Wheatley *Cornw.* 4 C1
South Wheatley *Notts.* 51 K4
South Whiteness 109 C8
South Widcombe 19 J6
South Wigston 41 H6
South Willesborough 15 F3
South Willingham 52 E4
South Wingate 63 F3
South Wingfield 51 F7
South Witham 42 C4
South Wonston 11 F1
South Woodham Ferrers 24 E2
South Wootton 44 A3
South Wraxall 20 B5
South Yardley 40 D7
South Zeal 6 E6
Southall 22 E4
Southam *Glos.* 29 J6
Southam *Warks.* 31 F2
Southampton 11 F3
Southampton Airport 11 F3
Southbar 74 C4
Southborough 23 J7
Southbourne *Bourne.* 10 C5
Southbourne *W.Suss.* 11 J4

Southburgh 44 E5
Southburn 59 F4
Southchurch 25 F3
Southcott 6 D6
Southdean 70 B3
Southease 13 H6
Southend *Aber.* 99 F6
Southend *Arg. & B.* 66 A3
Southend *W.Berks.* 21 K4
Southend Airport 24 E3
Southend-on-Sea 24 E3
Southerndown 18 B4
Southerness 65 K5
Southery 44 A6
Southfleet 24 C4
Southgate *Gt.Lon.* 23 F2
Southgate *Norf.* 44 E3
Southgate *Norf.* 44 A2
Southgate *Swan.* 17 J7
Southill 32 E4
Southington 21 J7
Southleigh 8 B5
Southminster 25 F2
Southmuir 82 E2
Southoe 32 E2
Southolt 35 F2
Southorpe 42 D5
Southowram 57 G7
Southport 48 C1
Southrepps 45 G2
Southrey 52 E6
Southrop 20 E1
Southrope 21 K7
Southsea *Ports.* 11 H5
Southsea *Wrex.* 48 B7
Southstoke 20 A5
Southtown *Norf.* 45 K5
Southtown *Ork.* 107 D8
Southwaite *Cumb.* 61 J6
Southwaite *Cumb.* 61 G2
Southwark 23 J4
Southwater 12 E4
Southway 19 J7
Southwell *Dorset* 9 F7
Southwell *Notts.* 51 K7
Southwick *Hants.* 11 H4
Southwick *Northants.* 42 D6
Southwick *T. & W.* 62 E1
Southwick *W.Suss.* 13 F6
Southwick *Wilts.* 20 B6
Southwold 45 K7
Southwood *Norf.* 45 H5
Southwood *Som.* 8 E1
Sowerby *N.Yorks.* 57 K1
Sowerby *W.Yorks.* 57 F7
Sowerby Bridge 57 F7
Sowerby Row 60 E2
Sowton 7 H6
Soyal 96 C2
Spa Common 45 G2
Spadeadam 70 A6
Spalding 43 F3
Spaldington 58 D6
Spaldwick 32 E1
Spalefield 83 G7
Spalford 52 B6
Spanby 42 D2
Sparham 44 E4
Spark Bridge 55 G1
Sparkford 9 F2
Sparkwell 5 F5
Sparrowpit 50 C4
Sparrow's Green 13 K3
Sparsholt *Hants.* 11 F1
Sparsholt *Oxon.* 21 G3
Spartylea 61 K2
Spaunton 63 J7
Spaxton 8 B1
Spean Bridge 87 J6
Speddoch 68 D5
Speen *Bucks.* 22 B1
Speen *W.Berks.* 21 H5
Speeton 59 H2
Speke 48 D4
Speldhurst 23 J7
Spellbrook 33 H7
Spelsbury 30 E6
Spen Green 49 H6
Spencers Wood 22 A5
Spennithorne 57 G1
Spennymoor 62 D3
Spetchley 29 H3
Spetisbury 9 J4
Spexhall 45 H7
Spey Bay 98 B4
Speybridge 89 H2
Speyview 97 K7
Spilsby 53 H6
Spindlestone 77 K7
Spinkhill 51 G5
Spinningdale 96 D2
Spirthill 20 C4
Spital *High.* 105 G3
Spital *W. & M.* 22 C4
Spital in the Street 52 C3
Spitalbrook 23 G1
Spithurst 13 H5
Spittal *D. & G.* 64 E4
Spittal *D. & G.* 64 D5
Spittal *E.Loth.* 76 C3
Spittal *Northumb.* 77 J5
Spittal *Pembs.* 16 C3
Spittal of Glenmuick 90 B6
Spittal of Glenshee 82 C1
Spittalfield 82 C3
Spixworth 45 G4
Spofforth 57 J4
Spondon 41 G2
Spooner Row 44 E6
Spooney 39 F2
Sporle 44 C4
Sportsman's Arms 47 H7
Spott 76 E3
Spratton 31 J1
Spreakley 22 B7
Spreyton 6 E6
Spridlington 52 D4
Springburn 74 E4
Springfield *Arg. & B.* 73 J3
Springfield *D. & G.* 69 J7
Springfield *Fife* 82 E6
Springfield *Moray* 97 H6
Springfield *P. & K.* 82 C4
Springfield *W.Mid.* 40 C7
Springholm 65 J4
Springkell 69 H6
Springleys 91 F1
Springside 74 B7
Springthorpe 52 B4
Springwell 62 D1
Sproatley 59 H6

Sprotbrough 51 H2
Sproughton 35 F4
Sprouston 77 F7
Sprowston 45 G4
Sproxton *Leics.* 42 B3
Sproxton *N.Yorks.* 58 C1
Spurstow 48 E7
Square Point 65 H3
Squires Gate 55 G6
Sròndoire 73 G3
Sronphadruig Lodge 88 E7
Stableford 40 A2
Stackhouse 56 D3
Stackpole 16 C6
Stacksteads 56 D7
Staddiscombe 5 F5
Staddlethorpe 58 E7
Stadhampton 21 K2
Stadhlaigearraidh 84 C1
Staffield 61 G2
Staffin 93 K5
Stafford 40 B3
Stagden Cross 33 K7
Stagsden 32 C4
Stagshaw Bank 70 E7
Stain 105 J2
Stainburn 57 H5
Stainby 42 C3
Staincross 51 F2
Staindrop 62 C4
Staines 22 D4
Stainfield *Lincs.* 42 D3
Stainfield *Lincs.* 52 E5
Stainforth *N.Yorks.* 56 D3
Stainforth *S.Yorks.* 51 J1
Staining 55 G6
Stainland 50 C1
Stainsacre 63 J2
Stainton *Cumb.* 55 J1
Stainton *Cumb.* 61 F4
Stainton *Dur.* 62 B5
Stainton *Middbro.* 62 D5
Stainton *N.Yorks.* 62 B7
Stainton *S.Yorks.* 51 H3
Stainton by Langworth 52 D5
Stainton le Vale 52 E3
Stainton with Adgarley 55 F2
Staintondale 63 J3
Stair *Cumb.* 60 D4
Stair *E.Ayr.* 67 J1
Staithes 63 J5
Stake Pool 55 H5
Stakeford 71 H5
Stalbridge 9 G3
Stalbridge Weston 9 G3
Stalham 45 H3
Stalham Green 45 H3
Stalisfield Green 14 E2
Stalling Busk 56 E1
Stallingborough 53 F1
Stalmine 55 G5
Stalybridge 49 J3
Stambourne 34 B5
Stamford *Lincs.* 42 D5
Stamford *Northumb.* 71 H2
Stamford Bridge 58 D4
Stamfordham 71 F6
Stanborough 33 F7
Stanbridge *Beds.* 32 C6
Stanbridge *Dorset* 10 B4
Stanbridge Earls 10 E2
Stanbury 57 F6
Stand 75 F4
Standburn 75 H3
Standeford 40 B5
Standen 14 D3
Standford 12 B3
Standish 48 E1
Standlake 21 G1
Standon *Hants.* 11 F2
Standon *Herts.* 33 G6
Standon *Staffs.* 40 A2
Stane 75 G5
Stanfield 44 D3
Stanford *Beds.* 32 E4
Stanford *Kent* 15 G4
Stanford Bishop 29 F3
Stanford Bridge 29 G2
Stanford Dingley 21 J4
Stanford in the Vale 21 G2
Stanford on Avon 31 G1
Stanford on Soar 41 H3
Stanford on Teme 29 G2
Stanford Rivers 23 J1
Stanford-le-Hope 24 C3
Stanghow 63 H5
Stanground 43 F6
Stanhoe 44 C2
Stanhope *Dur.* 62 A3
Stanhope *Sc.Bord.* 69 G1
Stanion 42 C7
Stanley *Derbys.* 41 G1
Stanley *Dur.* 62 C1
Stanley *P. & K.* 82 C4
Stanley *Staffs.* 49 J7
Stanley *W.Yorks.* 57 J7
Stanley *Wilts.* 20 C4
Stanley Common 41 G1
Stanlow 48 D5
Stanmer 13 G6
Stanmore *Gt.Lon.* 22 E2
Stanmore *W.Berks.* 21 H4
Stannersburn 70 C5
Stanningfield 34 C3
Stannington *Northumb.* 71 H6
Stannington *S.Yorks.* 51 F4
Stansbatch 28 C2
Stansfield 34 B3
Stanstead 34 C4
Stanstead Abbotts 33 G7
Stansted 24 C5
Stansted Airport 33 J6
Stansted Mountfitchet 33 J6
Stanton *Derbys.* 40 E4
Stanton *Glos.* 30 B5
Stanton *Northumb.* 71 G4
Stanton *Staffs.* 40 D1
Stanton *Suff.* 34 D1
Stanton by Bridge 41 F3
Stanton by Dale 41 G2
Stanton Drew 19 J5
Stanton Fitzwarren 20 E2
Stanton Harcourt 21 H1
Stanton Hill 51 G6
Stanton in Peak 50 E6
Stanton Lacy 28 D1
Stanton Long 38 E6
Stanton Prior 19 K5

Stanton St. Bernard 20 D5
Stanton St. John 21 J1
Stanton St. Quintin 20 C3
Stanton Street 34 D2
Stanton under Bardon 41 G4
Stanton upon Hine Heath 38 E3
Stanton Wick 19 K5
Stanton-on-the-Wolds 41 J2
Stanwardine in the Fields 38 D3
Stanway *Essex* 34 D6
Stanway *Glos.* 30 B5
Stanwell 22 D4
Stanwell Moor 22 D4
Stanwick 32 C1
Stanwix 61 F1
Stanydale 109 B7
Staoinebrig 84 C1
Stape 63 J7
Stapehill 10 B4
Stapeley 39 F1
Staple 15 H2
Staple Fitzpaine 8 B3
Staplecross 14 C5
Staplefield 13 F4
Stapleford *Cambs.* 33 H3
Stapleford *Herts.* 33 G7
Stapleford *Leics.* 42 B4
Stapleford *Lincs.* 52 B7
Stapleford *Notts.* 41 G2
Stapleford *Wilts.* 10 B1
Stapleford Abbotts 23 H2
Stapleford Tawney 23 J2
Staplegrove 8 B2
Staplehurst 14 C3
Staplers 11 G6
Stapleton *Bristol* 19 J4
Stapleton *Cumb.* 70 A6
Stapleton *Here.* 28 C2
Stapleton *Leics.* 41 G6
Stapleton *N.Yorks.* 62 D5
Stapleton *Shrop.* 38 D5
Stapleton *Som.* 8 D2
Stapley 7 K4
Staploe 32 E2
Staplow 29 F4
Star *Fife* 82 E7
Star *Pembs.* 17 F2
Star *Som.* 19 H6
Starbotton 56 E2
Starcross 7 H7
Starkigarth 109 D10
Starling's Green 33 H5
Starr 67 J4
Starston 45 G7
Startforth 62 B5
Startley 20 C3
Statham 49 F4
Stathe 8 C2
Stathern 42 A2
Station Town 63 F3
Staughton Green 32 E2
Staughton Highway 32 E2
Staunton *Glos.* 28 E7
Staunton *Glos.* 29 G6
Staunton Harold Hall 41 F3
Staunton on Arrow 28 C2
Staunton on Wye 28 C4
Staveley *Cumb.* 61 F7
Staveley *Derbys.* 51 G5
Staveley *N.Yorks.* 57 J3
Staveley-in-Cartmel 55 G1
Staverton *Devon* 5 H4
Staverton *Glos.* 29 H6
Staverton *Northants.* 31 G2
Staverton *Wilts.* 20 B5
Staverton Bridge 29 H6
Stawell 8 C1
Stawley 7 J3
Staxigoe 105 J3
Staxton 59 G2
Staylittle 37 H6
Staynall 55 G5
Staythorpe 51 K7
Stean 57 F2
Steane 31 G5
Stearsby 58 C2
Steart 19 F7
Stebbing 33 K6
Stebbing Green 33 K6
Stedham 12 B4
Steel Cross 13 J3
Steele Road 70 A4
Steen's Bridge 28 E3
Steep 11 J2
Steep Marsh 11 J2
Steeple *Dorset* 9 J6
Steeple *Essex* 25 F1
Steeple Ashton 20 C6
Steeple Barton 31 F6
Steeple Bumpstead 33 K4
Steeple Claydon 31 H6
Steeple Gidding 42 E7
Steeple Langford 10 B1
Steeple Morden 33 F4
Steeton 57 F5
Stein 93 H6
Steinmanhill 99 F6
Stella 71 G7
Stelling Minnis 15 G3
Stemster *High.* 105 G2
Stemster *High.* 105 G4
Stemster House 105 G2
Stenalees 4 A5
Stenhousemuir 75 G2
Stenigot 53 F4
Stenness 108 B5
Stenscholl 93 K5
Stenton *E.Loth.* 76 E3
Stenton *P. & K.* 82 B3
Steornabhagh (Stornoway) 101 G4
Stepaside 16 E5
Stepney 23 G3
Steppingley 32 D5
Stepps 74 E4
Sternfield 35 H2
Sterridge 6 D1
Stert 20 D6
Stetchworth 33 K3
Stevenage 33 F6
Stevenston 74 A6
Steventon *Hants.* 21 J7
Steventon *Oxon.* 21 H2
Stevington 32 C3
Stewartby 32 D4
Stewarton *D. & G.* 64 D6
Stewarton *E.Ayr.* 74 C6
Stewkley 32 B6
Stewton 53 G4
Steyning 12 E5

Steynton 16 C5
Stibb 6 A4
Stibb Cross 6 C4
Stibb Green 21 F5
Stibbard 44 D3
Stibbington 42 D6
Stichill 77 F7
Sticker 3 G3
Stickford 53 G6
Sticklepath 6 E6
Stickney 53 G7
Stiffkey 44 D1
Stifford's Bridge 29 G4
Stillingfleet 58 B5
Stillington *N.Yorks.* 58 B3
Stillington *Stock.* 62 E4
Stilton 42 E7
Stinchcombe 20 A2
Stinsford 9 G5
Stirchley *Tel. & W.* 39 G5
Stirchley *W.Mid.* 40 C7
Stirkoke House 105 J3
Stirling *Aber.* 99 K6
Stirling *Stir.* 75 F1
Stirton 56 E4
Stisted 34 B6
Stithians 2 E5
Stittenham 96 D4
Stivichall 30 E1
Stix 81 J3
Stixwould 52 E6
Stoak 48 D5
Stobo 75 K7
Stoborough 9 J6
Stoborough Green 9 J6
Stobwood 75 H5
Stock 24 C2
Stock Green 29 J3
Stock Lane 21 F4
Stock Wood 30 B3
Stockbridge *Hants.* 10 E1
Stockbridge *Stir.* 81 J7
Stockbury 24 E5
Stockcross 21 H5
Stockdalewath 60 E2
Stockerston 42 B6
Stocking Pelham 33 H6
Stockingford 41 F6
Stockland 8 B4
Stockland Bristol 19 F7
Stockleigh English 7 G5
Stockleigh Pomeroy 7 G5
Stockley 20 C5
Stocklinch 8 C3
Stockport 49 H4
Stocksbridge 50 E3
Stocksfield 71 F7
Stockton *Here.* 28 E2
Stockton *Norf.* 45 H6
Stockton *Shrop.* 39 G6
Stockton *Warks.* 31 F2
Stockton *Wilts.* 9 J1
Stockton Heath 49 F4
Stockton on Teme 29 G2
Stockton on the Forest 58 C4
Stockton-on-Tees 63 F4
Stockwood 8 E4
Stodday 55 H4
Stodmarsh 25 J5
Stody 44 E2
Stoer 102 C6
Stoford *Som.* 8 E3
Stoford *Wilts.* 10 B1
Stogumber 7 J2
Stogursey 19 F7
Stoke *Devon* 6 A3
Stoke *Hants.* 21 H6
Stoke *Hants.* 11 J4
Stoke *Med.* 24 E4
Stoke *W.Mid.* 30 E1
Stoke Abbott 8 D4
Stoke Albany 42 B7
Stoke Ash 35 F1
Stoke Bardolph 41 J1
Stoke Bliss 29 F2
Stoke Bruerne 31 J3
Stoke by Clare 34 B4
Stoke Canon 7 H6
Stoke Charity 11 F1
Stoke Climsland 4 D3
Stoke D'Abernon 22 E6
Stoke Doyle 42 D7
Stoke Dry 42 B6
Stoke Ferry 44 A6
Stoke Fleming 5 J6
Stoke Gabriel 5 J5
Stoke Gifford 19 K4
Stoke Golding 41 F6
Stoke Goldington 32 B4
Stoke Hammond 32 B6
Stoke Heath 39 F3
Stoke Holy Cross 45 G5
Stoke Lacy 29 F3
Stoke Lyne 31 G6
Stoke Mandeville 22 B1
Stoke Newington 23 G3
Stoke on Tern 39 F3
Stoke Orchard 29 J6
Stoke Poges 22 C3
Stoke Prior *Here.* 28 E2
Stoke Prior *Worcs.* 29 J2
Stoke Rivers 6 E2
Stoke Rochford 42 C3
Stoke Row 21 K3
Stoke St. Gregory 8 C2
Stoke St. Mary 8 B2
Stoke St. Michael 19 K7
Stoke St. Milborough 38 E7
Stoke sub Hamdon 8 D3
Stoke Talmage 21 K2
Stoke Trister 9 G2
Stoke Wake 9 G4
Stoke-by-Nayland 34 D5
Stoke-on-Trent 40 A1
Stokeford 9 H6
Stokeham 51 K5
Stokeinteignhead 5 K3
Stokenchurch 22 A2
Stokenham 5 J6
Stokesay 38 D7
Stokesby 45 J4
Stokesley 63 G5
Stolford 19 F7
Ston Easton 19 K6
Stonar Cut 25 K5
Stondon Massey 23 J1
Stone *Bucks.* 31 J7
Stone *Glos.* 19 K2
Stone *Kent* 23 J4
Stone *Kent* 14 E5
Stone *Staffs.* 40 A2
Stone *Worcs.* 29 H1
Stone Allerton 19 H6
Stone Cross *E.Suss.* 13 K6
Stone Cross *Kent* 15 F4

Stone Cross *Kent* 13 J3
Stone House 56 C1
Stone Street *Kent* 23 J6
Stone Street *Suff.* 45 H7
Stonebridge *E.Suss.* 13 J4
Stonebridge *Warks.* 40 E7
Stonebroom 51 G7
Stoneferry 59 H6
Stonefield *Arg. & B.* 73 G3
Stonefield *S.Lan.* 75 F6
Stonegate 13 K4
Stonegrave 58 C2
Stonehaugh 70 C6
Stonehaven 91 G6
Stonehouse *D. & G.* 65 J4
Stonehouse *Glos.* 20 B1
Stonehouse *Northumb.* 61 H1
Stonehouse *Plym.* 5 F5
Stonehouse *S.Lan.* 75 F6
Stoneleigh 30 E1
Stonely 32 E2
Stoner Hill 11 J2
Stones Green 35 F6
Stonesby 42 B3
Stonesfield 30 E7
Stonestreet Green 15 F4
Stonethwaite 60 D5
Stoney Cross 10 D3
Stoney Middleton 50 E5
Stoney Stanton 41 G6
Stoney Stoke 9 G1
Stoney Stratton 9 F1
Stoney Stretton 38 C5
Stoneyburn 75 H4
Stoneygate 41 J5
Stoneyhills 25 F2
Stoneykirk 64 A5
Stoneywood 91 G3
Stonganess 108 E2
Stonham Aspal 35 F3
Stonnall 40 C5
Stonor 22 A3
Stonton Wyville 42 A6
Stony Houghton 51 G6
Stony Stratford 31 J4
Stonybreck 108 A1
Stoodleigh 7 H4
Stopham 12 D5
Stopsley 32 E6
Stoptide 3 G1
Storeton 48 C4
Stornoway (Steornabhagh) 101 G4
Stornoway Airport 101 G4
Storridge 29 G4
Storrington 12 D5
Storth 55 H1
Storwood 58 D5
Stotfield 97 K4
Stotfold 33 F5
Stottesdon 39 F7
Stoughton *Leics.* 41 J5
Stoughton *Surr.* 22 C6
Stoughton *W.Suss.* 12 B5
Stoul 86 D5
Stoulton 29 J3
Stour Provost 9 G2
Stour Row 9 H2
Stourbridge 40 A7
Stourpaine 9 H4
Stourport-on-Severn 29 H1
Stourton *Staffs.* 40 A7
Stourton *Warks.* 30 D5
Stourton *Wilts.* 9 G1
Stourton Caundle 9 G3
Stove 106 F4
Stoven 45 J7
Stow *Lincs.* 52 B4
Stow *Sc.Bord.* 76 C6
Stow Bardolph 44 A5
Stow Bedon 44 D6
Stow cum Quy 33 J2
Stow Longa 32 E1
Stow Maries 24 E2
Stowbridge 44 A5
Stowe *Glos.* 19 J1
Stowe *Shrop.* 28 C1
Stowe *Staffs.* 40 C3
Stowell *Glos.* 30 B7
Stowell *Som.* 9 F2
Stowey 19 J6
Stowford 6 C7
Stowlangtoft 34 D2
Stowmarket 34 E3
Stow-on-the-Wold 30 C6
Stowting 15 G3
Stowupland 34 E3
Stracathro 83 H1
Strachan 90 E5
Strachur 80 B7
Stradbroke 35 G1
Stradishall 34 B3
Stradsett 44 A5
Stragglethorpe 52 C7
Straiton *Edin.* 76 A4
Straiton *S.Ayr.* 67 H3
Straloch *Aber.* 91 G2
Straloch *P. & K.* 82 B1
Stramshall 40 C2
Strang 54 C6
Strannda 93 F3
Stranraer 64 A4
Strata Florida 27 G2
Stratfield Mortimer 21 K5
Stratfield Saye 21 K5
Stratfield Turgis 21 K6
Stratford 29 H5
Stratford St. Andrew 35 H3
Stratford St. Mary 34 E5
Stratford sub Castle 10 C1
Stratford Tony 10 B2
Stratford-upon-Avon 30 C3

Strath 105 H3
Strathan *High.* 102 C6
Strathan *High.* 87 F5
Strathaven 75 F6
Strathblane 74 D3
Strathcarron 95 F7
Strathdon 90 B3
Strathgirnock 90 B5
Strathkanaird 95 H1
Strathkinness 83 F6
Strathmiglo 82 D6
Strathpeffer 96 B6
Strathrannoch 95 K4
Strathtay 82 A2
Strathwhillan 73 J7
Strathy 104 D2
Strathyre 81 F6
Stratton *Cornw.* 6 A5
Stratton *Dorset* 9 F5
Stratton *Glos.* 20 D1
Stratton Audley 31 H6
Stratton St. Margaret 20 E3
Stratton St. Michael 45 G6
Stratton Strawless 45 G3
Stratton-on-the-Fosse 19 K6
Stravanan 73 J5
Stravithie 83 G6
Streat 13 G5
Streatham 23 F4
Streatley *Beds.* 32 D6
Streatley *W.Berks.* 21 J3
Street *Lancs.* 55 J4
Street *N.Yorks.* 63 J6
Street *Som.* 8 D1
Street Dinas 38 C2
Street End *Kent* 15 G2
Street End *W.Suss.* 12 B7
Street on the Fosse 9 F1
Streethay 40 D4
Streetlam 62 E7
Streetly 40 C6
Strefford 38 D7
Strensall 58 C3
Strensham 29 J4
Stretcholt 19 F7
Strete 5 J6
Stretford 49 G3
Stretford Court 28 D3
Strethall 33 H5
Stretham 33 J1
Strettington 12 B6
Stretton *Ches.* 48 D7
Stretton *Derbys.* 51 F6
Stretton *Rut.* 42 C4
Stretton *Staffs.* 40 A4
Stretton *Staffs.* 40 E3
Stretton *Warr.* 49 F4
Stretton en le Field 41 F4
Stretton Grandison 29 F4
Stretton Heath 38 C4
Stretton Sugwas 28 D4
Stretton under Fosse 41 G7
Stretton Westwood 38 E6
Stretton-on-Dunsmore 31 F1
Stretton-on-Fosse 30 D5
Stribers 55 G1
Strichen 99 H5
Stringston 7 K1
Strixton 32 C2
Stroat 19 J2
Stromeferry 86 E1
Stromemore 86 E1
Stromness 107 B7
Stronachlachar 81 F7
Strone *Arg. & B.* 73 K2
Strone *High.* 88 C2
Strone *High.* 87 H6
Strone *Stir.* 81 F6
Stronechrubie 102 E7
Stronenaba 87 J6
Stronlonag 73 K2
Stronmilchan 80 C5
Strontian 79 K1
Strontoiller 80 A5
Stronvar 81 F6
Strood 24 D5
Strood Green 12 D4
Stroquhan 68 D5
Stroud *Glos.* 20 B1
Stroud *Hants.* 11 J2
Stroud Common 22 D7
Stroud Green 24 E2
Stroul 74 A2
Stroxton 42 C2
Struan *High.* 85 J1
Struan *P. & K.* 81 K1
Strubby 53 H4
Strumpshaw 45 H5
Struthers 82 E7
Struy 96 B7
Stryd-issa 38 B1
Stryt-yr-hwch 38 C1
Stuartfield 99 H6
Stub Place 60 B7
Stubbington 11 G4
Stubbins 49 G1
Stubhampton 9 J3
Stubley 51 F5
Stubton 42 B1
Stuck *Arg. & B.* 73 J4
Stuck *Arg. & B.* 73 J4
Stuckbeg 74 A1
Stuckgowan 80 E7
Stuckindroin 80 E6
Stuckreoch 73 J1
Stuckton 10 C3
Stud Green 22 B4
Studdon 61 K1
Studfold 56 D2
Studham 32 D7
Studholme 60 D1
Studland 10 B6
Studley *Warks.* 30 B2
Studley *Wilts.* 20 C4
Studley Common 30 B2
Studley Roger 57 H2
Stuggadhoo 54 C6
Stump Cross 33 J4
Stuntney 33 J1
Stunts Green 13 K5
Sturbridge 40 A2
Sturmer 34 B4
Sturminster Common 9 G3
Sturminster Marshall 9 J4
Sturminster Newton 9 G3
Sturry 25 H5
Sturton by Stow 52 B4
Sturton le Steeple 51 K4
Stuston 35 F1
Stutton *N.Yorks.* 57 K5
Stutton *Suff.* 35 F5
Styal 49 H4
Styrrup 51 J3
Suainebost 101 H1
Suardail 101 G4
Succoth *Aber.* 90 C1
Succoth *Arg. & B.* 80 D7
Succothmore 80 C6
Suckley 29 G3
Sudborough 42 C7
Sudbourne 35 J3
Sudbrook *Lincs.* 42 C1
Sudbrook *Mon.* 19 J3
Sudbrooke 52 D5
Sudbury *Derbys.* 40 D2
Sudbury *Gt.Lon.* 22 E3

Sudbury *Suff.* 34 C4
Sudgrove 20 C1
Suffield *N.Yorks.* 63 J3
Suffield *Norf.* 45 G2
Sugarloaf 14 E4
Sugnall 40 A2
Suie Lodge Hotel 81 F5
Sulby 54 C4
Sulgrave 31 G4
Sulham 21 K4
Sulhamstead 21 K5
Sullington 12 D5
Sullom 108 C5
Sullom Voe Oil Terminal 108 C5
Sully 18 E5
Sumburgh 109 G10
Sumburgh Airport 109 F9
Summer Bridge 57 H3
Summercourt 3 F3
Summerfield 44 B2
Summerhill 48 C7
Summerhouse 62 D5
Summerleaze 19 H3
Summerseat 49 G1
Summertown 21 J1
Summit 49 J1
Sunadale 73 G6
Sunbury 22 E5
Sundaywell 68 D5
Sunderland *Cumb.* 60 C3
Sunderland *T. & W.* 62 E1
Sunderland Bridge 62 D3
Sundhope 69 J1
Sundon Park 32 D6
Sundridge 23 H6
Sundrum Mains 67 J1
Sunhill 20 E1
Sunipol 78 E2
Sunk Island 53 F1
Sunningdale 22 C5
Sunninghill 22 C5
Sunningwell 21 H2
Sunniside *Dur.* 62 C3
Sunniside *T. & W.* 62 D1
Sunny Bank 60 D7
Sunnylaw 75 F1
Sunnymead 21 J1
Sunnyside *Aber.* 91 G5
Sunnyside *Northum.* 70 E7
Sunnyside *W.Suss.* 13 G3
Sunwick 77 G5
Surbiton 22 E5
Surfleet 43 F3
Surfleet Seas End 43 F3
Surlingham 45 H5
Sustead 45 F2
Susworth 52 B2
Sutcombe 6 B4
Suton 44 E6
Sutors of Cromarty 97 F5
Sutterton 43 F2
Sutton *Beds.* 33 F4
Sutton *Cambs.* 33 H1
Sutton *Gt.Lon.* 23 F5
Sutton *Kent* 15 J3
Sutton *Lincs.* 52 B7
Sutton *Norf.* 45 H3
Sutton *Notts.* 42 A2
Sutton *Notts.* 51 J4
Sutton *Oxon.* 21 H1
Sutton *Pembs.* 16 C4
Sutton *Peter.* 42 E6
Sutton *S.Yorks.* 51 J1
Sutton *Shrop.* 39 G7
Sutton *Shrop.* 39 F2
Sutton *Shrop.* 38 E4
Sutton *Staffs.* 40 A1
Sutton *Suff.* 35 H4
Sutton *W.Suss.* 12 C5
Sutton Abinger 22 E7
Sutton at Hone 23 J4
Sutton Bassett 42 A7
Sutton Benger 20 C3
Sutton Bonington 41 H3
Sutton Bridge 43 H3
Sutton Cheney 41 G5
Sutton Coldfield 40 D6
Sutton Courtenay 21 H2
Sutton Crosses 43 H3
Sutton Grange 57 H2
Sutton Green 22 D6
Sutton Holms 10 B3
Sutton Howgrave 57 J2
Sutton in Ashfield 51 G7
Sutton in the Elms 41 H6
Sutton Lane Ends 49 J5
Sutton le Marsh 53 J4
Sutton Leach 49 G3
Sutton Maddock 39 G5
Sutton Mallet 8 C1
Sutton Mandeville 9 J2
Sutton Montis 9 F2
Sutton on Sea 53 J4
Sutton on the Hill 40 E2
Sutton on Trent 51 K6
Sutton Poyntz 9 G6
Sutton St. Edmund 43 G4
Sutton St. James 43 H4
Sutton St. Nicholas 28 E4
Sutton Scarsdale 51 G6
Sutton Scotney 11 F1
Sutton upon Derwent 58 D5
Sutton Valence 14 D3
Sutton Veny 20 B7
Sutton Waldron 9 H3
Sutton Weaver 48 E5
Sutton Wick 19 J6
Sutton-in-Craven 57 F5
Sutton-on-Hull 59 H6
Sutton-on-the-Forest 58 B3
Sutton-under-Brailes 30 D5
Sutton-under-Whitestonecliffe 57 K1
Swaby 53 G5
Swadlincote 41 F4
Swaffham 44 C5
Swaffham Bulbeck 33 J2
Swaffham Prior 33 J2
Swafield 45 G2
Swainby 63 F6
Swainshill 28 D4
Swainsthorpe 45 G5
Swainswick 20 A5
Swalcliffe 30 E5
Swalecliffe 15 H5
Swallow 52 E2
Swallow Beck 52 C6
Swallowcliffe 9 J2
Swallowfield 22 A5

Swalwell 71 H7
Swampton 21 H6
Swan Street 34 C6
Swanage 10 B7
Swanbach 39 F1
Swanbourne 32 B6
Swanbridge 18 E5
Swancote 39 G6
Swanland 59 F7
Swanlaws 70 C2
Swanley 23 J5
Swanmore 11 G3
Swannington *Leics.* 41 G4
Swannington *Norf.* 45 F4
Swanscombe 24 C4
Swansea (Abertawe) 17 K6
Swanton Abbot 45 G3
Swanton Morley 44 E4
Swanton Novers 44 E2
Swanwick *Derbys.* 51 G7
Swanwick *Hants.* 11 G4
Swarby 42 D1
Swardeston 45 F5
Swarkestone 41 F3
Swarland 71 G3
Swaton 42 E2
Swavesey 33 G2
Sway 10 D5
Swayfield 42 C3
Swaythling 11 F3
Swaythorpe 59 G3
Sweetshouse 4 A4
Sweffling 35 H2
Swell 8 C2
Swepstone 41 F4
Swerford 30 E5
Swettenham 49 H6
Swffryd 19 F2
Swiftsden 14 C5
Swilland 35 F3
Swillbrook 55 H6
Swillington 57 J6
Swimbridge 6 E2
Swimbridge Newland 6 E2
Swinbrook 30 D7
Swincliffe 57 H4
Swinderby 52 B6
Swindon *Staffs.* 40 A6
Swindon *Swin.* 20 E3
Swindon Village 29 J6
Swine 59 H6
Swinefleet 58 D7
Swineshead *Beds.* 32 D2
Swineshead *Lincs.* 43 F1
Swineshead Bridge 43 F1
Swiney 105 H5
Swinford *Leics.* 31 G1
Swinford *Oxon.* 21 H1
Swingfield Minnis 15 H3
Swinhoe 71 H1
Swinhope 53 F3
Swining 109 D6
Swinithwaite 57 F1
Swinscoe 40 D1
Swinside Hall 70 C2
Swinstead 42 D3
Swinton *Gt.Man.* 49 G2
Swinton *N.Yorks.* 58 D2
Swinton *N.Yorks.* 57 H1
Swinton *S.Yorks.* 51 G3
Swinton *Sc.Bord.* 77 G6
Swintonmill 77 G6
Swithland 41 H4
Swordale 96 C5
Swordland 86 D5
Swordle 79 G1
Swordly 104 C2
Sworton Heath 49 F4
Swyddffynnon 27 F2
Swyncombe 21 K2
Swynnerton 40 A2
Swyre 8 E6
Syde 29 J7
Sydenham *Gt.Lon.* 23 G4
Sydenham *Oxon.* 22 A1
Sydenham Damerel 4 E3
Syderstone 44 C2
Sydling St. Nicholas 9 F5
Sydmonton 21 H6
Syerston 42 A1
Syke 49 H1
Sykehouse 51 J1
Sykes 56 B4
Sylen 17 J5
Symbister 109 E6
Symington *S.Ayr.* 74 B7
Symington *S.Lan.* 75 H7
Symonds Yat 28 E7
Symondsbury 8 D5
Synod Inn 26 D3
Syre 103 J4
Syreford 30 B6
Syresham 31 H4
Syston *Leics.* 41 J4
Syston *Lincs.* 42 C1
Sytchampton 29 H2
Sywell 32 B2

T

Taagan 95 G5
Tabost *W.Isles* 101 F6
Tabost *W.Isles* 101 H1
Tacher 105 G4
Tackley 31 F7
Tacleit 100 D4
Tacolneston 45 F6
Tadcaster 57 K5
Tadden 9 J4
Taddington 50 D5
Taddiport 6 C4
Tadley 21 K5
Tadlow 33 F4
Tadmarton 30 E5
Tadworth 23 F6
Tafarnaubach 28 A7
Tafarn-y-bwlch 16 D2
Tafarn-y-Gelyn 47 K6
Taff's Well (Ffynnon Taf) 18 E3
Tafolwern 37 H5
Taibach *N.P.T.* 18 A3
Tai-bach *Powys* 38 A3
Taicynhaeaf 37 F4
Tain *High.* 96 E3
Tai'n Lôn 46 C7
Tai'r Bull 27 J6
Tairgwaith 27 G7
Tairlaw 67 J3
Takeley 33 J6
Takeley Street 33 J6
Talachddu 27 K5
Talacre 47 K4

Talardd 37 H3
Talaton 7 J6
Talbenny 16 B4
Talbot Green 18 D3
Talerddig 37 J5
Talgarreg 26 D3
Talgarth 28 A5
Taliesin 37 F6
Talisker 85 J1
Talke 49 H7
Talkin 61 G1
Talla Linnfoots 69 G1
Talladale 95 F4
Talladh-a-Bheithe 81 G2
Tallarn Green 38 D1
Tallentire 60 C3
Talley 17 K2
Tallington 42 D5
Talmine 103 H2
Talog 17 G3
Tal-sarn 26 E3
Talsarnau 37 F2
Talskiddy 3 G2
Talwrn *I.o.A.* 46 C5
Talwrn *Wrex.* 38 B1
Talybont *Cere.* 37 F7
Tal-y-bont *Conwy* 47 F6
Tal-y-bont *Gwyn.* 36 E3
Talybont *Gwyn.* 37 F2
Talybont-on-Usk 28 A6
Tal-y-Cae 46 E6
Tal-y-cafn 47 F5
Tal-y-llyn *Gwyn.* 37 G5
Talyllyn *Powys* 28 A6
Talysarn 46 C7
Tal-y-wern 37 H5
Tamavoid 74 D1
Tamerton Foliot 4 E4
Tamworth 40 E5
Tandridge 23 G6
Tanerdy 17 H3
Tanfield 62 C1
Tangiers 16 C4
Tanglandford 91 G1
Tangley 21 G6
Tangmere 12 C6
Tangwick 108 B5
Tangy 66 A1
Tankerness 107 E7
Tankersley 51 F2
Tan-lan 37 F1
Tannach 105 J4
Tannachie 91 F6
Tannachy 96 E1
Tannadice 83 F2
Tannington 35 G2
Tannochside 75 F4
Tansley 51 F7
Tansor 42 D6
Tantobie 62 C1
Tanton 63 G5
Tanworth in Arden 30 C1
Tan-y-fron 47 H6
Tan-y-graig 36 C2
Tangyrisiau 37 F1
Tan-y-groes 17 F1
Tan-y-pistyll 37 K3
Taobh a' Deas Loch Baghasdail 84 C3
Taobh Siar 100 D7
Taobh Tuath (Northton) 92 E3
Tapeley 6 C3
Taplow 22 C3
Taraphocain 80 B3
Tarbat House 96 E4
Tarbert *Arg. & B.* 73 G4
Tarbert *Arg. & B.* 72 E2
Tarbert *High.* 79 H1
Tarbert (An Tairbeart) *W.Isles* 100 D7
Tarbet *Arg. & B.* 80 E7
Tarbet *High.* 86 D5
Tarbet *High.* 102 D4
Tarbolton 67 J1
Tarbrax 75 J5
Tardebigge 29 J2
Tardy Gate 55 J7
Tarfside 90 C6
Tarland 90 C4
Tarleton 55 H7
Tarlogie 96 E3
Tarlscough 48 D1
Tarlton 20 C2
Tarnbrook 55 J4
Tarnock 19 G6
Tarporley 48 E6
Tarr 7 K2
Tarrant Crawford 9 J4
Tarrant Gunville 9 J3
Tarrant Hinton 9 J3
Tarrant Keyneston 9 J4
Tarrant Launceston 9 J4
Tarrant Monkton 9 J4
Tarrant Rawston 9 J4
Tarrant Rushton 9 J4
Tarrel 97 F3
Tarring Neville 13 H6
Tarrington 29 F4
Tarrnacraig 73 H7
Tarsappie 82 C5
Tarskavaig 86 B4
Tarves 91 G1
Tarvie *High.* 96 B6
Tarvie *P. & K.* 82 B1
Tarvin 48 D6
Tarvin Sands 48 D6
Tasburgh 45 G6
Tasley 39 F6
Taston 30 E6
Tatenhill 40 E3
Tatham 56 B3
Tathwell 53 G4
Tatsfield 23 H6
Tattenhall 48 D7
Tatterford 44 C3
Tattersett 44 C2
Tattershall 53 F7
Tattershall Bridge 52 E7
Tattershall Thorpe 53 F7
Tattingstone 35 F5
Tatworth 8 C4
Tauchers 98 B5
Taunton 8 B2
Tavelty 91 F3
Taverham 45 F4
Tavernspite 16 E4
Tavistock 4 E3
Taw Bridge 6 E5
Taw Green 6 E6
Tawstock 6 D3
Taxal 50 C5
Tayburn 74 D6
Taychreggan 80 B5
Tayinloan 72 E6
Taylors Cross 6 A4
Taynafead 80 B6
Taynish 73 F2
Taynton *Glos.* 29 G6

Taynton *Oxon.* 30 D7
Taynuilt 80 B4
Tayock 83 H2
Tayovullin 72 A3
Tayport 83 F5
Tayvallich 73 F2
Tealby 52 E3
Team Valley 71 H7
Teanamachar 92 C5
Teangue 86 C4
Teasses 83 F7
Tebay 61 H6
Tebworth 32 C6
Tedburn St. Mary 7 G6
Teddington *Glos.* 29 J5
Teddington *Gt.Lon.* 22 E4
Tedstone Delamere 29 F3
Tedstone Wafre 29 F3
Teeside International Airport 62 E5
Teeton 31 H1
Teffont Evias 9 J1
Teffont Magna 9 J1
Tegryn 17 F2
Teigh 42 B4
Teigngrace 5 J3
Teignmouth 5 K3
Telford 39 F5
Telham 14 C6
Tellisford 20 A6
Telscombe 13 H6
Telscombe Cliffs 13 H6
Tempar 81 H2
Templand 69 F5
Temple *Cornw.* 4 B3
Temple *Midloth.* 76 B5
Temple Bar 26 E3
Temple Cloud 19 K6
Temple Ewell 15 H3
Temple Grafton 30 C3
Temple Guiting 30 B6
Temple Hirst 58 C7
Temple Normanton 51 G6
Temple Sowerby 61 H4
Templecombe 9 G2
Templeton *Devon* 7 G4
Templeton *Pembs.* 16 E4
Templeton Bridge 7 G4
Templewood 83 H1
Tempsford 32 E3
Ten Mile Bank 43 J6
Tenbury Wells 29 F2
Tenby (Dinbych-y-Pysgod) 16 E5
Tendring 35 F6
Tenga 79 G3
Tenterden 14 D4
Tepersie Castle 90 D2
Terally 64 B6
Terling 34 B7
Ternhill 39 F2
Terregles 65 K3
Terrington 58 C2
Terrington St. Clement 43 J3
Terrington St. John 43 J4
Tervieside 89 K1
Teston 14 C2
Testwood 10 E3
Tetbury 20 B2
Tetbury Upton 20 B2
Tetchill 38 C2
Tetcott 6 B6
Tetford 53 G5
Tetney 53 G2
Tetney Lock 53 G2
Tetsworth 21 K1
Tettenhall 40 A5
Tettenhall Wood 40 A6
Tetworth 33 F3
Teuchan 91 J1
Teversal 51 G6
Teversham 33 H3
Teviothead 69 K3
Tewel 91 G6
Tewin 33 F7
Tewkesbury 29 H5
Teynham 25 F5
Thainston 90 E1
Thainstone House 91 F3
Thakeham 12 E5
Thame 22 A1
Thames Ditton 22 E5
Thames Haven 24 D3
Thamesmead 23 H3
Thanington 15 G2
Thankerton 75 H7
Tharston 45 F6
Thatcham 21 J5
Thatto Heath 48 E3
Thaxted 33 K5
The Apes Hall 43 J7
The Bage 28 B4
The Balloch 81 K6
The Banking 91 F1
The Bar 12 E4
The Belfry 40 D6
The Birks 91 F4
The Bog 38 C6
The Bourne 22 B7
The Bratch 40 A6
The Bryn 19 G1
The Burf 29 H2
The Burn 90 D7
The Camp 20 C1
The Chequer 38 D1
The City 22 A2
The Common 10 D1
The Craigs 96 B2
The Cronk 54 C4
The Den 74 B5
The Dicker 13 J5
The Drums 82 E1
The Eaves 19 K1
The Flatt 70 A6
The Folly 32 E7
The Grange *Shrop.* 38 C2
The Grange *Surr.* 23 G7
The Green *Arg. & B.* 78 A3
The Green *Wilts.* 9 H1
The Haven 12 D3
The Headland 63 G3
The Hermitage 23 F6
The Howe 54 A7
The Isle 28 D4
The Knowle 23 H4
The Laurels 45 H6
The Leacon 14 E4
The Lee 22 C1
The Lhen 54 C3
The Lodge 78 D2
The Marsh 38 C6
The Moor *E.Suss.* 14 D6
The Moor *Kent* 14 C5
The Mumbles 17 K7

The Mythe 29 H5
The Neuk 91 F5
The Node 33 F7
The Oval 20 A5
The Rhos 16 D4
The Rowe 40 A2
The Sands 22 B7
The Shoe 20 B4
The Smithies 39 F6
The Stocks 14 E5
The Vauld 28 E4
The Wrythe 23 F5
The Wyke 39 G5
Theakston 57 H1
Thealby 52 B1
Theale *Som.* 19 H7
Theale *W.Berks.* 21 K4
Thearne 59 G6
Theberton 35 J2
Thedden Grange 11 H1
Theddingworth 41 J7
Theddlethorpe All Saints 53 H4
Theddlethorpe St. Helen 53 H4
Thelbridge Barton 7 F4
Thelnetham 34 E1
Thelveton 45 F7
Thelwall 49 F4
Themelthorpe 44 E3
Thenford 31 G4
Therfield 33 G5
Thetford 44 C7
Theydon Bois 23 H2
Thickwood 20 B4
Thimbleby *Lincs.* 53 F5
Thimbleby *N.Yorks.* 63 F7
Thirkleby 57 K2
Thirlby 57 K1
Thirlestane 76 D6
Thirn 57 H1
Thirsk 57 K1
Thistleton *Lancs.* 55 H6
Thistleton *Rut.* 42 C4
Thistley Green 33 K1
Thixendale 58 E3
Thockrington 70 E6
Tholomas Drove 43 G5
Tholthorpe 57 K3
Thomas Chapel 16 E5
Thomastown 90 D1
Thompson 44 D6
Thomshill 97 K6
Thong 24 C4
Thoralby 57 F1
Thoresby 51 J5
Thoresway 52 E3
Thorganby *Lincs.* 53 F3
Thorganby *N.Yorks.* 58 C5
Thorgill 63 J7
Thorington 35 J1
Thorington Street 34 E5
Thorlby 56 E4
Thorley 33 H7
Thorley Street *Herts.* 33 H7
Thorley Street *I.o.W.* 10 E6
Thormanby 57 K2
Thornaby-on-Tees 63 F5
Thornage 44 E2
Thornborough *Bucks.* 31 J5
Thornborough *N.Yorks.* 57 H1
Thornbury *Devon* 6 C5
Thornbury *Here.* 29 F3
Thornbury *S.Glos.* 19 K3
Thornby 31 H1
Thorncliff 50 C7
Thorncombe 8 C4
Thorncombe Street 22 C7
Thorncote Green 32 E4
Thorndon 35 F2
Thorndon Cross 6 D6
Thorne 51 J1
Thorne St. Margaret 7 J3
Thorner 57 J5
Thornes 40 C5
Thorney *Bucks.* 22 D4
Thorney *Notts.* 52 B5
Thorney *Peter.* 43 F5
Thorney *Som.* 8 D2
Thorney Hill 10 D4
Thornford 9 F3
Thorngrove 8 C1
Thorngumbald 59 J7
Thornham 44 B1
Thornham Magna 35 F1
Thornham Parva 35 F1
Thornhaugh 42 D5
Thornhill *Cardiff* 18 E3
Thornhill *D. & G.* 68 D4
Thornhill *Derbys.* 50 D4
Thornhill *S'ham.* 11 F3
Thornhill *Stir.* 81 H7
Thornhill *W.Yorks.* 50 E1
Thornholme 59 H3
Thornicombe 9 H4
Thornley *Dur.* 62 E3
Thornley *Dur.* 62 C3
Thornliebank 74 D5
Thorns 34 B3
Thornsett 50 C4
Thornthwaite *Cumb.* 60 D4
Thornthwaite *N.Yorks.* 57 G4
Thornton *Angus* 82 E3
Thornton *Bucks.* 31 J5
Thornton *E.Riding* 58 D5
Thornton *Fife* 76 A1
Thornton *Lancs.* 55 G5
Thornton *Leics.* 41 G5
Thornton *Lincs.* 53 F6
Thornton *Mersey.* 48 C2
Thornton *Middbro.* 63 F5
Thornton *Northumb.* 77 H6
Thornton *P. & K.* 82 B3
Thornton *Pembs.* 16 C4
Thornton *W.Yorks.* 57 G6
Thornton Curtis 52 D1
Thornton Hough 48 C4
Thornton le Moor 52 D3
Thornton Park 77 H6
Thornton Rust 57 F1
Thornton Steward 57 G1
Thornton Watlass 57 H1
Thorntonhall 74 D5
Thornton-in-Craven 56 E5
Thornton-le-Beans 62 E7
Thornton-le-Clay 58 C3
Thornton-le-Dale 58 E1
Thornton-le-Moor 57 J1

Thornton-le-Moors 48 D5
Thornton-le-Street 57 K1
Thorntonloch 77 F3
Thornwood Common 23 H1
Thornylee 76 C7
Thoroton 42 A1
Thorp Arch 57 K5
Thorpe *Derbys.* 50 D7
Thorpe *E.Riding* 59 G5
Thorpe *Lincs.* 53 H4
Thorpe *N.Yorks.* 57 F3
Thorpe *Norf.* 45 J6
Thorpe *Notts.* 51 K7
Thorpe *Surr.* 22 D5
Thorpe Abbotts 35 F1
Thorpe Acre 41 H3
Thorpe Arnold 42 A3
Thorpe Audlin 51 G1
Thorpe Bassett 58 E2
Thorpe Bay 25 F3
Thorpe by Water 42 B6
Thorpe Constantine 40 E5
Thorpe Culvert 53 H6
Thorpe End Garden Village 45 G4
Thorpe Green 34 D3
Thorpe Hall 58 E2
Thorpe Hesley 51 F3
Thorpe in Balne 51 H1
Thorpe in the Fallows 52 C4
Thorpe Langton 42 A6
Thorpe Larches 62 E4
Thorpe le Street 58 E5
Thorpe Malsor 32 B1
Thorpe Mandeville 31 G4
Thorpe Market 45 G2
Thorpe Morieux 34 D3
Thorpe on the Hill *Lincs.* 52 C6
Thorpe on the Hill *W.Yorks.* 57 J7
Thorpe St. Andrew 45 G4
Thorpe St. Peter 53 H6
Thorpe Salvin 51 H4
Thorpe Satchville 42 A4
Thorpe Thewles 62 E4
Thorpe Tilney Dales 52 E7
Thorpe Underwood 57 K4
Thorpe Waterville 42 D7
Thorpe Willoughby 58 B6
Thorpe-le-Soken 35 F6
Thorpeness 35 J3
Thorpland 44 A5
Thorrington 34 E7
Thorverton 7 H5
Thrandeston 35 F1
Thrapston 32 D1
Threapland 56 E3
Threapwood 38 D1
Three Bridges 13 F3
Three Burrows 2 E4
Three Chimneys 14 D4
Three Cocks 28 A5
Three Crosses 17 J6
Three Cups Corner 13 K4
Three Holes 43 J5
Three Leg Cross 13 K3
Three Legged Cross 10 B4
Three Mile Cross 22 A5
Threekingham 42 D2
Threemilestone 2 E4
Threlkeld 60 E4
Threshers Bush 23 H1
Threshfield 56 E3
Threxton Hill 44 C5
Thriepley 82 E4
Thrigby 45 J4
Thringarth 62 A4
Thringstone 41 G4
Thrintoft 62 E7
Thriplow 33 H4
Throcking 33 G5
Throckley 71 G7
Throckmorton 29 J3
Throphill 71 G5
Thropton 71 F3
Throwleigh 6 E6
Throwley 14 E2
Throws 33 K6
Thrumpton 41 H2
Thrumster 105 J4
Thrunton 71 F2
Thrupp *Glos.* 20 B1
Thrupp *Oxon.* 31 F7
Thrushelton 6 C7
Thrussington 41 J4
Thruxton *Hants.* 21 F7
Thruxton *Here.* 28 D5
Thrybergh 51 G3
Thulston 41 G2
Thunder Bridge 50 D1
Thundergay 73 G6
Thundersley 24 E3
Thunderton 99 J6
Thundridge 33 G7
Thurcaston 41 H4
Thurcroft 51 H4
Thurdistoft 105 H2
Thurgarton *Norf.* 45 F2
Thurgarton *Notts.* 41 J1
Thurgoland 50 E2
Thurlaston *Leics.* 41 H6
Thurlaston *Warks.* 31 F1
Thurlbear 8 B2
Thurlby *Lincs.* 42 E4
Thurlby *Lincs.* 52 C6
Thurleigh 32 D3
Thurlestone 5 G6
Thurloxton 8 B1
Thurlstone 50 E2
Thurlton 45 J6
Thurlwood 49 H7
Thurmaston 41 J5
Thurnby 41 J5
Thurne 45 J4
Thurnham 14 D2
Thurning *Norf.* 44 E3
Thurning *Northants.* 32 D1
Thurnscoe 51 G2
Thursby 60 E1
Thursford 44 D2
Thursley 12 C3
Thurso 105 G2
Thurstaston 48 B4
Thurston 34 D2
Thurstonfield 60 E1
Thurstonland 50 D1
Thurton 45 H5
Thurvaston 40 E2
Thuster 105 H3
Thuxton 44 E5
Thwaite *N.Yorks.* 61 K7
Thwaite *Suff.* 35 F2
Thwaite Head 55 G1
Thwaite St. Mary 45 H6
Thwing 59 G2

Tibbermore 82 B5
Tibberton *Glos.* 29 G6
Tibberton *Tel. & W.* 39 F3
Tibberton *Worcs.* 29 J3
Tibbie Shiels Inn 69 H1
Tibenham 45 F6
Tibertich 79 K7
Tibshelf 51 G6
Tibthorpe 59 F4
Ticehurst 13 K3
Tichborne 11 G1
Tickencote 42 C5
Tickenham 19 H4
Tickhill 51 H3
Ticklerton 38 D6
Ticknall 41 F3
Tickton 59 G5
Tidcombe 21 F6
Tiddington *Oxon.* 21 K1
Tiddington *Warks.* 30 D3
Tiddleywink 20 B4
Tidebrook 13 K4
Tideford 4 D5
Tidenham 19 J2
Tidenham Chase 19 J2
Tideswell 50 D5
Tidmarsh 21 K4
Tidmington 30 D5
Tidpit 10 B3
Tidworth 21 F7
Tiers Cross 16 C4
Tiffield 31 H3
Tifty 99 F6
Tigerton 83 G1
Tigh a' Gearraidh 92 C4
Tighachnoic 79 H3
Tighnabis 81 J6
Tighnabruaich 73 H3
Tighnacomaire 80 A1
Tigley 5 H4
Tilbrook 32 D2
Tilbury 24 C4
Tile Cross 40 D7
Tile Hill 30 D1
Tilehurst 21 K4
Tilford 22 B7
Tillathrowie 90 C1
Tillers' Green 29 F5
Tillery 91 H2
Tilley 38 E3
Tillicoultry 75 H1
Tillingham 25 F1
Tillington *Here.* 28 D4
Tillington *W.Suss.* 12 C4
Tillington Common 28 D4
Tillyarblet 83 G1
Tillybirloch 90 E4
Tillycairn Castle 90 E3
Tillycorthie 91 H2
Tillydrine 90 E5
Tillyfar 99 G6
Tillyfour 90 D3
Tillyfourie 90 E3
Tillygreig 91 G2
Tillypronie 90 C4
Tilmanstone 15 H2
Tilney All Saints 43 J4
Tilney High End 43 J4
Tilney St. Lawrence 43 J4
Tilshead 20 D7
Tilstock 38 E2
Tilston 48 D7
Tilstone Fearnall 48 E6
Tilsworth 32 C6
Tilton on the Hill 42 A5
Tiltups End 20 B2
Timberland 52 E7
Timberland Dales 52 E6
Timbersbrook 49 H6
Timberscombe 7 H1
Timble 57 G4
Timperley 49 G4
Timsbury *B. & N.E.Som.* 19 K6
Timsbury *Hants.* 10 E2
Timsgearraidh 100 C4
Timworth Green 34 C2
Tincleton 9 G5
Tindale 61 H1
Tingewick 31 H5
Tingley 57 H7
Tingrith 32 D5
Tingwall 106 D5
Tinhay 6 C7
Tinney 4 C1
Tinshill 57 H6
Tinsley 51 G3
Tinsley Green 13 F3
Tintagel 4 A2
Tintern Parva 19 J1
Tintinhull 8 D3
Tintwistle 50 C3
Tinwald 69 F5
Tinwell 42 D5
Tippacott 7 F1
Tipperty *Aber.* 91 F6
Tipperty *Aber.* 91 H2
Tiptoe 10 D5
Tipton 40 B6
Tipton St. John 7 J6
Tiptree 34 C7
Tiptree Heath 34 C7
Tirabad 27 H4
Tirdeunaw 17 K6
Tiree Airport 78 B3
Tirindrish 87 J6
Tirley 29 H6
Tirphil 18 E1
Tirril 61 G4
Tir-y-dail 17 K4
Tisbury 9 J2
Tissington 50 D7
Tister 105 G2
Titchberry 6 A3
Titchfield 11 G4
Titchmarsh 32 D1
Titchwell 44 B1
Titley 28 C2
Titlington 71 G2
Titsey 23 H6
Titson 6 A5
Tittensor 40 A2
Tittleshall 44 C3
Tiverton *Ches.* 48 E6
Tiverton *Devon* 7 H4
Tivetshall St. Margaret 45 F7
Tivetshall St. Mary 45 F7
Tixall 40 B3
Tixover 42 C5
Toab *Ork.* 107 E7
Toab *Shet.* 109 F9
Tobermory 79 G2
Toberonochy 79 J7
Tobha Mòr 84 C1

Tobson 100 D4
Tocher 90 E1
Tockenham 20 D4
Tockenham Wick 20 D3
Tockholes 56 B7
Tockington 19 K3
Tockwith 57 K4
Todber 9 G2
Toddington Beds. 32 D6
Toddington Glos. 30 B5
Toddington W.Suss. 12 D6
Todenham 30 D5
Todhills Angus 83 F4
Todhills Cumb. 69 J7
Todlachie 90 E3
Todmorden 56 E7
Todwick 51 G4
Toft Cambs. 33 G3
Toft Lincs. 42 D4
Toft Shet. 108 D5
Toft Hill 62 C4
Toft Monks 45 J6
Toft next Newton 52 D4
Toftcarl 105 J4
Toftrees 44 C3
Tofts 105 J2
Toftwood 44 D4
Togston 71 H3
Tokavaig 86 C3
Tokers Green 22 A4
Tolastadh 101 H3
Tolastadh a' Chaolais 100 D4
Tolastadh Ur 101 H3
Toll of Birness 91 J1
Tolland 7 K2
Tollard Royal 9 J3
Tollcross 74 E4
Toller Down Gate 8 E4
Toller Fratrum 8 E5
Toller Porcorum 8 E5
Toller Whelme 8 E4
Tollerton N.Yorks. 58 B3
Tollerton Notts. 41 J2
Tollesbury 25 F1
Tollesby 63 G5
Tolleshunt D'Arcy 34 D7
Tolleshunt Knights 34 D7
Tolleshunt Major 34 C7
Tolpuddle 9 G5
Tolvah 89 F5
Tolworth 22 E5
Tom an Fhuadain 101 F6
Tomatin 89 F2
Tombreck 88 D1
Tomchrasky 87 J3
Tomdoun 87 H4
Tomdow 97 H7
Tomich High. 87 K2
Tomich High. 96 D4
Tomich High. 96 D1
Tomintoul 89 J3
Tomnacross 96 C7
Tomnamoon 97 H6
Tomnaven 90 C1
Tomnavoulin 89 K2
Tomvaich 89 H1
Ton Pentre 18 C2
Tonbridge 23 J7
Tondu 18 B3
Tonfanau 36 E5
Tong 39 G5
Tong Norton 39 G5
Tong Street 57 G6
Tonge 41 G3
Tongham 22 B7
Tongland 65 H5
Tongue 103 H3
Tongue House 103 H3
Tongwynlais 18 E3
Tonna 18 A2
Ton-teg 18 D3
Tonwell 33 G7
Tonypandy 18 C2
Tonyrefail 18 D3
Toot Baldon 21 J1
Toot Hill 23 J1
Toothill 10 E3
Top End 32 D2
Topcliffe 57 J2
Topcroft 45 G6
Topcroft Street 45 G6
Toppesfield 34 B5
Toppings 49 G1
Topsham 7 H7
Topsham Bridge 5 H5
Torastan 78 D1
Torbain 89 J3
Torbeg Aber. 90 B4
Torbeg N.Ayr. 66 D1
Torbryan 5 J4
Torcastle 87 H7
Torcross 5 J6
Tordarroch 88 D1
Tore 96 D6
Toreduff 97 J5
Toremore High. 89 J1
Toremore High. 105 G5
Torgyle 87 K3
Torksey 52 B5
Torlum 92 C6
Torlundy 87 H7
Tormarton 20 A4
Tormisdale 72 A2
Tormore 73 G7
Tormsdale 105 G3
Tornagrain 96 E6
Tornahaish 89 K4
Tornaveen 90 E4
Torness 88 C2
Torpenhow 60 C3
Torphichen 75 H3
Torphins 90 E4
Torpoint 4 E5
Torquay 5 K4
Torquhan 76 C6
Torr 5 F5
Torran Arg. & B. 79 K7
Torran High. 96 E4
Torran High. 94 B7
Torrance E.Dun. 74 E4
Torrance S.Lan. 74 E5
Torrancroy 90 B3
Torrich 97 F6
Torridon 95 F6
Torrin 86 B2
Torrisdale Arg. & B. 73 F7
Torrisdale High. 103 J2
Torrish 104 E7
Torrisholme 55 H3
Torroble 96 C1
Torry Aber. 98 C6
Torry Aberdeen 91 H4
Torryburn 75 J2
Torsonce 76 C6
Torterston 99 J6
Torthorwald 69 F6

Tortington 12 C6
Tortworth 20 A2
Torvaig 93 K7
Torver 60 D7
Torwood 75 G2
Torworth 51 J4
Tosberry 6 A3
Toscaig 86 D1
Toseland 33 F2
Tosside 56 C4
Tostarie 78 E3
Tostock 34 D2
Totaig 93 H6
Totamore 78 C2
Tote 93 K7
Totegan 104 D2
Totford 11 G1
Tothill 53 H4
Totland 10 E6
Totley 51 F4
Totnes 5 J4
Toton 41 H2
Totronald 78 C2
Tottenham 23 G2
Tottenhill 44 A4
Totteridge 23 F2
Totternhoe 32 C6
Tottington Gt.Man. 49 G1
Tottington Norf. 44 C6
Totton 10 E3
Touchen-End 22 B4
Toulton 7 K2
Toux 99 H5
Tovil 14 C2
Tow Law 62 C3
Toward 73 K4
Towcester 31 H4
Towednack 2 B5
Towersey 22 A1
Towie Aber. 99 G4
Towie Aber. 90 D2
Towie Aber. 90 C3
Towiemore 98 B6
Town End Cambs. 43 H6
Town End Cumb. 55 H1
Town Green 48 D2
Town Row 13 J3
Town Street 44 B7
Town Yetholm 70 D1
Townend 74 C3
Townhead 65 G6
Townhead of Greenlaw 65 H4
Townhill 75 K2
Townshend 2 C5
Towthorpe E.Riding 59 F3
Towthorpe York 58 C4
Towton 57 K6
Towyn 47 H5
Toynton All Saints 53 G6
Toynton Fen Side 53 G6
Toynton St. Peter 53 H6
Toy's Hill 23 H6
Trabboch 67 J1
Traboe 2 E6
Tradespark High. 97 F6
Tradespark Ork. 107 D7
Trafford Centre 49 G3
Trafford Park 49 G3
Trallong 27 J6
Trallwn 17 K6
Tranch 19 F1
Tranent 76 C3
Trantlebeg 104 D3
Trantlemore 104 D3
Tranwell 71 G5
Trap 17 K4
Traprain 76 D3
Traquair 76 B7
Trawden 56 E6
Trawsfynydd 37 G2
Trealaw 18 C2
Treales 55 H6
Trearddur 46 A5
Treaslane 93 J6
Trebanog 18 D2
Trebanos 18 A1
Trebarrow 4 C1
Trebartha 4 C3
Trebarwith 4 A2
Trebetherick 3 G1
Treborough 7 J2
Trebudannon 3 F2
Trebullett 4 D3
Treburley 4 D3
Trebyan 4 A4
Trecastle 27 H6
Trecwn 16 C2
Trecynon 18 C1
Tredavoe 2 B6
Tre-ddiog 16 B3
Tredegar 18 E1
Tredington Glos. 29 J6
Tredington Warks. 30 D4
Tredinnick Cornw. 3 G1
Tredinnick Cornw. 4 C5
Tredomen 28 A5
Tredrissi 16 D1
Tredunnock 19 G2
Treen 2 A6
Treeton 51 G4
Trefaldwyn (Montgomery) 38 B6
Trefasser 16 B2
Trefdraeth 46 C5
Trefecca 28 A5
Trefeglwys 37 J6
Trefenter 27 F2
Treffgarne 16 C3
Treffynnon (Holywell) Flints. 47 K5
Treffynnon Pembs. 16 B3
Trefgarn Owen 16 B3
Trefil 28 A7
Trefilan 26 E3
Treflach 38 B3
Trefnanney 38 B4
Trefnant 47 J5
Trefonen 38 B3
Trefor Gwyn. 36 C1
Trefor I.o.A. 46 B4
Treforest 18 D3
Treforest Industrial Estate 18 D3
Trefriw 47 F6
Trefynwy (Monmouth) 28 E7
Tregadillett 6 B7
Tregaian 46 C5
Tregare 28 D7
Tregaron 27 F3
Tregarth 46 E6
Tregavethan 2 E4
Tregear 4 C2
Tregeare 4 C2
Tregeiriog 38 A2

Tregele 46 B3
Tregidden 2 E6
Treglemais 16 B3
Tregolds 3 F1
Tregole 4 B1
Tregonetha 3 G2
Tregony 3 G4
Tregoyd 28 A5
Tre-groes 17 H1
Treguff 18 D4
Tregurrian 3 F2
Tregynon 37 K6
Trehafod 18 D2
Treharris 18 D2
Treherbert 18 C2
Trekenner 4 D3
Treknow 4 A2
Trelash 4 B1
Trelassick 3 F3
Trelawnyd 47 J5
Trelech 17 F2
Trelech a'r Betws 17 G3
Treleddyd-fawr 16 A3
Trelewis 18 E2
Treligga 4 A2
Trelights 3 G1
Trelill 4 A3
Trelissick 3 F5
Trelleck 19 J1
Trelleck Grange 19 H1
Trelogan 47 K4
Trelystan 38 B5
Tremadog 36 E1
Tremail 4 B2
Tremain 17 F1
Tremaine 4 C2
Tremar 4 C4
Trematon 4 D5
Tremeirchion 47 J5
Tremethick Cross 2 B5
Trenance 3 F2
Trenarren 4 A6
Trench Tel. & W. 39 F4
Trench Wrex. 38 C2
Treneglos 4 C2
Trenewan 4 B5
Trent 8 E3
Trentham 40 A1
Trentishoe 6 E1
Treoes 18 C4
Treorchy 18 C2
Tre'r-ddol 37 F6
Tre-Rhys 16 E1
Trerulefoot 4 D5
Tresaith 26 B3
Trescott 40 A6
Trescowe 2 C5
Tresham 20 A2
Treshnish 78 E3
Tresillian 3 F4
Tresinney 4 B2
Tresinwen 16 C1
Treskinnick Cross 4 C1
Tresmeer 4 C2
Tresparrett 4 B1
Tresparrett Posts 4 B1
Tressait 81 K1
Tresta Shet. 108 F3
Tresta Shet. 109 C7
Treswell 51 K5
Trethurgy 4 A5
Tretio 16 A3
Tretire 28 E6
Tretower 28 A6
Treuddyn 48 B7
Trevalga 4 A2
Trevalyn 48 C7
Trevanson 3 G1
Trevarren 3 G2
Trevarrick 3 G4
Tre-vaughan Carmar. 17 H3
Trevaughan Carmar. 17 F4
Trevellas 2 E3
Trevelmond 4 C4
Treverva 2 E5
Trevescan 2 A6
Trevethin 19 F1
Trevigro 4 D4
Trevine Arg. & B. 80 B5
Trevine Pembs. 16 B2
Treviscoe 3 G3
Trevone 3 F1
Trevor 38 B1
Trewalder 4 A2
Trewarmett 4 A2
Trewarthenick 3 G4
Trewassa 4 B2
Trewellard 2 A5
Trewen 4 C2
Trewern 38 B4
Trewidland 4 C5
Trewilym 16 E1
Trewint 4 B1
Trewithian 3 F5
Trewoon 3 G3
Treworga 3 G1
Treyarnon 3 F1
Treyford 12 B5
Triangle 57 F7
Trickett's Cross 10 B4
Trimdon 62 E3
Trimdon Colliery 62 E3
Trimdon Grange 62 E3
Trimingham 45 G2
Trimley St. Martin 35 G5
Trimley St. Mary 35 G5
Trimpley 29 G1
Trimsaran 17 H5
Trimstone 6 D1
Trinafour 81 J1
Trinant 19 F2
Tring 32 C7
Trinity 83 H1
Trisaig 87 G7
Trispen 3 F3
Tritlington 71 H4
Trochry 82 A3
Troedyraur 17 G1
Troedyrhiw 18 D1
Trondavoe 108 C5
Troon Cornw. 2 D5
Troon S.Ayr. 74 B7
Trosaraidh 84 C3
Troston 34 C1
Troswell 4 C1
Trottiscliffe 23 K6
Trotton 12 B4
Troughend 70 D4
Troustan 73 J3
Troutbeck 61 F6
Troutbeck Bridge 61 F6
Trow Green 19 J1
Trowbridge 20 B6
Trowle Common 20 B6
Trowley Bottom 32 D7
Trows 76 E7
Trowse Newton 45 G5

Trudernish 72 C5
Trudoxhill 20 A7
Trull 8 B2
Trumaisge Arraidh 92 D4
Trumpan 93 H5
Trumpet 29 F5
Trumpington 33 H3
Trunch 45 G2
Trunnah 55 G5
Truro 3 F4
Trusham 7 G7
Trusley 40 E2
Trusthorpe 53 J4
Truthan 3 F3
Trysull 40 A6
Tubney 21 H2
Tuckenhay 5 J5
Tuckingmill 2 D4
Tuddenham Suff. 35 F4
Tuddenham Suff. 34 D1
Tudeley 23 K7
Tudhoe 62 D3
Tudweiliog 36 B2
Tuffley 29 H7
Tufton Hants. 21 H7
Tufton Pembs. 16 D3
Tugby 42 A5
Tugford 38 E7
Tughall 71 H1
Tuirnaig 94 E3
Tulchan 82 A5
Tullibody 75 G1
Tullich Arg. & B. 80 B6
Tullich Arg. & B. 79 K6
Tullich High. 97 F4
Tullich High. 88 D7
Tullich Moray 98 B6
Tullich Stir. 81 G4
Tullich Muir 96 E4
Tulliemet 82 A2
Tulloch Aber. 91 G1
Tulloch High. 96 D1
Tulloch Moray 97 H6
Tullochgorm 73 H1
Tullochgribban High 89 G2
Tullochvenus 90 D4
Tulloes 83 G3
Tullybannocher 81 J5
Tullybelton 82 B4
Tullyfergus 82 C3
Tullymurdoch 82 C2
Tullynessle 90 D3
Tumble 17 J4
Tumby 53 F7
Tumby Woodside 53 F7
Tummel Bridge 81 J2
Tunbridge Wells 13 J3
Tundergarth Mains 69 G5
Tunga 101 G4
Tunstall E.Riding 59 K6
Tunstall Kent 24 E5
Tunstall Lancs. 56 B2
Tunstall N.Yorks. 62 D7
Tunstall Norf. 45 J5
Tunstall Stoke 49 H7
Tunstall Suff. 35 H3
Tunstead 45 H3
Tunworth 21 K7
Tupsley 28 E4
Tupton 51 F6
Tur Langton 42 A6
Turbiskill 73 F2
Turclossie 99 G5
Turgis Green 21 K6
Turin 83 G2
Turkdean 30 C7
Turnastone 28 C5
Turnberry 67 G3
Turnchapel 4 E5
Turnditch 40 E1
Turner's Green 30 C1
Turners Hill 13 G3
Turners Puddle 9 H5
Turnford 23 G1
Turnworth 9 H4
Turret Bridge 87 K5
Turriff 99 F5
Turton Bottoms 49 G1
Turvey 32 C3
Turville 22 A2
Turville Heath 22 A2
Turweston 31 H5
Tutbury 40 E3
Tutnall 29 J1
Tutshill 19 J2
Tuttington 45 G3
Tuxford 51 K5
Twatt Ork. 106 B5
Twatt Shet. 109 C7
Twechar 74 E3
Tweedmouth 77 H5
Tweedsmuir 69 F1
Twelveheads 2 E4
Twenty 42 E3
Twerton 20 A5
Twickenham 22 E4
Twigworth 29 H6
Twineham 13 F4
Twinhoe 20 A6
Twinstead 34 C5
Twiss Green 49 F3
Twitchen Devon 7 F2
Twitchen Shrop. 28 C1
Twizell House 71 G1
Two Bridges 5 G3
Two Dales 50 E6
Two Gates 40 E5
Twycross 41 F5
Twyford Bucks. 31 H6
Twyford Derbys. 41 F3
Twyford Dorset 9 H3
Twyford Hants. 11 F2
Twyford Leics. 42 A5
Twyford Norf. 44 E3
Twyford Oxon. 31 F5
Twyford W'ham 22 A4
Twyford Common 28 E5
Twynholm 65 G5
Twyning 29 H5
Twyning Green 29 H5
Twynllanan 27 G6
Twyn-yr-odyn 18 E4
Twyn-y-Sheriff 19 H1
Twywell 32 C1
Tyberton 28 C5
Tyburn 40 D6
Tycroes 17 K4
Tycrwyn 38 A4
Tydd Gote 43 H4
Tydd St. Giles 43 H4
Tydd St. Mary 43 H4
Tyddewi (St. David's) 16 A3
Tye Common 24 C2
Tye Green 34 B6
Ty-hen 36 A2
Tyldesley 49 F2
Tyle-garw 18 D3

Tyler Hill 25 H5
Tylers Green Bucks. 22 C2
Tyler's Green Essex 23 J1
Tylorstown 18 D2
Tylwch 27 J1
Ty-Mawr Conwy 37 J1
Ty-mawr Denb. 38 A1
Ty-nant Conwy 37 J1
Ty-nant Gwyn. 37 J3
Tyndrum 80 E4
Tyneham 9 H6
Tynehead 76 B5
Tynemouth 71 J7
Tynewydd 18 C2
Tyninghame 76 E3
Tynron 68 D4
Tyn-y-cefn 37 K1
Tyn-y-Cwm 37 H7
Tyn-y-ffridd 38 A2
Tynygraig Cere. 27 F2
Tyn-y-graig Powys 27 K4
Ty'n-y-groes 47 F5
Tyringham 32 B4
Tythegston 18 B4
Tytherington Ches. 49 J5
Tytherington S.Glos. 19 K3
Tytherington Som. 20 A7
Tytherington Wilts. 20 C7
Tytherleigh 8 C4
Tytherton Lucas 20 C4
Ty-uchaf 37 J3
Tywardreath 4 A5
Tywardreath Highway 4 A5
Tywyn 36 E5

U

Uachdar 92 D6
Uags 86 D1
Ubbeston Green 35 H1
Ubley 19 J6
Uckerby 62 D6
Uckfield 13 H4
Uckinghall 29 H5
Uckington 29 J6
Uddingham 74 E4
Uddington 75 G7
Udimore 14 D6
Udny Green 91 G2
Udny Station 91 H2
Udstonhead 75 F6
Uffcott 20 E4
Uffculme 7 J4
Uffington Lincs. 42 D5
Uffington Oxon. 21 G3
Uffington Shrop. 38 E4
Ufford Peter. 42 D5
Ufford Suff. 35 G3
Ufton 30 E2
Ufton Nervet 21 K5
Ugborough 5 G5
Uggeshall 35 J1
Ugglebarnby 63 K6
Ugley 33 J6
Ugley Green 33 J6
Ugthorpe 63 J5
Uig Arg. & B. 78 C2
Uig Arg. & B. 73 K2
Uig High. 93 J5
Uig High. 93 G6
Uigen 100 C4
Uiginish 93 H7
Uigshader 93 K7
Uisgebhagh 92 D7
Uisken 78 E6
Ulbster 105 J4
Ulcat Row 61 F4
Ulceby Lincs. 53 H5
Ulceby N.Lincs. 52 E1
Ulceby Cross 53 H5
Ulcombe 14 D3
Uldale 60 D3
Uldale House 61 J7
Uley 20 A2
Ulgham 71 H4
Ullapool 95 H2
Ullenhall 30 C2
Ullenwood 29 J7
Ulleskelf 58 B5
Ullesthorpe 41 H7
Ulley 51 G4
Ullingswick 28 E4
Ullinish 85 J1
Ullock 60 B4
Ulpha 60 C7
Ulrome 59 H4
Ulsta 108 D4
Ulting 24 E1
Uluvalt 79 G5
Ulverston 55 F2
Ulwell 10 B6
Ulzieside 68 C3
Umberleigh 6 E3
Unapool 102 E7
Underbarrow 61 F7
Underhoull 108 E2
Underriver 23 J6
Underwood Newport 19 G3
Underwood Notts. 51 G2
Undy 19 H3
Unifirth 109 B7
Union Croft 91 G5
Union Mills 54 C6
Unstone 51 F5
Unthank 61 F3
Up Cerne 9 F4
Up Exe 7 H5
Up Hatherley 29 J6
Up Holland 48 E2
Up Marden 11 J3
Up Nately 21 K6
Up Somborne 10 E1
Up Sydling 9 F4
Upavon 20 E6
Upchurch 24 E5
Upcott Devon 6 C6
Upcott Here. 28 C3
Upend 33 K3
Uphall Dorset 8 E4
Uphall W.Loth. 75 J3
Uphall Station 75 J3
Upham Devon 7 G5
Upham Hants. 11 G2
Uphampton 29 H2
Uphill 19 G6
Uplawmoor 74 C5
Upleadon 29 G6
Upleatham 63 H5
Uplees 25 G5

Uploders 8 E5
Uplowman 7 J4
Uplyme 8 C5
Upminster 23 J3
Upottery 7 K5
Upper Affcot 38 D7
Upper Ardroscadale 73 J4
Upper Arley 39 G7
Upper Arncott 31 H7
Upper Aston 40 A6
Upper Astrop 31 G5
Upper Basildon 21 K4
Upper Beeding 12 E5
Upper Benefield 42 C7
Upper Bighouse 104 D3
Upper Boat 18 E3
Upper Boddington 31 F3
Upper Borth 37 F7
Upper Boyndlie 99 H4
Upper Brailes 30 E4
Upper Breakish 86 C2
Upper Breinton 28 D4
Upper Broughton 41 J3
Upper Bucklebury 21 J5
Upper Burgate 10 C3
Upper Burnhaugh 91 G5
Upper Caldecote 32 E4
Upper Camster 105 H4
Upper Catshill 29 J1
Upper Chapel 27 K4
Upper Chute 21 F6
Upper Clatford 21 G7
Upper Coberley 29 J7
Upper Cotton 40 D1
Upper Cound 38 E5
Upper Cwmbran 19 F2
Upper Dallachy 98 B4
Upper Dean 32 D2
Upper Denby 50 E2
Upper Derraid 89 H1
Upper Diabaig 94 E5
Upper Dicker 13 J5
Upper Dovercourt 35 G6
Upper Dunsforth 57 K3
Upper Eastern Green 40 E7
Upper Eathie 96 E5
Upper Elkstone 50 C7
Upper End 50 C5
Upper Farringdon 11 J1
Upper Framilode 29 G7
Upper Froyle 22 A7
Upper Gills 105 J1
Upper Glendessarry 87 F5
Upper Godney 19 H7
Upper Gornal 40 B6
Upper Gravenhurst 32 E5
Upper Green Essex 33 H5
Upper Green Mon. 28 C7
Upper Green W.Berks. 21 G5
Upper Gylen 79 K5
Upper Hackney 50 E6
Upper Halliford 22 D5
Upper Halling 24 C5
Upper Hambleton 42 C5
Upper Hardres Court 15 G2
Upper Hartfield 13 H3
Upper Hawkhillock 91 J1
Upper Hayton 38 E7
Upper Heath 38 E7
Upper Helmsley 58 C4
Upper Hergest 28 B3
Upper Heyford 31 F6
Upper Hill 28 D3
Upper Hopton 50 D1
Upper Horsebridge 13 J5
Upper Hulme 50 C6
Upper Inglesham 21 F2
Upper Kilchattan 72 B1
Upper Killay 17 J6
Upper Knockando 97 J7
Upper Lambourn 21 G3
Upper Langwith 51 H6
Upper Largo 83 F7
Upper Lochton 90 E5
Upper Longdon 40 C4
Upper Longwood 39 F5
Upper Ludstone 40 A6
Upper Lybster 105 H5
Upper Lydbrook 29 F7
Upper Maes-coed 28 C5
Upper Midhope 50 E3
Upper Minety 20 D2
Upper Mitton 29 H1
Upper Muirskie 91 G5
Upper North Dean 22 B2
Upper Norwood 23 G4
Upper Obney 82 B4
Upper Oddington 30 D6
Upper Ollach 86 B1
Upper Poppleton 58 B4
Upper Quinton 30 C4
Upper Ridinghill 99 J5
Upper Rissington 30 D6
Upper Rochford 29 F2
Upper Sanday 107 E7
Upper Sapey 29 F2
Upper Scolton 16 C3
Upper Seagry 20 C3
Upper Shelton 32 C4
Upper Sheringham 45 F1
Upper Skelmorlie 74 A4
Upper Slaughter 30 C6
Upper Sonachan 80 B5
Upper Soudley 29 F7
Upper Stoke 41 F7
Upper Stondon 32 E5
Upper Stowe 31 H3
Upper Street Hants. 10 C3
Upper Street Norf. 45 H4
Upper Street Suff. 35 F5
Upper Sundon 32 D6
Upper Swell 30 C6
Upper Tean 40 C2
Upper Thurnham 55 H4
Upper Tillyrie 82 C7
Upper Tooting 23 F4
Upper Town 19 J5
Upper Tysoe 30 E4
Upper Upham 21 F4
Upper Victoria 83 G4
Upper Wardington 31 F4
Upper Weald 32 B5
Upper Weedon 31 H3
Upper Welson 28 B3
Upper Wield 11 H1
Upper Winchendon 31 J7
Upper Woodford 10 C1
Upper Wootton 21 J6
Upper Wraxall 20 A4
Upper Wyche 29 G4

Upperthong 50 D2
Upperton 12 C4
Uppertown 105 J1
Uppingham 42 B6
Uppington Dorset 10 B4
Uppington Shrop. 38 E5
Upsall 57 K1
Upsettlington 77 G6
Upshire 23 H1
Upstreet 25 J5
Upton Bucks. 31 J7
Upton Cambs. 32 E1
Upton Ches. 48 D6
Upton Cornw. 4 C3
Upton Cornw. 7 J3
Upton Devon 7 J5
Upton Devon 5 H6
Upton Dorset 9 J6
Upton Hants. 21 G6
Upton Hants. 10 E3
Upton Lincs. 52 B4
Upton Mersey. 48 B4
Upton Norf. 45 H4
Upton Northants. 31 J2
Upton Notts. 51 K5
Upton Notts. 51 K7
Upton Oxon. 21 J3
Upton Peter. 42 E5
Upton Slo. 22 C4
Upton Som. 7 H3
Upton W.Yorks. 51 G1
Upton Bishop 29 F6
Upton Cheyney 19 K5
Upton Cressett 39 F6
Upton Cross 4 C3
Upton End 32 E5
Upton Green 45 H4
Upton Grey 21 K7
Upton Hellions 7 G5
Upton Lovell 20 C7
Upton Magna 38 E4
Upton Noble 9 G1
Upton Pyne 7 H6
Upton St. Leonards 29 H7
Upton Scudamore 20 B7
Upton Snodsbury 29 J3
Upton upon Severn 29 H4
Upton Warren 29 J2
Upwaltham 12 C5
Upware 33 J2
Upwell 43 J5
Upwey 9 F6
Upwood 43 F7
Uradale 109 D9
Urafirth 108 C5
Urchany 97 F7
Urchfont 20 D6
Urdimarsh 28 E4
Ure 108 C5
Urgha 93 G2
Urlay Nook 62 E5
Urmston 49 G3
Urquhart High. 96 C6
Urquhart Moray 97 K5
Urra 63 G6
Urray 96 C6
Ushaw Moor 62 D7
Usk 19 G1
Usselby 52 D3
Utley 57 F5
Uton 7 G6
Utterby 53 G3
Uttoxeter 40 C2
Uwchmynydd 36 A3
Uxbridge 22 D3
Uyeasound 108 E2
Uzmaston 16 C4

V

Valley (Dyffryn) 46 A5
Valley Truckle 4 B2
Valleyfield D. & G. 65 G5
Valleyfield Fife 75 J2
Valsgarth 108 F1
Vange 24 D3
Vardre 17 K5
Varteg 19 F1
Vatersay (Bhatarsaigh) 84 B5
Vatten 93 H7
Vaul 78 B3
Vaynor 27 K7
Vaynor Park 38 A5
Veaullt 28 A3
Veensgarth 109 D8
Velindre Pembs. 16 E2
Velindre Powys 28 A5
Vellow 7 J2
Veness 106 E5
Venn 5 H6
Venn Ottery 7 J6
Vennington 38 C5
Ventnor 11 G7
Vernham Dean 21 G6
Vernham Street 21 G6
Vernolds Common 38 D7
Verwood 10 B4
Veryan 3 G5
Vicarage 8 B6
Vickerstown 54 E3
Victoria 3 G2
Vidlin 109 D6
Viewfield 105 F2
Viewpark 75 F4
Vigo 40 C5
Vigo Village 24 C5
Villavin 6 D4
Vinehall Street 14 C5
Vine's Cross 13 J5
Viney Hill 19 K1
Virginia Water 22 C5
Virginstow 6 B6
Virley 34 D7
Vobster 20 A7
Voe Shet. 109 D6
Voe Shet. 108 C4
Vowchurch 28 C5
Voy 107 B6

W

Wackerfield 62 C4
Wacton 45 F6
Wadborough 29 J4
Waddesdon 31 J7
Waddingham 52 C3
Waddington Lancs. 56 C5
Waddington Lincs. 52 C6
Waddingworth 52 E5
Wadebridge 3 G1
Wadeford 8 C3
Wadenhoe 42 D7

Wadesmill 33 G7
Wadhurst 13 K3
Wadshelf 51 F5
Wadsley Bridge 51 F3
Wadworth 51 H3
Wadworth Hill 59 J7
Waen 47 K6
Waen-fach 38 B4
Waen-wen 46 D6
Wag 105 F6
Wainfleet All Saints 53 H7
Wainfleet Bank 53 H7
Wainhouse Corner 4 B1
Wainscott 24 D4
Wainstalls 57 F7
Waitby 61 J6
Wakefield 57 J7
Wakerley 42 C6
Wakes Colne 34 C6
Walberswick 35 J1
Walberton 12 C6
Walcot Lincs. 42 D2
Walcot Lincs. 52 E7
Walcot N.Lincs. 59 J7
Walcot Shrop. 38 C7
Walcot Tel. & W. 58 F7
Walcot Green 45 F7
Walcote Leics. 41 H7
Walcote Warks. 30 C3
Walcott 45 H2
Walcott Dales 52 E7
Walden 57 F1
Walden Head 56 E1
Walden Stubbs 51 H1
Walderslade 24 D5
Walderton 11 J3
Walditch 8 D5
Waldley 40 D2
Waldridge 62 D1
Waldringfield 35 G4
Waldron 13 J5
Wales 51 G4
Walesby Lincs. 52 E3
Walesby Notts. 51 J5
Walford Here. 28 C1
Walford Here. 28 E6
Walford Shrop. 38 D3
Walgherton 39 F1
Walgrave 32 B1
Walhampton 10 E5
Walk Mill 56 D6
Walkden 49 G2
Walker 71 H7
Walker Fold 56 B5
Walkerburn 76 B7
Walkeringham 51 K3
Walkerith 51 K3
Walkern 33 F6
Walker's Green 28 E4
Walkhampton 5 F4
Walkington 59 G6
Walkwood 30 B2
Wall Northumb. 70 E7
Wall Staffs. 40 D5
Wall Bank 38 E6
Wall Heath 40 A7
Wall under
  Heywood 38 E6
Wallacehall 69 H6
Wallacetown 67 G3
Wallasey 48 B3
Wallbottle 71 G7
Wallend 24 E4
Waller's Green 29 F5
Wallingford 21 K3
Wallington Gt.Lon. 23 F5
Wallington Hants. 11 G4
Wallington Herts. 33 F5
Wallis 16 D3
Wallisdown 10 B5
Walliswood 12 E3
Walls 109 B8
Wallsend 71 J7
Wallyford 76 B3
Walmer 15 J2
Walmer Bridge 55 H7
Walmersley 49 H1
Walmley 40 D6
Walpole 35 H1
Walpole Cross
  Keys 43 J4
Walpole Highway 43 J4
Walpole
  St. Andrew 43 J4
Walpole St. Peter 43 J4
Walsall 40 C6
Walsall Wood 40 C5
Walsden 56 E7
Walsgrave on
  Sowe 41 F7
Walsham le
  Willows 34 E1
Walsoken 43 H4
Walston 75 J6
Walsworth 32 E5
Walterstone 28 C6
Waltham Kent 15 G3
Waltham
  N.E.Lincs. 53 F2
Waltham Abbey 23 G1
Waltham Chase 11 G3
Waltham Cross 23 G1
Waltham on the
  Wolds 42 B3
Waltham
  St. Lawrence 22 B4
Walthamstow 23 G3
Walton Bucks. 32 B7
Walton Cumb. 70 A7
Walton Derbys. 51 F6
Walton Leics. 41 H7
Walton M.K. 32 B5
Walton Mersey. 48 C3
Walton Peter. 42 E5
Walton Powys 28 B3
Walton Som. 8 D1
Walton Staffs. 40 A2
Walton Suff. 35 G5
Walton Tel. & W. 38 E4
Walton W.Yorks. 51 F1
Walton W.Yorks. 57 K5
Walton Warks. 30 D3
Walton Cardiff 29 J3
Walton East 16 D3
Walton on the Hill 23 F6
Walton on the
  Naze 35 G6
Walton on the
  Wolds 41 H4
Walton Park 65 H3
Walton West 16 B4
Walton-in-Gordano 19 H4
Walton-le-Dale 55 J7
Walton-on-Thames 22 E5
Walton-on-the-Hill 40 B3
Walton-on-Trent 40 E4

Walwen Flints. 47 K5
Walwen Flints. 48 B5
Walwick 70 E6
Walworth 62 D5
Walwyn's Castle 16 B4
Wambrook 8 B4
Wanborough
  Surr. 22 C7
Wanborough
  Swin. 21 F3
Wandel 68 E1
Wandon 71 F1
Wandsworth 23 F4
Wangford Suff. 35 J1
Wangford Suff. 44 B7
Wanlip 41 J4
Wanlockhead 68 D2
Wannock 13 J6
Wansford
  E.Riding 59 G4
Wansford Peter. 42 D6
Wanstead 23 H3
Wanstrow 20 A7
Wanswell 19 K1
Wantage 21 G3
Wapley 20 A4
Wappenbury 30 E2
Wappenham 31 H4
Warblebank 60 D2
Warbleton 13 K5
Warborough 21 J2
Warboys 33 G1
Warbstow 4 C1
Warburton 49 F4
Warcop 61 J5
Ward End 40 D7
Ward Green 34 E2
Warden Kent 25 G4
Warden
  Northumb. 70 E7
Wardgate 40 E1
Wardhouse 90 D1
Wardington 31 F4
Wardle Ches. 49 F7
Wardle Gt.Man. 49 J1
Wardley 42 B5
Wardlow 50 D5
Wardy Hill 43 H7
Ware Herts. 33 G7
Ware Kent 25 J5
Wareham 9 J6
Warehorne 14 E4
Waren Mill 77 K7
Warenford 71 G1
Warenton 77 K7
Wareside 33 G7
Waresley 33 F3
Warfield 22 B4
Wargrave 22 A4
Warham 44 D1
Wark Northumb. 70 D6
Wark Northumb. 77 G6
Warkleigh 6 E3
Warkton 32 B1
Warkworth
  Northants. 31 F4
Warkworth
  Northumb. 71 H3
Warlaby 62 E7
Warland 56 E7
Warleggan 4 B4
Warley 40 C7
Warley Town 57 F7
Warlingham 23 G6
Warmfield 57 J7
Warmingham 49 G6
Warmington
  Northants. 42 D6
Warmington
  Warks. 31 F4
Warminster 20 B7
Warmlake 14 D2
Warmley 19 K4
Warmsworth 51 H2
Warmwell 9 G6
Warndon 29 H3
Warnford 11 H2
Warnham 12 E3
Warningcamp 12 D6
Warninglid 13 F4
Warren Ches. 49 H5
Warren Pembs. 16 C6
Warren House 6 E7
Warren Row 22 B3
Warren Street 14 E2
Warrenby 63 G4
Warrington M.K. 32 B3
Warrington Warr. 49 F4
Warroch 82 B7
Warsash 11 F4
Warslow 50 C7
Warter 58 E4
Warthill 58 C4
Wartle 90 D4
Wartling 13 K6
Wartnaby 42 A3
Warton Lancs. 55 J2
Warton Lancs. 55 H7
Warton Northumb. 71 F3
Warton Warks. 40 E5
Warwick Cumb. 61 F1
Warwick Warks. 30 D2
Warwick Bridge 61 F1
Wasbister 106 C4
Wash Common 21 H5
Washaway 4 A4
Washbourne 5 H5
Washfield 7 H4
Washfold 62 B6
Washford 7 J1
Washford Pyne 7 G4
Washingborough 52 D5
Washington
  T. & W. 62 E1
Washington
  W.Sussex 12 E5
Washmere Green 34 D4
Wasing 21 J5
Waskerley 62 B2
Wasperton 30 D3
Wass 58 B2
Watchet 7 J1
Watchfield Oxon. 21 F2
Watchfield Som. 19 G7
Watchgate 61 G7
Watendlath 60 D5
Water 56 D7
Water Eaton 31 G7
Water End Herts. 23 F1
Water End Herts. 32 D7
Water Newton 42 E6
Water Orton 40 D6
Water Stratford 31 H5
Water Yeat 55 F1
Waterbeck 69 H6
Waterfall 50 C7

Waterfoot E.Renf. 74 D5
Waterfoot Lancs. 56 D7
Waterford 33 G7
Waterhead Cumb. 60 E6
Waterhead D. & G. 68 C5
Waterhill of Bruxie 99 H6
Waterhouses Dur. 62 C2
Waterhouses
  Staffs. 50 C7
Wateringbury 23 K6
Waterloo Aber. 91 J1
Waterloo Mersey. 48 C3
Waterloo N.Lan. 75 G5
Waterloo Norf. 45 G4
Waterloo P. & K. 82 B4
Waterloo Pembs. 16 C5
Waterloo Poole 10 B5
Waterloo Cross 7 J4
Waterloo Port 46 C6
Waterlooville 11 H3
Watermeetings 68 E2
Watermillock 61 F4
Waterperry 21 K1
Waterrow 7 J3
Watersfield 12 D5
Waterside Aber. 90 B3
Waterside Aber. 91 J2
Waterside Bucks. 22 C1
Waterside E.Ayr. 67 J3
Waterside E.Ayr. 74 E7
Waterside E.Dun. 74 E3
Waterstock 21 K1
Waterston 16 C5
Waterthorpe 51 G4
Watford Herts. 22 E2
Watford
  Northants. 31 H2
Wath N.Yorks. 57 J2
Wath N.Yorks. 57 G3
Wath Brow 60 B5
Wath upon Dearne 51 G2
Watlington Norf. 44 A4
Watlington Oxon. 21 K2
Watnall 41 H1
Watten 105 H3
Wattisfield 34 E1
Wattisham 34 E3
Watton E.Riding 59 G5
Watton Norf. 44 D5
Watton at Stone 33 G7
Watton Green 44 D5
Wattston 75 F4
Wattstown 18 D2
Wattsville 18 E2
Waun Fawr 37 F7
Waun y Clyn 17 H5
Waunarlwydd 17 K6
Waunclynda 17 K2
Waunfawr 46 D7
Wavendon 32 C5
Waverbridge 60 D2
Waverton Ches. 48 D6
Waverton Cumb. 60 D2
Wawne 59 G6
Waxham 45 J3
Waxholme 59 K7
Way Gill 56 E3
Way Village 7 G4
Wayford 8 D4
Waytown 8 D5
Wdig (Goodwick) 16 C2
Weachyburn 98 E5
Weald 21 G1
Wealdstone 22 E3
Weare 19 H6
Weare Giffard 6 C3
Wearhead 61 K2
Wearne 8 D2
Weasenham
  All Saints 44 C3
Weasenham
  St. Peter 44 C3
Weat*hercote 62 E4*
Weatheroak Hill 30 B1
Weaverham 49 F5
Weaverthorpe 59 F2
Webheath 30 B2
Webton 28 D5
Wedderlairs 91 G1
Weddington 41 F6
Wedhampton 20 D6
Wedmore 19 H7
Wednesbury 40 B6
Wednesfield 40 B5
Weedon 32 B7
Weedon Bec 31 H3
Weedon Lois 31 H4
Weeford 40 D5
Week 7 F4
Week Orchard 6 A5
Week St. Mary 4 C1
Weekley 42 B7
Weeley 35 F6
Weeley Heath 35 F7
Weem 81 K3
Weeping Cross 40 B3
Weethley 30 B3
Weeting 44 B7
Weeton E.Riding 59 K7
Weeton Lancs. 55 G6
Weeton N.Yorks. 57 H5
Weir Essex 24 E3
Weir Lancs. 56 D7
Weirbrook 38 C3
Welbeck Abbey 51 H5
Welborne 44 E5
Welbourn 52 C7
Welburn 58 D3
Welbury 62 E6
Welby 42 C2
Welches Dam 43 H7
Welcombe 6 A4
Weldon 42 C7
Welford Northants. 41 J7
Welford W.Berks. 21 H4
Welford-on-Avon 30 C3
Welham Leics. 42 A6
Welham Notts. 51 K4
Welham Green 23 F1
Well Hants. 22 A7
Well Lincs. 53 H5
Well N.Yorks. 57 H1
Well End 22 B3
Well Hill 23 H5
Well Town 7 H5
Welland 29 G4
Wellbank 83 F4
Welldale 69 G7
Wellesbourne 30 D3
Wellhill 97 G5
Welling 23 H4
Wellingborough 32 B2
Wellingham 44 C3
Wellingore 52 C7
Wellington Cumb. 60 B6
Wellington Here. 28 D4
Wellington Som. 7 K3
Wellington
  Tel. & W. 39 F4

Wellington Heath 29 G4
Wellington Marsh 28 E4
Wellow
  B. & N.E.Som. 20 A6
Wellow I.o.W. 10 E6
Wellow Notts. 51 J6
Wells 19 J7
Wellsborough 41 F5
Wells-next-the-Sea 44 D1
Wellwood 75 J2
Welney 43 J6
Welsh Bicknor 28 E7
Welsh End 38 E2
Welsh Frankton 38 C2
Welsh Hook 16 C3
Welsh Newton 28 D7
Welsh St. Donats 18 D4
Welshampton 38 D2
Welshpool
  (Y Trallwng) 38 B5
Welton
  B. & N.E.Som. 19 K6
Welton Cumb. 60 E2
Welton E.Riding 59 F7
Welton Lincs. 52 D4
Welton Northants. 31 G2
Welton le Marsh 53 H6
Welton le Wold 53 F4
Welwick 59 K7
Welwyn 33 F7
Welwyn Garden
  City 33 F7
Wem 38 E3
Wembdon 8 B1
Wembley 22 E3
Wembury 5 F6
Wembworthy 6 E5
Wemyss Bay 73 K4
Wenallt 37 J1
Wendens Ambo 33 J5
Wendlebury 31 G7
Wendling 44 D4
Wendover 22 B1
Wendron 2 D5
Wendy 33 G4
Wenhaston 35 J1
Wenlli 47 G6
Wennington
  Cambs. 33 F1
Wennington
  Gt.Lon. 23 J3
Wennington
  Lancs. 56 B2
Wensley Derbys. 50 E6
Wensley N.Yorks. 62 B7
Wentbridge 51 G1
Wentnor 38 C6
Wentworth
  Cambs. 33 H1
Wentworth
  S.Yorks. 51 F3
Wentworth Castle 51 F2
Wenvoe 18 E4
Weobley 28 C3
Weobley Marsh 28 D3
Wepham 12 D6
Wepre 48 B6
Wereham 44 A5
Wergs 40 A5
Wernrheolydd 28 C7
Werrington Cornw. 6 B7
Werrington Peter. 42 E5
Werrington Staffs. 40 B1
Wervil Brook 26 C3
Wervin 48 D5
Wesham 55 H6
Wessington 51 F7
West Aberthaw 18 D5
West Acre 44 B4
West Allerdean 77 H6
West Alvington 5 H6
West Amesbury 20 E7
West Anstey 7 G3
West Ashby 53 F5
West Ashling 12 B6
West Ashton 20 B6
West Auckland 62 C4
West Ayton 59 F1
West Bagborough 7 K2
West Barkwith 52 E4
West Barnby 63 K5
West Barns 76 E3
West Barsham 44 D2
West Bay 8 D5
West Beckham 45 F2
West Benhar 75 G4
West Bergholt 34 D6
West Bexington 8 E6
West Bilney 44 B4
West Blatchington 13 F6
West Boldon 71 J7
West Bradenham 44 D5
West Bradford 56 C5
West Bradley 8 E1
West Bretton 50 E1
West Bridgford 41 H2
West Bromwich 40 C6
West Buckland
  Devon 6 E2
West Buckland
  Som. 7 K3
West Burrafirth 109 B7
West Burton
  N.Yorks. 57 F1
West Burton
  W.Suss. 12 C5
West Butterwick 52 B2
West Byfleet 22 D5
West Cairncake 99 G6
West Caister 45 K4
West Calder 75 J4
West Camel 8 E2
West Cauldcoats 74 E6
West Challow 21 G3
West Charleton 5 H6
West Chelborough 8 E4
West Chevington 71 H4
West Chiltington 12 D5
West Chiltington
  Common 12 D5
West Chinnock 8 D3
West Chisenbury 20 E6
West Clandon 22 D6
West Cliffe 15 J3
West Clyne 97 F1
West Coker 8 E3
West Compton
  Dorset 8 E5
West Compton
  Som. 19 J7
West Cross 17 K7
West Curry 4 C1
West Curthwaite 60 E2
West Dean
  W.Suss. 12 B5
West Dean Wilts. 10 D2
West Deeping 42 E5
West Derby 48 C3
West Dereham 44 A5

West Ditchburn 71 G1
West Down 6 D1
West Drayton
  Gt.Lon. 22 D4
West Drayton
  Notts. 51 K5
West Dullater 81 G7
West Dunnet 105 H1
West Edington 71 G5
West Ella 59 G7
West End Beds. 32 C3
West End E.Riding 59 G3
West End Hants. 11 F3
West End Kent 25 H5
West End Lancs. 55 H3
West End Lincs. 53 G3
West End N.Som. 57 G4
West End Norf. 45 J4
West End Oxon. 21 H1
West End S.Lan. 75 H6
West End Suff. 45 J7
West End Surr. 22 C5
West End Surr. 22 C5
West End Green 21 K5
West Farleigh 14 C2
West Farndon 31 G3
West Felton 38 C3
West Firle 13 H6
West Fleetham 71 G1
West Garforth 57 J6
West Ginge 21 H3
West Glen 73 J3
West Grafton 21 F5
West Green 22 A6
West Grimstead 10 D2
West Grinstead 12 E4
West Haddlesey 58 B7
West Haddon 31 H1
West Hagbourne 21 J3
West Hagley 40 B7
West Hall 70 A7
West Hallam 41 G1
West Halton 59 F7
West Ham 23 H3
West Handley 51 F5
West Hanney 21 H2
West Hanningfield 24 D2
West Hardwick 51 G1
West Harptree 19 J6
West Harting 11 J2
West Hatch 8 B2
West Heath
  Hants. 22 B6
West Heath
  W.Mid. 30 B1
West Helmsdale 105 F7
West Hendred 21 H3
West Hesleton 59 F2
West Hill Devon 7 J6
West Hill N.Som. 19 H4
West Hoathly 13 G3
West Holme 9 H6
West Horndon 24 C3
West Horrington 19 J7
West Horsley 22 D6
West Horton 77 J7
West Hougham 15 H3
West Huntspill 19 G7
West Hyde 22 D2
West Hythe 15 G4
West Ilsley 21 H3
West Itchenor 11 J4
West Keal 53 G6
West Kennett 20 E5
West Kilbride 74 A6
West Kingsdown 23 J5
West Kington 20 B4
West Kirby 48 B4
West Knapton 58 E2
West Knighton 9 G6
West Knoyle 9 H1
West Kyloe 77 J6
West Lambrook 8 D3
West Langdon 15 J3
West Langwell 96 D1
West Lavington
  W.Suss. 12 B4
West Lavington
  Wilts. 20 D6
West Layton 62 C5
West Leake 41 H3
West Lexham 44 C4
West Lilling 58 C3
West Lingo 83 F7
West Linton 75 K5
West Littleton 20 A4
West Lockinge 21 H3
West Looe 4 C5
West Lulworth 9 H6
West Lutton 59 F3
West Lydford 8 E1
West Lyng 8 C2
West Lynn 44 A4
West Mains 77 J6
West Malling 23 K6
West Malvern 29 G4
West Marden 11 J3
West Markham 51 K5
West Marsh 53 F2
West Marton 56 D4
West Melton 51 G2
West Meon 11 H2
West Meon Hut 11 H2
West Mersea 34 E7
West Milton 8 E5
West Minster 25 F4
West Molesey 22 E5
West Monkton 8 B2
West Moors 10 B4
West Mostard 61 J7
West Muir 83 G1
West Ness 58 C2
West Newton
  E.Riding 59 J6
West Newton
  Norf. 44 A3
West Norwood 23 G4
West Ogwell 5 J3
West Orchard 9 H3
West Overton 20 E5
West Park Aber. 91 F5
West Park Mersey. 48 D3
West Parley 10 B5
West Peckham 23 K6
West Pennard 8 E1
West Pentire 2 E2
West Perry 32 E2
West Porlock 7 G1
West Putford 6 B4
West Quantoxhead 7 K1
West Rainton 62 E2
West Rasen 52 D4
West Raynham 44 C3
West Rounton 63 F6
West Row 33 J2
West Rudham 44 C3
West Runton 45 F1
West Saltoun 76 C4

West Sandwick 108 D4
West Scrafton 57 F1
West Shinness
  Lodge 103 H7
West Somerton 45 J3
West Stafford 9 G6
West Stockwith 51 K3
West Stoke 12 B6
West Stonesdale 61 K6
West Stoughton 19 H7
West Stour 9 G2
West Stourmouth 25 J5
West Stow 34 C1
West Stowell 20 E5
West Stratton 21 J7
West Street 14 E2
West Tanfield 57 H2
West Taphouse 4 B4
West Tarbert 73 G4
West Tarring 12 E6
West Thorney 11 J4
West Thurrock 23 J4
West Tilbury 24 C4
West Tisted 11 H2
West Tofts Norf. 44 C6
West Tofts P. & K. 82 C4
West Torrington 52 E4
West Town Hants. 11 J5
West Town N.Som. 19 H5
West Tytherley 10 D1
West Walton 43 H4
West Walton
  Highway 43 H4
West Wellow 10 D2
West Wemyss 76 B1
West Wick 19 G5
West Wickham
  Cambs. 33 K4
West Wickham
  Gt.Lon. 23 G5
West Williamston 16 D5
West Winch 44 A4
West Winterslow 10 D1
West Wittering 11 J5
West Witton 57 F1
West Woodburn 70 D5
West Woodhay 21 G5
West Woodlands 20 A7
West Worldham 11 J1
West Worlington 7 F4
West Worthing 12 E6
West Wratting 33 J3
West Wycombe 22 B2
West Yell 108 D4
Westbere 25 H5
Westborough 42 B1
Westbourne
  Bourne. 10 B5
Westbourne
  W.Suss. 11 J4
Westbrook 21 H4
Westbury Bucks. 31 H5
Westbury Shrop. 38 C5
Westbury Wilts. 20 B6
Westbury Leigh 20 B6
Westbury on Trym 19 J4
Westbury-on-
  Severn 29 G7
Westbury-sub-
  Mendip 19 J7
Westby 55 G6
Westcliff-on-Sea 24 E3
Westcombe 9 F1
Westcote 30 D6
Westcott Bucks. 31 J7
Westcott Devon 7 J5
Westcott Surr. 22 E7
Westcott Barton 31 F6
Westdean 13 J7
Westdowns 4 A2
Wester Aberchalder 88 C2
Wester Badentyre 99 F5
Wester Culbeuchly 98 E4
Wester Dechmont 75 J3
Wester Fintray 91 G3
Wester Foffarty 83 F3
Wester
  Greenskares 99 F4
Wester Gruinards 96 C2
Wester Lealty 96 D4
Wester Lonvine 96 E4
Wester Newburn 83 F7
Wester Ord 91 G4
Wester Quarff 109 D9
Wester Skeld 109 B8
Westerdale
  High. 105 G3
Westerdale
  N.Yorks. 63 H6
Westerfield Shet. 109 C7
Westerfield Suff. 35 F4
Westergate 12 C6
Westerham 23 H6
Westerleigh 19 K4
Westerton Aber. 91 F5
Westerton Angus 83 H2
Westerton Dur. 62 D3
Westerton P. & K. 81 K6
Westerwick 109 B8
Westfield Cumb. 60 A4
Westfield E.Suss. 14 D6
Westfield High. 105 F2
Westfield Norf. 44 D5
Westfield W.Loth. 75 H3
Westgate Dur. 62 A3
Westgate N.Lincs. 51 K2
Westgate Norf. 44 D1
Westgate
  Northumb. 71 G6
Westgate Hill 57 H7
Westgate on Sea 25 K4
Westhall Aber. 90 E2
Westhall Suff. 45 J7
Westham Dorset 9 F7
Westham E.Suss. 13 K6
Westhampnett 12 B6
Westhay 19 H7
Westhead 48 D2
Westhide 28 E4
Westhill Aber. 91 G4
Westhill High. 96 E7
Westhope Here. 28 D3
Westhope Shrop. 38 D7
Westhorpe Lincs. 43 F2
Westhorpe Suff. 34 E2
Westhoughton 49 F2
Westhouse 56 B2
Westhumble 22 E6
Westing 108 E2
Westlake 5 G5
Westleigh Devon 6 C3
Westleigh Devon 7 J4
Westleigh Gt.Man. 49 F2
Westleton 35 J2
Westley Shrop. 38 C5
Westley Suff. 34 C2
Westley Heights 24 C3
Westley Waterless 33 K3

Westlington 31 J7
Westlinton 69 J7
Westloch 76 A5
Westmarsh 25 J5
Westmeston 13 G5
Westmill 33 G6
Westminster 23 F4
Westmuir 82 E2
Westness 106 C5
Westnewton
  Cumb. 60 C2
Westnewton
  Northumb. 77 G7
Weston
  B. & N.E.Som. 20 A5
Weston Ches. 49 G7
Weston Devon 7 K7
Weston Dorset 9 F7
Weston Halton 48 E4
Weston Hants. 11 J2
Weston Herts. 33 F5
Weston Lincs. 43 F3
Weston Moray 98 C4
Weston N.Yorks. 57 G5
Weston Northants. 31 G4
Weston Notts. 51 K6
Weston Shrop. 38 E3
Weston Shrop. 38 E6
Weston Staffs. 40 B3
Weston W.Berks. 21 H4
Weston Beggard 28 E4
Weston by Welland 42 A6
Weston Colville 33 K3
Weston Corbett 21 K7
Weston Coyney 40 B1
Weston Favell 31 J2
Weston Green
  Cambs. 33 K3
Weston Green
  Norf. 45 F4
Weston Heath 39 G4
Weston Hills 43 F3
Weston Jones 39 G3
Weston Longville 45 F4
Weston
  Lullingfields 38 D3
Weston Patrick 21 K7
Weston Point 48 D4
Weston Rhyn 38 B2
Weston Subedge 30 C4
Weston Turville 32 B7
Weston under
  Penyard 29 F6
Weston under
  Wetherley 30 E2
Weston Underwood
  Derbys. 40 E1
Weston Underwood
  M.K. 32 B4
Westonbirt 20 B3
Westoning 32 D5
Weston-in-Gordano 19 H4
Weston-on-the-
  Green 31 G7
Weston-on-Trent 41 G3
Weston-super-
  Mare 19 G5
Weston-under-
  Lizard 40 A4
Westonzoyland 8 C1
Westow 58 D3
Westport
  Arg. & B. 66 A1
Westport Som. 8 C3
Westrigg 75 H4
Westruther 76 E5
Westry 43 G6
Westside 91 G5
Westward 60 D2
Westward Ho! 6 C2
Westwell Kent 14 E3
Westwell Oxon. 30 D7
Westwell Leacon 14 E3
Westwick Cambs. 33 H2
Westwick Dur. 62 B5
Westwick Norf. 45 G3
Westwood Devon 7 J6
Westwood Wilts. 20 B6
Westwood Heath 30 D1
Westwoodside 51 K3
Wether Cote Farm 58 C1
Wetheral 61 F1
Wetherby 57 K5
Wetherden 34 E2
Wetheringsett 35 F2
Wethersfield 34 B5
Wethersta 109 C6
Wetherup Street 35 F2
Wetley Rocks 40 B1
Wettenhall 49 F6
Wettenhall Green 49 F6
Wetton 50 D7
Wetwang 59 F4
Wetwood 39 G2
Wexcombe 21 F6
Weybourne 45 F1
Weybread 45 G7
Weybridge 22 D5
Weycroft 8 C4
Weydale 105 G2
Weyhill 21 G7
Weymouth 9 F7
Whaddon Bucks. 32 B5
Whaddon Cambs. 33 G4
Whaddon Glos. 29 H7
Whaddon Wilts. 10 C2
Whaddon Gap 33 G4
Whale 61 G4
Whaley 51 H5
Whaley Bridge 50 C4
Whaligoe 105 J4
Whalley 56 C6
Whalton 71 G5
Wham 56 C3
Whaplode 43 G4
Whaplode Drove 43 G4
Whaplode
  St. Catherine 43 G4
Wharfe 56 C3
Wharles 55 H6
Wharncliffe Side 51 F3
Wharram le Street 58 E3
Wharram Percy 58 E3
Wharton Ches. 49 F6
Wharton Here. 28 E3
Whashton 62 C6
Whatcote 30 D4
Whatfield 34 E4
Whatley 20 A7
Whatlington 14 C6
Whatstandwell 51 F7
Whatton 42 A2
Whauphill 64 E6
Whaw 62 A6
Wheatacre 45 J6
Wheatcroft 51 F7
Wheathampstead 32 E7

Wheathill	39	F7
Wheatley Hants.	11	J1
Wheatley Oxon.	21	K1
Wheatley Hill	62	E3
Wheatley Lane	56	D6
Wheaton Aston	40	A4
Wheddon Cross	7	H2
Wheelerstreet	22	C7
Wheelock	49	G7
Wheelton	56	B7
Wheen	90	B7
Wheldrake	58	C5
Whelford	20	E2
Whelpley Hill	22	D1
Whelpo	60	E3
Whenby	58	C3
Whepstead	34	C3
Wherstead	35	F4
Wherwell	21	G7
Wheston	50	D5
Whetley Cross	8	D4
Whetsted	23	K7
Whetstone	41	H6
Whicham	54	E1
Whichford	30	E5
Whickham	71	H7
Whiddon Down	6	E6
Whifflet	75	F4
Whigstreet	83	F3
Whilton	31	H2
Whim	76	A5
Whimple	7	J6
Whimpwell Green	45	H2
Whin Lane End	55	G5
Whinburgh	44	E5
Whinnyfold	91	J1
Whippingham	11	G5
Whipsnade	32	D7
Whipton	7	H6
Whisby	52	C6
Whissendine	42	B4
Whissonsett	44	D3
Whistley Green	22	A4
Whiston Mersey.	48	D3
Whiston Northants.	32	B2
Whiston S.Yorks.	51	G4
Whiston Staffs.	40	C1
Whiston Staffs.	40	A4
Whitbeck	54	E1
Whitbourne	29	G3
Whitburn T.&W.	71	K7
Whitburn W.Loth.	75	H4
Whitby Ches.	48	C5
Whitby N.Yorks.	63	K5
Whitchurch		
B. & N.E.Som.	19	K5
Whitchurch Bucks.	32	B6
Whitchurch Cardiff	18	E4
Whitchurch Devon	4	E3
Whitchurch Hants.	21	H7
Whitchurch Here.	28	E7
Whitchurch Pembs.	16	B3
Whitchurch Shrop.	38	E1
Whitchurch		
Canonicorum	8	C5
Whitchurch Hill	21	K4
Whitchurch-on-		
Thames	21	K4
Whitcombe	9	G6
Whitcott Keysett	38	B7
White Colne	34	C6
White Coppice	49	F1
White Cross Cornw.	3	F3
White Cross Devon	7	J6
White Cross Here.	28	D4
White End	29	H6
White Lackington	9	G5
White Ladies Aston	29	J3
White Mill	17	H3
White Moor	41	F1
White Notley	34	B7
White Pit	53	G5
White Roding	33	J7
White Waltham	22	B4
Whiteacen	97	K7
Whiteash Green	34	B5
Whitebog	99	H5
Whitebridge High.	105	H1
Whitebridge High.	88	B3
Whitebrook	19	J1
Whiteburn	76	D6
Whitecairn	64	C5
Whitecairns	91	H3
Whitecastle	75	J6
Whitechapel	55	J5
Whitechurch	16	E2
Whitecraig	76	B3
Whitecroft	19	K1
Whitecrook	64	B5
Whitecross	2	C5
Whiteface	96	E3
Whitefield Aber.	90	E1
Whitefield Gt.Man.	49	H2
Whitefield High.	88	C2
Whitefield High.	105	H3
Whitefield P.&K.	82	C4
Whiteford	91	F2
Whitegate	49	F6
Whitehall	106	F5
Whitehaven	60	A5
Whitehill Hants.	11	J1
Whitehill Kent	14	E2
Whitehill N.Ayr.	74	A5
Whitehills	98	E4
Whitehouse Aber.	90	E1
Whitehouse		
Arg. & B.	73	G4
Whitekirk	76	D2
Whitelackington	8	C3
Whitelaw	77	G5
Whiteleen	105	J4
Whiteleys	74	B7
Whiteley	11	G4
Whiteley Bank	11	G6
Whiteley Village	22	D5
Whiteleys	64	A5
Whitemans Green	13	G4
Whitemire	97	G6
Whiteparish	10	D2
Whiterashes	91	G2
Whiterow	105	J4
Whiteshill	20	B1
Whiteside		
Northumb.	70	C7
Whiteside W.Loth.	75	H4
Whitesmith	13	J5
Whitestaunton	8	B3
Whitestone Aber.	90	E5
Whitestone		
Arg. & B.	73	F7
Whitestone Devon	7	G6
Whitestripe	99	H5
Whiteway	29	J7
Whitewell Aber.	99	H4
Whitewell Lancs.	56	B5
Whiteworks	5	G3
Whitewreath	97	K6

Whitfield Here.	28	D5
Whitfield Kent	15	H3
Whitfield		
Northants.	31	H4
Whitfield		
Northumb.	61	J1
Whitfield S.Glos.	19	K2
Whitford Devon	8	B5
Whitford (Chwitffordd)		
Flints.	47	K5
Whitgift	58	E7
Whitgreave	40	A3
Whithorn	64	E6
Whiting Bay	66	E1
Whitkirk	57	J6
Whitlam	91	G2
Whitland	17	F4
Whitland Abbey	17	F4
Whitletts	67	H1
Whitley N.Yorks.	58	B7
Whitley Read.	22	A5
Whitley Wilts.	20	B5
Whitley Bay	71	J6
Whitley Chapel	62	A1
Whitley Lower	50	E1
Whitley Row	23	H6
Whitlock's End	30	C1
Whitminster	20	A1
Whitmore Dorset	10	B4
Whitmore Staffs.	40	A1
Whitnage	7	J4
Whitnash	30	E2
Whitney	28	B4
Whitrigg Cumb.	60	D1
Whitrigg Cumb.	60	D3
Whitsbury	10	C3
Whitsome	77	G5
Whitson	19	G3
Whitstable	25	H5
Whitstone	4	C1
Whittingham	71	F2
Whittingslow	38	D7
Whittington		
Derbys.	51	F5
Whittington Glos.	30	B6
Whittington		
Lancs.	56	B2
Whittington Norf.	44	B6
Whittington Shrop.	38	C2
Whittington Staffs.	40	D5
Whittington Staffs.	40	A7
Whittington Worcs.	29	H3
Whittlebury	31	H4
Whittle-le-Woods	55	J7
Whittlesford	33	H4
Whitton N.Lincs.	59	F7
Whitton Northumb.	71	F3
Whitton Powys	28	B2
Whitton Shrop.	28	E1
Whitton Stock.	62	E4
Whitton Suff.	35	F4
Whittonditch	21	F4
Whittonstall	62	B1
Whitway	21	H6
Whitwell Derbys.	51	H5
Whitwell Herts.	32	E6
Whitwell I.o.W.	11	G7
Whitwell N.Yorks.	62	D7
Whitwell Norf.	45	F3
Whitwell Rut.	42	C5
Whitwell-on-the-		
Hill	58	D3
Whitwick	41	G4
Whitwood	57	K7
Whitworth	49	H1
Whixall	38	E2
Whixley	57	K4
Wholton Dur.	62	C5
Whorlton		
N.Yorks.	63	F6
Whygate	70	C6
Whyle	28	E2
Whyteleafe	23	G6
Wibdon	19	J2
Wibsey	57	G6
Wibtoft	41	G7
Wichenford	29	G2
Wichling	14	E2
Wick Bourne.	10	C5
Wick High.	105	J3
Wick S.Glos.	20	A4
Wick V. of Glam.	18	C4
Wick W.Sus.	12	D6
Wick Wilts.	10	C2
Wick Worcs.	29	J4
Wick Airport	105	J3
Wick Hill Kent	14	D3
Wick Hill W'ham	22	A5
Wick St. Lawrence	19	G5
Wicken Cambs.	33	J1
Wicken Northants.	31	J5
Wicken Bonhunt	33	H5
Wickenby	52	D4
Wickersley	51	G3
Wickford	24	D2
Wickham Hants.	11	G3
Wickham W.Berks.	21	G4
Wickham Bishops	34	C7
Wickham Heath	21	H5
Wickham Market	35	G3
Wickham St. Paul	34	C5
Wickham Skeith	34	E2
Wickham Street		
Suff.	34	B3
Wickham Street		
Suff.	34	E2
Wickhambreaux	15	H2
Wickhambrook	34	B3
Wickhamford	30	B4
Wickhampton	45	J5
Wicklewood	44	E5
Wickmere	45	F2
Wickwar	20	A3
Widdington	33	J5
Widdrington	71	H4
Wide Open	71	H6
Widecombe in the		
Moor	5	H3
Widegates	4	C5
Widemouth Bay	6	A5
Widewall	107	D8
Widford Essex	24	C1
Widford Herts.	33	H7
Widmerpool	41	J3
Widnes	48	E4
Widworthy	8	B5
Wigan	48	E2
Wiggaton	7	K6
Wiggenhall		
St. Germans	44	A4
Wiggenhall St. Mary		
Magdalen	44	A4
Wiggenhall St. Mary		
the Virgin	43	J4
Wiggenhall		
St. Peter	44	A4

Wiggington	58	C4
Wigginton Herts.	32	C7
Wigginton Oxon.	30	D5
Wigginton Staffs.	40	E5
Wigglesworth	56	D4
Wiggonby	60	D1
Wiggonholt	12	D5
Wighill	57	K5
Wighton	44	D2
Wightwizzle	50	E3
Wigley	10	E3
Wigmore Here.	28	D2
Wigmore Med.	24	E5
Wigsley	52	B5
Wigsthorpe	42	D7
Wigston	41	J6
Wigston Parva	41	G6
Wigthorpe	51	H4
Wigtoft	43	F2
Wigton	60	D2
Wigtown	64	E5
Wilbarston	42	B7
Wilberfoss	58	D4
Wilburton	33	H1
Wilby Norf.	44	E6
Wilby Northants.	32	B2
Wilby Suff.	35	G1
Wilcot	20	E5
Wilcott	38	C4
Wilcrick	19	H3
Wildboarclough	49	J6
Wilden Beds.	32	D3
Wilden Worcs.	29	H1
Wildhern	21	G6
Wildhill	23	F1
Wildsworth	52	B3
Wilford	41	H2
Wilkesley	39	F1
Wilkhaven	97	G3
Wilkieston	75	K4
Willand	7	J4
Willaston Ches.	48	C5
Willaston Ches.	49	F7
Willen	32	B4
Willenhall W.Mid.	40	B6
Willenhall W.Mid.	30	E7
Willerby E.Riding	59	G7
Willerby N.Yorks.	59	G2
Willersey	30	C4
Willersley	28	C4
Willesborough	15	F3
Willesborough Lees	15	F3
Willesden	23	F3
Willesley	20	B3
Willett	7	K2
Willey Shrop.	39	F6
Willey Warks.	41	G7
Williamscot	31	F4
Williamthorpe	51	G6
Willian	33	F5
Willimontswick	70	C7
Willingale	23	J1
Willingdon	13	J6
Willingham		
Cambs.	33	H2
Willingham Lincs.	52	B4
Willington Beds.	32	E4
Willington Derbys.	40	E3
Willington Dur.	62	C3
Willington T.&W.	71	J7
Willington Warks.	30	D5
Willington Corner	48	E6
Willisham	34	E3
Willitoft	58	D6
Williton	7	J1
Willoughby Lincs.	53	H5
Willoughby Warks.	31	G2
Willoughby		
Waterleys	41	H6
Willoughby-on-the-		
Wolds	41	J3
Willoughton	52	C3
Willows Green	34	B7
Willsworthy	6	D7
Wilmcote	30	C2
Wilmington Devon	8	B4
Wilmington		
E.Suss.	13	J6
Wilmington Kent	23	J4
Wilmslow	49	H4
Wilnecote	40	E5
Wilpshire	56	B6
Wilsden	57	F6
Wilsford Lincs.	42	D1
Wilsford Wilts.	20	E6
Wilsford Wilts.	20	D6
Wilsill	57	G3
Wilsley Green	14	C4
Wilson	41	G3
Wilstead	32	D4
Wilsthorpe	42	D4
Wilstone	32	C7
Wilton Cumb.	60	B5
Wilton N.Yorks.	58	E1
Wilton R.&C.	63	G4
Wilton Sc.Bord.	69	K2
Wilton Som.	8	B2
Wilton Wilts.	21	F5
Wilton Wilts.	10	B1
Wimbish	33	J5
Wimbish Green	33	K5
Wimblebury	40	C4
Wimbledon	23	F4
Wimblington	43	H6
Wimborne Minster	10	B4
Wimborne St. Giles	10	B3
Wimbotsham	44	A5
Wimpole	33	G4
Wimpstone	30	D4
Wincanton	9	G2
Wincham	49	F5
Winchburgh	75	J3
Winchcombe	30	B6
Winchelsea	14	E6
Winchelsea Beach	14	E6
Winchester	11	F2
Winchet Hill	14	C3
Winchfield	22	A6
Winchmore Hill		
Bucks.	22	C2
Winchmore Hill		
Gt.Lon.	23	G2
Wincle	49	J6
Wincobank	51	F3
Winderton	30	E4
Windhill	96	C7
Windlesham	22	C5
Windley	41	F1
Windley Meadows	41	F1
Windmill Hill		
E.Suss.	13	K5
Windmill Hill Som.	8	C3
Windrush	30	C7
Windsor	22	C4
Windy Yet	74	C5
Windygates	82	E7
Wineham	13	F4
Winestead	59	K7

Winfarthing	45	F7
Winford	19	J5
Winforton	28	B4
Winfrith Newburgh	9	H6
Wing Bucks.	32	B6
Wing Rut.	42	B5
Wingate	63	F3
Wingates		
Gt.Man.	49	F2
Wingates		
Northumb.	71	F4
Wingerworth	51	F6
Wingfield Beds.	32	D6
Wingfield Suff.	35	G1
Wingfield Wilts.	20	B6
Wingham	15	H2
Wingmore	15	G3
Wingrave	32	B7
Winkburn	51	K7
Winkfield	22	C4
Winkfield Row	22	B4
Winkhill	50	C7
Winkleigh	6	E5
Winksley	57	H2
Winksley Banks	57	H2
Winkton	10	C5
Winlaton	71	G7
Winlaton Mill	71	G7
Winless	105	H3
Winmarleigh	55	H5
Winnards Perch	3	G2
Winnersh	22	A4
Winscombe	19	H6
Winsford Ches.	49	F6
Winsford Som.	7	H2
Winsham	8	C4
Winshill	40	E3
Winsh-wen	17	K6
Winskill	61	G3
Winslade	21	K7
Winsley	20	A5
Winslow	31	J6
Winson	20	D1
Winsor	10	E3
Winster Cumb.	61	F7
Winster Derbys.	50	E6
Winston Dur.	62	C5
Winston Suff.	35	F2
Winstone	20	C1
Winswell	6	C4
Winterborne Came	9	G6
Winterborne		
Clenston	9	H4
Winterborne		
Houghton	9	H4
Winterborne		
Kingston	9	H5
Winterborne		
Monkton	9	F6
Winterborne		
Stickland	9	H4
Winterborne		
Whitechurch	9	H4
Winterborne		
Zelston	9	H5
Winterbourne		
S.Glos.	19	K3
Winterbourne		
W.Berks.	21	H4
Winterbourne		
Abbas	9	F5
Winterbourne		
Bassett	20	D4
Winterbourne		
Dauntsey	10	C1
Winterbourne Earls	10	C1
Winterbourne		
Gunner	10	C1
Winterbourne		
Monkton	20	D4
Winterbourne		
Steepleton	9	F6
Winterbourne		
Stoke	20	D7
Winterburn	56	E4
Wintercleugh	68	E2
Winteringham	59	F7
Winterley	49	G7
Wintersett	51	F1
Wintershill	11	G3
Winterslow	10	D1
Winterton	52	C1
Winterton-on-Sea	45	J4
Winthorpe Lincs.	53	J6
Winthorpe Notts.	52	B7
Winton Bourne.	10	B5
Winton Cumb.	61	J5
Wintringham	58	E2
Winwick Cambs.	42	E7
Winwick		
Northants.	31	H1
Winwick Warr.	49	F3
Wirksworth	50	E7
Wirswall	38	E1
Wisbech	43	H5
Wisbech St. Mary	43	H5
Wisborough Green	12	D4
Wiseton	51	K4
Wishaw N.Lan.	75	F5
Wishaw Warks.	40	D6
Wisley	22	D6
Wispington	53	F5
Wissett	35	H1
Wissington	34	D5
Wistanstow	38	D7
Wistanswick	39	F3
Wistaston	49	F7
Wiston Pembs.	16	D4
Wiston S.Lan.	75	H7
Wistow Cambs.	43	F7
Wistow N.Yorks.	58	B6
Wiswell	56	C6
Witcham	33	H1
Witchampton	9	J4
Witchburn	66	B2
Witchford	33	J1
Witcombe	8	D3
Witham	34	C7
Witham Friary	20	A7
Witham on the Hill	42	D4
Withcote	42	B5
Witherenden Hill	13	K4
Witherhurst	13	K4
Witheridge	7	G4
Witherley	41	F6
Withern	53	H4
Withernsea	59	K7
Withernwick	59	H5
Withersdale Street	45	G7
Withersfield	33	K4
Witherslack	55	H1
Witherslack Hall	55	H1
Withiel	3	G2
Withiel Florey	7	H2
Withington Glos.	30	B7
Withington		
Gt.Man.	49	H3
Withington Here.	28	E4
Withington Shrop.	38	E4

Withington Staffs.	40	C2
Withington Green	49	H5
Withleigh	7	H4
Withnell	56	B7
Withybrook	41	G7
Withycombe	7	J1
Withycombe		
Raleigh	7	J7
Withyham	13	H3
Withypool	7	G2
Witley	12	C3
Witnesham	35	F3
Witney	30	E7
Wittering	42	D5
Wittersham	14	D5
Witton	83	G1
Witton Bridge	45	H2
Witton Gilbert	62	D2
Witton Park	62	C3
Witton-le-Wear	62	C3
Wiveliscombe	7	J3
Wivelsfield	13	G4
Wivelsfield Green	13	G5
Wivenhoe	34	E6
Wiveton	44	E1
Wix	35	F6
Wixford	30	B3
Wixoe	34	B4
Woburn	32	C5
Woburn Sands	32	C5
Wokefield Park	21	K5
Woking	22	D6
Wokingham	22	B5
Wolborough	5	J3
Wold Newton		
E.Riding	59	G2
Wold Newton		
N.E.Lincs.	53	F3
Woldingham	23	G6
Wolfelee	70	A3
Wolferlow	29	F2
Wolferton	44	A3
Wolfhampcote	31	G2
Wolfhill	82	C4
Wolfpits	28	B3
Wolf's Castle	16	C3
Wolfsdale	16	C3
Woll	69	K1
Wollaston		
Northants.	32	C2
Wollaston Shrop.	38	C4
Wollaston W.Mid.	40	A7
Wollerton	39	F3
Wolsingham	62	B3
Wolstenholme	49	H1
Wolston	31	F1
Wolvercote	21	H1
Wolverhampton	40	B6
Wolverley Shrop.	38	D2
Wolverley Worcs.	29	H1
Wolverton Hants.	21	J6
Wolverton M.K.	32	B4
Wolverton Warks.	30	D2
Wolvesnewton	19	H2
Wolvey	41	G7
Wolviston	63	F4
Wombleton	58	C1
Wombourne	40	A6
Wombwell	51	G2
Womenswold	15	H2
Womersley	51	H1
Wonastow	28	D7
Wonersh	22	D7
Wonson	6	E7
Wonston	11	F1
Wooburn	22	C3
Wooburn Green	22	C3
Wood Burcote	31	H4
Wood Dalling	44	E3
Wood End Beds.	32	D4
Wood End Herts.	33	G6
Wood End Warks.	40	E6
Wood End Warks.	30	C1
Wood Enderby	53	F6
Wood Green	23	G2
Wood Hayes	40	B5
Wood Norton	44	E3
Wood Street		
Village	22	C6
Woodale	57	F2
Woodbastwick	45	H4
Woodbeck	51	K5
Woodbine	16	C4
Woodborough		
Notts.	41	J1
Woodborough		
Wilts.	20	E5
Woodbridge	35	G4
Woodbury	7	J7
Woodbury Salterton	7	J7
Woodchester	20	B1
Woodchurch Kent	14	E4
Woodchurch		
Mersey.	48	B4
Woodcote Oxon.	21	K3
Woodcote		
Tel.&W.	39	G4
Woodcott	21	H6
Woodcroft	19	J2
Woodcutts	9	J3
Woodditton	33	K3
Woodeaton	31	G7
Woodend Aber.	90	E3
Woodend Cumb.	60	C7
Woodend High.	88	B2
Woodend High.	79	J1
Woodend		
Northants.	31	H4
Woodend P.&K.	82	B4
Woodend W.Suss.	12	B6
Woodfalls	10	D2
Woodford Cornw.	6	A4
Woodford Gt.Lon.	23	H2
Woodford Gt.Man.	49	H4
Woodford		
Northants.	32	C1
Woodford Bridge	23	H2
Woodford Green	23	H2
Woodford Halse	31	G3
Woodgate Norf.	44	E4
Woodgate W.Mid.	40	B7
Woodgate W.Suss.	12	C6
Woodgate Worcs.	29	J2
Woodgreen	10	C3
Woodhall	62	A7
Woodhall Spa	52	E6
Woodham Dur.	62	D4
Woodham Surr.	22	D5
Woodham Ferrers	24	D2
Woodham		
Mortimer	24	E1
Woodham Walter	24	E1
Woodhaven	83	F5
Woodhead	91	F1
Woodhill	39	G7
Woodhorn	71	H5
Woodhouse		
Cumb.	55	J1

Woodhouse Leics.	41	H4
Woodhouse		
S.Yorks.	51	G4
Woodhouse Eaves	41	H4
Woodhouses	40	D4
Woodhuish	5	K5
Woodhurst	33	G1
Woodingdean	13	G6
Woodland Devon	5	H4
Woodland Dur.	62	B4
Woodlands Dorset	10	B4
Woodlands Hants.	10	E3
Woodlands Shrop.	39	G7
Woodlands Park	22	B4
Woodleigh	5	H6
Woodlesford	57	J7
Woodley	22	A4
Woodmancote		
Glos.	20	D1
Woodmancote		
Glos.	29	J6
Woodmancote		
W.Suss.	13	F5
Woodmancote		
W.Suss.	11	J4
Woodmancott	21	J7
Woodmansey	59	G6
Woodmansterne	23	F6
Woodminton	10	B2
Woodmoor	38	B5
Woodnesborough	15	J2
Woodnewton	42	D6
Woodplumpton	55	J6
Woodrising	44	D5
Woodseaves		
Shrop.	39	F2
Woodseaves		
Staffs.	39	G3
Woodsend	21	F4
Woodsetts	51	H4
Woodsford	9	G5
Woodside		
Aberdeen	91	H4
Woodside Brack.F.	22	C4
Woodside D.&G.	69	F6
Woodside Fife	83	F7
Woodside Fife	82	D7
Woodside Herts.	23	F1
Woodside N.Ayr.	74	B7
Woodside P.&K.	82	C4
Woodside Shrop.	28	C1
Woodside W.Mid.	40	B7
Woodstock	31	F7
Woodstock Slop	16	D3
Woodston	42	E6
Woodthorpe		
Derbys.	51	G5
Woodthorpe		
Leics.	41	H4
Woodton	45	G6
Woodtown	6	C3
Woodville	41	F4
Woodwalton	43	F7
Woodyates	10	B3
Woofferton	28	E2
Wookey	19	J7
Wookey Hole	19	J7
Wool	9	H6
Woolacombe	6	C1
Woolage Green	15	H3
Woolaston	19	J1
Woolavington	19	G7
Woolbeding	12	B4
Wooler	70	E1
Woolfardisworthy		
Devon	7	G5
Woolfardisworthy		
Devon	6	B3
Woolfords Cottages	75	J5
Woolhampton	21	J5
Woolhope	29	F5
Woolland	9	G4
Woollage Green	15	H3
Woollard	19	K5
Woollaton	6	C4
Woolley		
B. & N.E.Som.	20	A5
Woolley Cambs.	32	E1
Woolley W.Yorks.	51	F1
Woolmer Green	33	F7
Woolmere Green	29	J2
Woolmersdon	8	B1
Woolpit	34	D2
Woolscott	31	F2
Woolstaston	38	D5
Woolsthorpe Lincs.	42	B2
Woolsthorpe Lincs.	42	C3
Woolston S'ham.	11	F3
Woolston Devon	5	H6
Woolston Shrop.	38	D7
Woolston Warr.	49	F4
Woolston Green	5	H4
Woolstone M.K.	32	B5
Woolstone Oxon.	21	F3
Woolton	48	D4
Woolton Hill	21	H5
Woolverstone	35	F5
Woolverton	20	A6
Woolwich	23	H4
Woonton	28	C3
Wooperton	71	F1
Woore	39	G1
Wootton Beds.	32	D4
Wootton Hants.	10	D5
Wootton Kent	15	H3
Wootton N.Lincs.	52	D7
Wootton		
Northants.	31	J3
Wootton Oxon.	31	F7
Wootton Oxon.	21	H1
Wootton Shrop.	28	D1
Wootton Staffs.	40	A3
Wootton Staffs.	40	D1
Wootton Bassett	20	D3
Wootton Bridge	11	G5
Wootton Common	11	G5
Wootton Courtenay	7	H1
Wootton Fitzpaine	8	C5
Wootton Green	32	D4
Wootton Rivers	20	E5
Wootton		
St. Lawrence	21	J6
Wootton Wawen	30	C2
Worcester	29	H3
Worcester Park	23	F5
Wordsley	40	A7
Wordwell	34	C1
Worfield	39	G5
Work	107	D6
Workington	60	B4
Worksop	51	H5
Worlaby	52	D1
Worlds End		
Hants.	11	H3
World's End		
W.Berks.	21	H4
Worle	19	G5
Worleston	49	F7
Worlingham	45	J6
Worlington	33	K1

Worlingworth	35	G2
Wormbridge	28	D5
Wormegay	44	A4
Wormelow Tump	28	D5
Wormhill	50	D5
Wormiehills	83	H4
Wormingford	34	D5
Worminghall	21	K1
Wormington	30	B5
Worminster	19	J7
Wormiston	83	H7
Wormit	82	E5
Wormleighton	31	F3
Wormley Herts.	23	G1
Wormley Surr.	12	C3
Wormshill	14	D2
Wormsley	28	D4
Worplesdon	22	C6
Worrall	51	F3
Worsbrough	51	F2
Worsley	49	G3
Worstead	45	H3
Worsthorne	56	D6
Worston	56	C5
Worswell	5	F6
Worth Kent	15	J2
Worth W.Suss.	13	G3
Worth Matravers	9	J7
Wortham	34	E1
Worthen	38	C5
Worthenbury	38	D1
Worthing Norf.	44	E4
Worthing W.Suss.	12	E6
Worthington	41	G3
Wortley Glos.	20	A2
Wortley S.Yorks.	51	F3
Worton	20	C6
Wortwell	45	G7
Wotherton	38	B5
Wotton	22	E7
Wotton		
Underwood	31	H7
Wotton-under-		
Edge	20	A2
Woughton on the		
Green	32	B5
Wouldham	24	D5
Wrabness	35	F5
Wrae	99	F5
Wrafton	6	C2
Wragby	52	E5
Wragholme	53	G3
Wramplingham	45	F5
Wrangham	90	E1
Wrangle	53	H7
Wrangle Lowgate	53	H7
Wrangway	7	K4
Wrantage	8	C2
Wrawby	52	D2
Wraxall N.Som.	19	H4
Wraxall Som.	9	F1
Wray	56	B3
Wray Castle	60	E6
Wraysbury	22	D4
Wrea Green	55	G6
Wreay Lancs.	61	F4
Wreay Cumb.	61	F2
Wrecclesham	22	B7
Wrecsam (		
Wrexham)	38	C1
Wrekenton	62	D1
Wrelton	58	D1
Wrenbury	38	E1
Wreningham	45	F6
Wrentham	45	J7
Wrenthorpe	57	J7
Wrentnall	38	D5
Wressle	58	D6
Wrestlingworth	33	F4
Wretham	44	D7
Wretton	44	A6
Wrexham		
(Wrecsam)	38	C1
Wrexham Industrial		
Estate	38	C1
Wribbenhall	29	G1
Wrightington Bar	48	E1
Wrightpark	74	E1
Wrinehill	39	G1
Wrington	19	H5
Writhlington	19	K6
Writtle	24	C1
Wrockwardine	39	F4
Wroot	51	K2
Wrotham	23	K6
Wrotham Heath	23	K6
Wrotham Hill	23	F2
Wrotham Park	23	F2
Wroughton	20	D3
Wroxall I.o.W.	11	G7
Wroxall Warks.	30	D1
Wroxeter	38	E5
Wroxham	45	H4
Wroxton	31	F4
Wstrws	17	G1
Wyaston	40	D1
Wyberton	43	G1
Wyboston	32	E3
Wybunbury	39	F1
Wych Cross	13	H3
Wychbold	29	J2
Wyck	11	J1
Wyck Rissington	30	C6
Wycliffe	62	C5
Wycoller	56	E6
Wycomb	42	A3
Wycombe Marsh	22	B2
Wyddial	33	G5
Wye	15	F3
Wyke Dorset	9	G2
Wyke Shrop.	39	F5
Wyke W.Yorks.	57	G7
Wyke Regis	9	F7
Wykeham N.Yorks.	59	F1
Wykeham N.Yorks.	58	E2
Wyken	39	G6
Wykey	38	C3
Wylam	71	G7
Wylde Green	40	D6
Wyllie	18	E2
Wylye	10	B1
Wymering	11	H4
Wymeswold	41	J3
Wymington	32	C2
Wymondham		
Leics.	42	B4
Wymondham		
Norf.	45	F5
Wyndham	18	C2
Wynford Eagle	8	E5
Wynnstay Park	38	C1
Wynyard	63	F4
Wyre Piddle	29	J4
Wyresdale Tower	56	B4
Wysall	41	J3

Wyson 28 E2
Wythall 30 B1
Wytham 21 H1
Wythburn 60 E5
Wyton 33 F1
Wyverstone 34 E2
Wyverstone Street 34 E2
Wyville 42 B3
Wyvis Lodge 96 B4

Y
Y Bryn 37 H3
Y Drenewydd (Newtown) 38 A6
Y Fan 37 J7
Y Felinheli 46 D6
Y Fenni (Abergavenny) 28 C7

Y Fflint (Flint) 48 B5
Y Ffôr 36 C2
Y Trallwng (Welshpool) 38 B5
Yaddlethorpe 52 B2
Yafford 11 F6
Yafforth 62 E7
Yalding 23 K7
Yanworth 30 B7
Yapham 58 D4
Yapton 12 C6
Yarburgh 53 G3
Yarcombe 8 B4
Yardley 40 D7
Yardley Gobion 31 J4
Yardley Hastings 32 B3
Yardro 28 B3
Yarkhill 29 F4
Yarlet 40 B3
Yarley 19 J7
Yarlington 9 F2
Yarm 63 F5

Yarmouth 10 E6
Yarnacott 6 E2
Yarnbrook 20 B6
Yarnfield 40 A2
Yarnscombe 6 D3
Yarnton 31 F7
Yarpole 28 D2
Yarrow 69 J1
Yarrow Feus 69 J1
Yarrowford 69 K1
Yarsop 28 D4
Yarwell 42 D6
Yate 20 A3
Yateley 22 B5
Yatesbury 20 D4
Yattendon 21 J4
Yatton Here. 28 D2
Yatton N.Som. 19 H5
Yatton Keynell 20 B4
Yaverland 11 H6
Yaxham 44 E4
Yaxley Cambs. 42 E6
Yaxley Suff. 35 F1

Yazor 28 D4
Yeading 22 E3
Yeadon 57 H5
Yealand Conyers 55 J2
Yealand Redmayne 55 J2
Yealmpton 5 F5
Yearby 63 H4
Yearsley 58 B2
Yeaton 38 D4
Yeaveley 40 D1
Yedingham 58 E2
Yelford 21 G1
Yelland Devon 6 C2
Yelland Devon 6 D6
Yelling 33 F2
Yelvertoft 31 G1
Yelverton Devon 5 F4
Yelverton Norf. 45 G5
Yenston 9 G2
Yeo Vale 6 C3
Yeoford 7 F6
Yeolmbridge 6 B7

Yeomadon 6 B5
Yeovil 8 E3
Yeovil Marsh 8 E3
Yeovilton 8 E3
Yerbeston 16 D5
Yesnaby 107 B6
Yetlington 71 F2
Yetminster 8 E3
Yetts o'Muckhart 82 B7
Yielden 32 D2
Yiewsley 22 D4
Ynys 36 E2
Ynysboeth 18 D2
Ynysddu 18 E2
Ynyshir 18 D2
Ynyslas 37 F6
Ynysmeudwy 18 A1
Ynystawe 17 K5
Ynysybwl 18 D2
Yockenthwaite 56 E2
Yockleton 38 C4
Yokefleet 58 E7

Yoker 74 D4
Yonder Bognie 98 E6
York 58 C4
Yorkletts 25 G5
Yorkley 19 K1
Yorton 38 E3
Youldon 6 B5
Youldonmoor Cross 6 B5
Youlgreave 50 E6
Youlthorpe 58 D4
Youlton 57 K3
Young's End 34 B7
Yoxall 40 D4
Yoxford 35 H2

Ystrad 18 C2
Ystrad Aeron 26 E3
Ystrad Meurig 27 G2
Ystrad Mynach 18 E2
Ystradfellte 27 J7
Ystradffin 27 G4
Ystradgynlais 27 G7
Ystradowen N.P.T. 27 G7
Ystradowen V. of Glam. 18 D4
Ythanwells 90 E1
Ythsie 91 G1

Z
Zeal Monachorum 7 F5
Zeals 9 G1
Zelah 3 F3
Zennor 2 B5

INDEX TO PLACE NAMES IN IRELAND

Abbreviations

Ant. Antrim	Kilk. Kilkenny	Tyr. Tyrone	Wexf. Wexford
Dub. Dublin	Tipp. Tipperary	Water. Waterford	

A
Aasleagh 112 B6
Abbeyfeale 110 C3
Abbeyleix 111 F2
Achill 112 B5
Adare 110 C2
Annahilt 113 G4
Annalong 113 H5
Antrim 113 G3
Ardara 112 D3
Ardee 113 G5
Ardglass 113 H4
Arklow (Antinbhear Mór) 111 G2
Armagh 113 G4
Armoy 113 G2
Arvagh 113 E5
Ashbourne 113 G6
Athboy 113 F6
Athenry 110 D1
Athleague 112 D6
Athlone (Baile Átha Luain) 113 E6
Athy 111 F1
Augher 113 F4
Aughnacloy 113 F4
Aughrim 111 G2
Avoca 111 G2

B
Balbriggan 113 G6
Bailieborough 113 F5
Ballaghaderreen 112 D5
Ballina (Béal an Átha) 112 C5
Ballinafad 112 D5
Ballinalack 113 E6
Ballinamore 113 E5
Ballinasloe (Béal Átha na Sluaighe) 110 D1
Ballindine 112 C6
Ballinrobe 112 C6
Ballon 111 F2
Ballybay 113 F5
Ballybofey 113 E3
Ballybrack 110 A4
Ballybunnion 110 B3
Ballycanew 111 G2
Ballycastle Ant. 113 G2
Ballycastle Mayo 112 C4
Ballyclare 113 G3
Ballyconnell 113 E5
Ballycroy 112 B5
Ballydesmond 110 C3
Ballygar 112 D6
Ballygawley 113 F4
Ballygorman 113 F2
Ballyhale 111 F3
Ballyhaunis 112 D6
Ballyheigue 110 B3
Ballyjamesduff 113 F5
Ballykelly 113 F3
Ballylynan 111 F2
Ballymacarberry 111 E3
Ballymacmague 111 E4
Ballymacoda 111 E4
Ballymahon 113 E6
Ballymakeery 110 C4
Ballymena 113 G3
Ballymoney 113 G3
Ballymote 112 D5
Ballymurphy 111 F2
Ballynahinch 113 H4
Ballyragget 111 F2
Ballyshannon 112 D4
Ballyvaughan 110 C1
Ballyward 113 G4
Baltinglass 111 G2
Banagher 111 E1
Banbridge 113 G4
Bandon 110 D4
Bangor 113 H4
Bangor Erris 112 B5
Banteer 110 C3
Bantry 110 B5
Belcoo 113 E4

Belderg 112 B4
Belfast 113 H4
Belfast City Airport 113 H4
Belfast International Airport 113 G4
Belmullet 112 B5
Beragh 113 F4
Bessbrook 113 G5
Bettystown 113 G6
Birr 111 E1
Blackrock 113 G5
Blackwater 111 G3
Blarney 110 D4
Blessington 111 G1
Bohola 112 C5
Borris 111 F2
Borrisokane 110 D1
Borrisoleigh 111 E2
Boyle 112 D5
Bray (Bré) 111 G1
Broadford 110 C3
Broughshane 113 G3
Bunbeg 112 D3
Bunclody 111 G2
Buncrana 113 E2
Bundoran 112 D4
Burtonport 112 D3
Bushmills 113 G2
Butlers Bridge 113 F5
Buttevant 110 D3

C
Cahermore 110 B5
Cahir 111 E3
Cahirciveen 110 A4
Callan 111 F3
Cappoquin 111 E3
Carlingford 113 G5
Carlow (Ceatharlach) 111 F2
Carndonagh 113 F2
Carnlough 113 G3
Carraroe 110 B1
Carrick-on-Shannon 113 E5
Carrick-on-Suir (Carraig na Sivire) 111 F3
Carrickfergus 113 H3
Carrickmacross 113 F5
Carrigallen 113 E5
Carrigtwohill 113 D4
Carrowdore 113 H4
Carrowkeel 113 F2
Cashel 111 E3
Castlebar (Caisleán an Bharraigh) 112 C5
Castlebellingham 113 G5
Castleblayney 113 F5
Castlebridge 111 G3
Castlecomer 111 F2
Castleconnell 110 D2
Castlederg 113 E3
Castledermot 111 F2
Castlegregory 110 B3
Castleisland 110 B3
Castlemaine 110 B3
Castlemartyr 111 E4
Castlepollard 111 F6
Castlerea 112 D6
Castletown 111 E1
Castletown Bere 110 B5
Catherdaniel 110 A4
Cavan 113 F5
Celbridge 111 G1
Charlestown 112 D5
Cheekpoint 111 F3
City of Derry Airport 113 F3
Clady 113 E3
Clane 111 G1
Clara 111 E1
Clarecastle 110 C2
Claregalway 110 C1
Claremorris 112 C6
Clashmore 111 E4
Claudy 113 F3
Clifden 112 B6
Cliffony 112 D4

Cloghan 111 E1
Clogheen 111 E3
Clonakilty 110 C5
Clonbern 112 D6
Clones 113 F5
Clonmel (Cluain Meala) 111 E3
Clonroche 111 G3
Clonygowan 111 F1
Cloonbannin 110 C3
Clooneagh 113 E5
Cobh (An Cóbh) 110 D4
Coleraine 113 F2
Collooney 112 D5
Comber 113 H4
Cong 112 C6
Cookstown 113 F4
Cootehill 113 F5
Cork (Corcaigh) 110 D4
Cork Airport 110 D4
Corofin 110 C2
Courtmacsherry 110 D5
Courtown 111 G2
Craanford 111 G2
Craigavon 113 G4
Creeslough 113 E2
Cregganbaun 112 B6
Crookhaven 110 B5
Croom 110 D3
Crossgar 113 H4
Crosshaven 110 D4
Crossmaglen 113 G5
Crumlin 113 G4
Crusheen 110 C2
Cullybackey 113 G3
Cushendall 113 G3
Cushendun 113 G2

D
Delvin 113 F6
Dingle 110 A3
Donaghadee 113 H4
Donaghmore 113 F4
Donegal 112 D4
Donoughmore 110 D4
Dooagh 112 B5
Downpatrick 113 H4
Draperstown 113 F3
Drimoleague 110 C5
Drogheda (Droichead Átha) 113 G6
Dromod 113 E5
Dromore Down 113 G4
Dromore Tyr. 113 E4
Dromore West 112 C5
Drumfree 113 E2
Drumkeeran 112 D5
Drummin 111 F3
Dublin (Baile Átha Cliath) 111 G1
Dublin Airport 113 G6
Dún Laoghaire 111 G1
Dunboyne 113 G6
Duncannon 111 F3
Duncormick 111 G3
Dundalk (Dún Dealgan) 113 G5
Dundonald 113 H4
Dundrum 113 H4
Dungannon 113 F4
Dungarvan Kilk. 111 F2
Dungarvan (Dún Garbhán) Water. 111 E4
Dungiven 113 F3
Dunglow 112 D3
Dunlavin 111 G1
Dunleer 113 G5
Dunloy 113 G3
Dunmanway 110 C4
Dunmore 112 D6
Dunmore East 111 F3
Dunmurry 113 G4
Dunquin 110 A3
Durrow 111 F2

E
Edenderry 111 F1
Edgeworthstown 113 E6

Eglinton 113 F3
Ennis (Inis) 110 C2
Enniscorthy (Inis Córthaidh) 111 G3
Enniskean 110 C4
Enniskerry 111 G1
Enniskillen 113 E4
Ennistymon 110 C2

F
Farranfore 110 B3
Fermoy 110 D3
Ferns 111 G2
Fethard 111 E3
Fintona 113 F4
Fintown 112 D3
Fivemiletown 113 F4
Foxford 112 C5
Foynes 110 C2
Frenchpark 112 D5
Freshford 111 F2

G
Galbally 110 D3
Galway (Gaillimh) 110 C1
Galway Airport 110 C1
Garvagh 113 F3
Glenamaddy 112 D6
Glengarriff 110 B4
Glengavlen 113 E5
Glenties 112 D3
Gorey 111 G2
Gort 110 C2
Gortahork 112 D2
Graigue 111 F2
Graiguenamanagh 111 F2
Granard 113 E6
Grange 111 E4
Greenore 113 G5
Greystones 111 G1
Gweedore 112 D3

H
Halfway 110 D4
Headford 112 C6
Holycross 111 E2
Horseleap 112 D6
Hospital 110 D3
Howth 113 G6
Hurler's Cross 110 C2

I
Inch Kerry 110 B3
Inch Wexf. 111 G2

J
Johnstown 111 E2

K
Kanturk 110 C3
Keady 113 F5
Kells Kilk. 111 F3
Kells (Ceanannus Mór) Meath 113 F6
Kenmare 110 B4
Kerry Airport 110 B3
Kilbeggan 111 E1
Kilcolgan 110 C1
Kilcommon 111 E3
Kilcoole 111 G1
Kilcormac 111 E1
Kilcullen 111 F1
Kildare 111 F1
Kilkee 110 B2
Kilkeel 113 G5
Kilkenny (Cill Chainnigh) 111 F2
Killala 112 C4
Killaloe 110 D2
Killarney (Cill Airne) 110 B4
Killenaule 111 E2
Killimor 110 D1

Killinchy 113 H4
Killinick 111 G3
Killorglin 110 B4
Killurin 111 G3
Killybegs 112 D4
Kilmacrenan 113 E3
Kilmaine 112 C6
Kilmallock 110 D3
Kilmona 110 D4
Kilmore Quay 111 G3
Kilrea 113 G3
Kilrush 110 B2
Kilteel 111 G1
Kiltimagh 112 C5
Kiltullagh 110 D1
Kingscourt 113 F5
Kinnegad 113 F6
Kinsale 110 D4
Kinvara 110 C1
Kircubbin 113 H4
Knock 110 C6
Knock International Airport 112 C5
Knockalough 110 C2
Knocktopher 111 F3

L
Lanesborough 113 E6
Larne 113 H3
Lauragh 110 B4
Laytown 113 G6
Leap 110 C5
Leighlinbridge 111 F2
Leixlip 111 G1
Letterkenny 113 E3
Lifford 113 E3
Limavady 113 F3
Limerick (Luimneach) 110 D2
Lisbellaw 113 E4
Lisburn 113 G4
Lisdoonvarna 110 C1
Lismore 111 E3
Lisnarrick 113 E4
Lisnaskea 113 E5
Listowel 110 B3
Londonderry (Derry) 113 F3
Longford 113 E6
Loughrea 110 D1
Louisburgh 112 B6
Lucan 111 G1
Lukeswell 111 F3
Lurgan 113 G4

M
Macroom 110 C4
Maghera 113 G3
Magherafelt 113 G3
Malahide 113 G6
Malin More 112 D3
Mallow (Mala) 110 D3
Manorhamilton 112 D4
Markethill 113 G4
May's Corner 113 G4
Middletown 113 F4
Midleton 110 D4
Milestone 111 E2
Milford 113 E3
Millstreet 110 C3
Milltown Malbay 110 C2
Mitchelstown 110 D3
Moate 111 E1
Mohill 113 E5
Moira 113 G4
Monaghan (Muineachán) 113 F5
Monasterevin 111 F1
Moneygall 111 E2
Moneymore 113 G3
Monivea 112 D1
Mount Bellew 112 D6
Mountmellick 111 F1
Mountrath 111 E1
Mountshannon 110 D2
Moville 113 F2
Moyvalley 111 F1
Muine Bheag 111 F2

Mullany's Cross 112 C5
Mullingar (An Muileann gCearr) 113 F6
Mulrany 112 B5
Murrisk 112 B6
Murroogh 110 C1

N
Naas (An Nás) 111 G1
Navan (An Uaimh) 113 G6
Nenagh (An tAonach) 110 D2
New Ross 111 F3
Newbridge (Droichead Nua) 111 F1
Newcastle Down 113 H5
Newcastle Dub. 111 G1
Newcastle West 110 C3
Newinn 111 E3
Newmarket 110 C3
Newmarket-on-Fergus 110 C2
Newport Mayo 112 B5
Newport Tipp. 110 D2
Newry 113 G5
Newtown 110 D3
Newtownabbey 113 H4
Newtownards 113 H4
Newtownbutler 113 F5
Newtownmount-kennedy 111 G1
Newtownstewart 113 F3
Ninemilehouse 111 E3
Nobber 113 F5

O
Oldcastle 113 F6
Omagh 113 F4
Oranmore 110 C1

P
Pallas Green 110 D2
Park 113 F3
Partry 112 C6
Pettigo 113 E4
Pomeroy 113 F4
Pontoon 112 C5
Portadown 113 G4
Portaferry 113 H4
Portarlington 111 F1
Portavogie 113 H4
Portlaoise 111 F1
Portlaw 111 F3
Portmagee 110 A4
Portrane 113 G6
Portrush 113 G2
Portsalon 113 E2
Portstewart 113 F2
Portumna 110 D1
Poulgorm Bridge 110 C4

R
Randalstown 113 G3
Raphoe 113 E3
Rathangan 111 F1
Rathdowney 111 E2
Rathdrum 111 G2
Rathfriland 113 G5
Rathkeale 111 E3
Rathkeevin 111 E3
Rathluirc (Charleville) 110 D3
Rathvilly 111 G2
Recess 112 B6
Ringsend 113 F3
Roscommon 112 D6
Roscrea 111 E2
Ross Carbery 110 C5
Rosslare 111 G3
Rosslare Harbour 111 G3
Rosslea 113 F5
Rush 113 G6

S
Saintfield 113 H4

Schull 110 B5
Shanacrane 110 C4
Shannon Airport 110 C2
Shercock 113 F5
Shillelagh 111 G2
Sion Mills 113 E3
Sixmilebridge 110 D2
Sixmilecross 113 F4
Skerries 113 G6
Skibbereen 110 C5
Slane 113 G6
Sligo (Sligeach) 112 D4
Sneem 110 B4
Strabane 113 E3
Stradbally 111 F1
Strangford 113 H4
Stranorlar 113 E3
Strokestown 112 D6
Swinford 112 C5
Swords 113 G6

T
Taghmon 111 G3
Tallow 111 E4
Tandragee 113 G4
Tarbert 110 C2
Templemore 111 E2
Templetuohy 111 E2
Thomastown 111 F3
Thurles (Durlas) 111 E2
Timolin 111 F1
Tipperary 110 D3
Tower 110 D4
Tralee (Trá Lí) 110 B3
Tramore (Trá Mhór) 111 F3
Trim 113 F6
Tuam 112 C6
Tubbercurry 112 D5
Tulla 110 D2
Tullamore (Tulach Mhór) 111 E1
Tullow 111 F2
Tully 113 E4
Tulsk 112 D6

U
Urlingford 111 E2

V
Virginia 113 F5

W
Warrenpoint 113 G5
Waterford (Port Láirgé) 111 F3
Waterford Regional Airport 111 F3
Watergrasshill 110 D4
Wellington Bridge 111 F3
Westport 112 B6
Wexford (Loch Garman) 111 G3
Whitehall 111 F2
Whitehead 113 H3
Wicklow (Cill Mhantáin) 111 H1

Youghal (Eochaill) 111 E4